EUROPE BY EURAIL 2017

TOURING EUROPE BY TRAIN

FORTY-FIRST EDITION

Written by
LaVerne Ferguson-Kosinski

Edited by
C. Darren Price

Rail Schedules by
C. Darren Price

Guilford, Connecticut

Globe
Pequot

An imprint of Rowman & Littlefield

Distributed by NATIONAL BOOK NETWORK

The author and the publisher gratefully acknowledge the kind permission of Eurostar Passenger Services and its website, Deutsche Bahn and its website, Brittany Ferries, Hoverspeed UK Limited, Irish Ferries U.K. Limited, P&O Stena Line, SeaFrance Limited, DFDS Seaways, and Stena Line to use their resources in the compilation of the timetables in this text.

The "International Services" rail map on pp. x–xi is reproduced courtesy of the *European Rail Timetable Ltd;* www.europeanrailtimetable.com.

British Library Cataloguing-in-Publication Information is available on file.

ISSN 1081-1125
ISBN 978-1-4930-1819-2 (pbk.)
ISBN 978-1-4930-1820-8 (e-book)

∞™ The paper used in this publication meets the minimum requirements of American National Standard for Information Sciences—Permanence of Paper for Printed Library Materials, ANSI/NISO Z39.48-1992.

Train schedules, prices, and conditions of use appearing in this edition are updated at press time and are subject to change without notice by the railways. Prices are estimates and are based on exchange rate at the time of printing. The information is to assist with trip planning only. We cannot be held responsible for its accuracy. Please check with the railways for the most recent information.

EUROPE BY EURAIL 2017

HELP US KEEP THIS GUIDE UP TO DATE

We would love to hear from you concerning your experiences with this guide and how you feel it could be improved and kept up to date. Please send your comments and suggestions to:

editorial@GlobePequot.com

Thanks for your input, and happy travels!

In Loving Memory
of
Our Son
Matthew Carlo Palma
1972–2007

A loving friend to so many
A world traveler and adventurer
A heart and soul filled with kindness
And uncommon generosity . . .

Editor of *Europe by Eurail*
And *Britain by BritRail*

ABOUT THE AUTHOR

LaVerne Ferguson-Kosinski and her late husband, Lt. Col. George Ferguson, first coauthored this unique and comprehensive how-to guide in 1980.

After battling a long illness, George, who was globally and affectionately known as "Mr. Eurail," passed away in 1997 and was buried at Arlington National Cemetery.

LaVerne wanted to ensure that accurate British and European rail travel information would continue to be available. She is devoted to producing comprehensive, practical, yet friendly guidebooks for the independent rail traveler or armchair dreamer. Her technical writing and editorial background; academic education in English, world history, and communications; and experience in research and development for an international research institute have added considerable substance to her three decades of traveling the rails in Britain and Europe.

Her dream of exploring the world began in third-grade geography class when she first began collecting travel brochures. After attending Ohio State University, LaVerne lived in and traveled throughout Europe. She resides in Fort Myers Beach, Florida, with her husband, Joe "Cool" Kosinski, a structural engineer.

Heartfelt thanks and appreciation go to you, the readers, whose comments, suggestions, and corrections help keep both guidebooks accurate and up to date.

ACKNOWLEDGMENTS

Researchers for *Europe by Eurail* also included the late Matthew Palma, **Major Robert Bean,** Margaret Keith, Joseph Kosinski, and C. Darren Price. Major Robert Bean, a true train enthusiast, has played an ongoing, much appreciated role with both *Europe by Eurail* and *Britain by BritRail* for several years. His attention to minute details and knowledge of rail travelers' needs is superb. **Margaret Keith,** a certified Red Badge Guide for France, an artist, and a longtime European rail expert, has provided her invaluable input to *Europe by Eurail* since 1982. **Joseph Kosinski,** aka "the Steel Man," has been instrumental in Internet research, setting up databases, and accompanying his wife/author, LaVerne Ferguson-Kosinski, on her treks throughout Europe. Foremost a top structural design engineer in Florida with his own firm, J.C. Kosinski Engineering, Inc., Joe's creativity and attention to details are unsurpassed as can be seen in his design of the Pentagon renovations in Washington, DC.

We also wish to extend thanks to Raffaela Essayan, Frank Berardi, David Brever, Bill Schroeder, and the entire staff of CIT Tours; Jean Heger of Rail Europe Group; our many, many friends in the European tourist offices; and our travel partner professionals throughout Europe.

CONTENTS

Introduction 1
Why Eurail? 2
How to Use *Europe by Eurail* 3
Planning a Eurail Trip 5
How to Get There 8
European Rail Passes 9
Europe's Passenger Trains 14
Trip Tips 23

AUSTRIA 35
Vienna (Wien) 38
Austrian Alps Tour 43
Baden 45
Melk 47
Salzburg 50

BELGIUM 53
Brussels (Bruxelles) 56
Antwerp (Antwerpen) 64
Bruges (Brugge) 66
Ghent (Gent) 68
Namur 70

CZECH REPUBLIC 73
Prague (Praha) 76
Brno 80
Pilsen (Plzeň) 82
Kutná Hora 84

DENMARK 87
Copenhagen (København) 91
Aarhus (Århus) 97
Helsingør (Elsinore) 99
Hillerød 101
Odense 103
Roskilde 105

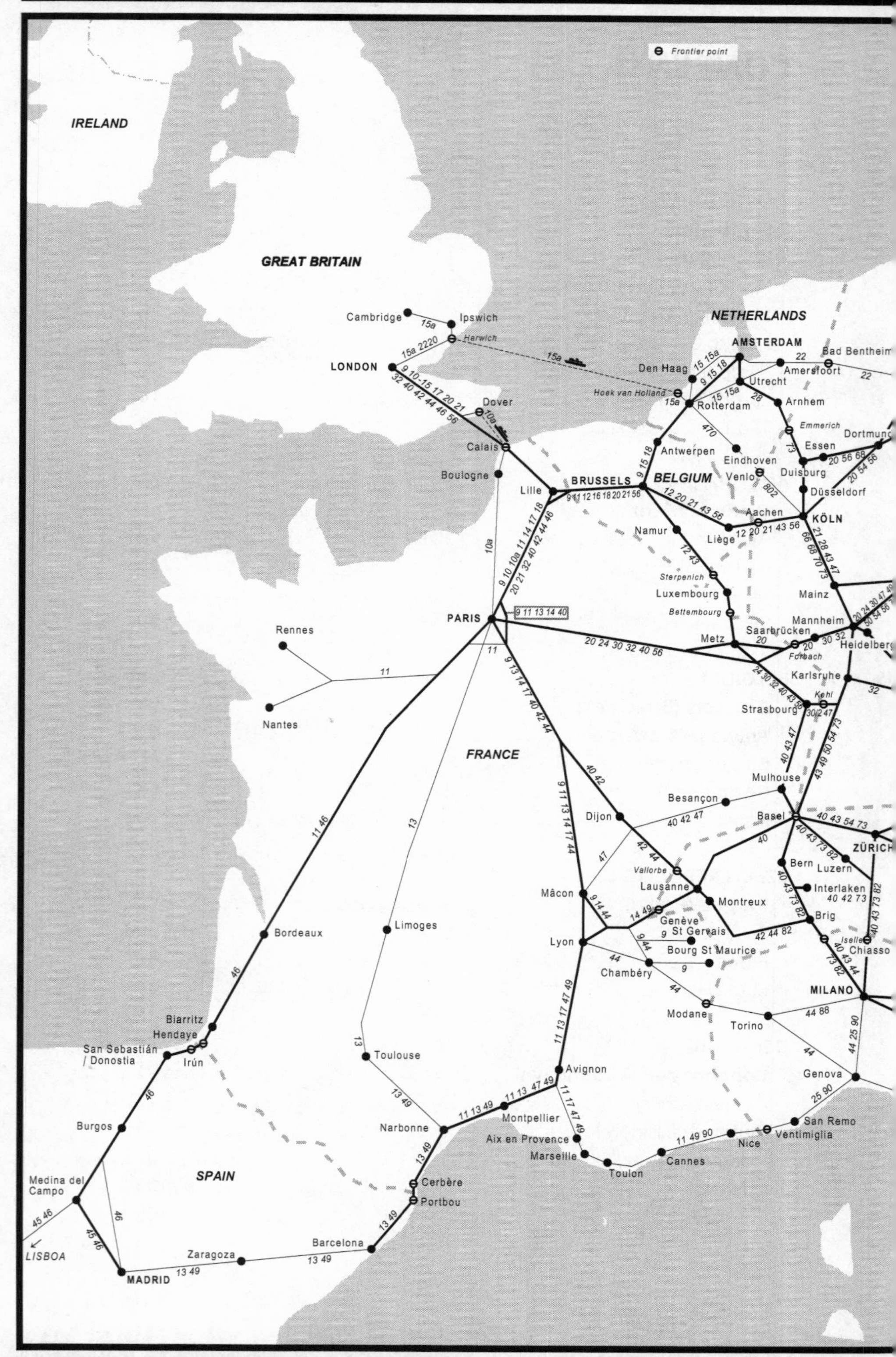

Frontier point
IRELAND
GREAT BRITAIN
NETHERLANDS
BELGIUM
FRANCE
SPAIN
LONDON
Cambridge
Ipswich
Harwich
Dover
Calais
Boulogne
Lille
BRUSSELS
AMSTERDAM
Den Haag
Hoek van Holland
Rotterdam
Utrecht
Amersfoort
Bad Bentheim
Arnhem
Emmerich
Antwerpen
Eindhoven
Venlo
Essen
Duisburg
Düsseldorf
Dortmund
Aachen
KÖLN
Namur
Liège
Sterpenich
Luxembourg
Bettembourg
Mainz
Mannheim
Heidelberg
Saarbrücken
Forbach
Metz
Karlsruhe
Kehl
Strasbourg
PARIS
Rennes
Nantes
Mulhouse
Besançon
Basel
ZÜRICH
Dijon
Bern
Luzern
Interlaken
Vallorbe
Lausanne
Montreux
Mâcon
Genève
St Gervais
Brig
Iselle
Chiasso
Lyon
Bourg St Maurice
Chambéry
MILANO
Modane
Torino
Bordeaux
Limoges
Biarritz
Hendaye
San Sebastián / Donostia
Irún
Toulouse
Avignon
Genova
Montpellier
Narbonne
Aix en Provence
Marseille
Toulon
Cannes
Nice
Ventimiglia
San Remo
Burgos
Cerbère
Portbou
Medina del Campo
LISBOA
Zaragoza
Barcelona
MADRID

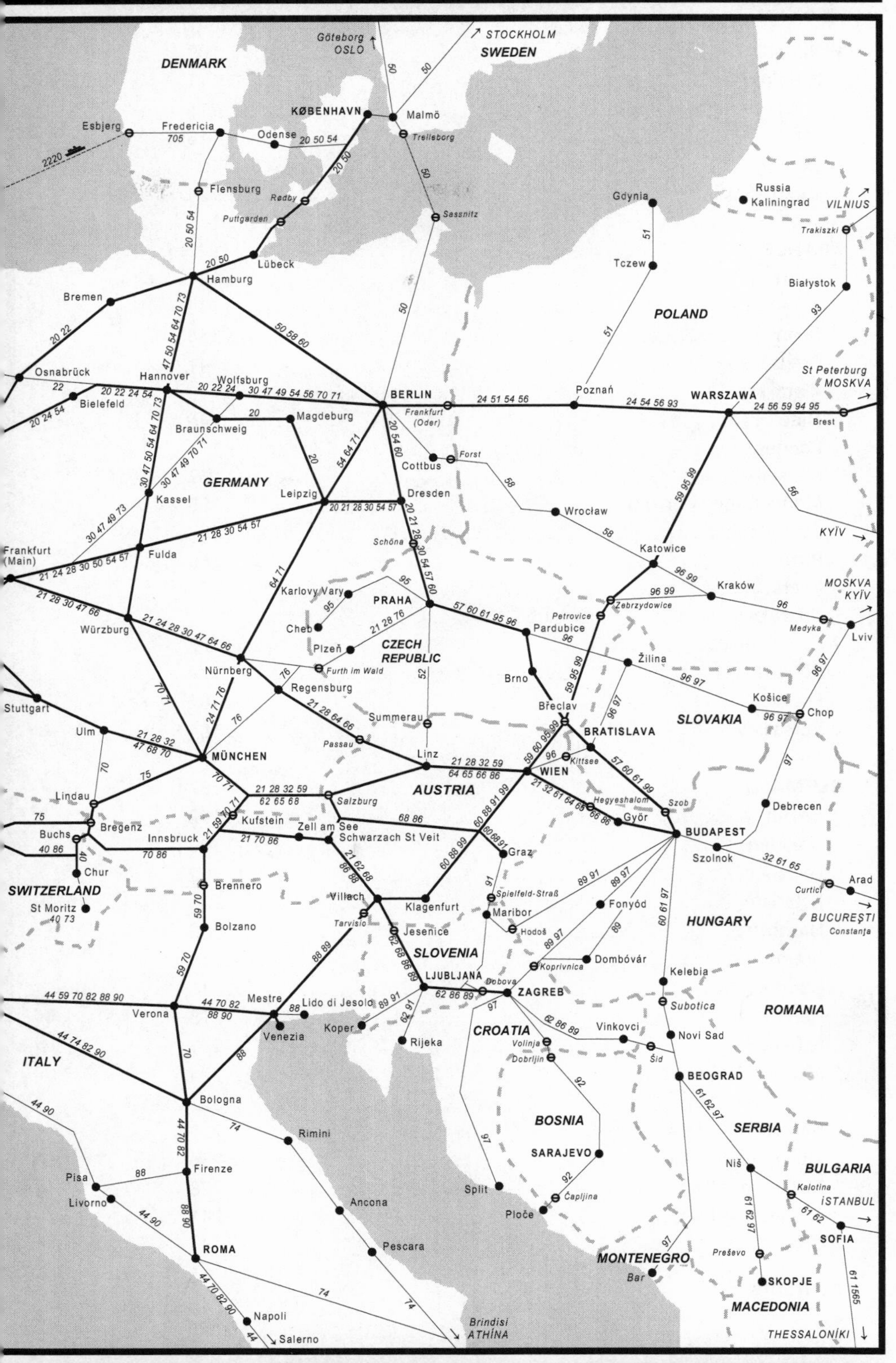
DENMARK
SWEDEN
POLAND
GERMANY
CZECH REPUBLIC
SLOVAKIA
AUSTRIA
HUNGARY
ROMANIA
SWITZERLAND
SLOVENIA
CROATIA
BOSNIA
SERBIA
BULGARIA
MONTENEGRO
MACEDONIA
ITALY
Russia
Göteborg OSLO
STOCKHOLM
KØBENHAVN
Malmö
Trelleborg
Esbjerg
Fredericia
Odense
Flensburg
Rødby
Puttgarden
Sassnitz
Lübeck
Hamburg
Bremen
Osnabrück
Hannover
Bielefeld
Wolfsburg
Braunschweig
Magdeburg
BERLIN
Frankfurt (Oder)
Cottbus
Forst
Kassel
Leipzig
Dresden
Schöna
Frankfurt (Main)
Fulda
Würzburg
Karlovy Vary
Cheb
PRAHA
Plzeň
Furth im Wald
Nürnberg
Regensburg
Stuttgart
Ulm
MÜNCHEN
Passau
Summerau
Linz
Lindau
Bregenz
Buchs
Chur
St Moritz
Innsbruck
Kufstein
Salzburg
Zell am See
Schwarzach St Veit
Brennero
Bolzano
Villach
Tarvisio
Klagenfurt
Jesenice
Graz
Spielfeld-Straß
Maribor
Hodoš
WIEN
Kittsee
Hegyeshalom
Győr
BRATISLAVA
Břeclav
Brno
Pardubice
Petrovice
Zebrzydowice
Katowice
Kraków
Wrocław
Poznań
Gdynia
Tczew
Kaliningrad
VILNIUS
Trakiszki
Białystok
WARSZAWA
St Peterburg MOSKVA
Brest
KYÏV
MOSKVA KYÏV
Medyka
Lviv
Žilina
Košice
Chop
Szob
BUDAPEST
Debrecen
Szolnok
Curtici
Arad
BUCUREŞTI Constanţa
Fonyód
Dombóvár
Koprivnica
Dobova
LJUBLJANA
ZAGREB
Kelebia
Subotica
Novi Sad
Vinkovci
Šid
BEOGRAD
Volinja
Dobrljin
SARAJEVO
Čapljina
Split
Ploče
Bar
Niš
Kalotina
İSTANBUL
SOFIA
Preševo
SKOPJE
THESSALONÍKI
Verona
Mestre
Venezia
Lido di Jesolo
Koper
Rijeka
Bologna
Rimini
Firenze
Pisa
Livorno
Ancona
Pescara
ROMA
Napoli
Salerno
Brindisi ATHÍNA

FINLAND 109
Helsinki 111
Hanko (Hangö) 116
Lahti 118
Tampere 121
Turku 124

FRANCE 127
Lyon 131
Annecy 136
Dijon 138
Grenoble 141
Vienne 143
Nice 146
Cannes 151
Marseilles 153
Monte Carlo (Monaco) 155
Saint-Raphaël 157
Paris 160
Caen 171
Chartres 174
Fontainebleau 177
Rennes 179
Rouen 182
Versailles 184

GERMANY 187
Berlin 192
Dresden 200
Leipzig 202
Potsdam 205
Hamburg 208
Bremen 214
Hameln 216
Hannover 218
Lübeck 221
Munich (München) 224
Berchtesgaden 231
Garmisch-Partenkirchen 233
Innsbruck, Austria 236
Nuremberg (Nürnberg) 238
The Romantic Road 241
Ulm 244

GREECE . . . 247
Athens (Athinai) . . . 251
Argos (Arghos) . . . 256
Corinth (Korinthos) . . . 258
Patras . . . 261
Piraeus . . . 263

HUNGARY . . . 267
Budapest . . . 269
Lake Balaton . . . 273
Siófok . . . 273
Kecskemét . . . 274
Szeged . . . 274

IRELAND . . . 277
Dublin . . . 281
Cork . . . 287
Galway . . . 289
Kilkenny . . . 291
Killarney . . . 293

ITALY . . . 295
Milan (Milano) . . . 298
Bologna . . . 304
Genoa (Genova) . . . 307
Lake Lugano . . . 309
Venice (Venezia) . . . 311
Rome (Roma) . . . 314
Anzio . . . 320
Florence (Firenze) . . . 322
Naples (Napoli) . . . 325
Pisa . . . 327

LUXEMBOURG . . . 331
Luxembourg City . . . 333
Clervaux . . . 339
Koblenz . . . 341
Metz . . . 343
Trier . . . 345

THE NETHERLANDS 349
Amsterdam 353
Alkmaar 361
Enkhuizen 363
Haarlem 365
Hoorn 367

NORWAY 371
Oslo 374
Bergen 379
Hamar 381
Larvik and Skien 384
Lillehammer 387

POLAND 391
Warsaw (Warszawa) 393
Kraków 398
Gdańsk 400
Lublin 402

PORTUGAL 405
Lisbon (Lisboa) 408
Cascais and Estoril 412
Coimbra 414
Setúbal 415
Sintra 417

SPAIN 419
Barcelona 424
Blanes 429
Lleida (Lerida) 431
Sitges 433
Tarragona 434
Madrid 437
Aranjuez 442
Avila 444
Burgos 446
El Escorial 447
Toledo 449

SWEDEN 451
Stockholm 455
Eskilstuna 460
Norrköping 462
Uppsala 464

SWITZERLAND 467
Bern (Berne) 473
The Golden Pass 479
Interlaken 482
Lucerne (Luzern) 485
Rheinfelden 488
Zermatt 490
Zürich 492

TURKEY 499
Istanbul 500
Ankara 502
Cappadocia 503

APPENDIX 505
Rail-Tour Itineraries 505
Base-City Hotels and Information 515
Ferry Crossings 520
International Calling 527
Communicating on the Go 527
Train Travel Terminology 531
Passport Information 533
European Tourist Offices in North America 534
To Purchase Passes 538
Airline Numbers and Websites 539
Hotel Reservation Numbers 540
Airport–City Connections 541
Eurail Passes 545
Eurail Select Pass 546
Eurail Regional Passes 547
Eurail Country Passes 554
Security 561
BritRail Passes 562
BritRail Family Passes 562

INTRODUCTION

"To travel by train is to see nature and human beings, towns and churches and rivers, in fact to see life."

—AGATHA CHRISTIE

This 41st edition of *Europe by Eurail* reflects the "new" Europe and the energy and exuberance of its rail system. It's dynamic, it's futuristic, and it's on the move—accelerating with the high-tech boldness and immense speed of the world's finest transportation system.

Train travel is an enigma for most non-Europeans who either have forgotten or have never had an opportunity to learn what travel by train is like. *Europe by Eurail* takes the puzzlement out of European rail travel—like having a friend along who takes you by the hand and shows you how to use the world's finest transportation network to see and learn about European life and culture. Toward that end, this guide provides specific, pragmatic information with step-by-step directions.

Europe by Eurail is a train traveler's how-to book. *Europe by Eurail* deals primarily with the necessities of train travel in Europe and offers guidance for appreciating the educational and cultural sites and events that abound along the right-of-way of the Continent's magnificent rail system. It is not a hotel/restaurant guide but rather tells you how to locate them. Certain hotels and restaurants do occasionally gain mention, however, especially if they add to the graciousness and enjoyment of a train trip or a stay in a city.

"See Europe by Train" has been a favorite slogan of Europe's railways for decades, but never has it been as full of meaning as it is today. You will never be bored traveling on a high-speed train because rail travel is still leisurely enough to fully enjoy the constantly changing scenes of hills and hamlets, farms and forests, and cities and countrysides. Each country has its own special attractions to offer rail travelers as they speed through, ensconced in comfort and free from worry. Added to the passing scenes is the opportunity for leisurely dining and drinking while chatting with fellow passengers, most of whom are the Europeans you hoped to meet.

Travel by train in Europe is a unique and pleasurable experience. All aboard—and take your imagination with you.

Why Eurail?

Many visitors to Europe fail to realize that the European rail network (which we refer to simply as "Eurail") can take you to practically every nook and cranny on the Continent, so they assume they must rent a car. At first glance, those European fly-drive packages might appear enticing, but the more you investigate them, the less appealing they become. In general, car rentals have one basic fault—the price you are quoted may not be the price you pay; it usually is higher. One important facet of a fly-drive package is the VAT (value-added tax), which ranges from 15 to 25 percent in European countries. In some countries, foreign tourists are eligible for refunds on certain purchases [contact 800-KNOW-VAT (800-566-9828) or visit www.globalrefund.com for more information], but there are no VAT refunds on car rentals. Reference to the VAT may be tactfully avoided in car rental information or perhaps hidden in the fine print of the terms. After determining the low cost of a rental car with unlimited mileage privileges (which also includes the privilege of buying unlimited gasoline), don't forget to multiply the bottom line by the VAT of the country and add that figure to the cost.

Another item frequently overlooked is insurance. As a general rule, add to the quoted rental cost another 20 percent for personal accident insurance, collision insurance, and taxes. After that, prepare yourself for another shock—the price of gasoline in Europe is about three times what you'd pay in the United States, plus gasoline stations are not nearly as numerous as they are stateside.

Also consider that the number of European road-traffic fatalities is more than four times that in North America, and that watching the road ahead is not really what most folks go to Europe to do, nor is deciphering the signs an easy feat. Most European automobiles are small, compact vehicles. That four-passenger economy car you're thinking of renting could never carry four passengers and their luggage—so, bring on the Mercedes at three times the price and double the gas. By now, you will realize why Europeans park their own cars and ride the trains themselves.

The more you open your eyes to rail travel, we think, the more you'll find there is no better way to go. One key reason for going to Europe is to mingle with Europeans. Traveling day after day in a motor coach filled with other American tourists or riding for hours in a small rental car with your spouse helping you navigate and the kids crammed in with the suitcases is not, in our opinion, the best way to mingle. Europeans use their trains. They will be sitting next to you or across from you in the diner. You will be sharing the same experiences, so conversation will come easily. It's a great way to make new friends.

Those traveling with children across the Continent will find the trains to be a fun and intriguing blessing. The kids can eat, get a drink, take a nap, or go to the restroom just as often as their little hearts desire while you enjoy the scenery en route.

Trains have always held an aura of romance and charm that cannot be experienced in any other mode of transportation. The mere mention of The Orient Express, for example, sparks visions of glamour, intrigue, mystery—and sumptuous dining.

Although many of the original famous trains have been replaced by high-speed, high-tech international express trains, that special thrill of rail travel is still there.

The Europeans know how to run a railroad. The Eurail network connects more than 30,000 cities, villages, and hamlets with more than 96,000 daily train departures on more than 174,000 miles of track. And the system is getting faster, more efficient, and more elegant. Unlike the airlines' sardinelike accommodations, European trains are comfortable, stylish, and loaded with amenities to please the tourist and business traveler alike.

Originally, the idea of purchasing a pass for unlimited travel by train within a specified time period, for example, one month, on the Eurail system was a simple one. One type of rail pass, called a **"Eurail pass,"** was offered to non-European residents as a way to encourage independent travelers to use Europe's rail network.

Although today's European rail passes encompass a wide variety of options, time periods, and countries, using a rail pass is still the most economical, convenient, and flexible way to get the most out of the European rail network. A point-to-point ticket enables you to travel from one point to another but does not provide the flexibility to change your plans. Rail passes, on the other hand, provide unlimited rail travel each day within a specified time frame. They eliminate the hassle of standing in long lines to purchase single tickets, and they can save you a bundle of money if you are making long or frequent journeys.

For details on the various kinds of European rail passes available to non-European residents, please consult the European Rail Passes section later in this introduction, or contact one of the companies listed under "To Purchase Passes" in the Appendix.

 *Remember . . . purchase **your** rail passes before leaving for Europe!*

The Base City–Day Excursion Concept combined with the appropriate rail pass provides greater flexibility to see more of Europe at its best—by train. Many of our cost-conscious readers modify the concept by using the less expensive suburban area of a major city or one of our day-excursion points as their "base." With any one of the various types of rail passes available today, it's easy to modify our comfortable rail travel concept to suit your budget and itinerary. Armed with a rail pass and a current copy of *Europe by Eurail*, you become your own tour guide, packing and moving on only when you want to. For the experienced traveler or the novice, it's the only way to go.

How to Use *Europe by Eurail*

Base City–Day Excursion Concept

In 1976 *Europe by Eurail* first launched a new concept for easy, comfortable, hassle-free train travel by combining the economy of a Eurail pass with the Fergusons' Base City–Day Excursion method of touring Europe. Now proudly in its 41st edition,

Europe by Eurail has proven to be a most useful tool for travelers using any type of rail pass that allows access to any or all of the Eurail system.

Currently, the Eurail system includes a total of 28 countries, stretching from Ireland to Turkey and from Portugal to Finland.

We identify base cities throughout Europe in which you may stay in comfort and from which you may make numerous day excursions to interesting places, returning each night to the same hotel room. This concept eliminates the hassles of daily packing and unpacking and luggage lugging. This more relaxed approach to rail travel is not only an enjoyable way to visit Europe but also affords the time to see and do a delightful variety of things outside of the major cities.

You do not have to be a geographer to use *Europe by Eurail*. It is conveniently arranged alphabetically—first by country, then by base city. Rail system maps accompany each country chapter.

Europe by Eurail picks up the traveler disembarking from the train on arrival from another base city (or at the airport if it is the traveler's entry point to Europe) and leads him or her step-by-step through the essentials of European rail travel.

We take a pragmatic approach to European rail travel by providing explicit walking directions and explanations based from rail stations. For example, a bewildered tourist standing on a train platform in one of Brussels's three train stations needs practical, no-nonsense information—in a hurry:

The Grand'Place? How do I get there?
Where's the tourist information office?

Europe by Eurail leads you with specific directions: "To reach the Grand'Place from Gare Centrale (Central Station), walk downhill in the direction of the Town Hall's spire until you reach the square. The tourist office is to the right of the spire when you are facing the Town Hall."

Country sections explain what types of tourist rail passes are accepted, specify what kinds of bonuses are available, and provide specific information about rail travel within that country. These sections also list each country's tourist information office locations in North America, their telephone/fax numbers, and, where applicable, websites and e-mail addresses.

Some base cities have a single train station; others have multiple stations. Under train station descriptions are the subsections concerning

- Exchanging money and using ATMs
- Locating tourist information
- Locating and using luggage facilities
- Securing hotel accommodations
- Obtaining train information and reservations
- Obtaining rail pass validation

Base city **tourist information offices** and **hotel reservation information** are listed with addresses, telephone and fax numbers, websites and e-mail addresses (if available), hours of operation, and, of utmost importance, how to reach those offices from the rail station.

Connections from each base city to others are listed at the end of each base city section. Not all base cities can be reached from another in the same day, although most can.

A **sightseeing, attractions,** and **special tour** information section for each base city provides a general introduction to what to see and do and how to do it.

Day excursions begin with the distance and average train time and include train schedules to/from the base city. Trains departing a base city are usually in the morning, and trains returning from the day excursions are usually in the late afternoon or early evening.

A brief history and highlights of each day excursion enable you to decide which ones are of the most interest. Then, *Europe by Eurail* again provides step-by-step directions on how to get from the rail station to the tourist information offices and to the various day-excursion sights and attractions.

Special Features

Special features in the Appendix of this edition of *Europe by Eurail* include:

- **Sample 15-Day Itineraries**
- **International Calling & Dialing Codes**
- **Glossary of Rail Terminology**—In four languages
- **U.S. Passport Offices**
- **European Tourist Offices in North America**—Where to get advance destination information
- **Airline and Hotel Information**

Planning a Eurail Trip

Planning Pays Off

Depending on who you are, your concept of a "plan" can vary. We have observed two general types of rail travelers—one conservative, the other adventurous. One traveler may require a detailed, hour-by-hour schedule for a day's activities; another may merely get up in the morning and see what happens that day.

The first questions to answer when planning a trip are, "When can I go and how much time can I spend there?" April through October are the most popular months for touring in Europe and for many events. When planning your trip, take bank holidays into consideration, since banks, postal services, most shops, and many attractions are closed, and some transportation services are reduced.

Whether or not you admit it, everyone has a problem budgeting vacation time. It's human nature to try to see as much as possible in as little time as possible. This "sightseer's syndrome" could be dangerous to your vacation. Avoid it by planning an itinerary that allows ample "free time." Also, vary the day excursions by going on a short one following a particularly long outing away from the base city. Try to see and do too much on your vacation, and you will return home looking as if you desperately need another one.

How long should your Eurail tour be? There are many factors bearing on such a determination, the most important being the individual. How much annual vacation time do you have? How do you use it—all at one time or in two or more segments? Rail passes can accommodate just about anyone's personal needs, with Eurail Global Passes ranging from 15 consecutive days to 3 months of travel and "design-your-own" Eurail Select Passes valid for rail travel within any 3, 4, or 5 adjoining countries out of 28 European countries that are connected by trains or ships. When you add the wide variety of regional and individual country rail passes available, it may, at first, seem confusing. But *Europe by Eurail* can help you.

Even if you don't have two weeks or more for that grand tour of Europe, travel magazines and the travel sections of the Sunday newspapers plus the Internet are usually loaded with one-week bargain fares to almost anywhere, mainland Europe included. By coupling our Base City–Day Excursion mode with a rail pass, you can maximize the time you do have to spend in Europe.

After determining the length of time you will have for your European rail trip, the next step is to develop a clear idea of **where you want to go,** what you want to see, and what you want to do. Develop your objectives well before your departure date. We disagree with those who believe that anticipation of travel is more rewarding than its realization. But we do agree that the planning phase can also be a fun part of your trip. Properly done, this "homework" will pay substantial dividends when travel actually begins.

To get things started, visit websites and telephone or e-mail the **tourist offices** of each country you plan to visit (addresses in North America are listed in the Appendix). Be specific. Indicate when you will be going, where you wish to go, and what in particular you would like to see. If you have any special disabilities or interests and hobbies, be sure to mention them. By spelling out your information needs, you will obtain better responses.

You may want to start your research with some basic websites about each country in general and then do city-specific searches. For example, to obtain general information on Germany, start with the German National Tourist Office website: **www.germany-tourism.de.** Other sources of information can be found in each country chapter, or see the Appendix.

Seek out friends and neighbors who have been to Europe. No doubt you'll find their experiences flavored with their own likes and dislikes, but their stories may just spark some new ideas for your plans.

You are now ready for the decisive phase of your trip planning—**constructing an itinerary.** First, draw a blank-calendar–style form or use a calendar form on your computer covering a period from at least one week prior to your departure to a few days following your return. (Make extra copies of the form—you'll need them. Changes are common in this project!) Now begin to block your itinerary into the calendar form, being mindful that the itinerary can be changed but the number of days in a week remains fixed. Possibly by the third time through the exercise, you'll begin to see the "light at the end of the tunnel." It's only human to try to cram too many activities into a day, but it's better to discover your planning errors before starting your trip rather than in the middle of it.

With your itinerary in a calendar format, you can now determine your housing requirements, seat and sleeper reservations, and other facets of your forthcoming trip. The days blocked out in advance of your departure can show your "count-down" items—stopping the newspaper, having mail held at the post office, and so on. Make several copies of your completed itinerary, and leave some behind for the folks with whom you want to stay in touch. Above all, take copies of your itinerary with you—you'll be surprised how beneficial they are, and you will refer to them frequently.

One item that you can't leave home without is a **passport.** U.S. citizens are admitted to European countries with only a passport; a visa is not required. If you do not have one or if yours has expired, write immediately to one of the U.S. passport offices listed in the Appendix (www.travel.state.gov). Allow a minimum of one month to obtain your passport. There are ways to expedite the process, but be safe by planning ahead and making this the first order of business when you've decided to make your trip abroad.

"Know before you go"—the slogan of the U.S. Customs Service that pertains to what you can return with—also applies to the financial aspects of vacation planning. The fluctuation of the dollar's purchasing power in Europe over the past few years has left a lot of us wondering whether we can afford a vacation on the other side of the Atlantic. It is sometimes difficult to determine what effect Europe's inflation will have on your dollars once you're there. Planning in advance and purchasing most of your vacation needs in advance (particularly transportation) in American dollars are probably the most effective ways to combat inflation and price fluctuations. Buy as many of your vacation needs as you can before you go, and plan to limit your out-of-pocket costs paid in foreign currency to a minimum. This way, you are protected against fluctuating currency values.

Accommodations usually account for the greatest share of a traveler's budget. Low-cost airfare and transportation bargains, like rail passes, can get the traveler to and around Europe, but the real bite out of the buck comes when the visitor opens his or her wallet to pay for a night's lodging. Attractively priced accommodations packages are being offered by some tour operators, but too few suit the needs of independent travelers, as is the case for travelers on a rail vacation. With advance planning and advance payment, however, you can realize significant savings if you are willing to put forth the extra time and effort to do your "homework."

Well ahead of your intended departure date—preferably two months in advance, but no less than six weeks—write or e-mail the tourist offices listed in the Appendix and request information regarding lodging in the areas you intend to stay during your rail journey. The best assurance that you will have a room waiting upon arrival is to make an advance deposit directly to the hotel, then take care of the balance with the hotel's cashier when checking out. And always ask the hotel to confirm the room rate when you check in; doing so will avoid delays and possible financial embarrassment when leaving.

One final bit of advice on reducing the cost of accommodations in Europe: **Use your rail pass.** A rail pass can provide exceptional savings in housing costs by permitting you to stay *outside* the base city's center, where hotel rooms, pensions, bed-and-breakfast housing, and the like are far less expensive than their downtown counterparts. Lodgings in the suburbs, a la rail pass, can be more economical and just as convenient as those in the base cities.

Keep in mind that tourist information offices maintain extensive lists of all types of accommodations, from hostels, bed-and-breakfast establishments, and pensions to five-star luxury hotels.

When inquiring as to availability, you will be asked the inevitable question, "What do you want to be near?" Naturally, when you're traveling by rail, your response will be, "Near the rail station." You are in for a surprise—most major cities have multiple primary rail stations. A better site-selection statement might be to ask for a hotel near one of the major lines of the metro, or subway.

The budget-minded traveler may write to the European tourist offices in North America listed in the Appendix and ask for information about budget accommodations in the countries to be visited while in Europe. The plenitude of modestly priced lodgings and inexpensive restaurants, even in Europe's most expensive cities, will amaze you.

Those interested in staying in hostels must join **Hostelling International.** Adult (age 18 to 54), $28; senior citizen (age 55 and older), $18; age 17 and younger, free. For further details contact HI-AYH at (301) 495-1240 or visit www.hiayh.org.

Note: We recommend having a confirmed *accommodations reservation in your European arrival city where you will be spending the first night.*

How to Get There

Transatlantic air traffic is so frequent and varied today that no description—short of an entire book—could do it justice. Excursion fares are available in a multitudinous variety. Charter flights are available, too, and they are still mostly money savers. But some excursion rates are less expensive than charters. It is not uncommon on a regularly scheduled airliner winging its way to Europe to find that every passenger in your row of seats paid a different fare for the same flight on the same schedule with the same service!

Travel agents keep tabs on the rapidly changing airline industry. If you've dealt with a reputable travel agency over the years, contact them for air-excursion-fare options. Since many airlines no longer pay commissions to travel agents, you may have to pay a service fee. We think it's worth it, but if you have lots of leisure time, call the various airlines' toll-free telephone numbers and ask them for fare information or visit their websites. You may also use one of the various online fare services. Be sure you use a well-known, reputable site, and remember that some charter and low-cost airlines may not have fares listed on these sites. We have listed the contact information for a few airlines in the Appendix. Don't be disturbed if you receive a variety of responses and be willing to spend some time to get the best fare.

Regarding charter flights, inquire about them, but investigate thoroughly before making any final decisions. Here again, get your travel agent involved, even if it's only to obtain the tickets. Even some of the most reputable air-charter carriers still operate on a "Go–No Go" basis. This means that if enough passengers sign up for the flight, it will go as scheduled; if not enough passengers are booked, the flight will be scrubbed.

European Rail Passes

A rail pass provides flexibility and economy if you are making several trips, especially any over long distances. A point-to-point ticket is, of course, good for travel from one city to another. You can, though, consult the fares between major cities listed on the websites of the companies in the "To Purchase Passes" section of the Appendix. Add up the cost of each leg of your journey, and then compare it to the cost of a rail pass to see what economically works best for your trip.

Today's rail traveler has a wide choice of rail passes available, from the 28-country Eurail Global Pass to regional passes encompassing groups of countries and individual, or national, country passes.

Note: A comprehensive list of prices and types of rail passes can be found in the Appendix of this edition.

How Long Is a Rail Pass Day?

There are many different types and price ranges of rail passes available that provide *unlimited* rail transportation for a specified number of days. A "rail pass day" runs from midnight to midnight, during which time it is possible to make unlimited on-and-off-the-train journeys. Those with flexible rail passes can extend the use of their passes by taking advantage of the overnight bonus. This allows passengers on overnight *direct* trains departing after 1900 to count the trip toward the next day of train travel. This is a great way to get the most out of your pass on long treks, plus be rested for a full day of sightseeing. Flexible passes are described later in this section.

Rail Pass Validation

You have six months from the issue date of the rail pass (the date of purchase stamped on your pass) in which to begin using it. Prior to boarding your first train in Europe, present your pass for validation at the rail station. Allow for a little extra time for the validation process, but once your pass is validated, that ends standing in line to buy another ticket—a real convenience.

- Do not make any entries (such as filling in your passport number) prior to validation.
- Although it is not a part of the validation process, write the starting and ending dates of your pass validation period on a piece of paper and hand it to the clerk along with your pass and passport. (Remember, Europeans write the day before the month; thus, 10/07/16 would mean July 10, 2016.)
- Be certain the clerk agrees to the dates before he or she enters the validity period on your pass.
- Double-check the validation dates before accepting the pass. If an error is made in either the dates or your passport number, have it corrected immediately.
- The clerk then enters your passport number and stamps the pass.
- Do not remove the pass from its cover.

Note: Once validated, your rail pass is neither refundable nor replaceable, so guard it with the same attention you give to your cash, traveler's checks, and passport.

Eurail Global Passes

Eurail Global passes are valid for unlimited rail travel (in the class indicated on the pass) on the national railways and some private railway companies in the following 28 countries: Austria, Belgium, Bosnia, Bulgaria, Croatia, Czech Republic, Denmark, Finland, France, Germany, Greece, Hungary, Ireland (Republic of), Italy, Luxembourg, Macedonia, Montenegro, the Netherlands, Norway, Poland, Portugal, Romania, Serbia, Slovakia, Slovenia, Spain, Sweden, Switzerland.

Some premier trains, such as AVE, Eurostar, and Thalys, require a supplement. Eurail passes, however, provide a substantial discount on the fare, as well as free or reduced-rate travel on selected ferries, lake steamers, and some buses. More information on travel bonuses offered by each country is listed in the individual country chapters of this edition. A complete list of bonuses, a Eurail map, and timetable also come free with your rail pass.

There are two basic types of Eurail Global passes: consecutive-day and flexible-day passes. **Consecutive-day passes** are valid for an unlimited number of rail journeys during the number of rail pass days you purchase, which constitutes the pass's "validity" period. For example, if you purchased a 15-day Eurail Global Pass and took your first train trip on January 1, your pass would be valid for use as many times as you want in any of the aforementioned countries until midnight on January 15. We call it the "tick-tock" pass.

Flexible-type Eurail Global passes provide exactly what the "Eurail Global Pass Flexi" name implies—flexibility. Flexipasses work especially well if you plan to stay in one place and not travel for a few days. You choose the number of travel days, either 10 or 15, and use any or all of them within a two-month validity period. Thus, while you're not traveling, your rail pass is not "ticking" away. For example, if you purchase a 10-day Eurail Global Pass Flexi, you will have 10 boxes on your pass to write the dates of the days on which you use the train(s). We recommend, however, that you write in the date on the date that you travel, rather than in advance, just in case you want to change your travel plans at the last minute. When entering the date, remember the format: day first and then the month.

Eurail Global Pass

Valid for unlimited first-class rail travel. Choose from five consecutive-day durations: 15 days, 21 days, one month, two months, or three months. Go as you please, stop where and when you want. This pass is an excellent value for anyone visiting several countries.

Eurail Global Pass Saver

Unlimited first-class rail travel for two to five people traveling together at all times in any or all of the previously listed 28 European countries, with the same privileges and choice of validity periods as the basic Eurail Global Pass.

Eurail Global Pass Youth

For those who are still younger than age 26 but at least age 12 on their first day of train travel, this pass provides unlimited second-class rail travel in any or all of the aforementioned 28 countries. It entitles you to the same privileges and choice of validity periods as the first-class Eurail Global Pass, except it is valid for second-class travel only.

Eurail Global Pass Flexi

Unlimited first-class rail travel in any or all of the aforementioned 28 countries. Buy either 10 or 15 travel days and use them within two months.

Eurail Global Pass Saver Flexi

Unlimited first-class rail travel for two to five people traveling together at all times in any or all of the aforementioned 28 countries. Purchase either 10 or 15 travel days to be used within two months.

Eurail Global Pass Youth Flexi

Unlimited second-class rail travel for passengers younger than age 26 but at least age 12 on their first day of travel. Purchase either 10 or 15 days of travel to be used within two months.

Eurail Select Pass

This rail pass is versatile but somewhat more complicated than other passes. It provides unlimited first-class rail travel for 4, 5, 6, 8, or 10 days within a two-month validity period in any 2 to 4 adjoining countries in the Eurail system. The travel days may be used consecutively or nonconsecutively. The countries you choose must be adjoining by country border and must be connected by direct train service (i.e., not by rail service through another country) or by ship. Confused? The following list clarifies which countries qualify.

Country	Connected by train or ship to
Austria	Germany, Hungary, Italy, Switzerland, Slovenia/Croatia*
Benelux*	Germany, Ireland
Bulgaria/Serbia/ Montenegro*	Croatia/Slovenia*, Hungary, Romania, Greece
Croatia/Slovenia*	Austria, Bulgaria/Serbia/Montenegro*, Hungary, Italy
Czech Republic	Austria, Germany
Denmark	Germany, Norway, Sweden
Finland	Germany, Sweden
Germany	Austria, Benelux*, Denmark, Finland, Switzerland, Sweden
Greece	Italy, Bulgaria/Serbia/Montenegro*

Hungary	Austria, Bulgaria/Serbia/Montenegro*, Romania, Croatia/Slovenia*
Ireland	Benelux*
Italy	Austria, Croatia/Slovenia*, Greece, Spain, Switzerland
Norway	Denmark, Sweden
Portugal	Spain
Romania	Bulgaria/Serbia/Montenegro*, Hungary
Spain	Italy, Portugal
Sweden	Denmark, Finland, Germany, Norway
Switzerland	Austria, Germany, Italy

* For the purposes of this pass, these country combinations are considered one country: Benelux (Belgium, the Netherlands, and Luxembourg), Croatia/Slovenia, and Bulgaria/Serbia/Montenegro.

Eurail Select Pass Saver

This offers the same benefits and conditions as the aforementioned Eurail Select Pass but is designed for two or more persons traveling together. Each person receives a 15 percent discount.

Eurail Select Pass Youth

Travelers must be under the age of 26 but at least age 12 on the first day of travel. Valid for unlimited second-class rail travel in three adjoining countries of your choice. Other benefits and conditions are the same as the first-class Eurail Select Pass.

Eurail also offers many other types of rail passes: single-country, two-country, and regional passes. For a full listing of passes and prices, please refer to the Appendix.

Europe's Passenger Trains

Europe's passenger trains range from perky little cogwheel cars that ascend the Alps to the sleek, high-tech, high-speed trains that whisk you to your destination at an average speed of 186 mph. In between are international **EuroCity** (EC) express trains running on the main lines, national **InterCity** (IC) and regional trains providing express services within a country's borders, and the extensive collection of railcars that ply suburban lines.

The basis of Western Europe's high-speed rail traffic is a flawless rail bed equipped with endless-welded track, which enables the trains to glide smoothly enough to permit dining without fear that the next curve might slosh your coffee. The newer high-speed passenger trains include a whole stable full of various passenger car (carriage) types, including plush compartment interiors, comfortable seats, a children's play area, and businesslike amenities such as computer hookups and telephones.

TGVs (*train à grande vitesse*, or train of great speed) and **Thalys** trains are at the very heart of the European high-speed rail network connecting France with Belgium, the Netherlands, Germany, and Switzerland. The **TGV Atlantique** cruises at speeds up to 186 mph to link Paris with western and southwestern France. France's **TGV Méditerranée** (TGV Med) connects Paris with Avignon in 2 hours 40 minutes, Marseilles in only 3 hours, Montpellier in 3 hours 15 minutes, and Nice in 5 hours 36 minutes. Travel time to 140 cities was reduced by up to one hour and frequency of service increased on the Paris to Marseilles route from 11 to 17 trains per day and on the Paris to Nice route from 3 trains per day to 6. TGV Med is a double-decker train that can accommodate up to 1,056 passengers in total comfort. The newest "superstar" among the TGV lines is the **TGV Est Europeén** which broke the TGV's previous world speed record (320 mph, or 515 km/h) in April 2007 by traveling at 357 mph! The TGV Est slashed rail travel times not only between Paris and cities in eastern France but also to cities such as Luxembourg City; Frankfurt, Munich, and Stuttgart in Germany; and Basel and Zurich in Switzerland. TGV high-speed lines also connect Paris's Charles de Gaulle Airport and Disneyland Paris with many other major French cities.

Germany's **InterCity Express** (ICE) service provides cars with increased legroom, headphones, and even some video systems built into the seat backs. The ICE 3 train was unveiled in Berlin at Expo 2000. This new member of the ICE family is now the fastest not only in speed but also in acceleration.

Italy has not only a "tilting tower" (the Leaning Tower of Pisa) but also "tilting" trains termed **Eurostar Italia.** You can sit back and relax with snacks and an espresso while the comfortable ETR 500 Pendolino trains whisk you to your destination at an operating speed of more than 150 mph.

The British-Belgian-French–modified TGVs, known as **"Eurostar"** trains, connect Britain with Continental Europe. Connecting through London and the English Channel tunnel (Chunnel) to Paris or Brussels, the Eurostar trains make the British connection between St. Pancras International Station and Paris's Gare du Nord in 2 hours 15 minutes, and to Brussels Midi Station in 1 hour 15 minutes, and London to Lille in only 1 hour 20 minutes. Even the airlines can't get you there any faster if you consider the amount of time it takes from city center to the airport, going through security and customs, and then transportation from the arrival airport to city center.

The "Chunnel" and Eurostar Trains

On May 6, 1994, England's Queen Elizabeth II and France's President François Mitterand inaugurated a new era in European train travel—the linking of England and France via a tunnel that runs underground and beneath the English Channel. More than 17 million tons of earth were moved to build the two rail tunnels (one for northbound and one for southbound traffic) and one service tunnel. The Chunnel has proven to be one of the world's largest undertakings. The project cost more than $13 billion and took seven years to complete.

Napoleon's engineer, Albert Mathieu, planned the first tunnel in 1802, incorporating an underground passage with ventilation chimneys above the waves. For obvious reasons the British were nervous. Later, in 1880, the first real attempt at a tunnel was undertaken by Colonel Beaumont, who bored 2,000 meters into the earth before abandoning the project. When work on another tunnel began in 1974, the Beaumont tunnel was found to be in good condition. Construction of the current tunnels began in 1987; they are 38 kilometers in length undersea and have an average depth of 40 meters under the seabed.

Operated by a British railway operating company (Eurostar) and by the French (SNCF) and Belgian (SNCB) railways, the Eurotunnel provides three different types of service between England and the Continent. Eurostar provides passenger service, and Le Shuttle provides automobile, coach, and lorry service between Folkstone and Calais. International rail freight rounds out the list.

Travel times from London to Paris were reduced from more than 9 and a half hours to 2 hours 15 minutes, and Brussels is only 1 hour and 15 minutes away, thus making a European Capitals tour nothing more than a day excursion. Eurail pass holders receive a discount on Eurostar tickets. Eurostar also serves Lille and Calais in Northern France, Marne-la-Valle to Euro Disney just east of Paris, and Ashford in England. There are also some additional ski trains during the winter months.

The sleek **Eurostar** trains (Trans Manche Super Trains) each carry nearly 800 passengers (25 in premium first class, 206 in first class, and 548 in second class) and reach speeds of 186 mph in France and 100 mph through the Chunnel and in England. The train is based primarily on the TGV but was redesigned to accommodate the three different voltage types encountered en route. The trains are accessible to disabled passengers and those with special needs. Arrangements may be made up to 48 hours prior to departure by calling Eurostar Complimentary Assistance Service in the United Kingdom at +44 (1233) 617575. Sufficient storage for luggage is provided.

Families traveling with children may opt for coaches 1 or 18, where facilities are offered for baby changing and flip-up seats allow more room for kids. Ask the train manager for a children's pack of things to do while traveling.

For security reasons, you are required to check in at the Eurostar terminal at least 30 minutes prior to departure. We suggest allowing a bit more time. This train is long (nearly a quarter of a mile) and the walk to your seat may be a lengthy one. After check-in and passing through the security and passport control, you will find a boarding-area lounge, cafeteria, bar, and shops.

Those taking advantage of a trip from Paris or Brussels to London on a Eurostar train are in for a treat. The trains offer the comfort and amenities comparable to few other trains in the world. From departure you're in store for a smooth, quiet ride, and even when you enter the tunnel, the only noticeable change is the sudden darkness outside the windows. Those concerned with changes in air pressure needn't worry. Air flow through the tunnel is regulated to minimize changes in pressure, and few passengers, if any, notice discomfort.

Eurostar staff are multilingual and are available to provide assistance from the minute you enter the terminal to the minute you exit the platform. You'll notice them right away, dressed in navy blue uniforms accented with yellow scarves or ties. If you have any questions, don't be shy—they're there to serve you, and serve you they do.

Passengers traveling first class are treated to an onboard gourmet meal with wine ranging from breakfast to dinner, depending upon the time of day. Second-class passengers won't starve either, as a buffet car and roving refreshment-cart services are available at reasonable costs.

Given the frequency of rail service and the speed of travel, it's easy to see how a "quick trip" to Paris, Brussels, or any Continental destination can be accomplished. On the following pages are the schedules for Eurostar trains running between London, Paris, and Brussels.

Notes

- Holders of any of the varieties of Eurail, Benelux, BritRail or French rail passes receive discounts on Eurostar services.
- Only BritRail passes may be used for rail travel within Britain.
- All Eurostar trains are nonsmoking.

To purchase one-way or round-trip Eurostar tickets or for scheduling information on trains to other cities, visit www.eurostar.com.

London—Paris*

DEPART LONDON St. Pancras International	ARRIVE PARIS Gare du Nord	TRAIN NUMBER	NOTES
0540	0917	9080	M–F
0701	1017	9004	M–F
0755	1117	9008	M–Sa
0819	1147	9010	Su
0917	1247	9014	M–F
1024	1347	9018	Exc. Sa
1224	1547	9024	Daily
1331	1647	9028	Daily
1531	1847	9036	Daily
1631	1947	9040	Daily
1731	2047	9044	Daily
1801	2117	9046	M–F
1901	2217	9050	Exc. Sa
2001	2317	9054	Daily

* Local time. Continental Europe is 1 hour ahead of the United Kingdom. No service on December 25.

Paris—London*

DEPART PARIS Gare du Nord	ARRIVE LONDON St. Pancras International	TRAIN NUMBER	NOTES
0713	0832	9007	M–Sa
0813	0930	9011	Sa–Su
0913	1039	9015	Daily
1013	1130	9019	M–F
1113	1239	9023	Daily
1313	1439	9031	Daily
1513	1630	9039	Daily
1613	1739	9043	Daily
1713	1832	9047	Daily
1813	1939	9051	Exc. Sa
1913	2039	9055	Daily
2013	2139	9059	Daily
2113	2239	9063	Exc. Sa

* Local time. Continental Europe is 1 hour ahead of the United Kingdom. No service on December 25.

London—Brussels*

DEPART LONDON St. Pancras International	ARRIVE BRUSSELS Midi	TRAIN NUMBER	NOTES
0650	1007	9110	M–F
0657	1005	9110	Sa Only
0855	1205	9116	Daily
1058	1405	9126	Exc. Su
1258	1608	9132	Daily
1504	1805	9140	Exc. Sa
1604	1905	9144	Sa
1704	2005	9148	Exc. Sa
1804	2105	9152	M–F
1904	2208	9156	Sa–Su

* Local time. Continental Europe is 1 hour ahead of the United Kingdom. No service on December 25.

Brussels—London*

DEPART BRUSSELS Midi	ARRIVE LONDON St. Pancras International	TRAIN NUMBER	NOTES
0656	0759	9109	M Only
0756	0857	9113	Exc. Su
0852	0957	9117	Daily
1056	1157	9125	M–F
1252	1405	9133	Exc. Su
1456	1605	9141	Daily
1656	1803	9149	Exc. Su
1756	1903	9153	M–F
1856	1957	9157	Exc. Sa
1952	2103	9161	Daily

* Local time. Continental Europe is 1 hour ahead of the United Kingdom. No service on December 25.

London—Disneyland Paris

DEPART LONDON St. Pancras International	ARRIVE DISNEYLAND PARIS Marne-La-Vallee	TRAIN NUMBER
1014	1402	9074

DEPART DISNEYLAND PARIS Marne-La-Vallee	ARRIVE LONDON St. Pancras International	TRAIN NUMBER
1649	1847	9057

Night Trains/Hotel Trains

Although we usually advocate going to Europe to see it, not sleep through it, today's European overnight trains provide a most comfortable and convenient means of transport across long distances. And there's an aura of romance on Europe's luxurious hotel trains.

There is a great variety of accommodations (and prices) on night trains, ranging from comfortable reclining seats in second class on certain trains, termed "sleeperettes," to luxurious hotel-style trains complete with a lobby area, concierge, and restaurant car.

All night trains require reservations, and rail passes do not cover the cost of sleeping accommodations. You must pay a supplement, which varies according to the type of accommodations and type of train. For example, the supplemental cost per person to rail pass holders for a reclining seat with a headrest and reading lamp on the CityNightLine trains connecting Germany with Switzerland and Austria is only about $32.

Traditional night trains usually do not have full restaurant service, but the steward can provide drinks and snacks, or, of course, you can bring your own. Night trains are normally composed of standard sleeping cars, couchette cars (with six berths per compartment in second class and four-berth compartments in first), plus seats.

EuroNight (EN) trains are usually air-conditioned and provide additional comfort and services with the same basic facilities as the traditional sleeping-car trains. EN trains offer a wash basin with soap, towels, and a power plug; a real bed with sheets, pillows, and blankets; complimentary mineral water, snacks, and a continental breakfast served in the cabin.

For luxury, comfort, and privacy, Europe's high-tech, high-comfort **hotel trains** are top of the line. There are three main categories of accommodations on hotel trains: Tourist, First, and Luxury Class. Tourist Class provides four beds in one compartment. First Class has one- or two-bed compartments. Both Tourist and First Class have toilet facilities at the end of each rail car. Luxury Class features one- and two-bed compartments with toilet and shower facilities inside the compartment.

CityNightLine trains are first-class night trains featuring high-quality, double-decked, hotel-style sleeping accommodations and single-level sleeperette cars with reclining seats. The Deluxe category provides spacious two-bed compartments with shower, toilet, wash basin, closet, table and chairs, down covers, a welcome drink and breakfast, and panoramic windows. The Economy category consists of two- and four-bed compartments and quads with washing facilities, a closet, down covers, mineral water, and breakfast. These trains also feature reclining seats. CityNightLine routes include Zürich to Berlin (via Frankfurt), Dresden (via Leipzig), Hamburg (via Dortmund) and Norddeich; and Dortmund to Vienna (via Cologne–Frankfurt). All cars are nonsmoking, except in the bar and service car.

DB-Nachtzugs (German Rail) are high-quality overnight hotel trains connecting major cities in Germany and Denmark. Four categories are available: Deluxe and Economy compartment amenities are the same as CityNightLine trains. DB-Nachtzugs also include couchette cars, reclining seats, and a lounge car. Popular international routes include Berlin–Amsterdam; Berlin/Hamburg–Brussels, Munich, and Paris; Hamburg–Frankfurt–Stuttgart; and Munich/Stuttgart/Frankfurt–Copenhagen.

The tilting Spanish **Elipsos** trains operate within Spain and internationally into Portugal, France, Italy, and Switzerland. The Gran Clase sleeping cars include private toilet and shower facilities; Turista Class offers four-berth compartments; or, for economy, choose the sleeperette seats. Trains carrying the Gran Clase cars include the famous *Pau Casals* (Barcelona–Geneva, Bern, and Zürich), the *Antonio Machado* (Barcelona–Seville/Malaga), the *Joan Miro* (Barcelona–Paris), *Francisco de Goya* (Paris–Madrid), *Salvador Dali* (Barcelona–Milan), and the *Lusitania* (Madrid–Lisbon).

Generally speaking, the least expensive trains with sleeping accommodations are in southern and eastern Europe; northern and central Europe are the most expensive. The sleeperette, or reclining seat, is the least expensive type of accommodation, and Luxury (or Deluxe) Class on hotel trains is the most expensive.

The **OverNight Express** (Dutch) runs from Amsterdam to Munich daily, departing at 2031, and from Munich to Amsterdam daily. Choose from three options: the traditional sleeper, a couchette (four per compartment), or the more economical reclining seat. You can have dinner on the train, sleep, and have breakfast the following morning—a great way to arrive refreshed, well rested, and ready to explore your new destination.

Seat Reservations

Most international and long-distance trains *require* seat reservations, including TGVs, Eurostars, InterCity and AVEs, EuroCity trains, some ICEs, and specialty sightseeing trains such as those in Switzerland (*Glacier Express, Bernina Express, Crystal Panoramic,* and the *William Tell Express*).

A computerized reservation system linking the European rail routes is available in every major rail terminal in Europe. Check the train departure board—if there is an **"R"** next to that train, seat reservations are mandatory, and you should not board without one. Seat reservations for TGVs and many other types of trains can be made at automatic reservation-ticket dispensers in the rail stations.

Eurostar Fares: London—Paris or Brussels

Eurostar fares are provided in U.S. dollars, one-way in either direction, and are subject to change at the discretion of the railways.

Fare Type	1st Class	Standard Class	Conditions
Passholder*	$193	$116	Exchangeable before travel; nonrefundable
Full Fare	$336	$285	Exchangeable and partially refundable before travel
Business Premier	$480	NA	Refundable up to 2 mo after travel date; exchangeable
Economy	$193	$93	Min. 1 night stay
Senior	$108	$65	Age 60 and older
Youth	$108	$65	Younger than age 26 on day of travel; nonrefundable
Child	$105	$62	Age 4–11
Wheelchair Adult†	$41	NA	
Wheelchair Companion†	$41	NA	
Wheelchair Child†	$41	NA	

*Holders of Eurail, BritRail, France, and Benelux passes, and holders of the Eurail Benelux–Germany Pass. Nonrefundable; may be exchanged once prior to departure; exchange only in Europe.

† 100% refundable up to 2 months after travel date; exchangeable.

- Seat reservations are mandatory on all Eurostar trains
- Tickets issued include reservation on the same voucher (inclusive price)
- 1st Class includes meal served at your seat

Seat reservations in Europe cost about $5 each, and this cost is not included in a rail pass. Advance seat reservations may be made from North America; however, they are more expensive and nonrefundable. If you choose to make seat reservations from North America, you may make them through the same place you purchase your rail pass. We do recommend making them for long-distance/express trains during high season and if traveling on or near a holiday.

The farther south you travel in Europe, the more important it becomes to have seat reservations, even if they are not required. Always have seat reservations when traveling in Italy and Greece. Seat reservations are not, however, accepted for most local trains, nor for trains traveling within the borders of Belgium, the Netherlands, Luxembourg, or Switzerland, with the exception of specialty trains.

To ensure that you receive the proper reservation:

- **Determine the day and date of your travel.** Remember, Europeans reverse the order of the month and day when writing dates. Day, month, and then year is the standard reading. For example, June 15, 2008, appears as 15/06/08 and not as 06/15/08.
- **Check the train schedules** posted in the rail stations for the train number, its departure time, and arrival time at your destination.
- **Print this information** on a piece of paper, starting with the date, the train number, and the departure time. Draw a short arrow, and then add the arrival time of the train and the name of your destination.
- **Indicate the number of seat reservations required.** Your seat reservation will identify the class of travel (first or second), smoking or nonsmoking, car number, and, in most cases, the seat number(s).

Plan to be on the train platform several minutes prior to scheduled departure. European trains stop only for a short time at intermediate stations to let passengers on and off, and stops of only one or two minutes are usual. To save a lot of scurrying around when the train arrives, **check the illustrated train composition diagrams** displayed on the platforms to determine the approximate positioning of your train's first- and second-class coaches.

Then, as your train approaches, look for *either* a large number **"1"** on or near the doors or a yellow stripe above the train windows to indicate first-class cars if you have a first-class rail pass and/or a first-class seat reservation. Second-class cars are indicated with a large **"2"** on or near the doors.

Train Schedules

Most European rail stations have train arrival and departure times prominently posted, usually by huge digital display boards. The printed ones posted are easily recognized by their background color—**departure times are printed on yellow; arrival times on white.** Intermediate stops, train platform, and track numbers are posted as well. In case of discrepancy, the digital display boards take precedence. Although the time schedules may change, the track numbers seldom change.

Schedules are listed chronologically in 24-hour time from 0001 (one minute after midnight) to 1200 (noon) and to 2400 (midnight)—for instance, a departure time of 1843 would be equal to 6:43 p.m. *Note:* Arrival times for overnight/sleeper train schedules in this book show "+1" after the arrival time. This means your train arrives at the listed time on the following day.

Train information and reservation offices in the stations also provide printed mini-schedules listing rail services between two specific points. They're free. These offices have national and international schedules as well.

Train schedules presented in this edition of *Europe by Eurail* are updated to press time. They are, however, *for planning purposes only.* When purchasing a rail pass, you are entitled to receive a **free timetable and map** of the major rail connections. Depending on the amount of travel you will be doing, we would also suggest purchasing a European Rail Timetable as a companion to this book, www.europeanrailtimetable.eu.

Train Splitting

When international trains in Europe have multiple destinations, sometimes passenger coaches are "split" en route, with cars going to different cities. To make certain you end up where you want to be:

- **Check the train sideboards** displaying the departure point, stops en route, and the final destination.
- **Announce your destination** to the conductor as he or she checks your rail pass.
- **Stay in your seat** when the train halts at a terminal for "splitting" the coaches. Since the splitting process occurs quickly, if you are in another part of the train you could easily end up at the wrong destination—sans suitcase and your fellow travelers.

There may also be times when two trains are scheduled to depart on the same track—one in each direction, of course. Check for your train's departure position; otherwise, you might be standing at the wrong end of the track as your train pulls away.

Trip Tips

Before You Go

If there have been any break-ins in your neighborhood, you should take steps to ensure that a break-in doesn't happen to you while you are gone. Alert the neighbors to keep a watchful eye for suspicious people and their activities. Many professional thieves have been known to park in a driveway in broad daylight with a moving van. The police should be advised regarding your absence: depending on where you live, they may conduct regular checks of your house. Also, check with the insurance agency that writes your homeowner's policy. Ask the same question they ask in those television commercials: "Am I covered?" You may need additional coverage during your absence. One final caution: Don't announce your forthcoming vacation plans in the newspapers or on any social media site. You may trust all of your online friends, but do you trust all of their friends, who may also be able to see your information? Thieves can read, too. Save the social column, and the posting of pictures for your friends to be jealous of, for your return.

What to Take?

Half the clothes and twice the money! Obviously, the practical answer to this question is, "As little as possible." We usually tend to pack everything we might conceivably use during a vacation, lug it everywhere, use it very little, and return home with longer arms. In these days of wash-and-wear fabrics (and deodorants), such an approach is not necessary. A good recommendation is to take **one medium-size suitcase with wheels** and a shoulder bag or two small bags. Hold to this rule, and you will have a more comfortable trip. Regardless of how comfortably warm you expect the weather to be at your destination, pack a sweater. Brief cold spells in Europe are not uncommon. Stow a small pocket flashlight in your shoulder bag together with a collapsible umbrella or rain hat in the "unlikely event" that you may need them.

Bring a washcloth if you normally use one, since they generally are not found in European hotels. Take an **electrical converter** and **adapter plugs** for your electrical appliances, such as electrical razors and hair dryers. Travel-size, dual-voltage hair dryers are more convenient—you only need to switch the voltage to the European 220 and add the appropriate adapter plug.

If you must take expensive jewelry with you (which we do not recommend), take a copy of its **insurance appraisal** as proof of purchase to customs officials upon your return. The same for watches produced by foreign manufacturers. You may have bought that solid-gold Rolex in a St. Louis pawnshop for a song, but the customs inspector could have you singing a different tune if you can't come up with the paperwork! Also bring **proof of purchase** on any expensive items you are traveling with, such as your laptop computer or video camera.

If you wear prescription eyeglasses or contact lenses, take a copy of the **eyeglass or contact lenses prescription** with you. The same applies for **prescription medications.** Even if you use only over-the-counter drug products, we suggest taking an adequate supply of the item in its original container. Many such products are not available in Europe or are sold under a different label or packaging.

Cash, Currencies, and Cards

On January 1, 2002, the **euro** (abbreviation is EUR; symbol €) became the legal tender for 12 of the countries in *Europe by Eurail*: Austria, Belgium, Finland, France, Germany, Greece, Republic of Ireland, Italy, Luxembourg, the Netherlands, Portugal, and Spain. Based on the decimal system, 100 "cents" equals 1 euro and there are eight different coins and seven different banknotes. Each country may use a different term for the subunit "cents." For example, France is permitted to use the term "euro-centimes" and Germany to use "euro-pfennig." Coins are issued in 1, 2, 5, 10, 20, and 50 euro cents, as well as 1-euro and 2-euro coins. Banknotes are issued in 5, 10, 20, 50, 100, 200, and 500 euro denominations.

At press time, $1.00 U.S. = 0.90 EUR. For more information on converting from U.S. dollars to euros and to other countries' national currencies, visit the website **www.xe.com/ucc** or create your own "Cheat Sheet for Travelers" online at

www.oanda.com/currency/travel-exchange-rates. You can print out the conversion rates in a wallet-size format for each country you intend to visit. You can also purchase an electronic foreign exchange rate converter to carry with you.

Don't carry more cash than you can afford to lose; use **ATMs** (automated teller machines) or carry traveler's checks. You will, of course, need some cash on your flight to pay for tips, snacks, refreshments, and taxi fares at your arrival city. U.S. currency will usually do, but don't carry it all in one big roll—distribute it around in pockets, briefcase, money clip, and/or money belt. A money belt is an ideal way to carry larger notes. Getting some smaller denominations of the local currency is always a great idea for tipping.

ATMs offer the best exchange rate on foreign currencies, but if you plan to use them, do your homework first. Ask your bank for a list of ATM locations in the countries where you plan to travel and whether your magnetic imprint needs to be modified to work in foreign ATMs. Be certain to know your PIN number, and inquire if the bank will charge you per overseas cash withdrawal. Also, remember that ATM PIN numbers in Europe are four digits; six digits will not work. The two largest international ATM networks are Visa/Plus and MasterCard/Cirrus. To find out which network your bank uses, you can look on the back of your card for the network logo. To find the ATM locations abroad for Visa/Plus, write to Visa International, 900 Metro Center Boulevard, M1-9C, Foster City, CA 94404, or access the website at www.visa.com; for MasterCard/Cirrus, call (800) 4-CIRRUS, or access its website at www.mastercard.com.

Although U.S. banks levy surcharges for the luxury of using their machines, these charges do not extend to U.S.-issued cards at machines overseas. Remember, though, that a cash withdrawal on a credit card is like a "temporary mini-loan," and there is an interest charge.

You can avoid interest charges by using a **debit card** (whereby cash withdrawals and purchases are deducted from your checking account). Debit cards have a major drawback, however; it is far more difficult to refute billing errors when the money has already been withdrawn from your checking account. You probably will still pay a fee of around $2 per withdrawal with a debit card. If you do carry traveler's checks, cash them at the branch-bank facilities located in or near railway stations and airports. Banks and official currency-exchange services are required to pay the official exchange rates. Hotels and stores seldom give you the full exchange value and often add substantial service fees. Credit cards are handy for paying the larger expenses, such as hotels and restaurants. The charge is converted into dollars at the applicable exchange rate on the date the charge is posted.

Make a list of credit card, traveler's check, airline ticket, and rail pass numbers that you plan to take. With a computer and a scanner, you can put copies of your documents on a USB thumb drive. When purchasing your rail pass, inquire about Pass Protection, a type of travel insurance covering any unused portion of the pass in case of loss or theft while abroad. Leave a copy of your list at home and pack one in your suitcase or carry-on bag. Make **two copies of your passport.** Leave one copy at home and take the other one with you. Carry a certified copy of your birth certificate and a few extra passport photos. Taking the time to do this will save you days of delay on your trip if your passport is lost or stolen. If your passport is lost or stolen, report it to the local police and contact the nearest U.S. embassy or consulate.

Cameras

If you plan to take an expensive foreign-made camera that you purchased in the United States, bring the sales slip. Otherwise, go to a U.S. Customs Office before leaving the country and have your equipment registered. Carry a copy of the sales slip or the registration form with your passport, and keep a spare copy tucked away in the camera case or your shoulder bag.

Some quick thoughts for those of you considering bringing or buying a digital camera. Unless you are serious about cameras, don't get caught up in buying the newest, best camera, with the most megapixels. Find a reasonably sized camera which is easy to use and fits your budget. (Currently, $200–$300 will buy you an excellent portable model, without expensive extra features you are unlikely to use.) Spend time before your trip getting comfortable with at least the basic features of your camera. You don't want to be desperately fumbling with your camera while speeding by a shepherd with his flock in the highlands of Scotland! Your digital camera will probably take a memory card of some kind. Given that taking your laptop abroad is probably not a good idea, our suggestion is to buy four or five smaller cards instead of one or two larger cards. This reduces the number of pictures that you lose if your camera is lost or stolen, or if a card goes bad. Several companies make small padded wallets that carry your extra cards independent of your camera and camera bag, and can stay on your person to keep your pictures from being lost. If your camera uses rechargeable batteries, an extra set is recommended. Also, be sure to have the necessary adapters for charging the camera battery in your hotel room.

En Route Tips

Something about flying makes it more demanding on your system than a similar amount of time spent at home or in the office. For North Americans, it takes an entire day to reach Europe by air and an entire day to return. A transatlantic trip with a minimum of inconveniences is what we're after. Here are some suggestions that we've found helpful on our flights.

In-Flight Comfort. If you plan to catch some shut-eye en route, ask for a seat alongside a bulkhead. Bulkheads don't mind being leaned on, but passengers do. If you need more legroom, sit in an emergency exit row, but only if you are physically capable of standing and opening the exit hatch if necessary. Also, be sure your seat reclines. On some planes the seats in front of the emergency exits do not recline.

Opt for seats in the forward section of the airplane; passengers in the forward section generally experience less vibration and engine noise.

Wear loose clothing. Unfasten your shoes, but don't take them off. Your feet will swell following several hours of immobility at airplane altitudes. The best remedy is to walk the length of the aisle in the airplane every hour or so. Try deep knee bends. To reduce swelling, consider wearing elastic stockings.

Flying dehydrates your body. Drink lots of water and watch what you mix with it—alcohol and soda drinks dehydrate, too. Special meals for special diets are no problem with the airlines, but requests should be made at the same time as reservations and reconfirmed 48 hours prior to departure.

Jet Lag—What to Do about It. Although the flying time aboard most commercial jet airliners ranges from seven to eight hours, airport to airport, it will be Day 2 before you arrive in Europe. (There are a few daytime eastbound transatlantic flights, but most depart in the evening during Day 1 and arrive the following morning; that is, Day 2.) During the flight you will be exposed to a cocktail hour, a dinner hour, and a break for an after-dinner drink, followed by a full-length feature movie.

In the morning, as the sun rises in the east over Europe, you'll be awakened for breakfast an hour or so before landing.

Add up the time consumed by all the scheduled events while en route, and you'll quickly conclude that your night spent in the sky over the Atlantic Ocean consisted of many things—except sleep. Even if you did manage to sleep during the entire trip instead of eating, drinking, and watching movies, your body and all its functions will be arriving in Europe a few hours after midnight by North American time. You will crave adjustment to the phenomenon known as jet lag, which will be trying its best to interrupt your plans for a carefree vacation.

The following explanation of what jet lag is and some means to combat it should prove helpful to any traveler undergoing four or more hours of time change.

The human body has numerous rhythms; sleep is one of them. Even without sunlight, as in a cave, the body will still maintain a twenty-four-hour awake/asleep cycle. The heart rate falls to a very low ebb in the early hours of the morning, when you are usually asleep. Body temperature, which affects the mental processes, also drops during this time. Consequently, if an air traveler is transported rapidly to a time zone five or six hours ahead of that of the departure point, even though it may be 8:00 or 9:00 a.m. at the arrival point in local time, the traveler's body functions are at a low ebb. As a result, the traveler feels subpar, and this feeling can persist for as long as two or three days unless something is done to correct it.

To cope effectively with jet lag, start varying your normal sleep-eat-work pattern a week or so before your departure. If you are normally up by 7:00 a.m. and in bed around 11:00 p.m. or so, get up earlier and go to bed later for a few days. Then reverse the procedure by sleeping in a bit in the morning and going to bed ahead of your normal time. Vary your mealtimes, possibly putting off breakfast until lunchtime. This will condition your body to accept changes in routines. In turn, when the big transatlantic change comes, it won't be as much of a shock on your system.

Remember, to lessen the effects of jet lag en route, avoid excessive drinking of alcohol and soda and eating. Set your watch to local time at your destination as you descend on your flight. By doing this, you subconsciously accelerate your adjustment to the new time zone. For example, how many times have you looked at your watch and then realized you were hungry? After your arrival, exercise the first day by taking a vigorous walk, followed by a long nap. Then take it easy for the rest of your arrival day. From now on begin doing everything you normally do back home according to the new local time.

Some seasoned transatlantic travelers take even stronger precautions to avoid jet lag. They follow the rule of "no coffee, tea, food, wine, beer, or liquor" on the day of the flight to Europe. They do, however, advocate lots of fruit juices, vegetable juices, and water (no carbonated drinks). This method follows the theory that your body clock will then go on hold, waiting for you to restart it with breakfast the day you arrive in Europe.

Resist the temptations of the airlines up to the point of breakfast, and try to get some sleep. Some current studies have shown the hormone melatonin to be useful in combating jet lag, but as with any other over-the-counter drug, you should first consult your physician. And then there's the "light theory"—that using a blue light source behind your elevated kneecaps will eliminate jet lag. Regardless of which remedies you choose, respect jet lag by taking some precautions and taking it easy on yourself, and you'll enjoy your vacation.

Tax-Free Purchases. Tax-free shopping in Europe ended in 1999 between European Union (EU) countries. This change has little if any effect on U.S. and other non–EU travelers as long as travel is to or from a non–EU destination. At press time, the EU consists of 28 member countries: Austria, Belgium, Bulgaria, Croatia, Cyprus, Czech Republic, Denmark, Estonia, Finland, France, Germany, Greece, Hungary, Ireland, Italy, Latvia, Lithuania, Luxembourg, Malta, the Netherlands, Poland, Portugal, Romania, Slovakia, Slovenia, Spain, Sweden, and the United Kingdom. Turkey, and the former Yugoslav Republic of Macedonia are two other candidate countries. Every international airport, as well as many ferry ports and train stations, currently has a "tax-free" shopping service. The routine is generally the same: You select your purchase, pay for it and add it to your carry-on luggage, find safe storage for it during the flight, and then haul it off the airplane. There are variations.

For example, at JFK in New York you select the items from a sample or catalog. The items are then delivered "for your convenience" to your departure gate for pickup. The hazards of this system are many. If the delivery person gets things mixed up and fails to make the right gate at the right time, you'll be off into the wild blue yonder sans purchases. Or if you are late passing the pickup point, sometimes an unknown "benefactor" will try to help by taking your purchases onboard the plane ahead of you—then finding this so-called benefactor can prove to be difficult.

Solution? Buy your "booty" aboard the airplane while en route. Most international airlines carry aboard a good stock of "tax-free" items that you can purchase from the cabin crew. It's always best to check at the airline counter, however, to be certain that this in-flight service will be available on your particular flight. *Tax-free,* by the way, is a misused term. Most items, with the exception of alcohol and tobacco, normally may be purchased more cheaply in the arrival city. Many airports have specialty shopping outlets to compensate for revenue losses.

Keep in mind that everything you purchase, "tax-free" or otherwise, is subject to customs duty when returning home. Shipped items are processed separately. Consequently, know your quotas and attempt to stay within them to avoid paying duty and experiencing delays.

Prior to Landing. Fill out all the customs and immigration forms your flight attendant may give you, and keep them with your passport and airline ticket. Keep this packet handy but secure, until your credentials are required by the customs or immigration officials at the arriving airport.

Train Travel Tips

"What affects men sharply about a foreign nation," wrote G. K. Chesterton, "is not so much finding or not finding familiar things, it is rather not finding them in the familiar place."

Going to Europe for the first time can mean a confusion of terminology that causes us to learn too late that what we sought was actually available throughout our visit. Our problem can be merely not knowing where to look and what to ask for. The following tips should help you enjoy your rail adventures:

Travel for the Disabled. Rail travel is becoming more and more a chosen method of transportation and recreation for disabled persons. Many aids for the disabled have been incorporated into rail-station design. Trains are being designed with wider doors for wheelchair access; some even have a removable seat to make room for a wheelchair. Ramp access to toilets, buffets, and other facilities is being provided. Folding wheelchairs are also available at main stations so that occupants can be transferred to a regular seat once aboard the train.

The European railways are eager to provide as comfortable a journey as possible for the disabled passenger. To do this, advise authorities of your intended travel plans before departure.

In the United States contact Mobility International USA, 132 E. Broadway, Suite 343, Eugene, OR, 97401 (*Tel:* 541-343-1284; *Fax:* 541-343-6812); visit www.miusa.org or e-mail info@miusa.org for information about services and referrals to international affiliates. They also produce helpful publications.

If you plan to travel in Europe with a disabled person, as soon as you establish your itinerary, contact one of the tourist offices listed in the Appendix and begin making arrangements. The same applies to the airline you'll be using for your transatlantic flight. Give details of your itinerary, the nature of the disability, and any other information that will help them to help you, such as whether a wheelchair is needed at departures and arrivals. Specifically, provide information regarding special diets, medications, and toilet and medical-attention requirements. With these details attended to, you can look forward to a pleasant journey.

Baggage Carts. Many otherwise able train visitors to Europe impose a severe disadvantage upon themselves by arriving with more luggage than anyone could possibly carry. Train porters are nearly an extinct species, and their demise was expedited by the luggage trolley—Europe's version of our baggage cart—an elusive device that, whatever your position on the train platform, haunts the extreme opposite end and often requires insertion of coins to use.

Our number one trip tip to all train travelers is to "go lightly." We repeat: At most, take **one medium-size suitcase with wheels or two small bags,** augmented by a modest shoulder bag. There will still be times when you wish you could discard your suitcase. Pack lightly and leave room for souvenirs, or you'll just need to purchase another piece of luggage.

If you have purchased a model with built-in wheels, however, it usually will follow at your heels like a well-trained dog as you apply minimum pulling power. Unlike a dog, the wheeled suitcase cannot climb stairs by itself, so be prepared to lift it on and off the train and in some stations without elevators. Consider investing in your own baggage cart to take with you if your luggage does not have wheels. There are many types available.

When loading your luggage onto a baggage cart or station trolley, keep the load as narrow as possible. The trolleys provided by the station should not be taken aboard the train, although we've seen it tried. Again, if you are taking your own cart with you, fold it before boarding. If you don't, you may spend an embarrassing ten minutes or so on the station platform extracting a hapless fellow traveler from it as your train eases out of the station without you.

Porter Services. Porter service is on the wane but still available in some train stations, particularly the larger ones. The best way to locate a porter is to inquire at the Left Luggage (baggage storage) area. Most stations also offer luggage lockers (some stations have stopped this service and, for security reasons, have even removed trash containers). If your luggage has been checked in at the station, there will be a handling charge, but the tip remains a personal transaction between you and the porter.

Most porters will take your bags to the train and place them aboard in the luggage racks over your seat. Porters are rather scarce on arrival platforms. If you must have assistance, approach the stationmaster's office or the train conductor prior to departure, with the request that a porter be asked to meet your train upon arrival at your destination.

If you are transferring between base cities or changing hotels from one city to another, you can request the hall porter at the hotel you are leaving to arrange for the arriving hotel's hall porter to meet your train upon arrival. A small tip should arrange everything.

A Few More Train Travel Tips

- Show your pass or rail ticket, upon request, and in the case of the pass, have your passport handy should the conductor want to see it.
- Don't place your feet on the seats of the train unless you have removed your shoes or have provided a protective covering for the seat.
- Place your luggage in the overhead racks (or the luggage vestibules) provided for that purpose—not on the seats so that other passengers won't be able to crowd you.
- Observe the smoking/nonsmoking areas and rules. There are rather stiff fines for smokers who violate the nonsmoking regulations.
- Observe seat reservations. Seating that has been reserved is marked, usually by a ticket inserted at the top of the seat. Even though it is apparent that a seat is unoccupied, if there are other passengers seated opposite, ask whether the seat is open—doing so will avoid embarrassment later if the person holding the reservation happens to return.
- Arrange dining-car reservations on long-distance trains soon after boarding. Ask the conductor. If he or she cannot make the reservations for you, a member of the dining-car crew will do so. Generally, these crew members pass through the train prior to the first serving for that purpose. Usually there are two servings, so be prepared to select the one to your liking. You can also ask about the menu at the same time. The second serving is scheduled so that the dining-car crew has time to tidy up before the train reaches its destination. Therefore, the first serving is preferred by many because it does not seem to be as rushed.
- If you plan an overnight journey on a sleeper, ask the attendant to explain how the equipment in your compartment operates. For example, newer sleeping cars have electric shades. A push of the button and they open; another push of the same button and they close. If you did not know the button's function, you just might try pushing the button while the train was standing in a station and you were not properly dressed for the occasion!
- Tip the attendant on a sleeper for his or her services; the appropriate time to do so is when breakfast is served.

Not by Bread Alone

Oddly enough, the reader who exists on hamburgers and milk shakes back home will find such a diet expensive to maintain in Europe. Europe abounds in good, wholesome food. Practically every major railway station has a cafeteria where the food is displayed along with the prices. "Order the spaghetti Bolognese," was the advice of one tourist official in Switzerland. "You can't go wrong," he declared, and he was right.

Many of the railway stations have cafes and dining-room facilities, and some even have gourmet restaurants. Most European restaurants offer a tourist menu at a fixed cost. Look for the menu sign, posted outside, showing the prices and food selections.

If you are puzzled by foreign menus, take heart. Many European restaurants have menus that have been translated into your language. Although the translated versions may take some of the "adventure" out of eating in a foreign country, they may save an embarrassing moment—such as ordering the poulet and ending up with a whole roasted chicken!

To help hold the food price line, determine whether your hotel includes breakfast with the accommodations and, if so, what kind of breakfast and how much the room is without it.

On day excursions, pack a picnic-style lunch. Bread, cheese, pastry, cold cuts, fruits, soft drinks, and beer or wine—all are available from local shops. If you give advance notice, perhaps the hotel will prepare a basket lunch for you.

For the most part, meals served aboard the trains are, naturally, on the expensive side. In many cases, though, the food is excellent and well worth the premium you pay for enjoying it as you speed along through the scenic countryside. Many trains provide buffet and cafeteria services, and you can usually count on a food trolley being aboard for drinks and sandwiches. On some premium trains, such as the TGV, gourmet meals are served at your seat—airline style. One fact remains: The least expensive food aboard a train is that which you brought. Again, plan ahead and save.

Dos & Don'ts Safety Tips

- Picking pockets is an art that is seemingly practiced throughout the world and most commonly occurs in crowded public places. Be leery of being bumped or of someone causing a distracting incident. Don't carry anything more valuable than a handkerchief in hip pockets. Money belts, holster wallets, or pouches that can be hidden are the safest way to carry cash and other valuables.
- If you do not have a concealable money belt, holster wallet, or pouch, women should place the straps of their purses across their chests and carry the purses in front—not on the side with the straps only on the shoulder.

Motorcycle thieves can grab the purse from your shoulder very easily. Men should modify the inside pocket of a coat or jacket with a zipper or Velcro. Or sew a medium-size button both above and below the pocket opening. Loop a piece of shoestring or other strong string around the buttons when carrying valuables. Don't let the thought of someone picking your pocket alarm you. Just be aware of it, and take the proper precautions.

- Don't leave cash, cameras, and other valuables in the hotel room or locked up in a suitcase. Take them with you, or leave them in the hotel safe. We advocate leaving expensive jewelry at home, but if you must take it with you, leave it in the hotel safe when you're not wearing it.
- Don't dangle your camera from around your neck or wrist; keep it in an inexpensive-looking camera bag.
- Don't designate one individual to carry everyone's passport or other valuables, and don't carry all of your own valuables in one place. Split up documents and money in various safe holding locations.
- Do stay alert and be cautious when in crowded places, including rail stations. Ask questions and seek help from official personnel.

For further peace of mind, review the website www.travel.state.gov/content/passports/english/go.html for insightful tips and suggestions for "A Safe Trip Abroad." It contains ideas on what to bring and leave behind, what to learn and arrange before you go, as well as helpful tips for public transport safety.

Remember, visitors are always subject to the law of the land, so pay attention to media reports and research some of the local laws and customs prior to departure. Also consider visiting the U.S. State Department's Internet site, www.state.gov, which contains up-to-date information on foreign affairs. You may also contact the U.S. Department of State Bureau of Consular Affairs for information on travel warnings and public announcements by calling (202) 647-5225; *Fax:* (202) 647-3000; or visit www.travel.state.gov, where several helpful documents are available, such as *A Safe Trip Abroad, Tips for Americans Residing Abroad, Tips for Older Americans,* and *Tips for Students*.

AUSTRIA

Austria's central location in Europe and its six international airports of the Imperial Cities—Vienna (Wien), Graz, Innsbruck, Klagenfurt, Linz, and Salzburg—make it a convenient gateway country for European travelers. Although German is the native language of Austria, most tourism officials also speak English. With a smile on your face, try the informal German greeting "Grüss Gott," and ask slowly and distinctly, "Do you speak English?" A smile almost always elicits a cooperative attitude.

Austria is more than museums and antiques; it is also "the sound of music," spectacular scenery, and gourmet foods. Austria is a country where one can easily overindulge in temptingly tasty pastries and piles of schlagobers (whipped cream)—and what a way to go. We discovered why the schlagobers is so delicately delicious—it's the real thing.

Sports enthusiasts can enjoy a variety of summer activities, including hang gliding, hiking, mountain climbing, water sports, and a dip in Austria's largest "hot tub," Kopeiner See, where lake water temperatures climb to 82.4 degrees Fahrenheit in summer.

As the Austrian National Tourist Office succinctly states: "Austria is more than 1,000 years old. So far, so good." For more information and pretrip planning tips, be sure to visit Austria's website, **www.austria.info,** or contact the Austrian Tourist Office in North America:

New York: P.O. Box 1142, New York, NY 10108. *Tel:* (212) 575-7723; *Fax:* (212) 730-4568; *E-mail:* travel@austria.info

Toronto: 2 Bloor Street West, Suite 400, Toronto, Ontario M4W 3E2, Canada. *Tel:* (416) 967-3381; *Fax:* (416) 967-4101; *E-mail:* travel@austria.info

Banking

Currency: Euro (€)

Exchange rate at press time: 0.90 = U.S. $1

Hours: 0800–1230 and 1330–1500 Monday–Friday; closing at 1730 on Thursday; closed Saturday and Sunday. Banks in most airport and rail terminals are open 0800–2000 seven days a week; until 2200 in Vienna.

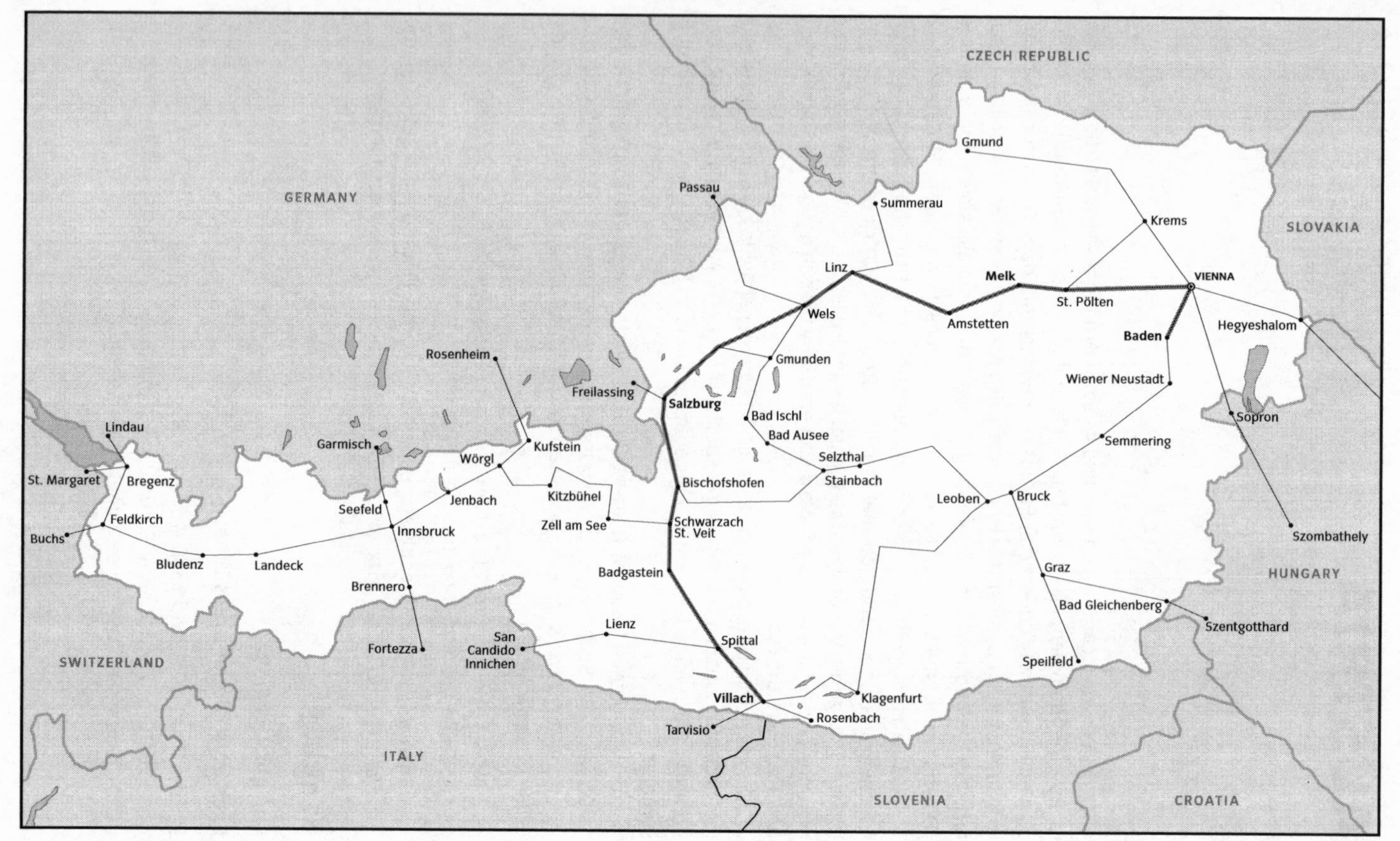
CZECH REPUBLIC
GERMANY
SLOVAKIA
HUNGARY
SWITZERLAND
ITALY
SLOVENIA
CROATIA
Gmund
Passau
Summerau
Krems
Linz
Melk
VIENNA
St. Pölten
Wels
Amstetten
Hegyeshalom
Baden
Rosenheim
Gmunden
Wiener Neustadt
Freilassing
Salzburg
Bad Ischl
Sopron
Lindau
Bad Ausee
Garmisch
Kufstein
Semmering
Selzthal
Wörgl
St. Margaret
Bregenz
Bischofshofen
Stainbach
Kitzbühel
Jenbach
Leoben
Bruck
Seefeld
Feldkirch
Zell am See
Schwarzach
St. Veit
Innsbruck
Buchs
Szombathely
Bludenz
Landeck
Badgastein
Graz
HUNGARY
Brennero
Bad Gleichenberg
Lienz
Szentgotthard
San
Candido
Innichen
Spittal
Fortezza
Speilfeld
Villach
Klagenfurt
Rosenbach
Tarvisio

Communications

Country Code: 43

For telephone calls within Austria, dial a zero (0) preceding area code.

Major Mobile Phone Companies: A1, T-Mobile, Orange, 3

Rail Travel in Austria

The Austrian Federal Railways, or Österreichische Bundesbahnen (ÖBB), operates the 5,800-kilometer rail system and accepts a variety of **Eurail passes;** the **European East Pass;** the regional passes combining Austria with Croatia-Slovenia, Czech Republic, Germany, Hungary, or Switzerland; and the national **Austria Pass.** (See the Appendix for a list of rail pass types and prices.) Remember to purchase your rail passes prior to your departure for Europe. Visit www.oebb.at.

The aforementioned rail passes include the following discounts within Austria:

- 50 percent discount on boats operated by BSB, SBS, and ÖBB on Lake Constance (from May to October)
- Various discounts on boat day trips operated by Wurm & Köck Steamers on the Danube between Linz and Passau (Germany). *Note:* Reservations are mandatory
- 20 percent discount on boats operated by DDSG–Blue Danube Schiffahrt between Melk and Krems, and between Dürnstein and Vienna (on Sunday)
- 20 percent discount on sightseeing trips on the Danube River in Vienna operated by DDSG–Blue Danube Schiffahrt

Additional Discounts:

- Pay only a reservation fee on ÖBB intercity buses from Klagenfurt–Graz and Klagenfurt–Villach–Venice
- Free entrance to ÖBB lounges
- 10 percent discount at Meininger Hotels or Hostels in Vienna or Salzburg
- 10 percent discount on daily rate at A&O Wien Stadthalle, A&O Wien Hauptbahnhof, and A&O Graz Hauptbahnhof

The basic **Austria Pass** is valid for 3 days of rail travel within a 15-day period. First class, $260; second class, $184. Additional rail days (up to 5) available for approx $30, first class; approx $20+, second class. Child rates are half of the adult fare for ages 4 to 11; younger than age 4 travel free—only if sharing a seat. Youth pass for 12–25 are $143 second class.

Seat reservations for both national and international travel may be made at any rail station. Eurail Aid offices are located in Innsbruck Hauptbahnhof, Salzburg Hauptbahnhof, and Wien Westbahnhof (Vienna West Station).

Base City: **VIENNA** **(Wien)**

www.info.wien.at
City Dialing Code: 1

Arriving by Air

Schwechat Airport, *Tel:* (01) 7007 22233 for information, including transport to the city center; www.viennaairport.com.

Located 19 kilometers from the city center, Schwechat Airport is the home base for Austrian Airlines, which offers nonstop flights between the United States (New York) and Vienna and serves more than 30 other international airlines. Tourist information is available in the "Arrivals Hall."

Airport–City Links: Trains run from 0453 then approximately every 30 minutes (Schnellbahn, Line S7) from the airport into Wien Mitte Station. The price is €4.20; journey time, 24 minutes. The City Airport Train direct to Wien Mitte takes only 16 minutes; fare: €12, children under 14 free. The first train to the airport departs at 0536 and then runs every 06 and 36 minutes past the hour. The first train from the airport departs at 0606 and then every 6 and 36 minutes past the hour. Last departure train is 2306 and 2339, respectively. During heavy morning and evening traffic, the train is the best way to go. At other times, you can take the airport bus service, which connects with the Westbahnhof (West Station), as well as with the city air terminal (next to the Hilton Hotel). The fare is €8; time en route, 25 to 35 minutes. The bus-departure point is immediately outside and to the left of the arriving-passenger exit. Purchase tickets on the bus. Buses depart every 30 minutes.

If you purchase a Vienna Card at the tourist information office in the Arrivals Hall of the airport ("Tourist Board"), you'll pay only €11 on the City Airport Train and only €2.00 to purchase an additional zone for the Line S7 train. See "Getting Around in Vienna" for details.

Taxis are available just outside the arrivals area. Fare to city center is about €33; journey time, 20 to 30 minutes.

Arriving by Train

The new Vienna Hauptbahnhof (Main) Station has now completely opened, and is now handling most long-haul routes to and from Vienna. Additional major train stations in the city include Westbahnhof, Mitte and Nord, most of which now handle primarily local and commuter traffic. For train information visit www.oebb.at.

Hauptbahnhof has four levels, marked as levels 1, 0, -1 and -2, with trains arriving on the lowest level, and commuter and local trains one level above. There is also a large connected mall area, with many amenities and shopping choices.

- **Baggage storage** located on the commuter train level (Level -1).
- **Money exchange** on the platform level (Level -2)
- **Train information,** reservations and rail pass validation is on the Main Concourse (Level 0)

Tourist Information/Hotel Reservations

- City center **main tourist office:** Albertinaplatz on the corner of Maysedergasse (behind the Vienna State Opera House). *Tel:* (01) 21114-0; *Fax:* (01) 216 84 92; www.info.wien.at; *E-mail:* info@vienna.info. *Hours:* 0900–1900 daily.

  To get there from the Westbahnhof (West Station) by public transport, take the U-Bahn (underground) Line U3 to Volkstheater and on the Ringstrasse, take Tram 2, D, or J for the two stops to the Opera House. From the Südbahnhof (South Station), take Tram D.
- Schwechat Airport, located opposite the baggage carousels in the Arrivals Hall. *Hours:* 0600–2300.
- **Hotel reservations** may be made at the tourist information offices and by: *Tel:* (01) 24 555 (*Hours:* 0900–1900 daily); *Fax:* (01) 24 555 666; www.info.wien.at; *E-mail:* info@vienna.info.

Getting Around in Vienna

The most economical and convenient way to discover Vienna is with the **Vienna Card.** For only €19.90, you'll have free access to Vienna's public transportation network for 72 hours (excluding night buses), plus discounts at 210 museums and attractions, concerts, shops, theaters, restaurants, cafes, and *Heurigen* (wine taverns). All the benefits are described in the 120-page Vienna Card coupon book.

Purchase the Vienna Card at tourist information offices, your hotel, or **Vienna Transport** (Wiener Linien) information offices, located in many underground stations. Or order the Vienna Card with your credit card by telephoning 011 +43 1 798 44 00 148 from the United States. Order online at www.wienkarte.at/card-order/order.php.

Vienna's efficient transportation network includes the U-Bahn underground, trams, S-Bahn (rapid-transit intracity trains), and bus service. The best bargain is the Vienna Card that covers more than just the transportation network. But there are other choices for transportation only: A single ticket is €2.10, a 24-hour network pass is €7.10, and a 72-hour network pass is €15.40. Children younger than age 6 travel free.

These transportation tickets can be purchased from tobacconists, at vending machines in the underground stations, or even at reception desks in many Viennese hotels. Single-trip tickets from vending machines in trams and buses cost €2.10. A punched single ticket is valid for one trip, including changing lines. Purchase a public transportation map.

Sights/Attractions/Tours

Vienna tourist-office personnel are highly qualified professionals who can help you find a variety of ways to see Vienna, and one of the best ways to really get to know the city is on foot. Ask for the brochure ***Walks in Vienna*** (www.wienguide.at). Choose from 11 guided walking tours; each has a different theme. Reservations are not required; just show up at the point mentioned in the brochure for the particular tour you choose. Cost: €15 per person (with a Vienna Card, €13); younger than age 14, €8. Duration of the walking tours is 1½–2 hours. Private guided tours may also be arranged through Vienna Guide Service [*Tel:* 43 1 587 363362; www.viennaguideservice.at]. For a real moving experience, tour Vienna by bicycle on more than 800 kilometers of bicycle paths. Call Bike & Guide at 43 0 6991 17582 61. *E-mail:* office@bikeandguide.com; www.bikeandguide.com.

You can see Vienna at your own pace with the "Hop-on, Hop-off" bus tours (discount with the Vienna Card). *Tel:* (01) 712 46830; *E-mail:* office@viennasightseeingtours.com; www.viennasightseeingtours.com. Short city tour (about 60 minutes): €14 adults; €7 children. One-day ticket: €25 adults; €12 children.

For a leisurely view of Vienna, take a cruise aboard the ship MS *Vindobona* from the Danube Canal onto the Danube. The ship departs from Schwedenplatz for a cruise to Reichsbrucke. You can return to the city via the underground or the MS *Vindobona*. Departures are at 1130 and 1500. One-way, €19.90; round-trip €26 (10 percent discount with Vienna Card; children under 10 free, 10–15 years old half price). Ask the tourist office for the DDSG Blue Danube Ships' brochure detailing their cruise programs or call (01) 588 80 0; *Fax:* (01) 588 80 440; www.ddsg-blue-danube.at; *E-mail:* info@ddsg-blue-danube.at.

Vienna is many things, but primarily it is music. Visit the **Vienna State Opera House,** a preeminent point of European music. The Schoenbrunn Palace, former summer residence of the Hapsburg Empire, is truly worth seeing. Get there by taking the U4 line on the Underground. See operas and operettas performed at the **Court Theatre at Schoenbrunn.** On the palace grounds, wander through the New Maze that was patterned as closely as possible to the original design created between 1698 and 1740.

Visit the Strauss home where the "Blue Danube Waltz" was written. Thrill to the harmonious voices of the famous **Vienna Boys' Choir** (www.wsk.at), or marvel at the white Lipizzaner stallions as they dance to music in the **Spanish Riding School.** For information and tickets: *Tel:* (01) 533 90 31; www.srs.at.

Vista of Vienna

The pace is slower in Vienna; Vienna developed the waltz, and the city's tempo has moved in leisurely three-quarter time ever since.

Vienna's coffeehouses are oases of good living at a leisurely pace. Visiting them during your stay is a must. Our favorite coffeehouse happens to be the original one in Vienna, the **Sacher Café,** a part of Hotel Sacher immediately behind the Opera House. It has a semiformal but friendly atmosphere. By all means, try the *Sachertorte* (chocolate cake) and don't miss the *Apfelstrudel* (apple cake). Expensive? Well, yes, but it's worth it.

The Viennese "invented" coffee. According to legend, in 1683 the Turks were defeated and abandoned their three-centuries' quest to conquer the heart of Europe at the gates of Vienna. In their hasty departure, they left some bags of coffee beans behind. The local folks swarmed out of the city and carried the bags back behind its protective walls and began experimenting. A gentleman by the name of Kolschitzky evolved a clear brew—unlike the Turks who, to this day, serve it with the grounds—and the people of Vienna were so elated that they erected a bronze statue to his memory.

The Viennese like to eat well. Choose from a dazzling array of eateries from stand-up snack bars and simple little pubs, known as Beisel, to ethnic specialties and gourmet restaurants. Since good food deserves good libation, try the tasty and strong Austrian beer or some of Austria's great vintages. These are bottled and aged; but young, fresh wine is rushed to the taverns, where locals and visitors alike consume it as though it might lose its freshness between sips.

Since Hungary accepts Eurail passes, many Eurail travelers transit Vienna on through trains such as the *Wiener Walzer* without stopping. Take advantage of the frequent rail service, and stop for a few hours in Vienna en route to Budapest. Baggage can be stored in the *Gepackaufbewahrung* (temporary baggage storage facility) in the Westbahnhof main concourse level.

Train Connections to Other Base Cities from Vienna (Wien)

Depart from Vienna Hauptbahnhof Station, unless otherwise noted.

DEPART	TRAIN NUMBER	ARRIVE	NOTES
		Amsterdam Centraal	
2139	EN 420	1127+1	R, 4, Sleeper
		Berlin Hauptbahnhof	
0909	RJ 72	1858	R, 3
2250	EN 60406	0911+1	R, Sleeper
		Bern (Berne)	
0930	RJ 162	1828	1
2325	EN 60466	0928+1	R, 1, Sleeper
		Brussels (Bruxelles) Midi/Zuid	
2139	EN 420	0935+1	R, 4, Sleeper
		Budapest Keleti	
0642	EN 463	0924	R
0942	RJ 49	1219	
1342	RJ 63	1619	
1542	EC 65	1819	
1942	D 347	2220	R
		Hamburg Hauptbanhof	
1250	ICE 90	2153	R
2039	EN 490	0751+1	R, Sleeper
		Munich (München) Hauptbahnhof	
0630	RJ 260	1025	
0830	RJ 262	1225	
1630	RJ 66	2025	
2325	EN 462	0610+1	R, Sleeper
		Paris Gare de l'Est	
2325	EN 462	1235+1	R, 2, Sleeper
		Prague (Praha)	
0709	RJ 70	1108	
0909	RJ 72	1308	
1309	RJ 76	1708	
2250	EN 60406	0408+1	Sleeper
		Rome (Roma) Termini	
1923	EN 235	0922+1	R, Sleeper
		Warsaw Centralna	
0809	EC 104	1505	R
1409	EC 102	2105	R
2250	D 406	0700+1	R, Sleeper

DEPART	TRAIN NUMBER	ARRIVE	NOTES
		Zürich Hauptbahnhof	
0730	RJ 160	1520	
0930	RJ 162	1720	
2225	EN 60466	0820+1	R, Sleeper

Daily, including holidays, unless otherwise noted
R Reservations required
+1 Arrives next day
1. Change trains in Zurich.
2. Change trains in Munich (München).
3. Change trains in Prague (Praha).
4. Change trains in Frankfurt.

Day Excursions from Vienna

Because of its location on the Danube River and the eastern reaches of the Alps, Vienna can offer some unusual day-excursion opportunities. Among them are cruises on the Danube to **Melk** or tours through the Vienna Woods and the **Austrian Alps** by train.

Local trains can take you to **Baden,** one of the most famous sulfur-bath spas in Austria. Express trains can whisk you from Vienna to **Salzburg** in time for lunch—followed by dinner—and still return you in time to slumber in your base city of Vienna.

Day Excursion to

Austrian Alps Tour

Via Villach and Salzburg

Depart from Vienna Meidling Station
Distance by Train: 541 miles (871 km)
Average Train Time: 4 hours, 40 minutes

The Austrian Alps probably provide more beauty than all of the fine-art masterpieces in the world laid end to end. The fact that you can watch the splendor of their alpine panorama unfold from the comfort of a train compartment makes this a most unusual and thrilling day excursion.

Take an adequate, large-scale map of Austria along, and try to select a day when good visibility is forecast. For the latter, your hotel should be able to provide a weather forecast, and an ideal map is the one published by Kummerly and Frey. You'll find it in newspaper kiosks or station newsstands.

This day excursion requires changing trains in Salzburg with the option of changing trains en route to Salzburg at Villach. The time between trains in Villach and Salzburg varies according to the schedule you select. Consider having lunch in Villach followed by dinner in Salzburg. Dining aboard is also possible, since all of the trains listed on the schedule haul dining cars.

The Alps in Austria are divided from north to south into three chains: the **northern limestone Alps,** the **central high Alps,** and the **limestone Alps of the south.** These chains are separated from each other by the great furrows that form the river valleys of the Inn, the Salzach, and the Enns in the north and the Drava and Mur in the south. The route we have selected for this day excursion takes you through all three alpine chains.

Vienna (Wien)—Austrian Alps Tour

DEPART Vienna Meidling	TRAIN NUMBER	ARRIVE Villach
0632	EC 31	1046
0832	RJ 533	1246
1032	RJ 535	1446

DEPART Villach	TRAIN NUMBER	ARRIVE Salzburg
1316	IC 691	1548
1516	IC 591	1748
1716	EC 110	1948

DEPART Salzburg	TRAIN NUMBER	ARRIVE Vienna Meidling
1508	RJ 67	1723
1608	RJ 165	1823
1708	RJ 69	1923
1808	RJ 167	2023
1908	RJ 261	2123
2012	OIC 841	2258
2108	RJ 663	2323

Daily, including holidays
Distance: 541 miles (871 km)

Even if the weather is good when you leave Vienna, the climate of the Alps varies considerably with differences in altitude. Expect some changes in the temperature and visibility while en route. It is not unusual to enter a tunnel with the landscape bathed in sunlight only to emerge at the other end into a storm.

Vienna is 580 feet above sea level. Leaving the city, the train moves along the edge of the Vienna Woods. Before arriving in Bruck, you will get an occasional glimpse of the **Raxalpe Peak** (6,630 feet). This steep-sided limestone massif, due to its proximity to Vienna, has become very popular with city-based mountain climbers. Here, the train follows the first mountain railway **(Semmeringbahn)** built in Europe (1848 to 1854), which runs between Gloggnitz and Murzzuschlag.

From Murzzuschlag to Bruck, the train parallels the Murz River through the last really mountainous pass leading out of the Alps and on to the broad plains fed by the Danube. Bruck lies at the confluence of the Mur and the Murz Rivers in the pleasant setting of the **Styrian Alps.** After passing Unzmarkt, the peaks of the Zinken (7,255 feet) and the Greimberg (8,115 feet) Alps are visible. You then arrive in **Klagenfurt,** 1,472 feet above sea level. Summers here are extremely hot, for the town lies in a basin shielding it from the moderating effects of the Mediterranean.

Between Klagenfurt and Velden, the train passes along Lake Woerth before arriving in Villach. Leaving Villach and approaching the Tauern Tunnel (5 miles long), you will be able to view Mount Hochalm (11,020 feet). As you exit the tunnel, Edelweiss-Spitz (8,453 feet) stands guard on the left while Mount Gamskarspitze (9,296 feet) looms on the right.

After pausing briefly at **Badgastein**—the highest en route station, at 2,838 feet above sea level—the train gradually descends into Schwarzach and parallels the Salzach River, which flows past Bischofshofen and the city of Salzburg. Your return train to Vienna arrives at Westbahnhof (West Station).

Day Excursion to

Baden

Baths, Cures, and Casino

Depart from Vienna Meidling Station
Distance by Train: 17 miles (27 km)
Average Train Time: 20 minutes
City Dialing Code: 2252
Tourist Information Office: Brusattiplatz 3 (Leopoldsbad), A-2500 Baden bei Wien
Tel: (02252) 22 60 06 00; **Fax:** (02252) 80 733
www.baden.at
E-mail: info@baden.at
Hours: May 1–September 30: 0900–1800 Monday–Friday, 0900–1400 Saturday, closed Sunday; October 1–April 30: 0900–1700 Monday–Friday; closed Saturday and Sunday
Notes: Proceed to level 3 for trains departing on tracks 11 and 19 for Baden in direction of Graz. To get to the tourist information office from the rail station, use the station underpass to the town side of the tracks. Walk directly through

the park in front of the station and bear right onto Bahnstrasse (Station Street) at the end of the park. Two blocks farther along, you will see a Fussgängerzone (pedestrian area). Turn right and walk to the town square. Pass the Rathaus (city hall) on its left side and proceed toward the end of the pedestrian area through Grüner Markt (the marketplace). The tourist office is just behind Grüner Markt.

Baden is situated on the eastern edge of the Vienna Woods and surrounded by extensive vineyards and woodlands. Because it also lies on the edge of Europe's great eastern Pannonian plain, it enjoys a moderate climate, much sunshine, and favorable temperatures. In fact, Baden is in the warmest part of Austria, and it is well-known as a health resort.

Baden sits on 15 ancient **thermal water springs**—with a regular temperature of 36 degrees Celsius (97 degrees Fahrenheit). These sulfurous thermal springs form the basis for treatments and cures; some four million liters of it are used daily. The early Romans were always keen on baths, and they spent hours soaking in the medicinal, hot sulfur springs of the area they called "Aquae." In the 19th century, Baden became the center of social life for Vienna's growing sphere of influence. Today, it is a world-renowned spa full of charm, flowers, and more swimming pools than one can possibly enter in a single day excursion.

Swimming is a year-round pastime, either outdoors in the thermal and mineral pools or indoors at **Römertherme.** The thermal public swimming pool (*Thermalstrandbad*), with its Art Deco–style, 5,000-square-meter pool area and extensive sandy beach, is an adventure-bath for the whole family. In 1930 a section of the parklands of Castle Weilburg was added, making it one of the largest open-air baths in Austria.

Baden offers other forms of relaxation, ranging from quiet paths leading in and around the eastern edges of the Vienna Woods to a lively game of blackjack in the **Casino Baden** opposite Kurpark. The casino is open daily 1500–0300. Visit www.casinos.at. Baden is also ideal for shopping—its entire center is a pedestrian zone filled with small specialty shops. When you tire of bargain hunting, retreat to the city rose garden in **Doblhoff Park** to watch chess played on a larger-than-life chessboard.

Another interesting pastime is visiting the informal **wine taverns** scattered throughout the town. Since the Middle Ages, every citizen of Baden has had the right to sell self-produced wine, as well as meat and sausage specialties. These "taverns" are identified by a pole decorated with fir twigs, or you can seek them out by following the tavern signs displayed throughout the town. Visitors engaged in "researching" taverns might do well to come to Baden as early as possible and leave only when they have discovered the best vintage—or spend the night in Baden, depending upon how much research they conducted.

Vienna (Wien)—Baden

Trains depart Vienna Meidling for Baden daily at 37 minutes past the hour beginning at 0637. Plus commuter trains departing at 07 minutes past the hour, plus other frequent service. Most trains departing for Graz stop at Baden.

Trains depart Baden for Vienna Meidling daily at 02 and 32 minutes past the hour until 2302, plus other frequent service. Check schedules in Baden railway station.

Distance: 17 miles (27 km)

Day Excursion to

Melk

Alternative Cruise up the Danube

Depart from Vienna West Station (Westbahnhof)
Distance by Train and Boat: 102 miles (192 km)
Total Time: 7 hours, 40 minutes
City Dialing Code: 2752
Tourist Information Office: Kremser StraBe 5, 3390 Melk
Tel: 02 7 5252 3074 10; **Fax:** 43 0 2752 51160 30
www.tiscover.at/melk
E-mail: melk@donau.com
Hours: April–October 0900–1800 Monday–Saturday; November–March 0900–1700 Monday–Thursday, 0900–1430 Friday
Brandner ship line: Tel: (07433) 2590 21; **Fax:** (07433) 2590 25; **E-mail:** schif fahrt@brandner.at; www.brandner.at
DDSG ship line: Tel: (01) 588 80 0; **Fax:** (01) 588 80 440; **E-mail:** info@ddsg-blue-danube.at; www.ddsg-blue-danube.at
Notes: As you emerge from the bahnhof (rail station), walk toward the abbey, which dominates the foreground. The tourist office is in the town hall, which sits at the base of the abbey, 3 blocks from the station.

The Danube is Europe's grand river, second in length only to the Volga and stretching almost 1,800 miles across eight countries. As plains, hills, and mountains succeed one another along its course, the Danube can be sluggish, swift, or even wild. The Danube rises in Germany's Black Forest—the length of a football field away from the watershed of the Rhine. By the time its waters reach the German city of Ulm, the Danube becomes navigable by river craft. Between Ulm and Vienna, the Danube takes on an alpine character. The Danube is unusual among the rivers of the world in that it flows from west to east. At its delta, it empties into the Black Sea.

The "Blue Danube Waltz" is a musical expression of the attractiveness and charm of Austria along the banks of the Danube. The vast countryside—fringed by the Austrian Alps on the south—offers a vista of natural beauty. Although the waters of the river, especially in times of flood, do not always display the color of which the song sings, the beauty of the countryside through which the Danube flows makes it easy to forget that the waters are actually milky white throughout most of the spring and summer.

Vienna (Wien)—Melk—Up the Danube (Donau)

There is no longer a regular Danube (Donau) steamer service between Vienna and Melk.

Instead, take the train to Melk, steam downriver to Krems, and then return to Vienna from Krems by train. Between April and October, steamers depart Melk at 1100, 1350, and 1625. November to March, steamers depart Melk at 1350. Alternately, take the train to Krems, go upriver, and return to Vienna from Melk by train. Between April and October, steamers depart Krems at 1015, 1315, and 1545. November to March, steamers depart Krems at 1015. Note that trains to/from Krems terminate in the Vienna Franz-Josefs-Bahnhof station.

DEPART **Vienna Westbahnhof**	TRAIN NUMBER	ARRIVE **Melk**	NOTES
0554	REX 1606	0721	
0720	REX 1912	0822	M–F
0820	REX 1914	0922	
1054	REX 1626	1222	
1420	REX 1920	1522	
DEPART **Melk**	**TRAIN NUMBER**	**ARRIVE** **Vienna Westbahnhof**	**NOTES**
1436	REX 1941	1540	
1736	REX 1923	1840	
1836	REX 1659	2006	Exc. Sun
2236	REX 1675	0032+1	
DEPART **Vienna Franz-Josefs-Bahnhof**	**TRAIN NUMBER**	**ARRIVE** **Krems**	**NOTES**
0805	REX 2810	0914	
1105	REX 2818	1214	
1405	REX 2826	1514	

DEPART	TRAIN NUMBER	ARRIVE	NOTES
Krems		Vienna Franz-Josefs-Bahnhof	
1551	REX 2843	1658	
1750	REX 2849	1858	
1951	REX 2855	2058	
2151	REX 2859	2258	

Daily, unless otherwise noted

We recommend taking the 0600 train to Melk, the point from which the cruise down the Danube begins. It will bring you to Melk in time for unhurried connections with the ship, but Melk itself is steeped in history and warrants your visit. The earlier train will permit you to wander about Melk's ancient streets, guarded by the watchtowers of its town wall, and to visit Melk's **Benedictine Abbey,** the epitome of Baroque architecture in Austria. To book a guided tour of the abbey: *Tel:* (02752) 555 0; *Fax:* (02752) 555 249; *E-mail:* tours@stiftmelk.at; www.stiftmelk.at.

Have lunch and sample the fine regional wines in one of Melk's charming *Heurigen* taverns before you walk or taxi to the DDSG pier, known locally as "Schiff Station." Check with the information desk on the pier for boarding instructions.

Carry a map of the Danube and refer to it often, for it's one fine scene after another. The market town of **Spitz,** on the Danube's left bank, is readily recognizable because it nestles at the base of the *Tausendeimer* mountain. The name of the mountain ("a thousand vessels") doesn't refer to the river traffic—it refers to the fact that the vineyards on its sides, in a good year, can produce a thousand vessels of wine.

When the ship calls at **Durnstein,** with its red roofs, you should recall that it was here that King Richard I, the Lionhearted of England, was captured and held prisoner when he returned from the Third Crusade. The next port of call will be **Krems,** which marks the eastern area of the Wachau. Since olden times, Krems has been the hub of the Wachau wine trade. Here, the Danube becomes dotted with islands as the ship draws nearer to Vienna.

Day Excursion to

Salzburg

Fortress City

Depart from Vienna Hauptbahnhof*
Distance by Train: 196 miles (315 km)
Average Train Time: 3 hours, 11 minutes
City Dialing Code: 662
Tourist Information Offices:
Mozartplatz Information Office, Mozartplatz 5; **Tel:** (0662) 88 98 73 30
Salzburg-Süd Information Office, Park & Ride Parkplatz, Alpensiedlung-Süd, Alpenstrasse; **Tel:** (0662) 88 98 73 60 (Easter–October)
Salzburg Main Station, Sudtiroler Platz l; **Tel:** (0662) 88 98 73 40
www.salzburginfo.at
E-mail: tourist@salzburg.info
Hours: 0900–1800 or 2000 daily (depending on time of the year)
*Salzburg is also a popular day excursion from Munich. Distance by train: 95 miles (153 km); average train time: 1 hour, 30 minutes

If Vienna gives you the impression that it is musically inclined, wait until you see and hear Salzburg. It has been described as a music festival that never seems to end. No wonder—Salzburg is the birthplace of Mozart. His home is now a museum, and his music has become the very soul of Salzburg.

Music isn't the only thing that makes Salzburg an interesting city. It has the largest completely preserved fortress in central Europe—the **Hohensalzburg Fortress** (circa 1077). You can reach it by taking the cable car from Festungsgasse 4, located right behind the **Neptune Fountain.** The cable car can whisk you to the top of Salzburg and the Hohensalzburg Fortress in a minute. There is a footpath leading to the top, but it takes a lot of huffing and puffing. Conducted tours include the State rooms, **Fortress Museum,** and **Rainer Museum.** The tour with an audio guide takes about 40 minutes. *Hours:* January–April, October–December: 0930–1700; May–September: 0900–1900; Advent weekends and Easter: 0930–1800. Visit www.salzburg-burgen.at/en/hohensalzburg/.

Vienna (Wien)—Salzburg

DEPART Vienna Hbf	TRAIN NUMBER	ARRIVE Salzburg
0555	IC 540	0848
0655	IC 542	0948
0755	IC 662	1048
0855	IC 690	1148
0955	IC 548	1248

Salzburg—Vienna (Wien)

DEPART Salzburg	TRAIN NUMBER	ARRIVE Vienna Hbf
1512	IC 741	1805
1612	IC 691	1905
1712	IC 745	2005
1812	IC 747	2105
1912	IC 749	2205
2012	IC 841	2305
2108	RJ 663	2330

Daily unless otherwise noted

There is a terrace restaurant on the fortress' south side where you may view the mountains as you dine (in summer).

The **Salzburg Card,** available at the tourist information offices and hotels, provides admission to all of the attractions in Salzburg, free access to public transportation, and many discounts. Choose a 24-, 48-, or 72-hour card for €23, €31, or €36, respectively. Find out more by visiting the Salzburg website or e-mailing cards@salzburginfo.at.

To conduct your own tour, begin in the old section of the city. Board bus No. 1, 5, 6, or 51 at the bus stop in front of the railway station and ride to the Staatsbrucke, the fifth stop. This places you on the perimeter of the Old Town, where most of the sightseeing is located. Orient yourself with the **Kapitelplatz** (Capital Place), and you are right in the center of everything.

The music-festival season starts in January and ends in December. In other words, it never ends. Afternoons in Salzburg may be spent in one of its comfortable coffeehouses watching theatergoers and opera buffs flocking to a performance—many in formal attire. Elegance is a way of life.

Salzburg has a charming narrow street, **Getreidegasse,** which is lined with gilt and wrought-iron trade signs, pictorial devices dating from the time when few people could read. This is one of the best areas in town to find authentic Austrian souvenirs.

Mozart's birthplace, **Mozarts Geburtshaus,** is located at No. 9 Getreidegasse [*Tel:* (0662) 873154; www.mozarteum.at] and is probably one of the most visited houses in the city. *Hours:* 0900–1730 daily (until 2000 in July and August). Birthplace of Wolfgang Amadeus Mozart in 1756, it is now a museum. The Mozart family lived in the third-floor apartment from 1747 to 1773. Here you will see paintings and original instruments belonging to Mozart, including his childhood violin. Only about five minutes from Mozart's birthplace is The Mozart Residence, or Mozart-Wohnhaus, open daily 0900–1730 (until 2000 in July and August), [*Tel:* (0662) 87 42 27 40; www.mozarteum.at], across the Salzach River at No. 8 Markartplatz. Special audio and visual exhibits document the life of the Mozart family. It was here that Mozart lived and composed until 1780. His famous pianoforte, Mozart family portrait, and instruments from that era are on exhibit in the Dancing Master's Hall. Both are included with the Salzburg Card.

Mozart died a pauper in Vienna at age 35, and his body was dumped into an unmarked grave. His life story supports the expression applicable to too many of the world's great artists: "To be appreciated, one must die first."

BELGIUM

Belgium may be small in size—about the size of Maryland in the United States—but it is large in its significance to the European Community. Belgium played an important role in creating the European Union. The Treaty on the European Union was signed in Maastricht in 1992 in an effort to safeguard peace in Europe and to move toward economic and monetary union with intergovernmental cooperation. Belgium's capital city, Brussels, is the seat of the European Union, NATO, and many other world trade and finance companies.

In 1830 Belgium gained its independence. No longer a part of the Netherlands, Belgium became a federal state of communities and regions. The three communities are based on the Dutch, French, and German languages and culture—the Flemish Community, the French Community, and the German-speaking Community. The three regions (Flanders, Brussels Capital, and Wallonia) were based on economic concerns.

Belgium has a hereditary constitutional monarchy, but the king does not "govern"; he serves as protector of the country's unity and independence. King Albert II became Belgium's sixth king in 1993.

Perhaps not as well known is Belgium's significant gastronomic role in western Europe. After all, it was the Flemish Benedictine monks who invented beer, and the beers considered to be "the best" are the ones still brewed traditionally in Belgian monasteries. Restaurants of the Ardennes are well-known for their wild game, and the coastal restaurants serve some of the finest North Sea fish and shellfish dishes. A not so well-known culinary fact about Belgium: The ratio of restaurants to population is equal to that of France.

For more information about Belgium, use the Internet address **www.visitbelgium.com** or contact the Belgian Tourist Office in North America:

New York: 300 East 42nd Street, 14th Fl, New York, NY 10017.
Tel: (212) 758-8130; *Fax:* (212) 355-7675
E-mail: info@visitbelgium.com

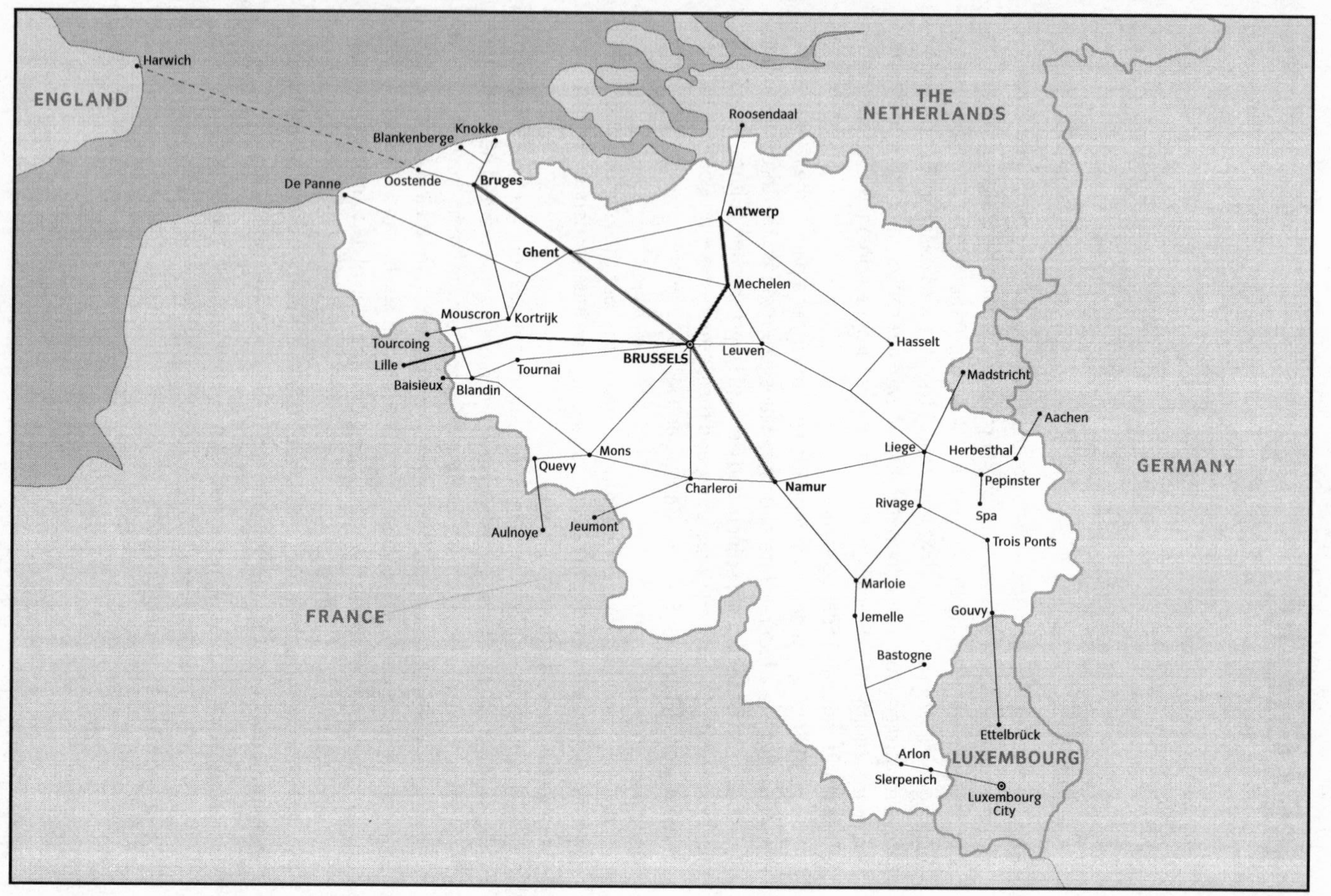
Harwich
ENGLAND
THE NETHERLANDS
Roosendaal
Knokke
Blankenberge
Oostende
De Panne
Bruges
Antwerp
Ghent
Mechelen
Mouscron
Kortrijk
Tourcoing
Lille
Tournai
BRUSSELS
Leuven
Hasselt
Baisieux
Blandin
Madstricht
Aachen
Herbesthal
Liege
GERMANY
Mons
Quevy
Pepinster
Charleroi
Namur
Rivage
Spa
Aulnoye
Jeumont
Trois Ponts
Marloie
FRANCE
Jemelle
Gouvy
Bastogne
Ettelbrück
Arlon
LUXEMBOURG
Slerpenich
Luxembourg City

Banking

Currency: Euro (€)

Exchange rate at press time: €0.90 = U.S. $1.00

Hours: 0900–1600 Monday–Friday; closed Saturday, Sunday, and holidays

Communications

Country Code: 32

For telephone calls within Belgium, dial a zero (0) preceding area code.

Major Mobile Phone Companies: Proximus, Mobistar, BASE

Rail Travel in Belgium

The Belgian railways were the first to be constructed on the continent of Europe, and Belgian Railways (NMBS/SNCB) is said to operate one of the densest rail networks in the world (3,454 kilometers). Visit www.b-rail.be. Brussels serves as an international crossroads. InterCity (IC) trains connect the main towns and regions of Belgium; the Inter-Regional (IR) trains include stops at local stations. Rail service is frequent—usually every hour between most major cities and towns, and with SNCB's integrated schedules, you need not wait long for train connections.

TGV Thalys trains link Brussels to Paris in 1 hour and 16 minutes and to Amsterdam in the Netherlands in only 2 hours and 40 minutes; the high-speed Eurostar trains can whisk you from Brussels to London in only 2 hours, 20 minutes.

The Belgian Railways accepts a variety of **Eurail passes,** including the **Eurail Benelux–Germany Pass,** as well as the regional **Benelux Pass,** which provides unlimited rail travel for any five days within a one-month period in Belgium, the Netherlands, and Luxembourg. If you are two adults traveling together, purchase the special **Benelux Saverpass** and save.

Benelux Pass in USD

5 days in 1 month	1st Class	2nd Class
Adult	$446	$358
Youth (age 4–25)	—	$234

Benelux Saverpass

5 days in 1 month	1st Class	2nd Class
2 people traveling together, price per person	$380	$304

Base City: **BRUSSELS** (Bruxelles)

www.brusselsinternational.be
City Dialing Code: 2

Brussels (Bruxelles) has stood for more than 1,000 years as a signpost of ideals and ideas, a crossroad of people and events. Less than 150 miles from Amsterdam and 200 miles from Paris, Brussels is a bonanza for travelers desiring to see Europe by train. Few people realize how short distances actually are in Belgium, of which Brussels is the capital. Its most opposite points are only 195 miles apart.

Latin and Nordic cultures meet in Brussels, making it a city of contrasts. French is spoken by the Walloon people of French origin, and Flemish is the tongue of the nation's Germanic inhabitants. French, German, and Flemish are official languages in Belgium. Consequently, most signs are trilingual in Brussels. English is spoken in all of the train stations, hotels, and the majority of public places.

Brussels is old; it celebrated its millennium in 1979. Brussels is new; it's the headquarters of the European Common Market and the North Atlantic Treaty Organization (NATO). It is amazing that the people of Brussels have been able to preserve the city's quaint atmosphere while immersed in all this international activity.

Arriving by Air

Brussels Airport, B-1930, Zaventem, *Tel:* (0) 2 753 7753 (0700–2200); www.brusselsairport.be. Located 14 kilometers from city center.

Airport–City Links: Airport City Express trains depart from the airport terminal basement level every 20 minutes for Brussels Gare du Midi (South Station), Gare du Nord (North Station), and Gare Centrale (Central Station). Journey time—about 20 minutes. Fares: €6.90 first class; €5.30 second class. (Eurail pass not accepted.)

Bus station located on ground floor, beneath Arrivals Hall. Take escalators/elevators through the Diamond Area of the terminal. Fare: €10 adults; €5 children. Three or four buses per hour.

Taxis about €45, tip included. Available outside Arrivals Hall. Look for yellow and blue logo on taxi. Save 20 to 50 percent by phoning for a Brussels taxi instead of using the vehicles waiting at the airport. *Tel:* (0) 27529800. Avoid using unmetered taxis!

Money exchange: "GWT" located in Arrivals Hall, Departures Hall, in the duty-free shopping area, and near the baggage carousels.

Arriving by Train

Brussels has three train stations along its main line: one in the north (Gare du Nord), one in the south (Gare du Midi), and a midcity underground station (Gare Centrale). EuroCity trains and the major express trains do not stop in the central station. Change at either the north or south station and then transfer to a local train if Gare Centrale is your destination. The Eurostar, Thalys, and TGV trains arrive at Brussels Midi.

North Station (Nord Bruxelles or Gare du Nord), Rue du Progrès 76. Primarily domestic commuter traffic. *Tel:* (02) 528 28 28 (general travel information).

- **Money exchange:** In a corridor to the left when exiting from the trains into the main station area. *Hours:* 0800–2000 daily, including Sunday.
- **Hotel reservations:** At the information booth in the departure hall. *Hours:* 0900–1700 Monday–Friday.
- **Train information:** In the corridor off the left-hand side of the main station area as you exit from the trains. *Hours:* 0600–2200 Monday–Saturday.
- **Train reservations** are available at ticket window No. 3 or No. 4 in the main station area.
- **Rail pass validation** is at window No. 3 or No. 4.

A railway museum is located on the mezzanine of the North Station. Turn right when entering the main station from the train area, and walk up the stairs at the end of the concourse. The museum holds an interesting collection of rail-transportation vehicles, ranging from the first Belgian steam locomotive to some of the present-day diesel and electric traction units. The museum is well worth the time of your visit. Admission is free.

Central Station (Gare Centrale), Carrefour de l'Europe 2. Links both North and South Stations via underground trackage. Many of the express trains do not stop here. You may, however, board any of the local trains as a shuttle to either of the main stations and vice versa. Therefore, it is possible to establish yourself in one of the downtown hotels or pensions quite near Central Station yet be able to make any train connection with a minimum of inconvenience.

- **Money exchange:** Center hall of the station. As you stand looking at the train information board above the ticket windows, the office is on your right. *Hours:* 0800–2000 daily.
- **Hotel reservations:** Can be made at the Reservations booth in the center hall of the station. Hotel accommodations can also be obtained by visiting the tourist information center in the town hall facing the Grand'Place. (Refer to the section "Tourist Information/Hotel Reservations.") *Hours:* 0900–1730 daily.

- **Train information:** Displayed in the main station area immediately above the ticket windows. This is hourly information. Regular printed schedules are also displayed.
- **Train reservations** are available only at North and South (Midi) Stations.
- **Rail pass validation** must be completed at either North or Midi Station.

South Station (Gare du Midi), Rue de France 2. Gateway to Great Britain (via Eurostar trains through the Channel Tunnel), France, and Spain. On the main floor you will find all the necessary train and tourist services. The tracks are located on the floor above, and each track has its own escalator leading to it. The underground metro station is underneath the rail station.

- **Money exchange:** Left side of the main hall as you enter from the street. *Hours:* 0700–2200 daily.
- **Hotel reservations:** "Information" booth in the center of the main hall. *Hours:* 0900–1800 Monday–Friday. If the information booth is closed, use the Brussels International Tourism & Congress in the Grand'Place.
- **Train reservations and rail pass validation:** Local trains, at the ticket counters in the main hall. Reservations for international trains must be made in the Relations Internationales Office on the far right-hand side of the main hall. Take a number from the ticket machine to wait for your turn. Rail passes may be validated at this office; Eurostar has its own terminal where its tickets are validated.
- **Eurostar Terminal:** Right side of the main hall as you enter from the street. Automatic ticket check-in (a simple insertion of your ticket into a machine) begins one hour prior to departure. Then enter the main terminal, which consists of a large waiting room, cafes, and duty-free stores. Keep in mind that you will carry your luggage onto the train as there is no baggage check-in. If you did not purchase your Eurostar tickets before departing for Europe, they may be purchased at the Relations Internationales Office.

Tourist Information/Hotel Reservations

- *Brussels International Tourist Information:* Hôtel de Ville (Town Hall), Grand'Place, 1000 Brussels *Tel:* (0) 2 513 89 40; *Fax:* (0) 2 513 83 20; www.visitbrussels.be; *E-mail:* info@visitbrussels.be. *Hours:* 0900–1800 daily in summer; 1000–1400 January–Easter. Hotel reservations available.

To reach the Grand'Place from Gare Centrale (Central Station), walk downhill in the direction of the Town Hall's spire until you reach the square. The tourist office is to the right of the spire when you are facing the Town Hall. The tourist office has everything you will need to make your visit to Brussels enjoyable. In addition to tourism information and hotel reservations for Brussels, this office can also provide guides to restaurants, museums, and monuments; tickets to shows; city tours; public transport information; and books and maps.

- *Belgian Tourist Office:* Rue du Marché-aux-Herbes 63, B-1000 Brussels. Information/hotel reservations for all of Belgium. *Tel:* (0) 2 504 03 90; *Fax:* (0) 2 513 04 75; www.opt.be. *Hours:* June 1–September 30, daily 0900–1900; November 1–March 30, Monday–Saturday 0900–1800 and Sunday 1300–1700; April–May and October, daily 0900–1800. Located 1 block north of the Grand'Place.

Getting Around in Brussels

Brussels boasts a highly efficient public transport system encompassing metro, tram, and bus (STIB, Societé des Transports Intercommunaux Bruxellois). **Transport information:** *Tel:* (0) 2 515 2000. A free map is available from the tourist office. The signs for the metro are blue with a white letter "M"; tram and bus stop signs are red and white. Many of the metro lines also have aboveground bus and tram connections. Note that the trams and buses stop "on request." This means you should raise your hand to signal the driver to stop.

Purchase transport tickets at metro stations; STIB offices, or newsstands: one single ticket, €2.00; card for 5 journeys, €8.00; card for 10 journeys, €12.50; one-day card for use on all STIB transport whenever you wish during the same day, €7.00. The one-day pass is also available at tourist information offices.

The **Brussels Card** is a good bargain. Valid for 24 hours (€24), 48 hours (€36), or 72 hours (€43), it provides free access to most of Brussels's 25 museums; free public transportation, including the blue double-decker buses; and a 25 percent reduction at the famous mussels restaurant Chez Leon. It also comes with an illustrated guide booklet. Purchase at tourist information offices, hotels, and museums, public transportation agencies, or online.

Sights/Attractions/Tours

The city abounds in things to see and do, ranging from its elegant Grand'Place to historic Waterloo. If you visit Brussels during the summer, sign up at the tourist office for what we believe is the best way to browse Brussels—"Summer Routes"—attractive, unique theme packages and tours incorporating trams, coaches, boats, or bikes, as well as feet. These are not the usual whistle-stop tours; you get off the beaten track, and you can choose the theme tour that appeals to you. The tourist office also conducts other city tours—in 14 languages!

If you want to conduct your own tour, arm yourself with maps and information from the tourist office. Then head for the **Grand'Place.** You can reach it from the Central Station (Gare Centrale) by walking downhill toward the spire of the Town Hall. When you reach the square, take a minute to drink in the splendor of the ornate medieval guild houses facing the square. You will realize immediately why it is

Train Connections to Other Base Cities from Brussels

Depart from Brussels (Bruxelles) Midi/Zuid South Station.

DEPART	TRAIN NUMBER	ARRIVE	NOTES
		Amsterdam Centraal	
0545	IC 9211	0905	1
0645	IC 9215	1005	
And then hourly at 45 minutes after the hour until 2045, plus Thalys* trains departing at 0752, 0852, 0952, 1152, 1352, 1552, 1652, 1752, 1952, and 2052.			
		Barcelona Sants	
1113	Thalys 9328*	2034	R, 2, Exc. Sa
		Berlin Hauptbahnhof	
0728	Thalys 9401*	1409	R, 3
0928	Thalys 9413*	1609	R, 3
1425	ICE 17	2106	R, 3
1928	Thalys 9473*	0653+1	R, 3, Sleeper
		Bern (Berne)	
0733	ICE 91	1556	R, 7
1233	IC 975	2056	R, 7
		Budapest Keleti	
1425	ICE 17	0919+1	R, 8, Sleeper
		Hamburg Hauptbahnhof	
0728	Thalys 9401*	1413	R, 3
0928	Thalys 9413*	1613	R, 3
1025	ICE 15	1713	R, 3
1425	ICE 17	2113	R, 3
1728	Thalys 9461*	0014+1	R, 3
		Luxembourg	
0633	IC 2106	0951	
And hourly at 33 minutes past the hour until 2033, plus other frequent service.			
		Lyon Part-Dieu	
0710	TGV 9810	1030	R, 5
0817	Thalys 9801*	1200	R
1031	TGV 9826	1400	R
1217	TGV 9828	1600	R
1617	TGV 9836	2000	R
		Milan (Milano) Centrale	
0813	Thalys 9310*	1750	1, 4
1217	Thalys 9334*	2237	R, 1, 2
1713	Thalys 9364*	0550+1	R, 2, Sleeper

DEPART	TRAIN NUMBER	ARRIVE	NOTES
		Munich (München) Hauptbahnhof	
0728	Thalys 9401*	1427	R, 3
0928	Thalys 9413*	1627	R, 3
1728	Thalys 9461*	0027+1	R, 3
1928	Thalys 9473*	0602+1	R, 3, Sleeper
		Nice Ville	
0843	Thalys 9412*	1654	R, 2
1031	TGV 9826	1905	R, 2
1217	TGV 9828	2037	R
2113	Thalys 9388*	1255+1	R, 2, Sleeper
		Paris Gare du Nord	
0843	Thalys 9412*	1005	R
And hourly at 43 minutes past the hour until 2043, plus other frequent service.			
		Prague (Praha)	
1928	Thalys 9473*	1128+1	R, 3, Sleeper
		Vienna (Wien) Westbahnhof	
0728	Thalys 9401*	1909	R, 3
1825	ICE 19	0820+1	R, 6, Sleeper
		Warsaw Centralna	
1928	Thalys 9473*	1215+1	R, 3, Sleeper
		Zürich Hauptbahnhof	
0625	ICE 11	1400	7
1425	ICE 17	2200	3
1928	Thalys 9473*	0805+1	R, 3, Sleeper

Daily, unless otherwise noted
R Reservations required
* Thalys high-speed train, supplement required
+1 Arrives next day
1. M–F.
2. Change trains in Paris.
3. Change trains in Cologne (Köln).
4. Change trains in Zurich.
5. M–Sa.
6. Change to sleeper train EN 421 in Frankfurt, departing 2233.
7. Change trains in Basel.
8. Change trains in Frankfurt and in Munich (München) to sleeper EN 463.

called the most beautiful square in all of Europe. If you are looking for a souvenir or a gift for someone, we can suggest pralines (hand-dipped chocolates), speculoos (brown sugar biscuits), or some fine Brussels lace. All three of these Belgian specialties are available from shops in and around the Grand'Place.

Following your map, proceed down C. Bulstraat (just to the left of the Town Hall as you face it). The name changes to Stoofstraat. At the corner of Eikstraat and Stoofstraat, you can view one of Brussels's most beloved, albeit somewhat irreverent, symbols—**Manneken Pis.** It's a fountain statue—sometimes costumed—doing just what its name implies.

Want to see Brussels and the rest of the European Community in one day? You can. Ask the tourist information office for details about **Mini-Europe** [*Tel:* (0) 2 478 05 50] in Bruparck (metro stop: Heysel). You'll see Europe in miniature—more than 300 models of famous buildings and monuments of the European members constructed on a scale of 1:25, complete with animation and sound effects. Watch a TGV glide by, an Airbus take off, or Mt. Vesuvius erupt simply by pushing a button. *Hours:* March 15–June 30, 0930–1800; July 1–August 31, 0930–2000; September 1–30, 0930–1800; October 1–January 4, 1000–1800; Closed January 5–March 14. Admission €14.30 (children younger than age 12, €10.70). Visit www.minieurope.com.

Bits and Bites of Brussels

Brussels's cosmopolitan population knows how to enjoy itself. Eating and drinking well in Brussels is not a problem. Succumbing too easily to gastronomic temptation is the real difficulty. Bruxellois, it is said, is like French cuisine served in German portions—although some lighter touches of the nouvelle cuisine have inched their way into Brussels's menus.

For the finest gourmet dining, experience the city's most famous culinary establishment, **Comme Chez Soi** at 23 Place Rouppe. For reservations call (0) 2 512 29 21 (closed Sunday and Monday). Visit www.commechezsoi.be; *E-mail:* info@commechezsoi.be. It's only a 15-minute walk from the Grand'Place, at the end of Rue du Midi.

In Belgium beer is not just beer; it's an art form, and the local cafes and bistros are as much an attraction as are the brews they dispense. In Brussels some offer more than 100 different labels of Belgian beer alone. Curious? Order a "gueuze," "lambic," or a "krik" (cherry beer).

For bistro-type dining with a modest price tag, we suggest that you head for the pedestrian-only **Rue des Bouchers** (Street of the Butchers), a stone's throw from the Grand'Place. For lobster with morels or shrimp served in an Art-Deco atmosphere, try **Aux Armes de Bruxelles** at No.13. *Tel:* (0) 2 511 5550; *Fax:* (0) 2 501 0185; www.armebrux.be; *E-mail:* arbrux@beon.be. Or, if you prefer quaint, rustic decor, try **Le Marmiton.** *Tel:* (0) 2 511 7910. Along with the gastronomy, in the evening the area presents numerous sidewalk displays by local artisans.

If you've never eaten a **Brussels waffle,** you haven't lived a full and rewarding life. We are not referring to the "Belgian waffle" that you'll find at concession stands at every state fair, nor do we refer to the highly touted desserts served by fancy restaurants using a waffle as a base piled high with candied fruits and buried in whipped cream. These confections are good, mind you, but nothing in the world can surpass the kind of waffle that Brussels offers. There's nothing fancy about a Brussels waffle. The vendor will hand it to you wrapped in a small napkin.

Brussels waffles are a part of the environment—you can buy them from several small waffle shops located in the area around the city's opera house, and you should only buy them from a shop that actually makes the waffles right on the premises. Look for the sign *gaufres* in French or *wafels* in Flemish.

Day Excursions

It is difficult to choose from the numerous day excursions Brussels has to offer. With its central location and plentiful trains available, a day excursion to Paris, Amsterdam, Luxembourg, or Köln (Cologne) is quite feasible. Via the Channel Tunnel and its Eurostar trains, even London becomes a day excursion. We, however, present four day excursions going to various points within Belgium itself. We offer **Antwerp,** city of diamonds and Rubens; **Bruges** and its famous Markt; **Ghent** with its flower show; and **Namur,** gateway to the beautiful Ardennes.

Day Excursion to

Antwerp (Antwerpen)

The Diamond City

Depart from Brussels Midi/Zuid Station
Distance by Train: 35 miles (57 km)
Average Train Time: 40 minutes
City Dialing Code: 3
Tourist Information Office: Grote Markt 13, B–2000 Antwerp
Tel: (0) 3 232 01 03; **Fax:** (0) 3 231 19 37
www.visitantwerp.be
E-mail: visit@stad.antwerpen.be
Hours: 0900–1745 Monday–Saturday, 0900–1645 Sunday
Notes: To walk to the tourist information office takes about 15 minutes. Antwerp's metro system can also get you there, but first stop at the metro office in the railway station for fare and routing information. In a hurry? Follow the pictograms to the taxi queue. Train-departure information for your return trip to Brussels can be found on the many train bulletin boards located throughout the station. A train information office is on the street side of the station, between the two main exits. The train information office does not dispense tourist information, but they can assist you in finding the tourist office.

If you are convinced that diamonds are a girl's best friend or the kids are hankering to see one of Europe's finest zoos, go to Antwerp. Be certain the train you take from Brussels is marked "Antwerp Central." EuroCity and other through trains continuing to Amsterdam stop only at stations on the edge of Antwerp. The central station is right in the city center near the diamond district. If you do end up in one of Antwerp's suburban stations, board an inbound local train.

The city's name is spelled three ways: "Antwerp" is the English version; in French it is "Anvers"; and its Flemish title is "Antwerpen." Call it what you will, this fine city with nearly half a million people is a marvelous place to visit. Its contrasts will amaze you. Antwerp is Belgium's second city, the third-largest port in the world, reputed to be the world's diamond center (for more than 500 years) and a Renaissance treasure house.

Because Antwerp is one of the world's major seaports, it offers an unusual harbor tour that the entire family can enjoy. With more than 3,000 acres of docks, 17 dry docks, and 6 locks (including the largest in the world), the harbor is a spectacle you should not miss. There is a variety of waterborne tours to select from, and a short trip on the River Scheldt takes 50 minutes. The port sightseeing tour that we recommend takes 2½ hours (www.flandriaboat.com; departs 1000 and 1430, €8.00 adult, €7.00 children). A combination zoo–harbor ticket is available, too.

Many guided or self-directed walking tours of the city and sites are available. Ferries, tourist trams, bicycles, horse-drawn trams and carriages, and rickshaw tours are among the choices offered as well. Consider using the Antwerp City Card, good for 48 hours for €25. It includes free entry to all museums and churches, a free guide, and significant discounts on other venues and attractions. The card is available from the Tourist Office.

Antwerp boasts 20 museums, among them the **Plantin-Moretus,** featuring a 16th-century printing press. Most of Antwerp's museums are closed on Monday, but the zoo, which is just to the right as you exit from the railway station, is open daily until sunset. If you are interested in the **Zoo-Harbor Tour** combo ticket, check with the city tourist information office and pick a time to participate.

Most seasoned travelers put **Rubens's House** (www.rubenshuis.be; *Hours:* 1000–1700 Tuesday–Sunday) at the top of their list of sightseeing "musts." Admission: €8. Rubens bought a beautiful patrician dwelling where he lived with his family from 1615 until his death in 1640. Works of the great Flemish master also are kept in many of the museums and churches in Antwerp. Rubens is buried in **St. James Church,** where you may view the painting ***Madonna with Child and Saints,*** which shortly before his death he directed be placed on the altar. Rubens and Antwerp remain inextricably linked.

Brussels (Bruxelles)—Antwerp (Antwerpen)

DEPART Brussels Midi/Zuid	TRAIN NUMBER	ARRIVE Antwerp Central	NOTES
0657	IC 3106	0751	Daily
0757	IC 3107	0851	Daily
0857	IC 3108	0951	M–F
0928	IC 3308	1020	Sa–Su
0957	IC 3109	1051	Daily
plus other frequent service.			

DEPART Antwerp Central	TRAIN NUMBER	ARRIVE Brussels Midi/Zuid	NOTES
1439	IC 3335	1532	M–F
1440	IC 3336	1532	Sa–Su
1517	IC 9240	1615	Daily
1539	IC 3336	1633	M–F
1609	IC 3137	1703	Daily
1739	IC 3338	1832	M–F
1909	IC 3140	2002	Daily
plus other frequent service until 2317.			

All departing trains en route to Antwerp also stop at Brussels Central Station, then at Brussels Nord Station; trains returning to Brussels from Antwerp stop first at Nord, then Central, and then Midi/Zuid Station.

Distance: 35 miles (57 km)

Other sightseeing musts are the **Cathedral of Our Lady** (largest Gothic church in Belgium), containing four Rubens masterpieces; the **Grote Markt** (marketplace); and the **Open Market** (known locally as the Birds Market). The Birds Market is open on Sunday morning, when miscellaneous wares are sold. All these city highlights will be on the map you receive at the city tourist office, and all are within reasonable walking distance.

The Flemish term *De Rubenswandeling* means **The Rubens Walk.** It's all laid out for you in a colorful brochure, its map detailing 11 points of interest associated with Rubens. For variety, there is a *Stadswandeling/Rondwandeling*—city round-trip walking tour—prepared in a similar format. Both are available at the tourist office.

According to legend, the site of Antwerp was once inhabited by a giant who extracted tribute from all who navigated the river and he cut off a hand of those who refused to pay. He was slain by a Roman soldier, who cut off the giant's hand and threw it into the river. Thus, the city's name: *Ant* (hand) and *werpen* (from the verb "to throw"). In support of the legend, the city fathers erected a statue of the Roman soldier, Silvius Brabo, in front of the city hall. Those not subscribing to the legend say the name was derived from *Aenwerpen* (higher land). There's always someone who doesn't believe in the tooth fairy.

Day Excursion to

Bruges (Brugge)

Old Lace and Church Spires

Depart from Brussels Nord Station
Distance by Train: 65 miles (105 km)
Average Train Time: 1 hour, 7 minutes
City Dialing Code: 50
Tourist Information Office: Toerisme Brugge, Burg 11, B–8000 Brugge
Tel: (0) 50 44 46 46; **Fax:** (0) 50 44 46 45
www.brugge.be
E-mail: toerisme@brugge.be
Hours: 0900–1800 Monday–Friday, 1000–1400 Saturday–Sunday
Notes: Arriving in Bruges, check schedules posted in the station for your return train to Brussels. The train information office is inside the station on the left side as you exit from the train platform [*Tel:* (0) 50 38 23 82]. Tourist information is available outside the station near the Video Palace, or go to the central tourist office in Burg Square.

Brussels (Bruxelles)—Bruges (Brugge)

Two or more trains per hour from Brussels Midi/Zuid to Bruges at 06 and 22 minutes after the hour; journey time 50 minutes. The same trains depart first from Nord Station, then Central, and finally Midi/Zuid.

Returning trains (2 or more each hour) depart Bruges at 32 and 57 minutes after the hour; journey time 50 to 55 minutes. Trains arrive first at Midi/Zuid, then Central, and then Nord.

Note: The rail route from Brussels to Bruges is the main line to the port of Oostende. Consequently, most of the trains going in that direction stop at all three of the main Brussels stations. Check departure information in the station you plan to depart from in Brussels.

Distance: 65 miles (105 km)

To get to the tourist office in Burg Square, board any bus stopping in front of the railway station that is marked *Centrum* at the entrance side of the bus. The bus will take you to the Markt. It stops in the center of the square in front of the Provincial Palace. To return to the station, board the bus marked O Station at the library on the square close to the Markt, which can be reached by walking through Kuiperstraat off the Markt.

Bruges is where the arts reign supreme. Venues range from the Japanese-designed pavilion for the Burg to the Concertgebouw—an arts center of distinction. Bruges has magnetic attractions—many of which date from the Middle Ages and the Renaissance—as well as picturesque canals, art treasures, and antiques shops. Probably the most interesting sight is the **Burg,** where history has been in the making since the ninth century. Surrounding the Burg are museums of all descriptions, spectacular church spires, peaceful canals, and fascinating alleyways. Next to the Burg is the **Markt** (Marketplace), where you will find the **Town Hall** and the **Belfry,** a remarkable building that dominates the Markt with its famous 280-foot-high octagonal tower. If you are up to it, climb up the Belfry for a panoramic view. The Brugge City Card provides free admission to over 20 attractions along with a visitors guide, discounts at some shops, and a free canal trip. Available at the tourist office, or online: www.bruggecitycard.be; €40 for 48 hours, €45 for 72 hours.

During the 13th and 14th centuries, Bruges stood at the crossroads of traffic between the Mediterranean and the Baltic. Rich cargoes piled high on its docks, and its warehouses held treasures of spices, cloth, and other luxuries. Bruges was bursting at the seams during this period. Hundreds of ships dropped anchor in its harbor. In its medieval magnificence, Bruges boasted a population double that of London. There was no equal to the grandeur of its court—and no one seemed alarmed that the estuary linking Bruges with the North Sea was growing more narrow and more shallow as the silt from the River Zwyn slowly oozed seaward.

Inexorably, the waterway began to close. Deep-draft ships could no longer navigate the estuary. The docks were abandoned, and Bruges became a victim of its own progress, a landlocked city. Today, Bruges is a museum of the Middle Ages, with gabled rooflines casting shadows on its cobblestone streets. Despite the loss of its commerce with the sea, Bruges has managed to maintain its former opulence.

Remnants of grand days past, the canals of Bruges, graced by a bevy of swans, weave in and around the city. Oddly enough, the birds' presence is attributable to a murder. In 1488 the good people of Bruges beheaded a tyrant named Langhals ("Long Neck"). Miffed by this deed, the counts of Flanders decreed that the "long necks," the symbolic swans, would be kept at public expense forever—and they are.

Although walking is the best way to see Bruges, there are other interesting ways. One is by canal boat—board behind the Belfry. The trip lasts 35 minutes. Or, if pedal power appeals to you, rent a bike at the station.

Yet another, and no less pleasant, way of seeing the city is by horse-drawn cab. The cabs wait at Markt Square.

In addition to all the sights of historic significance in Bruges, there are many stores selling exquisite, handmade Flemish lace; excellent reproductions of Flemish paintings; and colorful ceramics. In general, prices are slightly lower than in Brussels, and the quality is as high.

Day Excursion to

Ghent (Gent)

Historic Beauty

Depart from Brussels Nord Station
Most trains from Brussels to Ghent stop in all three of Brussels's metropolitan train stations. Check departure information in your station.
Distance by Train: 40 miles (64 km)
Average Train Time: 45 minutes
City Dialing Code: 9
Tourist Information Office: Ghent Old Fish Market, St. Veerleplein 5, 9000 Gent
Tel: (0) 9 266 56 60
www.gent.be or **www.visitgent.be**
E-mail: visit@gent.be
Hours: October 15–March 14: 0930–1630 daily; March 15–October 14: 0930–1830
Notes: To reach the tourist office, take tram No. 10, 11, 12, or 13 to the town center at Korenmarkt.

Ghent is one of the true Flemish water towns. Three rivers—the Schelde, the Lys, the Lieve—plus a canal flow through it. This accounts for its more than 100 bridges and its Celtic name, "Ganda," meaning a place of confluence. In the 14th century,

Ghent was the second-largest city north of the Alps after Paris. In 1827 the cutting of the Terneuzen canal made Ghent the second-largest seaport in Belgium. In more modern times, Ghent has become world famous for its flower show and the International Ghent Fair. Both are held in the Flanders Expo, a trade fair complex a few kilometers from the center of Ghent.

Brussels (Bruxelles)—Ghent (Gent)

At least three trains per hour depart Midi/Zuid at 06, 33, and 51 minutes after the hour; journey time approximately 30 minutes. Trains depart first from Nord, then Central, and then Midi/Zuid.

Returning trains (at least three each hour) depart Ghent at 24, 40, and 55 minutes after the hour; journey time approximately 30 minutes. Trains arrive first at Midi/Zuid, then Central, and then Nord.

Distance: 40 miles (64 km)

Ask for the free brochure *All Information for Tourists* at the tourist office. The brochure includes a map with different walking tours. Each is color-coded, and places of interest are indicated. During the summer season, guided walking tours for individuals start at the tourist office every day. Or what about enjoying a carriage trip or a boat excursion?

A museum pass is available from the tourist office, which at €35 for 72 hours provides free admission to 15 museums and monuments, as well as free city bus and tram use.

Saint Michael's Bridge, in the heart of the city, is a good place to begin your walking tour. The view from here is impressive, with church towers and guild houses rimming the skyline. In the distance you can see the **Castle of the Counts,** one of the most imposing feudal fortresses in Europe today. It played a prominent role in Ghent's history during feudal times. The tradespeople had united in a number of strong guilds and could offer armed resistance against their feudal lords, the counts, when said gentry came to collect the rent. The town hall and the Belfry, symbols of civic freedom, were also erected during that period. The Castle of the Counts was completely restored in 1887 and is well worth your inspection.

The **Kouter** is a favorite place for the citizens of Ghent to start their Sunday walks. Every morning there is a flower market here, which on a Sunday takes over the whole area. In the summer, bands from Ghent and the province play in the wrought-iron bandstand in the middle of the square. The vegetable and fruit markets are open Monday through Saturday at the **Groentenmarkt.** As the commercial activity diminishes, the social activities gain tempo.

In early times Ghent, like many other Flemish towns, was involved in warding off the Norse invaders coming off the beaches of the North Sea to loot and plunder. Later, Ghent was able to turn to more peaceful activities. Growing in opulence, Ghent fostered the emerging artists of Flanders and today is considered the cradle of Flemish art.

Each September and October, Ghent plays host to the **Flanders Festival of Music.** Some of the world's greatest musicians and the most celebrated Belgian orchestras and choirs perform. Many other annual events take place. International regattas are held every May at the **Watersportbaan.** From April 1 to October 31 daily and from November 1 to March 31 on Friday and Saturday, many of the city's historic places, such as the Castle of the Counts, are illuminated at night. Check with the tourist office for a list of events and festivals.

Hungry? With more than 350 restaurants to choose from, something will suit your taste buds—Italian, Greek, French, Chinese, vegetarian—you name it, you can find it. Opposite the town hall, try the **Hotel Cour St. Georges.** Although Ghent lies inland from the North Sea, it is, in fact, a seaport and offers some exceptional seafood. If you enjoy shellfish, order the Belgian specialty, moules mariniers (steamed mussels).

Day Excursion to

Namur

Gateway to the Ardennes

Depart from Brussels Midi Station
Distance by Train: 43 miles (69 km)
Average Train Time: 60 minutes
City Dialing Code: 81
Tourist Information Office: Maison du Tourisme de Namur, Square Leopold, 5000 Namur
Tel: (0) 81 24 64 49; **Fax:** (0) 81 26 23 60
www.namurtourisme.be or **www.ftpn.be**
E-mail: info@namurtourisme.be
Hours: 0930–1800 daily
Notes: In the Namur Station, leave the train-platform area via an underground ramp. Once on the ramp, walk past sortie 1 to sortie 2 and take the stairs to the street level. Bear toward the right around the "C & A" store and proceed to the park, where the tourist office will be in plain view.

If you would like to revisit the 18th century, go to Namur. It is one of the most attractive towns in Belgium. The tourist office offers several excellent walking tours and theme tours. It can also provide personalized tours upon request. For the footsore and those wanting to range farther afield, book an **"All-in-One"** ticket that includes boat tours, harborside attractions, and the Citadel of Namur, complete with underground explorations.

Brussels (Bruxelles)—Namur

At least 2 trains hourly depart Midi/Zuid at 3 and 33 minutes after the hour; journey time 1 hour. Trains depart first from Midi/Zuid, then from Central, and then from Nord.

Returning trains depart Namur at 14 and 45 minutes after the hour, until 2214; journey time 1 hour. Trains arrive first at Nord, then Central, and then Midi/Zuid. Last train departs at 2221.

Distance: 43 miles (69 km)

On Saturday morning, don't miss the colorful flower market at the **Place du Palais de Justice** and the Leopold Square shopping center. Probably you will not find such a concentration of museums and monuments anywhere else in Europe.

The dominating landmark of Namur—**the Citadel**—looms on its skyline. It is in the center of the **Parc du Champeau.** The walk there can be delightful. The tourist bureau will provide full details. You can also reach the Citadel by bus. Board bus No. 3 in the town square, adjacent to the railway station. A tour of the Citadel is included in the "All-in-One" ticket, along with a ride in the tourist office's shuttle.

The Citadel of Namur sits at the confluence of the Meuse and the Sambre. Two thousand years of history are contained within its walls. Originally a Celtic stronghold with primitive fortifications, it was altered into a strongly defensive castle. Underground fortifications were added in the 15th century and again expanded century after century until modern weaponry brought a cessation of such defenses in the 18th century. Throughout its history, however, the Citadel, as one of the most important strongholds of Europe, faced 20 sieges!

Namur's tourist office has a wide selection of excursions for you to select from. Here are but a few: **The Gardens of Annevoie,** famous for its 18th-century style of flowers and fountains, are open 0930 to 1730 (1830 July–August; www.annevoie.be); a visit can be made in minutes. A restaurant and tavern are on the grounds. **Cruises on the River Meuse** are available in a variety of schedules, including a picnic onboard or ashore.

For aquatic buffs, a kayak or boat trip down the River Lesse is available, with departures daily throughout the season at 1000 and 1400. Looking for something a bit less strenuous? Perhaps a water tour of the **Caves of Neptune** would fill the bill. It's a 45-minute tour and includes a 20-minute boat ride plus a sight and sound show. There are other ways to discover the Lesse and the valley area—try the rail/bike ride on an old railway line.

Namur is the gateway to the Ardennes, the forests and mountains of Belgium, with all the amenities of a holiday resort. Should you find yourself with time to spare (a very unlikely thing), take a stroll on the **Boulevard de la Sambre,** an attractive, tree-lined avenue. If, on the other hand, you are looking for exquisite gifts, the **Rue de l'Ange** has excellent shops. Or enjoy Brasseries (Breweries) du Bocp and des Fagnes.

Visit Namur during the summer season of festivals. This is the best way to experience the local folklore of the Stiltwalkers of Namur; the looming giants, the Royal Society of Moncrabeau; the bright-yellow uniformed Canaris regiment; or the choreographed lunacy of the dancing Chinels.

CZECH REPUBLIC

After emerging from behind the Iron Curtain with the fall of the Soviet Union in 1989, and splitting from Slovakia in 1993, the Czech Republic has rapidly modernized and is now generally considered to be on par with most countries in Western Europe. Given this rise and the historical and natural beauty of the region, it is no wonder that the Czech Republic has become one of the most visited countries in Europe.

Besides the many historical sites and outdoor activities, the country, and the Capital of Prague particularly, have become known as something of a "party country." The exchange rate has generally made it an inexpensive travel destination, and Prague has a large number of bars located close to each other and often open very late. While petty crime (mostly pickpocketing and overcharging on taxis) has been a problem, the country is generally safe, even if you're stumbling back to your hotel room late at night.

For more information and pretrip planning tips, be sure to visit the Czech Republic website, www.czechtourism.com, or contact the ***Czech Tourist Authority:*** 1109 Madison Avenue, New York, NY 10028. *Tel:* (212) 288-0830 ext.101; *Fax:* (212) 288-0971, *Email:* newyork@czechtourism.com

Banking

Currency: Koruna (CZK)

Exchange rate at press time: 23.9 CZK = U.S. $1.00

Hours: 0900–1530 Monday–Friday, closed Saturday and Sunday. In all but the smallest towns, ATMs available.

Communications

Country Code: 420

For telephone calls within the Czech Republic, dial a zero (0) preceding area code.

Major Mobile Phone Companies: T-Mobile, O2, Vodafone

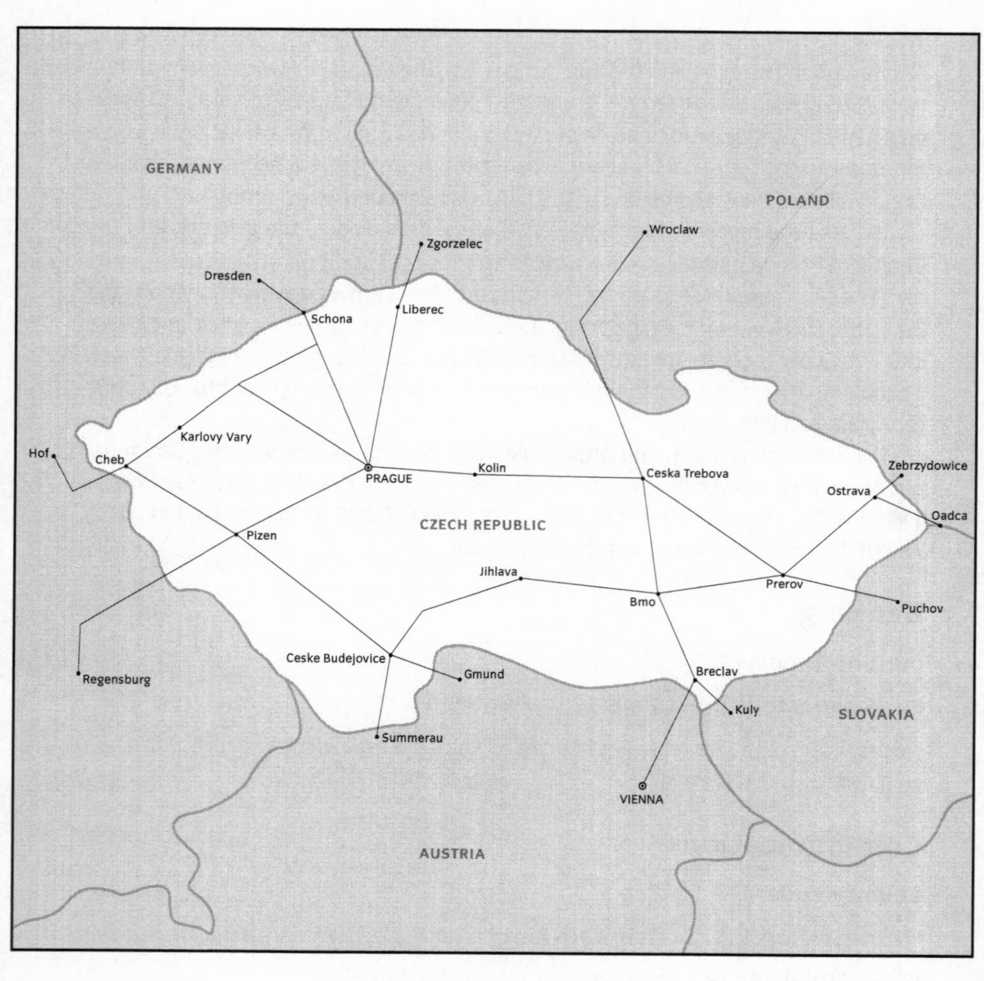
GERMANY
POLAND
Wroclaw
Zgorzelec
Dresden
Schona
Liberec
Karlovy Vary
Hof
Cheb
PRAGUE
Kolin
Ceska Trebova
Zebrzydowice
Ostrava
Oadca
CZECH REPUBLIC
Pizen
Jihlava
Bmo
Prerov
Puchov
Regensburg
Ceske Budejovice
Gmund
Breclav
Kuly
SLOVAKIA
Summerau
VIENNA
AUSTRIA

Rail Travel in the Czech Republic

Czech Railways, or České dráhy (ČD), owns and operates almost all of the more than 9,000 kilometers of rail in the Czech Republic and accepts the **European East Pass;** the **Czech Republic-Germany Pass;** the **Austria-Czech Republic Pass;** and the national **Czech Republic Pass.** (See the Appendix for a list of rail pass types and prices.) Remember to purchase your rail passes prior to your departure for Europe. Visit www.ceskedrahy.cz.

The aforementioned rail passes include the following discounts within the Czech Republic:

- Free access to the ČD lounges located in several railway stations for 1st class passholders
- Special ticket available on the Expressbus from Prague to Nürnberg. Reservations are required.
- Up to 20 percent discount at Orea Hotels

Czech Republic Pass

Valid for 3, 4, 5, or 8 days of rail travel in a 1-month period.

	ADULT 1st Class	ADULT 2nd Class	YOUTH 2nd Class
3 days	$173	$129	$87
4 days	$239	$179	$119
5 days	$336	$250	$167
8 days	$399	$296	$197

Children age 4–11 half adult fare; younger than age 4 travel free. Youth age 12–25.

Base City: **PRAGUE (Praha)**

www.praha.eu or www.praguewelcome.cz
City Dialing Code: 23

Arriving by Air

Ruzyně International Airport, *Tel:* (420) 220 111 888 for information, including transport to the city center; www.prg.aero.

Located 19 kilometers from the city center, Ruzyně Airport is the home base for Czech Airlines and serves more than 20 other international airlines. Direct flights are available to New York and Atlanta. Tourist information is available in the "Arrivals Hall."

Airport–City Links: Bus service every 30 minutes (Airport Express) from the airport into Prague Main Station. The price is 150 CZK; journey time, 35 minutes. Bus service is also available to other parts of the city.

Taxis are available just outside the arrivals area. Fare to city center is about 500–700 CZK; journey time, 30 to 40 minutes; be sure to use one of the licensed taxis.

Arriving by Train

Prague Main Station (Praha hlavní nádraž, Praha hl.n) is the main station in Prague, as well as the central station for all of the Czech Republic.

Prague Main Station is worth a visit by itself for the Art Nouveau design of the station and the original booking hall, now a restaurant. The more recent portion of the station has a currency exchange desk (open 0900–1600 weekdays), left luggage service, as well as restaurant and small shop services. An information desk (railpass validation also) is open 0400–0030 Monday–Friday and 0700–0030 Saturday and Sunday.

Tourist Information/Hotel Reservations

- Main Tourist Office, Staroměstské náměstí 1, just off the main square in Old Town. Open 0900–1900 daily, until 2000 in the summer. Accommodation service available, as well as tickets for various concerts and other events, tours, the Prague Card, and guidebooks.
- Ruzyně Airport, in Terminal 2, open 0800–2000 daily.
- Prague Main Station, Main Lobby, open 1000–1800 Monday–Saturday.

Getting Around in Prague

The most economical and convenient way to discover Prague is with the **Prague Card.** The card provides free access to Prague's public transportation, plus free entry at 44 attractions with discounts at more than 50 museums and attractions, concerts, shops, theaters, restaurants, cafes, and tours. All the benefits are described in the 150-page Prague Card coupon book. The card is 880 CZK for 48 hours, 990 CZK for 72 hours, and 1200 CZK for 96 hours, with discounted student rates also available. Purchase in any Tourist Office, or online at www.praguecitycard.com.

Prague has an efficient public transport system, including subway, trams, busses and ferries. All work on the same fare system, based around the time you need the pass rather than the route you are taking. The basic 90-minute pass is 32 CZK, with 24-hour passes 110 CZK. Tickets can be purchased from machines at all metro stops and many bus stops, as well as tourist offices and some tobacco shops. Using public transport in Prague is highly recommended, as unlicensed taxis that horribly overcharge tourists are notorious in the city. Prague is working hard to counter this problem, but you can easily avoid it by taking the bus or metro.

Sights/Attractions/Tours

Dominating the west bank of the Vltava is the enormous Prague Castle. Generally recognized as the largest castle in the world, parts of it were constructed from the 9th century, while major additions and alterations continued over the next 1,000 years. Built over this time frame, the castle represents almost every major style of architecture of the last millennium. The castle can easily be a full trip, as it now also houses museums dedicated to art, Czech history, and toys, and regularly hosts festivals, including the Summer Shakespeare Festival. The castle grounds are open summer tourist season April 1–October 31 0500–2400; premise regular tickets 0900–1700. Gardens open April and October 1000–1800 daily; May and September 1000–1900; June and July 1000–2100; and August 1000–2000. Winter tourist season is January 1–March 31, 0600–2300 daily. Premise regular tickets 0900–1600. Tickets are required for Old Royal Palace, St. George's Basilica, the National Gallery, Cathederal of St. Vitus, Golden Lane, Powder Tower, and Rosedberg. "Long Visit" tickets, covering all of the ticketed areas, are 350 CZK, with tickets for portions of the castle less; www.hrad.cz.

Old Town, centered on Old Town Square, is the center of the original town site of Prague. The cornerstone of the square is the **Orloj (Astronomical Clock).** Originally built in 1410, the clock plays an hourly show of the Apostles. It also demonstrates the location of the moon, the planets, and the sun, among other functions. There are numerous cafes and restaurants in the area, serving all types of food and drink. Be sure to check out the **Municipal House,** a large and striking Art Nouveau building completed in 1912, still in use as an event hall. Concerts of various types are held in the building, and guided tours of the amazingly decorated interior are available daily 1000–1900. **The Museum of Communism** tells the story of communism in the Czech Republic, from 1948 until 1989, and houses many interesting artifacts from this period of recent Czech history. Open 0900–2100 daily, admission 190 CZK adults, 150 CZK students. Visit www.muzeumkomunismu.cz.

Possibly the single most famous landmark in the Czech Republic, the **Charles Bridge** crosses the Vltava River, connecting Old Town with the Lesser Quarter, just below the Prague Castle. Construction on the almost 1,700-foot-long bridge started in 1357, and upon its completion in the early 15th century it immediately became an important trade route between eastern and western Europe. It is also famous for the three large bridge towers, especially the one on the Old Town side of the river, a massive Gothic-style structure. The bridge is decorated with 30 statues of saints along its length. The bridge is crowded during the day, with many artists and street vendors to serve the thousands of tourists that walk its length.

The **Prague Zoo** is consistently ranked among the best zoos in the world and is on the leading edge of research and breeding programs. It has contributed to the breeding and subsequent reintroduction to the wild of Przewalski's horse, a type of wild horse that was nearly extinct by 1945. Hours 0900–1900, shorter in winter; 200 CZK; www.zoopraha.cz. The zoo is located on the north side of the Vltava River and immediately next to the **Troja Castle.** This Baroque palace was built in the 17th century, but now is owned by the city of Prague and houses an impressive collection of Czech art. As impressive as the palace itself are the huge, immaculately maintained gardens, where you could easily spend hours wandering and relaxing.

Prague is the city of the Vltava River, and a steamboat trip on the river is an excellent way to see the city in a different way, or to travel to a different portion of the city. Most riverboats depart from Rašínovo Quay, southwest of Old Town, on the east bank of the river. (Take the Metro B-line to Karlovo náměstí.) Trips include a guide to point out the various sights along the way, and food and drinks are available on board. A 90-minute trip is 310 CZK for adults and 160 CZK for children under 12. Many other itineraries are available, including a dinner cruise and a trip from Karlovo náměstí upriver to the zoo. Visit www.praguesteamboats.com.

Since the fall of communism, Prague has become well known as a place with excellent nightlife, and drinking, especially beer, is an important part of Czech culture. There are many pubs throughout the city, and if you stay away from the tourist-heavy area around the Charles Bridge or Old Town square, they offer an excellent opportunity to meet the locals. It is common custom to join others, so if there are no tables available, don't hesitate to ask to join a group. There are several companies that offer "pub crawl" tours, which include some drinks, entry into several clubs, a guide and often a t-shirt, and generally are around 500 CZK. The area east of Old Town, also known as the Žižkov neighborhood, is well known for its high concentration of bars. This diverse neighborhood is also the home of many foreigners and artists, and also home to the **Žižkov Television Tower,** built on the hill of the same name. The communist-built tower, which dominates the skyline, was rumored to have been built to jam Western radio transmissions. It houses an observation deck; open daily 0800–2400, admission 150 CZK; www.towerpark.cz.

Train Connections to Other Base Cities from Prague (Praha)

Depart from Prague Main Station (Praha hlavní nádraž) unless otherwise noted.

DEPART	TRAIN NUMBER	ARRIVE	NOTES
		Amsterdam Centraal	
1827	CNL 456	0934+1	R, Sleeper
		Berlin Hauptbahnhof	
0627	EC 178	1058	
0827	EC 176	1258	
1027	EC 174	1458	
1227	EC 378	1658	
1427	EC 172	1858	
1627	EC 170	2058	
		Bern (Berne)	
1827	CNL 458	0824+1	R, 1, Sleeper
		Brussels (Bruxelles) Midi/Zuid	
1827	CNL 458	0935+1	R, 2, Sleeper
		Budapest Keleti	
0549	EC 273	1235	
0949	EC 277	1635	
1549	EC 175	2235	
		Copenhagen (København) H.	
0427	EN 406	1730	R, 4
		Hamburg Hauptbanhof	
0827	EC 176	1511	
1227	EC 174	1911	
1427	EC 172	2115	
		Munich (München) Hauptbahnhof	
0912	EX 354	1505	
1712	EX 356	2305	
		Paris Gare de l'Est	
1827	CNL 458	0950+1	R, 2, Sleeper
		Vienna (Wien) Westbahnhof	
0849	EC 73	1251	
1049	EC 75	1451	
1449	EC 79	1851	
1849	RJ 373	2251	
		Warsaw Centralna	
1424	EC 117	2214	R
2200	EN 445	0700+1	R, Sleeper
		Zürich Hauptbahnhof	
0912	EC 354	2053	R, 3
1827	CNL 458	0905+1	R, Sleeper

Daily, including holidays, unless otherwise noted
R Reservations required
+1 Arrives next day

1. Change trains in Basel.
2. Change trains in Köln.
3. Change trains in Munich (München).
4. Change trains in Berlin.

Day Excursions from Prague

From Prague, head to **Brno** to see churches and castles, as well as a world-renowned piece of modern architecture, all in an important university city. More interested in the history of beer? **Pilsen** should be high on your list, with several brewery tours (and great samples) available. For impressive churches and an interesting display of skeletons, be sure to make the quick trip to **Kutná Hora.**

You have other options if you plan to spend longer in the Czech Republic. Other cities to consider include **Ostrava,** known for its coal mining and steel works; **Olomouc,** a university town with an impressive collection of architecture; and **Carlsbad,** a large and historic spa. For outdoors sightseeing and activities, northeast of Prague is the **"Bohemian Paradise"** region, with its dramatic sandstone formations, old, crumbling castles, and many opportunities for outdoor recreation.

Day Excursion to

Brno

Centuries of Splendor

Depart from Prague Main Station
Distance by Train: 257 miles (413 km)
Average Train Time: 2 hours, 45 minutes
City Dialing Code: 5
Tourist Information Office: Radnická 8, 65878 Brno
Tel: 420542427150; **Fax:** 420542427151
www.ticbrno.cz
E-mail: info@ticbrno.cz
Hours: 0800–1800 Monday–Friday, 0900–1800 Saturday and Sunday

A smaller city in the southeast of the country, Brno is an important regional hub, as well as the center of the Czech Court system, and an educational center, with around ten percent of the city's population consisting of students. The center of the city holds **Freedom Square,** a large, vaguely triangular-shaped square that remains the center of city life. A pedestrian-only area (except for trams), the square is surrounded by small cafes and shops, as well as an impressive array of buildings. Barely a block north of the square is **St. James Church,** which, with its unmistakable 300-foot-tall spire, is the seventh tallest building in the Czech Republic, despite having been finished in 1592.

Just west of the city center, on a hill overlooking the center of the city, sits **Špilberk Castle.** Originally a royal castle from the 13th century, it gradually became a massive fortress and the most notorious prison of the Austro-Hungarian Empire. After World War II, the castle was purchased by the city of Brno and became the home of the city museum. The museum houses a gallery, library, various exhibits, and a very nice children's workshop area. The castle is open daily 1000–1800 in the summer, but closed Monday in the winter. Admission to view the castle, all exhibitions, and the casemates (an underground area originally built as fortifications, then converted to prison use) is 90 CZK. Visit www.spilberk.cz.

Located several blocks south of Freedom Square, **The Cathedral of St. Peter and Paul** sits on a hill, and dominates the skyline of Brno. It is considered one of the most important churches in the country, as well as an important cultural landmark. The church is open for tours 0815–1830 daily, unless services are underway, and the inside is a sight to behold, with magnificent stained glass, statues and woodwork, as well as displays of historic church objects. Guide services are available, and required to access the tower and crypt. Admission is 35 CZK; www.katedrala-petrov.cz.

A UNESCO World Heritage site, the **Villa Tugendhat** is a residence, built in the late 1930s, and generally considered one of the most important examples of functionalist architecture in the world. Designed by the famous German architect Ludwig Mies van der Rohe, who would later immigrate to the US and complete many works there, the house is the prototypical "glass house." Check www.tugendhat.eu for updates and information on visiting. Because of this site's popularity we recommend to all visitors to buy tickets at least 1 month in advance. Closed Monday.

If you intend to visit in late May or early June, check for the exact dates of the fireworks show **"Ignis Brunensis."** Brno is known across Europe for these shows, which are a competition between fireworks professionals with spectators reaping the benefits. The show is free, but expect crowds, and be sure of your accomodation plans with tens of thousands of spectators in town. Visit www.ignisbrunensis.cz.

The **Masaryk Circuit** racetrack, with a history dating back to the early 1930s, also attracts large crowds for various auto and motorcycle racing events. If you are feeling adventurous, tours and rides on the track are available.

Given the location of Brno in the Czech Republic, the possibility exists of stopping in Brno on your way out of the country, if you plan to continue to Vienna or Budapest. If you choose to do this, head to Brno in the morning, spend the day in

Brno (luggage lockers available), and then continue to Vienna (Wien), departing on RS 371 at 1924 to arrive Vienna at 2051. To head to Budapest, depart Brno at 1824 to arrive in Budapest at 2235.

Prague—Brno

DEPART Prague Main Station	TRAIN NUMBER	ARRIVE Brno
0649	EC 71	0922
0749	EC 275	1022
0849	EC 73	1122
0949	EC 277	1222

Hourly departures continue until 1949.

DEPART Brno	TRAIN NUMBER	ARRIVE Prague Main Station
1538	EC 276	1808
1638	EC 78	1908
1738	EC 274	2008
1838	EC 370	2108
1938	EC 272	2208
2038	EC 372	2308

Distance: 257 miles (413 km)

Day Excursion to

Pilsen (Plzeň)

History and Brews

Depart from Prague Main Station
Distance by Train: 71 miles (114 km)
Average Train Time: 1 hour, 40 minutes
City Dialing Code: 377
Tourist Information Office: nam. Republiky 41, 301 00 Plzeň
Tel: (420) 378 035 330; **Fax:** (420) 378 035 332
www.pilsen.eu
E-mail: info@icpilsen.cz
Hours: April–September: 0900–1900 daily; October–March: 0900–1800 daily
Notes: Tourist Office is on the north side of the Main Square, across from St. Bartholomew's Cathedral. Exit the train station and turn right onto Sirková, then left onto Pražská, and follow this to the main square. There is also a Tourist Office in the rail station, with slightly shorter hours.

The city of Pilsen is best known as having been the birthplace of the modern Pilsner style of beer, and the home of the Pilsner Urquell brewery. Officially established in 1295, Pilsen has historically been a scene of great conflict, besieged and captured repeatedly in the 17th century. Additionally, until most ethnic Germans were expelled post-World War II, the city was very much a mixed community, with a significant percentage of German-speakers in the area. Primarily a manufacturing center when the country was under Soviet domination, after a period of turmoil and uncertainty, the city has attracted Western investment and is again a manufacturing center for many goods, including trains, electronics, and heating and cooling equipment.

St. Bartholomew's Cathedral dominates the central square of Pilsen. The cathedral, finished in the 16th century, is the third tallest building in the Czech Republic, with its main spire rising to over 330 feet. The inside of the cathedral is filled with sacred art from the 17th century to the present, including a Madonna dated from 1390 that still sits next to the altar. The cathedral is open to the public when services are not being conducted. Just east of the main square on Pražská, look for **U Salzmannų**, one of the oldest beer restaurants in the country, which serves traditional Czech cuisine. On the north side of the main square is **Town Hall,** a Renaissance building that is generally considered one of the most beautiful city halls in the Czech Republic.

Be sure to visit the **Great Synagogue,** the second largest synagogue in Europe (and third largest in the world). Originally started in 1888, the building fell in disrepair under the Nazis, and then while the region was under communist rule. Reopened in 1988 after a massive restoration, it is primarily used as a concert and exhibition hall, although a small portion still fulfills its role as a place of worship. The building is a striking mix of styles, including Russian, Romantic, and Oriental design elements.

The Pilsen Municipal Armory is one of the best preserved medieval armories in Europe. Now the **Pilsen Historical Museum,** the armory houses an impressive display of early firearms and cannons and shows visitors what life was like in a fortified medieval town. Open 1000–1800 Tuesday–Sunday. Admission is 60 CZK; www.zcm.cz.

Originally a city-owned brewery, the **Pilsner Urquell Brewery** (now known as Plzensky Prazdroj) created the modern pilsner style in 1842. The golden, bottom-fermented beer was higher quality and much more drinkable than the beer produced in the area at the time, and it quickly caught on in central Europe. The style was also widely copied, and now the pilsner style and its descendants are a majority of the beer produced in the world. Brewery tours are available in English daily at 1245, 1415, and 1615; take about an hour and a half; and are 140 CZK per person. Reservations are recommended, but not required. Visiting will take you on both a historical and practical tour of the art and science of brewing and does include a sample at the end. Joint tickets are available for the brewery tour combined with admission to the **Brewery Museum,** located just a few blocks from the brewery. The brewery museum will take you deeper into the brewing craft and has exhibitions on the historical origins of beer and its serving. Another historic brewery, the **Gambrinus Brewery,** is also open for public tours. Information on all three beer stops can be found at www.prazdrojvisit.cz, or call (420) 377 062 888 for reservations. The Brewery Museum is also the access to the historic **Pilsen Underground,** a network of tunnels and cellars, some of which date to the 15th century. The guided tour takes around 50 minutes, and leads you through some 800 meters of the underground, with archeological finds and a narration of the building and various uses of the underground. Call (420) 377 235 574 or visit www.plzenskepodzemi.cz for reservations.

Prague—Pilsen (Plzeň)

DEPART Prague Main Station	TRAIN NUMBER	ARRIVE Plzen
0612	R 766	0748
0712	R 778	0848
0812	R 764	0948
0912	EX 354	1048
1012	R 762	1148

DEPART Plzeň	TRAIN NUMBER	ARRIVE Prague Main Station
1707	EX 355	1841
1907	R 779	2041
2007	R 767	2141
2109	EX 357	2241

Distance: 71 miles (114 km)

Day Excursion to

Kutná Hora

From Silver to Skeletons

Depart from Prague Main Station
Distance by Train: 45 miles (73 km)
Average Train Time: 1 hour
City Dialing Code: 420
Tourist Information Office: Palackého Square, 377 284 01 Kutná Hora
Tel: (420) 327 512 378; **Fax:** (420) 327 515 556
www.kh.cz
E-mail: infocentrum@kutnahora.cz
Hours: April–September: 0900–1800 daily; October–March: 0900–1700 Monday–Friday, 1000–1600 Saturday and Sunday

Notes: Change trains in Kutná Hora Main (hl.n.) Station, and continue to Kutná Hora mesto station, or take a bus (#1) to the center of town. Tourist Office is on the north side of the main square.

Once the second largest Czech city, Kutná Hora was a silver mining town between the 13th and 16th centuries, before the mines were tapped out. The city then suffered during several hundred years of poverty and many changes in control. While no longer the financial and industrial center it once was, the historical center of the town contains many extraordinary pieces of medieval and baroque architecture.

First head to the **Church of St. Barbara,** located south of the city center. The church, started in 1388, was not completed until 1905, with construction stopped repeatedly as the town's fortunes declined. The final structure is also believed to be significantly smaller than the original design. The structure is still a massive Gothic cathedral with huge flying buttresses and towering arches. Many internal features have survived in excellent shape, including stained glass, altars, and some medieval frescoes. Open November–December 1000–1700 Monday–Friday, 1000–1800 Saturday–Sunday; January–March 1000–1600 daily; April–October 0900–1800 daily. Located immediately next to the church is the Jesuit College. Originally built in the late 17th century as the Jesuits tried to bring Catholicism back to the area, the building is being converted for use as an art gallery and public space.

A symbol of Kutná Hora's prior importance, the **Italian Court** was once the royal mint, as well as the residence of the king when he came to Kutná Hora. After the end of the royal mint in 1770, the building was used for many years as the town hall. A **Museum of Minting** is now contained in the building, and many of the rooms that served the royal family are open for viewing. Open daily November–February 1000–1600, March and October 1000–1700, and April–September 0900–1800.

Located just west of the town center is the **Stone House,** an original 17th century residence that now is a living history museum, where visitors can learn what it was like to live in the Kutná Hora of the past. The house is also a silver museum and hosts other rotating exhibits throughout the year. It is open April and October 0900–1700 Tuesday–Sunday; May, June, and September 0900–1800; July and August 1000–1800; November 1000–1600; admission is 50 CZK; www.cms-kh.cz. Also available is a tour of a medieval silver mine. The mine, which was rediscovered in 1967, has replicas of the typical floors and other fittings that would have been used in a medieval mine. Not for the claustrophobic, but a unique perspective on what people have done in the name of precious metals.

For one of the stranger sites, but also one of the things that Kutná Hora is known for (although technically in the neighboring town of Sedlec), be sure to visit the **Sedlac Ossuary.** Located underneath the **Church of All Saints,** the area was originally a popular cemetery, as an abbott returning from the Holy

Land brought back dirt from where Jesus was crucified and sprinkled it over the cemetery. When the church was built over the existing cemetery starting around 1400, thousands of skeletons were uncovered and placed in the specifically designed ossuary underneath the church. In the late 1800s, a woodcarver was hired to bring some sort of order to the over 40,000 human skeletons. He created bizarre works of art out of the human bones, including garlands of skulls, and a giant chandelier that includes at least one of each bone in the human body. Ossuary hours: November–February 0900–1600, April–September 0800–1800, October and March 0900–1700; admission 60 CZK. Cathedral hours: April–October, 0900–1700 Monday–Saturday, 1100–1700 Sunday; November–March, 1000–1600 Monday–Saturday, 1100–1600 Sunday; admission 50 CZK. Additional charge for taking photographs. Visit www.kostnice.cz.

Prague—Kutná Hora

DEPART Prague Main	TRAIN NUMBER	ARRIVE Kutná Hora Main
0606	R 975	0655
0806	R 977	0855
1006	R 979	1055

DEPART Kutná Hora Main	TRAIN NUMBER	ARRIVE Prague Main
1701	R 980	1751
1801	R 978	1851
1901	R 976	1951
2101	R 972	2151

Other service available with change in Kolin.

Distance: 45 miles (73 km)

DENMARK

Danes are a fun-loving people, and their sparkling humor is unsurpassed. For example, the late Victor Borge, one of Denmark's leading exponents of such jocularity, explained that his ultra-expensive concert grand piano was "every bit as good as a Rolls-Royce, except," quipped Victor, "it has smaller wheels." This is typical Danish humor, and this fairy-tale land of Denmark abounds in it. No doubt you will find the Danes to be the most happy and humorous of all Europeans. Why are they that way? One of our Danish friends explains it in this manner: "For centuries, we Danes were the most feared of the Vikings, destroying and plundering at will. Now, we've got that all out of our system and have nothing left to do except to be happy!" This happy attitude seems to exist throughout the country.

Legend has it that the ancient Vikings, fierce as they were, never missed the chance to throw a party, and apparently their descendants are just as enthusiastic when it comes to having a good time. In summer there are festivals throughout Denmark where eating, drinking, singing, and dancing are the orders of the day. In winter the Danes go inside for their celebrations, where eating, drinking, singing, and dancing are the orders of the day. Oddly enough, this never seems to be monotonous to the Danes—or their visitors. With the completion of the Øresund Fixed Link—the bridge linking Copenhagen, Denmark, with Malmö, Sweden—it is even more convenient to visit both countries.

For more information about Denmark, contact the Danish and Swedish Tourist Board in North America:

New York: Grand Central Station; New York, NY 10163–4649;
Tel: (212) 885-9700; *Fax:* (212) 885-9710; www.goscandinavia.com or www.visitdenmark.com; *E-mail:* info@goscandinavia.com

Banking

Currency: Danish Kroner (DKK)

Exchange rate at press time: DKK 6.61 = U.S. $1.00

Hours: 0930/1000–1600; 1730 on Thursday; closed Saturday and Sunday

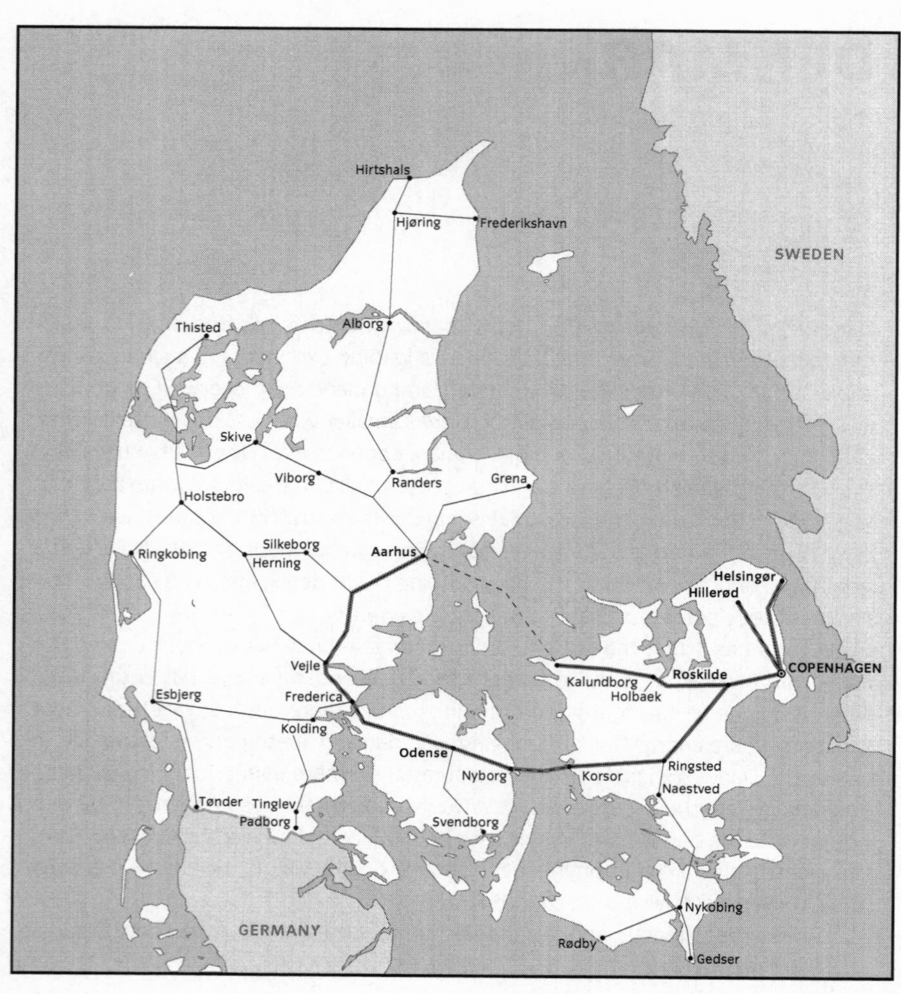
Hirtshals
Hjøring
Frederikshavn
SWEDEN
Thisted
Alborg
Skive
Viborg
Randers
Grena
Holstebro
Silkeborg
Herning
Aarhus
Ringkobing
Helsingør
Hillerød
COPENHAGEN
Vejle
Kalundborg
Roskilde
Holbaek
Esbjerg
Frederica
Kolding
Odense
Nyborg
Korsor
Ringsted
Naestved
Tinglev
Tønder
Padborg
Svendborg
Nykobing
GERMANY
Rødby
Gedser

Communications

Country Code: 46

No city codes required for calls within Denmark. Danish phone numbers are usually eight digits.

Major Mobile Phone Companies: TDC, Telenor, Telia

Shopping

Hours: 0900/1000–1730/1800 Monday–Thursday, 0900/1000–1900/2000 Friday, and 0900/1000–1300/1400 Saturday.

Denmark has a hefty 25 percent VAT (value-added tax). It may be avoided in two different ways: Have your purchases sent home; this way, you pay only the purchase price of the item plus shipping and insurance. Second plan, take the goods home yourself by paying the VAT; save your purchase slips and get the VAT refunded at the Copenhagen Kastrup Airport tax-free shop. In that case, plan to arrive at the airport an hour ahead of your original reporting time.

Rail Travel in Denmark

The dynamic Danish State Railways (DSB) is on the move (www.dsb.dk). In June 1997, the newly opened tunnel and bridge made crossing the Great Belt by train more than an hour faster than going by ferry. The "Lyntog" (high-speed diesel) trains cruise from Copenhagen to Aarhus in only 2½ hours instead of 4. In July 2000, the 16-kilometer rail and motorway tunnel/bridge complex connecting northeast Denmark and southern Sweden was completed. The Øresund Bridge connects Copenhagen and Malmö, creating the largest domestic market in northern Europe (equaling Berlin, Hamburg, and Amsterdam).

Denmark's InterCity and Lyntog trains feature seats with headphones for listening to music, 220-volt outlets for computers, and play areas for children. In first class, passengers can help themselves to tea, soft drinks, and newspapers. The DSB wants to make your trip fast but comfortable. It is advisable to have seat reservations on all IC and Lyntog trains.

The following bonuses apply if you have any of the **Eurail passes:**

- **Stena Line** ships, Frederikshavn–Göteburg (Sweden); 20 percent discount (no discount on cabins or couchettes)
- **DFDS Seaways** ships, Copenhagen–Oslo, 25 percent discount
- **Color Line** ships, 50 percent discount on day crossings: Frederikshavn/Skagen–Larvik (Norway); Hirtshals–Kristiansand (Norway)
- **Scandlines/DFO,** free ferry crossing Rødby Faerge to Puttgarden, Germany (rail pass must be valid in both Denmark and Germany)
- **Hjørring Privatbanen** railways, Hjørring–Hirtshals v.v.—50 percent discount

- **Skagensbanen** railway, 50 percent discount Frederikshavn–Skagen
- **Danish Railway Museum** in Odense—25 percent discount

For travel solely within Denmark, choose the Eurail Denmark Pass. If your European travels are within all of Scandinavia, consider the **Eurail Scandinavia Pass** that you can purchase in North America. It provides unlimited rail travel in Denmark, Finland, Norway, and Sweden, plus discounts on certain ferry crossings and private railways. Although you can purchase a Scandinavia Pass at train stations in Scandinavia, it is considerably more expensive than if you purchase it in North America. For ordering information, contact one of the companies listed under "To Purchase Passes" in the Appendix.

Eurail Denmark Pass

Available for 3 or 7 days of travel within a one-month period. Bonus: Discount at the Hilton Hotel in Copenhagen.

	ADULT	ADULT	YOUTH (12–25)	CHILD (11–YOUNGER)	
	1st Class	2nd Class	2nd Class	1st Class	2nd Class
3 days	$238	$156	$118	$120	$82
7 days	$327	$214	$162	$164	$110

Eurail Scandinavia Pass

Valid for unlimited rail travel in Denmark, Finland, Norway, and Sweden.

	ADULT	ADULT SAVER*	YOUTH	CHILD (4–11)
	2nd Class	2nd Class	2nd Class	
4 days in 2 months	$368	$313	$276	$159
5 days in 2 months	$406	$345	$304	$174
6 days in 2 months	$462	$394	$348	$198
8 days in 2 months	$510	$434	$383	$219
10 days in 2 months	$568	$483	$427	$243

Youth age 12–25. Younger than age 4 travel free.

*Price per person for 2 or more persons traveling together at all times.

Base City: **COPENHAGEN** (København)

www.visitcopenhagen.dk

Arriving by Air

Kastrup Airport: *Tel:* 32 31 32 31; *Fax:* 32 31 31 32; www.cph.dk. Located 8 kilometers southeast of Copenhagen. Most international flights to and from Denmark use Kastrup (Copenhagen) Airport. More than 60 airlines have regular services to Copenhagen, and there are several daily connections to/from all other major European airports.

Airport–City Links: The airport rail terminal links the airport to the Copenhagen main railway station (København H.) by train; departures every 10 minutes. The rail ticket office is located in Terminal 3 above the rail platforms. One-way ticket, DKK 36; journey takes 12 minutes.

Taxi service from the airport to city center costs DKK 250–300 depending on time of day (price includes taxes/tips). Nighttime rates are the most expensive. You can pay by credit card.

There are banks and ATMs in Terminal 3 (the Arrival Hall for all international flights); one is in the corridor leading to Terminal 2. *Hours:* 0600–2200 daily. There is a DSB (Danish Railways) ticket office near the escalators leading to the train platforms in Terminal 3, straight ahead after exiting from Customs. *Hours:* 0630–2330 daily. This office can validate your rail pass.

Arriving by Train

There are direct train connections from Copenhagen to major cities in Europe, including Stockholm, Oslo, Hamburg, and Basel.

Copenhagen has four major railway stations, but primarily the central station, **København Hovedbanegaard,** is of concern to rail pass travelers. Signs in and approaching the station are marked KØBENHAVN H. The abbreviation of Hovedbanegaard (Central Station), an "H," reflects the efficiency of this huge train complex right in the heart of the city. The tracks run below street level, and the architecture of the station blends well with the locale. København H. is suggestive of a great Viking hall with two great wooden archways that span its enclosed area.

The station is served by 12 tracks joined by 6 exits as you ascend from train level to the station's arrival area. For your orientation, upon arrival you may exit in a northerly or an easterly direction. Tivoli Gardens flank the station's east side, and a huge square fronts the station to the north. The Arrival Hall serves mainly for baggage handling. The lost-and-found office and the politi (police station) are alongside Tracks 11 and 12.

Most services are located in the north departure area: the SAS coach terminal, a cafeteria, and an excellent restaurant in the northwest corner. Taxi service is available at both the north and the east exits. City bus lines also serve the station, but inquire at the train information office before using one. Train arrival-and-departure information is displayed in bulletin form at both the arrival exits and the east and west entrances. Modern, airport-style digital displays give train-departure information automatically at each departure gate and on the train platforms. Elevator service and stairways are available between the station and the train platforms. If you are using a baggage cart, be certain to use the elevators.

- **Baggage storage:** Lockers are available in two sizes—the small one is DKK 25; the large one is DKK 35 for 24 hours. Baggage carts require a DKK 10 or DKK 20 coin (the carts accept either) refundable deposit.
- **Money exchange:** Den Danske Bank is located along the northwest side. It also has ATMs. *Hours:* 0600–2000 daily. A similar banking facility (FOREX) may be found in the row of shops on the ground level near the Bernsdorffsgade side. *Hours:* 0800–2100.
- **Train information:** Opposite McDonald's (near the bank). *Hours:* 0600–2230 daily. *Tel:* 33 14 17 01. For complicated questions, go to the train information office (RejseCenter) around the corner in the lobby leading to the Vesterbrogade exit. *Hours:* 0800–2000 daily. Take a numbered ticket from the distributor near the entrance. Push "Domestic" if your question refers to local travel within Denmark; push "International" for travel outside of Denmark or to have your rail pass validated. Small monitor screens at the top of the escalators leading to each platform give arrivals/departures from that track. Other monitors showing all arrivals/departures within the next hour or so are near the two main entrances to the station and along the wall between Tracks 6 and 7.
- **Train reservations:** RejseCenter on the north side of the station, just opposite the departure gates for Tracks 1/2 and 3/4. Inside the office, take a number for domestic or international assistance. *Hours:* 0930–1800 daily. International Reservations: *Tel:* 33 14 30 88; Domestic Reservations: *Tel:* 33 14 88 00.
- **Rail pass validation** is in the same office where international tickets are purchased, 0600–2230 daily.
- **Inter-rail center** is in the middle section of the south side of the station between Tracks 2 and 4. Enter by showing your rail pass. You can pick up information on what's going on in the *Copenhagen This Week* pamphlet, and the center personnel can help with reservations for youth hostels. For a few kroner you can even take a shower.

Tourist Information/Hotel Reservations

København Turistinformation: Vesterbrogade 4A, DK–1620 København V, Denmark. *Tel:* 70 22 24 42; *Fax:* 70 22 24 52; www.visitcopenhagen.dk; *E-mail:* touristinfo @woco.dk. *Hours:* January–April: Monday–Friday 0900–1600, Saturday 0900–1400, closed Sunday; May–June and September: Monday–Saturday 0900–1800, Sunday 0900–1400; July–August: Monday–Sunday 0900–1900, October–December: Monday–Friday 0900–1600, Saturday 0900–1400, closed Sunday. Closed Easter Sunday and Monday, Christmas Day, Boxing Day, December 31, and New Year's Day.

To reach the tourist office on foot, exit the central station and walk toward the corner on the right side, toward the front of the Tivoli Gardens. Cross the street at this point. The office is directly across from Tivoli Gardens' main entrance and readily identifiable by the familiar "i" sign.

Hotel reservations (*Tel:* 33 12 28 80; *Fax:* 33 12 97 23) can be made at the tourist office. The personnel are authorized to accept advance payments on behalf of the hotels to ensure reservations.

For luxury, convenience, and comfort, we can recommend the four-star Copenhagen Plaza at Bernstorffsgade 4, DK–1577 (*Tel:* 33 14 92 62; *Fax:* 33 93 93 62; www.profilhotels.se; *E-mail:* copenhagenplaza@profilhotels.dk). Room rates range from DKK 1595 and up for a standard room with one double bed. The Library Bar was cited as one of the best five bars in the world by *Forbes* magazine.

For a wide selection of less expensive hotels and hostels, visit www.hosteldenmark .com and www.dkhotellist.com.

Getting Around in Copenhagen

In Copenhagen an electrified metropolitan S-train railway network connects the city center with the suburban areas at frequent intervals. The metro, City Line, runs every 1½ minutes during rush hour.

A great convenience is the **Copenhagen Card,** which entitles you to unlimited travel by buses and trains in the entire metropolitan area, plus free entrances to more than 65 museums, attractions, and sights, including Tivoli and Tivoli Museum, Believe It or Not!, Danish Toy Museum, Frederiksborg Castle, and many more. A comprehensive guide booklet accompanies the card and includes a city map; 72-hour card: €75 adults; €34 children age 10 to 15; 24-hour card: €42 adults; €23 children. Up to two children under age 10 are allowed free with each adult card. Purchase at tourist offices or online.

Copenhagen has invested heavily in putting bicycle paths alongside many of its main streets, and the city provides more than 1,300 free bicycles for visitors to use while sightseeing. Look for one of the 125 Citybike parking areas located throughout the city center, deposit a DKK 20 coin, and start pedaling. When you return the bike, you get your money back. Check with the tourist office for more details.

Sights/Attractions/Tours

Tivoli Gardens (*Tel:* 33 15 10 01; *Fax:* 33 75 03 81; www.tivoli.dk) is generally open from mid-April through mid-September. *Hours:* 1100–2300 Sunday–Thursday, 1100–2400 Friday and Saturday. Check the Tivoli website for special Christmas Market dates and opening hours. It's not the world's largest amusement park, but it is unique. It has been in business since 1843. Each year, people come from all over the world to enjoy its very special blend of old and new attractions. Tree-lined walks, resplendent with flowers and sparkling illuminations, form the backdrop to its theaters and open-air amusement areas. Four evenings each week, the park closes with a fireworks display.

During its day of entertainment for young and old alike, international artists appear at the Tivoli Concert Hall, Gilbert & Sullivan scenarios are acted out at the Pantomime Theater, and the Tivoli Boys Guard parades frequently to the delight of all. There's also an impressive assembly of quality rides to thrill you, games to play, and more than 30 eating establishments to select from. Tivoli must be experienced. Prices: adults DKK 99; children under 7 free.

Amalienborg Palace is a beautiful example of Rococo architecture and has served as the permanent residence of the Danish royal family since 1794. See the changing of the Royal Guard at 1200 every day in the palace square.

Tour the colorful **Nyhavn canal** area with its quaint restaurants and cafes or take the city harbor tour—a comfortable way to see beautiful Copenhagen.

Want more? Tour the city's world-famous breweries, Carlsberg and Tuborg. Get details from the tourist office. Yes, they provide samples of their products. Contact Carlsberg in advance: *Tel:* 33 27 13 14; www.carlsberg.com.

The **New Museum of Modern Art Arken** (the Ark) is a favorite among those interested in contemporary art (www.arken.dk). The building itself is a fascinating structure. Open Tuesday–Sunday, 1000–1700, until 2100 on Wednesday. Prices: adults DKK 95, under 17 free.

Year-round, visit **Den Lille Havfrue ("The Little Mermaid"),** symbol of today's Copenhagen. It is an enchanting, soul-touching statue, and next to Queen Margrethe it is probably Denmark's most famous female.

Shopping? Copenhagen can accommodate you. You'll learn quickly about **Stroget** (pronounced "stroy-it"). It's not one but actually five different shopping areas, each designated pedestrian-only and lined with shops that might make you want to hide your credit cards. All the well-known Danish specialties are in profusion here. Just north of the Stroget in the Latin Quarter there are some good cafes and restaurants, so you can get anything from a hot dog to a five-course banquet. Try the world-famous Danish delicacy *smorrebrod*, which usually consists of rye bread topped with marinated herring or liver pâté and onion rings.

Train Connections to Other Base Cities from Copenhagen (København)

Depart from Copenhagen (København H.) Station.

DEPART	TRAIN NUMBER	ARRIVE	NOTES
		Amsterdam Centraal	
1137	ICE 34	2300	R, 1
		Berlin Hauptbahnhof	
0737	ICE 38	1419	R, 2
1137	ICE 34	1819	R, 2
1537	ICE 32	2223	R, 2
		Brussels (Bruxelles) Midi/Zuid	
0737	ICE 38	2032	R, 2, 3
1743	EC 30	0832+1	R, 3, Sleeper
		Hamburg Hauptbahnhof	
0737	ICE 38	1221	R
1137	ICE 36	1622	R
1537	ICE 32	2021	R
1737	EC 30	2223	R
		Munich (München) Hauptbahnhof	
0737	ICE 38	1857	R, 2
1137	ICE 34	2300	R, 2
1537	ICE 32	0710+1	R, 2, Sleeper
		Oslo Sentral	
0832	R 1026	1652	R, 4
1332	R 1056	2149	R, 4
		Paris Gare du Nord	
0737	ICE 38	2205	R, 2, 3
1713	EC 30406	1008+1	R, 2, Sleeper
		Prague (Praha)	
0737	ICE 38	1928	R, 2
1737	EC 30	0925+1	R, 2, Sleeper
		Stockholm Central	
0612	R 1012	1139	R, 7
1212	R 1048	1739	R, 7
1424	R 2000 542	1939	R
1824	X 2000 550	2339	R, Exc. Sa
2152	R 1106	0616+1	R, 6, Sleeper, Exc. Sa
		Vienna (Wien)	
1537	ICE 32	0816+1	R, 2, Sleeper

DEPART	TRAIN NUMBER	ARRIVE	NOTES
		Warsaw Centralna	
0937	ICE 36	2205	R, 5, Exc. Sa
		Zürich Hauptbahnhof	
0737	ICE 38	2200	R, 2
1737	EC 30	1200+1	R, 2, Sleeper

Daily, unless otherwise noted
R Reservations required
+1 Arrives next day
1. Change trains in Hamburg and Duisburg.
2. Change trains in Hamburg.
3. Change trains in Cologne (Köln).
4. Change trains in Göteborg.
5. Change trains in Berlin.
6. Change trains in Lund.
7. Change trains in Malmö.

For the best seafood specialties, we enjoyed the **Brasserie Le Coq Rouge** at Hotel Kong Frederik at Vester Voldgade 25. For reservations, *Tel:* 33 12 59 02; *Fax:* 33 93 59 01. If you have a sweet tooth, please, don't go home before you have tried the Danish waffle–ice cream combination.

Day Excursions

Five delightful day excursions await whenever you can break away from the charm that is distinctly Copenhagen's. Admittedly, this is a difficult thing to do because the Danish capital has so much to offer, what with its Tivoli Gardens and pedestrian-only shopping streets; but leave it you must. The entire country is a fairyland. Go out and enjoy it.

Jutland is the Danish mainland, the tip of the European continent that reaches northward toward the Scandinavian peninsula. **Aarhus** is Jutland's cultural center and Denmark's second-largest city. Fans of William Shakespeare will, no doubt, make **Helsingør** (Elsinore) their prime day-excursion choice. Castle buffs will head for **Hillerød** and its gracious Frederiksborg Castle. **Odense,** birthplace of Hans Christian Andersen, will delight day excursioners of all ages. **Roskilde** is loaded with Danish folklore and history, including a Viking-ship museum, Museum Island, and Denmark's most important medieval building—the Roskilde Cathedral—for centuries the final resting place of Denmark's royalty.

Day Excursion to

Aarhus (Århus)

World's Smallest Big City

Depart from København H. Station
Distance by Train: 139 miles (223 km)
Average Train Time: 2 hours, 36 minutes
No city code required
Tourist Information Office: Welcome Center, Banegårdspladsen 20, DK-8000 Aarhus
Tel: 8731 5010; **Fax:** 8612 9590
www.visitaarhus.com
E-mail: info@visitaarhus.com
Hours: September–June: 1000–1700 Monday–Friday; July–August: 1000–1800 Monday–Friday, 1000–1500 Saturday; closed Sundays
Notes: To reach the tourist office, exit the station and cross the street. Turn left and cross the street.

The Great Belt Tunnel decreased the travel time between Copenhagen and Aarhus from 4 hours to 2 hours and 36 minutes via express InterCityLyn service. And travel aboard the Danish Railways (DSB) InterCity trains is comfortable and a pleasant way to see the Danish countryside. When you arrive in Aarhus, disembark and follow the signs to the main rail station, where you mount stairs leading to the station's main concourse. Lift (elevator) service and escalators are available. After turning left, walk to the end of the corridor. The train information office is to the left at the end of the corridor. *Hours:* 0900–1900 daily.

People have lived in Aarhus ever since the Vikings settled at the mouth of the river, where it meets the bay. There the Norsemen constructed a harbor, built houses, and erected a church. During the 1960s, contractors excavating under a bank in Aarhus came upon the remains of a semicircular rampart that the Vikings of a thousand years ago used to protect their small community.

Today the site is a museum where you can see the reconstructed ramparts with a typical house of that time with tools and other belongings used by the first inhabitants of Aarhus. There is also a collection of 75 historic buildings that have been transferred there from every region of the country to re-create an entire 17th-century Danish market town, complete with narrow cobbled streets, shops, public squares—even a millrace. Known as The Old Town, it is the largest museum in Jutland. Here you can wander through Danish history from the Vikings to Hans Christian Andersen.

Copenhagen (København)—Aarhus (Århus)

DEPART Københaven H.	TRAIN NUMBER	ARRIVE Aarhus Station
0702	IC 125	1013
0755	Lyn 29	1043
0802	IC 129	1113
0855	Lyn 41	1143
0902	IC 133	1213
0955	Lyn 43	1243
1002	IC 137	1313
1055	Lyn 45	1343
1102	IC 141	1413

DEPART Aarhus Station	TRAIN NUMBER	ARRIVE Københaven H.	NOTES
1402	IC 153	1713	
1425	Lyn 44	1743	
1502	IC 157	1813	
1525	Lyn 259	1813	
1602	IC 161	1913	
1625	Lyn 61	1943	
1702	IC 165	2019	
1715	Lyn 58	2005	Th–Su
1815	Lyn 62	2105	
1845	IC 164	2156	
1915	Lyn 66	2205	
2015	Lyn 70	2305	

Daily, unless otherwise noted

Note: Reservations are recommended for travel on all IC and Lyntog trains in Denmark. Passengers may board the train without a reservation but are not guaranteed a seat.

Distance: 139 miles (223 km)

To reach **The Old Town,** follow the city map for a 10-minute walk, or take bus No. 3. *Hours:* January 2–February 7, 1100–1500; February 8–April 11, 1000–1600; June 28–August 10, 1000–1800; 1000–1700 rest of the year. Admission: DKK 60–135 adult, DKK 30–68 students, depending on time of year. Visit www.dengamleby.dk.

Admission to the **Viking Museum** is free, and it's only 3 blocks from the tourist office at Clemens Torv in the basement under Unibank. It is open only during banking hours, generally 1000–1800 Monday–Friday.

You may want to visit other attractions by taking the bus. If you plan to visit several attractions in Aarhus or if you plan to stay longer, purchase the **Aarhuscard** online at www.visitaarhus.com, at the tourist information/Welcome Center, at the bus station, at the youth hostel, or at hotels. It provides for free or discounted admission to most of the city's attractions as well as free transport on the yellow bus networks. Cost: one-day Aarhuscard DKK 129 adults, DKK 69 children; two-day Aarhuscard DKK 179 adults, DKK 79 children.

South of Aarhus you'll find the **Prehistoric Museum** at Moesgård, one of Denmark's top attractions. (*Hours:* 1000–1700 daily in summer; closed Monday during winter; DKK 60 adults, under 18 free.) Visit www.moesmus.dk. The museum contains collections from the Stone Age, the Bronze Age, the Iron Age, and the Viking period. To get there, take bus No. 6 from the railway station.

Between Odden and Aarhus, there is a hydrofoil ferry service that takes only 90 minutes. You can return to Copenhagen via this same route, but we recommend the "great circle" tour, which includes stops at the cities of **Frederica** and **Odense.**

Day Excursion to

Helsingør (Elsinore)

Hamlet's Hideaway

Depart from København H. Station
Distance by Train: 29 miles (47 km)
Average Train Time: 52 minutes
No city code required
Tourist Information Office: Helsingør Turistbureau, Havnepladsen 3, DK–3000 Helsingør
Tel: 49 21 13 33; **Fax:** 49 21 15 77
www.visithelsingor.dk
E-mail: info@visitnordsjaelland.com
Hours: January 2–June 27: 1000–1600 Monday–Friday; June 30–August 3: 1000–1700 Monday–Friday, 1000–1400 Saturday–Sunday; August 4–December 19: 1000–1600 Monday–Friday; 1000–1400 Saturday.
Notes: Located just across the street on the left side of the station. Look for the tourist agency sign at the end of Tracks 1 and 2 for more explicit directions. Words of caution: Obey the traffic signals when crossing to the tourist office, and use the designated walkway. A local, private railroad uses the street as a siding, and it could be hazardous to your health.

Helsingør (sometimes referred to by its older name, "Elsingore" or Elsinore) is one of Denmark's oldest populated places. Documents dating from 1231 record its development. In the vaults under **Kronborg Castle,** there is a statue of Holger Danske, a Viking chieftain who voyaged to the Holy Land as a crusader about A.D. 800, and there are many buildings of ancient vintage. For example, nearby No. 27 Strandgade is the oldest half-timbered house in town. It was built in 1577. Other structures date from the 15th century.

The lure of Shakespeare's *Hamlet* usually brings visitors to Helsingør. The town has many other attractions, however, not the least of which is the world's biggest and best ice-cream cone. Read on, Macbeth!

Local train service between Copenhagen and Helsingør runs every 20 minutes throughout the day and is interspersed with frequent express train service. The Helsingør railway station is the terminus for the train ferries that ply between Denmark and the town of Helsingborg in Sweden. The distance across the sound is less than 3 miles. This is why Helsingør was founded there and also why it flourished from 1426 through 1857 by the collection of the "sound dues" from all merchant ships that passed.

If you are interested in maritime ferry operations, Helsingør is the place to observe it. Arrivals and departures take place all day and into the night.

One of the tourist office's publications is *Helsingør Tourist Guide*. It describes, in great detail, Kronborg Castle, the churches of Saint Olai and Saint Mary, and the Carmelite monastery. These highlights are all nearby.

The **Kronborg Castle** (*Tel:* 49 21 30 78; www.ses.dk/kronborgcastle), the city's most famous landmark, was built by Christian IV between 1574 and 1582. *Hours:* January–March and November–December: 1100–1600 Tuesday–Sunday; April–May and September–October: 1100–1600 daily; June–August: 1000–1730 daily. Ticket prices vary depending on the tour but are generally DKK 75 for adults. With this formidable fortress came the rapid development of the town under its protective shelter. For several centuries Helsingør was the second-largest city in Denmark.

Hamlet's residency in the castle was imaginary, but the play was performed there from 1916 until 1954, when performances were curtailed for financial reasons. It was again performed in 1979, but there are no definite plans for the future. In the castle the King's Chamber, the Queen's Chamber, and the Great Hall must be seen to appreciate the once great splendor of this fortress. Cannons still stand along the seawall.

While admiring the Great Hall, you'll probably note that there are no fireplaces or other heating devices. Apparently, they were overlooked by the royal architect. This created no problem for the royal occupants, however, when they wanted to lay on a royal midwinter bash; they merely marched several thousand men of the royal guard into the area, and the troops' body heat sent the mercury soaring.

While in Helsingør, make certain that a part of your tour includes a stop at the **Raadhus** (town hall). In its council chamber, you can see a stained-glass window that depicts the history of the town. Outside of the town hall you will see a narrow street (Brostraede) leading to the sea. Follow it. The ice-cream shop is there.

Copenhagen (København)—Helsingør (Elsinore)

From Copenhagen to Helsingør:
Trains depart daily every 20 minutes at 12, 32, and 52 minutes past the hour 0513–1943. Journey time is approximately 49 minutes. Check with the train information office in the København H. Station.

From Helsingør to Copenhagen:
Trains depart daily every 20 minutes at 03, 23, and 43 minutes past the hour, 0543–1943; additional trains until 2245. Check with the train information office in the Helsingør train station.

Ferries between Helsingør, Denmark, and Helsingborg, Sweden:
Copenhagen–Helsingør trains connect with ferries to Sweden on Scandlines. Eurail pass is accepted for passage. Several ferries depart every 20 minutes beginning at 0640 until 2020, with less frequent service outside of these hours. Service in either direction takes about 20 minutes. If desired, you may combine a day excursion to Helsingør, Denmark, with a round-trip ferry crossing to Helsingborg, Sweden. Return trips are similar, beginning at 0600 and returning until 2300.

Distance: 29 miles (47 km)

Day Excursion to

Hillerød

Picture-Book Scenery

Depart from København H. Station
Distance by Train: 19 miles (30 km)
Average Train Time: 40 minutes
No city code required
Tourist Information Office: Frederiksvaerksgade 2A, 3400 Hillerød
Tel: 48 24 26 26; **Fax:** 48 24 26 65
www.visitnordsjaelland.com
E-mail: hnu@visitnordsjaelland.com
Hours: January 5–October: 0930–1600 Monday–Friday; June 29–September 10: 0930–1600 Monday–Friday, 0930–1330 Saturday
Notes: Follow the signs to the castle, starting just outside the station building (about a 20-minute walk). If you like, you can obtain a brochure in the railway station that contains a city map to help guide your way. Or take bus No. 701 or 702 in the direction of either Ullerød or Sophienborg, and ask the driver to let you off at the tourist information office. You can buy tickets on the bus for DKK 20.

Copenhagen (København)—Hillerød

Trains depart København H. at 0503 and then every 20 minutes thereafter.

Trains depart Hillerød at 1502, then every 20 minutes thereafter, last train at 2339.

Daily, including holidays

Distance: 19 miles (30 km)

Hillerød can become the crowning touch to your visit to Denmark. The town has an atmosphere distinctly its own with beautiful woodlands surrounding it. A picture-book lake rests in the town's center, faced on one side by the old town and its market square and on another by the majestic Frederiksborg Castle. There are few places in the world where nature and culture blend so perfectly.

No doubt the Frederiksborg Castle will be the first stopping point on your tour of Hillerød. A tour boat plies along the "most beautiful nautical mile in Denmark" between the castle and the marketplace from May 15 through September 15 (DKK 55 for adults, DKK 20 for children; www.dnm.dk).

The castle actually spans three islands. The first of its structures, erected by Frederik II in 1560, occupied the largest island. The balance of this imposing castle complex was built by Christian IV between 1600 and 1620. Between 1570 and 1840, Danish monarchs were anointed in the castle chapel, and it was used for the wedding of Danish Prince Joachim and Alexandra Manley from Hong Kong in 1995.

In 1859 a disastrous fire destroyed the interior of the main building, and irreplaceable treasures were lost forever. The chapel and all of its valuable contents, however, remained relatively undamaged. Among those items was the celebrated chapel organ built by Esaias Compenius in 1610. The chapel organist plays every Thursday between 1330 and 1400. The castle has been restored, at first by royal contributions and public donations, and, more recently, by philanthropic support from J. C. Jacobsen, former owner of the Carlsberg Brewery and the Carlsberg Foundation. *Hours:* April–October: 1000–1700 daily; November–March: 1100–1500 daily (admission: DKK 75, adults; DKK 20, children; www.frederiksborgmuseet.dk. There is an interesting museum of local and regional history, known as the **North Sealand Folk Museum,** by a small pond in a corner of the castle's gardens, and the castle itself now houses the Museum of Natural History.

The castle gardens, water canals, and fountains are among the most exquisite. In 1996 the reconstruction of the Baroque Garden was finished and inaugurated by Danish Queen Margrethe II; it resembles the original park from 1720. In another section of the castle garden, known as the *Indelukket,* you can inspect a charming little country house built in 1562 for the king to conduct informal entertainment. Several guided tours are offered of the sites, castles, museums, forest, and parklands of Hillerød. Contact the tourist center for arrangements.

The shop-'til-you-drop group will enjoy Hillerød's shopping center, the **"Slots Arkaderne"** (Castle Arcades), with more than 47 specialty shops. It, too, is conveniently located on Slotsgade. When you are coming from the railway station, the glass-covered Slots Arkaderne shopping mall is on the left-hand side of Slotsgade.

The **Money Historical Museum,** at No. 38 Slotsgade, is on your way to the castle. It should attract coin collectors of all ages as it comprises a very fine collection of Danish and foreign coins as well as other means of payment used in ancient times. Illustrations tell the story of political, historical, and cultural aspects of money and coinage.

Just outside Hillerød, you may want to visit the exhibit *Mode i Mini* of costumed dolls. You can reach it on bus No. 736. The display features 70 dolls with handmade costumes that present the history of dress as well as the history of humankind.

Day Excursion to

Odense

Home of Hans Christian Andersen

Depart from København H. Station
Distance by Train: 103 miles (165 km)
Average Travel Time: 1 hour, 17 minutes
No city code required
Tourist Information Office: Odense Turist Bureau, Vestergade 2, 5000 Odense C
Tel: 63 75 75 20; **Fax:** 63 75 75 39
www.visitodense.com
E-mail: otb@visitodense.com
Hours: July 1–August 31: 0930–1800 Monday–Friday, 1000–1500 Saturday, and 1100–1400 Sunday; September 1–June 30: 1000–1630 Monday–Friday and 1000–1300 Saturday
Notes: When you arrive in the Odense railway station, look for the train-information booth on the second floor. There you can obtain train information and a map of Odense showing how to get to the Turist Bureau at the Rådhuset (Town Hall). Information booth hours 0600–2100 Monday–Saturday, 0700–2200 Sunday.

Hans Christian Andersen, Denmark's famous teller of fairy tales, was born in a tiny yellow house in Odense on April 2, 1805. One hundred years later, the city bought the house and turned it into a museum. Tourists of all ages still flock to this magic point to see what his early life was like.

Many of Andersen's stories were set in or near Odense. Most of the locations can be seen today. The small, half-timbered house where he was born, now the nucleus of the **Hans Christian Andersen Museum,** is set in a cluster of other small houses from the same period. A visit there is like stepping back into the 19th century.

The Hans Christian Andersen house is near the tourist office, about a 10-minute walk from the rail station. *Hours:* July 1–August 31: 1000–1600 daily; rest of year: 1100–1500, except Monday. (Admission: DKK 30 adults, children free.) The area surrounding Hans Christian Andersen's home, with its little colored houses and cobblestone streets, is very attractive.

If you are visiting the museum area at mealtime, we suggest that you eat in a charming little restaurant nearby at Overgade 23, **Den Gamle Kro** ("The Old Inn"). *Tel:* 66 12 14 33; www.dengamlekro.eu. It's but one of a score of excellent restaurants in Odense. The tourist office has a handy pocket guide describing many of these eating establishments. You'll find an interesting selection—including such names as **Jensen's Boefhus** and **Den Lille Café Olivia.**

The house of Hans Christian Andersen is not the only attraction in Odense. With more than 185,000 inhabitants, the city is Denmark's third largest. Industrial and vigorous in its lifestyle, Odense has smart shops, spacious parks, and sparkling residential areas. Situated in the center of Denmark's second-largest island, the Isle of Funen, the city is the focal point for those wishing to explore the island's rolling countryside.

Copenhagen (København)—Odense

At least two trains depart København H. hourly at 32 and 55 minutes after the hour; journey time on IC trains is 1 hour 27 to 32 minutes (a few minutes faster Sa–Su). Lyntog trains (departing at 0655, 0755, and 0855) take only 1 hour 16 minutes.

At least two trains depart Odense hourly at 24 and 54 minutes after the hour; journey time for IC trains is 1 hour 33 minutes. Lyntog trains (departing at 51 minutes after the hour) take 1 hour 18 minutes.

Note: Seat reservations are recommended on all IC and Lyntog trains in Denmark. Passengers may board the train without a reservation but are not guaranteed a seat.

Distance: 103 miles (165 km)

The German emperor Otto III officially mentioned Odense for the first time in a letter dated March 18, 988. Although there were people living there at the time and a church had been previously erected, the present-day residents applied the emperor's date as a benchmark and declared 1988 as the "1,000th Anniversary of Odense."

A Hans Christian Andersen fairy tale is presented from mid-July through the first week in August at the **Open Air Theater** in Funen Village. The village is one of the largest open-air museums in Denmark, characterized by a coherent layout of landscape and a real village of 17th-century houses assembled from the Island of Funen and the surrounding islands. Here you will find farms with animals, a rectory, a school—even a brickyard and a forge. The theater seats 2,000 people. Open daily except Monday, 1000–1800 summer, closed in winter. Admission for adults DKK 60–85.

Odense has a museum for every interest—from art to transportation. **The Brandts Klaedefabrik Art Gallery, Danish Museum of Printing, Danish Press Museum,** and **Museum of Photographic Art** are all located in Brandts Passage. **The Danish Railway Museum** is next to the railway station at Dannebrogsgade 24 (*Tel:* 66 13 66 30; www.jernbanemuseum.dk). Experience 150 years of train and ferry history. *Hours:* 1000–1600 daily. Tickets: Adult DKK 60, children DKK 30.

The **Odense Adventure Pass** will provide free public transport within the Odense area and either free or reduced-price admission to Odense's museums, sights, and the zoo. A 24-hour pass costs DKK 169 for adults and DKK 100 for children; the 48-hour pass costs DKK 215 for adults and DKK 120 for children. The Adventure Pass can be purchased at the Odense Tourist Bureau. To reach the zoo, board one of Odense Aafart's covered cruise boats for a relaxing journey.

Day Excursion to

Roskilde

The Viking Ship Museum and the Cathedral

Depart from København H. Station
Distance by Train: 19 miles (31 km)
Average Train Time: 25 minutes
No city code required
Tourist Information Office: Staendertorvet 1, 4000 Roskilde
Tel: 46 31 65 65; **Fax:** 46 31 65 60
www.visitroskilde.com
E-mail: info@visitroskilde.dk
Hours: January–December: 1000–1300 Saturday; October–March: 1000–1600 Monday–Friday; April–September: 1000–1700 Monday–Friday
Notes: Ten-minute walk from the railway station. Exit the station and proceed downhill to the main street. Turn left at this point to the city square. The tourist office is only about 300 yards off the pedestrian street in Gullandsstraede.

Since Roskilde is so close to Copenhagen, you might think it would be so much like Denmark's capital city that a day excursion there would be pointless. On the contrary, Roskilde is as different from Copenhagen as night is from day. Known as the "Town of Viking Ships and Royal Tombs," Roskilde warrants a visit. In fact, it is difficult to see all that you might want to see in Roskilde in just one day. We recommend at least three things to do during your day excursion: (1) visit the cathedral, (2) take a guided tour, and (3) visit the Viking Ship Museum.

Roskilde's twin-spired, redbrick **Domkirke** (cathedral) dominates the skyline. Its construction was begun in 1170 on the same site where King Harald Bluetooth erected a church in A.D. 960. Today it's considered Denmark's most important medieval building and is inscribed on the World Heritage List. This international attraction has been the burial place of Danish royalty for centuries. Thirty-nine kings and queens of Denmark are buried there, representing the longest reign of family monarchy in the world. *Tel:* 46 31 65 65; www.roskildedomkirke.dk.

The cathedral is one of Denmark's first brick buildings, and it is said that it has as many tales to tell as it has bricks in its walls. Originally, a limestone edifice was erected on the foundation of Harald Bluetooth's church, only to be torn down and slowly replaced by the current brick structure, which was completed in 1280.

Some less significant but nevertheless interesting features of the cathedral are its granite measuring column and a 500-year-old clock. The column was used to measure the height of royal visitors. The tallest, Peter the Great of Russia, checked in at 6 feet 10 inches! The clock features Saint George and the dragon. For nearly 500 years, Saint George has mounted his trusty horse each hour and attacked the dragon, which screams in pain before going off to dragon heaven to be refurbished for the next hour's performance. Hours (except when services are being conducted): April–September: 0900–1700 Monday–Saturday, 1230–1700 Sunday; October–March: 1000–1600 Tuesday–Saturday, 1230–1600 Sunday. Admission is DKK 60 for adults; under 18 free. Guided tours available. *Tel:* 46 35 16 24.

If you visit Roskilde on a Wednesday or a Saturday morning, you will find the city's **market** in full operation. The market is unique in that it isn't limited to the sale of meats, poultry, fish, and produce—the usual bill of fare that you find throughout Europe. The market activities include a flea market that could rival the best American garage sale ever held. All of this activity takes place in the town square, the Staendertorvet, fronting the Town Hall.

Copenhagen (København)—Roskilde

Trains run about every 15 minutes from Copenhagen to Roskilde and vice versa all day beginning at 0500 through 0030; a couple of trains also run during the middle of the night. Travel time: 20–25 minutes.

Distance: 19 miles (31 km)

The **Viking Ship Museum** is an interesting addition to Roskilde's various attractions. *Hours:* 1000–1600 September–June, 1000–1700 July and August. In summer admission is DKK 115 for adults, DKK 100 for students; in winter DKK 80 for adults, DKK 70 for students (children younger than age 18, free). Proceed downhill from the cathedral. The museum island includes the Boat Yard, Visitor's and Archaeological Workshops, plus sailing trips from June through August are offered in Viking-ship replicas for all Viking wannabes. Viking ships, circa A.D. 1000 to 1050, have been restored piece by piece in this most modern of maritime museums, on the banks of the Roskilde fjord. For centuries legend had it that a barrier at the fjord's narrowest point actually had a Viking vessel beneath it. The legend was only partially correct in that a cofferdam operation in 1962 revealed that not one but five vessels had been sunk there to protect Roskilde's harbor from enemy fleets. Visit www.vikingeskibsmuseet.dk.

Just 6 miles west of Roskilde is the **Prehistoric Village–Historical–Archaeological–Experimental Centre** at Lejre, representing one of the most profound studies of prehistoric housing. Ask the tourist office about bus connections from the small station in Lejre to the center.

And if you visit during late June or early July, be sure to check out the **Roskilde Festival,** the greatest rock-and-jazz fest in northern Europe. Visit www.roskilde-festival.dk to keep up with the latest news and ticket information.

All ages will enjoy "one of the most beautiful houses in Scandinavia," **Ledreborg Palace,** an impressive example from the Rococo period. Tours of the palace are DKK 80 for adults and DKK 50 for children. *Tel:* 46 48 00 38; *Fax:* 46 48 04 80; www.ledreborgslot.dk. Admire exquisite landscape, architecture, paintings, and furnishings from more than 250 years ago; see the home's servant quarters, and even visit the dungeon. Don't forget your children (in the dungeon area, that is), as they will not want to miss the treasure hunt in and around the park or trying to find their way through one of Europe's most amazing mazes. During summer, enjoy concerts on the green.

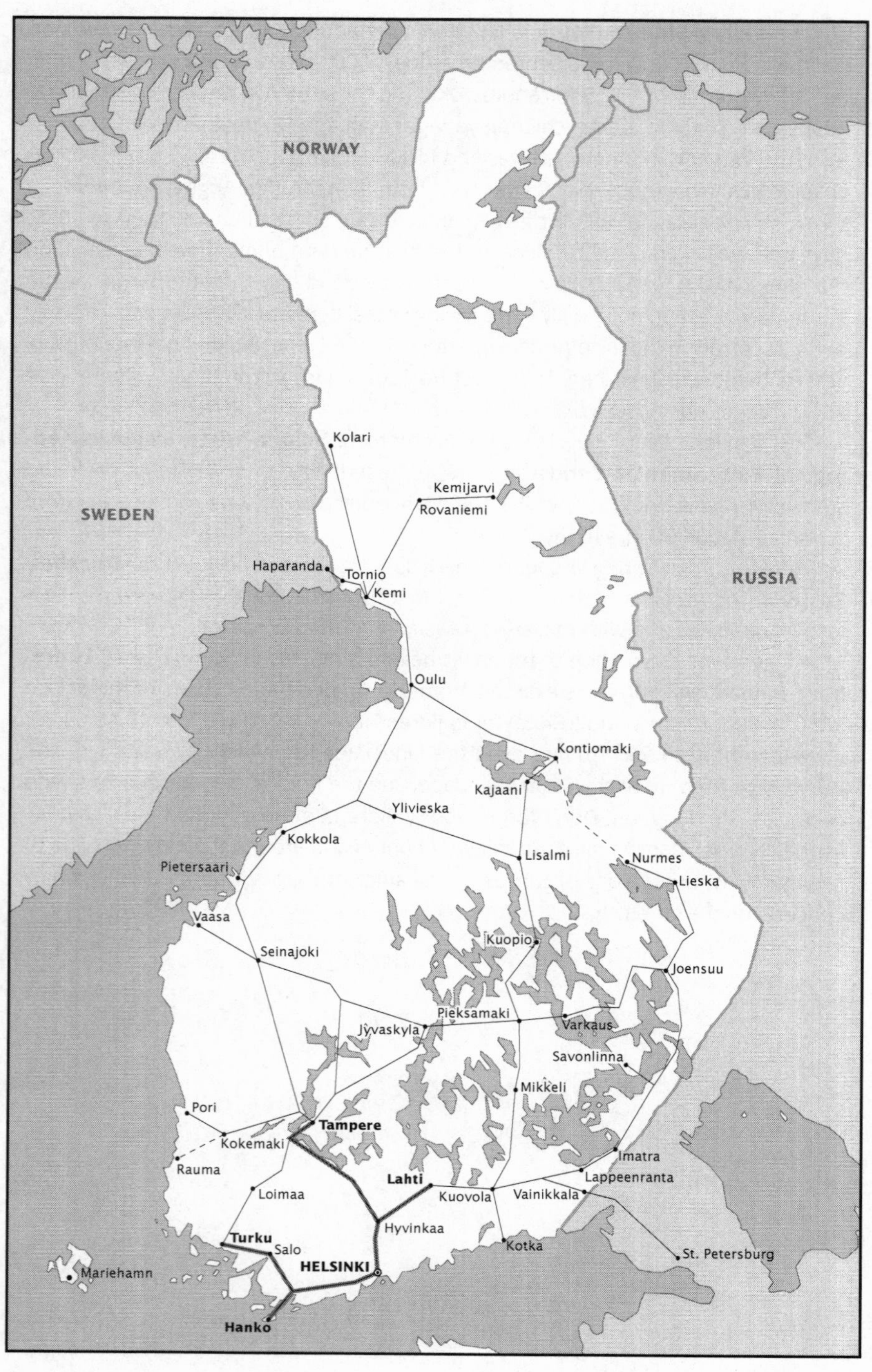
NORWAY
SWEDEN
RUSSIA
Kolari
Kemijarvi
Rovaniemi
Haparanda
Tornio
Kemi
Oulu
Kontiomaki
Kajaani
Ylivieska
Kokkola
Pietersaari
Lisalmi
Nurmes
Lieska
Vaasa
Seinajoki
Kuopio
Joensuu
Pieksamaki
Jyvaskyla
Varkaus
Savonlinna
Mikkeli
Pori
Tampere
Kokemaki
Rauma
Imatra
Lahti
Lappeenranta
Loimaa
Kuovola
Vainikkala
Hyvinkaa
Turku
Salo
Kotka
St. Petersburg
HELSINKI
Mariehamn
Hanko

FINLAND

Finland is well-known for its unique natural beauty, including 188,000 lakes, 179,000 islands, and Europe's biggest archipelago. Known as the "Land of the Midnight Sun" in summer, it is an artistic array of color in autumn, dazzling white in winter, and awash in green beauty in spring. Finland definitely is a country for all seasons.

Finnish and Swedish are the two languages spoken most frequently. English is a second language for many Finns, particularly for those involved in tourism and transportation, which is common in most European countries.

Because they share a common border, Finland and Russia have long been associated in one way or another. During the Napoleonic Wars, Russia invaded Finland, and it became a Russian grand duchy in 1809. Finnish nationalism grew, however, and the Finns proclaimed their independence in 1917. The Finns were again defeated by Soviet troops in the beginning of World War II. In the late 1980s the Soviet's political demise fostered development of closer relations with Western Europe and in 1995 Finland joined the European Union.

Finland is still considered a gateway between East and West. If you've always wanted to visit Russia, now's your chance. There are daily rail connections from Helsinki to Vyborg, St. Petersburg, and Moscow.

For tourist information, contact the Finnish Tourist Board Offices in North America:

> **New York:** 655 Third Ave., Suite 1810, New York, NY 10017; *Tel:* (800) 346-4636. *E-mail:* mek.usa@mek.fi or info@goscandinavia.com; www.goscandinavia.com or www.visitfinland.com

Banking

Currency: Euro (€)

Exchange rate at press time: €0.90 = U.S. $1.00

Hours: 0900–1600 Monday–Friday. Hours may vary regionally. Foreign currency and traveler's checks can also be exchanged in the following currency exchange offices: Katajanokka Harbor, Helsinki, open 0900–1800 daily and during the arrival and departure of ships, and the Helsinki-Vantaa Airport, open 0630–2300 daily.

Communications

Country Code: 358

For telephone calls within Finland, dial a zero (0) preceding area code.

Major Mobile Phone Companies: Sonera, Elisa, DNA

Rail Travel in Finland

The Finnish Railways (VR Ltd.; www.vr.fi) operate Finland's mass transportation system. High-speed Pendolino S 220 trains and InterCity and express trains provide long-distance services, and local and commuter trains provide connections for shorter routes. The variety of **Eurail passes** is accepted on the national rail network of Finland, and the group/student rate applies on the crossing by Finnjet from Helsinki to Rostock (Germany) and is available when reservations are made seven days before departure in Budget or Tourist IS class. Free transport is also offered on buses operating as train substitutes during certain hours. The national rail pass and the regional **Eurail Scandinavia Pass** are also accepted.

Eurail Finland Pass

Valid for any 3, 5, or 10 days of rail travel within 1 month.

	ADULT 1st Class	ADULT 2nd Class
3 days	$286	$193
5 days	$379	$256
10 days	$511	$345

Child fare (age 6–16) 50 percent off adult fare

Eurail Scandinavia Pass

Unlimited train travel in Denmark, Finland, Norway, and Sweden for a specified number of days. Also includes 20 to 50 percent discounts on certain ferries and bus connections.

See the Appendix for a detailed list of rail pass types and prices.

Base City: **HELSINKI**

www.hel.fi
City Dialing Code: 9

Arriving by Air

Vantaa Airport: *Tel:* 200 1 4636 (€0.57/min + local network charge); www.helsinki-vantaa.fi. Location: 20 kilometers north of Helsinki, 25 kilometers northeast of Espoo.

Airport–City Links: By bus: Finnair buses to Helsinki city center depart from Platform 1A outside the international terminal every 20–30 minutes 0545–0110; journey takes 35 minutes. Fare: €6.30. Local bus service: Operated by Sirolan Liikenne Oy; take bus No. 615, 616, or 617 from Platform 1B between the airport and the station square two to four times an hour; trip takes 40 minutes.

By taxi: Airport to the Central Railway Station takes 25 to 40 minutes. Fare €45–50. Airport Taxi is a share-the-ride service. Fare: €25 for one to four persons; €45 for five to seven persons; €60 for eight persons or private Airport Taxi.

Passengers should check in at the airport a minimum of 75 minutes before departure time for overseas flights. Contact Finnair several hours before flight time to check weather conditions at the airport. Duty-free shops at the airport are loaded with gifts of Finnish origins.

Arriving by Train

Helsinki is served by a single train terminal, the **Central Helsinki Railway Station,** which is considered one of the most famous works of Finnish-American architect Eliel Saarinen. The terminal lies right in the heart of Helsinki and is close to everything. The train platforms have a total of 19 covered tracks.

- **Baggage storage** is available on the far right of the main hall entering from the trains. Baggage lockers are available in various sizes at a standard charge. There is also a Left Luggage office on the left-hand side arriving from the trains. Pictograms will lead you to it.
- **Money exchange** is located in the main hall. There are two Forex money exchange desks open 0700 to 2100 daily. Banks are open 0915 to 1615 Monday through Friday.
- **Tourist information/hotel reservations** are available at the Helsinki Expert Hotel Booking Center. Pictograms will lead you. *Tel:* (09) 2288 1400; *Fax:* (09) 2288 1499; www.helsinkiexpert.fi; *E-mail:* hotel@helsinkiexpert.fi.

Hours: October–December: 0900–1500 Monday–Friday and 1000–1400 Saturday; January 2–April: 0900–1500 Monday–Friday and 1000–1400 Saturday; May: 0900–1600 Monday–Friday and 1000–1600 Saturday; June–August: 0900–1700 daily; September: 0900–1600 Monday–Friday and 1000–1600 Saturday.

- **Train information** is on the right-hand side of the station's main hall. *Tel:* 0307 20 900; www.vr.fi; *E-mail:* info@vr.fi.
- **Seat reservations** can be made at ticket counters 1 to 10 in the ticket office. *Hours:* 0630–2100 Monday–Saturday, 0830–2100 Sunday.
- **Rail pass validation** can be made at counters 14 to 17 at the VR International Tickets section.

There are many cafeterias and restaurants in the station. All information is in three languages—Finnish, Swedish, and English. Helsinki's Central Station connects with an underground shopping area—a great place to pick up a loaf of crusty bread, tasty cheese, and a beer when returning late from a day excursion.

Arriving by Ship

The Tallink-Silja Line ferries from Stockholm arrive at Helsinki's Eteläsatama dock. Tallink-Silja Finnjet and Viking Line ferries dock at Katajanokka Pier. Each ferry company maintains spacious passenger facilities complete with food services, lounges, currency exchanges, and connections to public transportation. Shipping activities in the harbor present many photographic opportunities. If you are continuing your Eurail journey back aboard the Tallink-Silja Line, a money exchange service is offered aboard by the ship's purser.

Tallink-Silja Line, Olympiaranta 1, Helsinki, FIN 00140. *Tel:* 040 547 541 222; *Fax:* 358 918 04311; www.tallinksilja.com/en/.

Viking Line, Katajanokanlaituri 8, Helsinki, FIN 00160. *Tel:* 358 91235300; *Fax:* 358 9647 075; www.vikingline.fi; *Email:* international.sales@vikingline.com

Tourist Information/Hotel Reservations

- *Helsinki City Tourist Information Office:* Pohjoisesplanadi 19, 00100 Helsinki; *Tel:* (09) 3101 3300; *Fax:* (09) 3101 3301; www.visithelsinki.fi; *E-mail:* tourist.info@hel.fi. *Hours:* Summer: 0900–2000 Monday–Friday and 0900–1800 Saturday and Sunday; October–April: 0900–1800 Monday–Friday and 1000–1600 Saturday and Sunday.

  Located in the market-square area of the harbor. To reach this office, board tram No. 3T immediately in front of the train station. Fare: €2.70 adult; €1.30 child. In about 10 minutes, the tram will pass the Tallink-Silja Line Terminal for Stockholm ferries. Disembark at the next stop, which is the market square on the harbor. Look for the green "i" sign.

Getting Around in Helsinki

The Helsinki Card is a veritable key to the city. This card not only grants you free travel on buses, trams, trains, and the Metro in the metropolitan area but also provides free entry to about 50 museums and other places of interest in and around Helsinki and includes a free guided sightseeing tour by bus. Showing the card in department stores brings you a free gift; it will spoil you in many of the city's restaurants, theaters, the opera, and concerts. A 96-page brochure describing the scores of opportunities the Helsinki Card provides may be obtained from the Helsinki City Tourist Office or in the Hotel Booking Centre at the railway station, as well as at some travel agencies, hotels, and department stores. Visit www.helsinkiexpert.fi.

Helsinki Card Prices

	ADULT	CHILD (7–16 YEARS)
24 hours	€39	€17
48 hours	€51	€20
72 hours	€61	€23

Sights/Attractions/Tours

During summer, Helsinki City Transport operates two unusual forms of sightseeing—the tomato-red pub-on-wheels tram, **Spårakoff,** and a tram named **2.** From mid-May to mid-August, Spårakoff departs from the stop at Mikonkatu near the rail station at 1400, 1500, 1700, 1800, 1900, and 2000. Fare: €8.00, drinks extra. Sip and sightsee all at the same time. Tram 2 takes you in a figure-eight loop around Helsinki center. Pick up a pamphlet with a map and descriptions of the sights from the tourist office. Board at Market Square, pay the driver €2.70 (only €2.20 when purchased in advance). Round-trip: about 60 minutes. Tram 3B follows the same route but in the opposite direction.

Another way to become acquainted with the city is to take a guided bus tour. Helsinki Experts' tours depart daily at 1100. Fare: €28 adult (€22 with Helsinki Card), €15 child (age 7–16). Visit www.helsinkiexpert.fi.

For a more intimate way to get to know Helsinki, ask the tourist office for the brochure *See Helsinki on Foot*. Tour No. 5—Market Square–Kaivopuisto–Eira—interested us. Just follow the route on the map in the brochure. The sights are numbered and explained. If you begin at Market Square, one of the first sights will be the ***Havis Amanda*** (a beautiful mermaid) fountain by the sculptor Ville Vallgren, created in 1908. Next you'll see the first public monument in Helsinki—the **Czarina's Stone,** designed by C. L. Engel to commemorate the Czarina Alexandra's visit. About midway through your tour, you may want to stop at the **Ursula Seaside Café** (No. 33 on the map). *Tel:* (09) 652 817; www.ursula.fi or kaivopuisto@ursula.fi.

Other tours originate at the Tallink-Silja Line or Viking Line terminals in the harbor area. These tours run two hours, and some schedules include lunch. Again, the tourist information office has the details.

Highlights of Helsinki

Helsinki is a city born of the sea, and it is from the sea that it draws its soul and nature. It is the beautiful daughter of the Baltic—a sparkling jewel with the blue sea as its setting. Helsinki is a modern city. Here the visitor does not come face-to-face with the past as he or she does in many other long-standing European capitals. Great fires destroyed the original Helsinki many times, but it was always rebuilt. The only original remains of the trade-and-seafaring town that Swedish king Gustav Vasa founded in 1550 at the mouth of the Vantaa River are the foundations of a church.

Helsinki did not become Finland's capital until 1812. It is very cosmopolitan, the heart of cultural and artistic experiences for the Finns. The city's colorful market square on the harbor is characterized by the glittering sea and an abundance of flowers and fruit, white seagulls, and busy salespeople. Helsinki has an ambience that is all its own, supported by a friendly population and the physical comforts to enable you to fully enjoy its many features.

Helsinki's market square, besides presenting flowers, fish, vegetables, fruits, and souvenirs, can also provide visitors with coffee and delicious sugared buns at the square's tent cafe. Market hours are 0630 to 1500 Monday through Saturday. From mid-May through August, the evening market hours are 1530 to 2000 Monday through Friday. Most shops in Helsinki are open 0900 to 1800 (or 2000) weekdays and 0900 to 1400 Saturday.

Surrounded as the city is by the sea, there is a lot of island hopping you can do while visiting Helsinki. A ride on a ferryboat will take you to **Korkeasaari Island,** Helsinki's zoo; by ferry you can also reach **Suomenlinna,** a fortress island started by the Swedes, captured by the Russians, and shelled by the British before being given to Finland, which used it as part of its sea defenses until 1973. Visit www.suomenlinna.fi. Should you tire of all this activity, you can plan to relax in one of Helsinki's excellent saunas.

Ferry Connections Helsinki—Stockholm

See Appendix, Ferry Crossings section, for detailed information.

Tallink-Silja Line ferries depart Helsinki Olympiaterminaali (Olympia Terminal), Eteläsatama port, at 1700 daily and arrive Stockholm Värtahamnen port at 0945 next day. The Stockholm to Helsinki trip leaves at 1645, arriving the next morning at 1030.*

Viking Line ferries depart Helsinki Katajanokka dock at 1730 daily. Arrive Stockholm Stadsgården dock 1000 next day. The Stockholm to Helsinki trip leaves at 1630, arriving the next morning at 1010.*

Train & Ferry Connections Helsinki—Stockholm via Turku

DEPART Helsinki	TRAIN NUMBER	ARRIVE Turku Harbor
0520	IC 941	0741
1702	IC 961	1900
Arrives Turku Satama (harbor train station)		

Tallink-Silja Line ferry MS *Silja Galaxy* departs Turku Silja Harbor daily at 0815, arrives Stockholm Värtahamnen port 1815; and MS *Silja Europa* departs at 2015 for arrival at 0610 the next day.*

Viking Line ferries depart Turku Linnansatama dock daily at 0845, arrive Stockholm Stadsgården dock at 1855, and depart at 2055 for arrival at 0630 the next day.* Bus connections between Stadsgården port and Cityterminalen (bus terminal) near Stockholm Central Station in connection with ship arrival/departure.

*Confirm sailing dates and make advance reservations by telephone, fax, or online.

Tallink-Silja Line
Olympiaranta
Helsinki FIN 0010
Tel: (09) 358 600 15700
Fax: (09) 358 918 04311
www.tallinksilja.com/en/

Viking Line
Katajanokanlaituri 8
Helsinki FIN 00160
Tel: (09) 12 351
Fax: (09) 647 075
www.vikingline.fi

Day Excursions

When you have finally broken the fine Finnish spell Helsinki casts over its visitors, you will want to venture forth into the Finnish countryside. We have selected four such adventures for your pleasure. They are **Hanko, Lahti, Tampere,** and **Turku.** Hanko, Finland's southernmost city, is a very popular summer resort with miles of wide beaches, good fishing, sailing, and all types of amusements. Lahti is about 65 miles north of Helsinki and provides an opportunity to ride trains between Helsinki and St. Petersburg. Also north of Helsinki lies Tampere, Finland's third-largest city. Both industrial and recreational, Tampere has much to offer visitors year-round. Turku, Finland's gateway to the west, was its former capital and an important cultural center before Helsinki was founded. Wherever you go, the friendly Finns will make you feel right at home. Enjoy Finland as the Finns do.

Day Excursion to

Hanko (Hangö)

Southernmost City

Depart from Helsinki Station
Distance by Train: 85 miles (137 km)
Average Train Time: 1 hour, 54 minutes
City Dialing Code: 19
Tourist Information Office: 5 Raatihuoneentori, P.O. Box 14, 10900 Hanko
Tel: (019) 2203 411; **Fax:** (019) 2203 261
www.hanko.fi
E-mail: tourist.office@hanko.fi
Hours: January 1–May 31 0900–1600 Monday–Friday; June 1–August 31 0900–1800 Monday–Friday, 1000–1600 Saturday–Sunday; September 1–December 31 0900–1600 Monday–Friday
Notes: To get to the Hanko tourist office, depart the station and proceed along the overpass crossing the railroad, which will be on your left as you arrive. Walk over the bridge and continue past the market square on your right. Turn left on Bulevardi Street. The tourist office is in the town hall, on the corner of Bulevardi Street and Vuorikatu. ("Katu" means "street.")

Hanko (Hangö) is Finland's southernmost town. It is best known as a summer resort, but because the climate in this part of Finland often is very mild, you can visit Hanko in any season. In September, for example, the seawater is still warm enough for swimming. If you do not want to swim, you can lie on the beach, take a walk in the surrounding area, go for a bicycle tour, hire a horse, or just relax. Hanko in autumn is an unusually peaceful place. No matter when you go there, you will find clean water, lots of fresh air, and lots of things to do. The peninsula where Hanko lies, known long ago among seafarers, was used for centuries as a harbor where sailing vessels could seek refuge from storms or winter ice packs. With time on their hands, many navigators, merchants, and soldiers kept themselves busy by carving their names or family coats of arms in the rocks along the shoreline of the harbor. More than 600 of these carvings have been found. Due to these inscriptions, the area gained the title "Guest Book of the Archipelago." You can inspect this handiwork during the sightseeing cruises available in the harbor area.

Hanko did not begin as a town until the 1870s. With the introduction of iron ships, winter navigation became possible, and Hanko's peninsula was found to be well suited as a year-round harbor. Both a railway and a harbor were constructed, and Hanko was well on its way to becoming an important part of the Finnish economy.

Helsinki—Hanko (Hangö)

DEPART Helsinki	TRAIN NUMBER	ARRIVE Hanko	NOTES
0656	IC 943/382	0850	R, 1
0902	IC 945/384	1050	R, 1
1202	IC 951/386	1350	R, 1

DEPART Hanko	TRAIN NUMBER	ARRIVE Helsinki	NOTES
1410	387/IC960	1558	R, 1
1610	389/IC 964	1758	R, 1
1810	391/IC 968	1958	R, 1
2040	393/IC 972	2226	R, 1

Daily, including holidays

R Reservations required, supplement required

1. Change trains in Karjaa.

Distance: 85 miles (137 km)

By the end of the 19th century, Hanko was a fashionable summer resort, especially among the Russians coming from the St. Petersburg area. The Russian influence is visible in the architecture of many wooden villas in Hanko, most of which are in the **Spa Park.** The peninsula on which Hanko lies was ceded to the Soviet Union in 1940 but was regained in 1941.

Hanko is inseparably linked to the sea. The sunny south of Finland has about 90 islands just within its town limits! The town has four small boat harbors, including the largest harbor for visiting boats in all of Finland, two commercial harbors, and four industrial harbors. None of this activity is detrimental to tourism; in fact, it attracts it. More than 200,000 tourists visit Hanko annually. They come not only for the long sandy beaches and aquatic sports but also for the various events that take place every year.

The day excursion to Hanko requires a change of trains at **Karjaa,** which you reach in a little more than an hour from Helsinki. In Karjaa you will transfer to a local train that makes an interesting trip through southern Finland's woods and quaint little rail stations before reaching Hanko. The Hanko station is the last stop on the line, so there's no chance of missing it.

Between 1880 and 1930 thousands of emigrants set off from Hanko for the United States, Canada, and Australia. In 1967 a statue commemorating this period was erected near the beach, a short distance from the tourist office. Depicting wild birds in free flight, this **"emigration monument"** is well worth the visit. Also worthwhile is the **Fortress Museum** [*Tel:* (040) 1359 228] in the Eastern Harbor and the **Municipal Art Gallery** [*Tel:* (019) 2203 270], which features exhibitions from local, Finnish, and foreign artists.

To experience Hanko's spa history, visit the famous **Summer Restaurant Casino,** one of the largest summer restaurants in Finland. To get there, head down Bulevardi toward the sea. Turn left onto Appelgrenintie. As you enter the Spa Park, you will see the beaches on your right. The villas in the park once housed Russian nobles and their families as guests.

Hanko has several other interesting restaurants, some of which are open year-round in the Eastern Harbor area. You can find Italian-style entrees, seafood, or homemade Finnish fare.

Other tours of Hanko and its surroundings can be arranged through the City Tourist Office. Brochures, maps, and special information leaflets are available; guides can be hired. Sea cruises operate every day from mid-June to the end of August. You can visit the highest lighthouse in the Nordic countries by a tour to **Bengtskär** [six to seven hours; *Tel:* (02) 466 7227; *Fax:* (02) 466 7228; www.bengtskar.fi] or take a shorter trip to **Pike's Gut** (Hauensuoli), the "Guest Book of the Archipelago." This is a narrow strait between two islands, Tullisari and Kobben. Sea tours start at the Eastern Harbor. Tickets are sold onboard. Fishing trips may also be arranged, but before angling off, check with the tourist office and obtain a general fishing permit from the town's post office. Hanko is packed with exciting as well as relaxing things to do.

Day Excursion to

Lahti

Ski, Skate, Sail, or Cycle

Depart from Helsinki Station
Distance by Train: 81 miles (130 km)
Average Train Time: 1 hour, 30 minutes
City Dialing Code: 3
Tourist Information Office: Askonkatu 9F, 15100 Lahti
Tel: (02) 0728 1750; **Fax:** (02) 0728 1751
www.lahtitravel.fi
E-mail: info@lahtiregion.fi
Hours: 1000–1700 Monday–Friday, 0900–1600 Saturday and Sunday
Notes: When you arrive in Lahti from Helsinki, exit on the left side of the train. Use the underground exit and walk toward track No. 4 to the station. Exit the terminal and proceed north along Rautatienkatu. Tourist office is located on the left-hand side of the street. Tourist information is available in the rail station, as well as in the Sports Centre and the Passenger Harbour, throughout the summer.

Lahti is the seventh-largest city in Finland, with nearly 100,000 inhabitants. It is particularly noted for its timber and wooden furniture, brewers' products, and clothing and is equally famous as a winter sports center. Sporting events have always played a prominent role in Lahti's lifestyle. The **Salpausselkä Ski Games,** as well as the **Finlandia** and other skiing events, have made Lahti world famous.

Perhaps the most spectacular sight in Lahti is its 116-meter ski jump, located in the **Lahti Sports Centre.** The jump is about a 15-minute walk from the tourist information office and merits everyone's inspection. An observation platform on top of the jump can be reached by elevator and is accessible to visitors daily during summer months and on weekends during low season. In addition to the 116-meter ski jump, there are smaller ski jumps and practice areas nearby. The ski-jump area actually is a year-round attraction for tourists. In addition to the observation platform, there is an open-air, heated swimming pool at the foot of the ski-jump complex and the complex houses a ski museum.

The Sports Centre is not the sole attraction in Lahti. In the 1920s and 1930s, the city had the most powerful broadcasting station in Finland. The station now stands as a Radio and TV Museum. The museum contains more than 1,000 items of great interest in the field of radio technology.

In Lahti general fitness is a feature of everyday life. There are illuminated trails for walking, jogging, and skiing—about 40 kilometers of them—as well as nonilluminated trails. Summer weekly events include outdoor theater, concerts, a lively marketplace, and hiking.

The city is unique in that it is one of the few metropolitan areas where you can live in a one-family house in the center of the city on the shore of a lake. (We suggest that the city planners of America go to Lahti to pick up a few pointers.) Much of Lahti's housing is spread over a wide area, along the city's green hillsides and lakeshores. Many visitors are surprised to find Lahti so sophisticated and versatile. The infrastructure of quality department stores, good hotels, and good restaurants coupled with civic convention centers capable of handling large numbers of people are the elements of Lahti's success. Lahti is modern yet traditional.

The old Vesijarvi Harbor has turned into a second living room for Lahti citizens and visitors with its musical and cultural events. There you can find the new **Sibelius Hall Congress and Concert Centre,** the largest wooden building constructed in Finland. This is where the world-famous Lahti Symphony Orchestra may be heard.

Shopping for excellent Finnish glassware can be a full-time occupation. Numerous Lahti department stores, as well as specialty shops, feature fine Finnish glassware and other high-quality items. The city is well-known for its ready-to-wear garments for both men and women. The Finnish furniture industry is centered here, and Lahti bread and beer are known all over Finland for their quality.

Helsinki—Lahti

DEPART Helsinki	TRAIN NUMBER	ARRIVE Lahti
0812	IC 71	0906
1012	IC 3	1104
1041	R 73	1142
1312	IC 5	1404

DEPART Lahti	TRAIN NUMBER	ARRIVE Helsinki
1456	IC 68	1548
1556	IC 8	1648
1756	IC 114	1848
1856	IC 10	1948
2054	IC 78	2148

Daily

Distance: 81 miles (130 km)

In summer Lahti's cultural life includes performances in the **Kariranta open-air theater** and the open-air concerts at the **Mukkula Tourist Centre.** Lahti provides an interesting as well as relaxing day-excursion site; it's a year-round attraction you shouldn't miss.

Sights to see while in town include the **Historical Museum,** the **Museum of Military Medicine,** the **Ski Museum,** and the **Museum of Art.** The Lahti Tourist Office conducts a two-hour city tour every Wednesday starting at 1800 from June 1 through August 2.

Lahti has been described as Finland's most American city. Founded in 1905, Lahti is, historically speaking, a young city, but it has grown more rapidly than towns of similar age or older. One reason for its vigorous development is its geographic position in the center of southern Finland, at the junction of major traffic routes. Another, we might add, is its friendly, courteous people.

Day Excursion to

Tampere

City of Theaters

Depart from Helsinki Station
Distance by Train: 116 miles (187 km)
Average Train Time: 1 hour, 55 minutes
City Dialing Code: 3
Tourist Information Office: Railway Station, Rautatienkatu 25A, Tampere
Tel: (03) 5656 6800; **Fax:** (03) 5656 6463
www.tampere.fi or **www.gotampere.fi**
E-mail: visittampere@visittampere.fi
Hours: June–August: 0900–1800 Monday–Friday and 1000–1500 Saturday–Sunday; September–May: 0900–1700 Monday–Friday
Notes: The main tourist office is now located inside the train station, making it easy to find.

Known as "the cradle of Finnish industry," Tampere is the youngest of the "triangle towns" of Finland, the others being Helsinki and Turku. The reference to a triangle comes from the fact that all three cities are approximately 93 miles (150 kilometers) apart from each other. The town of Tampere was granted its charter in 1779 by Gustavus III, who was king of both Sweden and Finland at that time. From a modest start, Tampere developed into an industrial and resort center early in the 19th century. Today, with its 210,000 inhabitants, it is the third-largest city in Finland.

Tampere is a city of lakes and parks. Its two major lakes are connected by rapids flowing over three waterfalls. Tampere is considered to be a "small" city. The city center is located on a narrow isthmus that is divided by the rapids. The "smallness" actually means that all shops, stores, restaurants, hotels, and other sights are within easy reach of one another, which makes Tampere an easy city to explore on foot.

Many tours are offered through the tourist office, such as the **Rapids Walk,** through the heart of the city, and the **Pispala Walk,** to the top of the ridge for a spectacular view, then to the bohemian historical district. Learn about Finland's Grand Duchy past during the **In the Footsteps of the Tsar** tour, or take the **Art Tour,** the **Guided Shopping Tour,** or the **Tour of Churches.** Visit the website of the tourist board for more listings. Many lake cruises are offered as well.

Among the noteworthy places to see and visit in Tampere is the **Sarkanniemi Adventure Park,** which contains an amusement park and a children's zoo, both of which are open daily in summer. An aquarium, a dolphinarium, a planetarium, an observation tower, and the **Sara Hilden Modern Art Museum** are also located in the complex. These attractions are open daily throughout the year, and the hours and prices depend on the time of year and how much of the park you are taking advantage of. Visit www.sarkanniemi.fi.

In the Sarkanniemi aquarium you will find some 3,000 fish and sea animals of more than 200 species from all over the world. See Eevertti and the other dolphins play games with their trainers. In the multimedia planetarium, a veritable galaxy of 6,000 twinkling bodies will open up before you. Here you will see both past and future movements in space projected on the planetarium's dome ceiling in a 30-minute space adventure.

The Sarkanniemi amusement park area also contains roller-coaster rides, big and small bumper cars, and many other attractions. The ultimate experience is the Rapids Ride, a 490-meter-long track excavated out of the rock. For more thrills and chills, try the Tornado roller coaster. The little ones in the family will love getting to know all of the fluffy animals in the children's zoo.

Art lovers will enjoy the Sara Hilden Modern Art Museum, with its outstanding collection of contemporary art. The paddle wheel boat ***Finlandia Queen*** starts its 1½-hour cruises from the quay nearby from June through August, running several days a week. Need we say more—except that the Sarkanniemi is the place to be?

Another place of interest in Tampere is the revolving auditorium of the **Pyynikki Summer Theater.** It is world renowned and was the first of its kind when it opened in 1959. Nearby Pispala Ridge, with its old timbered houses and Pyynikki Park, is also worth visiting.

The **Museum Centre Vapriikki** is located in a former engineering plant by the Tammerkoski Rapids, the site of the 1999 preliminary European Union (EU) summit meeting. Collections of five formerly separate museums form the basic exhibition in addition to international exhibitions. Open daily 1000–1800, closed Monday, admission €9 adults, €3 children.

Tallipiha (Stable Yards) is a family attraction located right in the heart of idyllic old Tampere. Formerly stables for the Nottbeck family horses, horsemen, and carriages, the area has been restored and houses a cafe, artisans' shops, and a chocolate shop. Horse-drawn carriage rides, among other activities, are offered. *Hours:* 1000–1800 Monday–Friday, 1000–1700 Saturday, and 1100–1700 Sunday in summer; 1000–1700 Tuesday–Friday and 1100–1600 Saturday–Sunday in winter. Visit www.tallipiha.fi.

In Tampere you can find a good cross section of Finnish architectural history. It ranges from charming wooden houses and Art Nouveau houses in the center of the city to the most modern designed office buildings and redbrick factory buildings at the city's rapids. Tampere's oldest building is the **Messukyla stone church,** which dates from the 15th century. The city's cathedral, with its architecture and frescoes, is an outstanding example of Finland's Art Nouveau period. A newer place of worship is the **Kaleva Church,** a strikingly modern construction completed in 1966. Another fine example of modern Finnish architecture is the city's main library, the **City Library Metso.** The **Moomin-Valley Museum,** in the same building, is also

Helsinki—Tampere

DEPART Helsinki	TRAIN NUMBER	ARRIVE Tampere	NOTES
0706	IC 63	0852	1
0806	IC 165	0952	1, Exc. Sa
0906	IC 85	1052	1
and later service at hourly intervals until 2006.			

DEPART Tampere	TRAIN NUMBER	ARRIVE Helsinki	NOTES
1507	IC 50	1652	1
1600	S 52	1730	
1707	IC 180	1852	1
1737	S R 342	1941	
1807	IC 54	1952	1
1907	IC 90	2052	1
2007	IC 184	2152	1
2107	IC 58	2252	1
2307	S 94	0052+1	

Daily, unless otherwise noted

+1 Arrives next day

1. A supplemental fare is charged on all IC trains. If the supplemental fare is paid in advance of boarding the train, a seat reservation is included at no extra charge; the supplemental fare may be paid aboard the train, but such payments do not guarantee seat availability.

Distance: 116 miles (187 km)

worth a visit. The Moomin collection includes more than 1,000 fairy-tale sketches and illustrations by the author-artist Tove Jansson and can be enjoyed by all ages. If you are interested in architectural design, Tampere can come up with a good serving of it.

In the center of Tampere, there is the **Verkaranta Arts and Crafts Center,** with Finnish articles of high quality on exhibition. Close by, you can browse about in Tampere's colorful old market hall and the outside markets that surround it. If you happen to be in town during the summer (June through August), there's a concert at 1900 at the Old Library Park in the city center on Tuesday and Thursday. Folk dance groups perform at 1900 on Wednesday.

Day Excursion to

Turku

Finland's First Capital

Depart from Helsinki Station
Distance by Train: 124 miles (200 km)
Average Train Time: 2 hours
City Dialing Code: 2
Tourist Information Office: Turku Touring, Aurakatu 4, Turku–20100
Tel: (02) 262 7444; **Fax:** (02) 262 7679
www.turku.fi or **www.turkutouring.fi**
E-mail: tourist.info@turku.fi
Hours: April 1–September 30: 0830–1800 Monday–Friday and 0900–1600 Saturday and Sunday; remainder of the year, Saturday and Sunday hours are 1000–1500
Notes: Turku's tourist information office can be reached by proceeding from the rail station down Humalistonkatu (Humlegardsgatan). Turn left at Eerikinkatu and proceed for 2 blocks, then turn right onto Aurakatu. The tourist information office will be at your right near the city hall. If arriving at the harbor from Stockholm, check with the Tallink-Silja Line desk for city information and directions to the city.

Turku is a city of contrasts, where past and present meet and blend. Finland's oldest established town, Turku celebrated its 785th anniversary in 2004. Turku was never founded; it seems it was always there. It developed naturally at the crossing of the northern trade routes at the mouth of the Aura River. The current population of approximately 170,000 is hardworking, industrious, and friendly.

With a rail pass, you can choose from two forms of traveling to Turku. You can go by train on a day excursion from Helsinki, or you can take the Tallink-Silja ferry from Stockholm. Whether you go by train or ferry, Turku deserves an extended examination because it has many interesting sights to offer.

Turku has three rail stations. Arriving from Helsinki, your train will make a brief stop at the Kupittaa suburban station before arriving in the city's main station. Do not detrain at Kupittaa. If you arrive in Turku on a day excursion from Helsinki and your train is scheduled to terminate at the ferry port (the third stop), rather than getting off at the main station (second stop), stay aboard the train and ride to the end of the line. There you can, time permitting, visit the nearby Great Castle of Turku. Farther along the river Aura, by the Martinsilta Bridge, is the retired sailing ship *Suomen Joutsen* (the "Swan of Finland"), the best-known tourist attraction in Turku. If you prefer a taxi, the fare is approximately €8 to €10; the walk from the port to the station should take about 20 to 30 minutes, and there's a lot to see en route. Bus service is also available. Bus No. 1 plies between the town's marketplace and the port. The bus fare is €2.50.

Helsinki—Turku

DEPART Helsinki	TRAIN NUMBER	ARRIVE Turku	NOTES
0520	IC 941	0732	continues to Turku Harbor, arriving 0741
0656	IC 943	0900	M–Sa
0902	IC 945	1100	
1202	IC 951	1400	
1402	IC 955	1600	
1502	IC 957	1700	
1602	IC 959	1800	continues to Turku Harbor, arriving 1819
1702	IC 961	1900	Exc. Sa
1802	IC 963	2000	continues to Turku Harbor, arriving 2016
2037	IC 967	2230	Exc. Sa

DEPART Turku	TRAIN NUMBER	ARRIVE Helsinki	NOTES
0537	IC 942	0734	
0625	IC 944	0825	M–F
0800	S 948	0958	M–F
0900	IC 950	1058	departs from Turku harbor at 0828
1100	IC 954	1323	
1200	IC 956	1358	
1400	IC 960	1558	
1500	IC 962	1658	
1600	IC 964	1758	
1700	IC 966	1858	
1800	IC 968	1958	
1830	IC 970	2023	
2130	IC 933	0052+1	departs from Turku Harbor at 2110

Daily, unless otherwise noted
IC InterCity train. Conveys Business Plus, Business, and 2nd class
S Pendolino S 220 train (high-speed train). Conveys Business Plus, Business, and 2nd class

Tours depart the Aurakatu tourist office Monday through Saturday from mid-June through August. Check with either of the city's tourist information offices for full details regarding sightseeing opportunities in and around Turku. Also available at the Tourist Office is the Turku card, good for free museum admission, free local buses, and other discounts. The card is €21 for 24 hours and €28 for 48 hours; a 24 hour family card is available for €45.

The **Great Castle of Turku,** which is only a brief walk from the Tallink-Silja Line, was begun in the 1280s. It is the largest castle in Finland and once served as a prison, but now it provides a magnificent banquet hall for state and civic functions. Also of interest to visitors is the historical museum that is housed in the Great Castle. Its collection provides insight regarding 400 years of Finnish history. *Hours:* 1000–1800 Tuesday–Sunday; closed Monday, admission €9.00 adults, €5.00 children.

An interesting museum combination is the **Aboa Vetus Museum** and the **Ars Nova Museum** (www.aboavetusarsnova.fi). The Aboa Vetus tells of how life in Turku developed since the 14th century, while Ars Nova focuses on 20th-century art. Multimedia programs help guide you through the museums. *Hours:* 1100–1900 daily.

The **Turku Cathedral,** another 13th-century structure, is open throughout the year. *Hours:* summer: 0900–2000 daily; winter: 0900–1900 daily. Turku Cathedral, the major medieval ecclesiastical building in Finland, is regarded as the national shrine. You will see many interesting Neoclassical buildings surrounding the cathedral. Turku boasts two major universities—one Finnish and one Swedish—with a combined student body exceeding 20,000.

During the early hours of the day, the bustling marketplace is full of life. There you will see brisk bargaining amid a brilliant display of flowers, fruit, vegetables, and fresh fish. Fire destroyed a major part of Turku in 1827, but Cloister Hill, a neighborhood of carpenters and stonemasons, escaped damage. Today the area houses the unique **Luostarinmäki Handicrafts Museum,** with some 30 workshops that reflect the 18th and 19th centuries. *Hours:* May–September: 1000–1800 Tuesday–Sunday; August–April 15: 1000–1600 Tuesday–Sunday.

The word *turku* means "marketplace." The city, born out of the needs of commerce, is still one of the largest commercial centers in Finland. The **Hansa Shopping Center,** the country's largest, is adjacent to the city's marketplace and features more than 100 shops and boutiques—plus a supermarket. Also there are hotels, theaters for movies and live performances, more than 100 restaurants, and four banks.

If you, too, are a rail travel enthusiast, be certain to stop at **The Blue Train Café** in the market hall. Its decor originates from a wooden long-distance Finnish railway car built in 1952 and is typical of the Finnish passenger railcars of the 1950s.

FRANCE

"How can you be expected to govern a country that has 246 kinds of cheese?"

—CHARLES DE GAULLE, 1962

Now, France has more than 500 different kinds of cheese and more than 450 types of wine. France is western Europe's largest and probably its most diverse country. Each of France's 22 regions has its own culture and scenery, its own style of architecture and art, its own gastronomy and lifestyle, and, in many cases, its own dialect. This delightful diversity makes travel in France so intriguing.

The primary language is, of course, French, but most tourism officials and rail personnel speak at least un peu (a bit) of English. The best way to obtain the most help and cooperation in France is to first of all smile and then ask in French, "Excusez moi, parlez-vous Anglaise?" Even if your pronunciation makes the French language unrecognizable, the idea that you at least attempted to ask in French makes a big impression.

For more information on France, contact the French Government Tourist Offices. *Hotline:* (514) 288-1904; **http://us.franceguide.com;** *E-mail:* info.us@franceguide.com.

New York: 825 Third Avenue, 29th Floor, New York, NY 10022. *Tel:* (212) 745-0952; *Fax:* (212) 838-7855

Chicago: Consulate General of France, 205 North Michigan Avenue, Suite 3770, Chicago, IL 60601. *Tel:* (312) 327-0290

Los Angeles: 9454 Wilshire Boulevard, Suite 210, Beverly Hills, CA 90212-2967. *Tel:* (310) 271-6665; *Fax:* (310) 276-2835

Montreal: 1800 McGill College Avenue, Suite 1010, Montreal, Quebec H3A 3J6, Canada. *Tel:* (514) 288-2026; *Fax:* (514) 845-4868

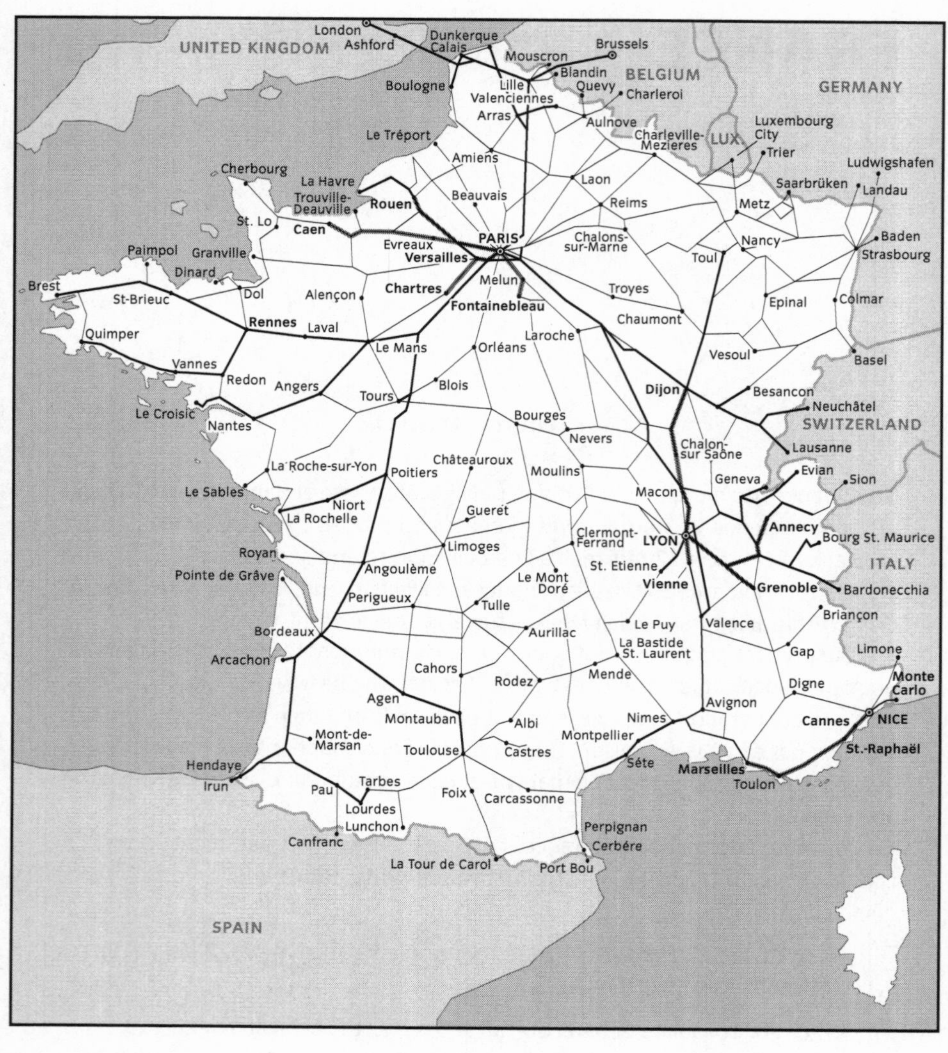

UNITED KINGDOM
London
Ashford
Dunkerque
Calais
Boulogne
Mouscron
Brussels
Blandin
Lille
Quevy
BELGIUM
Charleroi
GERMANY
Valenciennes
Arras
Aulnove
Le Tréport
Charleville-Mezieres
LUX.
Luxembourg City
Trier
Amiens
Ludwigshafen
Cherbourg
La Havre
Laon
Saarbrüken
Landau
Trouville-Deauville
Rouen
Beauvais
Reims
Metz
St. Lo
Caen
PARIS
Chalons-sur-Marne
Nancy
Baden
Evreaux
Strasbourg
Paimpol
Granville
Versailles
Toul
Dinard
Melun
Brest
Dol
Alençon
Chartres
Troyes
St-Brieuc
Fontainebleau
Epinal
Colmar
Rennes
Chaumont
Laval
Laroche
Quimper
Le Mans
Orléans
Vesoul
Basel
Vannes
Redon
Angers
Blois
Dijon
Besancon
Tours
Neuchâtel
Le Croisic
Bourges
SWITZERLAND
Nantes
Nevers
Chalon-sur Saône
Lausanne
Châteauroux
La Roche-sur-Yon
Poitiers
Moulins
Evian
Le Sables
Geneva
Sion
Niort
Macon
La Rochelle
Gueret
Annecy
Clermont-Ferrand
LYON
Bourg St. Maurice
Royan
Limoges
St. Etienne
ITALY
Angoulême
Pointe de Grâve
Le Mont Doré
Vienne
Grenoble
Bardonecchia
Perigueux
Tulle
Briançon
Bordeaux
Le Puy
Valence
Aurillac
La Bastide St. Laurent
Gap
Arcachon
Limone
Cahors
Mende
Rodez
Digne
Monte Carlo
Agen
Avignon
Nimes
Montauban
Cannes
NICE
Albi
Mont-de-Marsan
Montpellier
Toulouse
Castres
St.-Raphaël
Séte
Marseilles
Hendaye
Toulon
Irun
Tarbes
Pau
Foix
Carcassonne
Lourdes
Perpignan
Lunchon
Canfranc
Cerbère
La Tour de Carol
Port Bou
SPAIN

Banking

Currency: Euro (€)

Exchange rate at press time: €0.90 = U.S. $1.00

Hours: 1000–1300/1500–1700 Monday–Friday (some are open Saturday and closed Monday)

Communications

Country Code: 33

For telephone calls within France, dial the two-digit prefix applicable for the area as listed below and then the eight-digit phone number:

01—for Paris numbers
02—for the northwest of France
03—for the northeast of France
04—for the southeast of France
05—for the southwest of France

All calls within France must use the full 10 digits. When placing calls to France from another country, use the country code 33 and drop the initial zero. (For example, to call the Lyon Tourist Information Office from the United States, you would dial 011 +33 4 72 77 69 69.)

Major Mobile Phone Companies: Orange, SFR, Bouygues Telecom

Rail Travel in France

Seemingly, France has more varieties of trains than it has cheeses. The French lead the world in rail technology, and their TGV (*train à grande vitesse*) trains hold the world's friction rail speed record at 320 mph.

French National Railroads (Société Nationale des Chemins de Fer Français, or SNCF) operates some 21,100 miles of rail lines, supplemented by SNCF buses in mountainous areas. For train information and reservations for all of France, call 33 9 70 609970; www.sncf.com.

French National Railroads accepts the variety of **Eurail passes, France Rail-pass, Eurail France–Italy Pass, Eurail France–Spain Pass,** and **Eurail France–Switzerland Pass.** Eurail bonuses in France include:

- Paris, France–London, England, via Eurostar thru the Chunnel—Special discounted fares (about 50 percent) for rail pass holders
- SeaFrance—50 percent discount on Calais–Dover (England) ferry crossing
- Irish Ferries: Cherbourg and Roscoff–Rosslare, Republic of Ireland: 30 percent discount on standard foot passenger fares (advance booking recommended). Sailings April through September.

- 50 percent discount on Chemins de Fer de la Corse between Ajaccio, Calvi, and Bastia
- 50 percent discount on Chemins de Fer de la Provence between Digne and Nice (private railroad)
- 30 percent discount on ferry crossings from Marseilles/Nice/Toulon to Ajaccio/Bastia/Calvi (Corsica) operated by SNCM and Ferry France
- 20 percent discount on Chemins de Fer du Montenvers—Mer de Glace

France Railpass

	ADULT 1st Class	ADULT 2nd Class	SAVERPASS* 1st Class	SAVERPASS* 2nd Class
3 days in 1 month	$312	$253	$274	$222
Additional days	$44	$37	$39	$34

	YOUTH 1st Class	YOUTH 2nd Class
3 days in 1 month	$225	$191
Additional days	$31	$27

Maximum of 6 additional days. Youth age 12–25; children age 4–11, half adult fare; younger than age 4 travel free.

*Price per person based on 2 or more people traveling together at all times, includes 40% companion discount.

France Railpass Special Bonuses

- Reduced rates on the Museum of Peace in Caen and the D-Day landing beaches pass
- 20 percent discount on admission to many French National Monuments
- Valid on the RER–lines B & C (Airport Charles de Gaulle–Paris Nord rail station)
- Special pass holder fares on Premier Trains: Eurostar, Elipsos, TGVs, and some night trains
- 50 percent discount on 1 hour Seine River cruises with Bateaux Parisiens
- 10–20 percent discount on many city passes (including Nancy, Strasbourg, Lyon and Pontpellier)

See the Appendix for additional rail passes valid in France.

Base City: **LYON**

www.lyon-france.com

Lyon bustles with industry, trade fairs, and business. Its origins, however, go back to Roman times. Founded in A.D. 43, its old town stands on a hillside of volcanic soil containing some of the richest archaeological sites in France and still contains an unspoiled area of 14th- and 15th-century houses.

Lyon also claims to be the gastronomic capital of the world, and it has some impressive credentials to back its claim. The gastronomic tradition comes from its geographic position in the center of such great culinary areas as Bourgogne, Savoy, Beaujolais, and many others. With tongue in cheek, Lyon citizens say that the whole world cannot come from Lyon—there has to be at least a little from elsewhere. With our tongue in cheek, we note that Lyon also has several American-style fast-food establishments. Touché!

Although proud of its history and devoted to preserving its antiquity, Lyon has forged ahead with a continuous modernizing, building-and-expansion program that rivals even that of Paris. Part-Dieu, a complete and separate metropolis on the left bank of the Rhône, rises like a modern phoenix above the rest of Lyon, most of which was built during the 18th century. Lyon's contrasts are great. By virtue of these contrasts, Lyon is becoming one of the great cities of France and of Europe.

Arriving by Air

Lyon Saint Exupéry International Airport (*Tel:* [334] 2600 7007; www.lyon.aeroport.fr), 15 miles (25 kilometers) to the east of Lyon. International air service between Lyon and New York is provided by Air France and Delta Airlines. A TGV station provides high-speed rail service from Saint Exupéry to many other French destinations.

Airport–City Links: Airport tram (rhônexpress) service to Lyon Part-Dieu station, every 30 minutes, 0600 to 0000. To the airport, 0500 and 0530, then every 15 minutes 0600–2100, and every 30 minutes 2100–0000. Journey time: around 30 minutes; fare, €14.50 one way; €25.50 round-trip.

Limousine service is also available direct to most of the city's hotels. Journey time: about 45 minutes.

Taxis: €40 to €50 (daytime) and about €55 to €60 (nighttime) to Gare Part-Dieu. A taxi stand is in front of Terminal 1, level 1.

Arriving by Train

Most of the TGV Duplex (double-decker) trains from Paris to Lyon terminate at Part-Dieu, but a few continue on to terminate at Perrache.

The facilities provided by **Gare de Perrache** have been expanded by the ultramodern annex appended to the front of the current station building. This annex houses a bus terminal, the terminal for the city's Metro system, and a bevy of offices, shops, snack bars, and restaurants. The terminal for the airport bus and local taxi services is also located in the annex.

Access to the annex is gained by escalators immediately in front of the station's main doors. Pedestrian traffic, moving from the station through the annex and into the city, uses another escalator system to exit into Lyon's **Place Carnot.** The square, with its statues, fountains, and waterfalls, is one of the city's showplaces.

Gare de Perrache, together with its annex, is a large and sprawling complex. Access to train platforms is through two underground passageways—Sortie Nord and Sortie Sud (north and south exits)—and escalators that descend from the ticket office and the waiting-room areas. Use of either passageway will take you to platform No. 1 and, in turn, to exits leading to the street side of the station. Fortunately, there's an abundance of pictographs throughout the station.

If you have baggage, be prepared to carry it. Baggage carts for passenger use are not available, probably due to the platform stairways. The escalators serve only the tracks reserved for express-train service.

Train-departure signs are displayed in the underground passageways at the bottom of the platform stairways. The north passageway, however, will not list a southbound departure, nor the south a northbound one, unless it is a train running through Lyon Perrache and not originating there. All train departures are displayed over the ticket windows in the main station hall.

Money exchange: Available at the Bureau de Change in the Perrache Station. *Hours:* 0630–2130 daily. ATMs are also available. Starting at the train-information area, follow the pictographs and proceed by either escalator or elevator to the station's TGV departure lounge on the second level.

Train information: The office is located within the main building of the Perrache Station. Use the main entrance, turn right once you have entered the hall, and proceed through an archway to the train information office. *Hours:* 0600–2000 Monday–Saturday, 0900–1830 Sunday/holidays.

The French National Railroads produces *Le Fiches Horaires* (minitimetables), which are free. A selection is normally kept immediately outside the train information office door and inside the office on the left-hand wall. These timetables may eliminate standing in line to make inquiries.

Train reservations may be made in the train information office at any one of the operating windows. We did not find the train information staff too adept at English. Consequently, we recommend submitting your reservation requests in writing.

Rail pass validation is handled at any window in the train information office. Write the starting and ending dates on a piece of paper, and obtain concurrence from the attendant before the entry is made on your rail pass.

Lyon's ultramodern Metro (subway) system serves both Gare de Perrache and Gare Part-Dieu rail stations.

Tourist Information/Hotel Reservations

Lyon Tourist Information (central office): Lyon Convention and Visitors Bureau, Place Bellecour, BP 2254, 69214 Lyon cedex 02 (two Metro stops from Gare de Perrache); *Tel:* 04 72 77 69 69; *Fax:* 04 78 42 04 32; *Reservations Desk:* 04 72 77 72 50; www.lyon-france.com.

Hours: 0900–1800, 7 days a week.

Hotel reservations for within the city of Lyon may be made at the tourist information office Reservations Desk.

Getting Around in Lyon

Lyon has an ultramodern Metro (subway) system. One of its main terminals is in Gare de Perrache; there's another in the rail terminal at Part-Dieu. Trains run every 3 to 10 minutes from 0500 to 2400 daily. A single-ride ticket costs €2.80; a book of 10 tickets, €14.00; 1-day tourist ticket, €5.20.

The best way to discover Lyon is with the tourist office's **"Lyon City Card."** Valid for one, two, or three days (at €21, €31, and €41; reduced rates for those younger than age 18), this card covers city transport on buses, metro, and trams as well as entrance to museums, guided tours, and river cruises. You can even save 10 percent on shopping (excluding some promotional items) at Galeries Lafayette Part-Dieu.

Sights/Attractions/Tours

Cityrama Lyon operates a 1½-hour sightseeing bus tour of Lyon. *Tel:* 04 44 55 61 00; www.pariscityrama.com. The buses are equipped with headsets providing explanations of the tour sights in six languages, including English. Fare for adults, €18; one child rides free for each paying adult. Buses depart daily every hour from 1000–1815 April through October, and at 1000, 1130, 1400, and 1600 November through March. Hop on and off whenever you want at any of the nine stops. Ask for a folder at the tourist office.

Or join the Lyon Tourist Office's guided tour, "A Stroll Through Old Lyon," which is conducted on foot over a two-hour period. Departures are daily throughout the tourist season at a charge of €10. An evening tour is also available. The tourist office also offers self-guided audio tours to discover Lyon at your own pace in about three hours for €7 (available in English, German, Italian, and Spanish).

Le Vieux Lyon (Old Lyon) is a charming area to visit. For your convenience use the *funiculaires* (funicular) to gain the summit. Take bus No. 44 from the station annex and ask the driver to let you off at the St. Jean bus stop. The funicular station is located at rue St. Jean and avenue Max, immediately to the left of **place St. Jean.**

Old Lyon is said to be the most extensive Renaissance area in France. It covers about 1 mile along the right bank of the Saone River at the foot of Fourvière Hill. The historic area of Lyon, the **Fourvière Hill,** Croix-Rousse Hill, Renaissance Quarter, and the Peninsula were recognized as UNESCO World Heritage architectural sites. While visiting the Fourvière Hill area, check out Lyon's answer to Paris's Eiffel Tower, located behind the basilica. The Lyonese claim their tower is 5 feet higher than the Parisians', and it is—above sea level, that is.

Day Excursions

Contrasts continue in the selection of day excursions from Lyon, the third-largest city in France. A scant 25 miles short of Geneva, the town of **Annecy** and its crystal-clear lake wait to charm you. Annecy's old quarter, lying back from the lake, has one of Europe's finest marketplaces.

Dijon vies with Lyon for gastronomic honors. During your visit to Dijon, you will want to shop for its world-renowned product, mustard. But that's not all it has to offer. The history of Burgundy breathes in Dijon, its capital, and you will want to catch its scent.

Grenoble is situated in the midst of a breathtaking panorama of mountains. A ride on its téléphérique will provide an even more remarkable view of the city and the countryside surrounding it.

Vienne, 20 miles to the south, is almost a suburb of Lyon, but it is very different. It has some of the best-preserved Roman buildings and amphitheaters in all of Europe and one of the world's finest restaurants, La Pyramide.

Train Connections to Other Base Cities from Lyon Part-Dieu

DEPART	TRAIN NUMBER	ARRIVE	NOTES
		Amsterdam Centraal	
0704	TGV 6604	1342	R, 1, M–Sa
1104	TGV 6614	1742	R, 1
1134	TGV 6616	1842	R, 1
1504	TGV 6622	2142	R, 1
1700	TGV 9868	2242	R, 2
		Barcelona Sants	
0704	TGV 6809	1238	R, 3, Exc. Su
2010	TGV 9837	1131+1	R, 3, Sleeper
		Bern (Berne)	
0636	RE 96500	1026	R, 4, Exc. Su
0834	RE 96502	1226	4
1234	RE 96510	1626	R, 4
1534	TGV 9750	1926	R, 4
1836	RE 96520	2256	R, 4
2034	RE 96522	0101+1	R, 4
		Brussels (Bruxelles) Midi/Zuid	
0550	TGV 9852	0943	R
1100	TGV 9860	1458	R
1700	TGV 9868	2043	R
1900	TGV 9864	2256	R
		Madrid Puerta de Atocha	
0704	TGV 6809	1545	R, 3, Exc. Su
		Milan (Milano) Centrale	
0831	TGV 9241	1350	R
1635	RE 96514	2237	R, 4, Exc. Sa
		Nice Ville	
0636	TGV 6805	1106	R, M–F
1106	TGV 6821	1537	R
1436	TGV 9757	1905	R
1806	TGV 6815	2237	R
		Paris Gare de Lyon	
0634	TGV 6642	0831	R, M–F
0704	TGV 6690	0901	R, M–Sa
0804	TGV 6608	1015	R
0904	TGV 6610	1103	R
and then hourly service until 2104, plus 1734.			
		Rome (Roma) Termini	
1150	RE 17905	2129	R, 6
1916	RE 17816	1040+1	R, 5, Sleeper

DEPART	TRAIN NUMBER	ARRIVE	NOTES
		Zürich Hauptbahnhof	
0834	RE 96502	1328	4
1034	RE 96506	1528	4, Exc. Sa
1534	TGV 9750	2028	R, 4
1635	RE 96514	2128	4, Exc. Sa
1804	TGV 6868	2226	R, 4

Daily, unless otherwise noted

R Reservations required

+1 Arrives next day

1. Change trains in Paris.
2. Change trains in Brussels.
3. Change trains in Montpellier.
4. Change trains in Geneva.
5. Change trains in Dijon.
6. Change trains in Chambéry.

Day Excursion to

Annecy

Alpine Lake

Depart from Lyon Part-Dieu Station
Distance by Train: 99 miles (160 km)
Average Train Time: 2 hours, 25 minutes
Tourist Information Office: Bonlieu Center, 1 rue Jean Jaurés, 74000 Annecy
Tel: 04 50 45 00 33; **Fax:** 04 50 51 87 20
www.annecytourisme.com
E-mail: info@lac-annecy.com
Hours: January–mid-May: 0900–1230/1345–1800 Monday–Saturday and 0930–1230 Sunday; mid-May–mid-September: 0900–1830 Monday–Saturday and 0900–1230/1345–1830 Sunday; mid-September–December: 0900–1230/1345–1800 Monday–Saturday and 0930–1230 Sunday. If this office is closed, go to the bureau of information in the city hall, which is open until 1900 daily, except Sunday and holidays.
Notes: Reach the information office via bus No. 1 from in front of the station to place de la Liberation, where you'll find the office in the Bonlieu Center. On foot, use the underground pedestrian passageway to the left of the station as you exit. Continue to walk a block ahead to rue Vaugelas. Here, turn left and walk 4 blocks to where rue Vaugelas ends at place de la Liberation (a large open area).

Annecy (pronounced "Ahn-see") still remains largely undiscovered by North Americans, although it has long been a retreat of the French themselves. A crystal-clear lake, a spectacular view of the Alps, foothills that touch the town, an old quarter where quaint canals cross arcaded lanes, an engaging market selling everything from apples to zinnias—these are Annecy.

Annecy is a health spa and a popular holiday center. It has innumerable hotels, casinos, and, best of all, the lake. The basin in which the lake lies is so protected against pollution that the latter is almost transparent in its purity. The Thiou River, flowing out of the lake and through the old quarter of Annecy, runs through canals and meanders around islands en route to the Rhône and the Mediterranean.

Tour-boat operators offer a wide variety of tours around the "sea" of Annecy. Rapid tours, lasting a little more than an hour, have frequent departures. The more vigorous traveler can opt to cycle around it. Either mode will provide a spectacular view of alpine meadows, rivers, waterfalls, and the bountiful natural riches surrounding the lake.

Visit the town hall, **Hôtel de Ville,** just a short walk along **quai Chappuis.** But exercise caution when crossing the street—the locals stage a "Grand Prix" on occasion.

The tourist information office has several brochures describing the city and its lake, including an illustrated booklet, *Through the Old Town.* The office also contains bulletin boards with numerous announcements of cultural events in Annecy.

From the bridge crossing the Thiou River, you will catch your first glimpse of the **Palais de l'Isle** sitting astride the river. As its name suggests, this curious palace was an island stronghold, and it remains one of the most arresting monuments of Annecy. Its oldest sections date from the 12th century. At one time it housed Annecy's municipal offices and the high judges' private apartments and also served as a dungeon.

Beyond the Palais de l'Isle lies the enchanting marketplace of Annecy's **Old Quarter.** A network of narrow streets filled with every type of shop imaginable is augmented on market days by hundreds of stands erected in the streets, where only pedestrians are allowed to pass.

Along with the chic boutiques and appliance shops, the marketplace vends every imaginable food product, pastry, flower, and condiment. Lavender, picked in the Alps, and locally manufactured culinary wares are also available.

The picturesque medieval appeal of Annecy stems from both the French and Italian civilizations as a result of having changed sides several times during its more than 2,000-year existence. The area became a part of the French empire in 1792, although it reverted to the Italian Kingdom of Sardinia in 1815. It was not until 1860 that all of Savoy, where Annecy is situated, was again reunited with France as a reward to the French for helping Italy in its war with Austria.

Lyon—Annecy

DEPART Lyon Part-Dieu	TRAIN NUMBER	ARRIVE Annecy
0708	RE 17970	0902
0808	RE 17972	1007
1208	RE 17978	1407

DEPART Annecy	TRAIN NUMBER	ARRIVE Lyon Part-Dieu
1553	RE 17958	1752
1653	RE 17960	1852
1853	RE 17964	2052

Daily, including holidays
Distance: 99 miles (160 km)

Annecy slipped quietly into the 20th century with the introduction of TGV train service directly from Paris. The distance from the Gare de Lyon Station in Paris to Annecy is covered in about 3¾ hours—a trip that formerly consumed at least 8 hours. Currently, there are four trains daily that depart in the morning, making the possibility of a day excursion to Annecy from Paris a reality.

Departing Paris Gare de Lyon Station on TGV 6601 at 0550, you would arrive in Annecy at 1007; boarding TGV 6984 departing Annecy at 1831, you would be back in Paris by 2212 (does not run on Saturday). It's a full day but a fun-packed one, too.

Day Excursion to

Dijon

Cutting the Mustard

Depart from Lyon Gare de Perrache or Part-Dieu Station
Distance by Train: 122 miles (197 km)
Average Train Time: 1 hour, 30 minutes
Tourist Information Office: 15 Cour de la Gare, Tourist Pavillon, Place Darcy, 21000 Dijon
Tel: 08 92 70 05 58; **Fax:** 08 80 42 18 83
www.dijon-tourism.com
E-mail: info@dijon-tourism.com
Hours: April–September: 0930–1830 Monday–Saturday, 1000–1800 Sunday; October–March: 0930–1300 and 1400–1800 Monday–Saturday, 1000–1600 Sunday
Notes: Exit through the main doors of the station and bear to the right onto avenue Maréchal Foch. Average walking time: 5 minutes. Use the Hotel Climat de France as a landmark. Proceed along avenue Foch for 1 block. As you

approach place Darcy, you will find the tourist information office on the left-hand side of the street.

Say "Dijon" to any American who likes to eat well, and the response will be "mustard." Mention Dijon to any Frenchman, and his eyes will roll and his hands will fly as he describes the gastronomic wonders of the Burgundian city's pastry shops, restaurants, cassis (black-currant liquor), and mustard—but not necessarily in that order. Dijon, the ancient capital city of Burgundy, has something for everyone. It sets a fine table, lives its history, and preserves its art.

Dijon is the gateway to France's most famous wine region, the Côte d'Or. Important historically in 1015 when Robert I, Duke of Burgundy, made it the capital of his duchy, today it produces more than 40 million bottles each year. The city's most brilliant era, however, was from the 14th through the 18th centuries, when it gained most of its art and beautiful monuments.

Dijon cannot be visited in a hurry. An entire day can easily be spent visiting its **Palace of the Dukes of Burgundy** and the **Museum of Fine Arts,** which is housed in the palace. The museum, founded in 1783, is the most important in France after the Louvre in Paris. Don't miss the huge banquet room of the palace, known as the Guards Room. The tombs of the dukes are located here. The tombs provide some descriptive background as to how the populace rated the four "Valois" Dukes of Burgundy: Philip the Bold, Jean the Fearless, Philip the Good, and Charles the Rash. Visit www.dijon.fr.

Modern art has made an entry in the palace in the form of a department housing an exhibition of Impressionist works from the Granville collection. There's also a gallery devoted completely to the works of local artists from the Burgundy area.

The city is particularly proud of its artists, among them François Pompon (1855–1933). Sculptor Pompon began his career as a Burgundy marble cutter. He attended Dijon's school of fine arts before further studies and apprenticeships in Paris. He sculpted 300-plus works, almost all depicting animals. His fresh, clear style has astonishing simplicity.

Engrossing as Dijon's works of art can be, don't forget to break for lunch—another Dijon work of art that can't be hurried. Whatever entree you select, we are certain that you will want to enhance it with a dab or so of Dijon mustard. A word of caution—make that dab a small one, and determine first if it suits your palate. Dijon's favorite condiment has some varieties that exceed the fire power of any Mexican pepper.

Dijon's railway station is unique in that its main hall is circular. Train information is available in the area marked INFORMATION VOYAGEURS on the right as you enter the main hall of the station. *Hours:* 0800–1915 Monday–Friday, 0900–1700 Saturday–Sunday. A map showing the location of the city's tourist information office in relation to the rail station is displayed prominently in the station's foyer.

Lyon—Dijon

DEPART Lyon Part-Dieu	TRAIN NUMBER	ARRIVE Dijon	NOTES
0558	TGV 6880	0739	
0616	RE 17800	0819	M–F
0716	RE 17756	0919	
1016	RE 17806	1219	M–F
1216	RE 17808	1419	R
1416	RE 17810	1619	R

DEPART Dijon	TRAIN NUMBER	ARRIVE Lyon Part-Dieu	NOTES
1345	RE 17813	1547	M–F
1440	RE 17815	1644	
1621	TGV 6815	1756	R
1640	RE 17761	1844	
1840	RE 17763	2048	
1943	RE 17823	2144	M–F
2040	RE 17767	2244	

Daily, unless othwise noted
R Reservations required
Distance: 122 miles (197 km)

The tourist office displays a room-availability list immediately outside the office entrance. This depicts the number of vacancies existing in the various hotels of Dijon and its surrounding areas. Within the tourist office, you will find hotel-reservations facilities and money exchange services. There is a nominal fee for each call within Dijon to secure hotel reservations.

The **Saint Benigne Cathedral** probably holds the record for being destroyed and rebuilt more times than any other place of worship in France—four times since its origins back in the sixth century! The current church was built between 1281 and 1325. Also constructed in the 13th century, the **Church of Notre Dame** in Dijon fared better over the centuries. Both edifices are typical Burgundian Gothic.

One of the newer attractions in Dijon includes the **University of Bourgogne.** The Centre International d'Etudes Françaises attracts students from all over the world to study the French language and culture.

Day Excursion to

Grenoble

And the Bastille Cableway

Depart from Lyon Part-Dieu Station
Distance by Train: 80 miles (129 km)
Average Train Time: 1 hour, 30 minutes
Tourist Information Office: 14, rue de la République, 38000 Grenoble
Tel: 04 76 42 41 41; **Fax:** 04 76 00 18 98
www.grenoble-tourisme.com
E-mail: info@grenoble-isere-tourisme.com
Hours: October–April: 0900–1800 Monday–Saturday, 1000–0000 Sunday; May–September: 0900–1900 Monday–Saturday, 1000–0000 Sunday
Notes: Located some distance from the railway station in a labyrinth of winding streets. Reach the tourist office by either tramway in the direction of Grand Place, Universités, or Auguste Delaune. Your stop is Hubert Dubedout/Maison du Tourisme. MAISON DU TOURISIME signs are displayed at many intersections.

Grenoble will remind many North Americans of Denver, Colorado. Lodged on a wide plain, butted against the swift waters of the Isere River, and backdropped by the French Alps, it is a breathtaking scene of man and nature in concert.

Known as "the capital of the French Alps," Grenoble lies at the feet of three majestic mountain ranges at the crossroads of a number of large valleys. Its Isere River was first bridged by Roman legion engineers in 43 B.C.; Napoleon employed the concealment of the area to move his armies into the Italian campaign. Modern mountaineering was born on its towering peaks.

Grenoble unfolds the past as well as the present in its monuments and art. The **Musée de Grenoble** houses one of the finest collections of old and modern masters in France. The classics of Rubens and Watteau, along with those of Utrillo and Picasso, adorn its galleries. The **Cathedral of Grenoble** dates from the 12th century. In the center of Grenoble, in the oldest part of the town, you will find the **Musée de l'Ancien Evêché.** Begin by exploring an area below the surface of the outside square to see the remains of the town wall and Grenoble's first baptistery, then continue on to the old bishop's palace. The early **Renaissance Palace of Justice** was built in the 16th century.

The University of Grenoble was founded in 1339—making it one of the oldest in Europe—and is considered by many academics to be one of the best in France. Grenoble's student population exceeds 50,000, more than 8,000 of whom are foreigners from 150 different countries. With university students near snow-covered slopes, it was inevitable that winter sports should develop. The 1968 Winter Olympics were hosted by Grenoble, and many other sports gatherings, including the Davis Cup finals, have taken place in the city's magnificent Sports' Hall.

Lyon—Grenoble

DEPART Lyon Part-Dieu	TRAIN NUMBER	ARRIVE Grenoble
0642	RE 17603	0808
0814	RE 17609	0938
0944	RE 17687	1108
1114	RE 17615	1238
1214	RE 17617	1338

DEPART Grenoble	TRAIN NUMBER	ARRIVE Lyon Part-Dieu
1252	RE 17692	1414
1320	RE 17622	1446
1452	RE 17696	1614
1550	RE 17648	1720
1650	RE 17630	1820
1752	RE 17634	1915
1852	RE 17638	2014
1922	RE 17640	2044
2022	RE 17642	2146

Daily
Distance: 80 miles (129 km)

To ride the **Téléphérique de la Bastille,** wend your way to the banks of the Isere River and then to the Jardin de Ville (city garden). From practically any point on the riverfront, you can see the "bubbles" of the cableway flying up and down the hillside in groups of three. A photographic hint: Ride the rear "bubble" up and the front one down for better views of Grenoble and its environs. Visit www.bastille-grenoble.fr, round-trip: €7.50.

The terminal at the top of **Guy Pape Park** provides a spectacular view of the city and its surrounding countryside. Dominating the heights is the **Bastille,** a 19th-century fortress housing a military museum and a restaurant featuring traditional, regional cuisine. On a suitable day, you may opt to descend on foot through Guy Pape Park to the **Jardin des Dauphins** (Dauphins' garden) on the banks of the Isere. Contact the tourist office for bicycle-rental information, then search for and explore the gardens, the fountains, or the famous "grey gold" (concrete) buildings of Grenoble.

TGV service makes a Grenoble day excursion from Paris practical. Departing Paris Gare de Lyon at at 0641 on TGV 6901 places you in Grenoble at 0942, or leave at 0741 on TGV 6905 to arrive at 1042. There are six TGVs departing from Paris Gare de Lyon Monday through Friday, four TGVs on Saturday, and five on Sunday. The last daily TGV returning to Paris departs Grenoble at 1916 and arrives at Gare de Lyon in Paris at 2219.

Day Excursion to

Vienne

Of Roman Origin

Depart from Lyon Gare de Perrache or Part-Dieu Station
Distance by Train: 20 miles (32 km)
Average Train Time: 24 minutes
Tourist Information Office: No. 3 Cours Brillier, 38200 Vienne
Tel: 04 74 53 80 30; **Fax:** 04 74 53 80 31
www.vienne-tourisme.com
Email: contact@vienne-tourisme.com
Hours: 0900–1200 and 1330–1800 Monday–Saturday, 1000–1200 and 1400–1700 Sunday
Notes: About a 10-minute walk from the railway station. Depart from the statue in front of the rail station down Cours Brillier to the tourist pavilion on the left-hand side of the street.

Turn a corner in Vienne, and you turn a page of history. Roman in origin, this charming city lies on the Rhône River to the south of Lyon but so close (20 miles) that it could be mistaken easily for a Lyon suburb. Such is not the case. Vienne is distinctly different.

Among the remains of this once great city of the Roman Empire, and dating from the first century B.C. to the end of the third century A.D., stand a temple, an amphitheater, and a pyramid that was once the center of a Roman circus. Roman Vienne spread to both sides of the Rhône River, where ruins of a warehouse and baths have been uncovered.

A statue in memory of the fallen during 1914 and 1940 stands in the square fronting the railway station. Take a moment to pause and reflect here. Note, too, that many of the names have family extensions in North America.

Attendants at the tourist office will assist by marking a suggested walking tour on your map. The majority of the city's sights, concentrated in the old north quarter, allow visitors to move quickly from one attraction to another.

Collections of bronze, ceramics, and jewels are on display at the **Museum of Fine Arts.** Perhaps the most impressive Roman ruin of Vienne is the **Temple of Augustus and Livia,** which is perfectly preserved. One almost expects toga-clad senators to step through its portals and into a local pastry shop. The temple is surrounded by more modern structures in the center of the city. No doubt the proximity of other buildings has helped shield and preserve the temple through the ages.

The great **amphitheater of Vienne** was cleverly built into the slope of the hillside on which the town now stands. In its original state, it could hold 13,000 spectators. It was covered entirely by soil in the first century A.D., but excavations between 1922 and 1938, when activities were curtailed by World War II, have brought to life some very beautiful remnants of statuary, coins, and jewels from the era. The

Lyon—Vienne

DEPART	TRAIN NUMBER	ARRIVE	NOTES
Lyon Gare de Perrache		Vienne	
0719	RE 87105	0754	
0819	RE 87109	0854	
0919	RE 86113	0954	
1419	RE 87127	1454	

DEPART	TRAIN NUMBER	ARRIVE	NOTES
Vienne		Lyon Gare de Perrache	
1219	RE 17704	1259	
1419	RE 17714	1509	
1521	RE 86118	1609	Exc. Sa
1705	RE 86142	1739	
1758	RE 86126	1820	Exc. Sa
1905	RE 87150	1940	Exc. Su
2019	RE 17724	2101	
2151	RE 86194	2212	

Daily, unless otherwise noted
Distance: 20 miles (32 km)

amphitheater, modernized with stage lighting, is now the scene of many fine theatrical presentations in Vienne for thousands of spectators throughout the summer season, including the Vienne Jazz Festival. Similar lighting of the Temple of Augustus and Livia makes an evening visit to the city a memorable one.

The **pyramid** was erected in the center of a Roman circus to guide the racing chariots, but it was never completed. For centuries it was believed to be the tomb of Pontius Pilate, who, according to a 12th-century legend, had died in Vienne while living there in exile. Little else remains of the circus site, but it stirs your imagination.

The city's famous restaurant, **La Pyramide** (named for its location on boulevard Fernand-Point at the former Roman circus), has been endorsed by many gourmets as the world's finest. Reservations are recommended at La Pyramide, which is closed every Tuesday and Wednesday at noon in season and annually from November through mid-December. Call ahead at 04 74 53 01 96 or fax the restaurant at 04 74 85 69 73; www.lapyramide.com. It's expensive, but you only live once!

When departing from the main part of town, you can reach Vienne's pyramid and the restaurant La Pyramide by taking the main road that runs to the south, cours de Verdun (RN 7), to boulevard Fernand-Point, on your right. When proceeding from the tourist information office at cours Brillier, head south on quai Riondet, and turn left onto boulevard Fernand-Point.

Vienne also has its share of medieval buildings. Most of them are still being lived in and look very much as they probably did back in the 15th and 16th centuries.

Although its industrial history is not as well known, for more than 200 years Vienne was an important center for textiles, especially carded wool and a cloth called "Renaissance." The **Musée de la Draperie,** housed in the Saint Germain building, is worth a visit. *Hours:* April 1–September 30: 1400–1800; closed Monday and May 1. Still a center of a lively wool trade, the town manufactures chemicals and flourishes from other industries, too. The people of Vienne are justly proud of their industrial endeavors, set in the midst of a richly wooded countryside.

Base City: **NICE**

en.nicetourisme.com

Nice, "the gateway to southern Europe," has changed more in 50 years than it did over the past two centuries. According to Nice's Convention and Visitors' Bureau, Nice's "history advances, but its past remains."

In the days before World War I, the Riviera was a haven for rich Russian dukes and English lords seeking escape from the rigors of a more northerly winter. When such aristocracy, particularly the Russian version, began to fade from the scene, summer became the popular season, bringing with it hordes of Americans and others seeking the sun and all sorts of fun, including the nocturnal varieties.

The Riviera began to change. Towns and fishing villages that earlier visitors knew have grown together into an almost continuous resort town stretching from Saint-Raphaël to the Italian border. Nice, the largest community in the area, lies about halfway between these two points and is our base city for numerous day excursions in either direction. However, because of the relatively short distances between points and excellent rail service, one could select any one of the day excursions (Cannes, Monte Carlo, or Saint-Raphaël) as a base city.

Arriving by Air

Nice Côte d'Azur Airport, 4 miles (9 km) west of the city. Visit www.nice.aeroport.fr.

The airport has a convenient Rendezvous (meeting place) just beyond the arrival gates and an American Express Bureau de Change (**money exchange**) and **information desk** farther into the international terminal, Terminal 1. Terminal 2 is for flights within France. If you are not certain of your transportation mode to your final destination, inquire at the airport's information desk or at one of the airline counters inside.

- **Airport–City Links:** An **airport bus** and **limousine service** are available between the airport and the Nice Ville railway station. Bus fare: €6; departs every 20 minutes. Journey time is about 20 minutes. Connections can be made in the front-left section of the airport building as you exit.
- **Taxis** are available at the exit from the airport terminals. Fare between airport and rail station: about €25. Journey time: about 15 minutes. Taxis and intercity bus service between the airport in Nice and the resorts of Cannes and Monte Carlo are also available.

Several resort hotels offer free or reduced-rate transportation to their locations along the Riviera. Inquire at the airport information desk.

Arriving by Train

Nice Ville Station—Gare SNCF Centrale, avenue Thiers. *Tel:* 04 92 14 82 52/53

Nice is a major rail terminus for the Mediterranean region, with 20 daily connections from France's largest cities and 11 from other countries.

The exterior of the central station in Nice is deceptive. There is a lot more activity and more facilities than those you see. Although it is smaller than most major train terminals in Europe, it seems to function equally well, with the exception of long ticket lines. Here again, a rail pass will prove to be an invaluable convenience.

Manual lockers are available (*Tel:* 04 92 14 82 68).

If your luggage is lost or stolen, if you missed your train, or if you need help with a disabled or elderly passenger, don't panic. The railway station provides a helpful service—the **SOS Voyageurs SNCF** (Travelers' SOS Service). *Tel:* 04 93 16 02 61 Monday through Friday, 0900 to 1200 and 1500 to 1800 for assistance. (Closed Saturday and Sunday.)

Money exchange office is outside the main station and on the right as you exit from the trains (*Tel:* 04 93 82 13 00). *Hours:* June–September: 0700–2130 daily; remainder of the year, 0800–2000 daily.

Train information, reservations, and **rail pass validation** office is inside the main station on the extreme left side when exiting from the trains. The office is marked RESERVATION INFORMATION—RENSEIGNEMENTS. *Hours:* 0800–1900 Monday–Saturday, 0900–1900 Sunday/holidays.

Remember, when having your pass validated, write out the starting and ending dates on a piece of paper and get the railroad clerk to agree to the correctness of the dates before the validation information is entered onto your rail pass.

Tourist Information/Hotel Reservations

There are three Offices du Tourisme (tourist information offices) in the city of Nice, plus one in the international terminal at the airport. *Tel:* 08 92 70 74 07 (main information line); www.nicetourism.com; *E-mail:* info@nicetourism.com:

Avenue Thiers (in the railway station)
Fax: 04 92 14 46 49
Hours: June–September: 0800–2000 Monday–Saturday, 0900–1900 Sunday; October–May: 0800–1900 Monday–Saturday, 1000–1700 Sunday

5, Promenade des Anglais
Fax: 04 92 14 46 49
Hours: June–September: 0800–2000 Monday–Saturday; 0900–1900 Sunday; October–May: 0900–1800 Monday–Saturday
To get there, take avenue Jean Medecin to Massena Square, then turn to the right to reach avenue de Verdun and the Promenade.

Nice Côte d'Azur Airport—Terminal 1
Fax: 04 93 21 44 50
Hours: June–September: 0800–2100 daily; October–May: 0800–2100 Monday–Saturday

Hotel reservations may be booked at any of the tourist offices or via the website: www.nicetourism.com. Room vacancies in Nice and throughout the Riviera are extremely hard to come by during June, July, and August, as well as during the winter holiday period. If possible, reserve your accommodations well in advance.

Hotel rates in Nice and the rest of the Riviera vary according to season, so be specific when requesting reservations. The most expensive time of the year is between late March and the end of October. If you are looking for bargain rates, late October through January is when the rates are lowest.

Getting Around in Nice

The best way to get around in Nice is on foot, by bicycle/scooter, or by bus or minivan.

- Nice Location Rent, 12 rue de Belgique (*Tel:* 04 93 82 42 71; *Fax:* 04 93 87 76 36) for bikes, mopeds, scooters, roller blades
- The Nice Côte d'Azur public bus transport network links 24 towns with a single fare system. Tickets are sold onboard the buses. Single fare: €1; one-day pass €4.

Sights/Attractions/Tours

Nice boasts more than 200 hotels and 1,000 restaurants. Most of these facilities are located in the modern section of Nice, west of the Paillon River, which divides the town in two.

The Riviera is noted for its spectacular scenery. Every proper ingredient of sea, shore, cliffs, and mountains is present. Grapes and flowers are the predominant crops of its highly cultivated farmlands. It is one of the great flower-growing areas of Europe and probably the most famous center in the world for perfume production.

Train Connections to Other Base Cities from Nice

DEPART	TRAIN NUMBER	ARRIVE	NOTES
		Amsterdam Centraal	
1104	TGV 6176	2142	R, 2, Exc. Sa
2000	05774	1342+1	R, 1
		Barcelona Sants	
1024	IC 4760	1931	5
		Berlin Hauptbahnhof	
1202	TGV 6170	0709+1	R, 2, Sleeper
		Brussels (Bruxelles) Midi/Zuid	
0704	TGV 6172	1547	R, 1
1104	TGV 6176	1947	R, 1
		Luxembourg	
0702	TGV 6172	1653	R, 3
2000	NZ 5774	1059+1	R, 2, Sleeper
		Lyon Part-Dieu	
0724	TGV 6852	1158	R
1223	TGV 6864	1654	R
1724	TGV 6806	2200	R
		Madrid Chamartin	
1055	TGV 9750	2320	R, 5, 6
		Milan (Milano) Centrale	
0949	RE 86019	1450	R, 4
1809	EC 147	2250	R
		Munich (München) Hauptbahnhof	
0808	EC 139	2021	R, 7
		Paris Gare de Lyon	
0702	TGV 6172	1241	R
1101	TGV 6176	1641	R
1359	TGV 6178	1941	R
1551	TGV 6168	2145	R
1702	TGV 6180	2242	R
2000	NZ 5774	0738+1	R, 8, Sleeper
		Rome (Roma) Ostiense	
0526	RE 86001	1433	4, M–F
0808	EC 139	1640	R, 7
1807	EC 147	0554+1	R, 7, Sleeper

Daily, unless otherwise noted

R Reservations required

+1 Arrives next day

1. In Paris, transfer to Nord station.
2. In Paris, transfer to Est station.
3. Change trains in Metz.
4. Change trains in Ventimiglia.

5. Change trains in Montpellier.
6. In Barcelona, transfer to Sants station.
7. Change trains in Milano.
8. Arrive Paris Austerlitz.

The Riviera is also a center for modern art. The works of many 20th-century artists can be found in its numerous museums and exhibition halls. Picasso spent the last years of his life in a villa overlooking the Mediterranean.

In selecting Nice as the base city for the day excursions in the Riviera area, we considered the variety of features and attractions that the city has to offer, and they are many.

In the maze of Old Nice's narrow streets, you will discover, in variations of light, shade, and fragrances, the **fish market,** the **Palais Lascaris,** the **public squares** of the city—each one different in function but all with an air of grace—and, in a sudden burst of sunlight, the beaches.

To the east, the old town and port offer many attractions to those who have a feeling for the past. At 300 feet above the **Old Town,** in a public park where once a fortress stood, the views are unforgettable. Streets and houses in the Old Town date from the 16th century.

The **Marché aux Fleurs** (Flower Market), one of the most beautiful and truly native sights in the Old Town of Nice, is held daily except Monday in the **Cours Saleya,** a block south of the **Prefecture Palace** near the opera. At Cours Saleya, you'll discover what makes Nice so fragrant and colorful. You will also discover what makes the cuisine of the area so appetizing: A fruit-and-vegetable market flourishes right in the midst of the floral beauty. Mondays are a bit different in the Cours Saleya, since that's when the market is reserved for antiques dealers. But here again is another opportunity to delve into the priceless things that make Nice so nice.

There are 10 casinos within 40 miles of Nice and three international ski resorts only two hours away. The world-famous **Nice Carnival** takes place every February. Other festive events, however, are to be found in Nice throughout the year. The King Carnival takes place just before Lent and rivals New Orleans's Mardi Gras.

Turn from the sea in Nice, and your eyes confront **Mont Alban** and its fortress overhanging the harbor. If you choose to go to the alpine area behind the city, there's a charming private narrow-gauge railroad, **Chemin de Fer de Provence** (Railroad of Provence), that will transport you through rocky gorges and sheer cliffs and Lingostiere, on the invasion route used by Napoleon, to an exceptional panorama of the Alps and the Mediterranean Sea. Visit www.trainprovence.com.

For another train ride, this one within the city, board the **Nice "little train"** at its station on the Promenade des Anglais for a scenic ride through the shady, narrow streets of the Old Town to **Castle Hill** for a vista of the Baie des Anges (Bay of Angels) and the Port of Nice.

Day Excursions

With Nice as their pivot point, four wonderful day excursions have been selected. **Cannes** was picked for its beaches and bikinis (or something even less); **Marseilles,** melting pot of the Mediterranean, because of its flair for bouillabaisse and its Bogart background; **Monte Carlo (Monaco)** for its coastline and casino; and **Saint-Raphaël,** the resort on the Riviera with something for everyone, and at popular prices.

Day Excursion to

Cannes

Top of the Riviera

Depart from Nice Ville Station
Distance by Train: 19 miles (31 km)
Average Train Time: 25 minutes
Tourist Information Office: 1 boulevard de la Croisette, 06400 Cannes
Tel: 33 0492998422; **Fax:** 33 0492998423
www.cannes-on-line.com or **www.cannes.travel**
E-mail: tourisme@palaisdesfestivals.com
Hours: 0900–1200 and 1400–1830 Monday–Saturday
Notes: Reach the tourist information office by turning left in the main station hall, then take the stairs located immediately outside. Elevator service is also available. Look for the sign that reads SERVICE DU TOURISIME DE LA VILLE DE CANNES, SYNDICAT D'INITIATIVE ACCUEIL DE FRANCE, SYNDICAT DES HOTELIERS.
Cannes Tourisme Information Office, Palais des Festivals, boulevard de la Croisette, across from the Majestic Hotel. *Hours:* Open daily 1000–1900, November–February, 0900–1900 March–September.
Croisette Change (money exchange), 3 boulevard de la Croisette, 06400 Cannes *Hours:* 0900–1800 Monday–Friday.

Cannes has been described as a magnet that attracts the famous, the rich, and the dreamers. It also has a reputation of being impossibly expensive. No doubt this is true of **La Croisette**—the waterfront boulevard of Cannes lined with sandy beaches, extravagant restaurants, and elegant hotels. But this reputation does not apply to all of Cannes.

Cannes is a large resort with nearly 5,000 hotel rooms within its city limits and that many again in its suburbs. A hundred yards or so back from the waterfront, hotels charge a fraction of the rates extracted from the famous, the rich—and the dreamers—who insist on living at the water's edge.

Nice—Cannes

There are at least 3 trains per hour in each direction throughout the day from 0602 to 2239; journey time, 25–35 minutes.

Distance: 19 miles (31 km)

The Cannes railway station is modern and efficient. All services are grouped conveniently in or near its main hall. As you exit from the track area, you can reach the **train information and reservations office** via the escalator to your right. *Hours:* summer: 0900–1230 Monday–Saturday and 1400–1830 Sunday; winter: 0900–1900 Monday–Friday. Coin-operated baggage lockers are available on the main level at either end of the station.

Walking through Cannes is enjoyable and easy. Certainly no one would want to miss a stroll along the Promenade de la Croisette, one of the most beautiful and highly celebrated seaside walks on the Riviera. It borders the Bay of Cannes for about 2 miles until you reach its extreme eastern end at the Palm Beach Casino—with its gaming rooms and gala evenings—on place Franklin D. Roosevelt.

Along the way, you will see some of the world's finest yachts berthed close by magnificent rose gardens in the Port Pierre-Canto and the famous **Palais des Festivals et des Congrés,** home of the International Film Festival. Walk along the old port to the old part of town called **"Le Suquet,"** which overlooks the harbor and offers a marvelous view of the bay.

Except for the brief period in the late fall when the Mistral winds make things a bit uncomfortable, the climate of Cannes is wonderfully mild and temperate. Because of a few canes and reeds growing in the bay, the Romans named the spot "Castrum de Canois," and for centuries Cannes remained a small village inhabited only by fishermen.

History relates that in 1834 the Lord Chancellor of England, Lord Brougham, "whilst" en route to Nice, was prevented from reaching there due to a cholera quarantine and paused briefly in Cannes. Taken by the place, his lordship decided on the spur of the moment to build a house in Cannes and did so, straightaway—the transaction in real estate taking a matter of only eight days. For the next 34 years, until the time of his death, Lord Brougham left the winter fogs of London for the sunshine of Cannes. His lordship's example was quickly followed by other English aristocracy, and Cannes' population began to swell accordingly. Alluding to the eight days required to get Cannes under way, locals point out that God took only seven days to create the universe—so Cannes, necessarily, is a cut above all else.

The center of Cannes is ideal for strolling and shopping. Locals claim that you get more than what you pay for because the area has a theatrical atmosphere about it, and the show is free. Not so on the Croisette, the waterfront. Here the most elegant of shops extol the virtues of high fashion at equally high prices. Window-shopping, however, is free to all.

Excursion-boat services from the main port take you to the islands of **Sainte-Marguerite** and **Saint-Honorat.** Sainte-Marguerite's prison incarcerated the Man in the Iron Mask, and the island named after Saint Honorat has the remains of the monastery the saint started in the fourth century. Boats run daily throughout the year.

Another very delightful boat ride provides an unequaled panorama of the Mediterranean and the Alps each afternoon from June through September. This excursion departs at 1430, cruises the Bay of Cannes and the **Esterel Coast,** and returns at 1730. If you don't happen to be one of the millionaires with a yacht tied up in Port Pierre-Canto, now's your chance to enjoy the same exhilarating view that they enjoy—at a more reasonable price.

Day Excursion to

Marseilles

City of Intrigue

Depart from Nice Ville Station
Distance by Train: 140 miles (225 km)
Average Train Time: 2 hours, 15 minutes
Tourist Information Office: 11, La Canebiere–13001 Marseilles
Tel: 33 0 826 500 500; **Fax:** 33 04 91 138920
www.marseille-tourisme.com
E-mail: info@marseille-tourisme.com
Hours: 0900–1900 Monday–Saturday, 1000–1700 Sunday and holidays
Notes: The tourist information office is located adjacent to the municipal docks. Via Metro, take Line 1 in the direction "La Timone" to stop "Vieux Port–Hôtel de Ville." You may taxi there just by showing the driver the address. To reach it on foot—about a 15-minute walk—leave the railway station by descending the steps to street level. Directly in front is the boulevard d'Athens (a promenade from the original settlers, no doubt). Follow this street to the third traffic signal, including the one at the foot of the train station steps. Turn to the right onto boulevard La Canebiere, and just beyond the second traffic light now in front of you, look for the tourist office in the last building on the left-hand side of the street just before the small boat harbor.

Also, there is a small tourist office in the train station on the track level that is open 1000 to 1800.

Nice—Marseilles

DEPART Nice Ville	TRAIN NUMBER	ARRIVE Marseilles St-Charles	NOTES
0555	17470	0833	M–F
0655	17474	0929	R
0854	17478	1133	Sa, Su
1055	TGV 9750	1329	R, Exc. Su
1223	TGV 6864	1459	R
1354	14786	1633	

DEPART Marseilles St-Charles	TRAIN NUMBER	ARRIVE Nice Ville	NOTES
1431	RE 17487	1707	R
1631	TGV 9757	1905	R
1831	RE 17495	2106	
2001	TGV 6815	2237	R

Daily, unless otherwise noted
R Reservations required
Distance: 140 miles (225 km)

Marseilles, the great port of France, is second only to Paris in population and is one of the oldest surviving towns in the world. Although French in character, Marseilles is distinctly Mediterranean, with an international flair. There is much to compare in the character of Marseilles to the contents of its epicurean delicacy, bouillabaisse, and the three ingredients so essential in its making.

Greeks, fleeing out of Asia Minor from the Persians, founded Massalia (Marseilles) in 600 B.C. Their enterprising nature disturbed the Ligurians, who came from Italy, as well as the Iberians coming from Spain, and a lot of head smashing took place until the Greeks appealed to Rome for help. Romans came by the legions and promptly named the area a Roman province. Hannibal and his elephants created some disturbance but nothing like that of 360,000 Teutonic warriors in 102 B.C. who were seemingly bent on destroying the civilized world and all that was in it.

Rome, again to the rescue, dispatched Caius Marius to the province; he, in turn, disposed of 100,000 Teutons near Aix-en-Provence, just north of Marseilles, thus saving the day for the province and impacting the future of modern-day France. Even today, the most popular name for men in this region is Marius.

The French national anthem, "The Marseillaise," was composed in Strasbourg by a young French military officer, Rouget de Lisle. The battle song was published and reached Marseilles just at the time when the city was giving a send-off banquet to 500 volunteers bound for Paris and the revolution. Someone sang the new song, and immediately the banquet room picked it up in chorus.

The song was an immediate success, and the volunteers sang it in unison at every stopping place en route to Paris. By the time they reached Paris they had become somewhat of an accomplished choir, which electrified the Parisians as they marched through the streets of Paris singing the stirring words at the tops of their voices.

All the foregoing was given to set the mood for your arrival in Marseilles. Although the city is not famous as a tourist center, it is a very enjoyable place to visit. Its unusual character and mixture of peoples cannot be found anywhere else in the world.

Not far from the tourist office, you will find the **Vieux-Port** and its fish market, which defies description. This is one of the few places in the world where you can obtain those three essential ingredients for bouillabaisse: red gurnet, conger eel, and a Mediterranean fish known locally as *rascasse.* Nearby restaurants serve it to perfection.

Here in the Vieux-Port, from a pier known as the quai des Belges (Belgian Wharf), you can take a ferry for the 15-minute crossing to the island of **Chateau d'If,** made famous in *The Count of Monte Cristo,* by Alexandre Dumas. The castle is interesting to visit, and your guide will dramatically conclude your tour by showing you the opening through which the count was said to have made his escape. The visit to the island takes about 1½ to 2 hours, including the tour of the dungeons where the Man in the Iron Mask and many other political prisoners were imprisoned.

Day Excursion to

Monte Carlo (Monaco)

Roulette and Relaxation

Depart from Nice Ville Station
Distance by Train: 9 miles (14 km)
Average Train Time: 20 minutes
Monaco Country Dialing Code: 377
Tourist Information Office: Monte Carlo Tourist Information, 2a Boulevard des Moulins, Monte Carlo, MC 98030 Monaco
Tel: 92 16 61 16; **Fax:** 92 16 60 00
www.visitmonaco.com
E-mail: dtc@gouv.mc
Hours: 0900–1900 Monday–Saturday, 1000–1200 Sunday
Notes: The bus terminal is a short distance downhill from the railway station. Board bus No. 4, and ask the driver to let you off at the Office National du Tourisme (the National Tourist Office). From June 15 to September 30, there's a small tourist information kiosk in the station lobby open daily 0800 to 2000.

The Principality of Monaco lies 4,092 miles east of Philadelphia—two cities inexorably linked by the memories of their princess, Grace Patricia Kelly, who died as the result of a tragic accident in 1982. Monaco consists of 0.7 square mile (453 acres) of rocky coastline along the Riviera. It has been ruled by members of the Grimaldi family for the past 10 centuries. Its famous gambling casino is located in Monte Carlo, one of four sections that make up the principality. The other three are Monaco-Ville itself (the capital and site of the palace), La Condamine (a commercial and residential area), and Fontvieille (a residential and light-industries section).

Monaco operates a highly efficient bus system consisting of five major lines: No. 1 (Red), No. 2 (Blue), No. 4 (Gold), No. 5 (Brown), and No. 6 (Green), which serves the Fontvieille-Larvotto (beach) area. These are augmented by Line No. 3, serving the beach area during the summer.

Euros are the legal tender in Monaco, so there is no need to change your currency. Traveler's checks can be cashed at "La Credit Lyonnais" or "LCL," a bank opposite the train station. *Hours:* 0845–1200 and 1330–1700 Monday–Friday. The American Express office is just to the west of the casino at 2 avenue de Monte Carlo.

If cracking casinos is your cup of tea, Monte Carlo's public gambling rooms open at 1000 daily. You must be at least age 21 to enter. Youngsters are not barred, however, at the **National Museum and Collection of Dolls and Automatons of Yesteryear,** located at 17 avenue Princesse Grace. *Hours:* Easter–September: 1000–1800 daily; October–Easter: 1000–1215 and 1430–1800 daily. Admission, adults €6.00, children age 6 to 14 and students €4.00. Visit www.monte-carlo.mc/musee-national.

Pomp and ceremony still prevail in Monte Carlo. The changing of the guard takes place daily in front of the **Place du Palais** exactly at 1155. The charge for visiting the Prince's **Palace State Apartments** is €8.00; children age 8 to 14, €4.00. Tours are conducted daily April through September, 1000 to 1800, and during October, 1000 to 1800. Visit www.palais.mc. One of Europe's greatest aquariums, the **Musée Oceanographique,** lies near the palace on the seaside. *Hours:* January–March, October–December: 1000–1800; April–June, September: 1000–1900; July–August: 0930–2000. Admission: adults, €14; children, €7.00. Visit www.oceano.mc.

While at the Place du Palais, you should visit the **Museum of Napoleonic Souvenirs and Collections of the Palace Historic Archives.** *Hours:* June–September: 0930–1830 daily; reduced hours during the balance of the year. Admission: adults, €4; children age 8 to 14, €2. Visit www.palais.mc.

Nice—Monte Carlo

There are at least 2 trains per hour—often 3 or 4—from 0605 to 2305 throughout the day in both directions; journey time is about 20 minutes.

Distance: 9 miles (14 km)

Other attractions include the **Wax Museum of the Princes of Monaco,** the **Museum of Old Monaco,** and the **Museum of Prehistoric Anthropology,** the last featuring the Exotic Gardens and the Observatory Cave. The tourist office publishes a brochure listing all places of interest, opening times, and admission fees. Also available is a map showing the city's "semi-pedestrianized" zone, public lifts, and the bus system.

The grandeur of the Monaco yacht harbor may be viewed from many vantage points. The view from the casino's restaurant Le Prive is impressive—expensive, too. Probably the best site (at popular prices) is a canopy-covered table at the Portofino Restaurant, which clings to the cliff just above the quai President Kennedy.

Day Excursion to

Saint-Raphaël

"In" Place on the Riviera

Depart from Nice Ville Station
Distance by Train: 37 miles (59 km)
Average Train Time: 50 minutes
Tourist Information Office: Office de Tourisme 99, Quai Albert 1er, B.P. 210, 83 702 Saint-Raphaël
Tel: 04 94 19 52 52; **Fax:** 04 94 83 85 40
www.saint-raphael.com
E-mail: information@saint-raphael.com
Hours: September–June: 0900–1230 and 1400–1830 Monday–Saturday; July and August: 0900–1900 daily
Notes: Located across the street and to the left of the main entrance to the railway station. It is identified by a white "i" sign together with TOURISME in brown letters. If you arrive late, there is also a tourist information stand available on the Veillat Beach, 1 block from the main tourist information office. It is open 1400 to 2200.

Saint-Raphaël is the Riviera resort that has something for everyone—and at popular prices. Its primary asset is its delightful weather, which is mild in the winter and moderate throughout the entire summer.

Nice—Saint-Raphaël

DEPART Nice Ville	TRAIN NUMBER	ARRIVE Saint-Raphaël	NOTES
0655	RE 17474	0744	
0724	TGV 6852	0820	R
0854	RE 17478	0946	
and continuing with 3 to 4 trains each hour until 2034.			

DEPART Saint-Raphaël	TRAIN NUMBER	ARRIVE Nice Ville	NOTES
1613	RE 17487	1707	
1712	EC 147	1803	R
1810	TGV 9757	1905	R
1919	RE 81229	2033	
2014	RE 17495	2106	R
2141	TGV 6815	2237	R

Daily
R Reservations required
Distance: 37 miles (59 km)

Before leaving the railway station, check the departure schedules for trains returning to Nice. There is a train information office in the station on your right as you exit the train platform. *Hours:* 0800–1900 Monday–Saturday.

With such a richly diverse area, Saint-Raphaël is a year-round destination. Sports enthusiasts are attracted by water sports, sailing, diving, and four beautiful golf courses—two 18-hole courses and two 9-hole courses located in three different areas. Situated between the Mediterranean Sea and Limestone Provence, the Esterel mountain—a volcanic range encompassing 79,000 acres—offers many nature activities such as hiking, horseback riding, and mountain biking.

The fishing-boat dock in Saint-Raphaël is not far from the railroad station. The tourist office can point the way. Here you will find some unusually fine local restaurants where, in the summer, you can dine at tables set under trees close to the boats. It is a relaxing atmosphere.

Saint-Raphaël has an interesting history. Its modern origins stem from the era of the Roman Empire, when it was a fashionable suburb of the Roman port of Frejus. Napoleon passed through Saint-Raphaël in both victory and defeat. In 1799 the emperor and his generals disembarked there upon returning from Egypt; a pyramid standing in the town still commemorates the event. In 1814 he sailed again from Saint-Raphaël, this time for Elba and exile. On April 28, as Napoleon, overcome with emotion, was saying good-bye to the soil of France, the English frigate he was to sail in fired a salute of 21 guns.

The site where Saint-Raphaël now stands has played an exciting part in the history of the Mediterranean. Because of its natural harbor, which is deep enough to accommodate even the deepest-draught warships, the Romans developed it first as a holiday center. The town's casino is built over the original foundations of the Roman baths and a fish-holding tank. Villas of the rich Romans who had come to Saint-Raphaël to "take the sea air" were destroyed by Saracen pirates. By the time the pirates were driven from the area in the 10th century, the land lay deserted.

Much of Saint-Raphaël's modern development has been due in great part to the establishment of the cut-flower industry started there in 1880 by Alphonse Karr. Although its biggest revenues today are developed by the tourist industry, Saint-Raphaël is still a large and prosperous center for cut flowers.

An excellent excursion-boat service operates from Saint-Raphaël. The tourist information office will have to provide you with schedules and fares, as they are too varied to mention here. There are short cruises on the Mediterranean as well as full-day excursions to many ports of call on the Riviera.

Saint-Tropez, summer home of Brigitte Bardot and one of the better "topless" beaches of France, can be reached from Saint-Raphaël by bus (*Tel:* 04 94 83 87 63) or boat (*Tel:* 04 94 95 17 46). Journey time: 1 hour and 25 minutes in each direction, but connections can be made that allow almost seven hours of visiting and sightseeing in this quaint resort town. For details on bus service between Saint-Raphaël and Saint-Tropez, consult the rail information office in Nice or Saint-Raphaël or ask for assistance from the tourist office in Saint-Raphaël. There is no rail service between Saint-Raphaël and Saint-Tropez.

Base City: **PARIS**

www.parisinfo.com

"Every traveler has two cities," wrote Edna St. Vincent Millay, "his own and Paris." Besides being one of the most beautiful and captivating cities in Europe, Paris is the center of one of the most interesting regions of France. Local people call the area around Paris the **Ile de France** (Island of France), for it is here that the nation began in the forested lands stretching out in all directions around Paris. The city is not only the political capital of France; it's the country's industrial and commercial center as well. To understand and appreciate it, follow the suggestion of British poet and novelist Lawrence Durrell and watch it "quite quietly over a glass of wine in a Paris bistro."

Arriving by Air

Roissy-Charles de Gaulle Airport (Roissy-CDG), 17 miles (23 km) north of the city center (*Tel:* 0 892 68 1515; €0.34/min.). Two major terminals; Terminal 2 is split into six major sections with the recent completion of the newest terminal. The majority of flights from North America arrive at Terminals 2A, 2B, 2C, or 2D. Signs are posted in both French and English, and information is available in other languages.

Money exchange: TRAVELEX just outside customs area in Terminal 2C. *Hours:* 0730–1900. ATM at Sortie (Exit) 6.

SNCF (French Rail) office hours: 0730–1900. You can board a train to Lyon, Avignon, or Nice without having to transfer to Paris.

Roissy-CDG Airport–City Links

RER (Regional Express Railway) Line B trains run every 7 to 15 minutes 0450 to 2356 to Paris stations Gare du Nord, Chatelet-Les Halles, Saint-Michel-Notre-Dame, Port-Royal, and Denfert-Rochereau; journey time 35–45 minutes; fare €9.50. Plenty of luggage space. RER station is to the right of the customs area, Terminal 2C.

Roissybus departs every 15 minutes 0600 to 2300 between Roissy Terminal 2A and 2C (take Exit 9 from Terminal 2A) and Place de l'Opera (rue Scribe); 0600 to 2300 (from Terminals 2A and 2C; take Exit 5); journey time about 45 minutes; fare €10.50 payable on board.

Air France Coach Line 2 departs every 15 minutes 0545 to 2300 to Metro/RER stations Charles de Gaulle-Etoile (Avenue Carnot) and Porte Maillot (Boulevard Gouvion Saint-Cyr). From Terminals 2A and 2C, take Exit 2. Terminals 2B and 2D, take Exit 3. Journey time: about 50 minutes. Fare: €17 one way and €29 return.

Air France Coach Line 4 departs every 30 minutes 0600 to 2200 to stations Gare Montparnasse and Gare de Lyon. Terminals 2A and 2C, Exit C2; Terminals 2B and 2D, Exit B1. Journey time: about 50 minutes. Fare €17 one way and €29 return.

Taxis take about 45 minutes; fares average €80, depending on traffic and destination.

Orly Airport, 10 miles (14 km) south of Paris (*Tel:* 01 49 75 15 15). Terminal West (Ouest) for Air France, Iberia, and TAP flights; Terminal South (Sud) for most airlines.

Orly Airport–City Links

RER (Regional Express Railway) Line C trains GOTA or NORA depart every 20 minutes from 0545 to 2315 from Pont de Rungis Aeroport d'Orly Station. A free shuttle bus runs every 15 minutes between the Pont de Rungis Aeroport d'Orly Station and Orly Ouest (West) (use Exit G) and Orly Sud (South) (use Exit F) Terminals from 0545 to 2315. Journey time to Gare d'Austerlitz 35 minutes; RER Line C fare: €6.40.

Orlyval (automatic metro train) **+ RER Line B:** From Orly Ouest Terminal, take exit A, Departure Level. From Orly Sud, take exit K. Orlyval trains run every 4 to 8 minutes 0600 to 2300 daily. At Antony station, board RER Line B in the direction of Mitry-Claye or Aeroport Charles de Gaulle 2 TGV. Journey time to Chatelet Les Halles, 35 minutes; to Charles de Gaulle-Etoile, 40 minutes; to La Defense, 50 minutes; combined Orlyval + RER Line B ticket: €10.90.

Air France Coach Line 1 departs from Orly Sud (take exit L) and Orly Ouest (take exit D, Arrivals Level) every 20 minutes 0600 to 2200 to Gare Montparnasse (rue du Commandant Mouchotte, Metro Montparnasse-Bienvenue) and Invalides (Air France terminal, Metro/RER Invalides); fare: €12.50.

Orlybus departs every 15 to 20 minutes 0600 to 2330 to and from the Metro/RER stop Place Denfert-Rochereau. Journey time 25 minutes. From Orly Ouest Terminal, take exit D, Arrivals Level. From Orly Sud, take exit H. Fare: €7.50.

Aeroports Limousine, Chauffeur-driven Car, fixed fare: €95 Orly-Paris. *Tel:* 01 40 71 84 65.

Taxis: Average fare €40 to €55 to the center of Paris.

Roissy-CDG–Orly Airport Connections

RER Line B and OrlyVal (connect in Antony). Departures every 4 to 8 minutes 0600 to 2300; fare: €9.85.

Air France Coach Line 3 departs every 30 minutes 0600 to 2220 (weekdays), 0700 to 2230 (weekends). Arrivals in Terminals 2A and 2C, take Exit 2 from 2C. Arrivals in 2B and 2D, take Exit 1 from 2B. Departs Orly for Roissy-CDG same times and frequency. Arrivals in Orly Ouest Terminal, take Exit D; Orly Sud, take Exit K; fare: €11.

Taxis cost about €75 between Roissy-CDG and Orly.

Arriving by Train

Paris has six major railway stations, but arriving there by train from one of the other base cities listed in this edition of *Europe by Eurail* will place you either in Gare du Nord (North), Gare de l'Est (East), Gare de Lyon, Gare d'Austerlitz, or Gare Montparnasse. Details of these stations follow.

Transfers between rail stations in Paris may be made by bus, Métro, or taxi. If you have baggage, a taxi is your best bet. There are, however, inter-station buses that provide baggage storage. Rule out the Métro unless you are without baggage. Suggestion: Consult the conductor on your train at least 30 minutes prior to arrival. If you are transferring between stations to continue your journey, the railroad is obliged to assist you. For train information in France, call 08 90 036 10 10.

The Railway Stations

Gare du Nord (North Station), 18 rue de Dunkerque, 75010 Paris
The terminal for Eurostar and Thalys trains. Gateway to the channel ports of Calais and Boulogne plus Belgium, Germany, the Netherlands, and London via Eurostar.

Money exchange office: In the station concourse area across from Platform 3. *Hours:* 0615–2215 daily, except holidays. ATM, Point Argent, across from Platforms 3 and 4.

Train information: Displayed in digital format throughout the station. A rail information office is located across from Platform 1. *Hours:* 0630–2000 daily, including holidays.

Seat reservations, including TGV and sleeping cars, may be made in the train information office. A layout of the station can be seen on a chart across from Platform 5.

Eurostar has its own terminal, reservations, and waiting room upstairs from the main part of the station. The well-marked signs will direct you to it.

Gare de l'Est (East Station), place du 11 Novembre 1918, 75010 Paris
Gateway to eastern France, Germany, Luxembourg, Austria, and Switzerland. Located a short distance from Gare du Nord and can be reached on foot or by the Métro.

Money exchange: In the main reception-hall area opposite Platforms 25 and 26. ATMs available. *Hours:* 0745–2200 daily.

Train information: Displayed in digital format throughout the station. A rail information office is located on the left-hand side of the station coming from the trains, between Platforms 6 and 7. *Hours:* 0545–2045 every day, although on Sunday for information only (no reservations).

Seat reservations: May be made in the train information office.

Gare de Lyon (Lyon Station), 20 boulevard Diderot, 75012 Paris
Gateway to the Riviera, southern France, Italy, and western Switzerland. Located on the right bank of the Seine, some distance south of the north and east terminals.

Money exchange: On the left side of Sortie (Exit) 1 as you enter the station and proceed toward Platform A. *Hours:* 0745–2200 daily.

Train information: In digital format throughout the station. The office for train information, marked information and reservations, is in the center of the station, to the left of the *Billets Grandes Lignes* area. *Hours:* 0545–2045 daily. **Train reservations** at the same office.

Tourist information/hotel reservations: In the Paris Convention and Visitors Bureau, located in the main ticket hall. *Hours:* 0800–1800 Monday–Saturday.

Restaurant le Train Bleu is located on the mezzanine of Gare de Lyon. *Tel:* 01 43 43 09 06; *Fax:* 01 43 43 97 96; www.le-train-bleu.com. Without doubt, it is the most elegant restaurant of any train station in the world. Opened in 1901, it was originally called the *Buffet de la Gare de Lyon.* Quickly, however, it became the fashionable place for well-heeled passengers to partake of a late supper prior to boarding *Le Train Bleu,* the stylish sleeper that traveled between Paris and the French Riviera, and so it was renamed.

The food is good, and the decor is France at the beginning of the 20th century at its opulent best: crystal chandeliers, shimmering brass, and mahogany.

Gare d'Austerlitz (Austerlitz Station), 55 quai D'Austerlitz, 75013 Paris
Gateway to central and southwest France as well as Spain and Portugal. Located on the left bank of the Seine, a short distance from Gare de Lyon, which may be reached on foot or by the Métro.

Money exchange: Within the main hall of the station, close to the ticket windows. *Hours:* 0800–2000 daily.

Train information: A rail information office is located in the foyer of the station just before entering the main hall. *Hours:* 0600–2315 Monday–Saturday, 0700–2215 Sunday.

Seat reservations: May be made in the train information office.

Other major railway stations in Paris include **Gare Saint Lazare** (north and west of France) and **Gare Montparnasse** (west of France). There are four Métro stations (Routes 4, 6, 12, and 14) in or adjacent to the Montparnasse railway station. Consequently, it is easy to reach from other parts of the rail network. Route 4 connects directly with Gare du Nord (North Station) and Gare de l'Est (East Station). Trains departing Paris for Chartres from Montparnasse also stop in Versailles, but this station is some distance from the Palace of Versailles and should not be used for that day excursion.

In these railway stations the **reservation offices** are open 0800 to 2000 daily. Train information and reservations for all France: *Tel:* 08 36 35 35 39.

In addition to the six major railway stations of Paris, listed above, there are five smaller or suburban-type stations of importance to *Europe by Eurail* readers.

- **Gare des Invalides,** another station that begins underground with its trackage until well past the Eiffel Tower, is exclusively for trains running to the Palace of Versailles.
- **Gare Bercy** and **Gare Charolais** are two auxiliary stations serving the Gare de Lyon complex on the right bank of the Seine.
- On the Rive Gauche (Left Bank) side, **Gare Tolbiac** serves the Austerlitz station network, and **Gare Vaugirard** performs the same function for the extensive train trackage terminating in the Montparnasse station compound.

A system of buses connects the major Paris stations, Gare Saint Lazare, Gare du Nord, Gare de l'Est, Gare de Lyon, Gare Montparnasse, and Gare d'Austerlitz. Operated privately, the system charges a fare slightly higher than that of the Métro, but it is much more convenient for passengers with luggage than the Métro or regular city buses.

Tourist Information/Hotel Reservations

Office du Tourisme et des Congrès de Paris, 25, rue des Pyramides 75001 Paris; *Tel:* 08 92 68 30 00 (€0.34/min.); *Fax:* 01 49 52 53 00; www.parisinfo.com; *Metro stop:* Pyramides.

Hours: Summer: 0900–1900 daily (closed May 1); Winter: 1000–1900 daily.

Branch office at Eiffel Tower open 1000 to 1900 daily May through October 14.

Notes: Free maps of Paris are available at most hotels, or you can purchase one at tourist offices. You may also consult the Galeries Lafayette travel agency, 40 boulevard Haussman. *Hours:* 0930–2000 Monday–Saturday (until 2100 on Thursday). *Tel:* 01 42 82 34 56.

Getting Around in Paris

The mainstay of transportation within Paris is its subway system, the Métro. It has 16 lines, several with rubber-tired coaches that sort of sneak up on you in the station. The system has about 300 stations, covering all of the city and much of its suburbs. You can reach all the railway stations in Paris via the Métro. Visit www.ratp.fr.

Obtain a map of the Métro system from one of the tourist offices and ask for a brief explanation of its operation. Many of the Métro stations have an illuminated map in their entrances, where, by pushing the button of your desired destination, the entire route will light up showing what line to take, in what direction, and, when necessary, where to make transfers.

The French refer to transfers as *correspondances*. Although the lines are numbered, the reference you should remember is the direction, which refers to the last station on the end of the line in the direction in which you are traveling. For example, Line No. 1 has two directions: Grande Arche de la Défense in the west, Château de Vincennes in the east. If you were visiting the Louvre and wanted to see the Place de la Concorde next, look for the direction Grande Arche de la Défense because your destination lies to the west.

At transfer points, watch for the orange CORRESPONDANCE sign, then disembark and look for the direction sign for the line you want to transfer to. Proceed to that platform and there determine from the line map how many stops to your destination.

Purchase a **Paris Visite** (tourist pass) valid for one, two, three, or five consecutive days, which provides for travel on public transportation in Paris and surrounding areas using the Métro, bus, tram, Montmartre funicular, or RER and SNCF (French National Railways) lines within Ile-de-France as far as Euro-Disneyland, Versailles, Fontainebleau, and the airports. The Paris Visite also includes discounts at many museums and attractions, and many other valuable perks. Prices vary according to the number of zones selected.

If you are staying in Paris for the prescribed number of days and plan to make more than three one-way trips on the Métro or bus systems per day, the pass will definitely save you money, and the convenience is invaluable. These passes may be purchased in all of the main Métro and train stations in Paris, at the international airports, Paris tourist offices, and wherever you see the RATP logo. They can also be purchased in the United States.

Paris Visite Pass Prices in Euros

	1–3 Zones	1–6 Zones
1 day	€12	€25
2 days	€20	€38
3 days	€27	€54
5 days	€38	€66

For the ultimate sightseeing and transportation combination, the **Paris Pass** offers free entry to more than 60 major tourist attractions, a range of special offers and discounts, and unlimited use of Paris public transport within zones 1–3, all for one affordable price. Visit www.parispass.com. As well as free entry, the Paris Pass normally allows you to avoid long queues at the busiest tourist sights, including the Louvre, Panthéon, Arc de Triomphe, Musée d'Orsay, Centre Pompidou, and many more. Simply show the attendant your Paris Pass.

Paris Pass Prices in Euros

	Adult	Teen (Age 12–17)	Child (Age 4–11)
2 days	€112	€70	€40
4 days	€163	€91	€45
6 days	€195	€100	€56

Acquaint yourself with the **Paris RER** (Regional Express Railway), the high-speed, limited-stop rail service that runs *under*—that's right, *under*—the regular Paris Métro. If you need to get somewhere in a hurry, the RER's the way to go. For example, we have ridden from Gare de Lyon to the Arc de Triomphe (the Étoile) in less than 10 minutes. Call 08 36 68 41 41 for information. The RER consists of five lines. RER color-coded lines appear on maps as follows: Line A = Red, Line B = Blue, Line C = Yellow, Line D = Green, and Line E = Purple. *Line A* goes west to east from St. Germain-en Laye, La Défense, the Étoile, Auber, Châtelet, Gare de Lyon, and the Marne Valley. *Line B* goes north to south from Roissy-Charles de Gaulle Airport to Gare du Nord, Châtelet, Pont St. Michel, Luxembourg, and the Chevreuse Valley. *Line C* runs from Versailles and follows the Seine through Paris to Orly Airport. *Line D* runs from Orry-la-Ville Coye through central Paris then splits at the Villeneuve-St-Georges to Meluri or around to Malesherbes. *Line E* runs from central Paris at Hausann Saint-Lazare east to Chelles-Gournay and southeast to Tournan.

Note: *Eurail passes are not accepted on RER lines within the Paris region.*

Bus information: *Tel:* 01 43 46 14 14.

Taxi: *Tel:* 01 47 39 47 39, 01 45 85 85 85, *or* 01 49 36 10 10. To reserve a taxi for the airport, call before 2100 the night before.

Train Connections to Other Base Cities from Paris

Depart from Paris Gare du Nord Station, unless otherwise noted.

DEPART	TRAIN NUMBER	ARRIVE	NOTES
		Amsterdam Centraal	
0625	Thalys 9303*	0942	R, M–F
0825	Thalys 9315*	1142	R, Exc. Su
1225	Thalys 9339*	1542	R
1525	Thalys 9357*	1842	R
1925	Thalys 9381*	2242	R
		Barcelona Estacion de Franca	
0715	TGV 9711	1353	R, 1, 2
2252	NZ 3751	1121+1	R, 3, Sleeper
		Berlin Hauptbahnhof	
0601	Thalys 9401*	1409	R, 5
1155	Thalys 9437*	2009	R, 5
1550	Thalys 9461*	0010+1	R, 5
1749	Thalys 9473*	0653+1	R, 5, Sleeper
		Bern (Berne)	
0723	TGV 9203	1124	R, 1, 7, M–Sa
1023	TGV 9211	1426	R, 1, 7
1211	TGV 9773	1726	R, 1, 6
1423	TGV 9215	1824	R, 1, 7
1823	TGV 9225	2250	R, 1
1911	TGV 9785	0101+1	R, 1, 6
		Brussels (Bruxelles) Midi/Zuid	
0625	Thalys 9303*	0747	R, M–F
0725	Thalys 9309*	0847	R, Exc. Su
0825	Thalys 9315*	0947	R
plus hourly Thalys* train service at 25 min past each hour (but not 1325) until 2225. Arrive in Brussels at 47 min past each hour (but not 1447) until 2347.			
		Budapest Keleti	
0725	TGV 9571	2119	R, 8, 10
		Copenhagen (København) H.	
0725	TGV 9571	2222+1	R, 11, Sleeper, Exc. Sa
1906	ICE 9559	1222+1	R, 8, 12, Sleeper
		Hamburg Hauptbahnhof	
0601	Thalys 9401*	1413	R, 5
0755	Thalys 9413*	1613	R, 5
1155	Thalys 9437*	2026	R, 5
1550	Thalys 9461*	0008+1	R, 5
1906	TGV 9559	1651+1	R, 5, 8, Sleeper

DEPART	TRAIN NUMBER	ARRIVE	NOTES
		Lisbon (Lisboa) Oriente	
1228	TGV 8537	0720+1	R, 13, Sleeper
		Luxembourg	
0840	TGV 2809	1059	R, 8
1340	TGV 2827	1548	R, 8
1540	TGV 2821	1748	R, 8
1840	TGV 2835	2048	R, 8
		Lyon Part-Dieu	
0658	TGV 6603	0856	R, 1, Exc. Su
0753	TGV 6605	0956	R, 1
0858	TGV 6607	1056	R, 1
0958	TGV 6609	1156	R, 1
then hourly until 2058.			
		Madrid Chamartin	
0728	TGV 8531	1942	R, 13, Sleeper
1407	TGV 9715	0012+1	R, 3, Sleeper
		Milan (Milano) Centrale	
0911	TGV 9765	1737	R, 1, 6
1023	TGV 9211	1935	R, 1, 9
1511	TGV 9775	2237	R, 1, 6
1911	EN 221	0550+1	R, 1, Sleeper
		Munich (München) Hauptbahnhof	
1525	TGV 9575	2136	R, 8
1755	TGV 9579	2341	R, 8
		Nice Ville	
0719	TGV 6171	1300	R, 1
0915	TGV 6173	1455	R, 1
1119	TGV 6165	1654	R, 1
1237	TGV 6163	1835	R, 1
1519	TGV 6179	2055	R, 1
1719	TGV 6181	2255	R, 1
2122	NZ 5773	0837+1	R, 3, Sleeper
		Prague (Praha)	
1910	TGV 9553	1918	R, 4, 8, Sleeper
1906	ICE 9559	0928+1	R, 4, 8, Sleeper
		Rome (Roma) Termini	
0629	TGV 9241	1755	R, 1, 14
1441	TGV 9249	0717+1	R, 1, 14, Sleeper
1911	EN 221	0959+1	R, 1, Sleeper
		Vienna (Wien) Hauptbahnhof	
0555	Thalys 9401*	1909	R, 5
1525	Thalys 9575*	0635+1	R, 10, Sleeper
		Warsaw Centralna	
1755	Thalys 9473*	1205+1	R, 11

DEPART	TRAIN NUMBER	ARRIVE	NOTES
		Zürich Hauptbahnhof	
0723	TGV 9203	1126	R, 8, Exc. Su
1023	TGV 9211	1426	R, 8
1423	TGV 9215	1826	R, 8
1823	TGV 9223	2226	R, 8

Daily, unless otherwise noted
R Reservations required
*Thalys high-speed train, supplement required
+1 Arrives next day
1. Departs Paris Gare de Lyon Station.
2. Change trains in Figueres.
3. Departs Paris Austerlitz Station.
4. Change trains in Mannheim.
5. Change trains in Cologne (Köln).
6. Change trains in Geneva.
7. Change trains in Basel.
8. Departs Paris Gare de l'Est (East) Station.
9. Change trains in Zurich.
10. Change trains in Munich (München).
11. Change to sleeper train in Cologne (Köln).
12. Change trains in Hamburg.
13. Departs Paris Montparnasse Station. Change to sleeper train in Irún.
14. Change trains in Milan (Milano).

Sights/Attractions/Tours and Paris Potpourri

Musts during your stay in Paris include:

- A visit to the **Louvre** to view the *Mona Lisa* and *Venus de Milo.*
- A cable-car ride up to **Montmartre** for a view of the "City of Light" or by elevator up the **Eiffel Tower** to the highest point in Paris.
- Walk the **Champs Elysées** to the **Arc de Triomphe** and look deep into its "flame of remembrance" for the faces of France and its allies who fought and died in the two world wars.
- Lunch at a sidewalk cafe.
- Ride the **Seine** on a ***bateau*** (boat).
- Get a gargoyle's point of view from high atop **Nôtre Dame.**
- Dine at **Maxim's** (if your waistline and wallet can afford it).
- Take in a dazzling dinner/show at the great Parisian cabaret **Paradis Latin.**

Paris has triumphed once again in the arts—this time in a museum that served the city as a train station for nearly 40 years. **Gare du Quai d'Orsay** was inaugurated on Bastille Day 1900 and included a 400-room hotel. By 1939 the Gare d'Orsay was obsolete, its platforms too short to accommodate the longer, electrified trains of the day. In 1971 the city of Paris reluctantly scheduled the structure for demolition, creating an uproar from its citizens. Under pressure, the government reversed itself and saved both the station and the hotel, which became the **Musée** (museum) **d'Orsay.**

Located at 1 rue de la Légion d'Honneur (at entry to Quai d'Orsay RER station and near Solférino Métro stop), Musée d'Orsay boasts a glorious collection of 19th-century French painting and sculpture. *Hours:* Tuesday, Wednesday, Friday, Saturday and Sunday 0930–1800; Thursday 0930–2145. Galleries start closing at 1730 (2115 Thursday). Admission: €11.00. It is usually most crowded on Thursday night and the weekend. Reduced price, €8.50, on Sunday. Visit www.musee-orsay.fr.

An interesting mix of Egyptian and European art can be found at the **Musée du Louvre.** Its glass-pyramid entrance, designed by I. M. Pei, has sparked much controversy, similar to that brought about by Gustave Eiffel and his tower. Referred to by the writer Guy de Maupassant as the "disgraceful skeleton," the Eiffel Tower became the city's most recognizable landmark. *Hours:* 0900–1800 daily except Tuesday and certain public holidays. Evening hours are extended to 2145 Wednesday and Friday. (*Tel:* 01 40 20 51 77; www.louvre.fr.) Admission: €16. Reduced price (€6) after 1800. Free admission to youths younger than age 18.

To avoid queuing up and having to buy a separate ticket for each museum and monument, consider purchasing the **Paris Museum Pass,** which covers an unlimited number of visits within the validity period to more than 55 museums and monuments in Paris and Ile de France.

2-day pass	€42
4-day pass	€56
6-day pass	€69

Purchase the pass at any of the museums, at more than 100 Métro stations, or at tourist offices.

No stay in Paris is complete without a visit to one of its great cabarets. Our favorite is **Paradis Latin,** at 28 rue du Cardinal Lemoine (*Tel:* 01 43 25 28 28; *Fax:* 01 43 29 63 63; www.paradislatin.fr). This beautiful and elegant theater–dining hall played an interesting role in Parisian history. Its foundation dates from the 12th century, and its walls date from 1803 when Bonaparte decided to construct his "Theatre Latin." It burned down during the siege of Paris in 1870, and Gustave Eiffel (the Eiffel Tower architect) was appointed to design and rebuild it. It reopened with great success in 1889. Then, in the early 20th century, it was transformed into industrial workshops.

The theater was accidentally rediscovered in 1972 and meticulously restored to its former glory by 1977. According to Harold Israel, "At the Paradis, we decided that not only should the show be enchanting but also the cuisine should be of excellent quality as well," and it is. Dinner's at 2000 and the dazzling show starts at 2130. Enjoy!

The Champs-Elysées is the most famous thoroughfare in Paris, but you should also see Paris from its most beautiful avenue, the River Seine. Aboard a *bateau* (boat) sights such as the Louvre, Nôtre Dame, and the Eiffel Tower take on a different perspective—particularly at night, when the floodlights of the *bateaux* illuminate the passing scenes. Bateaux Parisiens, Port de la Bourdonnais (at the foot of the Eiffel Tower). *Tel:* 01 71 67 01 70 for schedules, rates, and reservations. Visit www.bateauxparisiens.com. Bon voyage!

Day Excursions

Three of the six Paris day excursions have been selected to introduce the traveler to Ile de France: **Chartres, Fontainebleau,** and **Versailles.**

These places are every bit as important to what Paris is today as are the Louvre, the Place de la Concorde, or the Eiffel Tower. The three remaining day excursions venture farther afield in express trains to visit **Caen and the Normandy Beaches, Rennes,** and **Rouen.**

Day Excursion to

Caen

And the Normandy Beaches

Depart from Paris St. Lazare Station
Distance by Train: 148 miles (239 km)
Average Train Time: 2 hours
Tourist Information Office: Office de Tourisme Place Saint-Pierre, F-14000 Caen
Tel: 02 31 27 14 14; **Fax:** 02 31 27 14 13
E-mail: maire@caen.fr
www.ville-caen.fr or the Normandy Tourism Board at **www.normandie-tourisme.fr**
E-mail: info@normandy-tourism.org
Hours: July–August: 0900–1900 Monday–Saturday, 1000–1300 and 1400–1700 Sunday; September–June: 0930–1300 and 1400–1800 Monday–Saturday

Paris—Caen

DEPART Paris St. Lazare	TRAIN NUMBER	ARRIVE Caen	NOTES
0707	3301	0858	M–F
0745	3333	0953	Sa
0845	3335	1053	M–F
0910	3303	1058	Sa–Su
1010	3305	1158	M–F
1145	3341	1353	Sa–Su
1210	3307	1400	M–F

DEPART Caen	TRAIN NUMBER	ARRIVE Paris St. Lazare	NOTES
1449	3308	1647	Daily
1702	3348	1916	Daily
1749	3351	1946	Exc. Sa
1854	3314	2046	M–F
and other frequent service until 2124 on Su, 1907 on Sa, 2025 M–F			
Distance: 148 miles (239 km)			

Seven decades have passed since one of the greatest battles in history took place in Normandy. At dawn on June 6, 1944, American, British, and Canadian forces, together with elements of the Free French, assailed the Normandy beaches along a broad spectrum of the coastline at five preselected landing points, Utah, Omaha, Gold, Juno, and Sword. Preceded by the drop of three airborne divisions during the predawn hours, between 0630 and 0730, 120,000 soldiers and about 20,000 vehicles were landed from the sea. The assault upon Adolf Hitler's "Fortress Europe" had begun.

By the night of August 21, 76 days later, the **Battle of Normandy** was over. The German Seventh Army had been encircled and forced to surrender. It had cost the Germans 640,000 soldiers—killed, wounded, or taken prisoner. Allied losses were tallied at 367,000 dead or wounded. American losses were set at 127,000 casualties—31,000 of that number died in battle.

The town of Caen was the pivot of the battle and paid heavily for its part in the conflict. By the second day of the invasion, the whole of the town center had been flattened by Allied bombing. The German garrison fought fiercely. It wasn't until July 9 that the British and Canadian troops were able to take the town. The Germans, however, retreated to the right bank of the Orne River, where they continued to direct mortar fire into the ruined town. Caen was not completely liberated until August 9. The Battle of Caen lasted more than two months. Seventy-five percent of the town was destroyed.

For years following the war, Caen was one vast building site in which life slowly began to return to normal. Reconstructed and restored, the town decreed that now is the time for all men of goodwill to be reconciled. To that purpose, the **Caen Memorial** was established on the site of one of the bloodiest battles in history to take you on a compelling journey from the dark years of world wars to a vision of peace.

The memorial is unlike any other museum devoted to the theme of warfare. It employs audiovisual presentations to explain the sequence of events that led up to the outbreak of hostilities in 1939, the suffering of the people involved, the preparation for the invasion, and the strategies behind it. Peace can never be taken for granted; consequently, the memorial ends its presentation with a powerful and moving film emphasizing the need for vigilance if we are to have peace in our world in our own time and in our children's.

Allow one day for the Caen Memorial and sightseeing in Caen—a typical day excursion. If you want to tour the landing beaches and the memorial, this may be a good place to consider renting a vehicle. Ask the tourist office for the brochure *The D-Day Landings and the Battle of Normandy.* The **Hertz** office in Caen is directly across from the rail station (closed Sunday). Reserve your first car rental on your rail/drive package at least seven days prior to your departure for Europe by calling Hertz at (800) 654-3001 or visiting www.hertz.com.

Another option is to take the train from Paris St. Lazare Station to Caen and purchase the Caen Short Break package, which includes a two-day pass for a visit of the Caen Memorial, guided tours of the D-Day Landing Beaches, a book on the D-Day Landing (in English), and one night in a one-, two-, or three-star hotel, including breakfast. Prices start at €108 per person, based on double occupancy. Make your reservations in advance with a credit card: *Tel:* 02 31 06 06 45 (0900 to 1800 Monday through Friday); telephone from the United States: 011 +33 2 31 06 06 44; www.memorial-caen.fr; *E-mail:* resa@memorial-caen.fr.

This is a pilgrimage that every American should make. Arriving in Caen, you can proceed directly to the memorial on city bus No.17 going in the direction of the memorial. It departs from the bus station outside the rail station on the right.

The memorial is open daily 0900 to 1900. A half-day tour time is recommended. Check at the information desk for the starting times of the English-language programs. A cafeteria is located on the second floor for refreshments.

Returning from the memorial to the station, take bus No. 17 in the direction of **Grace de Dieu.** The bus makes a stop in the center of the town at Tour Leroy near the tourist office (Office du Tourisme). Walk along **boulevard des Allies** and proceed 1 block to where it intersects rue Saint-Jean. From this point, the tourist office sign may be seen across the street to the right. The tourist office can advise on accommodations in Caen and the Normandy towns close to the beaches. For each full-priced ticket purchased at one of the museums, you get reduced rates at all the other ones in the D-Day Landings and the Battle of Normandy region.

Tours of the invasion beaches start in Caen and proceed west through the Anglo-Canadian sectors of Sword, Juno, and Gold before arriving in the American sectors of Omaha and Utah. With a Hertz rental car, proceed west from Caen on Route 13 past Bayeux, LaCambe, and Carentan until reaching Ste.-Mere-Eglise, the first town in France to be liberated on D-Day, June 6, 1944. Visit the Airborne Museum with its CG4-A glider and a C-47 airplane, and gaze in wonder at the Eighty-second Airborne paratrooper's predicament when his parachute caught on the church steeple opposite the museum.

Proceed from there to the **Utah Beach Landing Museum** at Ste. Marie-Du-Mont. An audiovisual presentation explains how Utah beach was used to land about one million soldiers on its shores. Your next stop should be **Pointe-Du-Hoc,** which was captured by the Second Ranger Battalion in a spectacular assault on June 6, 1944, scaling 100-foot cliffs to destroy a German battery of coastal guns. The Rangers made it, but they paid a high price for their valor—77 dead, with an overall casualty rate of about 60 percent.

Leaving Pointe-Du-Hoc, head east to **Colleville-St.-Laurent,** where on a summit overlooking Omaha beach, you enter the American cemetery. Pay your respects to the 10,000 Americans resting there. To paraphrase Sir Winston Churchill, "This part of a foreign field shall forever be American."

En route back to Caen, stop in Bayeux at the **Memorial Museum** that you passed earlier while en route to Ste.-Mere-Eglise—time permitting. Otherwise, plan to return there the following day, and visit the Anglo-Canadian sectors as well.

Day Excursion to

Chartres

Cathedral Country

Depart from Paris St. Montparnasse Station
Distance by Train: 55 miles (88 km)
Average Train Time: 1 hour
Tourist Information Office: 8 rue de la Poissonnerie-CS 10289 28008 Chartres Cedux
Tel: 02 37 18 26 26; **Fax:** 02 37 21 51 91
www.chartres.com or **www.chartres-tourism.com**
E-mail: info@otchartres.fr
Hours: January–April, October–December: 1000–1800 Monday–Saturday, 1000–1700 Sunday; April–September: 0930–1830 Monday–Saturday, 1000–1730 Sunday
Notes: Exit the station, cross the street in the direction of the cathedral, and continue straight ahead until you come to a large square. Bear left at the square and follow the cathedral signs that you will begin to see from that point onward.

The tourist information office is in a building at the far end of Cathedral Square. Its sign reads OFFICE DE TOURISME.

Mention Chartres and anyone who has been there recalls the Cathedral of Nôtre Dame but not much more. But Chartres has many other attractions. To mention a few, we start with the town itself. Beguiling, gabled houses line the streets. Make it a point to stroll through the **old quarter** of town along streets with the appealing names of rue du Soleil d'Or (Street of the Golden Sun) or rue des Ecuyers (Street of the Horsemen). The tourist office has a special walking-tour program for the Old Town that includes the rental of a headset and a prerecorded audio guide in English. The length of the walking tour is 1½ hours.

Food is another one of Chartres's attractions, so plan to dine there during your visit. There are many excellent restaurants—the one in the ancient **Inn of the Grand Monarque** at 22 place des Épars, for example.

On arrival in the Chartres station, check the train departures for Paris on the posters displayed in the main hall near the ticket windows. The cathedral is illuminated at night, so if you would like to see this, check for a later train departure.

The **Cathedral of Nôtre Dame** in Chartres is in plain view from the railway station and will draw you like a magnet. It is said to be the most beautiful Gothic cathedral in Europe. To get there, just follow the aforementioned directions from the station to the tourist office, which is located in the same area. The cathedral's stained-glass windows, the superb lines of its pillars and vaulting, and its interior are overwhelmingly beautiful. Fire destroyed the original 11th-century building. The current cathedral was rebuilt between 1194 and 1220.

It is interesting to note that the cathedral has two nonmatching spires. The plain one of simple architecture was built first; the elaborate spire in late Gothic followed later. On Sunday afternoons at 1645 during July and August, you can enjoy the organ recitals at the cathedral. Admission to these performances is free.

The district surrounding the cathedral is noted for its medieval houses. Time permitting, you should walk down to the river for a look at the old houses and bridges close to the restored Romanesque **Church of Saint André.**

The Cathedral of Chartres may be the most famous attraction in the city. There is a lot more to this ancient town, however. In addition to the Church of Saint André, there are others that warrant your inspection. The **Church of Saint Pierre** is a Gothic masterpiece. Its stained-glass windows dating from the 14th century, when added to those of the cathedral, make Chartres the metropolis of stained glass.

The **Episcopal Palace,** now the Museum of Fine Arts, has a lovely 17th-century facade in addition to its interesting contents. The exhibit includes a unique collection of harpsichords, painted wood carvings and art from Oceania, and many French, Flemish, and Italian paintings.

Paris—Chartres

DEPART Paris Montparnasse	TRAIN NUMBER	ARRIVE Chartres	NOTES
0609	RE 62403	0725	Exc. Su
0709	RE 62407	0825	Exc. Su
0809	RE 62411	0925	
0906	RE 16757	1007	
1009	RE 62413	1125	
1106	RE 16761	1207	
1209	RE 62417	1325	

DEPART Chartres	TRAIN NUMBER	ARRIVE Paris Montparnasse	NOTES
1453	RE 16770	1553	
1534	RE 62430	1650	
1634	RE 62432	1750	M–F
1734	RE 62434	1850	
1802	RE 62436	1920	M–F
1934	RE 62440	2050	
and other frequent service until 2134.			

Daily, unless otherwise noted
Distance: 55 miles (88 km)

Chartres is bountiful in its art and has many museums and galleries to enjoy, such as the **International Stained Glass Center, La Maison de l'Archeologie,** and the **Maison Picassiette,** as well as the **Natural History Museum,** the regional **School Museum,** and the **Agriculture Museum** (COMPA).

To see all of the city's attractions, hop aboard ***Le petit Chart' train*** (The little train of Chartres). From April through October, the "train" departs daily on the hour from in front of the cathedral on a 35-minute tour of "Old Chartres." The first departure is at 1030; the last departure is at 1800. Adults, €6.50; children, €3.50. All aboard!

Day Excursion to

Fontainebleau

Palace of Kings

Depart from Gare de Lyon
Distance by Train: 37 miles (60 km)
Average Train Time: 45 minutes
Tourist Information Office: Office de Tourisme, 4 rue Royale, 77300 Fontainebleau
Tel: 01 60 74 99 99; **Fax:** 01 60 74 80 22
www.fontainebleau-tourisme.com
E-mail: info@fontainebleau-tourisme.com
Hours: 1000–1700, except Tuesday; Royal Apartments tours 0930–1700 daily October–May, 0930–1800 daily June–September
Notes: To reach the palace from the railway station in Fontainebleau, take the No. 1 bus marked Château from the station to the palace. The ride takes 10 minutes. No admission charge to palace grounds. Admission to palace: €10 adults, free for children younger than age 18.

The **Palace of Fontainebleau** is most famous today as the residence of Napoleon Bonaparte, but the site attracted the presence of the kings of France and other royalty as far back in history as the 12th century. For many, Fontainebleau signifies the spirit of France more so than does Versailles.

In 1169 Louis VII had the chapel of his manor at Fontainebleau consecrated by Thomas à Becket, the famous English archbishop of Canterbury. The palace that stands today probably owes more to the imagination of Francis I of France than any other of its monarchs. In 1528 he had the remains of prior centuries torn down and rebuilt; he then filled the new structure with sumptuous jewels, weapons, statues, and pictures—among them the *Mona Lisa* (which graced the bathroom)—as a suitable reclining palace for his mistress, the Duchess d'Etampes. In 1539, with the place set in order, he received his great rival, Emperor Charles V, in the new digs.

The fortunes of Fontainebleau slumped under the reign of Louis XIV. He was giving more attention to his new project at Versailles and his dalliances with Madame de Maintenon; but his successors, Louis XV and Louis XVI, were faithful to the palace as an autumn residence. Slowly, Versailles became the "in place" with French courtiers, and only the old retainers showed up to probe the forest surrounding the château for wild game. Fortunately, Fontainebleau survived the French Revolution much better than did Versailles and other royal residences closer to Paris. (Suburban living had its advantages even then.)

Paris—Fontainebleau

In addition to the trains listed below, there is frequent commuter train service to and from Fontainebleau.

DEPART	TRAIN NUMBER	ARRIVE
Paris Lyon		Fontainebleau-Avon
0719	R 51807	0757
0919	R 51815	0957
1019	R 51819	1057
1149	R 52843	1226

DEPART	TRAIN NUMBER	ARRIVE
Fontainebleau-Avon		Paris Lyon
1500	RE 51958	1541
1700	RE 51964	1741
1900	R 51970	1941
2230	R 52978	2311

Daily

Distance: 37 miles (60 km)

Fontainebleau has probably bedded more queens, court favorites, and royal mistresses than other palaces in France. (Versailles had its headliners, like Pompadour and Du Barry, but Fontainebleau was more discreet.) Under the new management of Francis I, the Duchess d'Etampes was granted a chamber that later became known as the "King's Staircase" when Louis XV needed freer access to her apartments. Madame de Maintenon moved to Fontainebleau under the auspices of Louis XIV in 1686 and into a room that bears her name even today.

Since the beginning of the 17th century, every queen of France has slept in the queen's bedchamber within the palace. Marie Antoinette ordered the bed that now graces the chamber, but because of unfortunate developments, she never had the opportunity to lay her head upon its pillows.

When Napoleon Bonaparte became Emperor of France in 1804, he had Fontainebleau refurbished and refurnished to receive Pope Pius VII, who had come to crown him. From 1812 to 1814, the pope was also in residence in Fontainebleau—only this time he was not an invited guest but Napoleon's prisoner.

Not all of Napoleon's residence at Fontainebleau was surrounded with the fringe benefits befitting an emperor of his stature; he had some bad days, too. He signed his abdication in a room known now as the "Abdication Chamber" (formerly a bathroom) on April 6, 1814. Nineteen days later, he bade farewell to his officers and bodyguards in the Court of the White Horse from the horseshoe-shaped grand staircase that is now the main entrance to the palace.

Fontainebleau, unlike Versailles, possesses the secret of intimacy, no doubt due to the fact that each successive generation of kings or emperors added a wing of his own to the structure. The palace is full of nooks and crannies. There are back staircases and tapestries that pull aside to reveal secret hallways. Living in Fontainebleau, its occupants were surrounded by romance and intrigue. In a sense, it probably was the earliest version of the current "no-tell motel," but it had far more class!

The Germans used Fontainebleau as a military headquarters during World War II. Following the war, it served as a seat of the North Atlantic Treaty Organization (NATO) until 1965, when it became a public museum.

If you take the tour, and you should, your tour guide will lead you first through the Red Room, scene of Napoleon's abdication, then, in turn, through the Council Room, the Throne Room, and the Queen's Bedroom. From there, you pass through the Royal Apartments, then down the King's Staircase to the Oval Court, where the tour ends. It's intriguing.

The gardens and parks surrounding the palace are lovely throughout the year. You are invited to bring your own picnic lunch and spread it out on the royal grass as long as you don't litter the imperial landscape.

Day Excursion to

Rennes

Capital of Brittany

Depart from Paris Montparnasse Station
Distance by Train: 232 miles (374 km)
Average Train Time: 2 hours, 4 minutes
Tourist Information Office: Chapelle Saint-Yves, 11 rue Saint-Yves, CS 26410, F-35064 Rennes
Tel: 02 99 67 11 11; **Fax:** 02 99 67 11 10
www.ville-rennes.fr or **www.tourisme-rennes.com**
E-mail: infos@tourisme-rennes.com
Hours: July and August: 0900–1900 daily; September–June: 1000–1800 daily
Notes: From the rail station, take avenue Janvier to the river Vilaine, where a left turn puts the office in view 2 blocks farther on.

There's an expression that has been making the rounds of the travel trade for some time now: "Half the fun is in the going." Rennes fully qualifies as such a day excursion, since you can go there on the TGV *Atlantique,* the pride of the French rail fleet and holder of the friction-rail speed record.

Paris—Rennes

DEPART	TRAIN NUMBER	ARRIVE	NOTES
Paris Montparnasse		Rennes	
0704	TGV 8603	0916	M–Sa, 1
0736	TGV 8081	0952	M–F
0808	TGV 8091	1025	
0908	TGV 8611	1112	
1008	TGV 8083	1213	
1108	TGV 8617	1328	Exc. Sa, 1

DEPART	TRAIN NUMBER	ARRIVE	NOTES
Rennes		Paris Montparnasse	
1605	TGV 8063	1822	
1705	TGV 8643	1914	
1808	TGV 8657	2018	Exc. Sa
1835	TGV 8067	2054	M–Sa
1905	TGV 8663	2111	
2005	TGV 8090	2226	

Daily, unless otherwise noted
Reservations required on all TGVs
1. Runs from end of August through mid-July.
Distance: 232 miles (374 km)

Once outside of Paris and onto its special right-of-way, the TGV (*train à grande vitesse,* or train of great speed) cruises at 186 mph, and you will be experiencing some of the finest rail travel in the world. Be certain to have seat reservations. It's not a "seat belt" ride—it's smooth and totally enjoyable. Outbound in the morning, you can enjoy breakfast as the French countryside flashes by; inbound returning to Paris, you are in for a "Happy Hour" you'll never forget!

Rennes is unique in that it doesn't remind you so much of France as it does the area around Cornwall in Britain. As the cultural capital of the French province of Brittany, it has some strong ties to its Celtic origins in its architecture and gastronomy. Rennes stands at the confluence of the Ille and the Vilaine Rivers. This junction of waterways came to the attention of Julius Caesar, and in 56 B.C., his legions conquered its original Celtic settlers, the Riedones. After this flurry of activity, however, things settled down for the balance of the Middle Ages.

At the beginning of the 18th century, Rennes still looked as it had for several hundred years—with narrow alleys and houses constructed of lath and plaster and no running water for sanitation or firefighting. History records that in the evening of December 22, 1720, a drunken carpenter set fire to a pile of shavings, which, in turn, set fire to his house and then spread rapidly throughout much of the town, destroying more than a thousand other buildings before it burned itself out.

The part of the wooden town destroyed by that fire was rebuilt with granite arches and stone along well-ordered lines. Gabriel, architect to the French king Louis XV, then designed a new Town Hall. Thus, Rennes developed its "New Town" that stands yet today and awaits your inspection following your arrival in its ultramodern train station designed specifically for the high-speed TGV *Atlantique*. Rennes's aesthetic value embraces its vibrant past, present, and future by offering visitors a wealth of architectural variety. It rightfully claims to be one of the prettiest cities in Brittany.

With a population of 200,000, Rennes describes itself as youthful, well established, and dynamic. Well equipped with prestigious theater and museum facilities and augmented with a city orchestra and the **National Centre for Dramatic Art,** the city plays a major role in the cultural activities of the region.

In the first week of July, during the *Tombées de la Nuit* (Summer Festival), Old Rennes is illuminated with spotlights while ballets, songs, plays, or visual-arts presentations are performed. Daytime attractions include the contemporary architecture of the Law Courts, *Le Triangle,* and the cultural center. Saturday mornings are always special with the open-air market.

Guided tours depart from the main tourist information office at Pont de Nemours daily at 1100 (also at 2100 on Tuesday and Thursday) and at 1500 July 1 through August 31. City tours in English are offered Wednesday at 1500 during summer months.

Evenings in Rennes are pleasant. The city is home to numerous eating places offering a wide range of local or exotic cuisine—each establishment exhibiting a character all its own. Located close to the Atlantic Ocean as well as the English Channel, Rennes offers a selection of seafood second to none. For fine seafood served in an authentic 15th-century house, dine at **l'Auberge St. Sauveur,** at 6 rue St. Sauveur (*Tel:* 02 99 79 32 56). As this is a university city, the bars in rue Saint-Michel and rue Saint-Malo attract the younger set, and there are plenty of concerts, plays, or films to keep the elders fully occupied, too.

TGV *Atlantique* service to Rennes opens up another day-excursion opportunity, Mont-Saint-Michel, one of the great wonders of France. Operated by Les Courriers Bretons, a special luxury bus runs between the rail station in Rennes to Mont-Saint-Michel, taking only 1 hour and 10 minutes. The bus runs daily during summer and Friday through Sunday during the balance of the year. For details check with the House of Brittany in Paris, the Tourist Information Office in Rennes, or Les Courriers Breton in Saint Malo (*Tel:* 02 99 19 70 80); www.lescourriersbretons.com.

Day Excursion to

Rouen

Joan of Arc Memorial

Depart Paris St. Lazare Station
Distance by Train: 87 miles (140 km)
Average Train Time: 1 hour, 15 minutes
Tourist Information Office: Office de Tourisme et des Congres, 25 place de la Cathédrale, 76000 Rouen
Tel: 02 32 08 32 40; **Fax:** 02 32 08 32 44
www.rouentourisme.com
E-mail: otrouen@mcom.fr
Hours: May–September: 0900–1900 Monday–Saturday, 0930–1230 and 1400–1800 Sunday; rest of the year: 0930–1230 and 1330–1800 Monday–Saturday
Notes: The office is 5 minutes away from the station by taxi; 10 minutes on the underground, which stops at the Théâtre des Arts, just 2 blocks away from the office. Walking—and it's downhill all the way—takes about 20 minutes. Follow rue Jeanne d'Arc from in front of the station, turning left at rue du Gros Horloge (Big Clock). After walking under the clock, bear right at the cathedral plaza for a few yards to the tourist office.

Rouen was established by the Romans, who selected the site as the first point from the sea where a bridge could be built across the Seine. Rouen became the capital of Normandy at the beginning of the Christian era, and, despite many thrashings in many wars, it still contains a number of lovely churches, towers, and other reminders of its colorful past, such as half-timbered houses and town clocks.

Rouen is steeped in history and is considered one of the capitals of stained glass. We told you Rouen was colorful! During the Hundred Years' War, the city was held by the English from 1419 to 1449. **Joan of Arc** was burned at the stake in Rouen by the English in 1431. Her memory is commemorated during the last week of May every year during the Joan of Arc Festival. Highlights include music and street entertainment, a medieval market, parade, and fireworks.

Your train from Paris will arrive in Gare Rive-Droite, the rail station in Rouen on the right bank of the Seine. Several hotels, restaurants, and bars are clustered about the station's plaza. The city abounds with eating and drinking establishments—even McDonald's—so finding refreshments in Rouen during your visit will be no problem.

The tourist office has prepared an English-language pamphlet describing a tour itinerary that takes about two hours. It starts at the tourist office and takes the visitor to the principal points of interest within the boundaries of the historical town center. The railway station appears on the map, so you need not worry about finding your way back to the station.

Paris—Rouen

DEPART	TRAIN NUMBER	ARRIVE	NOTES
Paris St. Lazare		Rouen Rive-Droite	
0611	50003	0750	Exc. Su
0720	13101	0848	M–F
0820	13103	0948	
0850	3105	1000	
1020	13105	1148	Exc. Su
1050	3107	1200	Exc. Su
1220	13107	1348	
1250	3109	1400	Exc. Su

DEPART	TRAIN NUMBER	ARRIVE	NOTES
Rouen Rive-Droite		Paris St. Lazare	
1413	13120	1540	
1459	3120	1610	
1612	50004	1742	Exc. Sa
1712	13192	1840	
1759	3128	1910	
1859	3130	2010	Exc. Sa
2012	3132	2140	
2059	3134	2210	Exc. Sa

Daily, unless otherwise noted
Distance: 87 miles (140 km)

First stop on the tour is the city's **cathedral,** which stands as one of the most beautiful examples of French Gothic architecture. Construction began in the 12th century. It was leveled by a devastating fire in 1200, and it was not until the 15th century that it began to take on its current appearance. The cast-iron spire atop the cathedral's central tower is a 19th-century addition. Heavily damaged during World War II, the cathedral's restoration work still continues.

In order to rebuild the cathedral, Rouen had to revive the medieval skills of its original creators. The cathedral's structure was said to have gained its name from the fact that it was built with money paid by the faithful members of the parish for the privilege of consuming butter during Lent.

Following the tour itinerary suggested by the tourist office, the midway point of the tour will be the **Palace of Justice.** Three short blocks beyond, you will enter Rouen's **old market area,** with its narrow streets and half-timbered houses. There are more than 800 structures in Rouen that illustrate the typical architecture of the city from the Middle Ages to the end of the 18th century. The houses were termed half-timbered because their external and internal walls were constructed of timber frames, and the spaces between the structural members were filled with brick plaster or wattle—woven reeds covered and plastered with clay. You'll note that the upper stories of many half-timbered houses in Rouen project out over the ground level. This arrangement allows the lower part of the house to be protected against inclement weather.

Born a peasant in 1412, Joan of Arc believed she heard celestial voices. In 1429, during the Hundred Years' War when the English were about to capture Orleans, Joan convinced Charles VII (then Dauphin of France) of her divine mission and led the resistance against the English at Compiegne in 1430. Subsequently, she underwent fourteen months of interrogation by her captors and was then burned at the stake in the Old Market Square at Rouen on May 30, 1431. The Maid of Orleans, national heroine and patron saint of France, decisively turned the Hundred Years' War in France's favor.

The place in the old market where Joan of Arc met her fate is marked by a huge cross of concrete and metal. Towering over it is a modern church, completed in 1979, its roof representing the flames of the stake. It blends masterfully into the scene against a background of black-and-white timbered houses. The impact of history can be felt here.

Last stop is that huge clock you may have passed en route to the tourist office. It was positioned at ground level until 1527, when the people of Rouen asked that it be raised so they could see it better. The city council obliged by housing it in the elegant Renaissance structure you see today. The clock is unique in that it has only one hand. The globe at the top, which is no longer functioning, used to indicate the phases of the moon. Although the clock was converted to electricity in 1928, the original mechanism is still in place.

Day Excursion to

Versailles

Celebrated Site of France

Depart Paris for Versailles from any station on RER Line C
Distance by Train: 11 miles (18 km)
Average Train Time: 30 minutes
Tourist Information Office: Office de Tourisme, 2 bis, avenue de Paris
Tel: 01 39 24 88 88; **Fax:** 01 39 24 88 89
Tourist Office: www.versailles-tourisme.com.
Château: www.chateauversailles.fr.
Ville: www.mairie-versailles.fr
Hours: April–October: 0900–1900 Tuesday–Sunday, 1000–1800 Monday; November–March: 0900–1800 Tuesday–Saturday, 1100–1700 Sunday–Monday
Notes: To get to the tourist office, turn right as you exit the Rive Gauche Station. Walk about 100 yards to the next intersection, then turn left. You will find the tourist office and the palace about 20 yards farther on the left.

Paris's RER Line C runs between Orly Airport and Versailles. Suggested stations are Austerlitz, Orsay, Pont St. Michel, or Invalides, the railway station close to the Hotel des Invalides, which was founded by Louis XIV to serve as a military hospital and home for veterans. Gare Invalides can be reached via Métro line 8 or 13. Get off at the "Invalides" Métro stop.

Trains for Versailles also run from Montparnasse Station, but the station in Versailles to which this line connects is a considerable distance from the palace. Trains running from Gare Invalides, however, take you to within easy walking distance. Trains on RER Line C from Gare d'Austerlitz in Paris terminate in Versailles. Therefore, stay on the train until it reaches the end of the line. The main function of this station appears to be assisting visitors coming to Versailles to see **the palace.** Bilingual signs and voice announcements will assist you.

Hours: April–October: 0900–1830; November–March 0900–1730, closed Monday.

Admission:

Passport (day pass): Chateau, Trianons, Groves	€18.00
Chateau, Grand Apartments	€15.00
Grand Trianon & Petite Trianon	€10.00
Guided Tour of the Groves (1100 to 1600)	€8.00

Note: All prices subject to change. Reduced fares after 1530. Separate tickets required for the King's Bedchambers and Private Apartments, Royal Chapel, Opera (guided tours only), and the Museum of French History. Audioguides available for rent. You may purchase "e-Tickets" online at www.chateauversailles.fr, which enable you to use the express line. Just pick up your tickets at the e-Ticket booth on the day of your visit (present a photo ID).

The only way to understand the powerful influence that France exerted during the centuries of monarch rule is to visit Versailles. Here, only at Versailles, can you come to appreciate the spiritual, artistic, and political renown of France and its lineage of kings.

In 1623 Louis XIII (1601–1643) ordered a hunting lodge built on a hill named Versailles in place of a windmill that had occupied the site until then. The lodge was erected in 1624. Liking the spot so well, he then ordered the lodge replaced by a grand mansion, which was completed in 1634.

Paris—Versailles

Frequent service to/from Versailles: RER Line C trains depart Gare d'Austerlitz every 15–30 minutes and terminate in Versailles Rive Gauche (Chateau) Station; journey time about 40 minutes. Rive Gauche Station is significantly closer to the Palace of Versailles than the alternative RER Line C service to Versailles Chantiers or the SNCF station Versailles Rive Droite.

Distance: 11 miles (18 km)

His son, Louis XIV (1638–1715), the Sun King, liked the spot, too, hated the crowds in Paris with equal vigor, and envied his finance minister's fine home at Vaux le Vicomte to the extent that he came up with an order that put his dad's to shame—"Build a palace at Versailles to surpass all palaces!" Orders being orders, before long 36,000 laborers aided by 6,000 horses were at work building palace walls, digging lakes with canals to connect them, and transplanting a forest when the king and his gardener decided that God had planted it in the wrong place to begin with. Work continued on the **Palace of Versailles** over a period of 50 years.

The Sun King made certain that nothing from the outside world would be imported for Versailles if it could be created or found in France. The result was an extraordinary showcase of French culture.

Urged on, first by Madame de Pompadour and then by Madame du Barry, Louis XV (1710–1774) also ordered additions to the palace, including the Petit Trianon, which Louis XVI (1754–1793) gave to his wife, Marie Antoinette, when he came to the throne.

Despite the splendor of this edifice, Marie and her courtiers were drawn to the fantasies of a hamlet erected for her by her loving husband. There, among other rural objects, stood a dairy barn complete with cows, among which Marie and her companions would cavort—much to the consternation of the bovines, who had never observed such carefree antics before among the peasants of the land.

Versailles is an extraordinary complex of marvels where the kings of France were insulated from the distant horrors of the Revolution. Its restoration to the original is a marvel in itself—a testament to the heirs of its tradition.

Let your imagination run by visualizing throngs of court favorites, courtiers, teams of prancing horses pulling royal carriages over the cobblestones of the courtyard, chambermaids scurrying about, valets rushing about with the linens of the gentry, and butchers carving the roasts for the banquets under the surveillance of the king's hounds—all of this 17th-century tumult, cacophony, and frenzy taking place on a scale many times greater than that of any Cecil B. DeMille production.

It is impossible to see Versailles completely in one visit—three, perhaps, but nothing less than that. Consequently, set priorities (and this may sound silly) by going there the first time and just wandering around. Go back the second time and take the tour. Return the third time to see the things you missed or wanted to see again from the times before.

GERMANY

Germany's reunification, symbolized by the fall of the Berlin Wall in late 1989, had a great impact on the overall German economy and way of life; it also opened new doors to tourism. Of course unifying public transportation systems of the East and West played a major role in the total reunification process.

Germany is a land based on a rich, complex history on track to a vibrant future. In recent years Germany has seen an influx of refugees and foreigners that has fostered a political culture more tolerant of the customs and traditions of others.

Located in the heart of Europe, Germany makes a convenient starting point for travel, especially by rail, to nearly anywhere in Europe. Major airports for North Americans are Berlin, Dusseldorf, Frankfurt, Hamburg, and Munich, each of which is connected by rapid transit (S-Bahn) to the city's center.

The Germans are famous for brewing some of the tastiest beer in the world, and they love celebrating dozens of national, regional, and local holidays, holy or otherwise, with great passion, beer and wine tents, pageants, beer and wine, parades, beer and wine, festivals, beer and wine, markets, and lots of beer and wine.

The most well-known festivals include the German Mardi Gras, also known as Fasching, Fastnacht, or Fastnet, which includes masked balls; Munich's Octoberfest, which attracts people from all over the world; and the Hamburg Dom, Nuremberg's Christ Child's Market at Christmas, and the Onion Market in Weimar.

Don't let the guttural German language frighten you; many Germans, particularly tourism and train personnel, are multilingual. It's the majority of Americans who are "unilingual."

For more information on delightful Germany, contact the German Tourist Offices in North America: **www.germany-tourism.de** or **www.cometogermany.com.**

New York: 122 East 42nd Street, 52nd Floor, Suite 2000, New York, NY 10168-0072; *Tel:* (212) 661-7200; *Fax:* (212) 661-7174; *E-mail:* gntonyc@d-z-t.com

Chicago: P.O. Box 59594, Chicago, IL 60659-9594; *Tel:* (773) 539-6303; *Fax:* (773) 539-6378; *E-mail:* gntoch@aol.com

Beverly Hills: 8484 Wilshire Boulevard, Beverly Hills, CA 90211 *Tel:* (323) 655-6085; *Fax:* (323) 655 6086; *E-mail:* gntolax@aol.com

DENMARK
Westerland
Flensburg
Husum
Puttgarden
Sassnitz
Kiel
Heide
Rostock
Neurmüster
Travemünde
Cuxhaven
Elmshorn
Lübeck
Norden
Stasde
Wilhelmsh
Bremerhaven
HAMBURG
Schwerin
Emden
H. Harburg
Tanlow
Groningen
Leer
Neustrelitz
Oldenburg
Bremen
Dannenberg
Prenzlau
POLAND
Soltaur
Celle
Hengelo
Hannover
Potsdam
BERLIN
NETHERLANDS
Arnhem
Magdeburg
Hameln
Münster
Bad Harzburg
Eindhoven
Dortmund
Hamm
Bitterfeld
Elsterwerda
Essen
Göttingen
Halle
Düsseldorf
Hagen
Leipzig
Kassel
Dresden
Cärlitz
Madstricht
Köln
Erfurt
Aachen
Siegan
Chemnitz
Herbesthal
Bonn
Bad Schandau
Fuldo
BELGIUM
Limburg
Koblenz
Coburg
Frankfurt
Schirnding
Bingen
Mainz
Bamberg
Würzburg
LUX.
Trier
CZECH REPUBLIC
Luxembourg City
Lauda
Nuremberg
Apach
Rothenburg
Heidelburg
Firth im Wald
Crailsheim
Saarbrucken
Forach
Regensburg
Bayerisch
Treuchtlingen
Wissembourg
Lauterbourg
Plattling
Freyung
Aalen
Ingolstadt
Stuttgart
Pasau
Landshut
Strasbourg
Augsburg
FRANCE
Ulm
Mühldorf
MUNICH
Wels
Buchoe
Freiburg
Bad Totz
Salzburg
Weilheim
Kempten
Singen
Berchtesgaden
Bad Wiessee
Kufstein
Basel
Lindau
Bregenz
Oberstdorf
Seefeld
SWITZERLAND
Garmisch-Partenkirchen
Innsbruck
AUSTRIA

Toronto: 480 University Avenue, Suite 1500, Toronto, Ontario M5G 1V2, Canada; *Tel:* (416) 968-1685; *Fax:* (416) 968-0562; *E-mail:* info@gnto.ca

Banking

Currency: Euro (€)

Exchange rate at press time: €0.90 = U.S. $1.00

Hours: 0830–1230 and 1330–1600 Monday–Friday. Currency exchange offices are found at mainline railway stations and at airports. They are generally open 0600 to 2200.

Be aware that some establishments in Germany do not accept credit cards. Major hotels, restaurants, and department stores do, but have cash handy for the smaller establishments that do not.

Communications

Country Dialing Code: 49

Major Mobile Phone Companies: T-Mobile, Vodafone, E-Plus, O2

Rail Travel in Germany

Deutsche Bahn AG (www.bahn.de), or GermanRail, operates more than 25,000 miles of the unified rail networks of the former East and West Germany. Massive investments in infrastructure and train stock, including use of tilting trains, have benefited schedules and shortened journey times.

Germany's top-of-the-line, high-speed, long-distance **ICE** (InterCity Express) trains are big, bold, and beautiful, with an emphasis on passenger comfort and a wide range of services. There are 259 ICE trains of five different types, with the ICE3 being the fastest at 330 kilometers per hour, reducing the travel time between Cologne (Köln) and Frankfurt from 2 hours and 15 minutes to just more than 1 hour. ICEs, reaching speeds of up to 175 mph, depart hourly every day for major centers within Germany and into the Swiss cities of **Basel, Bern, Interlaken,** and **Zurich,** as well as **Vienna, Austria.** The network connects all major cities.

Each train has a restaurant car, termed **BordRestaurant,** with two sections—a traditional-style dining car and a self-service bistro. They're big on other amenities, too, such as headphones and private lockers in which to stow purses, cameras, or other valuables while you visit the BordRestaurant car. Some have video systems.

German Railpass

DAYS Within 1 Month	ADULT 1st Class Single	ADULT 1st Class Twin*	ADULT 2nd Class Single	ADULT 2nd Class Twin*	YOUTH 2nd Class
4 days	$403	$643	$298	$476	$239
5 days	$432	$691	$319	$512	$256
6 days	$476	$761	$352	$564	$282
7 days	$522	$835	$387	$619	$309
10 days	$658	$1,052	$486	$779	$390

*Twinpass prices are total for 2 people traveling together at all times.
Child (age 4–11) fare 50 percent of adult fare
Youth (age 12–25)
Bonuses for pass holders include free travel on KD River Steamers on certain Rhine, Main, and Moselle River sections and free travel on selected bus lines operated by Deutsche Touring/Europabus.

Changing trains in Germany is a snap. In many cities, platforms are designed in such a way that the train you need to transfer to may be standing immediately across the platform from the train in which you arrive. Since most GermanRail trains are often configured the same— first-class cars in the front, second-class cars in the rear—you merely cross the platform to find the same type of accommodation on the connecting train.

Train platforms are divided into sections A to E. If you are traveling on a long-distance train, consult the train configuration display to easily determine where you will be sitting.

Just when we thought porters went the way of the dinosaur, **porter service** is available in Dresden, Frankfurt am Main, Hamburg, Leipzig, Munich, Stuttgart, and Berlin Hbf Stations. The porters wear blue uniforms and red caps (€5 for first two items of luggage).

ICE2s have ample legroom, electronic destination indicators on the *outside* of the train cars, digital-display seat-reservation units above the seats, electronic 220V sockets for laptop computers, and increased facilities for the disabled; one car has a family compartment. The newer ICE3 (NeiTec, or tilting) trains are more high-tech and able to "tilt" to round curves at higher speeds.

Germany's **EuroCity (EC), InterCity (IC), D,** and **InterRegio (IR)** trains round out the mainline service. Regional services are provided by trains designated RE, RB, and SE. The **S-Bahn** ("Schnell," or "fast") rapid-transit system provides service to and from the suburban areas of Berlin, Cologne (Köln), Frankfurt, Hamburg, Hannover, Leipzig, Munich, Nuremberg, and Stuttgart.

The varieties of **Eurail Passes, German Railpass, Eurail Benelux–Germany Pass, Eurail Austria–Germany Pass, Czech Republic–Germany Pass,**

France–Germany Pass, Eurail Germany–Poland Pass, Eurail Germany–Switzerland Pass, and **Eurail Denmark–Germany Pass** are accepted by German Railways. Eurail bonuses include:

- Scandlines/DFO—Free transport on the Puttgarden–Rødby Faerge (Denmark). Rail pass must be valid in both Germany and Denmark.
- Free sailings on KD German Rhine Line boats between Cologne (Köln) and Mainz, and Koblenz and Cochem (extra charge for hydrofoil transport). Visit www.k-d.com.
- Europabus, 20 percent discount on the following routes (reservations in advance recommended highly): EB 189 Burgenstrasse (Castle Road): Mannheim–Heidelberg–Heilbronn–Rothenburg ob der Tauber–Ansbach–Nuremberg, *May to September.* EB 190/190A Romantische Strasse (Romantic Road): Frankfurt am Main–Rothenburg ob der Tauber–Augsburg–Munich–Füssen, *April to October.* Reservations via Deutsche Touring in Frankfurt am Main. *Tel:* 011 +49 69 7903 0 from the United States; *Fax:* 011 +49 69 7903 219. *E-mail:* incoming@touring.de.
- Mountain railroad Garmisch Partenkirchen–Grainau–Zugspitzplatt and on some cable cars in the summit area, 10 percent discount; plus reduced fare on the Freiburg–Schauinsland rack railway.
- 50 percent discount on boats operated by BSB, SBS, ÖBB, and URH on the Rhine River between Constance and Schaffhausen on Lake Constance, calling at Bregenz, Constance, Friedrichshafen, Kreuzlingen, Lindau, Romanshorn, Rorschach, Radolfzel, Ueberlingen, and the Isles of Reichenau and Mainau.
- No supplement required on ICE, IC, EC and CityNight Trains.

Base City: **BERLIN**

www.visitberlin.de
E-mail: information@visitberlin.de
City Dialing Code: 30

Although eons apart, the modern city of Berlin and the ancient city of Jericho shared a common occurrence—their walls "came a tumblin' down." The Bible (Joshua 6) is a bit vague concerning the actual date of the occurrence in Jericho, but we do know the Berlin Wall "fell" on November 9, 1989, 28 years after it was built. Berlin became a whole city; Germany became one country; Berlin is the capital of the new Germany; communism is on the wane worldwide; and this city again has the largest Jewish community in Germany.

For Berlin, World War II ended on the afternoon of May 2, 1945. Of the 245,000 buildings in Berlin before the war, 50,000 had been destroyed or rendered beyond repair. There was no electricity, no gas, no water. Before the war, Berlin had 4.3 million inhabitants; in May 1945, the remaining 2.8 million began the task of clearing away the debris.

In July of that year, Berlin became a four-power city with a joint Allied administration composed of Britain, France, Russia, and the United States. This division into zones turned the former German capital into an island of occupation surrounded completely by a sea of Soviets. East and West were in complete agreement about abolishing Nazism, but they had no common or precise answer as to what would replace it. Moreover, it quickly became evident that the Soviet intention was to gain complete control of the city.

On June 24, 1948, the Soviets sealed off the West's section of the city and, on the basis of "technical disorders," shut off their supply of electricity. They were left with a meager 36-day food supply. A disaster appeared imminent, but two days later the largest airlift in history began. From July 1948 to May 1949, the Western Allies transported, in some 213,000 flights, more than 1.7 million tons of food and other supplies to the beleaguered city. While operating the airlift, 70 members of the Allied Air Forces lost their lives. On May 12, 1949, the siege was lifted. Berliners began demonstrating their political choice by moving en masse to the Western sectors.

By August 1961, faced with mass evacuation of their sector, the Soviets began erecting the Berlin Wall. In 1989, after 28 years of division, the wall that Winston Churchill called the "Iron Curtain" was breached in one night. Before it "fell," more than 100 people lost their lives while attempting to cross it. The eastern part of Berlin, including its historic center, is once again easily accessible to visitors. The infamous Checkpoint Charlie was dismantled. Its guardhouse is now a museum piece.

Except for a small section that will stand as a mute reminder, every vestige of the Berlin Wall has been removed.

With the demise of the Wall, Berlin nearly doubled in size. The reunited metropolis rediscovered the traditional rhythm that made it famous throughout the world and added some new ones. This city offers incredible nightlife and never sleeps a wink. Hmm, did you pack your dancing shoes? Travelers from around the world are passing the word, "Berlin is worth the trip."

Arriving by Air

Tegel (TXL) and Schönefeld (SXL). Both airports are connected with the city center by buses and trains. Visit www.berlin-airport.de. Plans are to expand the Schönefeld site into a new international airport, the Berlin Brandenburg International Airport (BBI). Construction began in mid-2006 and is expected to be completed in early 2018. Tegal is expected to close in 2018, following the October 2008 closure of the old Tempelhof Airport. BBI's rail station will be under the terminal and provide 20-minute access to Berlin's city center.

Tegel Airport, 5 miles northwest, is your most likely arrival airport. Exiting from Customs, you'll see an information office between two rows of ticket counters. Go there for transportation information. From that position, look over your right shoulder and you will see the money-exchange office across the hall; open daily 0600 to 2200. ATMs are available near Gates 4, 10/11, and 15 and in the "Reisemarkt."

- **Airport–City Links:** TXL ExpressBus Nos. 128, 109, and X9 run to underground stations in Berlin, for connections to the city's underground, S-Bahn train, and bus network, at Jungfernheide, one stop from Jakob Kaizer Platz on the U7 line. A service also runs to city center destinations, including Unter den Linten and Französische Strasse, with connections to the U9 underground train at Turmstrasse, and ending at Alexanderplatz. Information is available from the BVG office in the main hall of the terminal [*Tel:* (0)30 19449]. **Taxis** are readily available outside the terminal. Journey time: 30 to 40 minutes. Fare: €25 to €35, depending on traffic.

Schönefeld Airport is served by many European airlines; you should check with the airline taking you into Berlin as to its landing airport. Schönefeld will become Berlin-Brandenburg International Airport sometime in late 2016. When the expantion to allow this is completed, almost all air traffic into and out of Berlin will be moved to the new airport, and Tegal will close. Airport Express train service to Berlin Hbf Station (RE7 and RB14) every half hour 0430 to 2300; journey time 31 minutes. City trains S9 and S45 take about 45 minutes. Fare: €3.10. ATMs are in Terminal A, ground floor, in the center.

- **Airport–City Links:** Subway line U6 (Platz der Luftbrücke Station) and bus lines 162 and 171.

Arriving by Train

On May 28, 2006, a new central train station opened in Berlin, combining most of the arrivals and departures that used to be separated between two other stations. These two stations, Zoologischer Garten (known as "Zoo Station" or "Zoobahnhof") and Ostbahnhof were replaced by the Berlin Hauptbahnhof (Hbf). Many trains that arrive at Hauptbahnhof also stop at either Zoobahnhof or Ostbahnhof, but the primary transfer point is Hauptbahnhof. There is a tourist information office on the ground floor, open daily 0800–2000. The S-Bahn trains and the city's U-Bahn (subway) connect the two stations. Money exchange is available on the first floor, near the luggage office, open 0800–2200. Train information for all of Berlin: *Tel:* (030) 19419; *Hours:* 0600–2215 daily, directly ahead from the main entrance.

Berlin Hauptbahnhof Station

The train station is centrally located in Berlin, only a few blocks from the Reichstag, the parliament building of Germany, used from 1894 until 1933 and then again since 1999, after its complete reconstruction; it is one of the most visited sites in Berlin.

On the ground floor of the station near the large clock there is the "Service-Point" customer service desk. The helpful personnel there are available 24 hours a day and able to assist with train schedules, hotel or car reservations, and any other questions. The station has a shopping mall attached to the terminal itself, with ATMs, money exchange, rental cars, and numerous other services available.

Berlin Zoo Station

Centrally located in the western sector of Berlin. The majority of the city's hotels, pensions, hostels, restaurants, shopping centers, and entertainment is also in this area.

- **Baggage storage:** Berlin Zoo is not a baggage-cart station, since ramps to the train level are nonexistent and elevators normally are not available for public use. Porters are available by prearrangement, but the best insurance for a no-hassle visit to Germany's capital is to observe the golden rule of rail travelers: Take one medium-size suitcase or two small ones—nothing else.
- **Money exchange:** Available at the Reisebank inside the station, in the arrival hall. *Hours:* 0600–2000 Monday–Saturday and 0800–1900 Sunday. An ATM is available outside the bank.
- **Train information, reservations, and rail pass validation:** As you descend from the trains into the main hall of the Berlin Zoo Station, there's a train information office in the *Reisezentrum* (Travel Center) to the far left. *Hours:* 0600–2200 daily. A rail schedule machine allows you to look up train schedules and receive a printout. Facing the Reisezentrum, you'll find lockers on the left-hand side. Train departure and arrival information is posted on boards above the stairway.

- **A EurAide office** is open daily during summer; closed on Sunday and holidays during the remainder of the year. This office (like the one in Munich) is designed specifically to assist English-speaking travelers.

Berlin Ostbahnhof

Deutsche Bahn AG (DB), or GermanRail, service counter is located in the center of the main hall. The personnel can give schedule information 24 hours a day, seven days a week, but don't count on their speaking English.

- For detailed information and to make reservations, go to the **Reisezentrum** (Travel Center), located on the street level in the main hall next to McDonald's. *Hours:* 0630–2200 daily. Lockers are to the right of the Reisezentrum as you face it.
- **Money exchange:** Facilities can be found on the street level near the coffee shop. *Hours:* 0700–1200 Monday–Friday, 0800–1200 and 1230–1600 Saturday, Sunday, and holidays. There's also an ATM in front of the travel center.

Tourist Information/Hotel Reservations

The city's main tourist information office is located conveniently on the ground floor of the Berlin Hauptbahnhof Station. *Tel:* 030 25 00 25. *Hours:* 0800–2200 daily.

Another tourist information office is located at Brandenburg Gate and offers the same services as the one in the Europa Center. *Address:* South Wing, Pariser Platz, 10117 Berlin Mitte. *Hours:* 0930–1800 daily. Both tourist offices can make hotel reservations.

For those interested in economical hostel-type accommodations, try **David's Cozy Backpackers Hostel,** five minutes from Zoobahnhof Station. *Tel:* from outside Germany 4917663197291; *Tel:* in Berlin (030) 21463156; www.david-berlin.de. It's privately owned, so there are no curfews and you get your own key. Smoke-free indoors. Prices: €11 to €17. Three other economical options are BaxPax Hostel Berlin, Mitte's Backpacker Hostel, and BaxPax Downtown Hostel Hotel. Rooms start at €17 (high season) and €11 (low season) and no curfew. Reservations can be made at www.baxpax.de for all three hostels.

Getting Around in Berlin

One of the first things visitors should do on arrival in Berlin is acquaint themselves with the city's phenomenal fast-train system—the S-Bahn ("S" is for *schnell*—fast) and the U-Bahn (underground train or subway). During rush hours, trains run every 3 to 5 minutes and approximately every 5 to 10 minutes at other times. The S- and U-Bahn systems are augmented by trams and buses. Standard tickets (*Ein-zelfahrschein*) for all forms of Berlin transportation cost €2.30; day ticket, €6.30.

The **Berlin Welcome Card** provides 48 or 72 hours of free travel on all buses and trains operating within the A, B, and C fare zones of the Berlin and Potsdam public transport network (BVG) for only €18.50 (48 hours) or €25.50 (72 hours). Purchase the card at all BVG ticket offices, tourist information offices, and at many Berlin hotels. The card also includes vouchers for discounts of up to 50 percent at more than 120 museums, sightseeing tours, theaters, restaurants, and other attractions.

Sights/Attractions/Tours

Those who are interested in politically relevant sites and buildings can take the **New Capital Tour** to learn more about the Reichstag (Parliament) and Bundeskanzleramt (Federal Chancellery), as well as many other sites worth seeing. Take Bus 85 from Berlin Hauptbahnhoff Station.

City-Circle-Tour has 14 hop-on/hop-off stops at various landmarks around the city and runs every 15 minutes in summer, every 30 minutes in winter. Start your tour at the corner of Rankestrasse and Kurfürstendamm, opposite the Kaiser-Wilhelm Church or at Alexanderplatz across from Hotel Park Inn Berlin-Alexanderplatz. Full-day fare: €20 adults; €10 children (age 7 to 13). If you choose to stay on the bus, the complete tour is two hours. All tours/tickets may be purchased at any of the tourist information centers.

If you happen to be in Berlin in July, ask about special rave tickets and trains for the Love Parade, the largest annual techno rave demonstration. Call the tourist office.

Berlin is such a fascinating, pulsating metropolis full of attractions, nonstop activities, and events that we can list but a few here. Don't miss a walk on Berlin's shopping and entertainment streets—**Kurfürstendamm** and **Friedrichstrasse.** Stop at No. 207–208 Kurfürstendamm for a journey through "A Story of Berlin," a multimedia presentation documenting the city's 800 years of history.

The **Friedrichstadtpalast** is Europe's largest light-entertainment theater that features gala performances, artistic displays, dancers and solo singers, and a live orchestra. The **Berlin Zoo** is one of the finest in Europe, and there's no better place to relax than in the attractive **English Gardens,** dedicated by Sir Anthony Eden. Berliners call it the "Garden of Eden."

The dome of the **Reichstag** has become one of the main attractions. At 23.5 meters high and 40 meters wide, it proudly stands in solitary splendor over the renovated Reichstag, which inaugurated the German Bundestag in April 1999. Climb to the top for an enjoyable view of the city.

Train Connections to Other Base Cities from Berlin

Many trains make stops at several Berlin train stations on arrival and departure from the city. The primary station used other than Berlin Zoobahnhof was the rebuilt Berlin Ostbahnhof that was named Berlin Hauptbahnhof by the German Democratic Republic government. After its reopening in 1998, the name reverted to the one used before 1945. Other stations used are Berlin Wannsee, Berlin Spandau, Berlin Lichtenberg, and Berlin Schönefeld. On May 26, 2006, a new station opened as the primary station in Berlin, again called Berlin Hauptbahnhof.

Depart Berlin Main (Hauptbahnhof) unless otherwise noted.

DEPART	TRAIN NUMBER	ARRIVE	NOTES
		Amsterdam Zuid	
0834	IC 148	1515	
1234	IC 144	1915	
1634	IC 140	2315	
		Brussels (Bruxelles) Midi/Zuid	
0652	ICE 654	1335	R, 1
0834	ICE 148	1708	R, 1, Exc. Su
1052	ICE 650	1735	R, 1
1349	ICE 858	2032	R, 1
1452	ICE 556	2135	R, 1
		Budapest Keleti	
0658	EC 171	1835	
1100	EC 379	2235	
1859	EN 477	0837+1	R, Sleeper
		Copenhagen (København) H.	
0506	ICE 1978	1222	R, 2, M–F
1039	ICE 1616	1822	R, 2
1307	ICE 176	2022	R, 2
		Hamburg Hauptbahnhof	
0526	ICE 1108	0724	M–F
0706	ICE 2070	0910	
0839	ICE 806	1021	
0942	ICE 906	1124	
and continuing service (ICE, EC, and IC trains) at about 1 hr intervals until 2245.			
		Luxembourg	
0652	ICE 654	1529	1, Exc. Su
2316	CNL 40458	1129+1	R, 2, Sleeper, Exc. Sa
		Munich (München) Hauptbahnhof	
0627	ICE 1505	1243	
0730	ICE 1005	1416	
1027	ICE 1589	1639	
1227	ICE 209	1841	
1428	ICE 1683	2105	

DEPART	TRAIN NUMBER	ARRIVE	NOTES
1627	ICE 1685	2250	
1949	ICE 842	0710+1	R, Sleeper
		Paris Gare du Nord	
0652	ICE 654	1605	1
1149	ICE 950	2005	1
1349	ICE 858	2205	1
2109	EN 452	1006+1	R, Sleeper, Exc. Sa
		Prague (Praha)	
0658	EC 171	1128	
0900	EC 173	1328	
1300	EC 175	1728	
1500	EC 177	1928	
1814	EN 60477	2378	
		Stockholm Central	
1928	D 300	1339+1	R, 3, Sleeper
		Warsaw Centralna	
0637	EC 41	1215	M–Sa
0937	EC 43	1515	
1237	EC 45	1815	
1637	EC 47	2205	Exc. Sa
		Vienna (Wien) Hauptbahnhof	
0903	EC 173	1851	
1300	EC 175	2251	
1814	EN 477	0702+1	R, Sleeper
		Zürich Hauptbahnhof	
0631	ICE 277	1500	4, Exc. Su
1035	ICE 371	1900	4
1231	ICE 373	2100	4
1431	ICE 375	2300	4
2150	CNL 471	0905+1	R, Sleeper

Daily, unless otherwise noted
R Reservations required
+1 Arrive next day
1. Change trains in Cologne (Köln).
2. Change trains in Hamburg.
3. Change trains in Malmö.
4. Change trains in Basel.

Berliners claim they have more museums than they have rainy days. You can obtain a three-day **Museum Pass** for €24 from the tourist information points in the Europa Center and at Brandenburg Gate. It provides entry to more than 50 museums and collections for three consecutive days. There are more than 170 museums housing collections of art, original artifacts, and other intriguing creations. Following Germany's reunification, the state museums were restored and new ones built, including the **Vitra Design Museum** and the **Jewish Museum.** The **Gemäldegalerie** reunited an internationally renowned collection of more than 1,300 paintings from the 13th to the 18th centuries that had been separated since the end of World War II. Part of the collection went to the United States and part to Russia. The **Old National Gallery** reopened as well. At some point during your visit, stand at the **Brandenburg Gate**—on either side—and feel democracy in action. Or take Europe's fastest lift up 90 meters to the platform on the **Kollhoff Tower** (formerly the **Daimler Chrysler Building**) for a spectacular panoramic view of this great city. Admission: €6.50. *Hours:* 1100–2000 daily.

Day Excursions from Berlin

Three day excursions have been selected. All of them—Dresden, Leipzig, and Potsdam—are typical German cities in their own right. Since the end of World War II, and until the "Fall of the Wall," they had been a part of the then German Democratic Republic, more often referred to as "East Germany." Consequently, tourist and transportation facilities are still being improved.

Dresden is an important city in the historic German state of Saxony and probably best known for its product Dresden china. **Leipzig** is also a part of Saxony and owes much of its prestige to its cultural accomplishments. **Potsdam** owes its appeal to Frederick the Great, who took the concept of *sans souci* (without care or worry) and transformed it into the reality of the delightful Sans Souci Palace. It was also the scene of the Potsdam Conference in 1945, where Harry (Truman) met "Old Joe" (Stalin) and got to like him—at least for a little while.

Day Excursion to

Dresden

China, Carillons, and Culture

Depart from Berlin Hauptbahnhof
Distance by Train: 117 miles (189 km)
Average Train Time: 2 hours, 30 minutes
City Dialing Code: 351
Tourist Information Office: Dresden Tourist Board, Prager Strasse 2b 01069 Dresden
Tel: (351) 501 501; **Fax:** (351) 501 509
www.dresden-tourist.de or **www.dresden.de**
E-mail: info@dresden.information.de
Hours: 1000–1900 Monday–Friday, 1000–1800 Saturday, and 1000–1500 Sunday
Notes: In the summer the center is open for longer hours. A five-minute walk on Prager Strasse, across the street from the rail station, will take you there.

Dresden's name is derived from *Drezdzane*, the old Slavic word for "forest people," who were the early settlers in the area. Dresden is situated in the wide, gentle valley of the Elbe River, about 19 miles (30 kilometers) from the northwest border of the Czech Republic. Although the city's fame comes mainly from its past cultural achievements, Dresden is also economically important and is best known for its Dresden china.

From its beginnings as a small Slavonic fishing village, Dresden developed a delightfully harmonious relationship with the river and the forest. As it grew, its scenic beauty was enhanced in the 17th and 19th centuries by builders who erected fine examples of Baroque and Rococo architecture. This, in turn, attracted a great number of artists and writers as Dresden grew into a modern, confident city of half a million citizens. With its architectural landmarks and its art treasures of Dutch, Flemish, and Italian collections, Dresden gained the well-deserved title "Florence of the Elbe."

On February 13, 1945, more than a half-million bombs rained down on Dresden from Anglo-American aircraft. Thirty-five thousand citizens died, and more than 15 square miles of the inner city were reduced to rubble. The air raid devastated nearly all of the city's cultural monuments. Dresden was declared dead. But Dresden is rising like a phoenix. Dust from the air raid scarcely settled before restoration began on the **Semper Opera House.** Forty years to the day, on February 13, 1985, Dresden's population celebrated the reopening of this world-famous theater, and many other cultural and historic edifices have been rebuilt.

Dresden's ***Altmarkt*** (old market) is the historic center of the city, which was rebuilt between 1953 and 1956. The city's botanical gardens, completely destroyed in 1945, were rebuilt in 1950. Only nine zoo animals survived the air attack, but

Berlin—Dresden

DEPART Berlin Hauptbahnof	TRAIN NUMBER	ARRIVE Dresden Hauptbahnof
0658	EC 171	0856
0900	EC 173	1056
1100	EC 379	1256
1300	EC 175	1458
1500	EC 177	1658

DEPART Dresden Hauptbahnof	TRAIN NUMBER	ARRIVE Berlin Hauptbahnof
1254	EC 174	1458
1456	EC 378	1658
1654	EC 172	1858
1854	EC 170	2058

Daily
All trains also stop at Dresden Neustadt
Distance: 117 miles (189 km)

in 1961 the zoo reopened with a stock of more than 2,000 animals representing nearly 500 species.

With typical Dresden determination, on February 13, 1992, the city announced that the **Frauenkirche** (Church of Our Lady)—decreed by the communists to stand in ruins forever—would be rebuilt. The church's dome dominates the scene. The Frauenkirche is the largest German Baroque and Protestant church and also the world's largest centrally planned Protestant church. After undergoing massive archaeological reconstruction, the church is now one of the most spectacular, and most visited, tourist spots in Dresden. Open Monday–Friday, 1000–1200 and 1300–1800, no charge for entry. The church's reconstruction site is near the **Albertinum Museum** at Brühlsche Terrace. The Albertinum houses the New Masters Picture Gallery, the "Green Vault," treasure chamber, and numismatic and sculpture collections. *Hours:* 1000–1800 Tuesday–Sunday. Admission €10.

Beginning with a group of only 55 dedicated members, the Society to Promote the Rebuilding of the Frauenkirche now numbers more than 5,000 members in Germany, with active supporters from more than 20 other countries. Out of the ruins long seen solely as an admonition against war, the Frauenkirche is rising again as beautiful as ever—a symbol of the healing of war's wounds, with a resounding message of a strong desire for peace.

Obtain the *Tourist City Guide* from the tourist office. It contains a city map, places of interest, sightseeing tours, and just about everything you might ever want to know about Dresden. The **Old Town** is on the left bank of the Elbe, and the **New Town** is across the river on its right bank. If you are an average sightseer, as we are, you can reach the Old Town area on foot from the city center in no more than 15 minutes.

Ask about the **Dresden Card** (€29.90; valid for 48 hours), which provides for free transportation on all tram and bus lines plus ferries on the Elbe, free entrance to many museums, and discounts on city tours. In typical German fashion, the city's ***Rathaus*** (town hall) has a ***Ratskeller*** (restaurant) in its cellar, where you may enjoy a cold draft and a sample of Saxon food before setting out to see Dresden.

One of the many magnificent edifices vying for your attention during your Dresden visit is the **Zwinger.** It is known as the most important Late Baroque building in Germany. The name "Zwinger" is a term used in the construction of fortresses and defines the space between the outer and inner ramparts. Heavily damaged in 1945, the Zwinger reconstruction was said to have begun "instantaneously" despite communist objections. It was restored to its current condition by 1963.

If you cross the Elbe, be sure to use Dresden's famous **Loschwitzer–Blasewitzer Bridge.** Opened in 1893, it was the only bridge to remain intact by 1945. The complex WWII German political and military organization known as the SS had the bridge set for destruction, but two Dresdeners, each unaware of the other's action, cut the wire to the explosives. The grateful populace of Dresden now refers to the bridge as the "Blue Miracle."

Day Excursion to

Leipzig

Bach and Mendelssohn Memories

Depart from Berlin Hauptbahnhof
Distance by Train: 113 miles (182 km)
Average Train Time: 2 hours
City Dialing Code: 341
Tourist Information Office: Katharinenstrasse 8, D–04109 Leipzig
Tel: (341) 710 4260; **Fax:** (341) 710 4271
www.leipzig.de
E-mail: info@ltm-leipzig.de
Hours: 0930–1800 Monday–Friday (1000–1800 November–February), 0930–1600 Saturday, 0930–1500 Sunday
Notes: The tourist office is 2 blocks out the front of the train station, directly across from the Art Museum—a five-minute walk.

Like many cities and towns in Europe, Leipzig has an old and a new section. Leipzig's old town is located between three rivers: the Parthe, the Elster, and the Pleisse. No doubt the site selection had much to do with safety, and the proximity to three navigable rivers also indicates an early interest in trade. Leipzig has been known for its great trade fairs that date from the Middle Ages and still attract businesspeople from all over the world.

The city's name is derived from Lipsk, the original Slav settlement named for the lime trees (*lipa*) growing there. Leipzig was built as a walled city in the 11th century; the walls surrounding the old town were replaced in the 18th century by a ring of parks and promenades. Subsequently, Leipzig expanded in all directions by gradually incorporating the suburbs that were growing up around it—a tactic followed by many American cities.

Reconstructed from 1996 to 1998, Leipzig's main rail terminal (Hauptbahnhof) has 23 platforms (plus 4 outside platforms) and is the largest rail terminal in Europe. The three-level station houses restaurants, shops, cafes, meeting rooms, travel agencies, money exchange, and other tourist facilities. More than 800 trains move through the terminus daily, carrying an estimated 75,000 passengers. There's no need to worry about navigating its size, since the Hauptbahnhof comes well equipped with pictographs.

The **Leipzig Card** provides transport on trams and buses and on the city railway to the **New Trade-Fair Centre.** There are also reductions on city tours, museums, concerts, Bach Festival tickets, and in selected restaurants. There are three types: one-day €9.90 (one person); three-day €19.90 (one person); three-day group €37.90 (two adults + up to three children younger than age 15). Purchase at the tourist office, rail station, and many hotels, or order online.

Berlin—Leipzig

DEPART Berlin Hauptbahnof	TRAIN NUMBER	ARRIVE Leipzig Hauptbahnof
0627	ICE 1505	0743
0827	ICE 1207	0943
1027	ICE 1509	1143
1227	ICE 209	1343

DEPART Leipzig Hauptbahnof	TRAIN NUMBER	ARRIVE Berlin Hauptbahnof
1615	ICE 1508	1733
1851	ICE 1506	1933
2015	ICE 1504	2133
2215	ICE 1582	2333

Daily
Distance: 113 miles (182 km)

The main attraction on the old town's market square is the **old town hall.** It was built in the record time of nine months in 1556 by Hieronymus Lotter. The building is one of the oldest Renaissance town halls still standing on German soil. Although severely damaged by fire during the Allied air raid on December 4, 1943, the building's facade remains almost unchanged from the 16th century. The city was governed from here until 1905, when a new town hall was erected in a more spacious area. Since 1909 the building has been the **Museum of History of the City of Leipzig.** Its attractions include the Old Council Chambers and special exhibits.

The new town hall, built between 1899 and 1905 on the foundations of earlier buildings, will also attract your attention with its 115-meter tower. It houses both the mayor and the city council.

Within the rim of the old town, the spires of the **Church of Saint Nicholas** (Nikolaikirche) and the **Church of Saint Thomas** (Thomaskirche) stand as sentinels over the scene. The first mention of Saint Nicholas was made in 1017; Saint Thomas was erected between 1212 and 1222 as the collegiate church of the Augustinian Choir. Its Late Gothic hall was added at the end of the 15th century.

The stained-glass windows of Saint Thomas, dating from the end of the 19th century, depict four historical personalities closely associated with Leipzig: Johann Sebastian Bach, Felix Mendelssohn Bartholdy, Martin Luther, and King Gustav Adolf II of Sweden. Saint Thomas became world famous from its association with Johann Sebastian Bach. The composer served as cantor of the church from 1723 to 1750. Since 1950, the remains of the great composer have lain in the church. For more information about the four-day Leipzig Bach Festival (in June), contact Bach-Archiv Leipzig, Thomaskirchof 16, PF 101349, D-04013 Leipzig; *Tel:* 49 341 9137 0 or *E-mail:* info@bach-leipzig.de, www.bach-leipzig.de. Contact the tourist office for a highlights list of other events in Leipzig.

The Church of Saint Nicholas, although containing some of the oldest building remains in Leipzig, recently played an important part in the reunification of Germany. From 1982, the prayers for peace held every Monday under the sheltering roof of the church "transmitted" loud and clear signals to the Leipzig demonstrators—impulses that, during the days of October and November 1989, brought about the "gentle revolution" that led to the downfall of the communist dictatorship.

Music lovers also will not want to miss the **Mendelssohn House,** where the innovative composer Felix Mendelssohn Bartholdy lived and died. The Mendelssohn House has been restored to its original grandeur. Visit www.mendelssohn-haus.de.

Outside Leipzig's old town you can visit the **Leipzig Zoo,** which was founded in 1878. Visit www.zoo-leipzig.de. The city information center will tell you it's "only a 15-minute walk," but perhaps a taxi would be better. Opened in 2011 is a tropical "Gondwanaland" area, with over 540 plant and animal species, and an option to tour the area by boat. It includes a jungle landscape, tropical hall, and a research camp for chimpanzees, gorillas, and orangutans. The zoo is noted for its lions and tigers, including the breeding of some 2,500 purebred Berber lions. An unusual feature of the zoo is its "shop-window," whereby spectators are separated from the animals only by a moat—a *deep* moat.

From the rubble left at the end of World War II, the city constructed a stadium seating 100,000 spectators. The stadium was the first major building project in Leipzig following the war. Three million cubic meters of rubble were used for the 23-meter-high terraces. The stadium has been modernized to hold 45,000 covered seats, and is now one of the premier soccer stadiums in Germany.

Day Excursion to

Potsdam

Where Harry Met Joe

Depart from Berlin Hauptbahnhof or Wannsee Station, or use S-Bahn
Distance by Train: 22 miles (36 km)
Average Train Time: 26 minutes
City Dialing Code: 331
Tourist Information Office: Inside the station (next to platform 6), Babelsberger Strasse 16, 14467 Potsdam
Tel: (0331) 27–8899; **Fax:** (0331) 275–5829
www.potsdam.de or **www.potsdam-tourism.com**
E-mail: tourismus-service@potsdam.de
Hours: April–October: 0930–2000 Monday–Saturday; November–March: 0930–1800 Monday–Saturday, 1000–1600 Sunday year-round
Notes: The office is located in the old market, a 5- to 10-minute walk from the railway station. Turn right out of the station and walk across the Lange Brucke (Long Bridge) and up the Friedrich-Ebert-Strasse to the center, which is located on the right side of the street. Ask for the illustrated pamphlet Info—*Stadtplan Potsdam.*

Originally a small settlement of Slavs, Potsdam first appeared in German chronicles under the name *Poztupimi* (Under the Oak Trees) in a Deed of Gift dated July 3, 993. There are virtually no oak trees left in present-day Potsdam, but from days gone by you will find a large number of handsome oak mansions and palaces surrounded by beautiful parks.

After a period of almost total insignificance during the Middle Ages, Potsdam eventually entered the sphere of German history in the 17th century when Frederick William, the Elector of Brandenburg, decided to make Potsdam his place of residence.

In the 18th century, during the reigns of King Frederick William I and his son Frederick II, known as Frederick the Great, Potsdam grew to be a prestigious royal seat and garrison town. Frederick William I established a military orphanage where the boys "learned to work" in nearby factories and also drilled in "square bashing," which came in handy whenever the impoverished peasants could no longer stand their plight and chose to demonstrate in the town square.

Unlike many towns emerging from the Middle Ages, Potsdam was not surrounded by a wall until the 18th century. Oddly enough, the wall served not so much as a military protection as it did a device to prevent soldiers from deserting and dishonest folks from smuggling. Whether the wall contributed to the growth of the town is not known, but Potsdam did flourish under the Fredericks. The *Alten Markt* (old market), the *Hollandisches Viertel* (Dutch quarters), the Brandenburger Strasse, and the **Sans Souci Park and Palace** date from the era of their reign.

Frederick II was growing a bit "long in the tooth" and decided he wanted to live "without cares" (*sans souci*). So, beginning in 1744 and during the following three decades, "Old Fritz" supervised the building of the palace and several other buildings, including his own tomb as a last resting place beside the palace.

The Rococo Sans Souci Palace was built from sketches by the king himself, together with designs by his architect, Knobelsdorff. With further additions made during the 19th century, Sans Souci stands today on a 717-acre complex as one of the largest and most significant parks in Europe.

But "Old Fritz" would not rest. After the Seven Years' War, in which he lost all the battles but won the war, he celebrated his "victory" by building another palace—the **Neues Palais** (New Palace).

The Potsdam Information Center conducts a bus tour from April through October that includes a tour of the **Sans Souci Palace** and its gardens. The tour (3½ hours) leaves the center at 1100. Cost: €27. Open year-round and closed Monday.

If you like palaces, you've come to the right place. **Charlottenhof Palace,** a part of the Sans Souci complex, comes complete with Roman baths. The baths, by the way, were not intended for the purpose of hygiene but formed a part of a museum-like dream world reflecting the romantic yearnings of Crown Prince Frederick William (Fat William).

The **Marble Palace** and the **New Garden**—called "new" in contrast with the "old" gardens at Sans Souci—were ordered built by "Fat William" when he was crowned in 1786. *Hours:* March–October: 1000–1800 daily; November–February: 1000–1700 weekends only. Guided tours are €8; self-guided visits are €3. *Tel:* (0331) 969 4200 for more information; www.spsg.de.

Potsdam's **old town** is a great place to browse. Right in the center of it you feel as though you've been transferred to Holland. To attract Dutch craftsmen to Potsdam, more than 100 middle-class Dutch Baroque–style houses were built between 1734 and 1742. The project failed in that it did not attract Dutchmen in the number expected, but the houses were inhabited, in turn, by Potsdam's craftsmen, artists, and military. Sometimes things just don't work out the way you want them to. Perhaps that is Potsdam's penchant—read on.

The son of Kaiser Wilhelm, Crown Prince William, built a second palace at the New Garden from 1913 to 1915. He named it **Cecilienhof** after his Crown Princess. Unlike his father, who never returned from his Dutch exile, the ex–Crown Prince did

Berlin—Potsdam

Berlin S-Bahn trains run frequently between many Berlin stations and Potsdam—4 or 5 trains each hour all day. In addition, Potsdam is a stop for many Deutsche Bahn mainline trains between Berlin and cities to the west—typically 3 or 4 trains each hour in both directions run from Berlin Zoobahnhof and from Berlin Hauptbahnhof (some also stop at Berlin Wannsee Station). Journey time from/to Berlin Hauptbahnhof is about 25 minutes, from/to Berlin Zoobahnhof about 20 minutes, and from/to Berlin Wannsee about 8 minutes.

Distance: 22 miles (36 km)

move back into Cecilienhof Palace in 1923 and stayed there until 1945, bringing a number of interesting guests.

From July 17 until August 2, 1945, Cecilienhof played host to the Potsdam Conference, the third and final meeting of Churchill, Stalin, and Truman. One of the conference aims was the unity of Germany, though what followed was actually its division. Harry Truman returned from the conference stating that he "liked old Joe." But just like the time when Harry met Sally, things didn't quite work out the way they wanted them to.

Base City: **HAMBURG**

www.hamburg-tourism.de
E-mail: info@hamburg-tourism.de
City Dialing Code: 040

The Free and Hanseatic City of Hamburg is an impressive title—for an equally impressive city. Its 1.7 million residents are proud of their city and are eager to show it. Hamburg is the largest in a league of "Hansa" cities in Germany that medieval merchants organized to secure greater safety and privileges in trading. For a long time nobility was barred from entering this affluent city, which sits poised between the Elbe River and Alster Lake.

Hamburg is full of surprises. It has more bridges than the combined total of Amsterdam and Venice. The city's harbor is one of the leading ports in Europe and ranks as one of the top 10 largest ports in the world—notwithstanding the fact that it is 68 miles inland from the North Sea!

Chartered in 1189, Hamburg occupies a 288-square-mile area, 20 percent of which is covered by water. To the delight of residents and visitors alike, about 10 percent of the city's total area has been landscaped into public parks. Many of these areas date from the 18th century, when landscaping was fostered by the city's wealthy residents as one of the arts.

Hamburgians have their port to thank for the development of their city to its current stature—an expansive metropolis of international business and culture. During the first weekend of May, the Hamburgians begin a three-day celebration to commemorate the year 1189, when Emperor Frederick Barbarossa granted Hamburg its "free port" status. The term free port means that transit cargo is exempt from custom duties. Not all of the harbor area, however, is classified as a free port.

Arriving by Air

Hamburg International Airport, 8 miles north of the city center at Fuhlsbüttel. Hamburg Airport officially opened its new facilities in 2005 with two state-of-the-art terminals.

Terminal 2 serves all Deutsche Lufthansa, Condor, and Star Alliance flights, including SAS, LOT, and their partner airlines. Terminal 1 handles all other airlines and charter flights. Airport information: *Tel:* (040) 5075-0; www.ham.airport.de. Tourist information is available in the arrivals area, Terminal 2.

Airport–City Links: Airport-Express busline 39 between the airport (Terminal 2) and Ohlsdorf U-Bahn station where frequent train service into Hamburg is available. Arrivals/departures every 10 minutes. If you are burdened with baggage, use the bus, Route S1; departures every 20 minutes, 0444 to 2344, for Hamburg's Hauptbahnhof (main rail station). Journey time: 25 to 30 minutes. Fare: €2.85. From city center to airport, service 0440 to 2020 every 15 minutes. Taxi stands in front of Terminals 1 and 4 (*Tel:* [040] 66 66 66, [040] 21 12 11, [040] 22 11 22); follow the pictographs. Average taxi fare to the city center, €20.

- **Money exchange: Reisebank:** Terminal 2, Level 0. *Hours:* 0900–2100 daily. Travelex: Terminal 2, Level 1. *Hours:* 0600–2100 daily. ATMs are available in Terminal 2, Level 0 and Terminal 1.

Arriving by Train

The Hamburg **Hauptbahnhof** (main rail station) appears as though it was constructed to handle the dirigible *Hindenburg*. Its immensity is impressive. There are 14 Gleise (tracks). Gleise 1 to 4 serve the S-Bahn, the suburban rail service; Gleise 5 to 14 are for regular train service. Most InterCity Express (ICE) trains glide in and out of the Hauptbahnhof on Gleise 13 and 14.

For a full-service restaurant, visit the InterCity Restaurant, accessible by elevator, on the station's second-floor front. The Gourmet Station on the main floor features national and international dishes. It's informal.

- **Baggage storage** carts are scarce. The baggage room is the best source for a cart or a porter.
- **Money exchange** hours: 0800–2200 daily.
- **Post office** hours: 0800–1800 Monday–Friday and 0800–1230 Saturday.
- **International telephones** are on the second floor of the post office.
- **Train information** is in the *Reisezentrum* (Travel Center) and is open 24 hours.
- **Rail passes** can be validated at window 20 or any window marked AUSLAND. Information windows are 21 to 24. If the attendant does not speak English, you will be referred to one who does.
- **Tourist office** in the main rail station open daily, 0800 to 2200 daily. *Tel:* 300 51 201 or 202.

Train Connections to Other Base Cities from Hamburg

Depart from Hamburg Hauptbahnhof, unless otherwise noted.

DEPART	TRAIN NUMBER	ARRIVE	NOTES
		Amsterdam Centraal	
0946	IC 1025	1500	1
1546	ICE 1029	2100	1
		Berlin Hauptbahnhof	
0648	ICE 173	0848	
0851	ICE 379	1055	
1051	ICE 809	1254	
and continuing hourly service until 2151.			
		Bern (Berne)	
0824	ICE 73	1556	3, Exc. Su
2029	CNL 479	0724+1	R, 3, Sleeper
		Brussels (Bruxelles) Midi/Zuid	
0746	IC 2023	1432	4
1046	IC 2217	1735	4
1346	ICE 2229	2032	4
1446	IC 2213	2135	4
		Budapest Keleti	
0648	EC 173	2035	
2052	EN 491	1119+1	R, 5, Sleeper
		Copenhagen (København) H.	
0724	EC 31	1222	
0928	ICE 33	1422	
1328	ICE 35	1822	
1728	ICE 39	2222	
		Milan (Milano) Centrale	
1024	ICE 75	2137	3
2029	CNL 479	1037+1	R, 3, Sleeper
		Munich (München) Hauptbahnhof	
0701	ICE 583	1239	
0901	ICE 585	1439	Exc. Sa
1001	ICE 787	1541	
and continuing ICE service at hourly intervals until 1901, then			
2246	IC 2021	0807+1	R, Sleeper, 4
		Paris Gare du Nord	
0746	IC 2023	1605	R, 4
1046	IC 2217	1935	R, 4
1346	ICE 2229	2205	R, 4

DEPART	TRAIN NUMBER	ARRIVE	NOTES
		Prague (Praha)	
0648	EC 173	1328	
0851	EC 379	1528	
1451	EC 179	2128	
		Rome (Roma) Termini	
1401	ICE 881	0922+1	R, 7, Sleeper
2001	CNL 479	1356+1	R, 6, Sleeper, M–F
		Stockholm Central	
0724	EC 31	1739	R, 2
0928	EC 33	2039	R, 2
1128	EC 1233	2339	R, 2, Exc. Sa
		Vienna (Wien) Südbahnhof	
0803	ICE 91	1709	R
2052	EN 491	0816+1	R, Sleeper
		Warsaw Centralna	
0738	ICE 703	1515	8
1436	ICE 1516	2205	R, 8, Exc. Sa
		Zürich Hauptbahnhof	
0824	ICE 73	1600	Exc. Su
1024	ICE 75	1800	
1224	ICE 77	2000	
1424	ICE 79	2200	
2024	CNL 479	0805+1	R, Sleeper

Daily, unless otherwise noted
R Reservations required
+1 Arrives next day
1. Change trains in Osnabrück.
2. Change trains in Copenhagen.
3. Change trains in Basel.
4. Change trains in Cologne (Köln).
5. Change trains in Vienna (Wien) Westbahnhof.
6. Change trains in Basel then Milan.
7. Change trains in Munich (München).
8. Change trains in Berlin.

Tourist Information/Hotel Reservations

- The *Hamburg Tourist Board* has an information office in the main rail station; exit Kirchenallee. *Hours:* 0800–2200 daily. For advance planning contact: Hamburg Tourist Board, Steinstrasse 7, 20095 Hamburg, Germany; *Tel:* from outside Germany, +49 (40) 3005 1300; *Fax:* +49 (40) 3005 1333; *E-mail:* info@hamburgtourism.de.

- Hotline for **hotel reservations** (0900 to 1900): (040) 3005 1300; or use the Internet hotel booking service: www.hamburgtourism.de.

In addition to general information, the board's information service can provide accommodation bookings; bookings for port tours and Alster cruises; arrangements for guides; and tips on sightseeing, dining, and shopping.

Getting Around in Hamburg

Purchase a **Hamburg-CARD** at tourist information offices, from U-Bahn (metro) station vending machines, and at most hotels. The CARD is a real bargain. It entitles you to travel free on the city's bus and train systems, subways, and port ferries at any time within the card's period of validity. It also provides unlimited admission to 11 museums and includes reductions up to 30 percent for such activities as the Alster tour, the Port tour, and the entrance fee to Hamburg's famous Hagenbucks Zoo.

The Hamburg-CARD is available as a daily card (€9.50 for one adult and up to three children younger than age 15, or €15.50 for up to five persons), a three-day card (€22.90 for one adult and three children or €39.90 for up to five persons), or a five-day card (€38.50 single, €64.90 group). The tourist information office will provide you with a brochure, *City Map and Tips from A to Z,* which explains the card's features.

Sights/Attractions/Tours—Hamburg Highlights

A tour of the harbor by launch is available year-round. (The launches are heated in winter.) In summer the tour operates every half hour from 0900 to 1800; for winter tours contact the tourist information office. The launches sail from St. Pauli pier. From the Hauptbahnhof, take either the U-Bahn line U3, or S-Bahn lines S1 or S3 to the Landungsbrücken station. Tickets: €9.50 adults; €6.00 children. Hamburg-CARD holders pay reduced rates. The tour takes about one hour. Ask for a launch with an English-speaking captain.

From April through October, leisure cruise boats depart from the quay at Jungfernstieg—Hamburg's elegant shopping street—to **cruise on Lake Alster.** Actually, the Alster is not really a lake. It is a tributary of the Elbe River that has been widened into a lake just before it flows into the Elbe River. This 460-acre lake, an area larger than the entire principality of Monaco, was created when the Alster was dammed in the early 13th century.

There is a wide selection of tours available on the Alster boats, including a one-hour trip along its shoreline, a tour of the city's canal system, a bridge tour where you'll see a sampling of the city's 2,400 bridges, and a twilight tour. A guided tour of the **Inner and Outer Alster** operates every half hour, 1000 to 1800; tour duration, about 50 minutes. Tickets: €12.00 adults, €6.00 children; Hamburg-CARD holders receive a discount. Even in winter the Alster boats cruise the lake for the popular "punch" cruises. To inquire, visit the **Alster-Touristik office** on the quay where the boats depart (*Tel:* 357 4240). Brochures are also available in all of the Hamburg tourist offices.

Take a ride on the **Hamburger Hummelbahn.** Hamburg-CARD holders get a substantial discount. *Hummel* is German for "bumble bee," and this amazing form of transportation literally "buzzes" all over town. The train does not run on tracks. Its open platforms are ideal for photographing. It's a fun trip.

Prefer a frightening one? Visit 2,000 years of terror and pain at the **Hamburg Dungeon** (€23.95 adults; €19 children younger than age 14. Children must be accompanied by an adult, and it might be better to not bring them at all. Perhaps a gruesome souvenir would suffice instead). *Hours:* 1000–1800 daily. *Tel:* (040) 3600 5520; www.thedungeons.com/hamburg. (€5 discount by ordering online.)

If you are in Hamburg on a Sunday, reserve a good part of the day for a visit to the **Fischmarkt** (fish market). Dating from about 1703, it is the oldest licensed market in Hamburg. Fish? Well, fish have become incidental to the market's activities; freshly caught fish, however, are still sold any day of the week from fishing boats at the city's pier.

On Sunday mornings, the pubs scattered around the fish market area draw crowds of early risers and late-night revelers alike. Take in the Sunday-morning auction activities held in the **Fischauktionshalle** (fish auction hall). The auction hall opens promptly at 0500 (0700 in winter) and lasts only until 1000, so hurry. Following the auction, treat yourself to a jazz breakfast right in the Fischauktionshalle.

Shopping is an international pastime, and Hamburg is a wonderful place to pursue such interests. No city on the Continent has so many covered shopping arcades. As a jumping-off place, start at the **Jungfernstieg,** where the white ferries depart for water tours of the Alster Lake. Here, you will find covered arcades where shoppers may stroll regardless of the weather. For big department-store shopping, head for **Monckebergstrasse,** directly east from the **Rathaus,** Hamburg's city hall. Or get off to a flying start right after arriving by train in Hamburg at the **Wandelhalle,** the covered mall above the train platforms in the Hauptbahnhof.

A unique memory will be a visit to the **Speicherstadt,** built in the late 19th century. This historic warehouse complex was built during the growth of the free port and served as storehouses along the crisscrossing canals of the day. Hamburg abounds in museums. Two museum ships are the ***Rickmer Rickmers,*** a reminder of bygone days when sailing ships ruled the waves, and the ***Cap San Diego,*** the "White Swan of the South Atlantic." Both offer discounts to Hamburg-CARD holders and are open daily starting at 1000.

At night, **St. Pauli,** the entertainment district, offers numerous pubs, restaurants, and discos along the (in)famous **Reeperbahn, Hans-Albers-Platz,** and **Grosse Freiheit.** Yes, this is the area the beer (St. Pauli Girl) is named after.

Day Excursions

Hamburg is situated in the center of a vast railway network. Consequently, the availability of day-excursion opportunities is virtually limitless.

Bremen, another great Hanseatic city of Germany, is quite a contrast to Hamburg, although jointly the two provide the largest operation of seaports within Germany today.

To the south of Hamburg, in the midst of the Weser Hills, stands the fascinating town of **Hameln,** where the tale of the legendary Pied Piper is reenacted every Sunday.

Ride the pride of the German fleet—the German ICE (InterCity Express)—to **Hannover** for a rewarding day of sightseeing amid the city's beautiful parks and gardens.

Lübeck is Germany's largest Hanseatic port on the Baltic and one of the oldest and most beautiful towns in Germany today. Go early and enjoy!

Day Excursion to

Bremen

And the Town Musicians

Depart from Hamburg Hauptbahnhof
Distance by Train: 76 miles (120 km)
Average Train Time: 55 minutes
City Dialing Code: 421
Tourist Information Office: Langenstrasse 2-4 28195 Bremen
Tel: (0421) 30 800–10; **Fax:** (0421) 30 800–30
www.bremen-tourismus.de
E-mail: info@bremen-tourism.de
Hours: 1000–1830 Monday–Saturday, 1000–1600 Sunday
Notes: A tourist information office is at the railway station. *Hours:* 0900–1900 Monday–Friday, 0930–1700 Saturday–Sunday

---

Bremen is Germany's oldest maritime city. Bremen got its start as a port city in the 10th century when Emperor Otto I approved the construction of its docks. It lies on the Weser River, 44 miles upstream from the mouth. Bremen is the second-largest port in Germany. With so much to see and do in Bremen, rail travelers visiting Bremen for the first time may want to confine their sightseeing to the area in and around the city's market square, then follow up with a second visit to the city's extensive harbor facilities. Certainly the charm of the market and its immediate surroundings will beckon the traveler to return again.

Finding your way from the Bremen railway station to the **market square** is an easy task. Attendants there can give you a considerable amount of information regarding Bremen. Particularly informative is a free brochure entitled *Bremen, Everything at a Glance*. The brochure contains background information on all aspects of Bremen.

Hamburg—Bremen

IC trains depart Hamburg Hauptbahnhof hourly at 46 minutes past the hour from 0746; journey time to Bremen Hbf is 56 minutes, last train at 2246.

Trains depart Bremen Hbf hourly at 18 minutes past the hour until 2218; then 2319; journey time is 54 minutes.

Distance: 76 miles (120 km)

The most direct route to the market square is down **Bahnhofstrasse,** which begins in front of the station. Proceed to where it intersects with Sogestrasse and crosses a former moat. A landmark at this point is a large windmill, seen in the distance on the right when crossing the bridge. Proceeding 2 blocks straight ahead on Sogestrasse brings you to the threshold of the old city center. A short walk through a shopping area and you are in the market square, where the **cathedral,** the **Rathaus** (city hall), and the **Liebfrauenkirche** are all clustered.

Bremen's oldest resident, the statue of *Roland,* which was erected in 1404, is the center attraction in the market square. Roland is a symbol of justice and freedom. Legend has it that Bremen will not pass away as long as the stone giant is still standing in the marketplace. Legend also has it that the city fathers have a replacement ready—just in case.

No one is quite certain as to Roland's origins. City history first mentions the existence of the knightly statue in the marketplace in 1366, but it was made of wood and went up in flames. So did its wooden replacement. The stone statue has fared better.

The 17th-century facade of the Rathaus makes it one of the most photographed public buildings in the world. Rising above the town hall are the twin towers of the 11th-century **Saint Peter's Cathedral,** site of an ancient sand dune where the earliest Bremeners sought refuge from the surging tides of the Weser River.

Seek out the cellar of the town hall. It is said that the people of Bremen are most at their ease in a cellar—and this cellar is one of the best. It's a Ratskeller with more than 650 varieties of German wines to sample. Chances are if you find it, it may be a while before you see the light of day again.

The bronze statue of Bremen's ***Four Musicians*** (the donkey, dog, cat, and rooster) is stashed away in a cranny between the Rathaus and the Liebfrauenkirche, the Church of Our Blessed Lady. Be certain you find and photograph it, or your kids will never forgive you. The *Four Musicians* is one of several statues erected in Bremen honoring the Brothers Grimm fairy tales. If you delve into the true origins of the odd assortment of these domestic animals, apparently they are symbolic of a peasants' revolt against aristocracy rather than the Grimms' version of frightening off robbers—but don't tell the kids. A free open-air stage performance at Liebfrauenkirchhof Square takes place on Sunday at noon and 1330 (May through September).

The **Böttcherstrasse,** a narrow street leading off the market square, was redeveloped as a center for arts and crafts, with shops, workshops, art collections, and fine restaurants—even a casino. At the end of the street you will come to the Martini Church on the banks of the Weser—the area known as "the **Schlachte Embankment.**" Here, the redesigned riverside promenade is inviting for leisurely strolls, and a myriad of restaurants and cafes offer national and international cuisine. Boat tours of the Bremen harbor, the Island of Heligoland (tax-free shopping), and other destinations depart from the piers immediately in front of the church.

Another area that you can reach on foot by walking upstream along the banks of the Weser is the **Schnoor.** The oldest surviving residential area within the city of Bremen, it boasts quaint little houses, inns, and workshops dating from the 16th, 17th, and 18th centuries.

City sightseeing tours depart daily (except Monday) from the bus station in front of the main railway station at 1100. Tickets (€13.90 adults; €9.90 children up to age 12) must be obtained beforehand at the tourist information office. Trips around the harbor depart the Martini Church jetty daily at frequent intervals from March through October. The trip lasts 1¼ hours.

Anywhere in Bremen, the marketplace, the Böttcherstrasse, and the Schnoor included, you may come upon a chimney sweep garbed in traditional swallow-tailed coat and high, black hat. Reach out and touch him, for it is said that doing so brings good luck. Everyone does, and it's quite an exciting time when one passes through a crowd. Legends old and new abound in Bremen. Enjoy your visit.

Day Excursion to

Hameln

Where the Pied Piper Played

Depart from Hamburg Hauptbahnhof
Distance by Train: 148 miles (233 km)
Average Train Time: 2 hours, 25 minutes
City Dialing Code: 5151
Tourist Information Office: Hameln Marketing and Tourismus GmbH, Deisterallee 1, D-31785 Hameln
Tel: (05151) 95 78 19; **Fax:** (05151) 95 78 40
www.hameln.com/tourism
E-mail: touristinfo@hameln.de
Hours: October–March: 0900–1800 Monday–Friday and 0930–1300 Saturday;

April: 0900–1800 Monday–Friday and 0930–1500 Saturday; May–September: 0900–1800 Monday–Friday, 0930–1500 Saturday, and 0930–1300 Sunday
Notes: The tourist office is a short walk from the Hameln railway station. Walk through the square in front of the station, turning right onto Bahnhofstrasse. At the first traffic light, turn left onto Deisterallee. When you note a modern glass building on the right of the main street (Deisterallee), you are in front of the tourist information office.

Hameln's Old Town will hold you spellbound with its cobblestone walks, ancient facades, and cozy eating places. If a time machine is ever invented, its first journey might well be to Hameln to confirm—or dispel—the Legend of the Pied Piper.

Fact or fable, the town's archives reflect that on June 26, 1284, an itinerant *Rattenfänger* (rat catcher) attired in a multicolored costume trilled his flute, and 130 children followed him out of town to an unknown fate. Only three children survived—one boy had returned for his coat and was left behind, a little blind lad lost his way, and a mute youngster returned but was unable to tell the story.

This most famous kidnapping supposedly happened in retribution for the town's elders' not paying the Pied Piper for his previous performance, when he trilled the town's burgeoning rat population to the Weser River, where they drowned. Moral of the story: You have to "pay the Piper."

The story of **Hameln's Pied Piper** is the most well-known of all German folklore. It appeared in the *Brothers Grimm German Legends* and has been translated into at least 30 languages. There are probably as many theories as to what actually happened as there are children who disappeared—maybe more. The most probable explanation relates to the colonization of an area in the Czech Republic to which many citizens of Hameln migrated after being recruited by wealthy nobles during the same time in history. Peasants were referred to frequently as the children of towns, so it is quite possible that the tales became tangled. The current citizens, however, appear to be happy that it worked out the way the Brothers Grimm recorded it.

Every Sunday from mid-May through mid-September, a live reenactment of the event is staged in the town square. The colorful Piper plus 50 or so of the town's

Hamburg—Hameln

Hamburg–Hannover–Hameln
Trains depart at 23 and 29 minutes past the hour between 0723 and 1923, then 2001 and 2158. Journey time 2 hours 15 minutes.

Hameln–Hannover–Hamburg
Trains depart at 20 and 50 minutes past the hour until 1920, then 2020, 2120, and 2220. Journey time averages 2½ hours.

Change trains in Hannover. S-Bahn trains for Hannover–Hameln.

Distance: 148 miles (233 km)

children (attired in charming "rat" costumes) and another 20 adults representing the town mayor and citizens of Hameln begin their performance promptly at noon.

You will have about 20 minutes to change trains in Hannover. You will realize you are approaching Hameln when you see the silhouette of the famous Piper on the railroad control tower. If you plan to arrive in Hameln for the performance at noon on Sunday, go directly to the town square.

Adjacent to the main tourist office at Deisterallee on the right is a beautiful park, the **Burgergarten.** The park is readily identified by its pleasant green gate with the silhouette of the Pied Piper. The tourist information office conducts one-hour guided walking tours (in German) every day from April through October at 1500 (cost €4.00 per person). Ask the tourist office for prices of English-speaking tours. You can even arrange for a tour with the Piper himself, including an autograph!

If you're making your own walking tour, turn right when leaving the tourist information office and take the pedestrian underground route. Follow the signs reading ALTSTADT (Old City). When you leave the underground passageway, you will be on Osterstrasse. The **Gaststatte Rattenfängerhaus** (Pied Piper House), which is a charming restaurant, will be to your immediate left. Either pause for refreshments here or proceed on Osterstrasse to the town hall, situated at the end of the street by the marketplace. En route, you will find several other attractive restaurants and cafes.

The Pied Piper isn't Hameln's only attraction—sightseeing in the Altstadt alone could fill your entire day. During the summer, it is possible to take a steamboat trip on the Weser River or stroll through the extensive woods surrounding Hameln. Visit **Museum Hameln** on Osterstrasse. *Hours:* 1100–1630 Tuesday–Sunday. *Tel:* (05151) 202 1215; *E-mail:* museum@hameln.de; admission: Adults €5, under 13 €3. It contains an extensive collection of civic art and culture dating from the origins of Hameln, including the Pied Piper legend.

You can observe the 2,000-year-old craft of glassblowing and engraving in the historical **Pulverturm** (glassworks). The old and the new have been blended successfully in Hameln.

Day Excursion to

Hannover

Follow the Red Thread

Depart from Hamburg Hauptbahnhof
Distance by Train: 111 miles (178 km)
Average Train Time: 1 hour, 30 minutes
City Dialing Code: 0511

Tourist Information Office: Hannover Tourist Service, Ernst-August-Platz 8, D-30159 Hannover
Tel: (0511) 12345 111; **Fax:** (0511) 12345 112
www.hannover-tourism.de
E-mail: info@hannover-tourismus.de
Hours: 0900–1800 Monday–Friday, 1000–1500 Saturday and Sunday between April and September
Notes: Exit the station and the tourist office is directly opposite the station.

Hannover is known throughout the world as a commercial center dating back almost 900 years. Ideally located in the center of Europe, it is well served by rail and air. As a world leader in hosting international events, Hannover hosted the first world's exposition ever to be held in Germany—EXPO 2000: Humankind–Nature–Technology—and unveiled Germany's ICE3 trains.

The history of Hannover is interesting in that it produced the lineage of Britain's modern royal family. George I of England was born in Hannover, as was his son and successor, George II. Thoroughly German in tastes and habits, both monarchs made frequent trips back to Hannover, where they also ruled under the title of "Elector." George III, who presided over the loss of Britain's American colonies, was the grandson of George II and the first English King George to be born on British soil.

Hannover's rail station, constructed initially between 1876 and 1879, has had numerous improvements, although it has retained its original 19th-century facade. Fourteen tracks serve passenger traffic from an elevated platform. A concourse at ground level connects all the tracks with the main station area. Running under the main station area and extending under the station's plaza and into the city is a shopping mall.

The **"Red Thread"** (the painted red line on the ground) is actually an unusual walking tour of the city. Follow the red line that runs through the city's sightseeing points, but do it with a *Red Thread* booklet that you can pick up at the tourist office for a nominal charge. The booklet fits easily in your hand—or it's small enough to slip into your pocket if you want to avoid looking like a tourist. It contains a map outlining the two-hour walking tour and describes 36 points of interest you will pass while following the Red Thread. Take a camera with a wide-angle lens. Each point of interest has been numbered and the number placed so that if you stand on the number while photographing the scene, you'll have the best shot possible.

Highlights of the Red Thread walking tour include the **Gallerie Luise,** a pedestrian shopping area; the city's **1852 Opera House;** the old city wall; and the new city hall. Hannover's oldest half-timbered building, dating from 1566, is also seen on the tour, which ends "under the stallion's tail"—unless you have succumbed on the tour route to the charm of the local fräuleins or bierstube.

Bus tours are conducted daily. The tour, which is described in English, takes 2½ hours; tickets, €15 for adults and €10 for children up to age 14 and college students. It starts at 1100 daily April–October; Saturday only the remainder of the year.

Purchase a one-day (€9.50) or three-day (€17.50) **HannoverCard** at the tourist information office and receive a 40 percent reduction on the tour. Group tickets for up to five persons are also available: one day €19.50, three days €33.50. Other benefits include free travel on all GVH buses and trams in fare zones 1 and 2 and myriad other sightseeing reduced fares, including a cruise on Hannover's downtown lake, Maschsee.

Hamburg—Hannover

Frequent service of at least two trains per hour in both directions from about 0700 to near midnight daily.

DEPART Hamburg	TRAIN NUMBER	ARRIVE Hannover
0618	ICE 71	0738
0701	ICE 583	0823
0729	ICE 2083	0859
0803	ICE 91	0921
0824	ICE 73	0938
0901	ICE 585	1023
0924	ICE 575	1038
1001	ICE 787	1121
1024	ICE 75	1138

DEPART Hannover	TRAIN NUMBER	ARRIVE Hamburg
1620	ICE 74	1735
1657	ICE 2082	1829
1720	ICE 576	1835
1820	ICE 72	1935
1836	ICE 786	1953
1909	IC 1094	2024
1936	ICE 584	2058
2020	ICE 70	2138
2036	ICE 90	2153
2122	ICE 572	2244
2136	ICE 582	2254

Distance: 111 miles (178 km)

Hannover's Zoo is less than five minutes from the central station by U-Bahn Line 6 or by bus No. 128 from the central station. With the Gorilla Mountain, Jungle Palace, Zoo Farm, and the Zambezi Savannah landscape, the Hannover Zoo has become one of the most attractive in Germany.

The **Great Herrenhausen Garden and Garden Theater** is one of Europe's greatest tourist attractions. In its 300-year-old landscaping, you will find the only example in Germany of early Baroque gardens that have survived in their original form. Herrenhausen Avenue, facing the gardens, is lined with 1,219 lime trees set in four rows; they link Hannover's inner city with the gardens of the former summer residence of the Royal House of Hannover in Herrenhausen. Many sections of the garden have remained unaltered through the centuries.

A highlight of the gardens is the unique **Regenwaldhaus (Rainforest House).** *Hours:* 0900–1800 in winter and until 2000 in summer. Throughout the summer, the ornamental fountains of the garden operate from 1100 to 1200 and 1500 to 1800 daily. Either U-Bahn No. 4 or No. 5 will take you to the Herrenhausen Garden, or you will be able to see a portion of the gardens during a stop on the city bus tour. Adult tickets cost €8.

Hannover has several museums spanning 6,000 years of history, including the **Sprengel Museum** (Modern Art), **Kestner Museum** (Egyptology, Greece, Middle Ages), **Hannover Museum of History** (local social history), and the **Busch Museum** in the **Georgengarten,** a natural park developed in the 18th century. In sharp contrast to the baroque world of the Herrenhausen Garden, the Georgengarten is a mature example of English landscape gardening.

Many of Hannover's residents believe that a day in their city should have 48 hours. The refurbished city center alone—an ambler's paradise (reserved entirely for pedestrians) with shops, cascading fountains, and cafes—can captivate you. With the frequent train service between Hamburg and Hannover, you can easily extend your stay into evening.

Day Excursion to

Lübeck

Renaissance and Rotspon

Depart from Hamburg Hauptbahnhof
Distance by Train: 39 miles (62 km)
Average Train Time: 38 minutes
City Dialing Code: 451
Tourist Information Office: Welcome Center, Bertlingstrasse 21
Tel: (0451) 889 9700; **Fax:** (0451) 122 5419
www.luebeck-tourism.de
E-mail: info@luebeck-tourismus.de
Tourist information: In the train station opposite track No. 1
Hours: June–September: 0930–1900 Monday–Friday, 1000–1700 Saturday, Sunday, and public holidays; January–May, October–November: 0930–1800 Monday–Friday; December: 0930–1800 Monday–Friday
Note: To get to the tourist office from the rail station, pass by the Holstentor and continue through Holstenstrasse to Holstentorplatz.

The Hanseatic City of Lübeck extends its hospitality in a phrase, "Welcome, to yesterday, today, and tomorrow." The city's origins go back to the year 1000, when "Liübice" was established as a royal seat, artisan settlement, and trading center on the banks of the Trave River near the Baltic Sea. Today, parts of the old town of Lübeck have become a UNESCO World Heritage Site, and tomorrow is well in the hands of its energetic citizens, who number more than 210,000.

Destroyed by fire in 1157, the city at present dates from 1159, when it was rebuilt. In 1358 it was chosen as the administrative headquarters for the Hanseatic League. Between 1806 and 1813 Napoleon I held Lübeck as a part of his empire. Until the turn of the 20th century, when it began to build its own industries, Lübeck was known only as a Baltic port. Its industrial strengths and strategic maritime location, however, brought destruction to Lübeck during World War II, when most of Lübeck's industrial complex and some one-fifth of its Old Town were destroyed by Allied aerial bombardment. In 1949 the reconstruction of Lübeck, including the historic Old Town, began. As Germany's largest Baltic port, this proud city has once again become a center of economic, cultural, and commercial interests.

Lübeck is noted for two culinary specialties that you should sample during your visit—marzipan and rotspon. Marzipan, a sweet specialty, is produced in a countless variety of forms. Try a piece of marzipan cake and visit the **Marzipan Museum** at Cafe Niederegger. The origins of marzipan are hidden in history. Lübeck's version is that during the famine of 1407, bakers produced a bread made from the stocks of almonds, since wheat flour was unavailable. Others believe that marzipan originated in Venice and the recipe came to Lübeck through trade links.

In the early days, when salt was used to preserve fish, ships sailing from Lübeck began carrying salt mined in the Lübeck area to fishing ports along the French coast of Biscay. Rather than return empty, the ships brought back casks of French wine to mature in Lübeck prior to bottling. A combination of sea climate and storage in Lübeck's wine cellars brought about an amazing improvement in the quality of the wine. This was first discovered in 1806 during Napoleon's occupation, when French officers found that the Bordeaux wine from Lübeck's wine cellars tasted considerably better than at home. Try a glass of *Lübeck er rotspon* and judge for yourself.

Lübeck's architecture ranges from Gothic to Neoclassical, and you can find typical examples of these as well as Renaissance, Baroque, and Rococo in almost every part of the town's old section. You can see all five styles mix in harmonic unity within 1 block, starting with the College of Music at the head of Grosse Petersgrube.

With Lübeck's illustrated brochure in hand, you can become your own tour guide, or you might want to opt for one of the town's regular guided walks that start from the tourist office in the marketplace. The guided walks take about two hours to complete. The tourist office in the train station can give you directions for finding the marketplace. For discounts and free public transportation, consider purchasing the Lübeck HappyDay Card, €11 for one day, €13 for two days, and €16 for three days.

Hamburg—Lübeck

DEPART Hamburg	TRAIN NUMBER	ARRIVE Lübeck	NOTES
0704	RE 21406	0748	
0734	RE 21456	0820	R, M–F
0804	RE 21408	0848	
0904	RE 21410	0948	
0928	ICE 33	1004	R
1004	RE 21412	1048	
1104	RE 21414	1148	
pattern continues until 2004, then 2108, 2208, and 2323.			

DEPART Lübeck	TRAIN NUMBER	ARRIVE Hamburg
Earlier trains with about the same frequency as these:		
1808	RE 21429	1853
1908	RE 21431	1951
2008	RE 21433	2051
2108	RE 21435	2151
2139	EC 30	2223
2308	RE 21439	2351

Daily, unless otherwise noted
R Reservations required
Distance: 39 miles (62 km)

After you leave the train station, your point of reference will be the **Holstentor,** an imposing structure perched prominently at the head of the harbor just before the bridge leading over the Trave River into Old Town. Built between 1464 and 1478, more as a prestige symbol for the town than to protect its harbor, the unique design of its twin towers has become the symbol of Lübeck. The museum of city history housed in the Holstentor is very interesting and features a model of Lübeck in 1650.

After crossing the river, follow **Holstenstrasse,** which leads directly to Lübeck's ***Rathaus*** (town hall), in the marketplace. It is one of the oldest town halls built in Germany between the 13th and 16th centuries and is certainly one of the most beautiful. The **Ratskeller Restaurant** in the basement of the Rathaus is a delightful place to pause for lunch or to sample a glass of rotspon. We can also recommend the **Schiffergesellschaft Restaurant** at No. 2 Breite Strasse, site of a meetinghouse built in 1535 for shipmasters and brimming with treasures from the world of shipping. Bring money—lots of it—the ambience and food are worth it. (Closed on Monday.) Visit www.schiffergesellschaft.de.

For an aerial view of Lübeck, cross Holstenstrasse from the marketplace to **Petrikirche** (St. Peter's Church). Here you can ride the elevator to a viewing platform 162 feet (50 meters) above the city.

Base City: **MUNICH** (München)

www.muenchen.de
E-mail: tourismus@muenchen.de
City Dialing Code: 089

Munich (München), the capital and heart of Bavaria, is situated in the center of a vast plain washed by the Isar River. Founded in 1158, it was given the status of a town in 1214. The immaculate and astonishing beauty of its countryside is visible in any direction. Rimmed by the Alps to the south and dark green pine forests in all other quadrants, Munich becomes the gateway to day excursions galore. With a population of more than a million, Munich is Germany's third-largest city, but it still retains its unmatched roisterous elegance.

Munich's mood is always festive, but twice a year the tempo soars even higher as the city observes Fasching and Oktoberfest. Fasching celebrations are held during January and February. The festivities could be compared to Mardi Gras, only Müncheners get a head start on everyone by cranking up just after New Year's Eve and never letting up until the sun sets on Ash Wednesday!

During this period of Fasching revelry, thousands of masked balls and parties are staged. Many are in fancy dress, and sometimes masks are worn because individuals don't wish to reveal their identities to their partners—who are seldom the ones they came in with. It's often a complete surprise when the inevitable unmasking takes place.

The coming of Lent doesn't dampen Munich's spirits one drop, for it marks the beginning of the strong beer season. Munich's monks, limited to one meal a day throughout Lent (but with no limit on their drinking), started this ancient custom that still prevails today. They asked the brewmasters if, during Lent, they could increase the regular alcoholic content of their product; the brewmasters agreed—and everyone apparently has lived happily ever after. There are six major breweries in Munich.

Oktoberfest, instituted by a Bavarian king in 1810 on the occasion of the marriage between Princess Therese von Sachsen-Hildburgshausen and Prince Ludwig (later King Ludwig I), actually takes place during the latter part of September and ends the first weekend in October. About six million liters of beer are produced by the city's breweries and dispensed directly from huge, chilled barrels in enormous tents serving as beer halls. Bands play throughout the day and long into the night while drinkers wash down sausages, roast chicken, and oxen with five to six million liter-size drafts of the world's finest brews.

Colorful road signs on just about every highway entering Bavaria declare it to be *Freistaat Bayern*, the Free State of Bavaria. Insurrection? Not really. It is the manifestation of the free and roisterous spirit of its citizens, who love their homeland and feel that there is no other place quite like it.

Arriving by Air

Munich International Airport is located 28 kilometers northeast of the city center. *Tel:* 49 89 975 00 (for flight information). Visit www.munich-airport.com. There is a 24-hour information area staffed by multilingual personnel on level 03.

Rail passes may be validated at the German Railways counter (MVV, Munich Integrated Transport System) in the central area of level 03.

Airport–City Links: Munich's rapid-transit rail system, S-Bahn No. 8 line, or No. 1 line, which stops at the Marienplatz (city center) and the Hauptbahnhof (main rail station). Journey time: 45 minutes. From the central area, descend to level 02. Trains depart every 10 minutes 0544 to 0024. Fare: €10.40 for a one-way ticket, which you can purchase from machines at the airport (near the escalators leading to the S-Bahn). Eurail passes and German Railpasses are valid on the S-Bahn, but if this is the only rail trip you'll be making that day, we suggest you purchase the one-way ticket and validate your rail pass when you're ready to journey out from Munich.

Lufthansa Airport Bus departs from the stop at Terminal Area A every 20 minutes for Munich Hauptbahnhof 0629 to 2229 daily; from the airport main concourse 0626 to 2148. From Munich Hauptbahnhof to the airport, buses depart every 20 minutes, 0515 to 1955. Tickets: €10.50; round-trip, €17.00. Travel time, about 40 minutes. *Tel:* 0049 1805 838426; *Fax:* (089) 323 2594.

Taxi stands in front of areas A, B, C, D, and E. Due to traffic congestion, travel time between the airport and the city by road can exceed one hour and can cost €50 to €60. Check at the taxi information desk in the central area of the airport. For advance taxi arrangements and information, *Tel:* (089) 97 59 68 87 in Munich.

Arriving by Train

Munich has several suburban stations, but most international trains stop only at the Hauptbahnhof.

Munich's railway station—the Hauptbahnhof is actually a city within a city. In addition to the regular rail station services, all you need do is descend one level on any one of the station's many escalators to discover a veritable city of shops, ranging from bakeries, *bier* (beer) *stubes,* and fruit stands to supermarkets, as well as the subway entrances to many of Munich's department stores. Most shops in the immediate Hauptbahnhof area are open late during the week as well as on weekends and holidays.

- **Money exchange** (Geldwechsel-Exchange-Cambio): Located in the far left corner (as you exit) of the main station hall next to the main entrance. *Hours:* 0700–2200 daily. This facility offers a service not usually found in other exchanges. It will accept foreign coins (except coins from eastern Europe). Most exchanges will accept only notes.

  An ATM is on the left-hand side as you face the bank. A walk-up currency exchange office is to the right when exiting the trains, by Track 11 at the street exit. *Hours:* 0730–1900 daily. There is also an ATM just before the Bayerstrasse exit.

  The EurAide office is in Room 3 next to Track 11. It is open primarily during the summer months: 0730 to 1630 daily in May; 0730 to 1800 daily from June 1 to the end of September.

- **Tourist information/hotel reservations** may be made in the tourist information office. To reach it, exit through the Bahnhof Platz exit and turn right. It is the second office on the right, next to the ABR Reisebüro. It is within the station complex but can only be reached from the outside. A nominal charge is made for reservations. *Hours:* 0900–2000 Monday–Saturday, 1000–1800 Sunday; *E-mail:* tourismus@muenchen.de.

  InfoPool–Young People's Guide lists youth accommodations and activities. For those on a budget, we recommend the **Euro Youth Hotel** (any age is welcome) at 5 Senefelderstrasse. *Tel:* (089) 59 90 88 11; *Fax:* (089) 59 90 88 77; www.euro-youth-hotel.de; *E-mail:* info@euro-youth-hotel.de. A double room with private shower/toilet facilities is €60 per person per night, including buffet breakfast; single with hallway shower/toilet facilities is €55 per night, including breakfast.

- **Train reservations** for EuroCity, InterCity, ICE, and express-train services can be made in the **Reisezentrum** (Travel Center), located in the center of the station in front of Tracks 21 and 22. *Hours:* 0700–2100 Monday–Friday, 0700–2000 Saturday. It can be very crowded, particularly on weekends and during the summer tourist season. You must make train reservations at least one day in advance. They can also be made at counters that have signs reading RESERVIERUNGEN.

- **Rail pass validation and train information** also can be obtained in the Reisezentrum. Use window 19, 20, or 47 for rail pass validation. For train schedules only (international or domestic), use window 2 or 3 or the service counter in the middle of the station across from Tracks 18 and 19. The sign reads DB SERVICE.

- **Food services** are available in several parts of the station. The most famous is the stand-up wiener-and-beer stube immediately to the right of the entrance into the main station concourse. Behind it, there are three full-service restaurants with posted prices and menus.

Train Connections to Other Base Cities from Munich

Depart from Munich Hauptbahnhof.

DEPART	TRAIN NUMBER	ARRIVE	NOTES
		Amsterdam Centraal	
0755	ICE 726	1527	1, M–Sa
0955	ICE 722	1727	1
1228	ICE 788	2100	1
1555	ICE 620	2327	1
2250	CNL 418	0934+1	R, Sleeper
		Berlin Hauptbahnhof	
0739	ICE 2300	1430	
0918	ICE 208	1533	
1117	ICE 1508	1733	
1320	ICE 1586	1933	
1716	ICE 1502	2333	
2228	CNL 40418	0918+1	R, Sleeper
		Bern (Berne)	
0717	EC 196	1258	4
1233	EC 194	1756	4
1833	EC 190	0002+1	4
		Brussels (Bruxelles) Midi/Zuid	
0527	ICE 614	1335	2
1055	ICE 720	1735	1
1128	ICE 518	1832	2
1455	ICE 622	2135	1
2250	CNL 418	0935+1	R, 2, Sleeper
		Budapest Keleti	
0934	RJ 63	1619	
2336	EN 463	0924+1	R, Sleeper
		Copenhagen (København) H.	
0641	ICE 1082	1822	5
1048	ICE 1158	2222	5
2228	CNL 40418	1422+1	R, 5, Sleeper
		Hamburg Hauptbahnhof	
0653	ICE 1162	1253	
0822	ICE 882	1354	
0905	ICE 680	1454	
1022	ICE 880	1554	
hourly departure pattern continues until 1822, then			
2228	CNL 40418	0836+1	R, Sleeper
		Luxembourg	
1346	EC 114	2129	2

DEPART	TRAIN NUMBER	ARRIVE	NOTES
		Milan (Milano) Centrale	
0734	EC 81	1525	R, 8, M–F
1338	EC 89	2055	R, 8
2108	CNL 485	0912+1	R, 8, Sleeper
		Nice Ville	
1411	ICE 1090	0937+1	R, 6, Su–Th
		Paris Gare de l'Est	
0625	TGV 9576	1235	R
1028	ICE 598	1635	3
1628	ICE 592	2235	R, 3, Exc. Sa
2250	CNL 40418	0924+1	R, Sleeper
		Prague (Praha)	
1702	ALX 357	2241	
		Rome (Roma) Termini	
0938	EC 85	1910	R, 7
1136	EC 87	2045	8
2108	CNL 485	0922+1	R, Sleeper
		Vienna (Wien) Hauptbahnhof	
0934	RJ 63	1330	
1534	RJ 69	1930	
1734	RJ 261	2130	
2336	EN 463	0635+1	R, Sleeper
		Warsaw Centralna	
0915	RJ 63	2107	9
1734	RJ 261	0700+1	R, 9, Sleeper
		Zürich Hauptbahnhof	
0717	EC 196	1153	
1233	EC 194	1653	
1633	EC 192	2053	
1833	EC 190	2253	

Daily, unless otherwise noted
R Reservations required
+1 Arrives next day
1. Change trains in Frankfurt.
2. Change trains in Cologne (Köln).
3. Change trains in Mannheim.
4. Change trains in Zürich.
5. Change trains in Hamburg.
6. Change trains in Mannheim and Marseille.
7. Change trains in Bologna.
8. Change trains in Verona.
9. Change trains in Vienna (Wien).

- **Luggage lockers** are available in four areas of the station. Look for signs reading SCHLIESSFÄCHER. There is also a luggage-checking office on the main floor under the Burger King. Open 0800–2000 Monday–Friday and 0800–1800 Saturday–Sunday.
- Another **tourist information office** is in the New Town Hall in Marienplatz (same building as the glockenspiel). *Hours:* 1000–1900 Monday–Friday, 1000–1700 Saturday, 1000–1400 Sunday. This office also will make hotel reservations.

Getting Around in Munich

Munich's fine S-Bahn (rapid train) system is operated by Deutsche Bahn (DB).

The German Railpass and the variety of Eurail passes that include Germany are accepted for travel throughout the entire S-Bahn system. The aforementioned rail passes are not accepted on the U-Bahn (underground or subway system) or on the trams (*Strassenbahnen*).

The S-Bahn has eight main operating lines, S-1 through S-8. All of these lines converge on the Marienplatz and Hauptbahnhof. You can obtain maps and fare information at the tourist information office. Visit www.mvv-muenchen.de.

A U-Bahn (subway) station is located directly under the plaza in front of the railway station. The Munich Hauptbahnhof is the center of train, tram, bus, suburban train, and subway services for the entire city.

A great value is the MVV-Single (valid for one person) or Partner (valid for two adults) Tageskarte (Day Tickets). The Day Ticket provides unlimited travel on the S-Bahn (rapid-transit line), U-Bahn (subway), streetcars, and buses on the date of validation until 0600 the following day. A Single Day Ticket for Munich's entire transport network costs €11.70; Partner Day Ticket, €21.30 (two adults). Remember to have your ticket "stamped/validated" by using any one of the machines near and in any station.

All of Munich's public transportation operates on the honor system. You must have a ticket for any conveyance you board, but you may not be asked to show it—then again, you may. If you are apprehended without a valid ticket, you will be fined €30 on the spot.

The **CityTourCard** is a great combination of city transport and sightseeing savings. It includes a day ticket for use on public transport in the MVV inner district (Munich city area) or in the entire network (Gesamtnetz) and a discount card that can be used at 30-plus tourist attractions (for example, Bavaria Filmstadt, Deutsches Museum, BMW Museum, Sea Life, Komödie im Bayerischen Hof, and much, much more). Visit www.citytourcard-muenchen.com for more details. Prices:

1-Day CityTourCard, Inner District	€10.90
1-Day CityTourCard, Inner District, Family (up to 5 persons)	€17.90

3-Day CityTourCard, Inner District	€20.90
3-Day CityTourCard, Entire Network	€32.90
3-Day CityTourCard, Entire Network, Family (up to 5 persons)	€53.90

Sights/Attractions/Tours

Munich's heart pulsates at the Marienplatz, the city's central square. From the tower of the new town hall in the center of the Marienplatz, a glockenspiel chimes every morning at 1100 and 1200 (again in summer at 1700) and is followed by a performance of mechanical figures, including knights on horseback and a crowing rooster. You will have to see it to believe it.

Dallmayr's Delicatessen is nearby—one of the finest delicatessens in the world. Facing the glockenspiel, walk around the right side of the town hall to the smaller square in the rear. Dallmayr's store will then be in plain view immediately across the street to your right, at 14–15 Dienerstrasse. *Tel:* (089) 213–5100; www.dallmayr.de. *Hours:* 0930–1900 Monday–Saturday, closed Sunday. Extravagant beyond description, it demands to be seen. If for no other reason, go to Munich to savor the sights and scents of Dallmayr's! A restaurant specializing in seafood and a unique gift shop are on the second floor. This is not your usual "deli"; you'll find rich German chocolates, caviar, lobster, fine wines—order a gourmet lunch "to go."

Munich has a great variety of things to see and do. There are approximately 100 historic buildings, two castles, 200 churches, 46 art collections and museums, and 58 performing theaters—all within the city limits and most of them within reasonable walking distance from the Marienplatz. Ask the tourist information office for the folder containing a city map showing the exact location of each of the points of interest, including the **1972 Olympic Park,** identified by color-coded squares. For admirers of the brewmaster's art, the map also pinpoints 12 of Munich's most famous beer gardens.

The **Hofbrauhaus** (the state-owned beer hall) is a short walk from the Marienplatz via Dallmayr's delicatessen. (It would be un-American not to stop!) The Hofbrauhaus dates from 1589. It is no longer operated as a brewery, but beer is drayed in to be consumed daily from 1-liter (1¾ pint) mugs while bands play lively tunes, often accompanied by the singing of the drinkers. There's a full-service restaurant on the second floor, where decorum is a bit more in evidence. **Planet Hollywood** is directly across the street from the Hofbrauhaus.

If you tire of city dining, take a southbound S-1 train on the S-Bahn from the main transfer station under the Marienplatz and get off in the **Village of Aying**—about a 30-minute ride. Walk 4 blocks toward the church steeple to the Brauereigasthof-Hotel Aying, where you'll find the best Bavarian food, beer, and atmosphere.

Those visiting Munich for the first time probably will want to take a guided tour by bus. A four-hour leisurely paced bicycle tour is also available for €25. For information call Mike's Bike Tours. *Tel:* (089) 255 43 988; www.mikesbiketours.com.

Day Excursions

South to the Alps and **Garmisch-Partenkirchen.** Into the Alps to **Berchtesgaden.** Through the Alps to Austria and beautiful **Innsbruck.** North to **Nuremberg, Ulm,** or **Rothenburg** and the **Romantic Road.** For a special adventure ascend the peak of Germany's highest mountain, the Zugspitze. Take your choice—and go at your leisure.

Day Excursion to

Berchtesgaden

Alps, Lakes, and Salt Mines

Depart from Munich Hauptbahnhof
Distance by Train: 112 miles (180 km)
Average Train Time: 2 hours, 40 minutes
City Dialing Code: 8652
Tourist Information Office: (Kurdirektion), Berchtesgadener Land, Königsseer Strasse 2, D-83471; opposite the railway station
Tel: (0) 86 52 96 70; **Fax:** (0) 86 52 96 74 00
www.tourismus-berchtesgaden.de or **www.berchtesgadener-land.com**
E-mail: info@tourismus-berchtesgaden.de or info@berchtesgadener-land.com
Hours: June 15–October 15: 0830–1800 Monday–Friday, 0900–1700 Saturday, 0900–1500 Sunday; October 16–June 14: 0830–1700 Monday–Friday, 0900–1200 Saturday, closed Sunday
Notes: To reach the tourist information office, cross the street in front of the station at the traffic light and incline to the left, following the KONIGSSEE sign. The office is located in a large cream-colored building on the right-hand side.

Don't let the train time to Berchtesgaden deter you from making this day excursion. The train follows a route that passes through some of the most beautiful countryside in the world, and the tours waiting for your arrival in Berchtesgaden are simply out of this world.

After Adolf Hitler seized power in 1934, he ordered the expansion of the facilities in **Obersalzberg,** an appendage to Berchtesgaden, with the intent of making it the equivalent of a summer White House. His dream was destroyed, however, when the greater part of Obersalzberg was demolished by an air attack on April 25, 1945.

If possible, take the early train out of Munich so you will have ample time to select a tour and have a relaxing lunch in one of Berchtesgaden's charming inns. Current schedules are always posted in the main hall of the station.

The village of Berchtesgaden has many attractions. Among them is the Folk Museum housed in the **Adelsheim Castle** (Schloss Adelsheim), where you will find displays of wood carvings and the famous Berchtesgaden wood-shaving boxes.

For one of the most spectacular scenic views in the world, take the Jennerbahn two-person cable cars to the top of Mount Jenner above **Lake Königssee** (literally translated "Royal Lake"). Start from the valley station at Lake Königssee. Your breathtaking, 20-minute ascent to 1,834 meters (6,017 feet) unveils vistas of mountain summits stretching as far as the eye can see. This wondrous landscape once caused Bavarian writer Ludwig Ganghofer to cry out: "Lord, if you love anyone, then set them down in this land!"

Munich (München)—Berchtesgaden

DEPART München Hbf	TRAIN NUMBER	ARRIVE Berchtesgaden	NOTES
0655	RE 79007	0930	1
0854	RE 79011	1130	1
0955	RE 79013	1230	1
1055	RE 79015	1330	1

DEPART Berchtesgaden	TRAIN NUMBER	ARRIVE München Hbf	NOTES
1331	BLB 84228	1606	1
1531	BLB 84236	1806	1
1831	BLB 84248	2115	1
2031	BLB 84254	2315	1

Daily, unless otherwise noted
1. Change trains in Freilassing.
Distance: 112 miles (180 km)

In addition to sightseeing in Berchtesgaden and its immediate surroundings, there are many interesting guided tours that can be taken outside of the village. The most popular ones for North Americans are visits to Obersalzberg, the Salt Mines, the Königssee, the Sound of Music/Salzburg Tour, and the Eagle's Nest. All tours are available year-round with the exception of the Eagle's Nest, which is open from mid-May to mid-October.

The **Obersalzberg tour** features a visit to the former location of the Berghof, Adolf Hitler's official home and the site of many pre–World War II conferences. Included on the tour is a trip through its air-raid shelters and bunkers, which provided protection to the conferees in the event that the Allied air forces wanted to disrupt the proceedings. Visit www.obersalzberg.de.

The **Salt Mines** are located a few miles outside the town of Berchtesgaden. If you have chronic respiratory problems, you may sigh a breath of relief in the specially treated air of the new curative salt mine tunnel. The guided tour is a thrilling experience. In miner's protective clothing, you ride a mine train, slide down chutes, and cross over subterranean lakes. What an adventure! Visit www.salzzeitreise.de. Open 0900–1700 in the summer, 1100–1500 November–April. Admission €16.00 adults, €9.50 children under 16.

The **Königssee** is considered the pearl of Berchtesgaden and provides some of the most romantic scenery in Upper Bavaria. In order to preserve the quietness of the lake and the clearness of its waters, electric boats have been the only crafts permitted to navigate there since 1909. A tour aboard an electric boat runs daily whenever the lake is ice-free. Midpoint in the cruise, the captain shuts down the motor and, in the silence of the lake, lets go with a blast on a trumpet that resounds and resounds for as many as seven times off the alpine palisades surrounding the lake.

The **Eagle's Nest** tour begins in May and is conducted daily in summer only. A bus conveys you to a height of 5,600 feet, where an elevator lifts you the final 400 feet to a never-to-be-forgotten experience. Despite the publicity gained by the Eagle's Nest's connection with Adolf Hitler, he visited there only about five times. The road running to the elevator that takes you to the summit is beyond doubt a uniquely daring feat of road building. It's a white-knuckle ride all the way. The tour itself is far less strenuous than that of the Salt Mines, but the weather is all important. Visit www.kehlsteinhaus.de.

Despite its ancient facade, Berchtesgaden is actually very modern in its tourist and recreational facilities. Should its charm overcome you—as it does many—consider an overnight stay. The Berchtesgadener Land tourist information office, opposite the rail station, can assist you in finding accommodations.

For lunchtime try the **Gasthof Neuhaus,** opposite the fountain in the town square. Its selection of *Schmankerl* (Bavarian specialties) is a treat, and its ice cream will make you forget all about Baskin-Robbins.

Day Excursion to

Garmisch-Partenkirchen

Bavaria at Its Best

Depart from Munich Hauptbahnhof
Distance by Train: 63 miles (101 km)
Average Train Time: 1 hour, 30 minutes
City Dialing Code: 8821
Tourist Information Office: Richard-Strauss-Str 2, 82467 Garmisch–Partenkirchen
Tel: (0) 88 21–180 700; **Fax:** (0) 88 21–180 755
www.garmisch-partenkirchen.de or **www.gapa.de**
E-mail: tourist-info@gapa.de
Zugspitze: www.zugspitze.de; *E-mail:* zugspitzbahn@zugspitze.de
Hours: Mid-October–mid-May: 0900–1700 Monday–Friday, 0900–1500 Saturday; mid-May–mid-October: 0900–1800 Monday–Saturday, 1000–1200 Sunday
Notes: Reach the information office by turning left outside the station and walking downhill about 300 yards to Bahnhof Strasse. Turn left, and walk about 150 yards to Richard Strauss Platz and the Kongresshaus (Congress Hall).

Bavaria's eccentric King Ludwig II spent lavishly, admired Wagner, and went mad—though not necessarily in that order. Two of his famous castles, Neuschwanstein and Linderhof, can be visited on tours from Garmisch-Partenkirchen, as well as the village of **Oberammergau** (home of the Passion Play) and the Zugspitze, Germany's highest mountain.

Munich (München)—Garmisch-Partenkirchen

DEPART München Hbf	TRAIN NUMBER	ARRIVE Garmisch
0732	RB 5411	0854
0832	RB 5413	0954
0932	RB 5415	1054
1032	RB 59449	1155
1132	RB 5419	1254
1232	RB 5421	1354

Zugspitze trains depart Garmisch at 15 minutes past the hour from 0815 to 1815.

DEPART Garmisch	TRAIN NUMBER	ARRIVE München Hbf
1507	RB 59476	1626
1607	RB 59460	1726
1705	RB 5422	1826
1805	RB 5426	1926
1905	RB 59478	2026
2005	RB 59462	2126
2107	RB 5432	2226
2207	RB 5434	2326
2307	RB 59480	0026+1

Zugspitze trains returning to Garmisch depart Zugspitzplatt Station at 30 minutes past the hour, 0930–1630.
All trains are daily, including holidays.
Distance: 63 miles (101 km)

DER, a German tour agency, offers a wide selection of tours in the Garmisch-Partenkirchen area, including tours of King Ludwig's **Neuschwanstein Castle** and his **Linderhof Castle.** The DER agency is immediately adjacent to the Garmisch-Partenkirchen rail station.

Proceed to track No. 1 by turning to the left at the bottom of the stairs leading from the arriving train platform. DER is visible from the rail-station lobby. Most tours are conducted daily.

Garmisch-Partenkirchen (actually two villages that united in 1935) hosted the 1936 Winter Olympics and the World Alpine-Ski Championship in 1978. Just visiting the Olympic facilities can consume an entire day. A downtown shopping spree can do the same, but with more injury to pocketbooks. In wintertime the Winter

Olympics ski jump provides spills and chills, and the Olympic Ice Stadium is open year-round.

The alpine ski runs extend 68 miles in length, and there are 93 miles of tracks for cross-country skiing. Two of the most popular alpine cable-car runs in summer are the **Eibsee-Zugspitze** system (9,678 feet) and the **Wank Bahn,** which takes you to the promontory of the Wank Alp (5,874 feet). There are others as well. One that is particularly convenient starts at the Olympic Ski Stadium on the fringe of Garmisch-Partenkirchen and scales the Eckbauer Alp to a height of 4,127 feet. From any of these points on a clear day, the view is extraordinary.

Near the Ski Stadium, you can hike through the Partnachklamm gorge, which has a trail cut into the rock. The trail follows the course of the Partnach Stream for more spectacular views. There's also the Hollentalklamm. Begin your hike at Hammersbach, about 3 kilometers west of Garmisch, a stop on the Zugspitzbahn. Hike a couple of kilometers up the mountain to the beginning of the gorge. The trail continues to the top of the Zugspitze. The tourist office can fill you in on all the details.

The **Zugspitze** is the highest mountain in Germany—9,718 feet, to be exact. A cog railway was completed in 1931 to the Zugspitzplatt, along with a cable car that scaled the last 2,000 feet to the top. Another cable car running from Eibsee, a station stop on the cog railway at the 3,500-foot level, was placed in operation during 1963. This system lifts passengers directly to the peak in a spectacular 10-minute ride.

These two systems make a circuitous routing possible—up one way and down another. The round-trip fare from Garmisch is €41.50 adults, €32 youth, and €22.50 children (discount for German Railpass and Eurail pass holders). The ticket entitles you to ride on any part of the total system. When you arrive in the Garmisch-Partenkirchen Station, walk about 100 yards to the cog-railway station on your right. The cog railway stops in Eibsee about 30 minutes after departing Garmisch. Transfer at this point to the Eibsee cable car.

The cable-car trip from Eibsee to the top of the Zugspitze takes about 10 breath-taking minutes. If you are in a hurry to return to Garmisch, you could retrace your trip by returning to Eibsee on the cable car, but we recommend that you proceed to the **Sonn Alpin Glacier Restaurant** via the "Gletscherbahn" cable car. At the Sonn Alpin, you join up with the cog railway, which terminates there in a huge vaulted hall blasted out of solid rock. Trains depart on the hour, and the trip back to Garmisch takes 1 hour and 10 minutes.

If you choose to stay in Garmisch, we can recommend the 3-star **Hotel Garmischer-Hof** at Chamonixtrasse 10. It's a charming hotel run by the Seiwald family for some 100 years. The food is excellent as well—Bavaria at its best. *Tel:* (0) 88 21 911 0; *Fax:* (0) 88 21 514 40; www.garmischer-hof.de; *E-mail:* hotel@garmischer-hof.de. Rates: €80 to €140 for a double.

Day Excursion to

Innsbruck, Austria

Jewel of the Alps

Depart from Munich Hauptbahnhof or **Ostbahnhof**
Distance by Train: 107 miles (172 km)
Average Train Time: 1 hour, 53 minutes
Austria Country Dialing Code: 43
City Dialing Code: 512
Tourist Information Office: Innsbruck Tourismus, Burggraben 3, A–6020 Innsbruck
Tel: (0512) 53560; **Fax:** (0512) 5356 314
www.innsbruck.info
E-mail: info@innsbruck.info
Hours: 0800–1800 daily
Notes: A tourist information office is located in the train station on the east side. To get to the office in town, follow Salurner Strasse to the Triumphal Arch; make a right and follow Maria-Theresien Strasse directly to the tourist office at the Burggraben crossroad entrance to the old town.

Located less than two hours away by train, Innsbruck is a convenient excursion to make from Munich. Innsbruck means "bridge over the Inn River." Situated at the junction of the Inn Valley and the Sill Gap, on the road and railroad route running into Italy through the Brenner Pass, the city is the cultural and tourist capital of the Austrian Tyrol and brings together nature, culture, sport, and tradition.

Innsbruck is surrounded theatrically by its mountains. There is a mountain view from nearly every street corner and every window in town. Looking northward from its main street, **Maria-Theresien Strasse,** you will confront the towering Alps, which seem to encroach upon the city. The scene is breathtaking.

This day excursion offers an opportunity to explore the **Tyrolean Alps** in a cable car—plus a visit to one of the most picturesque "old towns" in Austria. To top it off, a circuitous return on the **Mittenwald railroad** is possible; it takes you on a fantastically scenic rail route straight through the heart of the Austrian and Bavarian Alps en route back to Munich via Garmisch-Partenkirchen. Guided tours are offered twice daily from the main train station in the summer (1200 and 1400) and once daily at 1200 in winter. Rail pass holders get a 15 percent discount on the Seegrube-Hafelekar, Patscherkofel and the Mutterer Alm cable cars. The cost of a cable-car ride is equivalent to the Innsbruck Card, which includes a cable-car ride plus more.

Munich (München)—Innsbruck, Austria

DEPART	TRAIN NUMBER	ARRIVE
München Hbf		Innsbruck
0738	EC 81	0923
0938	EC 85	1123
1138	EC 87	1323
1338	EC 89	1523

DEPART	TRAIN NUMBER	ARRIVE
Innsbruck		München Hbf
1436	EC 80	1625
1636	EC 84	1823
1836	EC 86	2023
2036	EC 188	2223

Daily, including holidays
Distance: 107 miles (172 km)

You are in for an eye-filling day. Even the regular rail line running out of Munich is loaded with alpine scenery. Take a seat on the right side of your coach outbound from Munich for the best views.

The **Innsbruck Card** includes admission fees for many sights, museums, and other attractions (even a free welcome drink at the casino), and unlimited use of the public transportation network within the city. The card is a great bargain and is valid for a period of 24 hours at €33; 48 hours, €41; 72 hours, €47.

Also purchase the large guide map if you plan a walking tour of the city, then head west for a few blocks to Innsbruck's **Arc de Triumph.** From this point, turn north and wend your way slowly through the Altstadt (Old Town), which lines both sides of the street all the way to the **Goldenes Dachl** (Golden Roof) at the end of Herzog-Friedrich Strasse. Try your luck in the Casino, a tasty aperitif in the Piano Bar, or a culinary feast in the Guggeryllis Restaurant. It may come as a disappointment, but the so-called Golden Roof is made of heavy, gilded copper.

Bus tours of the city are available throughout the year. A city tour by bus departs the Central Bus Station daily at 1200 and 1400 June through September, free with your Innsbruck Card, or €6. Biking tours are a great way to see Innsbruck, too. Or take the 60-minute guided "City Walk" through the historic center of Innsbruck at 1100 and 1400; cost: €8.

We suggest you eat lunch in the **Goldener Adler** (Golden Eagle), the oldest inn in the city, founded in 1390! It is around the corner on the left and can best be described as a delicious experience. If you go there for dinner, enjoy Tyrolean music in the cellar restaurant. It will complete a perfect evening, although an expensive one. Another option is the **Ottoburg,** which is just past the Goldener Adler and serves good traditional meals. Here is an insider's tip on where many locals eat lunch: Try the **Fischerhäusl,** a cute little house with a garden located between the cathedral and congress center.

Every year on August 15, the Austrian Philharmonic Youth Orchestra performs in Innsbruck to celebrate the King of the Waltz—Johann Strauss—with the "hottest Strauss event in Austria," according to the 120 participating young musicians. For tickets: *Tel:* (0512) 5356; www.innsbruck-ticket-service.at; *E-mail:* office@innsbruck-ticket-service.at.

In the winter Innsbruck is an alpine sports paradise, with seven skiing regions, including the magnificent Stubai Glacier, 62 lifts, 55 marked ski runs, 130 kilometers of well-maintained ski trails, and 9.5 kilometers of high-altitude cross-country trails. Telephone, fax, or e-mail the Innsbruck Tourist Office for holiday and ski package information.

Day Excursion to

Nuremberg (Nürnberg)

Beer, Gingerbread, and Toys

Depart from Munich Hauptbahnhof or Pasing
Distance by Train: 125 miles (201 km)
Average Train Time: 1 hour, 40 minutes
City Dialing Code: 911
Tourist Information Office: Königstrasse 93, 90402 Nurnberg
Tel: (0911) 23 36-0; **Fax:** (0911) 2 33 61 66
www.nuernberg.de
E-mail: info@ctz-nuremberg.de
Hours: 0900–1900 Monday–Saturday, 1000–1600 Sunday
Notes: A tourist information pavilion is in front of the main railway station at Königstrasse 93.

Although Nuremberg (Nürnberg) is more than 950 years old, it is a lively, modern city. A mecca for lovers of markets, music, and museums, Nuremberg must have originated the "Day Excursion"!

On December 7, 1835, the first German train chugged its way from Nuremberg to Fürth, a neighboring city, with honored guests and two barrels of beer. But on this day excursion, ICE trains average 76 mph between Munich and Nuremberg—considerably faster than in 1835—and Nuremberg's brew is every bit the match for Munich's, for Nuremberg is a part of Bavaria, too. Get ready for an enjoyable day out.

When you arrive in Nuremberg, you will find the tourist office in front of the railway station. Another tourist information office is on the main market square at Hauptmarkt 18.

Munich (München)—Nuremberg (Nürnberg)

DEPART München Hbf	TRAIN NUMBER	ARRIVE Nuremberg Hbf
0755	ICE 726	0857
0855	ICE 724	0957
1022	ICE 880	1130
1117	ICE 1508	1227
1222	ICE 788	1330

DEPART Nuremberg Hbf	TRAIN NUMBER	ARRIVE München Hbf
1427	ICE 787	1541
1528	ICE 1509	1638
1627	ICE 789	1738
1728	ICE 209	1841

plus hourly service at 28 minutes past the hour until 2128, then 2202 and 2331.

Daily

Distance: 125 miles (201 km)

Conducted tours of the city from May to October and in the Christmas season depart daily at 1300, €10. Individual tours may be arranged at any time; one of the Tourist Board's experienced city guides will serve as escort. *Tel:* (0911) 2 33 61 23. Or put your own tour together with the **Nuremberg Cultour Ticket,** available at the tourist office. This two-day ticket offers entrance to many museums and sites. If you decide to stay over, hotel guests get free public transport in Nuremberg, Fürth, and Stein with the card as well. Ask about the Welcome Pack at the tourist office if you do book a hotel. You'll be in for a nice surprise.

One of the main gates of the old walled city of Nuremberg, the **Kingsgate,** is directly across from the railway station. Start at Königstrasse (King Street) and follow it to the heart of the old walled area known as the Hauptmarkt (Central Market). Plan to be there at noon; a mechanical clock will entertain you at the stroke of 12 with its seven electors paying homage to the emperor. Then look for a nearby pub . . . shouldn't be too hard, as they seem to be everywhere.

What goes better with beer than an authentic "Three in One"? Famous for their sausages, these Nuremberg minis may only be as big as your little finger, but they are spicy—and famous across Germany. Now, about that beer. . . .

Connoisseurs of the brewer's art won't want to miss a visit to Nuremberg's **Museum Brewery** and **Medieval Cellars.** The museum is really the Altstadthof brewery, whose motto, "Beer like our Forefathers," is observed today by the use of only the finest materials and brewing methods, which date from the 19th century. The cellars, going down 85 feet through solid rock, form a labyrinth of tunnels dug in the 14th century for the storage of beer. A guided tour is available.

Nuremberg offers not only beer but gingerbread and toys as well. The aroma of Nuremberg's special gingerbread, ***Lebkuchen,*** fills the Hauptmarkt every Christmas. At other times, including the pre-Christmas period (which starts in mid-August), the same aroma may be savored—and tasted—in the many pastry shops throughout the city. The traditional recipes of the original gingerbread are kept secret by the bakeries that produce it. Companies such as Lebkuchen Schmidt invite visitors to sample their products. Arrangements may be made by either of the tourist offices. Have the bakery shop ship some home for you.

Toy shops are in profusion, and the **Toy Museum** on Karl Street, 2 blocks from the Hauptmarkt via Augustinerstrasse, has a splendid display of dolls, puppets, and tin soldiers. The museum also houses an interesting model-railway layout, featuring—of all things—the train station in Omaha, Nebraska.

Nuremberg's most famous citizen was Albrecht Dürer, a man who towered above his time. The stately home in which he lived, from 1509 until his death in 1529, is located 2 blocks north of the Toy Museum, past the Wine Market, on Albrecht Dürer Strasse. The house holds a collection of the famed artist's works. The area surrounding it is probably the most interesting section within the walled city. Unfortunately, Dürer's most famous work, *The Four Apostles*, now rests in Munich, but a number of his paintings are exhibited along with a multilingual film presentation on his life and works. *Hours:* 1000–1700 Tuesday–Friday, (until 2000 Thursday), 1000–1800 Saturday–Sunday; also open Monday in summer. The New Museum features exhibits showing free form, applied arts, and modern design. Admission is €5.00 for adults, €4.00 children under 15.

If you have any doubt about that first day excursion by train originating in Nuremberg, check in at the **Verkehrsmuseum (Transportation Museum),** 3 blocks to the right of the train station as you face it. *Hours:* 0900–1700 Tuesday–Friday, 1000–1800 Saturday and Sunday. Admission: €5.00. There you will find the Adler (Eagle), the first German locomotive, complete with the two beer barrels mounted on its tender.

Day Excursion to

The Romantic Road

Delightfully Medieval

Depart from Munich Hauptbahnhof
Distance: 172 miles (276 km) by bus and 173 miles (278 km) by train
Total Journey Time: 12 hours, 36 minutes
City Dialing Code for Rothenburg ob der Tauber: 9861
Tourist Information Office: Rothenburg o.d. T. Tourist Office, Marktplatz 2, D-91541
Tel: (09861) 4 04 800; **Fax:** (09861) 404 529
www.rothenburg.de
E-mail: info@rothenburg.de
Hours: May–October: 0900–1800 Monday–Friday, 1000–1700 Saturday–Sunday; November–April: 0900–1700 Monday–Friday, 1000–1300 Saturday, closed Sunday
The Romantic Road: Deutsche Touring GmbH, Am Romerhof 17, 60486 Frankfurt/Main
Tel: (069) 7 90 35 01; **Fax:** (069) 7 90 32 19
www.deutsche-touring.de

Too long and too far? Not in the least. **The Romantic Road,** packed with superb scenery and delightful medieval villages, is worth every minute. The Deutsche Bahn (German Railroad) bus that takes you from Munich to **Würzburg** makes two stops en route: one in **Dinkelsbühl** for lunch and one in **Rothenburg** for sightseeing. After these pleasant interludes, plus a return trip to Munich on one of Germany's lightning-fast InterCity Express trains, you will wonder where the day has gone.

The Romantic Road bus carries an English-speaking guide. This trip has become so popular that seat reservations are necessary. Reservations can be made at the EurAide, Inc. office in the Munich railway station opposite track No. 11 in the main hall, three doors down from the line of four telephone booths. *Hours:* 0800–1600 Monday–Friday. *Tel:* (089) 59 38 89. Seat reservations are €7.00, and the Eurail pass and German Railpass provide a 20 percent discount.

The Romantic Road bus has no special markings. Ask for its departure position (which is usually No. 20/21) when you make reservations. Your reservation ensures you a seat on the bus, but not a specified seat. Be at the bus station at about 0830, therefore, to ensure getting a window seat.

Rothenburg is one of the most frequently visited places in Germany. Every year thousands of visitors from all parts of the world come to this ancient walled city. You will see why Rothenburg is picturesque and photogenic. Be sure to take a camera. Probably more photographs have been taken of its **Kobolzeller Tor** and **Siebers Tower** than of any other scene in Germany.

Munich (München)—The Romantic Road

Romantic Road excursion by bus from München to Dinkelsbühl to Rothenburg ob der Tauber to Würzburg; return to München by train.

Schedule shown is subject to change without notice.

EUROPA BUS TRIP 190:

Depart München Hbf Starnberger Bahnhof	1040
Arrive Dinkelsbühl (Schweinemarkt)	1435
Depart Dinkelsbühl (Schweinemarkt)	1505
Arrive Rothenburg ob der Tauber (Bahnhof)	1605
Depart Rothenburg ob der Tauber (Bahnhof)	1650
Arrive Würzburg (Busbahnhof)	1835

DEPART Würzburg Hbf	TRAIN NUMBER	ARRIVE München Hbf
1804	ICE 723	2004
1830	ICE 631	2038
1929	ICE 883	2138
2031	ICE 633	2239
2134	ICE 885	2346
2229	ICE 635	0040+1

+1 Arrive next day

Distance: 172 miles (276 km) by bus, plus 173 miles (278 km) by train

For detailed information and registration, contact:

Deutsche Touring GmbH
Am Römerhof 17
60486 Frankfurt (Main) Germany
Tel: (069) 7903 50
Fax: (069) 7903 219
www.touring.de
E-mail: service@touring.de

Touristik-Arbeitsgemeinschaft
Romantische Strasse
Marktplatz
D-91550 Dinkelsbühl
Tel: (098) 51 551387
Fax: (098) 51 551388
www.romantischestrasse.de
E-mail: info@romantischestrasse.de

Note: Eurail passes and German Railpasses are valid for a 20 percent discount on this excursion. Credit cards accepted.

The town is a museum piece of medieval character. Most of its 12,500 citizens living within or just outside the city's walls work to serve the tourist in some manner. This town has survived, even in the 21st century, as the "Jewel of the Middle Ages."

Enjoy your visit in Rothenburg, but keep your eye on the town clock, for the Romantic Road bus continues on its journey to Würzburg and its final destination, **Frankfurt,** promptly at 1630. If for some reason you do miss the 1630 bus departure, the German railroad also operates another bus line between Rothenburg and Steinach, where you can connect with train service back to Munich.

Arriving in Würzburg at 1800, you have the opportunity of returning to Munich at 1831 aboard ICE 631; or you might want to have dinner and linger. A later departure would allow you to stay in Würzburg for several hours. The last train departs Würzburg at 2331. There are several restaurants immediately across from the park fronting the east side of the Würzburg rail station where you could enjoy dinner.

Rothenburg is loaded with living legends. One concerns the salvation of the town from certain destruction by its wine-drinking mayor. In 1631, during the Thirty Years' War, the town was captured by imperial troops under the command of General Tilly. While the general toyed with the idea of destroying the town and executing its councilors, he was handed a tankard holding more than three quarts of heavy Franconian wine to aid his meditation.

The general promised mercy to Rothenburg if one of its councilors could drain the "bumper" in one mighty draft. Mayor Nusch did and thus saved the town. He slept for three days and nights following the mighty quaff, but apparently he suffered no other ill effects, for he lived another 37 years and died at the age of 80—with a smile on his face. The historic deed is reenacted daily by a glockenspiel installed in the gable of the Councilors' Tavern at 1100, 1200, 1300, 1400, 1500, 2000, 2100, and 2200. Be there!

Day Excursion to

Ulm

World's Tallest Cathedral

Depart from Munich Hauptbahnhof
Distance by Train: 92 miles (148 km)
Average Train Time: 1 hour, 13 minutes
City Dialing Code: 731
Tourist Information Office: Tourist-Information Ulm/Neu-Ulm, Stadthaus, Münsterplatz, D-89073 Ulm
Tel: (0731) 161 2830; **Fax:** (0731) 161 1641
www.tourismus.ulm.de
E-mail: info@tourismus.ulm.de
Hours: April–December: 0900–1800 Monday–Friday, 0900–1600 Saturday, 1100–1500 Sunday; January–March: 0900–1800 Monday–Friday, 0900–1600 Saturday
Notes: A display of tourist information is in the railway station to your left upon entering the station from the train platforms.

Silhouetted against a blue sky, the Gothic spire of the **Ulm Cathedral** is a scene you are not likely to forget. Poised on the banks of the swift-moving Danube, Ulm is a picturesque representation of a typical Swabian city. Birthplace of Albert Einstein, Ulm has withstood the onslaughts of many conflicts, including Napoleonic campaigns, with great dignity. Considered a miracle, its cathedral escaped damage throughout World War II, although serious damage was inflicted on the town by Allied bombing. Ulm's original facades have now been repaired or replaced.

With a skyward thrust of 528 feet, the spire of the cathedral is the tallest in the world. Although the foundation stone was laid in 1377, the two towers and the spire were not completed until 1890. When the central nave was completed in 1471, it could hold 20,000 people—twice as many as the town's population at that time. Truly, this was an ambitious undertaking right from the start. The clear vertical lines and the lightness of the cathedral's architecture are beautiful. The interior is open 0900 to 1700 daily with extended summer hours, except when services are being conducted. There is no entrance fee, but there is a small admission charge to ascend the spire.

Speaking of the spire, a breathtaking panorama of Ulm, the Danube, and the surrounding area rewards those who climb its 768 steps. A word of caution: The climb is rigorous and should not be attempted unless you have good physical stamina. Back on the Münster square in front of the cathedral, you will notice the remarkable contrast of the old Gothic style and the contemporary architecture of the **Stadthaus** (Town House), built by Richard Meier in 1993. This modern building offers a variety of activities, including exhibitions, concerts, conferences, and tourist information, plus magnificent views of the cathedral.

Munich (München)—Ulm

DEPART München Hbf	TRAIN NUMBER	ARRIVE Ulm Hbf
0727	ICE 612	0846
0746	IC 1296	0902
0828	ICE 690	0947
0848	ICE 1268	1002
0928	ICE 610	1045
1028	ICE 598	1147
1128	ICE 518	1249
additional trains hourly, or more frequently until 2301.		

DEPART Ulm Hbf	TRAIN NUMBER	ARRIVE München Hbf
1456	IC 219	1611
1509	ICE 517	1627
1609	ICE 597	1727
1656	EC 117	1811
1709	ICE 519	1827
1809	ICE 599	1927
1856	IC 391	2011
plus other frequent service until 2309.		

Daily
Distance: 92 miles (148 km)

You will get a brief view of the Danube and the cathedral when crossing the railroad bridge entering Ulm. Watch on the right-hand side of the train immediately after passing the Neu-Ulm (New Ulm) Station. The railroad bridge has a pedestrian crossing, so you may want to return to that vantage point again for a more prolonged observation. The bridge can be reached after leaving the station by walking to the right and following the railroad. Continue straight ahead, not turning with the trolleys, on the promenade to the river's edge and the approach to the bridge.

Cross onto the bridge to stand on the federal state borderline separating Bavaria and Baden-Württenberg right over the middle of the Danube.

Another route to the Danube is through the **Fischerviertel** (Fishermen's Quarter), which lies to the south of the cathedral. En route, you will pass the picturesque **Schiefes Haus** (Crooked House), which has settled over a canal. If you walk downstream on the Danube's left bank, the river promenade will bring you to the **Metzgerturm** (Butcher's Tower), another Ulm landmark. Walk on the ancient city wall, and see the old traditional Ulm river boat—the ***Ulmer Schachtel***—on the other bank of the Danube. Walking to the city center from the Metzgerturm, you'll reach the **Rathaus** (Town Hall) from 1370, famous for its opulent frescoes and ornamental carved figures. On the east gable is a beautiful astronomer's clock (1520).

Visit the **Ulm Museum,** where you will find displays of art and culture ranging from the Middle Ages to modern times. Notable features are the collections of modern graphics and important examples of Late Gothic art, as well as prehistoric finds such as the 30,000- to 40,000-year-old figure "Lion Man." There are also exhibits concerning some of Ulm's famous citizens, such as the physicist Albert Einstein, and Albrecht Berblinger, the "tailor of Ulm," who in 1811 made man's first serious attempt to fly. A model of his hang glider is on exhibit in the covered courtyard of the Rathaus. Visit www.museum.ulm.de. The funny Einstein Fountain, in front of the former Imperial city's arsenal ("Zeughaus") at the east of the old city center, merits a short visit.

Although the cathedral dominates the scene, a stroll through Ulm will reveal its other aspects—exclusive shops, boutiques, and department stores. For refreshment in between sightseeing, you will find traditional old taverns, pleasant restaurants, comfortable inns, and good hotels where you may enjoy Swabian specialty dishes accompanied by drafts of good Ulm beer.

Unique in the field of museums is Ulm's **Museum of Bread Culture** [Salzstadelgasse 10, D-89073 Ulm; *Tel:* (0731) 69955; *Fax:* (0731) 6021161; www.museum-brotkultur.de], situated in the beautifully restored salt warehouse from 1592. It presents an impressive display of the major ingredient of our daily diet for the last 8,000 years. *Hours:* 1000–1700 daily. It's only a 10-minute walk from the rail station. Not only does the museum effectively tell the story of breadmaking, it makes you aware of how serious hunger can be.

Very remarkable and to be noticed everywhere in Ulm and Neu-Ulm are the buildings and installations of the former Federal Fortification Ulm ("Bundesfestung"). Important landmarks of Europe's largest remaining 19th-century fortifications are the **Citadel Wilhelmsburg** on the "Michelsberg"—from where you have a splendid view of the city—Blaubeuren Gate or the "Glacis" bastion, now Neu-Ulm's municipal park.

Ulm University offers a Path of Art. More than 60 large works by artists of repute such as Niki de Saint-Phalle or Max Bill are presented along a 1½-kilometer tour around the university and Science Park Ulm. To get there, take bus line 3 or 5 from the central station to James-Franck-Ring.

Wiblingen Monastery (founded in honor of St. Martin in 1093), with its Baroque basilica and splendid Rococo library, is only 5 kilometers away (bus line 3 from Hauptbahnhof to Pranger). *Hours:* 0900–1800 daily except Monday (April–October). Church visit is €4.00 with an additional admission charge for the library and basilica.

With so much to see and do, the blue **Ulm Card** may be just the ticket for the day. It costs €12.00 per person or €10.50 per person for family of four or more. Prices include transport on buses and trams, discounts, and reduced prices for sites, guided tours, and a map of Ulm and Neu-Ulm. The Ulm Card is available at the tourist office, along with the monthly schedule of events.

GREECE

Inasmuch as Greece is most famous for its archaeological finds and significance in antiquity, many visitors are astounded to learn this scenic, sun-drenched country also includes about 1,400 islands and more than 7,500 caves, many of which contain subterranean rivers, lakes, and waterfalls. Complementing this varied geographic wonder are the mountain ranges such as the Pindus and, of course, the waters of the Mediterranean, the Aegean, and the Saronic Gulf linking Attica (Athens area and its port Piraeus) to the Peloponnese. *Note:* Due to the recent financial situation, be sure of your plans when visiting Greece. Call ahead and confirm specific plans whenever possible, and be aware that cash may be required. Check with the U.S. State Department for up-to-date travel advisories.

CHAT Tours, a leading tour operator in Greece, offers many delightful sightseeing tours and cruises to the Greek islands. The tour campus is located at 9 Xenofontos Street, Athens, Greece (*Tel:* 323 0827, 322 2886, or 322 3137; *Fax:* 323 1200; www.chatours.gr). For tourist information contact the Greek National Tourism Organization in North America:

New York: 305 E. 47th Street, New York, NY 10017. *Tel:* (212) 421-5777; *Fax:* (212) 826-6940; www.greektourism.com; *E-mail:* info@greektourism.com

Banking

Currency: Euro (€)

Exchange rate at press time: €0.90 = U.S. $1.00

Hours: 0800–1400 Monday–Thursday; 0800–1300 Friday

Communications

Country Code: 30

Major Mobile Phone Companies: Cosmote, Vodafone, Wind

Phone cards may be purchased at most kiosks and Greek Telecommunications offices. Public red phones and gray phones at kiosks are metered for long-distance calls. Pay the kiosk owner for number of units charged.

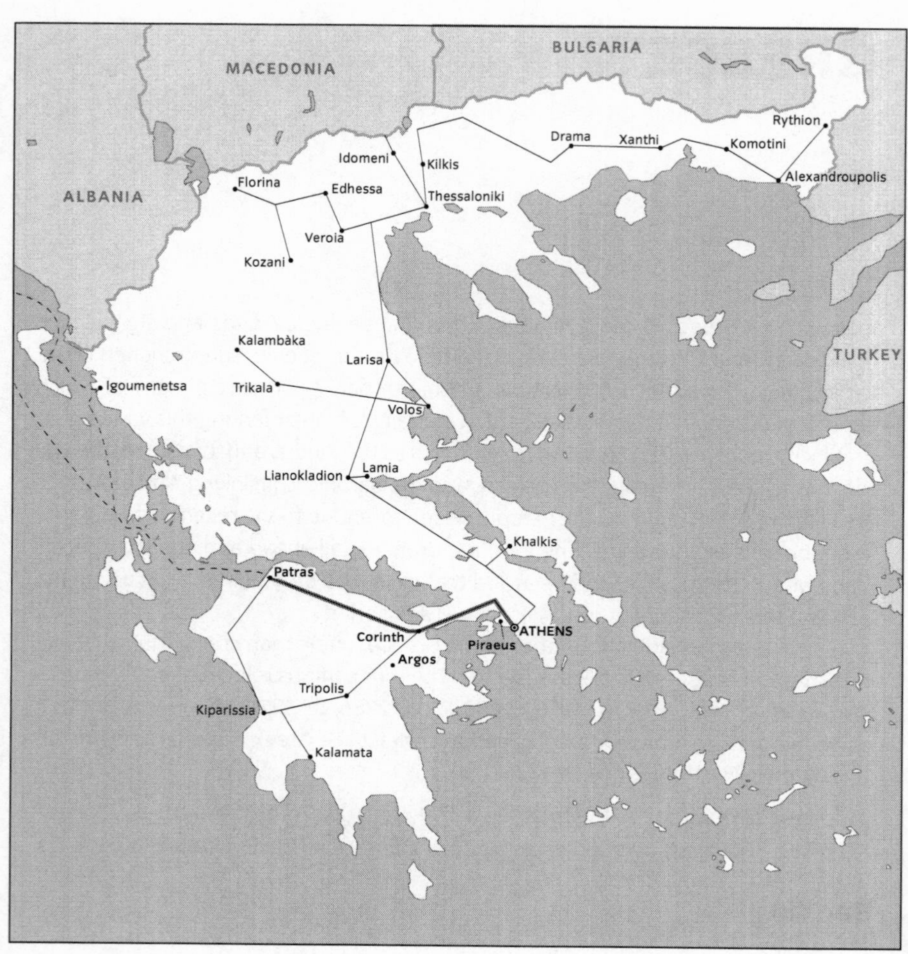
BULGARIA
MACEDONIA
ALBANIA
TURKEY
Rythion
Drama
Xanthi
Komotini
Alexandroupolis
Idomeni
Kilkis
Florina
Edhessa
Thessaloniki
Veroia
Kozani
Kalambàka
Larisa
Igoumenetsa
Trikala
Volos
Lianokladion
Lamia
Khalkis
Patras
Corinth
Piraeus
ATHENS
Argos
Tripolis
Kiparissia
Kalamata

Rail Travel in Greece

The Hellenic Railways Organization (OSE) has modernized its public transportation network considerably in the past few years, including adding new rail lines, upgrading existing ones, and introducing more modern, faster rolling stock. The line from Athens to Thessaloniki in the north has been modernized and several other ongoing modernization programs are under way by OSE. Visit www.ose.gr. Thanks to the 2004 Olympic Games being held in Athens, the Metro system in the Attica area is now connected with the suburban and Athens-Piraeus electric rail lines to create a more functional public transportation network.

The OSE accepts a variety of multicountry rail passes, including the variety of **Eurail passes,** the **Eurail Greece–Italy Pass,** the **Balkan Flexipass,** and the national rail pass—the **Greece Railpass**—for travel solely within Greece. (See the Appendix for prices and types of multicountry rail passes.)

Eurail bonuses include:

- Free ferry crossings (rail pass must be valid in Greece and Italy) from Patras, Igoumenitsa, and Corfu to Brindisi (Italy) on Hellenic Mediterranean Lines (HML) and Blue Star Ferries. A €20 surcharge applicable in July/August. Port taxes are extra.
- 20 percent discount on a one-day cruise—Athens to Aegina, Poros, and Hydra through Ionian Travel; plus reduced hotel rates in Athens. *Tel:* +30 1 523 9609 for reservations.
- 15 percent discount on some hotels and Athens attractions, when booked through Ionian Travel.

Greece Railpass

DAYS Within 1 Month	ADULT 1st Class	YOUTH 1st Class
3 days	$164	$146
4 days	$215	$193
5 days	$249	$222
6 days	$298	$266
7 days	$348	$310
8 days	$399	$355
9 days	$449	$401
10 days	$500	$445

Child fare (age 4–11) 50 percent off adult fare; younger than 4 travel free.
Youth younger than age 26.

Greece to Italy via Ferry—Crossing the Mediterranean

Attika Superfast Ferries operate daily, departing in the evening for arrival on the following day. The shortest journey time to Italy is Patras—Brindisi in only about 14 hours; to Bari, about 15 hours; and to Ancona, 19 hours. To reach the Patras Superfast ferry terminal from the rail station, turn left as you exit the station and walk along the street side of the quay about 300 yards.

Advance reservations are highly recommended, especially July 1 through August 31. Prices vary according to accommodations (from Pullman seats to deluxe cabins). For complete details, sailing dates, and fares, contact the individual ferry companies or their sales agent.

Superfast Ferries
123-125, Syngrou Avenue & 3, Torva Street 117 45, Athens, Greece
Tel: +30 (210) 891 9130; *Fax:* +30 (210) 891 9139
www.superfast.com
E-mail: info.athens@superfast.com

Superfast Ferries Sales Agent in U.S.:
Amphitrion Holidays
1506 21st Street NW, Suite 100 A
Washington DC 20036
Tel.: +1 202 872 9878
Fax: +1 202 872 8210
Email: amphitrion-us@superfast.com

Other ferry companies offering Eurail discounts (when valid in Greece) include:

Hellenic Mediterranean Lines
HSAP Building
P.O. Box 80057
GR-185 10 Pireaus, Greece
Tel: +30 (210) 422 5341; *Fax:* +30 (210) 422 5317
www.ferries.gr

Adriatica (Tirrenia Lines)
Zattere 1411
30123 Venice, Italy
Tel: +39 02 263 02803
www.tirrenia.it

Base City: **ATHENS** **(Athinai)**

www.breathtakingathens.com
City Dialing Code: 21

Arriving by Air

Athens International Airport—Eleftherios Venizelos. Athens International Airport (*Airport call center*: +30 210 353 0000; www.aia.gr) is located 33 kilometers southeast of Athens. The new airport met the goal of enhancing tourism to Athens in preparation for the Olympics in 2004.

- **Airport–City Links:** Airport Express Bus Line X95 connects the airport with Syntagma Square (Athens city center). Buses run every 20 minutes 0700 to 2130; less frequent service throughout the night. Fare €5.00. A suburban rail link connects the airport with downtown Athens' Larissa Station every hour from 0630 to 2330; journey time, 30 minutes.

- **Metro** Line 3 will take you from the airport to Athens Syntagma Square or Monastiraki Stations in about 36 minutes. At least two departures per hour. Fare: €8.

  Taxi queues are next to Door 3 of the Arrivals Level. Fares average about €35 to Syntagma Square; journey time, 30–40 minutes.

- **Money exchange, ATMs,** and **tourist information** are available in the Arrivals area, Level 0, of the main terminal.

  If you are departing Athens by air, the airport's tax-free shopping area offers a wide selection of Greek apparel, liquors, and delicacies. Unlike many tax-free shopping facilities, the one in Athens's airport has some reasonable values, but you can't bargain with the salespeople—leave that for shopping in the city.

Arriving by Train

Arrivals from eastern European countries and points in northern Greece terminate in Athens's Larissa Station, a standard-gauge facility. With the closure of the Peloponnese Station, if you are traveling via Attika's Superfast Ferries or Hellenic Mediterranean Lines ferries to the port of Patras, you will also arrive at Larissa station. The station has a train information booth with a limited amount of city information available. The station has taxi stands and bus service, but we recommend the taxi. The taxi fare from the station area to the tourist office on Syntagma (Constitution) Square is inexpensive, about €4 plus baggage charges, and well worth it.

Larissa Station serves the standard-gauge rail lines to the north.

- **Money exchange:** At the north end of the train platform. The sign reads BANK. *Hours:* 0800–2115 Monday–Friday, 0900–1400 Saturday, 0900–1300 Sunday.
- **Train information:** In a booth to your immediate left when entering the station from the train platform area. *Hours:* 0800–2200 daily. *Tel:* (0210) 823 7741.
- **Baggage storage:** In room marked LEFT BAGGAGE OFFICE located to the left as you enter the station from the track side (open 0700 to 2000).
- **Train reservations:** Are best obtained at the Greek Railways office at No. 1–3 Karolou Street or No. 6 Sina Street. Get taxi instructions from the tourist office on 2 Amerikis Street.
- **Rail pass validation:** Also available at the Greek Railways main office. Rail passes can also be validated at ticket windows in the stations, but only on your departure day.

Tourist Information/Hotel Reservations

The Greek National Tourism Organization has three offices in Athens:

- *Central Services,* Tsoha 7 Street, 11521 Athens. *Tel:* (210) 8707000; *Hours:* 0800–1500 Monday–Friday; *E-mail:* info@gnto.gr. Located in the vicinity of Syntagma Square. When you face the Parliament Building from the bottom of the square in the cafe area, the tourist information office is just across the street on the left. Money exchange is available here as well.
- *Athens International Airport* (Eleftherios Venizelos). *Tel:* (210) 3530445 8; *Hours:* 0900–2100 Monday–Friday, 1000–1600 Saturday–Sunday.
- *Athens Center,* 26A Amalias Street. *Tel:* (210) 3310392 and (210) 3310716; *Hours:* 0900–1900 Monday–Friday, 1000–1500 Saturday–Sunday.
- *Hotel and pension reservations:* Hellenic Chamber of Hotels, 24 Stadiou Str. 105 64 Athens–Hellas. *Tel:* (0210) 331 0022. Visit www.grhotels.gr.

Getting Around in Athens

Getting around in Athens is easy with its Metro and extensive bus and trolley-bus system. Obtain a public transport map showing routes and Metro stations at any of the tourist information offices. A single ticket is €1.40. A 24-hour ticket that covers the entire urban network (except airport bus lines) is €4.00. Visit www.ametro.gr. The Metro was modernized and expanded in preparation for the 2004 Olympics in Athens. Along with the "Athens-Piraeus Electric Railway" (ISAP), there are three lines. Additional services and expansions are still taking place. Progress was slowed somewhat by archaeological finds. You will marvel at the extensive use of marble in the Syntagma Station.

Sights/Attractions/Tours

Most of the tours offered are bus tours that include some walking. Consequently, you should inquire as to the tour's duration and terrain before signing up, and don't forget to wear comfortable walking shoes. To avoid the daytime heat, select an evening tour, when available. Most of the tourist attractions are illuminated.

The city tourist office is an excellent source for information concerning other areas of the country. Be certain to inform the attendant you speak with that you hold a Eurail pass. Otherwise you might find yourself signing up for a bus tour when a rail trip would suffice for the transportation to the site you want to see.

Although there is more to Athens than the **Acropolis,** it should be the first place to visit during your stay in the city. If you use the ISAP electric railway, detrain at Thission for the Acropolis. All else in and around Athens becomes secondary to this symbol of classic perfection that has stood majestically above Athens for about 2,500 years. Don't rush your visit, or you will regret it. Plan to spend an entire day, and if you go there during the summer months, go prepared with some sunscreen, sun hats, bottled water, and comfortable walking shoes.

The **Parthenon** is the focal point of the Acropolis, but there is much more to see. Study the **Propylaea,** the impressive entrance to the sanctuary, along with the **Temple of Athena-Niki** and the elegant row of maidens along the facade of the Erechtheion. You can peer down on the Theater of Dionysius from the rim of the Acropolis, but go there later to feel its "presence."

During the tourist season, a light-and-sound show of the Acropolis is presented in several languages. Don't miss it. The program in English starts at 2100. The tourist office can provide you with more details. You view the show from an opposite hillside, and it can cool down considerably. You may want to take a light sweater or pullover.

The Romans made their presence known in Athens, too. A group of ruins dating from the days of Julius Caesar clusters about the **Roman Forum** at the beginning of Aeolou Street. There are so many other sights to be seen that we recommend a guided tour as the only means of possibly scratching the surface of this wonderful city where Western civilization began.

With Athens's extensive history, expect to find a full retinue of museums. You won't be disappointed. Be aware that you may be required to check any bags, including purses, and that most museums charge a fee for videotaping within the museum. If your stay in the city is limited, visit the **Benaki Museum,** 1 Koumbari Street and Vassilissis Sofias Avenue, 10674 Athens. *Tel:* 0210 367 1000; *Fax:* 0210 367 1063; *Hours:* Monday–Saturday, 0900–1700, Sunday 0900–1500, and until 2400 Thursday. Admission: €7; www.benaki.gr. In its 28 chambers, you will see exhibits ranging from the Bronze Age to the beginning of the 20th century. As you pass through the centuries of statuary development, note the style by which the sculptors slowly developed the technique of depicting fingers and toes.

The modern city of Athens also holds much interest for visitors. You must visit the **Tomb of the Unknown Warrior,** with its colorful guards. Go to a cafe on **Syntagma Square** for coffee and pastry. Climb the timeworn steps leading through the **Plaka Quarter,** which hugs the base of the Acropolis. Take the Metro to Faliro Station, and sample the fruits of the sea at one of Mikrolimano's charming seafood restaurants.

Despite being one of the easternmost cities in Europe, Athens has a distinct Western appearance. Modern Athens surrounds the splendor of its ancient Acropolis, which has a nobility that survives time and change. That first glimpse of the Parthenon from the window of the plane or train that brought you to Athens remains a once-in-a-lifetime experience.

Addendum to Athens

Select one of Athens's "tavernas" and enjoy its food, music, and dancing. To experience a popular form of Greek entertainment, visit a bouzouki nightclub. Bouzouki music is similar to American blues in that the music reflects the pain and pathos often present in love and friendships. Before you participate in the traditional plate breaking, check with the management as to the cost per dozen. You could end up spending a lot of euros.

Train/Ferry Connections to Other Base Cities from Athens (Athinai)

Depart Athens Larissa Station by train to Patras (see rail schedule in "Day Excursion to Patras" section). Depart Patras by ferry to Brindisi, Italy (see Appendix "Ferry Crossings"), and then depart Brindisi by train to the selected base city.

Brindisi—Rome (Roma) Termini Trains

DEPART Brindisi	TRAIN NUMBER	ARRIVE Rome Termini
0611	ES 9350	1120
0846	IC 610	1902
1711	ES 9358	2220
2148	ICN 752	0956+1 (Sleeper)

Brindisi—Milan (Milano) Centrale Trains

DEPART Brindisi	TRAIN NUMBER	ARRIVE Milan Centrale
0626	IC 9814	1525
1226	IC 9826	2125
2148	ICN 752	0930+1 (Sleeper)

Reservations required on all the above listed trains
+1 Arrives next day
Note: Although rail travel is possible on the Athens (Athenai Larissa Station) Thessaloniki-to-Budapest route, Eurail passes do not cover travel through the former Yugoslavia and other eastern European countries (except Hungary and Romania). Also, travelers are warned of the hazards of traveling in politically unstable areas. The potential traveler choosing this route is urged to consult a European rail ticket agent for detailed schedule information and for information about procedures and visa requirements in eastern European countries.

Tourists are targets for ploys and pranks throughout the world. Athens is no exception. A waiter may suggest that you consume bottled water with your meal. After all, you may have been warned not to drink the regular water. Bottled water is a good idea, but insist that the waiter open the bottle at your table. Otherwise, you might receive an opened bottle of water that was just recently filled from the water tap in the kitchen. Or order a bottle of carbonated water. That's hard to bootleg!

Day Excursions

Riding a narrow-gauge train through areas steeped in the history of Western civilization is sufficiently stimulating to make the traveler overlook the lack of air-conditioning, posh dining cars, and other amenities. Our day excursion to **Argos,** the oldest continuously inhabited town in Greece, is one such adventure. **Corinth,** both modern and ancient, is rich in Greek history, from Alexander the Great down through Roman rule. **Patras,** port city and scene of the most spectacular carnival in Greece, is still another place to see on the Peloponnese. **Piraeus,** main port of Athens, provides culinary delights from the surrounding sea.

An InterCity train between Athens and **Larissa** provides an opportunity to spend several hours in Larissa during a day excursion out of Athens. Depart Athens at 0718, arrive in Larissa at 1118 on IC 50, and depart at 1759 on train 591 to arrive back in Athens by 2218. Or depart Larissa at 1926 on IC 61 for arrival in Athens at 2322. Although the IC 61 does not haul a restaurant car, there are beverages and some food available. Also, you will find an abundance of cafes and patisseries on the town square. Larissa, the "citadel," is the capital of Thessaly, and for a time it was the home of Hippocrates, the Father of Medicine.

Day Excursion to

Argos (Arghos)

Oldest Greek Town

Depart from Athens Peloponnese Bus Station
Distance by Bus: 89 miles (144 km)
Average Bus Time: 2 hours
City Dialing Code: 751

Argos does not have a tourist information office. Neither does it have a tourist police office such as one finds in many of the smaller towns throughout Greece. But these absences present no great hardship, for most of its sights are within the city limits. The area must be the birthplace of all Greeks who have ever worked in the United States as waiters. We met two of them by just standing on a corner and looking perplexed.

The station is about a kilometer from the town square in Argos. To reach the town square on foot, walk straight out of the station to the main road, where a road sign points to the right in the direction of town. Taxis are available for a nominal fare.

For sightseeing, orient yourself with the church in the town square. From its front door, you can reach the **Argos museum** by crossing the street, turning left, and proceeding to the first cross street, where you then turn right. The museum is half a block farther on the left-hand side of the street and is open daily except Tuesday. Admission is charged. This museum has an excellent collection of archaeological exhibits.

The **ancient theater and Roman ruins** lie on the outskirts of town, in the direction of the hillsides. They are a 5-minute taxi ride or a 15-minute walk from the museum. On foot, turn left at the next street beyond the museum and walk until

Athens (Athinai)—Argos (Arghos)

No train service is currently available to Argos. There are at least 5 buses a day from Athens to Argos, and additional buses from Corinth to Argos. Travel time from Athens to Argos is about 2 hours.

you reach the next main intersection. Turn right, and walk straight ahead to the site. If there is the slightest tinge of archaeology in your blood, you'll love this spot.

The theater has 90 tiers, which were cut into the hillside on a rather steep angle, making it possible for a perfect, uninterrupted view of the stage area from any seat in the house. Oddly enough, the 20,000 seating capacity of this amphitheater is more than adequate for the current 19,000 population of Argos.

History comes out to meet you on this day excursion. Argos lies in the plain of Argolis on the Peloponnese peninsula, land of myth and magic. Your mind can run rampant as you journey there. The *Iliad*, the *Odyssey*, and the beautiful Helen hover over all travelers who enter.

Modern history appears first as the train crosses the Isthmus of Corinth. Below the railroad bridge lies the canal connecting the Aegean and Ionian Seas. Alexander the Great, Caesar, and Nero all failed in their attempts to construct the waterway through 4 miles of solid rock. A French engineering firm finally succeeded in 1893. Watch for it about 1 hour and 20 minutes after leaving Athens. The best view is from the right side of the train. The railroad bridge is only 108 feet long; if you plan on taking pictures, have everything poised and ready to go, for it passes quickly.

Medieval history is next in line as you approach Argos, where the hillsides northwest of the city reveal at their highest point a Venetian fortress, which dominates the **White Chapel of the Prophet Elias** and **Our Lady of the Rocks Convent** lying below.

Ancient history unfolds in Argos itself, with the 20,000-seat theater, and 5 miles east of the town with the **Argive Heraeon** and the scattered remains of Greece's oldest recognizable temple (800 B.C.). **Tiryns,** legendary birthplace of Hercules, is also in the area. These last two sights are not on the bus line and are best visited by taxi from Argos.

Argos is the oldest continuously inhabited town in Greece. Many archaeologists suspect that it may be the oldest in all of Europe. Legends, many of them the basic stuff from which most of Greek mythology sprang, have their origins in Argos and the area surrounding it. In the legendary time of Danaus, storytellers relate how his 50 daughters slew their husbands on their wedding night and then tried to make amends with the devil by trying to fill a bottomless cask with water carried in sieves from the Lake of Lerna.

The legend does, however, have a happy ending. One of Danaus's daughters, realizing that it could ruin her honeymoon, let her spouse escape the murderous nuptial-night activities. For this she was rewarded by becoming the ancestral matriarch of a long line of mythological heroes.

The modern town of Argos was built up over ancient ruins from previous centuries of conflict. The last ethnic group to participate in that form of urban renewal was the Turks, who ravaged the town in 1397. As a result, Argos has scant visible remains of its ancient origins except the theater and the Roman baths.

Day Excursion to

Corinth (Korinthos)

And the Isthmian Canal

Depart from Athens Larissa Station
Distance by Train: 57 miles (91 km)
Average Train Time: 1 hour, 32 minutes
City Dialing Code: 741
www.ancientcorinth.net

This day excursion runs from modern Greece back through the millennia to the Bronze Age. You have the opportunity to see modern Corinth (Korinthos), a typical "new" Greek city, and its port on the Peloponnese. You may delve as well into the hillside of ancient Corinth, where Saint Paul established a church, Nero fiddled around with a canal, and Julius Caesar implemented an earlier version of the Marshall Plan.

En route to Corinth, the railroad skirts the Aegean Sea and crosses the Isthmian Canal. Watch for the canal when the train is about 1 hour out of Athens. The center of the canal runs 285 feet deep through solid rock. The railroad bridge passes 200 feet above the level of the water for a spectacular view.

Greek and Roman rulers (the infamous Nero included) periodically attempted to breach the isthmus with a canal, but until a French company using modern methods succeeded between 1882 and 1893, all had failed. The ancients hauled their small ships across the isthmus on rollers. Vestiges of the portage road are still visible just after the train crosses the bridge. Watch on the right side of the train for the best view. Have your camera poised and ready—the train traverses the area quickly.

Athens (Athinai)—Corinth (Korinthos)

DEPART Athens Larissa	ARRIVE Corinth
0555	0705
0726	0905
1125	1305
1544	1705

DEPART Corinth	ARRIVE Athens Larissa
1039	1152
1639	1752
1839	1952
2039	2152

Distance: 57 miles (91 km)

The current "new" city of Corinth, moved to its site in 1858 after an earthquake destroyed "old" Corinth, was leveled by an equally devastating earthquake in 1928. The site has had its share of earth tremors; ancient scribes record devastation in A.D. 522 and 551. Called an "undistinguished town," new Corinth is interesting in that it represents a community rebuilt on anti-seismic principles of low buildings that, paradoxically, give it an air of impermanence.

In fear of pirates, old Corinth was built well back from the sea. This strategic position served the city well. Corinth prospered and became one of the three great city-states of Greece, along with Athens and Sparta. Things went reasonably well until Corinth led the Achaean League against the Romans in 146 B.C. The Romans won the ball game and, a la Carthage (as was the custom in those days), laid waste to Corinth. After the city withstood a hundred years of total desolation, Julius Caesar decided to rebuild Corinth, and it blossomed into one of the great trading cities of the Roman Empire.

During his 18-month sojourn in Corinth, Saint Paul became alarmed about the sinful ways of the Corinthians and frequently "read the riot act" to the city fathers. Because of his violent condemnation of moral laxity, he was charged with inciting a riot. Instead of dispensing punishment, the city fathers issued Saint Paul a reprimand—and the suggestion that he leave town as soon as possible, which he did.

Historians estimate that at one time the ancient city of Corinth had a population of more than 460,000; today, its citizens number about 21,000. Although termed a citadel, the old city was attacked repeatedly and conquered through the ages. During their sweep through Greece, the Turks took over the city in 1458 and again in 1715. In 1458 the Turkish conquest ended when they retreated hastily in ships. The siege of the city in 1715 was described in prose by Lord Byron. There is little

Turkish architecture visible in the Corinthian area, due mainly to the short time they were on the premises.

There is excellent bus service between the city and the **archaeological site.** Departures are daily on the hour from 0600 to 2100. The bus terminal is on the south side of the city park. The sign over the terminal reads ΑΡΧΑΙΑ. A taxi will take you there from the railway station for a nominal fare.

To reach the bus station on foot, turn left after leaving the station and then right onto Damaskinou Street and right again onto Ermou Street, just before the Hotel Belle Vue. Turn left at this point and, 3 blocks later, you'll arrive at the bus terminal on the far left-hand corner of the city park. For further information check with the **"Tourist Police."** Walk through the park, past another bus terminal to a pharmacy on the right-hand side. Turn right, and find the police station half a block farther on the left-hand side.

Excavations have been in progress on the site of old Corinth for many years. Literature describing the excavations and the contents of the museum is available as you enter the site. Between 1925 and 1929, extensive excavations were made. Among the findings, an inscription was found that recorded the story of Androcles and the lion. According to Roman history, Androcles removed a thorn from a lion's paw. Later, when he was sentenced to death and thrown to the lions, the lion remembered Androcles's kindness and let him off without a scratch.

In ancient Corinth, you must pay for admission (€6) to the grounds and an additional fee to enter the museum. *Hours:* 0800–1900 daily June–October, 0830–1700 November–May. Plan to spend a minimum of four hours at the site. There is a lot of walking. Several canteens serve refreshments outside the main entrance.

Day Excursion to

Patras

Port City

Depart from Athens Larissa Station
Distance by Train: 138 miles (222 km)
Average Train Time: 3 hours, 49 minutes
City Dialing Code: 61
Tourist Information Office: Peloponnese and Western Greece Tourism Bureau, Othonos Amalias 6, Patras 26223. **Tel:** (261) 046-1740-1; **Fax:** (261) 046-1791
www.infocenterpatras.gr
Hours: 0800–2200 daily
Notes: Ask at the rail station or the ferry terminal for directions. Otherwise, turn right at the quay, and walk well beyond the ferry terminal and look for the signs leading to the office. There also is an information office at the entrance of the port of Patras (at Glyfada). The railway station in Patras lies on the quay, but it's about 500 yards from the pier where ferries depart for Brindisi. You'll spot the pier to the right as the train slows for its stop in the Patras Station. A **tourist information booth** is located at the entrance to the ferry terminal. For complete information regarding Patras and its surroundings, visit the Peloponnese and Western Greece Tourism Bureau at the aforementioned address.

Patras is the fourth-largest city in Greece. It is also the country's western gateway. Located at the entrance to the **Gulf of Corinth,** Patras has been a Greek seaport since the beginning of recorded history. Ships large and small are constantly arriving in, and departing from, its harbor. The ferry services of Adriatica (Tirrenia Line) and Hellenic Mediterranean Lines ply between Patras and Brindisi, Italy. Attika Enterprises (Superfast Ferries) ply between Patras and Bari. If you are traveling with a rail pass, no doubt you will either enter or leave Greece through the Port of Patras.

Patras is the port where the majority of Greek emigrants sailed for the United States. It is interesting to note that in 1922 refugees fleeing Asia Minor arrived at the pier in Patras penniless. Many of them paid for their passage to America by selling their Oriental carpets, which they had carried from their homelands. Since the early 1960s Patras has developed into a major Adriatic ferry port.

Spreading below its Venetian castle, Patras is where **Saint Andrew** taught Christianity and was crucified. The saint's head rests in a shrine following its return from Saint Peter's, Rome, in 1964. It was here in Patras in 1809 that Lord Byron first set foot on Greek soil.

The quay is an interesting part of Patras. The long mole, with its benches for resting, extends into the harbor and is a favorite place from which to watch the activity in the harbor. From it you can photograph the arrival of the ferryboats running between the ports of Patras and Brindisi. Patras is not just a busy harbor, however.

Athens (Athinai)—Patras

DEPART Athens Larissa	ARRIVE Patras
0555	0858
0855	1208

DEPART Patras	ARRIVE Athens Larissa
1630	1952
1830	2152

Distance: 138 miles (222 km)
Note: Due to construction work as the line from Athens to Patras is converted from narrow-gauge to standard gauge, you must switch to bus service in Kiato. Bus service is also available direct from Athens, travel time about 3 hours.

Its eucalyptus-soaked shorelines, topaz waters, and vast sandy beach at Kilini have made it well-known for its spas since antiquity.

Patras has two noteworthy celebrations: the stately procession of Saint Andrew on November 30 and a spectacular carnival during the last 10 days before Lent. The city also conducts a classic-theater season during the summer. We suggest a walking tour of Patras starting at the **Trion Symmahon Square,** across from the station and on the right. The long arcaded avenue leading off the park in the direction of the city's heights is studded with stores, restaurants, and specialty shops.

Continue walking on this avenue (Ayiou Nikolaou) to the foot of a broad flight of steps, which will bring you to the site of the ancient **Patras Acropolis.** Enjoy a wonderful view of the city, its harbor, and the surrounding hills and mountains from here. Return to the base of the steps, and proceed to the left on Yeoryiou Street, which will lead you to the **Odeum,** a characteristic Roman theater. It was discovered in 1889, but enterprising building contractors subsequently removed much of its marble, requiring the theater to be restored extensively in 1960.

Visitors seeking **Saint Andrews Church** should begin their quest at the Trion Symmahon Square and walk southwest along Andreou Avenue to the church, which stands by the sea at the avenue's end. A park dedicated to Andrew, the patron saint of Scotland, is across from the church.

To reach the city's museum, turn left at the Trion Fountain in Trion Symmahon Square and walk for 2 blocks, then turn right and walk for 2 more. The museum has an extensive collection of classic Greek and Roman statues plus a collection of prehistoric pottery. There is an admission charge.

The area surrounding Patras is steeped in history. Use Patras as a "base city" when visiting **Olympia,** original site of the Olympic Games. In Olympia you can visit the site of the Olympic flame, which is carried by runners to any point in the world where the games are to be held. Also of interest is the arch commemorating Nero's "victory" in a chariot race staged in A.D. 67. The emperor's chariot was pulled by 10 horses, while all other competitors had to make do with four—needless to say, Nero won.

Another interesting side trip can be made to the **Achaia Clauss Winery,** 5 miles outside Patras, to view the wine-making process and sample a bit of the product. If interested in either excursion, obtain information at one of the tourist offices.

Culinary delights abound in Patras. A sea-bass dish, *tsipoures*, is a specialty of the area. This and other Greek dishes are available in the tavernas scattered throughout the upper part of town. An American-style restaurant lies just before the Hellenic Lines office on the quay. Customers may stow their suitcases and backpacks there free of charge while waiting for the ferry.

Day Excursion to

Piraeus

Seafood by the Seaside

Depart from Athens Omonia Metro Station
Distance by Train: 5 miles (8 km)
Average Train Time: 20 minutes
City Dialing Code: 1
Tourist Information Office: Diikitirio Building, East Central Greece Islands, Marina Zeas, 18504
Tel: (010) 4522586; **Fax:** (010) 4522591
www.piraeusweb.com

You won't need your rail pass for this day excursion. You'll be traveling on Athens's privately owned electric line—ISAP. The line is the "subway" for the city. A major portion of the rails running to Piraeus, however, is aboveground.

Begin your journey from **Omonia Square** in the city. It connects with Syntagma (Constitution) Square via Stadhiou Street, which starts right outside the entrance to the tourist information office. The entrances to the underground terminal are clearly marked. Be certain to purchase and validate your tickets before boarding. The station uses a center platform for all trains, so check the directional signs for Piraeus before boarding.

Travel at off-peak hours to avoid the crowds. Service is frequent throughout the day. Train etiquette in Greece dictates that men relinquish their seats to the ladies and that the young do the same for elders. When in Greece, do as the Greeks do.

Athens (Athinai)—Piraeus

Frequent local trains run between Athinai Omonia Station and Piraeus on the ISAP Line; first train 0500, last train returning Omonia Station at 0030; journey time is approximately 20 minutes.

Distance: 5 miles (8 km)

Leave the electric train at the end of the line in Piraeus. The terminal lies right at the harbor. To stroll along the quay, exit the station straight ahead, turning left at the side along the sea. Commercial ships and ferries to hundreds of island points occupy the piers along the waterfront of the main harbor.

Throughout the centuries, Piraeus has had successes and failures. In 86 B.C. the Roman general Sulla destroyed the city and its docks, and for centuries Piraeus was considered an unimportant village. Reconstruction began only in 1834, when Athens became the capital of Greece. Resettled by islanders, Piraeus grew rapidly throughout the 19th century and played a large part in the revival of Athens.

Between 1854 and 1859, Piraeus was occupied by an Anglo-French fleet to prevent Greek nationalists' forays against Turkey, an Allied power in the Crimean War. During World War II the port was put out of action in April 1941 by a German air attack. The ammunition ship *Clan Fraser*, carrying 200 tons of TNT, together with two other ships loaded with ammunition, exploded and destroyed the port.

In addition to its main harbor, Piraeus has two small-craft harbors, **Zea** and **Mikrolimano.** Zea shelters pleasure craft, and Mikrolimano features fishing craft and seafood restaurants, the latter rimming its waterfront like pickets of a fence. Bus No. 20 will take you to either of the smaller ports. Board it from the bus terminal on the left side of the train station. Bus No. 20 stands in the far line, facing away from the sea.

After skirting the main harbor, the bus passes through a built-up area before it again sides with the sea at Zea. If Mikrolimano is your destination, ride four stops beyond Zea and dismount. **The Castella Hotel** is on the left side at the bus stop. From there, walk down to the harbor. If you're going for lunch, try to arrive before 1230, when the area is invaded by a horde of tour buses packed with hungry tourists. At night the tables in the restaurants overlooking the sea groan under their loads of fresh fish, luscious lobsters, and opulent oysters. Top off your evening by climbing the hill behind Mikrolimano for a magnificent view of the Mediterranean's Saronic Gulf.

Piraeus, main port of Greece, basks in the warm embrace of the Saronic Gulf, just a few miles and minutes outside the heart of Athens. Piraeus today is one of the principal ports of the Mediterranean and serves both commercial shipping and pleasure craft. Most tourists go to Piraeus not to view its remains of antiquity but, rather, to enjoy the picturesque atmosphere of its port and to indulge in some of the wonderful seafood served in its restaurants.

Many restaurants employ solicitors to influence your selection of eating places. You can ignore them. We have found that the better places lie to the right of the harbor. **Kanaris 2** is one of the more expensive restaurants, but it is well worth it. While on the subject of price, a word of caution: Check menu prices carefully before ordering. Many menu prices are given for 1 kilo (2.2 pounds) of fish—a price that the government requires the restaurants to list. Certainly, your platter won't hold that much, but some places will try to charge you on that basis. *Caveat emptor*—let the buyer beware.

During the summer, Piraeus is considerably cooler than Athens. Should the temperatures soar during your stay in the Greek capital, take a quick trip on the Athens subway to the seaside at Piraeus. In the evening the tavernas and nightclubs there provide a resort-type lifestyle. The city's nightspots feature popular singers.

Lacking museums, Piraeus's archaeological discoveries are displayed in the Athens National Museum. Of particular interest is a collection of statuary stored and forgotten by General Sulla in 86 B.C. Perhaps the general lost his claim check.

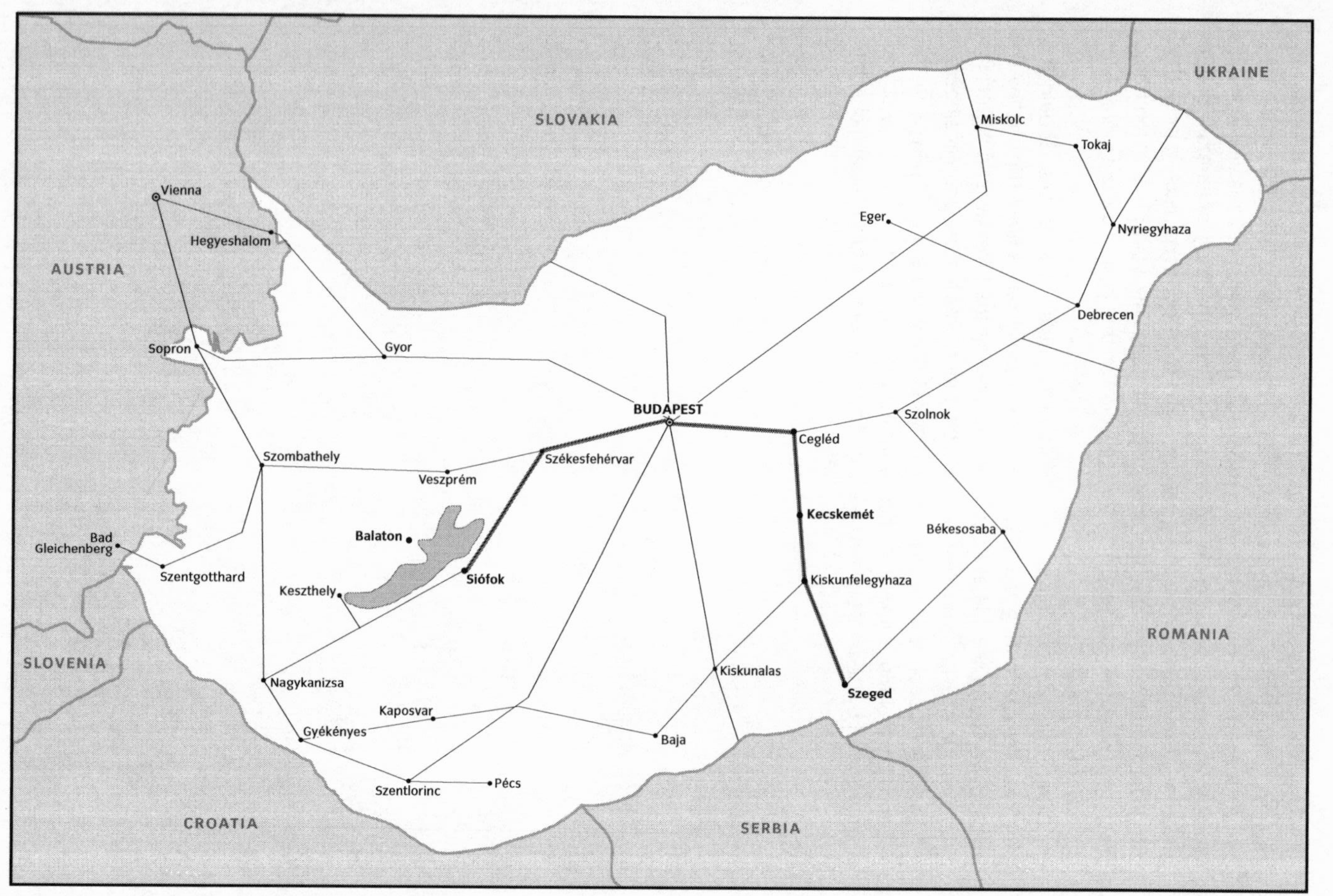

SLOVAKIA
UKRAINE
AUSTRIA
ROMANIA
SLOVENIA
CROATIA
SERBIA
Vienna
Hegyeshalom
Sopron
Gyor
Miskolc
Tokaj
Eger
Nyriegyhaza
Debrecen
BUDAPEST
Szolnok
Cegléd
Szombathely
Székesfehérvar
Veszprém
Kecskemét
Békesosaba
Balaton
Bad Gleichenberg
Szentgotthard
Siófok
Keszthely
Kiskunfelegyhaza
Kiskunalas
Nagykanizsa
Szeged
Kaposvar
Gyékényes
Baja
Szentlorinc
Pécs

HUNGARY

Hungary lies in the Carpathian Basin of Central Europe where the jewel of the Danube still shines with facets of multiple architectural styles. Hungary was the 17th member country to join the Eurail Community and the first Eastern European nation to do so. Of the country's 10.1 million inhabitants, 1.8 million live in its capital city of Budapest.

Present-day Hungarians descended from the Magyars, a nomadic, horse-riding people who conquered the land in the ninth century. The Magyars spoke a language unlike any other language of Europe, except Finnish, and even today other Europeans have difficulty understanding it. English and/or German, however, are spoken by many Hungarians in the tourism industry, particularly in hotels and restaurants.

Hungarian cuisine is hardy and flavorful. When dining on one of the many specialties made perhaps from cabbage, peppers, pork, and paprika, be sure to add a little Bull's Blood (wine) from Eger. For a marvelous treat do not pass up the fine pastries and baked goods of the region.

During World War II, the Hungarian government sided with the Axis powers. In April 1945 the country fell to Russian troops. Encouraged by the Polish defiance of the Soviet Union, Hungarians staged an uprising in 1956 that was quickly suppressed by Soviet troops and tanks. Hungary was under the "Iron Curtain" until 1989. The last Soviet troops left the country in June 1991. The Hungarian People's Republic became the Republic of Hungary with a newly elected democratic government—a coalition of six parties.

Hungary has six UNESCO World Heritage sites including the scientifically significant Baradla-Domica cave system of Aggtelek and Hortobágy's National Park, one of Europe's largest protected grasslands.

For more information on Hungary, visit **www.gotohungary.com,** e-mail info@hungarytourism.hu, or contact the Hungarian National Tourist Office in North America:

New York: 450 Fashion Avenue, #2601, New York, NY 10123; (212) 695-1221; www.gotohungary.com; *E-mail:* info@gotohungary.com

Banking

Currency: Hungarian Forint (HUF)

Exchange rate at press time: HUF 276.01 = U.S. $1.00

Communications

Country Code: 36

Major Mobile Phone Companies: T-Mobile, Telenor, Vodafone

Rail Travel in Hungary

The Hungarian State Railways (Magyar Allamvasutak, or MAV) includes more than 4,844 miles (7,750 kilometers) of rail lines with 1,423 miles (2,277 kilometers) electrified. Visit www.mavnosztalgia.hu. Fifty-four international trains per day arrive in Budapest, including Euronight (EN) service from Zürich and Bucharest. All international trains have dining and sleeping facilities; however, many of the Hungarian InterCity and express trains still do not offer all of the same amenities that can be found on the trains of Western Europe.

The Hungarian State Railways (MAV) accepts the variety of **Eurail** passes, the **European East Pass, Eurail Austria–Hungary Pass, Eurail Hungary–Croatia–Slovenia Pass, Eurail Hungary–Romania Pass,** and its own national pass—the **Eurail Hungary Pass.**

Eurail Hungary Pass

	ADULT 1st Class	SAVERPASS* 1st Class	YOUTHPASS** 2nd Class
3 days within 1 month	$138	$118	$91
8 days within 1 month	$258	$219	$169

Children age 4–11, half adult fare; children younger than age 4 travel free.

*Price per person based on 2–5 adults traveling together at all times

**Younger than age 26

For more detailed information on types and prices of other rail passes, please see the European rail passes listed in the Appendix.

Base City: **BUDAPEST**

www.budapestinfo.hu
City Dialing Code: 1

Budapest's tree-lined boulevards and spacious public squares bordered by magnificent buildings make it one of the most beautiful capitals of Europe. Hungary welcomes more than 24 million visitors annually, the majority of whom pass through Budapest, pausing to enjoy its special charm and atmosphere.

The city is actually a unification (in 1873) of three ancient towns: Óbuda with its Celtic and Roman ruins, Buda with its gently rolling hills on the west bank, and the community of Pest on the east bank. Buda stands on a terraced plateau and contains relics of a Turkish occupation; Pest rises from a plain and is the site of the Houses of Parliament, the Palace of Justice, the Museum of Fine Arts, and the National Museum. Buda and Pest are linked by six bridges over the Danube, including the beautiful Stone Chain Bridge.

Budapest's origins date from about 10 B.C. when the Romans established the colony of Aquincum on what is now Buda. The Vandals took it over from the Romans in A.D. 376, and, in turn, management changed hands frequently during invasions by the Tartars and the Turks until armies under Austrian leadership liberated what was left of the towns in 1686.

Some Roman ruins withstood the assaults and may be seen even today. You'll find many reasons to enjoy Budapest, known as the "Pearl of the Danube." Beyond the panorama (a UNESCO World Heritage Site), the healing waters of the springs, and the hospitality of the people, there is much to see and do and just take in. You'll be back.

Arriving by Air

Budapest's international airport, **Ferihegy,** has three terminals. Ferihegy 2A is about 20 kilometers southeast of the city center, and Ferihegy 2B is 24 kilometers. Terminal 1 serves low-cost carriers, terminal 2A handles flights for EU destinations, and terminal 2B is for flights outside of the EU. *Tel:* (01) 296 9696; www.bud.hu. *Flight information:* (01) 296 7000.

- **Airport–City Links:** Trains leave Terminal 1 every 15–20 minutes between 0542 and 2157, with less frequent service during the night.
- **Airport Minibus** (8- to 11-passenger minibuses) *Tel:* (01) 296 8555; *Fax:* (01) 296 8993. Operates between the two terminals and any address in Budapest.

Fare: HUF 3,200; discounted round-trip: HUF 5,500. Purchase tickets at the Welcome Desk in the Arrivals Hall.

- **Budapest Transport Enterprise** (BKV) services, bus No. 93 between Terminal 2 and terminus M3 metro line Köbánya-Kispest.

  The airport **taxi** stand is farther to the right, about 200 feet beyond the bus stop. Taxi service is available 24 hours a day. All taxis in Hungary must have yellow license plates and meters that print out receipts. Rates are fixed from the airport depending on the zone you are traveling to: HUF 6,500 to the city center. To reserve a taxi: Zona Taxi, *Tel:* (01) 222 2222.

- **Tourist information:** Inside all 3 terminals at the airport, near the terminal exits. *Hours:* 0800–2300 daily.

  Customs control uses the red-green corridor system just like the Western European countries. If you have nothing to declare, you should use the green corridor.

Arriving by Train

The Hungarian State Railways (MAV)
Tel: (01) 0640 49 49 49 Train information

Call for information on trains departing and arriving at Keleti, Deli, and Nyugati Stations. You can also visit www.mav-start.hu.

Keleti (East) **Station** is the terminus for most international express trains, with the exception of the *Adriatica, Agram, Maestral,* and *Graz* trains, which terminate in Budapest Deli (South) Station. Although it has undergone extensive improvements and restoration since its original construction in 1884, the old charm is still evident. Statues of George Stephenson, the inventor of the locomotive, and James Watt, creator of the steam engine, grace its entrance. The modern touch is found in the digital departure boards displayed at the platform entrances.

Stairs at the front of the station take you to the city's metro, a modern three-line subway system, but arrivals burdened with luggage should opt for the taxi queue immediately outside the station on the right. A word of caution: Be sure that the taxi you hail has a meter—and uses it. The best taxi service is City Taxi, and most drivers speak English. Call them at (01) 211 1111 and tell the English-speaking operator the telephone number you called from, and a taxi will arrive in just a few minutes. Any "no-name" taxi is almost certainly a rip-off.

Keleti Station has all of the usual tourist services. For rail reservations, proceed to the sign FOREIGN RAILWAY TICKETS—SEAT RESERVATIONS on your right when exiting from the trains. Note that window 2 is for currency exchange, window 3 for hotels, and window 6 is where you request tickets and seat reservations. Pay for all services in cash (U.S. dollars; forints not accepted).

Deli (South) **Station,** a modern concrete edifice on the Buda side of the Danube, features a huge supermarket on the ground level. Trains arrive overhead on uncovered platforms that lead to a covered concourse, with an enclosed waiting room and ticket office just beyond. The designation of Deli as Budapest's "south" station is a bit confusing in that it actually lies to the west of the city. A visit to the supermarket is a must. The products and produce selections offered may be fewer than those offered by even your local 7-Eleven store, but it's a great place to pick up the local flavor and mix with the citizens.

The Metro Line 2 (or Red) terminates at the Deli Station, with direct connections to the other two rail stations, Keleti and Nyugati. To access, follow the "M" pictographs leading from the train level; same for taxis.

Nyugati (West) **Station** stands at the head of Terèz Boulevard just before Nyugati Square. Nyugati Station has a Tourinform office as well as the usual amenities found at Keleti and Deli.

Tourist Information/Hotel Reservations

- *Tourism information office:* TourInform, Main Hall, Nyugati (West) Rail Station; *Tel:* (01) 302 8580; www.tourinform.hu; *E-mail:* nyugati@budapestinfo.hu. *Hours:* 0900–1800 daily.

The National Tourism Information Service has 754 travel offices in Hungary and offers information about its office hours and services for visitors, including money exchange, hotel reservations, travel reservations (including rail and air), tour bookings, and general tourist information. The main tourist office in Budapest is located at 1052 Süto u. 2 (Deák tér). *Tel:* (01) 438 8080; *Fax:* (01) 488 8661; *E-mail:* hungary @tourinform.hu. *Hours:* 0800–2000 daily.

If you are interested in organized tours, TourInform offers quite a selection of sightseeing and tour activities. The "City Tour" is a three-hour sightseeing adventure by bus to Budapest's famous spots, including Castle Hill for a panoramic view. Narrow-gauge train runs through gorgeous hillsides may be arranged through the offices, or you may also want to take a two-hour sightseeing cruise on the Danube.

For "the whole city in your pocket" do not pass up the **Budapest Card** (available for 24 hours for HUF 4,500, 48 hours for HUF 7,500 or 72 hours for HUF 8,900). The card offers free transportation around the city and discounts on shopping, restaurants, sightseeing, and cultural and folklore programs. Each card is valid for one adult and one child up to age 14. Pick up the card at the airport, metro ticket offices, tourist information offices, hotels, and underground ticket offices.

Train Connections to Other Base Cities from Budapest

Depart from Budapest Keleti Station unless otherwise noted.

DEPART	TRAIN NUMBER	ARRIVE	NOTES
		Amsterdam Centraal	
1540	RJ 68	0934+1	R, 6, Sleeper
		Berlin Hauptbahnhof	
0525	EC 280	1648	R
0925	EC 278	2058	R
1340	RJ 66	0610+1	R, 1, Sleeper
2005	EN 476	0911+1	R, Sleeper
2040	EN 462	1333+1	R, 6, Sleeper
		Bern (Berne)	
2040	EN 462	0928+1	R, 2, Sleeper
		Brussels Midi/Zuid	
2040	EN 462	1335+1	R, 3, 6, Sleeper
		Copenhagen (København) H.	
0525	EC 280	0029+1	R, 4
2040	EN 462	1822+1	R, 4, 6, Sleeper
		Hamburg Hauptbahnhof	
0525	EC 280	1911	R
0940	EC 62	7153	R
		Luxembourg	
0740	RJ 60	2229	R, 5
2040	EN 462	1500+1	R, 6, Sleeper
		Munich (München) Hauptbahnhof	
0740	RJ 60	1425	
1340	RJ 66	2025	R
2040	EN 462	0610+1	R, Sleeper
		Paris Est	
1540	RJ 68	1005+1	R, 6, Sleeper
2040	EN 462	1235+1	R, 6, Sleeper
		Prague (Praha)	
0925	EC 170	1628	
1525	EC 272	2208	
2005	EN 476	0408+1	R, Sleeper
		Rome (Roma) Termini	
1840	EC 148	1210+1	R, 1, 7, Sleeper
		Vienna (Wien) Hauptbahnhof	
0940	RJ 62	1218	R
1340	RJ 66	1618	R
1740	RJ 42	2018	R
2040	EN 462	2318	R

DEPART	TRAIN NUMBER	ARRIVE	NOTES
		Warsaw Centralna	
1125	EC 276	2108	
2005	EN 476	0700+1	R, Sleeper
		Zürich Hauptbahnhof	
0640	RJ 162	1720	R
2040	EN 462	0820+1	R, Sleeper

Daily
R Reservations required
+1 Arrives next day
1. Change trains in Vienna (Wien).
2. Change trains in Zürich.
3. Change trains in Frankfurt.
4. Change trains in Hamburg.
5. Change trains in Koblenz.
6. Change trains in Munich (München).
7. Change trains in Venezia.

For a night on the town, you have the option of a Goulash Party with wine and a show, or you can pull out all the stops with the "Budapest by Night" tour, which offers dinner, a floor show, dancing, and wine tasting accompanied by folk music. If visiting in August, plan ahead for the Buda-Fest by contacting the tourist office for a list of highlights for this summer cultural event. If you can work it in, the full-day Danube Bend bus tour on the right bank of the Danube to the towns of **Esztergom, Visegrád,** and **Szentendre** is well worth the expense for the experience. The area is not accessible by train, and the vistas along the river are captivating.

Day Excursions

Four day excursions from two of Hungary's nine tourism regions have been selected for your Hungarian explorations. (Call the Hungarian Tourist Board or visit their website for further information on the other regions.) Two excursions are to Balaton and Siófok, resort towns that border what the locals call the Balaton, the long, great lake lying south of Budapest. Two other excursions, Kecskemét and Szeged, take you south through the Great Plains region.

Although **Lake Balaton** is shallow (12.4 meters at the deepest point), it actually has waves created by the wind over the northern hills and offers water sports such as boating, yachting, sailing, fishing, and hunting, as well as horseback riding, and giant slides for kids of all ages. Visit www.balaton.gotohungary.com. You may explore a number of beautiful towns and villages, including **Siófok,** purportedly the best bathing resort on the Lake. Visit www.siofok.hu.

Considered "the capital of Lake Balaton," Siófok is 72 miles from Budapest and is easily reached by train. Siófok's railway station and harbor were built in 1863, nearly 800 years after the city was founded. Today green parks and flowering gardens transform the city into a paradise on and off shore. Notice the landscape of Millennium Park as soon as you step off the train in front of the station. Historic and modern structures provide an interesting mix while a variety of outdoor sculptures stand on public display in open-air exhibitions. The city has many organized programs and tours; check with the tourist office for offerings.

From the waters of Lake Balaton we go to the relaxing lifestyle of the Kiskunság region. **Kecskemét** is our next stop. The largest city of the Southern Great Plains (the area lying between the Danube and Tisza Rivers), Kecskemét has an impressive town square with a majolica-tile decorated Town Hall. The architecture is particularly stunning, with the Cifrapalota or Ornamental Palace, Katona Jozsef Theatre, and a 19th-century Moorish-style synagogue that today is the House of Science and Technology. Every August since 1934, the Hirös Festival has been held here. It highlights the traditional crafts, agriculture, and culture of the area.

Szeged, also in the Southern Great Plains, is often called the City of Sunshine, averaging 2,000 hours of sunshine a year—a bit warmer than the rest of the country. The city was devastated by a flood in 1879, but the Szeged Synagogue, the Votive Church, the Greek Orthodox Serbian Church, and other examples of architectural magnificence help this city shine in wonder. For a special treat visit during the open-air festival held July through August, but plan ahead as this festival is popular around the world.

The Southern Great Plains is abundant in traditional folk art such as motif painting, weaving, slipper crafting, egg painting, and the very popular and intricately decorated embroidery work and pottery. Contact the tourist boards for programming or shops to visit. You may even be lucky enough to experience a Hungarian folk-dance show.

We also encourage you to try the cuisine as testimony to the rich history and flavors of the different regions. Of course there is the *gulyás* (goulash) stew made with red paprika and multitudes of noodle dishes, but try the famous *halászlé* spicy fish soup and pike-perch of the Balaton; the wheat and vegetable dishes of the Great Plains made with cream; and desserts such as cottage cheese pie or cabbage strudel. Don't forget to try a glass of the king of wines, the wine of kings, *Tokaj* and a delicious apricot.

Prefer a different indulgence? The thermal bath is taken seriously in Hungary. More than 1,000 natural thermal springs throughout the country allow for a variety of spas to be incorporated into your stay. Whether enjoying the original Roman-built spas (three still exist today: Császár, Király, and Rudas), a modern hotel spa, or many of the resort spas in the countryside near Lake Balaton, a little pampering never harmed any traveler's soul. Besides, thermal bathing is part of the Hungarian culture and actually is quite affordable.

For more information on day excursions, contact:

Lake Balaton. There are several TourInform locations surrounding the lake, or visit www.balaton.gotohungary.com

Siófok, 8600 Víztorony, Pf.:75. *Tel:* (084) 315 355; *Fax:* (084) 310 117; *E-mail:* siofok@tourinform.hu; www.siofok.hu.

Kecskemét, 6000 Kossuth ter 1. *Tel/Fax:* (076) 481 065; www.kecskemet.hu.

Szeged, 6720 Victor Hugo u. 1. *Tel/Fax:* (062) 548 092, (062) 548 093; www.szegedvaros.hu.

Budapest—Balatonszentgyörgy

DEPART Budapest	TRAIN NUMBER	ARRIVE Balaton	DEPART Balaton	TRAIN NUMBER	ARRIVE Budapest
0735 Dél	D 850	1006	1547	D 853	1824 Dél
0935 Dél	D 852	1206	1747	D 851	2024 Dél
1135 Dél	D 854	1406	2027	R 8511	2359 Klt

Daily
Distance: 112 miles (180) km
Note: Budapest Keleti Station is designated as Klt and Budapest Déli Station is designated as Dél.

Budapest—Siófok

DEPART Budapest	TRAIN NUMBER	ARRIVE Siófok	DEPART Siófok	TRAIN NUMBER	ARRIVE Budapest
0600 Dél	IC 200	0721	1503	IC 201	1624 Dél
0735 Dél	D 850	0855	1703	D 853	1824 Dél
0935 Dél	D 852	1055	1903	D 851	2024 Dél
1135 Dél	D 854	1255	2205	D 8511	2359 Klt

Daily
Distance: 72 miles (115 km)

Budapest—Kecskemét

DEPART Budapest Nyugati	TRAIN NUMBER	ARRIVE Kecskemét	NOTES
0653	IC 702	0810	R
0753	IC 712	0910	R
0853	IC 722	1010	R
1153	IC 714	1310	R

DEPART Kecskemét	TRAIN NUMBER	ARRIVE Budapest Nyugati	NOTES
1548	IC 703	1707	R
1648	IC 713	1807	R
1848	IC 733	2007	R
1948	IC 701	2107	R
2048	IC 711	2207	R

Daily
R Reservations required
Distance: 66 miles (106 km)

Budapest—Szeged

DEPART Budapest Nyugati	TRAIN NUMBER	ARRIVE Szeged	NOTES
0653	IC 702	0915	R
0753	IC 712	1015	R
0853	IC 722	1115	R
1153	IC 714	1415	R

DEPART Szeged	TRAIN NUMBER	ARRIVE Budapest Nyugati	NOTES
1445	IC 703	1707	R
1545	IC 713	1807	R
1745	IC 733	2007	R
1845	IC 701	2107	R
1945	IC 711	2207	R

Daily
R Reservations required
Distance: 119 miles (191 km)

IRELAND

Known as "the Emerald Isle," Ireland is no doubt the greenest country of Europe. According to legend, a true Irishman can recognize at least 40 shades of green. The breeze that blows across the seas to Ireland drops its moisture from the time it touches the Irish shoreline on the Atlantic Ocean until it's well out into the Irish Sea. A raincoat or an umbrella—or both—is essential equipment for your visit, and a sweater, even in summer. But the sun also shines a bountiful bit of the time, and most of the time showers disappear as quickly as they come.

Today's tourists to Ireland are discovering a new Ireland. Tourism to Ireland is growing rapidly. To accommodate these increases, Ireland has expanded all forms of its public transportation. Ireland's five international airports—Dublin, Shannon, Cork, Knock, and Belfast (in Northern Ireland)—have undergone major expansions, reflecting the increase of air traffic from all parts of the world.

With all the enhancements in Ireland, one thing remains unchanged—Irish friendliness. Its citizens still seem to have the time to be genuinely interested in you and are wondrously literate when discussing almost any subject. Even if scurrying for a bus, the Irish will stop to chat when they spy a friend—after all, there's always another bus. In Gaelic *céad mile fáilte* means "one hundred thousand welcomes!" You'll hear it frequently.

For more information, contact the Irish Tourist Board offices in North America: **www.discoverireland.com**; *E-mail:* info@irishtouristboard.com.

New York: 345 Park Avenue, 17th Floor, New York, NY 10154; *Tel:* (800) 223-6470 or (212) 418-0800; *Fax:* (212) 371-9052

Toronto: 2 Bloor Street West, Suite 3403, Toronto, ON M4W 3E2, Canada; *Tel:* (800) 223-6470 or (416) 929-2777; *Fax:* (416) 929-6783

Northern Ireland Tourist Board:

59 North Street, Belfast, Ireland, BT1 1NB, *Tel:* 028 9023 1221, *Fax:* 028 902 40960; www.discovernorthernireland.com; *E-mail:* info@ntib.com

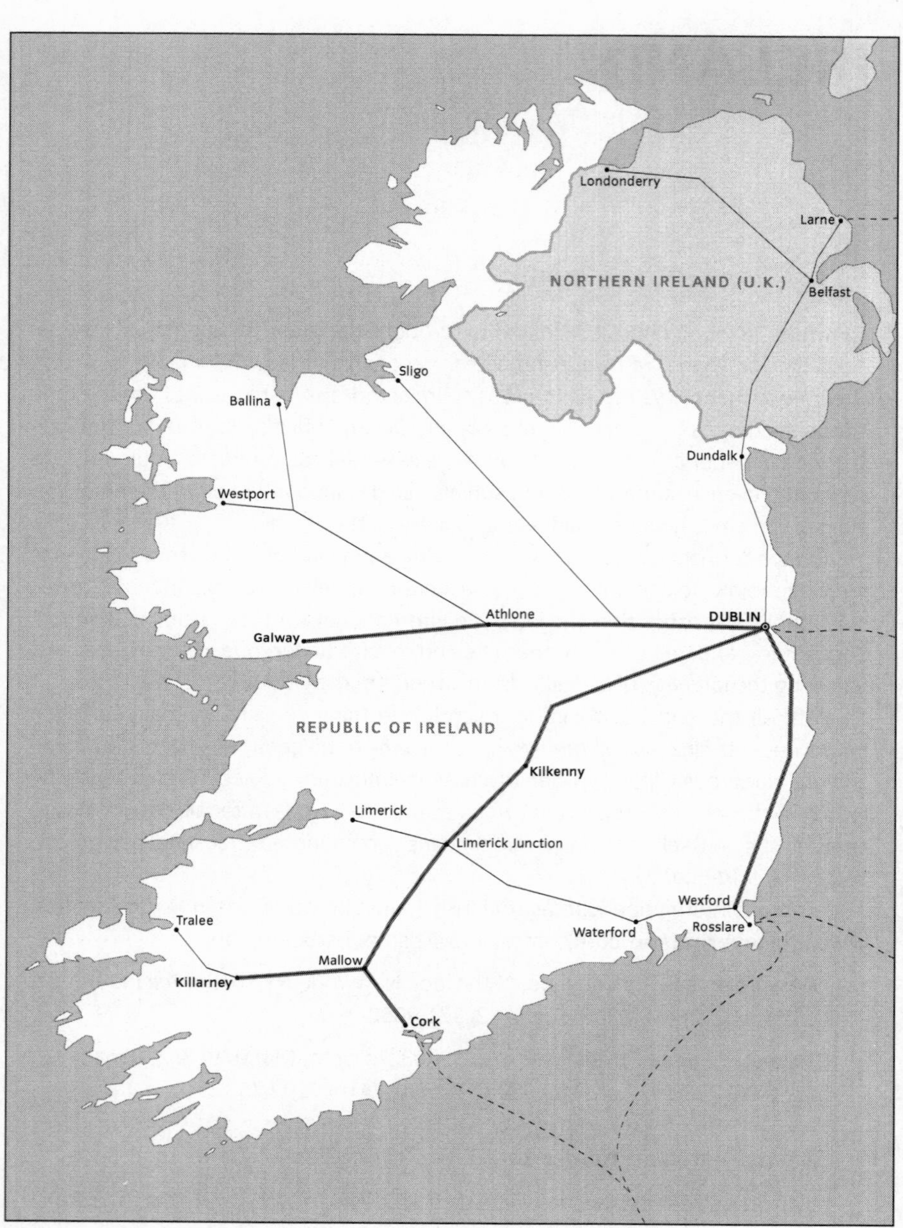
NORTHERN IRELAND (U.K.)
Londonderry
Larne
Belfast
Sligo
Ballina
Dundalk
Westport
Athlone
DUBLIN
Galway
REPUBLIC OF IRELAND
Kilkenny
Limerick
Limerick Junction
Wexford
Tralee
Waterford
Rosslare
Mallow
Killarney
Cork

Republic of Ireland

Currency: Euro (€)

Exchange rate at press time: €0.90 = U.S. $1.00

Communications

Country Code: 353

Major Mobile Phone Companies: Vodafone, O2, Meteor

Rail/Bus Travel in Ireland

Irish Rail (Iarnród Éireann)
www.irishrail.ie
Tel: (01) 850 366 222

Irish Bus (Bus Éireann)
www.buseireann.ie
Tel: (01) 836 6111

Dublin Bus
www.dublinbus.ie
Tel: (01) 873 4222

Northern Ireland Railways
www.translink.co.uk
Tel: (028) 9066 6630

Because the country is only about the size of the state of Pennsylvania in the United States, travelers can easily discover Ireland by using the rail and bus systems. **Irish Rail** (Iarnród Éireann)—a subsidiary of Coras Iompair Éireann (CIE), Ireland's transport company—has been upgrading its railroads and rail facilities as an essential part of Ireland's development plan, with the goal of reliable, convenient, and fast passenger travel throughout the country. Visit their website at **www.irishrail.ie.** Much of the equipment compares favorably with the InterCity trains operated on the Continent.

Ireland's high-speed trains are modeled after the futuristic TGV-style Eurostar trains and aptly dubbed "the trains of the future." The Enterprise is one of the high-tech trains that connects Dublin with Belfast in Northern Ireland. The air-conditioned carriages include digital displays and satellite route maps.

First class is referred to as "super-standard," and second class is known as "standard." First-class rail pass holders are entitled to travel in super-standard coaches without payment of supplements. First-class coaches are equipped with reclining seats, audio entertainment, wi-fi, and power ports to charge your devices. A facsimile service is provided, as are "Silver Service" meals served at the seats.

Standard-class coaches include a "family room" at one end of the car for those with children. Light meals are available from the mobile food-service cart and the buffet (pronounced "buffey" in Ireland) area of the coach.

Some trains operate with standard-class (second-class) coaches only. Standard-class seats are not reservable for individuals, only groups (no seat reservations on bank holidays or weekends). You are required to show your ticket (or rail pass) when entering the train platforms in Irish rail stations, so have it handy.

Food and beverages are served by Irish Rail's own catering service. The service varies according to the type of train. Full-service restaurant cars are hauled on main-line routes, but most catering consists of buffet cars or snack-bar service. Food carts are used on some routes. When traveling on a train hauling a restaurant car, super-standard passengers are provided with in-seat catering. In buffet cars you can obtain hot food, but trains equipped with snack-bar service offer only sandwiches and other prepared food. You may take your own food and beverages aboard. Take some candy treats with you—it's a good way to get acquainted with other passengers.

Eurail passes and **Eurail Select Passes** are accepted for rail travel in the Republic of Ireland, but not in Northern Ireland. Eurail bonuses include:

- 30 percent discount on Irish Ferries crossing Rosslare to Cherbourg and Roscoff (France) February through December. Advance booking recommended.
- 30 percent discount on Stena Line crossings, to and from Ireland. Advance booking recommended.
- 30 percent discount on Irish Ferries Line crossings, to and from Ireland. Advance booking recommended.
- 30 percent discount on Norfolkline Irish Sea Line crossings, to and from Ireland. Advance booking recommended.

The **BritRail Pass + Ireland** is accepted in both the Republic of Ireland and Northern Ireland, as well as in England, Scotland, and Wales, and covers a round-trip connection on your choice of three **Stena Line** ferry routes: between Dun Laoghaire and Holyhead, Rosslare and Fishguard, or Belfast and Stranraer. For more detailed information on travel in Britain, please read our other rail guidebook, *Britain by BritRail*, published by Globe Pequot.

Base City: **DUBLIN**

www.dublintourist.com or
www.visitdublin.com
City Dialing Code: 1

About one-third of the Republic of Ireland's population lives in or near Dublin. The city is as intoxicating as its national brew, Guinness, which is also lovingly referred to as Dublin's "water supply."

O'Connell Street is Dublin's somewhat tarnished "Main Street," the pulsating heart of the old city and Ireland's broadest boulevard. A grand statue of the Irish patriot Daniel O'Connell, *The Liberator,* stands at the foot of O'Connell Street, where O'Connell Bridge crosses the River Liffey. A new sculpture of James Joyce's river spirit, *Anna Livia,* is one of the many statues of national heroes posed along the way to the Garden of Remembrance at Parnell Square.

Art galleries, museums, shopping areas such as the Powerscourt Townhouse Center and Grafton Street, famous cathedrals, and elegant cafes are within walking distance of O'Connell Street. The best-preserved examples of 18th-century houses are also found nearby. **St. Stephen's Green,** at the top of Grafton Street, is ringed with magnificently restored, stately Georgian residences with solid-colored enameled doors and sparkling brass fixtures.

Arriving by Air

Ireland has two main gateways for air travelers from North America: **Shannon International Airport,** on the west side of the Republic (www.shannonairport.com), and **Dublin International Airport,** 12 kilometers northeast of the city's center (www.dublinairport.com). Aer Lingus, Air Canada, Continental, and Delta service both Shannon and Dublin. Other air carriers stop only in Shannon, which has a world-famous, duty-free shopping area featuring items produced in Ireland.

Shannon International Airport's Tourist Information and Reservations Centre is in the Arrivals Hall next to the main arrivals door. *Hours:* 0700–1730 daily.

- **Airport–City Links:** Shannon connects with the rail station in Limerick by airport bus service. Journey time: 45 minutes; fare: €5. Taxi fare to Limerick, about €35.

Dublin International Airport's Tourist Information and Reservations Centre is on the arrivals concourse next to the main arrivals door. *Hours:* 0800–1900 daily.

- **Airport–City Links:** Airlink Express bus service (Route 747) between Dublin Airport and Heuston and Connolly rail stations, as well as O'Connell Street (city center) and the Central Bus Station. Fare: €6 one way; €10 round-trip. Taxi fare, about €25.

Arriving by Train

Connolly Station and DART: Amiens Street (*Tel:* 01 703 2358). The Connolly Station is the terminal in Dublin for trains arriving from Northern Ireland and for boat trains connecting with the Irish ferries that sail from the port of Rosslare, south of Dublin, to the French ports of Cherbourg and Le Havre.

Coming from London by train requires a transfer to either a Stena Line or Irish Ferries ferry at Holyhead. The Stena Line ferries serve the port of Dun Laoghaire, a suburb of Dublin, where passengers can transfer to the center of the city by the local rapid-transit train service, DART.

The northwestern coastal city of Sligo is also reached by train service departing from Connolly Station, as are the towns of Wicklow and Wexford, located south of Dublin in the direction of Rosslare.

Heuston Station: west of city center on the River Liffey (*Tel:* 01 703 2132). Renovated in 2003, Heuston serves as the departure point for *Europe by Eurail* day excursions to Cork, Galway, Kilkenny, and Killarney.

City buses depart from the head of track No. 5 in Heuston Station and take passengers near the O'Connell Bridge. There is also a taxi stand on the opposite side of the station immediately beyond track No. 1 and outside the ticket-office entrance.

Heuston Station has eight main tracks. Ticket offices are located on the side of the station serving track Nos. 1 and 2. Train information and rail pass validation are available at any of the ticket windows.

Advance seat reservations may be obtained from the Iarnród Éireann (Irish Rail) ticket office at Connolly and Heuston Stations as well as at the Irish Rail Travel Centre at 35 Lower Abbey Street (*Tel:* 01 703 4058). Reservations can be made up to 1700 on the preceding day. If you don't have seat reservations, we suggest arriving in the station about a half hour before your train's scheduled departure time just in case the travel is heavy on the day you have selected for your excursion.

Shopping for Waterford crystal? Depart Heuston Station via Kilkenny to the town where it's made—and take money, lots of it!

Tourist Information/Hotel Reservations

- *Tourist Information Office:* Dublin Tourism Centre, Suffolk Street, Dublin 2; *Tel:* 00 3531 605 7700; reservations from the United States; *Tel:* 011 353 66 979 2083; www.visitdublin.com; *E-mail:* information@dublintourism.ie. *Hours:* 0900–1730 Monday–Saturday, 1030–1500 Sunday.

Dublin is well equipped to offer a wide range of accommodations to visitors. Two exceptions, however, come during the Dublin Horse Show in early August and St. Patrick's Day in March. The principal sporting and social event of the year in Ireland, the horse show attracts thousands of visitors from all parts of the world. Don't plan to be in Dublin during the horse show unless you have confirmed reservations. The city is filled to overflowing at that time. If you are planning a visit to Dublin on St. Patrick's Day or during the summer months, it would be wise to check well in advance with the Irish Tourist Board in New York for accommodation arrangements.

Travelers looking for homelike accommodations can purchase the Irish Tourist Offices' ***Self Catering Services Guide,*** which describes apartments or houses for short-term rent (for a few days, a weekend, or a week). For reservations, contact the Dublin Tourism Centre.

Bed-and-breakfast establishments are also a viable alternative to large, expensive hotels. Again, the Irish Tourist Offices maintain current descriptions. Noel and Deirdre Comer's extraordinary guesthouse, **Number 31,** at 31 Leeson Close, Lower Leeson Street, Dublin 2, is the former home of Sam Stephenson, one of Dublin's renowned architects. *Tel:* (01) 676 5011; *Fax:* (01) 676 2929; www.number31.ie; *E-mail:* info@number31.ie.

For those who wish to experience the ambience of one of Dublin's newest landmark hotels, we suggest the Brooks Hotel, 59–62 Drury Street, Dublin 2. *Tel:* (01) 670 4000; *Fax:* (01) 670 4455; www.brookshotel.ie; *E-mail:* reservations@brooks hotel.ie. Room rates range from standard to superior executive suites, and the location places you in the heart of the city, with Grafton Street, Temple Bar, and Trinity College only a short walk away.

Getting Around In and Outside Dublin

- **DART,** 35 Lower Abbey Street; *Tel:* 01 850 366 222; www.irishrail.ie.
- **Dublin Bus,** 59 Upper O'Connell Street; *Tel:* 01 873 4222; www.dublinbus.ie

DART, or Dublin Area Rapid Transit, is the electric commuter service running around Dublin Bay and provides the fastest way of getting around Dublin as well as convenient access to the many resorts and other attractions outside of Dublin.

Much of the route is coastal and gives many different views of the bay. It's excellent for short excursions to places such as the charming fishing village of Howth at its northern end or Dun Laoghaire, the busy harbor for the Stena Line ferry service to England via Holyhead. DART accepts Eurail passes, as well as the various Irish Rail and/or Bus combination passes.

Sights/Attractions/Tours—Discovering Dublin

Dublin, with a population of more than one million people in its greater metropolitan area, offers the excitement of a vital city yet the ambience of an Old World town. The **Dublin City Sightseeing Tour** (www.irishcitytours.com) provides an excellent introduction to the sights. Hop on and off the bus as you please. Purchase tickets at your hotel, tourist offices, or from the driver, €18 adult; €16 student.

The Dublin Tourism Centre (located in the former St. Andrew's Church) on Suffolk Street offers a plethora of city tours by bus and on foot, escorted and independent, and walking trails ranging from cultural tours to pub crawls.

Or, if you really want to "make a splash" in Dublin, try **Viking Splash Tours.** It's an unusual and fun way to see Dublin by land and water. You'll be aboard a vintage World War II amphibious military vehicle. Your sightseeing tour begins at Bull Alley Street beside the gardens of St. Patrick's Cathedral for the tour of Dublin and then becomes a "drive" into the Grand Canal Basin to continue the tour by water. Tour times: approximately every half hour 1000 to 1700 daily June through October; Saturday and Sunday only November; daily except Tuesday February through May. Price: €22 adults; €12 children younger than age 12; *Tel:* (01) 707 6000 for reservations. Visit www.vikingsplash.com.

If you plan to visit several attractions and/or museums, purchase the **Dublin Pass** for one, two, three, or six days. The Dublin Pass gives you free entry to more than 30 attractions and allows you to avoid queuing at Dublin's major attractions. It also includes a free map and 84-page guidebook, free transport on Aircoach from Dublin Airport, and discounts at various shops and restaurants. Prices: one-day: adult €39, child €21; two-day: adult €61, child €35; three-day: adult €71, child €42; six-day: adult €105, child €54. Purchase at tourist offices, at Dublin Airport, or online at www.dublinpass.ie.

One of Dublin's sights to see is **O'Connell Street.** A block away on the river's south bank stands **Parliament House** (now the Bank of Ireland), which faces the entrance to Trinity College, founded in 1592. The ***Book of Kells,*** considered its greatest treasure, is housed in the Collonades. Tourist trails lead from that point to **St. Stephen's Green,** at the top of Grafton Street, where its 22 acres are surrounded delightfully by splendid Georgian houses. Most shops in these areas are open Monday through Saturday from 0900 to 1730 or 1800, with extended hours on Thursday and many shops are now open on Sunday from 1200 to 1800.

For an insight into Irish life, visit a **Dublin pub.** In general, the Irish treat their pubs as a second home. The French seem to spend a relatively short time in a cafe before heading off. The English go to a pub for a chat with friends and the barmaid and perhaps a game of darts before heading homeward. But the Irish, when they have the time (and they generally seem to), are in the pub for the entire evening.

The main pub activities are drinking and talking, although many serve appetizing meals and snacks and provide entertainment in the form of traditional music and song. You are free to sit and watch or join in. To take the latter option, merely turn to your neighbor and mention the weather. With that, the ball's in play. What is revealed then is fascinating. You'll find that everyone has positive but sensible opinions about a myriad of subjects. Make certain that what you say about a topic is relevant, for unlike most bar conversationalists, the Irish listen when you speak.

Listening is an art that can be developed to a fine degree in a Dublin pub. Unless you are a Scot, try not to match the Dubliners' drinking ability or verbal athletics.

Suburban Dublin Day Excursions

Travelers can stay in Dublin, their "base city," and easily make day excursions to visit other areas outside of Dublin. Or they can use the "flip side" of the base city–day excursion concept by taking advantage of less expensive accommodations outside the city and making day excursions into Dublin.

One Dublin suburban-area day excursion is to **Dun Laoghaire** (www.dunlaoghaire.ie), a charming, lovely port on the Irish Sea that can be reached in only 15 minutes by DART from Dublin's Connolly Station. The ferry terminal and DART station are much more convenient for travelers than the former underground facility. The Stena Line's HSS (High-speed Seacat Service) catamaran provides inexpensive passage to and from Holyhead (England) in only 1 hour and 39 minutes. A variety of hotels, bed-and-breakfast establishments, hostels, and "self-catering" apartments and houses are available in Dun Laoghaire for those who prefer to stay just outside of Dublin.

Train Connections to and from Port of Rosslare for Ferry Connections to Cherbourg

Dublin—Rosslare Europort

DEPART Dublin Connolly	ARRIVE Rosslare Europort	NOTES	DEPART Rosslare Europort	ARRIVE Dublin Connolly	NOTES
0940	1226	Exc. Su	0720	1015	Exc. Su
1025	1310	Su	0940	1230	Su
1336	1626	Exc. Su	1255	1545	Exc. Su
1838 (1830 Su)	2128 (2115 Su)		1755 (1740 Su)	2044 (2035 Su)	

Daily, unless otherwise noted
For more information telephone (01) 850 366222 (outside Ireland: +353 1836 222)
Standard class only on all trains
Distance: 95 miles (168 km)

Other Dublin suburban areas within easy reach via DART, Suburban Rail, and the Arrow lines include:

Bray, 30 minutes from Dublin, is where writer James Joyce and artist Neil Jordan once lived and where rock star Bono of U2 makes his home. Connecting buses can take you to the quaint little village of **Enniskerry,** with its delightful cafes, coffee shops, and comfortable bed-and-breakfast facilities.

Howth, only 25 minutes from Connolly Station via DART, is a charming fishing village on the northern side of Dublin Bay.

Naas, southwest of Dublin, can be reached by the Arrow train line departing from Heuston Station. Naas is famous as a center for horse breeding, and race horse owners from all over the world attend the October yearling sales held nearby.

Kildare, also famous with the equestrian set as a center for horse breeding and home of the Irish National Stud, is only 48 kilometers away and is the last stop on the Arrow line trains departing from Dublin's Heuston Station. For luxurious resort-type accommodations (at resort-type prices, of course), the Kildare Hotel and Country Club is top-notch. The transformation of the former fifth-century Straffan mansion into a luxury hotel took more than two years to complete. The clubhouse and 18-hole golf course were designed by Arnold Palmer.

Waterford, a 12th-century Norman fortress positioned on the banks of the Suir, has been a significant port since the 16th century. Visit www.waterfordtourism.org; *E-mail:* info@southeasttourism.ie. The Dominican Blackfriars and ruins of the French Church are reminders of medieval times, as is the 12th-century Reginald's Tower, where the city's museum is located. In 1170 Strongbow was married to Princess Aoife, daughter of the King of Leinster, in Christ Church Cathedral, where today an audiovisual presentation using the excellent acoustics of the nave recreates a 1,000-year-old history of the area. Hook Tower, one of the oldest lighthouses in Europe, stands proudly at Hook Head at the beginning of the estuary in Waterford Bay.

Waterford is home to Waterford Crystal, the largest crystal factory in the world. Visit the **Waterford Prestige Manufacturing Facility,** *Tel:* +353 51 17000; www.waterfordvisitorcentre.com. *Hours:* March, Monday–Saturday 0900–1515, Sunday 0930–1515; April–October Monday–Saturday 0900–1615, Sunday 0930–1615; November–December: Monday–Friday 0900–1515, closed weekends. This new facility, opened June 2010, is a combination visitor center and high-end custom crystal manufacturing facility. Tours and audiovisual presentations are available March through December, and the gallery features some of the most valuable crystal pieces ever created.

Waterford Castle [*Tel:* (05) 187 8203; in the United States, *Tel:* (800) 221-1074; www.waterfordcastle.com; *E-mail:* info@waterfordcastle.com], located on its own private island, began as a monastic settlement in the 6th century. It ultimately became one of the estates of the Fitzgeralds, who were the kings of Ireland during the 15th and 16th centuries. Purchased by Eddie Kearns in 1987, it was developed into a luxurious hotel and country club. The castle's guest rooms are comfortable and bright, with beautiful views of the estate. Conference facilities are available, and special arrangements are made for business entertaining. The main dining room seats 65 guests and often hosts a resident pianist. Hunting and polo are available, as are deep-sea and freshwater fishing. Croquet is played on the castle lawns. An excellent country club, championship golf course, and luxurious leisure center also grace the island.

More Day Excursions

Other day excursions made conveniently with Irish Rail/Bus are **Cork, Galway, Kilkenny,** and **Killarney.** Cork provides a double treat when you tread its fascinating quays and kiss the renowned stone at nearby Blarney Castle. Galway, the western capital of Ireland, has all the charm of an ancient city, plus the vitality of expanding industries and popular holiday-resort attractions. The combination of Kilkenny Town and Kilkenny Castle offers a delightful variety of attractions, from cats and choir lofts to castle tours and witches' tales.

Day Excursion to

Cork

And the Blarney Stone

Depart from Dublin Heuston Station
Distance by Train: 165 miles (266 km)
Average Train Time: 2 hours, 20 minutes
City Dialing Code: 21
Tourist Information Office: Tourist House, Grand Parade
Tel: (021) 4255100; **Fax:** (021) 4255199
www.cometocork.com or **www.corkkerry.ie**
E-mail: corkkerryinfo@failteireland.ie
Hours: July–August: 0900–1900 Monday–Saturday; remainder of the year: 1000–1700 Monday–Friday, 1000–1500 Saturday; closed for lunch 1300–1415
Notes: To get to the tourist office on foot, exit the railway station and turn left onto Railway Street. Make a right onto Penrose's Quay to St. Patrick's Bridge. Turn left onto St. Patrick's Street until you come to Grand Parade on your left. Follow it past Oliver Plunkett Street, and you will see the tourist office on your left. To get to the bus station from the tourist office, go back to Oliver Plunkett Street, where you turn right. Turn left on Anglesea Street until you come to the bus station.

Cork, Ireland's second-largest city (about 200,000 residents) and commercial and passenger port, is easily accessible from both Dublin and Shannon (via train from Limerick). From Dublin a special executive car called "City Gold" is available, with special amenities for doing business, including fax and phone.

Cork City (*Corcach* in Irish, which means "marshy place") was built upon the marshes and wetlands of the River Lee. **Saint Finbarr's Cathedral** is located where Cork's first settlement and monastery was founded by the missionary in the seventh century. The **Guinness International Jazz Festival,** held in October, attracts world-famous musicians, including famous American stars.

The moist, temperate climate of Cork makes for splendid gardens and wonderful parks. And shopping the maze of streets between Patrick Street and South Mall provides a plethora of fashions and fashionable cafes and eateries offering finely prepared foods at various prices.

The village of **Blarney** is a short, 25-minute bus ride north of the city, where the "touristy" thing to do is visit **Blarney Castle** and kiss the legendary **Blarney Stone,** which promises the gift of eloquence to anyone believing enough to be lowered backward from the battlements on the roof of the castle to achieve it. You will, of course, be adding to the lip prints of thousands of other tourists who have attempted the same thing.

Board the bus marked Blarney in the city's bus terminal at Parnell Place. It's only a 10-minute walk down Glanmire Road to the river and the bus station. On Saturday and Sunday buses depart Cork every 1 hour and 15 minutes starting at 0900 and return on the same schedule. During the week, buses run about every 15 minutes. Travel time is 35 minutes. Check schedules with the Cork tourist office or call Bus Éireann at (353) 21 4508188. Plan to be back on the bus by 1800 to make your train back to Cork.

Dublin—Cork

DEPART Dublin Heuston	ARRIVE Cork	NOTES	DEPART Cork	ARRIVE Dublin Heuston
0700	0935	Exc. Su	1320	1555
0900	1145	Exc. Su	1520	1755
1000	1235		1620	1905
1100	1345	Exc. Su	1720	2000
1200	1435		1820	2105
1300	1535	Exc. Su	2020	2255

Distance: 165 miles (266 km)

There are many legends regarding the origins of the Blarney Stone. According to one, it was brought to Ireland from the Holy Land during one of the crusades. Another theory has the Blarney Stone originating from half of the Stone of Scone, with Robert the Bruce giving the mystical rock to Cormac MacCarthy, Lord of Blarney, in 1314. Legend has it that the gift of eloquence would be bestowed upon anyone who kissed it. It was not until Cormac MacCarthy saved an elderly woman from drowning that he learned of this magical secret. Visit www.blarneycastle.ie.

Day Excursion to

Galway

Roundstone

Depart from Dublin Heuston Station
Distance by Train: 129 miles (208 km)
Average Train Time: 2 hours, 40 minutes
City Dialing Code: 91
Tourist Information Center: Aras Failte, Foster Street, across from City Hall
Tel: (091) 537700; **Fax:** (091) 537733
www.discoverireland.ie/west
E-mail: irelandwestinfo@failteireland.ie
Hours: 0900–1745 Monday–Saturday
Notes: Emerging from the railway station, you'll see Eyre Square with the Kennedy Park in its center. Turn left onto the main street. The traditional green "i" signs will lead you to the tourist office. Fronting the square is the Great Southern Hotel. (Turn right and right again at Victoria Place to find the tourist office.)

Like some other Irish cities, Galway was established initially by foreigners. Since medieval times, it has been a significant port dominated by an oligarchy of 14 Norman and Welsh merchant families. As a thriving trade with Spain developed, the **Spanish Arch** was erected in 1594; it was created to protect the Spanish ships as they unloaded their cargo. It still remains below the Claddagh Bridge and has an adjacent museum. The avenue leading from the arch, known as the "Long Walk," is where Spanish merchants supposedly strolled into Galway City. The area is still resplendent with Spanish architecture.

Galway has become Ireland's fastest-growing city. A university town since the 14th century, Galway still has a huge student population and is a cultural center for writers and scholars. In October, March, and July, Galway (as in Dublin and Cork) hosts an **international film festival** to showcase new cinema.

Guided tours via double-decker buses depart **Eyre Square** every 30 minutes in the summer. Eyre Square, given to the city by Edward Eyre in 1710, is the heart of Galway City activity and the site where the John F. Kennedy Memorial Park is located. Fronting the square is the **Great Southern Hotel,** a hostelry combining the charm of both old and new and an ideal place to halt for a libation or a luncheon. The shopping center west of the square is also where the last section of the old wall has been preserved, along with the Penrice and Shoemaker Towers.

At 19 Eyre Square, the Bank of Ireland displays the priceless **Silver Sword** and **Great Mace**, the finest examples of Irish silver work remaining in the Republic.

Galway is a ferry port for the Aran Islands, which lie 30 miles offshore, as are Doolin and Rossaveal. Air service is available via Connemara Airport. The islands are a tribute to traditional Irish life and culture, and, as in Galway and Connemara, Gaelic is still proudly spoken among the natives.

The **Galway Bay Conference and Leisure Centre** (*Tel:* 091 520520) is a prime example of Galway City's growth. The deluxe facility is located on Galway's promenade, just minutes from Eyre Square and the City Center. It includes a fitness center with swimming pool, sauna, and steam room. Restaurant, bar, and lounge each have panoramic views of Galway Bay. With its proximity to **Leisureland,** the hotel is one of the most extensive conference and leisure centers in the country.

Or if you decide to base yourself in Galway for a night or two, try Jury's Galway City Hotel, a mere ½ mile from Ceannt Station. The inn overlooks Galway Bay and is located in the heart of the city beside the historic Spanish Arch. *Tel:* (091) 566444; *Fax:* (091) 568415; www.jurysinns.com.

Supposedly, the word *lynching* entered the English language through an act of Galway's chief magistrate, James Lynch-FitzStephen, elected to his post in 1493. According to a popular but dubious legend, his son, Walter, murdered a Spanish visitor and then confessed to the crime. He was condemned by his own father, but no one could be found to carry out the execution. So Judge Lynch, no doubt a firm believer in "spare the rod and spoil the child," hanged his own son and afterward retired into seclusion. **Lynch's Castle** stands today on Shop Street, and the Lynch Memorial attesting to this stern and unbending justice lies nearby, close to the **Church of St. Nicholas,** erected in 1320. Legend has it that Columbus worshiped in the church before setting out on his voyage of discovery to America.

An unusual feature of Galway is its downtown salmon weir, where shoals of salmon swim in the clear river en route to spawning grounds. This unique sight may be viewed from the **Salmon Weir Bridge,** which crosses the River Corrib by the city's cathedral.

Roundstone is a picturesque fishing village on the southern shores of Connemara. Already well known for superb seafood and quaint bed-and-breakfast-style hotels, Roundstone is also "the home of the bodhran"—a one-sided framed drum made from goatskin—Ireland's oldest product, made famous more recently when played by Christy Moore in *Riverdance*. A bus leaves daily during the summer from Foster Street in Galway City for Roundstone and Clifden.

Dublin—Galway

DEPART Dublin Heuston	ARRIVE Galway	NOTES	DEPART Galway	ARRIVE Dublin Heuston	NOTES
0735	1010	Exc. Su	1505	1742	Exc. Su
0800	1022	Su	1700	1935	Su
0925	1147	Exc. Su	1920	2147	Exc. Su
1125	1344		1800	2030	Su

Daily, unless otherwise noted

Distance: 129 miles (208 km)

If you have never seen *Riverdance* or heard the haunting tones of the bodhrans, you've missed one of the most exciting music and dance shows in the last 1,000 years. Visit master bodhran maker Malachy Kearns's (known locally as Malachy Bodhran) quaint craft and music shop. Malachy and artist-wife Anne are the only full-time bodhran makers in the world, and they've been making them for many years.

You can purchase the handmade bodhrans with Celtic designs, family crests, or names. *Hours:* 0900–1900 daily (closed Sunday in winter). Malachy Kearns mixes the goatskins with secret ingredients and soaks them for 7 to 10 days before stretching them over a beech-wood frame. Mr. Kearns attributes the bodhran's haunting tones to the goatskins; we think his secret ingredients have something to do with achieving such extraordinary sound. It is truly fascinating!

Roundstone Musical Instruments Ltd.
IDA Craft Centre, Roundstone
Co. Galway, Ireland
Tel: (095) 35808; *Fax:* (095) 35980
www.bodhran.com
E-mail: bodhran@iol.ie

Day Excursion to

Kilkenny

Ghosts and Gifts Galore

Depart from Dublin Heuston Station
Distance by Train: 81 miles (130 km)
Average Train Time: 1 hour, 49 minutes
City Dialing Code: 56
Tourist Information Office: Shee Alms House, Rose Inn Street, Kilkenny
Tel: (056) 51500; **Fax:** (056) 63955
www.kilkenny.ie
E-mail: info@kilkenny.ie
Hours: October–April: 0930–1700 Tuesday–Saturday; May–September: 0930–1730 Monday–Friday, 1000–1700 Saturday and Sunday
Notes: To reach the tourist office, turn left onto John Street after leaving the station, and walk to the bridge crossing the river. Cross the bridge, and John Street then becomes Rose Inn Street. Continue walking up Rose Inn Street, and you will find the office in the Shee Alms House on the right.

Kilkenny may be Ireland's smallest city, but it is one of the most popular destinations from Dublin. **Kilkenny Castle** (by guided tour only), a 12th-century grand stone fortress on the River Nore, dominates the scene and sets the theme. It was the chief residence of the Butler family from 1391 until 1935—almost 550 years. Recently restored to the majesty of the 1820s, it is now home to the National Furniture collection and the modern Butler Gallery. The castle is impressive and reminiscent of the great bastions along the Rhine River.

The **Kilkenny Design Centre** is a unique shopping experience with more than 200 craft shops under one roof offering the best in Irish design and workmanship in ceramics, glass, metal, clothing, jewelry, and other traditional and contemporary crafts. To add to the ambience, have a luscious Irish lunch at the upstairs restaurant overlooking the quaint cobbled courtyard of Kilkenny Castle.

Other sites include the 13th-century **St. Canice's Cathedral,** reputed to be one of the most beautiful in Ireland; **Rothe House,** home of the Kilkenny Archaeological Society; and **Shee Alms House,** a restored 16th-century building that houses the tourist information office.

Though small, Kilkenny is cosmopolitan, with a pub and club life that draws visitors from major cities. In fact, the **Paris Texas Café Bar** has to close its doors by 2100 because of the crowds. **Langton House Hotel,** a four-time winner of the National Pub of the Year award, is a traditional pub and restaurant in grand surroundings, with a disco club that stays open to the wee hours of the morning. (A hotel facility is adjacent to the disco; www.langtons.ie; *Tel:* [056] 77 65133.)

Dublin—Kilkenny

DEPART Dublin Heuston	ARRIVE Kilkenny	NOTES
0725	0901	Exc. Su
0910	1043	Su
1015	1140	Exc. Su

DEPART Kilkenny	ARRIVE Dublin Heuston	NOTES
1530	1706	Exc. Su
1843	2020	Su
1902	2040	Exc. Su

Daily, unless otherwise noted
Distance: 81 miles (130 km)

Another interesting landmark is **Kytler's Inn,** which has the distinction of being the oldest residence in the city and, by tradition, the house of the witch Dame Alice Kytler, born there in 1280. Dame Alice seems to have been a very nice lady except that she acquired and disposed of husbands—four in all—in rapid succession. This aroused the curiosity of the local folks, and in 1324 she was charged by Bishop de Ledrede with witchcraft, heresy, and criminal assaults upon her husbands. Brought to trial and condemned to burn at the stake as a witch, Dame Alice eluded her accusers and escaped across the Irish Sea to Scotland. Her maid, Petronilla, was not as fortunate; the bishop had her burned at the stake as a suitable substitute. Locals claim that Petronilla's ghost still haunts the cellar of what is now the Kytler Inn on St. Kieran Street—possibly asking for back wages?

Be sure to take advantage of the Kilkenny Culture Card, offering a 20 percent discount at heritage attractions, and a 20 percent discount on many crafts and gifts from area shops. The card is free if you are staying in Kilkenny, or inquire at the tourist office.

Day Excursion to

Killarney

Lakes and Jaunting Cars

Depart from Dublin Heuston Station
Distance by Train: 185 miles (298 km)
Average Train Time: 3 hours, 30 minutes
City Dialing Code: 64
Tourist Information Office: Beach Road, Killarney
Tel: (064) 6631633; **Fax:** (064) 34506
www.killarney-insight.com
Hours: July–August: 0900–2000 Monday–Saturday; June and September: 0900–1700 Monday–Saturday; October–May: 1000–1700 Monday–Saturday
Notes: To reach the tourist information office, turn left on Railway Road just after passing the Great Southern Hotel on your left as you leave the railway station. Railway Road crosses Muckross Road a short distance from the station. At the Cinema, cross to the other side of the road. The Killarney Plaza Hotel and the jaunting cars are on the right-hand side. Continue along Beech Road. Take a right turn into New Street Car Park. The tourist office is a short distance on the left-hand side.

Killarney is rivaled now by Dublin as the number one tourist attraction in the Republic of Ireland. Horse-drawn carriages known as jaunting cars take tourists to feature sights including **Muckross Abbey,** the ruins of a 15th-century Franciscan monastery; **Ross Castle,** on the banks of Lough Leane (which now offers memorable guided tours of the inner castle); and **Muckross House,** a 19th-century manor with a museum depicting local folk life and housing various crafts shops with blacksmiths, weavers, and potters. Muckross Traditional Farms is also a very fine attraction.

Jaunting-car rates are usually based on four passengers. If your party is fewer than four, the tourist office may be just the place to find other passengers willing to share the cost. The central jaunting-car stand in Killarney is a stone's throw from the tourist office, so you won't have to return to the railway station.

Killarney's **St. Mary's Cathedral** is an impressive Neo-Gothic structure worthy of a visit. The **Great Southern Hotel,** opposite the railway station, is a fashionable hostelry of great beauty, and its amicable Punch-bowl Bar is a good place to pause for a libation and friendly conversation.

There are many eating places to choose from. We found the food at the **Flesk Restaurant** at 14 Main Street to be tasty and satisfying. One of the favorite spots of the locals, too, the Flesk is known for its daily fresh fish specials, such as wild salmon, and its live Dingle Bay lobsters.

Dublin—Killarney

DEPART Dublin Heuston	ARRIVE Killarney	NOTES
0700	1016	1, Exc. Su
0900	1216	1, Exc. Su
1000	1337	1, Su
1100	1416	1, Exc. Su

DEPART Killarney	ARRIVE Dublin Heuston	NOTES
1538	1905	1
1737	2100	1
1826	2138	Su
1938	2255	1, Exc. Su

Daily, unless otherwise noted
1. Change trains at Mallow.
Distance: 185 miles (298 km)

A classic Killarney countryside excursion is by bus to **Kate Kearney's Cottage,** a coaching inn, where you are fortified with Irish coffee. Then, setting out by pony through the **Gap of Dunloe,** you are refreshed again at **Lord Brandon's Cottage** before returning by boat to Lough Leane and to Killarney by jaunting car. You can obtain information on prices from the tourist office. A comprehensive guide to Killarney is the *Killarney Area Guide,* which can be purchased at the Killarney tourist office.

ITALY

Why do we find Italy so inviting? Just ask any Italian—it can be summed up in three little words: *la dolce vita*, the sweet life. Italy is pasta, Pavarotti, and the Pope; it's fashion, Ferrari, and films; it's vino (wine), Venus, and villas—it's all of our favorite things that culminate in *la dolce vita*.

Most visitors are aware of Italy's predominantly Catholic heritage, but not many are aware that Italy also has a rich Jewish heritage dating as early as 140 B.C. Most Italian Jews are descendants of the group Sephardim, who were expelled from Spain and Portugal in the 15th and 16th centuries. Many outstanding synagogues and other Jewish sites are most evident in Florence, Rome, and Venice.

For more information about Italy, contact the Italian Government Tourist Boards (ENIT) in North America (**www.italiantourism.com** or **www.enit.it;** *E-mail:* sedecentrale@enit.it):

Chicago: 500 North Michigan Avenue, Suite 506, Chicago, IL 60611; *Tel:* (312) 644-9335; *Fax:* (312) 644-3019

New York: 630 Fifth Avenue, Suite 1965, New York, NY 10111; *Tel:* (212) 245-5618; *Fax:* (212) 586-9249

Los Angeles: 10850 Wilshire Boulevard, Suite 575, Los Angeles, CA 90024; *Tel:* (310) 820-1898; *Fax:* (310) 820-6357

Toronto: 110 Yonge Street, Suite 503, Toronto, Ontario M5C 1T4, Canada; *Tel:* (416) 925-4882; *Fax:* (416) 925-4799; *Brochure Hotline:* (416) 925-3870

Banking

Currency: Euro (€)

Exchange rate at press time: €0.90 = U.S. $1.00

Communications

Country Code: 39

For telephone calls within Italy, dial a zero (0) preceding area code.

Major Mobile Phone Companies: TIM, Vodafone, Wind, 3

SWITZERLAND
AUSTRIA
HUNGARY
SLOVENIA
CROATIA
SERBIA
BOSNIA
MONTENEGRO
FRANCE
Corsica (FRANCE)
TUNISIA
MALTA
Brennero
Merano
Lienz
Villach
Bolzano
Calalzo
St. Moritz
Brig
Lugano
Sondrio
Trento
Belluno
Udine
Aosta
Arona
Como
Bergamo
Treviso
Pordenone
Gorizia
Trieste
Novara
MILAN
Brescia
Vicenza
Modane
Vercelli
Verona
Padova
Venice
Pavia
Cremona
Bussoleno
Turin
Novi
Mantova
Rovigo
Asti
Piacenza
Parma
Ferrara
Cuneo
Genoa
Modena
Bologna
Breil
Savona
Ravenna
Nice
La Spezia
Rimini
Pistoia
Pesaro
Ventimiglia
Imperia
Pisa
Lucca
Florence
Senegallia
Ancona
Livorno
Empoli
Arezzo
Siena
Perugia
Chiusi
Assisi
Foligno
S. Benedetto
Grosseto
Ascoli
Terni
Viterbo
Orte
Rieti
L'Aquila
Pescara
Civitavecche
Isernia
Termoli
ROME
Roma Trastevere
Campobasso
Latina
Formia
Cassino
Foggia
Barletta
Anzio
Benevento
Caserta
Bari
Porto Torres
Olbia
Golfo Aranci
Naples
Brindisi
Sassari
Salerno
Potenza
Battipaglia
Taranto
Paestum
Chilivani
Metaponto
Sapri
Oristano
Maratea
Lecce
Paolo
Cosenza
Crotone
Cagliari
Lamezia Terme
Catanzaro
Messina
Villa S. Giovanni
Reggio di Calabria
Palermo
Trapani
Taormina
Cefalu
Marsala
Castelvetrano
Catania
Caltanisetta
Agrigento
Canicatti
Licata
Siracusa
Ragusa

Rail Travel in Italy

The **Italian State Railways** (*Ente Ferrovie Italiane dello Stato,* or *FS*) provides excellent and frequent train services linking all of Italy, including Sicily and Sardinia via train ferries, with Austria, France, and Switzerland (www.trenitalia.com). All main lines and many minor lines are electrified. Italy's principal express train service, the **Eurostar Italia** (not to be confused with the cross-Channel Eurostar trains and formerly referred to as the ETR Pendolino and ETR 500 trains) is among the best in Europe.

Keep in mind that Italian trains are not just for tourists; the Italians are heavily dependent upon their rail system, and second-class railcars are often crowded. We recommend traveling in first class when in Italy.

The Italian State Railways accepts the variety of **Eurail passes** (including the Eurail France–Italy, Greece–Italy, and Italy–Spain combination passes, and the Eurail Italy Pass). Eurail bonuses include:

- Free transport on Trenitalia-operated ferry crossings from Villa S. Giovanni to Messina (Sicily).
- 30–50 percent discount on Blue Star Ferries and Superfast from Brindisi to Patras, Corfu, and Igoumenitsa. Rail pass must be valid in both Italy and Greece.

The Eurail Italy Pass provides for unlimited rail travel on the entire Italian State Railways network for the specified number of days within a two-month period, including InterCity, EuroCity, and Rapido trains, with no surcharge. **Supplement required for Eurostar Italia, and some other premium trains.** Children younger than 12 years of age pay half adult fare; younger than 4 years of age, free.

Eurail Italy Pass

Valid for unlimited travel on the entire Italian State Railways network including InterCity, EuroCity, and the Rapido trains with no surcharge. Supplement required on Eurostar Italia, and ETR trains. First-class passes include the Leonardo Express (Rome Fumicino Airport–Roma Termini).

DAYS OF TRAVEL Within 2 months	ADULT 1st Class	ADULT 2nd Class	SAVERPASS* 1st Class	SAVERPASS* 2nd Class	YOUTH 2nd Class
3 days	$310	$253	$265	$215	$205
4 days	$345	$280	$294	$239	$229
5 days	$384	$311	$327	$266	$255
6 days	$418	$339	$356	$289	$277
7 days	$458	$372	$390	$317	$304
8 days	$493	$401	$420	$342	$327
9 days	$531	$431	$452	$368	$352
10 days	$569	$462	$485	$394	$377

*Saverpass for parties of 2–5 people traveling together at all times, price per person
Youth (younger than age 26)
Child (age 4–11) 50 percent off adult fare; children younger than age 4 travel free

Base City: **MILAN** (Milano)

www.ciaomilano.it
City Dialing Code: 02

Milan is fashionable and futuristic—as evidenced by the growing number of high-rise structures and the accelerating pace of its population. At the same time, Milan is ancient and respectful of its glorious past. For instance, the **Duomo** (cathedral) is the second-largest church in Italy, a beautiful example of Gothic stonework begun in 1386. *The Last Supper*, Leonardo da Vinci's famous painting, may be seen in the refectory of the **Santa Maria delle Grazie** convent. It was painted between 1495 and 1498. Like a typical Milanese, Leonardo was concerned with the future, and his drawings of machines in flight, together with some of his futuristic inventions, are exhibited in the **Leonardo da Vinci National Museum of Science and Technology,** Via San Vittore 21; metro stop San Ambrogio.

To promote its future, Milan created one of the most extensive fairgrounds in Europe; each year, thousands of businesses display or investigate products there. Milan does not live up to the stereotype of the Italian town. Lunches tend to be shorter, conversations seem more direct and to the point, and the Milanese appear to be in a bit of a hurry.

Transportation in Milan is abundant and unusually dependable. Several decades ago, the five o'clock train never left Milano Centrale on time; today, the five o'clock train leaves at five o'clock. Hotel services rival the finest in Europe; shops are sophisticated and efficient. In a word, Milan "works."

There is one crucial thing about Milan. It is virtually impossible to get a hotel room in the city when the major fairs and fall and spring fashion shows are in progress—September, October, and early March. Forget about August. That's when the Milanese go on vacation and the majority of the hotels are closed. The larger chains, however, are open year-round.

Arriving by Air

Milan has two airports serving international travelers. Milan's main international airport, **Malpensa,** is 28 miles northwest of the city, and 50 to 60 minutes is required to reach the downtown air terminal. Closer in, Milan's **Linate Airport** is located slightly more than 6 miles to the east of Milan. Check with your airline regarding which airport will be used for your flight. *Tel:* (02) 232323. Visit the website for both airports at www.sea-aeroportimilano.it/en/.

Airport–City Links: Malpensa Airport Bus service connects Malpensa Airport with Linate Airport (travel time of 1 hour 10 minutes) and Malpensa Airport with the Central Station (travel time of 50 minutes; fare: €10). Malpensa Express train service to the city departs every 30 minutes; journey time is 40 minutes. Fare: €12 one-way, €18 open return; office in Terminal 1.

A deluxe bus service [Air Pullman, *Tel:* (02) 58583202] runs every 10 minutes between Linate Airport and the Central Station from 0600 to 2300. Fare: €8.00. Purchase tickets on board the bus.

Bus, limousine, and taxi services are available at both air terminals. The taxi services are quite expensive, averaging about €65–€75 from Malpensa but only about €15 from Linate.

Arriving by Train

Milan has seven railway stations, but luckily, readers need be concerned with only one, the Milan Central Station **(Milano Centrale).** Milan's Central Station is enormous.

- **Money exchange** offices can be reached by going through the archway leading off *binari* (tracks) Nos. 10 to 15. Once through the archway and into the main hall of the station, you will see three Maccorp Italiana stands. *Hours:* 0730–2200 daily. Avoid the so-called money changers who frequent this area. Like the gypsies in the Paris Métro, their main purpose is to relieve you of your money. The gypsies do it by picking your pocket; the "money changers" are much more gentle in their approach—they just shortchange you. You will find the best rates at the official exchange offices.
- **Tourist information** (A.P.T.) is located on the platform (first) floor near the "Gran Bar" in the main hall. Maps and tour information are available. This office is not equipped to assist in locating hotel accommodations, but you can get directions to the central tourist office at Piazza del Duomo. *Hours:* 0900–1800 Monday–Friday and 0900–1300 and 1400–1700 Saturday–Sunday. *Tel:* (02) 77404318. A hallway on the left side of the tourist office will lead you to a public telephone.
- **Train information** office is marked with a black "i" sign, located at the extreme right end of the station as you come from the trains. Illuminated flags indicate what language is spoken at the windows. The British flag means English is spoken. *Hours:* 0700–2300.
- **Train reservations** for Eurostar Italia, EuroCity, InterCity, and Rapido express-train services are made in an office separate from the one dispensing train information. To reach it, go through the main station hall and descend to the station foyer on the street level. Turn left and look for a huge door marked BIGLIETTERIA EST (ticket office east). Go through the door, and take a number from the ticket machine to wait your turn. You will see counter Nos. 49 to 53, labeled PRENOTAZIONI (Reservations). *Hours:* 0550–2220 daily.

- **Rail pass validation** requires that you descend to street level via the escalator in the middle of the station, make a right turn, and look for a sign, BIGLIETTERIA OVEST. Then proceed to window 20 or 22, marked INTERNATIONAL TICKETS.
- **Food services** range from trackside vendors to a full-service restaurant. The restaurant, with a large and efficient self-service cafeteria next to it, is located on the far left side of the main hall as you exit from the trains. A snack bar is also there. Downstairs near the BIGLIETTERIA OVEST sign you will find an excellent cafeteria that serves traditional Italian hot entrees and sandwiches. Just behind the cafeteria is a supermarket.

  In this snack bar, as in the various smaller ones scattered throughout the main hall and track area, you need to purchase tickets for the particular food or beverage you desire from a cashier, then give the tickets to a counter attendant. The system works, but now you know how confused the Italian immigrant felt when ordering an American hamburger, especially if asked, "Would you like that with mustard, catsup, lettuce, tomato, pickles—and was that to go?"

  If this is your first rail trip into Italy, this will probably be your first acquaintance with the trackside vendors. Similar to the pushcarts that grace many of the streets in New York City, they offer a convenient variety of refreshments—and the price is right.
- **Baggage-checking** facilities may be reached by taking the exit at the end of Tracks 6 and 7. Across the main hall and to the right, you'll see a sign in red letters, DEPOSITO BAGAGLI. Rates vary according to what you store. The facility is open all the time.

  The main baggage room, located on the street level of the station, can be reached either from the plaza facing the Michelangelo Hotel or from the bottom of the main escalator, between the street level and the train concourse. *Hours:* 0600–2300 daily.
- **Station miscellany.** Milan's railway station has many other services. There is a large and rather comfortable first-class lounge leading off the street side of the main hall. Its entrance is just to the left of the tourist information office. Inside the lounge you will find a computer that can give you train information.

  Milano Centrale is a multilevel station, but elevator service from the train level to the street level is available. The entrance on the train level is inside the first-class lounge. If you have a first-class rail pass, you have full access to the passenger lounge and elevator service.
- **Taxi service** is available at both side entrances and the front, and **bus service** is in the Piazza Duca d'Aosta in front of the station. Pictographs of the station's facilities are located conveniently at the end of many tracks.

Double-check your departing train number and platform location. For example, when departing Milan for Munich aboard EuroCity 93 *Leonardo Da Vinci*, signs in the station will indicate the train's destination as MONACO. In Italian, this means "Monk," and Munich (in German) is the "City of Monks." So, you are on the right train, and you are not bound for Monaco, which, in French, means "Monte Carlo." InterCity 143 is the proper train to board if you are in fact going to Monaco and Monte Carlo via Genoa.

Emerging from the train platforms, if you detect the aroma of an American-style hamburger, it's coming from Wendy's. To get there, turn right in the station hall and take the escalator at the far end to the street level. Skirt the tram terminal to the left, then look for the Wendy's sign.

Tourist Information/Hotel Reservations

- *Tourist Information Office:* A.P.T., Via Marconi I, just off Piazza del Duomo; *Tel:* (02) 774 04343; *Fax:* (02) 774 04333

  Hours: Summer: 0900–1800 Monday–Saturday, 0900–1330 and 1400–1700 Sunday

  Notes: To reach the central tourist information office, take bus No. 60 in front of the station to Piazza del Duomo, site of Milan's cathedral. You can also take Line 3 of the metro to the Duomo stop. Attendants in the railway station information office will direct you.

Getting Around in Milan

Milan has an excellent underground transportation system (Metropolitana Milanese). A ticket costs €1.50 and is valid for 75 minutes on buses and trams or for one underground (metro) trip. There is also a day ticket available for €4.50 and a two-day ticket for €8.25.

The friendly Milanese devised the "Milano for You" *Welcome Card kit* to make your stay in Milan more convenient and enjoyable. The kit includes access to art tours, cultural theme dinners, Giuseppe Verdi Symphonic Orchestra tickets, a 24-hour public transportation ticket, city map, and an opera music compact disc. It's available at the tourist information office (€13).

There are times when Milan reaches the visitor saturation point and NO VACANCY signs go up all over town. Should you arrive in Milan without hotel reservations, you have two alternatives to consider.

If there is no housing in Milan, you can leave town. A EuroCity train can have you in Como in 30 minutes, where hotel rooms probably will be more plentiful. In fact, you may be taken with the idea of residing in this lovely lake location throughout your stay in the area. There is express-train service back to Milan every morning.

Another alternative is a fast but systematic search of the concentrated hotel area adjacent to the railway station. There is a covey of luxury and first-class hotels to the left of it. Dominating the scene is the 17-story Michelangelo, with the Bristol, the Anderson, the Andreola, and the Splendido close by.

For lower cost but comfortable lodgings, walk 2 blocks on Via Roberto Lepetit, beginning at the Michelangelo, to Piazza San Camillo. Within this distance, you pass the Florida, the Colombia, and the Boston hotels. No luck? Turn right at the Plaza onto Via Napo Torriani. Between this point and Piazza Duca d'Aosta 3 short blocks ahead (where you can again see the station), you pass several more hotels. If you have not found a room by this time, head back to Milano Centrale and take a train to Lake Como.

The main tourist office charges a nominal fee for making accommodations reservations, but they are not authorized to accept deposits to guarantee that your reservation will be honored on your arrival at the hotel or pension. If you have made a room reservation through the tourist office, proceed immediately to your hotel to confirm your reservation in person. Many Italian hoteliers operate on a "first-come, first-housed" basis, and even though you have a reservation, someone else may end up with your room.

Day Excursions

A total of four day excursions have been selected from Milan. The first two take you south of Milan into the Italian peninsula to Italy's gastronomic capital, **Bologna,** and the birthplace of Christopher Columbus, **Genoa.** Another day excursion takes you to where Switzerland meets Italy, **Lugano,** the Swiss city with an Italian flair. The remaining day excursion will take you east to "the Queen of the Adriatic," **Venice,** and the romance of its gondoliers and grand canals. You'll enjoy each of them.

Train Connections to Other Base Cities from Milan (Milano)

Depart from Milan (Milano) Centrale

DEPART	TRAIN NUMBER	ARRIVE	NOTES
		Amsterdam Centraal	
0845	TGV 9244	2042	R, 8
1823	EC 56	0934+1	R, 1, Sleeper
2305	EN 220	1542+1	R, 8, Sleeper
		Bern (Berne)	
0823	EC 32	1154	2
1123	EC 52	1423	
1223	EC 34	1554	2
followed by departures at 1425, 1723, 1823, 1923, and 2025.			
		Brussels (Bruxelles) Midi/Zuid	
0845	TGV 9244	1847	R , 8
2305	EN 220	1247+1	R, 8, Sleeper
		Copenhagen (København) H.	
1823	EC 56	1422+1	R, 1, Su–Th, Sleeper

DEPART	TRAIN NUMBER	ARRIVE	NOTES
		Hamburg Hauptbahnhof	
0723	EC 50	1935	R, 1
1123	EC 52	0014+1	R, 4
1510	EC 158	0550+1	R, 4, Sleeper
2105	CNL 40484	1253+1	R, 1, Sleeper
		Luxembourg	
0723	EC 50	1929	1
		Lyon Part-Dieu	
0845	TGV 9244	1510	R, 6
1223	EC 34	1924	R, 6
2305	EN 220	0944+1	R, 7, Sleeper
		Munich (München) Hauptbahnhof	
0705	ES 9703	1423	R, 3
0905	ES 9713	1624	R, 3
1305	IC 9723	2021	R, 3
2105	CNL 40481	0630+1	R, Sleeper
		Nice Ville	
0705	IC 141	1204	R
1510	IC 159	2004	R, 5
1705	IC 675	2306	R, 5
		Paris Gare de Lyon	
0845	TGV 9244	1611	R
1223	EC 34	1949	R, 6
2305	EN 220	0955+1	R, Sleeper
		Prague (Praha)	
1510	EC 158	0928+1	R, 4, Sleeper
		Roma (Roma) Termini	
0820	ES 9513	1140	R
0900	ES 9615	1155	R
1020	ES 9521	1340	R
and hourly service thereafter until 2020, then			
2317	ICN 797	0717+1	R, Sleeper
		Vienna (Wien) Hauptbahnhof	
0825	EC 12	2030	R, 4
2105	EN 481	0948+1	R, Exc. Fri, Sleeper
		Warsaw Centralna	
1225	EC 16	1215+1	R, 4, Sleeper

DEPART	TRAIN NUMBER	ARRIVE	NOTES
		Zürich Hauptbahnhof	
0825	EC 12	1228	R
1025	EC 14	1428	R
1225	EC 16	1628	R
1625	EC 20	2028	R
1825	EC 22	2228	R
2025	EC 2418	0028+1	R

Daily, unless otherwise noted
R Reservations required
+1 Arrives next day
1. Change trains in Basel.
2. Change trains in Brig.
3. Change trains in Verona Porta Nuova.
4. Change trains in Zürich.
5. Change trains in Ventimiglia.
6. Change trains in Geneva.
7. Change trains in Dijon-Ville.
8. Change trains in Paris.

Day Excursion to

Bologna

Italy's Gastronomic Capital

Depart Milano Centrale Station
Distance by Train: 136 miles (219 km)
Average Train Time: 1 hour, 42 minutes
City Dialing Code: 51
Tourist Information Office: No. 6, west side of Piazza Maggiore
Tel: (051) 23 9660; **Fax:** (051) 64 72253
Hours: 0900–1900 Monday–Saturday; 1000–1700 Sunday
www.bolognawelcome.com
E-mail: TouristOffice@comune.bologna.it
Notes: To reach this tourist office, turn left when exiting the rail station, and walk 2 blocks to Via Dell'Independenza, one of Bologna's main avenues. Turn right onto the avenue, and a delightful 15-minute walk will bring you to Neptune's Fountain. Then continue your walk in the same direction a short distance into Piazza Maggiore.

Bologna specializes in two areas—thinking and eating. When you think about it, you'll probably conclude, as we did, that it is not too bad a lifestyle to follow.

Bologna stands out historically and architecturally. Tourists can walk under the porticoes of the city while visiting the many monuments. If lined up, the porticoes would cover 40 kilometers!

Bologna's university, the oldest in Europe, was founded in 1088. By the 13th century, its student body numbered 10,000. One of its more recent students, Guglielmo Marconi (1874–1937), studied wireless telegraphy there. The university was noted for employing women professors. One professor, Novella d'Andrea, was said to be so beautiful in face and body that she had to give her lectures from behind a screen to avoid distracting her students.

Bologna is the capital of **Emilia-Romagna,** a northwest-to-southeast slice of the Italian peninsula just below its juncture with the European Continent. It is here that the "cultura villanoviana," better known as the Iron Age, began more than 4,000 years ago. After the fall of the Roman Empire, the city did not flourish again until after the 11th century. Marvelous Etruscan and Roman examples of history can be seen at the **Civic Archaeology Museum.**

Milan (Milano)—Bologna

DEPART Milano Centrale	TRAIN NUMBER	ARRIVE Bologna Centrale	NOTES
0542	ES 9507	0752	R
0720	ES 9609	0822	R
and hourly ES trains at 20 minutes past the hour until 2020, plus other non-ES trains; last train at 2050.			

DEPART Bologna Centrale	TRAIN NUMBER	ARRIVE Milano Centrale	NOTES
1438	ES 9528	1540	R
1538	ES 9532	1640	R
and hourly ES trains at 38 minutes past the hour, plus other non-ES trains; last train at 2238.			

Daily
R Reservations required
Distance: 136 miles (219 km)

An economically strong region, with the nation's highest employment rate, Emilia-Romagna holds the uncontested title of the "richest gastronomic region in Italy." Endless strings of sausages and thousands of cheese varieties adorn the windows of its delicatessen shops. Restaurants line the city's arcaded streets, filled with people devouring delicacies to the accompaniment of fine wines. Many of them are in the luxury class, but you can also dine very well in the less expensive restaurants. Many maintain an "open kitchen," which you're welcome to inspect and where you may chat with the cooks. The famous prosciutto of Parma is absolutely unlike any American prosciutto—and, like most Italian meat products, it cannot be sold in the United States.

Bologna is an ideal base for exploring the Emilia-Romagna area. Among the towns to visit are **Faenza,** for its ceramics; **Ferrara,** for its fortress; **Ravenna,** for its early Christian art; **Rimini,** for its Adriatic beach; and, of course, **Parma,** for its ham and Parmesan cheese. All are about one hour or less by rail from Bologna. All of these cities may be visited out of Milan, too. Consult the schedules in Milan's Central Station.

Bologna also has much to offer architecturally. Purchase a ticket (€18 adult) for the **City Tour** on the open-deck bus **Giro Tp** for an introduction to Bologna's sights and attractions. Board at the rail station and hop on and off as you please at any of the Giro Tp bus stops. You will see an ensemble of rare Italian beauty concentrated in its two enjoining squares, the **Piazza Maggiore** and the **Piazza del Nettuno.** Combined with the **Piazza di Porta Ravegnana,** the heart of Bologna even today reflects its Renaissance greatness.

Neptune's Fountain (Fontana del Nettuno) is the focal point of its piazza. Completed in 1566, it aptly depicts Bologna's vigorous nature. Saint Petronius Basilica, facing the Piazza Maggiore, was begun in 1390 but remains unfinished even today.

The Piazza Ravegnana contains not just one leaning tower but two. The taller, built by the Asinelli family between 1109 and 1119, stands 330 feet with a tilt exceeding 7½ feet. The other, the Garisenda Tower, is only 165 feet high, but it leans out 10 feet over its foundation. If you're in good physical condition and feel like climbing 498 steps, there's a fine view from the top of the Asinelli Tower.

And if you would like to experience more of the "culta Bononia" (the Latin name for Bologna), call the tourist office for the *Not Just for the Weekend* brochure. Rates and special offers on more than 50 hotels and inns, city and "pilgrim" tours; events year-round are also listed.

Day Excursion to

Genoa (Genova)

Great Port of Italy

Depart Milano Centrale Station
Distance by Train: 93 miles (150 km)
Average Train Time: 1 hour, 25 minutes
City Dialing Code: 010
Tourist Information Office: On the right-hand side of the Piazza Principe Station foyer after the second escalator coming from the trains
Tel: (010) 5572903
Hours: 0900–1820 daily
www.visitgenoa.it
E-mail: info@visitgenoa.it

Richard Wagner wrote, "I have never seen anything like this Genoa! It is something indescribably beautiful, grandiose, characteristic." According to its tourist office, Genoa is "a town that you have to know how to love . . . there can be no half measures." Genoa is a merchant town, a vertical city, a major Mediterranean port. It is a city of contrasts, mixing the ancient with the new.

To experience a taste of this interesting city, ride the InterCity 657 *Andrea Doria* out of Milan to Genoa at 0810 in the morning. Enjoy a leisurely walk along Genoa's avenues. Lunch in full view of the city's great harbor—largest in all of Italy. Board an InterCity late in the afternoon and be back in Milan for dinner that same day. Or fall in love with Genoa by lunchtime and return to Milan just before midnight. The relatively short time en route between these cities makes a "set your own pace" schedule ideal.

Be mindful that Genoa has two major railway stations, **Piazza Principe** and **Brignole.** If you come from Milan, Piazza Principe is the first stop after the train emerges from a tunnel. Digital schedule boards in both stations advise what time the next connecting train departs for the other station. To be certain, board your returning train to Milan from Piazza Principe because many through-trains do not call at Brignole. You can, however, ride any shuttle train from Brignole north to the next stop, which is Piazza Principe.

A boat tour of the city's harbor is a great way for visitors to acquaint themselves with Genoa. Tours by boat leave from the aquarium, in the old port area, daily at 1400. Organized boat trips from the Maritime Building may be arranged ahead of time. The tour runs every hour starting at 0930 and ending at 1730/1800 (or later, depending on the number of people asking for the trip), when a minimum of 10 persons is present. To reach the departure quay, proceed by bus or on foot to Piazza Caricamento, following the yellow signs to the aquarium. Cross the road and enter the old port area. You'll see the aquarium on your right. The tour boats are berthed just beside the aquarium building. Visit www.battellierigenova.it. Tickets €8.00.

Most visitors link Genoa with Christopher Columbus (1451–1505). This association begins as you leave the Piazza Principe Station fronted by **Piazza Acquaverde,** where a statue stands in honor of Columbus. A part of the city bus tour takes you to the Church of San Stefano, where Columbus was baptized, and into the Piazza della Vittoria—a vast expanse of lawns where the three ships of his fleet, the *Niña*, *Pinta*, and *Santa Maria*, are depicted in grass and flowers.

Plan a walking tour of Genoa. Depart Genova Piazza Principe Station and follow Via Balbi to Via Cairoli, which connects with "the street of Kings"—Via Garibaldi. At the end of Via Garibaldi, turn right (south), and proceed to the city's center, Piazza de Ferrari. From this point, you can continue along Via XX Settembre to the park in front of the Brignole Station or return on foot to the Piazza Principe Station by turning south and walking along the harbor. Both tourist information offices have maps to assist you in the walking tour. Be certain to include Genoa's great aquarium. The **Aquarium,** built in 1992 for the Columbus celebrations, is one of the biggest in Europe and should not be missed.

The city of Genoa lies beside a fine natural harbor at the foot of a pass in the Italian Apennines. It rivals Marseilles as the leading European port on the Mediterranean. Genoa's harbor facilities, which were damaged heavily during World War II, have been expanded and modernized. Shipbuilding is the leading industry of Genoa.

Ever since its birth, Genoa's calling has been the sea. Genoese ships transported Crusaders to the Middle East and returned laden with booty. Genoese merchants, profiting from the newly created demand in Europe for goods from the Middle East, expanded their operations throughout the Christian world. Genoese forts and trading posts soon spread throughout the Mediterranean and Aegean Seas, creating a rivalry between Genoese and Venetians. Ask the tourist office for hours and information on the sea and navigation museum called **Padiglione del mare e della Navigazione** in the Porto Antico Area.

Milan (Milano)—Genoa (Genova)

Milan (Milano)–Genoa (Genova)

Departures hourly alternating at 10 or 25 minutes past the hour beginning at 0610. Journey time: 93 minutes to 1 hour and 50 minutes.

Genoa (Genova)–Milan (Milano)

Departures at 21 and 44 minutes past the hour every other hour, until 1921, followed by 3 trains until 2146. Journey time: 1 hour 47 minutes.

Genoa is proud of its **Lanterna,** the lighthouse that has become the international symbol of the city. Built on the site of an ancient tower in the first half of the 16th century, it has guided mariners to its safe harbor for more than four centuries.

In the time of Christopher Columbus, another son of Genoa, Andrea Doria (1468–1560), did much to promote the development of the city's maritime power.

Serving as captain-general of Genoa's navy until defeated by Spanish forces in 1522, he served the French briefly before restoring the republic of Genoa as an ally of Holy Roman Emperor Charles V. Andrea Doria's palace can be seen during the city tour.

Those traveling with children will not want to skip **La Citta dei Bambini.** This children's town is fascinating to young ones and to the curious of any age who want to learn how scientific things work.

Day Excursion to

Lake Lugano

The Swiss Riviera

Depart Milano Centrale Station
Distance by Train: 48 miles (77 km)
Average Train Time: 1 hour, 15 minutes
Switzerland Dialing Code: 41
City Dialing Code: 91
Tourist Information Office: Palazzo Civico, Riva Albertolli, P.O. Box 2533, CH-6901 Lugano, Switzerland
Tel: (058) 866 6600; **Fax:** (058) 866 6609
www.luganotourism.ch
E-mail: info@luganotourism.ch
Hours: May–August: 0900–1900 Monday–Friday, 0900–1800 Saturday, 1000–1800 Sunday; November–March: 0900–1200 and 1330–1730 Monday–Friday, 1000–1230 and 1330–1700 Saturday; April and October: 0900–1900 Monday–Friday, 1000—1700 Saturday–Sunday
Notes: To reach the official tourist office of Lake Lugano, ride the funicolare (cable railway) to Piazza Cioccaro, and proceed on foot downhill to the center of Lugano, Piazza Riforma. As you continue downhill toward the lake, stop at the town hall, where the tourist office is located. Holders of Eurail passes need not purchase separate rail tickets to make excursions from Milan into Switzerland, since both Italy and Switzerland are included on these passes.

Lake Lugano, known as the Swiss Riviera, is sheltered from the north by the Lepontine Alps. It is favored with a climate that is exceptionally mild and is purportedly the sunniest of all central European resorts. Considered a year-round resort, the city of Lugano sponsors a multitude of events to attract visitors of all ages.

Although Lugano is a very short distance from Milan, you will be crossing the Swiss border on this day excursion. Don't forget your passport. There is a currency exchange desk in the railway station. *Hours:* 0600–2230 daily. The town abounds in banks and *cambio* (exchange) offices that offer official rates. As you leave the station, there is a

hotel-reservations-and-information office to your immediate right. Train information may be obtained in the office bearing the i sign to the left of the main exit.

When the lake beckons, there is a choice of eight round-trips by boat, each offering an opportunity for a special vista. If the mountains attract you, ascent is possible by cableways and funiculars in many different directions. Two funiculars, one at each end of Lugano, carry you swiftly up 3,000 feet to breathtaking views of either **Monte Bre** or **Monte San Salvatore.**

The list of things to do and see doesn't stop there. Take a motor coach to either **Sonvico** or **Tesserete,** typical Swiss mountain villages. Even a journey to the world-renowned resort of **St. Moritz** is possible. In fact, anything's possible—just ask at the Lugano tourist information office.

For a relaxing day on the lake, select the cruise to the **Swiss Miniature Village,** a unique exhibition of towns, hamlets, castles, mountains, and railways—all on a scale of 1:25. The model railway is centrally controlled and has a length of 186 miles! Realize that this is an all-day outing, but it has wooed millions of other visitors—why not you? *Hours:* 0900–1800 daily mid-March–October. *Tel:* (091) 640 10 60; www.swissminiatur.ch.

The tourist information office will gladly mark out a walking tour of the city and its interesting areas, or opt for a free guided walking tour every Monday morning from April until October.

For lunch in Lugano, you can make it a stand-up affair by selecting from a vendor's cart at lakeside or perhaps aboard a lake steamer. For an enjoyable sit-down meal, we recommend these quality restaurants in the center of Lugano: **Al Portone, Cantinone, Casino Kursaal, Commercianti, La Tinera, Parco Saroli, Olimpia, Orologio, Restaurant Scala,** and **Trani.** In Paradiso we can recommend **Osteria Calprino.**

Milan (Milano)—Lake Lugano

DEPART Milano Centrale	TRAIN NUMBER	ARRIVE Lugano	NOTES
0710	EC 25506	0818	R
0810	EC 25508	0926	R
1025	EC 14	1132	R
and further departures following the same pattern at 1225, 1425, 1625, and 1825.			

DEPART Lugano	TRAIN NUMBER	ARRIVE Milano Centrale	NOTES
1425	EC 17	1535	R
1625	EC 19	1735	R
1825	EC 21	1935	R
2026	EC 23	2135	R
2225	EC 25	2335	R

Daily
R Reservations required
Distance: 48 miles (77 km)

Shopping in Lugano is a pleasant experience. The place to do this is concentrated in the market area stretching from the bottom of the funicolare to the city square fronting the lake. Mouthwatering food vies for your attention along with a wide selection of Swiss products and crafts. We have yet to see a visitor enter the market area around lunchtime and not emerge a few minutes later with a sandwich in hand rivaling anything that Dagwood could concoct.

Shopping in this market area is, for the most part, in the shelter of overhead arcades. If you have been looking for specialty items of the Ticino area of Switzerland, you will find them here. Although firmly Swiss, the market in Lugano does have that piquant touch of Italy.

If you are longing for a Swiss-made watch, stop by **Bucherer's** in Lugano at Via Nassa 56. *Hours:* 0900–1830 Monday–Friday and Saturday until 1700. It carries its own styles as well as the other top Swiss names.

For a special treat be certain to visit our "secret hangout," **Gandria,** a small cliff-side village that clings precariously to the mountains descending from the east into Lake Lugano. Gandria has no streets, but there is a bus stop on the mountainside road above. The best, and more romantic, access is by lake steamer. If you want to share in our secret, inquire at any steamer pier regarding schedules to Gandria. You will want to take the Lugano-Porlezza Line and plan to have an early dinner at one of Gandria's superb restaurants.

Day Excursion to

Venice (Venezia)

Grand Canals and Gondolas

Depart Milano Centrale Station
Distance by Train: 166 miles (267 km)
Average Train Time: 2 hours, 45 minutes
City Dialing Code: 41
Tourist Information Office: In Santa Lucia rail station
Tel: (041) 529 87 11; **Fax:** (041) 523 03 99
www.turismovenezia.it
E-mail: info@turismovenezia.it
Hours: 0800–1830 daily
Notes: Proceed to the head of the train platform, and enter the main hall of the station. The train information office is on the immediate left. No tourist information is available at this office. Beyond that, you'll see a sign directing you to a self-service buffet. Digital train information is prominently displayed above the buffet sign. Telephones, ticket windows, newspaper stands, and specialty shops are on the right-hand side of the station hall. Just prior to exiting the station, you'll see tourist information.

Upon arrival in Venice (Venezia), the American humorist Robert Benchley telegraphed his publisher, "Streets are flooded, please advise." Things have changed little since. Venice is situated on 120 islands surrounded by 177 canals in a lagoon between the Po and Piave Rivers at the northern extremity of the Adriatic Sea. The islands on which the city is built are connected by 400 or so bridges. Not only by its site but also by its architecture and history, Venice is known as "the Queen of the Adriatic."

Venice was founded in A.D. 452 when the inhabitants of several northern Italian cities sought refuge there from the Teutonic tribes invading Italy during the fifth century. The Venetians improved their fortifications and erected bulwarks of masonry to protect their growing city from the sea and from their enemies.

During the Crusades, Venice developed trade with the Orient and quickly became the center for commerce with the East. Venice became the leading wartime power of the Christian world by the end of the 15th century. In 1797 Napoleon Bonaparte conquered Venice and turned its government over to Austria. Through subsequent political maneuvers, Venice became part of the newly established kingdom of Italy in 1866.

Be sure to obtain full details regarding the canal transportation system. Water taxis are expensive, with fares starting at €14.00, plus €0.26 for each additional 15 seconds. The public boats (*vaporetto*, *motoscafo*, or *motonave*) operated by ACTV are a far more affordable means of reaching the main parts of Venice. The most romantic way to traverse the canals is, of course, via Venice's famous gondolas.

Milan (Milano)—Venice (Venezia)

DEPART	TRAIN NUMBER	ARRIVE
Milan Centrale		Venice Santa Lucia
0635	IC 9701	0858
0805	IC 9709	1040
0905	IC 9711	1140

and at least hourly until 2035; journey time, 2 hours 35 minutes.

DEPART	TRAIN NUMBER	ARRIVE	NOTES
Venice Santa Lucia		Milan Centrale	
1502	ES 9730	1725	
1620	EC 42	1855	
1720	EC 9740	1955	R
1820	IC 9746	2055	
1950	IC 9750	2225	

Daily
R Reservations required
Distance: 166 miles (267 km)

Fares run €80 for about 40 minutes. For only €0.50, you could use one of the seven *traghetti* (ferries) to get from one side of the Grand Canal to the other. Also, ask for a map of Venice. You'll need it. Venetian addresses are somewhat peculiar in that they consist of a number and the name of a small area that could include several streets, thus making a particular restaurant or shop difficult to find. The canal navigation services (*Linee di Navigazione Lagunare*) are described in full detail on the reverse side of the map. If in Venice on a day excursion, purchase a one-way rather than a round-trip water-bus ticket from the rail station to **San Marco** on Line 1 and return to the station on foot.

Ticket in hand, board Line 1–Accelerata at Station 2, on the left side of the rail station. The dock and vessels are marked PIAZZALE ROMA–FERROVIA–LIDO, and the boat should be moving to your left as you come from the station. Boats proceeding to the right terminate at Station 1, Piazzale Roma, where you're required to disembark and purchase another ticket to get back on course!

Line 1 moves along the Grand Canal until emerging into open water from the canal at **Piazza San Marco** (St. Mark's), the center and most frequented part of Venice. The **Grand Canal** is Venice's principal traffic artery. It is lined with churches, museums, palaces—even a fish market—so keep your guidebook open so you can recognize these landmarks as you glide by.

Go ashore at St. Mark's and revel in the staggering sights before you. St. Mark's Bell Tower dominates the scene, but it won't be long before you'll find yourself standing in front of the cathedral. If time permits, take the elevator to the top of the bell tower for a spectacular view of vibrant Venice.

With so much to see, be mindful of the time or you will miss the train back to Milan. You can't hail a taxi at the last minute, since there are none, so allow at least 45 minutes for the return trip from St. Mark's to Santa Lucia Station by water bus. Or start ambling through Venice by following the signs, ALLA FERROVIA (to the rail station). They are posted everywhere and easy to follow. Allow two hours to reach the station on foot, although a reasonable pace should get you there about 30 minutes sooner.

En route, you will cross the **Rialto Bridge**—the best place to view the Grand Canal and a good place to shop, too. There are 24 shops right on the bridge and a variety of vendors selling their wares along both sides of the canal. Farther on, you will cross the **Ponte Degli Scalzi** (Station Bridge) and arrive at the rail station where you started.

We're sure you will return to Venice, but heed the plight of tourists burdened with too many bags on the water buses—come back with a minimum amount of luggage or stow it in the lockers at the Santa Lucia or Mestre Station.

Base City: **ROME (Roma)**

www. turismoroma.it
City Dialing Code: 06

Italians refer lovingly to Rome as the "Eternal City." In the days of the Caesars, all roads led to Rome. Today, the same may be said of Italian State Railways.

No one knows exactly when people first started living along the Tiber River where Rome developed. Archaeologists continue to find evidence of still earlier civilizations than that of the Romans buried under those remains they have already identified. Etruscans ruled the area long before the Romans. Remains of that earlier Mediterranean civilization continue to be discovered in and around Rome.

Rome has already had two periods of greatness in the civilized world, each of which had a significant impact. Two thousand years ago, Rome ruled a good part of Europe and the Middle East. Rome contributed roads, architecture, art, law, literature, and political experience to the entire area.

Conquered by barbarians during the fifth century A.D., the city managed to remain the home of the popes, and through them and their armies, political power was regained. During the Renaissance, Rome again became a great center of art and learning. Since 1870, when Italian troops captured the city from Pope Pius IX, Rome has been the capital of Italy.

Readers considering "open jaw" (arrive in one European city, depart from another) air transportation to and from Europe should give serious consideration to Rome as either their entry or exit point. For example, in the spring, enter Europe through Rome and wend your way northward as the weather improves. Leave from Amsterdam. In autumn, reverse the procedure. Follow those lingering fall days southward from Amsterdam to Rome. By planning a rail vacation itinerary in this manner, you can assure yourself of having more moderate weather.

As a matter of fact, the average daily temperatures of Amsterdam and Rome vary by 10 to 12 degrees Fahrenheit—Rome's, of course, being the higher. So, when in Rome, do as the Romans do—move north as the mercury soars in the summer, south again when it begins to sink.

Arriving by Air

Rome has two airports, but because Ciampino Airport is small and deals mainly with charter flights, we focus on the main airport, Leonardo da Vinci, also called Fiumicino. **Fiumicino Airport** is 22 miles southwest of Rome. *Tel:* (06) 65951; *Flight info:* (06) 65951; www.adr.it.

- **Airport–City Links:** Leonardo Express direct train service every 30 minutes from Fiumicino Airport to Rome's Stazione Termini (Central Station) in Rome runs 0550 to 2250. Journey time: 31 minutes. Fare: €14. It leaves and arrives at track No. 22 in Roma Termini Station.

  There is also an underground train service, FM1, from Fiumicino Airport to Tiburtina Station (total travel time, 46 minutes), with stops at local stations **Trastevere** and **Ostiense.** Trains run every 15 minutes 0505 to 2233, then half hourly until 2326; journey time, 42 minutes. Fare: €11.00. If you arrive at night, there is night bus service between Fiumicino Airport and Tiburtina Station. Buses run 0115 to 0500. Fare: €6.

  A taxi from Fiumicino Airport to the center runs about €40–€50, but we caution against using taxis unless your airline representative arranges it and determines the fare beforehand. Authorized taxis are white cars with meters.

Arriving by Train

When you arrive at the railway station in Rome, beware of the many willing "helpers" eager to carry your luggage and find you a cab. If you need a taxi, carry your own bag and get in the regular taxi line.

Roma Termini. Rome has several suburban stations, but the InterCity and express trains stop only in the main station—Roma Termini, which has undergone extensive renovation. It is like a city within a city. New signage is in both Italian and English. In its main concourse, the section separating the train platforms from the main hall, you will find a bar and restaurant. On the lower level of the station you will find services you normally associate only with the most modern airports—barbershops, hairdressers, showers, lounges, bookstore, drugstore, fast food, and clothing shops.

- **Money exchange** facilities are located throughout the railway station. In the main concourse, there is an office just to the left of *binari* (track) 12, between gateways 2 and 3. *Hours:* 0630–2200 daily.
- **Hotel reservations.** Hotel reservations in Rome and other Italian cities can be made Monday through Sunday 0700 to 2200 directly across from track No. 20.
- **Train information and reservations desks** are located across from Platforms 5 and 22. There is also an FS Information Office toward the Piazza dei Cinquecento exits, facing the bus station. *Hours:* 0630–2200. Visit www.trenitalia.com.

To ensure that you receive the proper reservation, determine the day and date of your travel, the number and departure time of your train, and its arrival time at your destination. This information can be taken from any of the train schedules posted throughout the station.

Print this information on a plain piece of paper, starting with the date, the train number, and the departure time. Draw a short arrow, then add the arrival time of the train and, finally, the name of the destination. Indicate the number of reservations required, then present the information to the attendant together with the rail pass you will use for the trip. Submission of this information may draw a small grin from the attendant making the reservations, but it will save time and lessen the possibilities of errors in completing your train reservations.

- **Rail pass validation** may be made at a window labeled in English in the FS Information Office located in the center of the train station near the main entrance facing the bus station. It is rather hidden away, and there are not any signs directing you. Just follow the signs for taxi and bus service, and right before you exit the station behind several tobacco shops you will see several windows, including the Eurail window and other windows that can provide you with information.

If you plan an early morning departure on the first day you use your rail pass, either allow an extra hour at the station that morning or inquire at one of the validating windows midevening the night before about the possibility of predating the validation.

Tourist Information/Hotel Reservations

- **Azienda di Promozione Turistica di Roma,** Via Parigi, 11–00185 (Piazza della Repubblica) Roma; *Tel:* (06) 48 89 91; *Fax:* (06) 42 13 81; *Call Center:* 36 004 399

  Hours: 0930–1900 Monday–Saturday, closed Sunday/holidays

  www.turismoroma.it; *E-mail:* turismo@comune.roma.it

  Notes: To visit this office, exit the main entrance of Roma Termini, skirt the left side of the city square in front of the station, and proceed past Museo Nazionale Romano (the National Roman Museum) to Via Parigi. Turn right at that point, then look for the office on the left-hand side of the street.

- **National Tourist Office, ENIT** (Head Office), Via Marghera 2/6, 00185 Roma, 1 block east of the railway station. *Tel:* (06) 49711; *Fax:* (06) 44 63 379; www.enit.it
- For tours in Rome and vicinity, the tourist office in the main hall of the railway station will be happy to oblige. There are several other "Tourist Information Points" including in Terminal B (International Arrivals) at Fiumicino Airport. *Hours:* 0800–1930 Monday–Saturday.

Getting Around in Rome

Rome's public transport is plentiful, with bus, metro (underground), and metropolitan rail systems. Visit www.atac.roma.it. **Metrebus Tickets** are valid for travel on all three forms. You must validate your ticket before boarding the metro and trains. Validate your ticket on buses at the orange stamping machine. The fine ranges between €50 and €500 if you're caught without a validated ticket. Metrebus Tickets are sold at tobacconists, bars, newsstands, travel agencies, and in the metro, bus, and railway stations. Single trip (€1.50), daily (€6), three-day (€16.50), and weekly (€24) tickets are available.

Legitimate taxis in Rome are moderate in price and equipped with meters. Beware of the "cab-and-coin" taxis. The driver is more than happy to take you where you want to go, but probably at three times the regular rate. Ask your hotel personnel to hail a taxi for you or telephone one of the radio-dispatched taxis: (06) 3570, (06) 6645, (06) 8822, (06) 4157, (06) 4994, or (06) 5551.

Sights/Attractions/Tours

Since Rome is so vast, you may want to take some organized tours to see all of it. **American Express Travel Service** conducts excellent tours, in English, of Rome and its surroundings. They also can assist in making train or hotel reservations in Rome or in any of the other base cities. There is an office conveniently located near the Spanish Steps, Piazza Di Spagna 38, Roma 00187. *Tel:* (06) 67641; *Fax:* (06) 67 82 456; *Hours:* 0900–1730 Monday–Friday, 0900–1230 Saturday (for financial services only). We can also recommend **CIT (Compagnia Italiano Turismo) Tours,** which can be booked through most hotels and pensions.

Another alternative is the **Bus 110 City Tour.** There are two versions: the "hop-on, hop-off" tour, which allows you to get off the bus at 10 different stops along the route, or nonstop. Departures are from the bus station (outside the Termini Station) every 15 minutes 0830 to 2030 April through September and 0900 to 2000 October through March. Purchase tickets at the ATAC kiosk, Piazza dei Cinquecento, in front of Termini Station or by cash only on the bus. Fare: €20 (hop-on, hop-off), €15 (nonstop).

For a romantic view of Rome at night, you may want to try a cruise on the Tiber River. From May to October, **Tourvisa Italia** offers an evening cruise, including dinner, live music, and dancing aboard the *Tiber II* motorboat. Depart from Ponte Umberto I on Wednesday, Friday, Saturday, and Sunday at 2000. Price: €52 per person. *Tel:* 06 44 87 41; www.tourvisa.it; *E-mail:* info@tourvisa.it.

If you prefer, roam around Rome on foot, but remember to keep purses and camera bags away from the curb side of the street. Motor-scooter thieves find them easy targets. The first step is to get a map from your hotel or the tourist office, then find your way to the **Spanish Steps.** Then, walk down Via Condotti—making some delightful detours down some of the side streets—to the Tiber River. Sightseeing musts during an initial visit include the **Pantheon,** the **Coliseum,** and, close by, the **Forum.** Set aside at least a couple of hours for a visit to the **Sistine Chapel** and **St.**

Peter's. You will be "touring" through history. Columns that looked down on the mighty Caesars, walls that Saint Peter and Saint Paul passed, statues sculpted by Michelangelo—these are Rome, where present-day life flourishes in the midst of monuments from past civilizations. Throw a coin in the **Trevi Fountain** as a down payment on your return trip, because you will certainly want to return.

For that once-in-a-lifetime splurge, dine in the rooftop restaurant of the **Hassler Hotel,** Rome's finest hostelry. It overlooks the Spanish Steps and the view of the city from the rooftop on a summer's evening is unmatched. *Tel:* (06) 69 93 40 for reservations. Ignore the cost. You only live once!

Train Connections to Other Base Cities from Rome

Depart from Rome Termini Station unless otherwise noted.

DEPART	TRAIN NUMBER	ARRIVE	NOTES
		Amsterdam Centraal	
1904	CNL 484	1527+1	R, 2, 3, Sleeper
		Bern (Berne)	
0800	ES 9610	1423	R, 1
1500	ES 9638	2123+1	R, 1
		Brussels (Bruxelles) Midi/Zuid	
1904	CNL 484	1335+1	R, 2, 3, Sleeper
		Budapest Keleti	
1904	EN 234	1219+1	R, 6, Sleeper
		Copenhagen (København) H.	
1904	CNL 484	1822+1	R, 3, 9, Sleeper
		Luxembourg	
1904	EN 484	1500+1	R, 4, Sleeper
		Lyon Part-Dieu	
1920	ES 9558	0944+1	R, 1, Sleeper, Exc. Sa
		Milan (Milano) Centrale	
0720	ES 9508	1040	R
0920	ES 9518	1240	R
1120	ES 9526	1440	R
1320	ES 9532	1640	R
1520	ES 9540	1840	R
then 1720, 1820, 1920 followed by			
2020	ES 9562	2340	R, Exc. Sa
		Munich (München) Hauptbahnhof	
0920	ES 9518	1821	R, 5
1904	CNL 484	0633+1	R, Sleeper

DEPART	TRAIN NUMBER	ARRIVE	NOTES
		Nice Ville	
0800	ES 9610	1600	R, 1
1357	ES 9774	2306	R, 1, 7
		Paris Gare de Lyon	
1220	ES 9528	2332	R, 1
1920	ES 9558	0907+1	R, 8, Sleeper
		Vienna (Wien) Hauptbahnhof	
1904	EN 234	0948+1	R, Sleeper
		Zürich Hauptbahnhof	
0700	ES 9606	1428	R, 1
1120	ES 9526	1951	R, 1
1320	ES 9532	2158	R, 1
1500	ES 9638	2328	R, 1

Daily
R Reservations required
ES (Eurostar Italia) high-speed trains require supplement
+1 Arrives next day

1. Change trains in Milan (Milano).
2. Change trains in Frankfurt.
3. Change trains in Munich (München).
4. Change trains in Paris.
5. Change trains in Bologna.
6. Change trains in Vienna (Wien).
7. Change trains in Ventimiglia.
8. Arrive Paris Bercy Station.
9. Change trains in Hamburg.

Day Excursions

Four interesting day excursions from Rome await your visit: **Anzio,** scene of an Allied beachhead during World War II; **Florence,** one of the most prominent art centers of the world; **Naples,** with its world-renowned **Isle of Capri**; and **Pisa,** where the tower really tilts.

Day Excursion to

Anzio

Historic Beachhead

Depart Rome Termini Station
Distance by Train: 35 miles (57 km)
Average Train Time: 1 hour
City Dialing Code: 06
Tourist Information Office: Regione Lazio Azienda Autonoma, Soggiorno e Turismo, Piazza Pia, 16
Tel: (06) 984 99406; **Fax:** (06) 984 99473
www.anzioturismo.com
E-mail: info@anzioturismo.com
Hours: June–September: 0900–1300 and 1600–1900 daily. Off-season hours: 0900–1300 and 1530–1800 Monday–Saturday. If the office is closed, directions will be posted on how to reach another office in the area.
Notes: To get to the tourist office on Pia Square: When leaving the Anzio railway station, walk downhill along the palm-lined avenue to Cesare Battisti Square. Then continuing on Via dei Fabbri, you will be in the main square of Anzio, Pia Square, where you will find the city's tourist information office to the left, near the church.

"Nothing more beautiful, nothing more agreeable, nothing more peaceful," wrote Cicero about Anzio. The Roman emperor Nero was born in Anzio. The villa where he spent his childhood and studied music still stands. Anzio's sandy beach attracted many important leaders over the centuries, which made it a VIP sanctuary, so to speak. Roman emperors such as Tiberius, Hadrian, Antoninus, and Commodus found escape from Rome and their affairs of state in Anzio.

American and British forces stormed ashore at Anzio and nearby Nettuno on January 22, 1944, to establish a beachhead, which they held until the taking of Rome on June 4, 1944. The devastated town that endured both the crossfire of the Germans and the bombardment of the Allied fleet offshore during that time has been restored completely, but row upon row of white crosses mark the graves in nearby military cemeteries, where lie 7,862 American and more than 6,000 British troops killed between Sicily and Rome. Those missing in action, 3,194 of them, sleep in unknown graves. A visit to these cemeteries is sobering.

If you, like the Roman emperors, want to escape the rigors of Rome or, on the other hand, wish to pay tribute to fallen comrades, Anzio extends a warm and pleasant welcome to all.

Rome (Roma)—Anzio

Depart Rome Termini

Monday–Saturday: 0507, 0607, 0714, 0821, 0942, then hourly until 2042, then 2136; Sunday: 0714, 0821, 0942, 1142, 1342, 1442, 1642, 1842, 1942, and 2136.

Depart Anzio

Monday–Saturday: 1312, 1412, then hourly until 2012, then 2202; Sunday: 1514, 1712, 1812, 2012, and 2202.

2nd class only
Journey time: 60–68 minutes
Distance: 35 miles (57 km)

Because of the city's proximity to Rome and frequent train connections, rail travelers might consider accommodations in the area during their visit. Anzio, together with the neighboring sea resorts stretching southward to it from **Lido dei Pini,** can offer a wide selection of housing amenities and accommodations. If interested, contact Anzio's tourist information office. For details and rates, *Tel:* (06) 9845147; *Fax:* (06) 9848135. For a longer stay, villas and apartments are available for rent at moderate rates.

Commuter trains depart the Roma Termini frequently for Anzio. For complete information regarding train service, check the *Partenze* (departure) information board in the main hall of Roma Termini.

Anzio is listed in the **Roma–Nettuno** section. It is one stop before Nettuno and the end of the line. Nettuno is where the American beachhead was established in World War II. Tell the train conductor about your destination, and he or she will be glad to alert you to the correct stop.

Upon arrival in Anzio, you will find directions for reaching Nettuno and the American Military Cemetery posted inside the train station; before proceeding, check with the Anzio tourist office and obtain the details on the bus service running between Anzio and Nettuno.

Places to visit in Anzio are, of course, the beach area and the harbor, where the Allied forces landed. The beach is now lined with cabanas, and the sand is excellent and the surf usually moderate. Be certain to visit the beachhead museum on **Via di Villa Adele** near the rail station.

The harbor holds many interesting places to investigate. Watercraft of all types are moored there, and the waterfront is lined with seafood restaurants to which fishermen sell their catch right from the dock. Deciding where to have lunch can be difficult—they all look inviting. On the street side of the harbor you will find a number of smart shops with eye-catching selections of nautical clothing.

Aside from the beach and the port area, places of particular interest are **Nero's Grottoes,** those ancient warehouses of the port located at the northern end of the Riviera Mallozzi. Beyond Anzio's western harbor wall lie the remains and mosaics of

Nero's villa, which runs from the beach up to the level of Via Fanciulla d'Anzio. It's an impressive sight.

At the foot of the **Innocenziano wharf** in Anzio, you can examine the remains of an 18th-century fort, and from the wharf itself, there is a view of the gulf with the Astura Tower and Circeo visible in the distance. The monument commemorating the Allied landings in 1944 is situated nearby on the western shore.

Nettuno, a seaside town of Saracen origins, is less than 3 miles distant. The American Military Cemetery is located there. The two British cemeteries are in Anzio. En route to Nettuno, you'll pass the Villa Colonna on the right and the **Villa Borghese,** with its magnificent gardens, on the left.

Anzio's involvement with the sea is reflected in its festivals. One such festival, the "Festa del Mare" (Feast of the Sea), is held in June in honor of Saint Antony of Padua, patron saint of the town.

Day Excursion to

Florence (Firenze)

City of Beauty

Depart Rome Termini Station
Distance by Train: 197 miles (317 km)
Average Train Time: 2 hours
City Dialing Code: 055
Tourist Information Office: Via Cavour, 1 rosso, 50129 Firenze
Tel: (055) 290832 or (055) 290833; **Fax:** (055) 2760383
www.firenzeturismo.it
E-mail: info@firenzeturismo.it
Hours: 0830–1830 Monday–Saturday, closed Sunday
Notes: Take a taxi there or board bus No. 1, 6, or 17. Tourist information also available in Piazza Stazione (the rail-station plaza), near the church Santa Maria Novella.

Florence (Firenze) as a day excursion is suggested for the traveler on a time-compressed itinerary. It is impossible to see all the beauty of Florence in one day. A week—or even a lifetime—could easily be devoted to such a pursuit. About 60 percent of the world's most significant artworks are in Italy, and about half of them are in Florence. No other city in the world pays better homage to human genius and creativity and, in turn, beauty appreciation than does Florence.

Aside from its buildings, art galleries, museums, and parks, Florence has had an interesting and rather hectic development as a municipality and seat of government. It was ruled by the Medici family until 1737, when the family died out and its leadership was assumed by Grand Duke Ferdinand III (1769–1824). Driven out by the French in 1799, the duke made several abortive attempts to resume power. He wasn't successful, however, until 1814.

Ferdinand's successor, Leopold II (1797–1870), held on until he was expelled in 1849. Florence was the capital of Italy under King Victor Emmanuel from 1865 to 1871, when the seat of government became Rome.

Although a part of Italian history since 200 B.C., it wasn't until the turn of the 11th century that Florence began to develop power and influence. Coincident with this growth came the development of the city's powerful guilds.

Florence was established on those banks of the Arno River spanned by the bridge of the Roman road Via Flaminia and where the Ponte Vecchio (old bridge) still stands today. With the single exception of Ponte Vecchio, all of the city's bridges were destroyed in 1944 during World War II. In 1966 a major flood damaged numerous art treasures in Florence, but many have since been restored by the use of sophisticated techniques.

Hotel reservations can also be arranged at the ITA tourist office in the railway station. The one at Via Cavour cannot make hotel reservations but gives the booking centers of Florence, which are Coopal, *Tel:* (055) 219525 and Promohotels, *Tel:* (055) 570481; www.promohotels.it. Maps are available at the tourist offices and at the CIT office (the Gray Line office) outside the station, or purchase the illustrated book *Florence, Pisa and Siena* at the newsstand inside the main hall of the station. An excellent map of Florence is contained in this informative book.

A **train-reservations office** (*Hours:* 0800–2000 daily) and **money exchange** are located inside the main station hall. *Hours:* 0830–1640 Monday–Saturday.

You can see most of the city's highlights by walking and, when needed, by taxi. Start by walking or taking a taxi to **Il Duomo** (the cathedral square) in the center of Florence. Here you can examine the three huge bronze doors of the **Battistero** (baptistery), enjoy the view from the top of the cathedral's dome, and enter the **Museo dell'Opera del Duomo** (cathedral museum), where you will find the priceless Altar of Saint John the Baptist displayed.

The **Galleria dell'Accademia** (Academy Gallery) is next. *Hours:* 0815–1850 Tuesday–Sunday; open until 2200 Tuesday and Wednesday July–September. Walk 3 blocks on Via Ricasoli, off Piazza Duomo's north side, to Piazza St. Marco. Michelangelo's *David* is displayed here. Visit www.polomuseale.firenze.it/accademia.

Take a taxi from here to **Piazza della Signoria,** which lies on the opposite side of the cathedral near the Arno River. (A brisk walk and some expert map reading will get you there in about 20 minutes.) This is the former center of Florence. The concentration of art treasures here is immense. The building with the tower is **Palazzo della Signoria** (Palace of the Lords), also known as **Palazzo Vecchio** (the Old Palace). Among its wealth of treasures is the little chapel of Eleonora of Toledo, with its magnificent frescoes by Bronzino (1503–1572). *Hours:* 0900–1900 daily; closes at 1400 Thursday. Admission: €6.00.

Rome (Roma)—Florence (Firenze)

DEPART Rome Termini	TRAIN NUMBER	ARRIVE Florence SMN	NOTES
0720	ES 9508	0851	R
0820	ES 9514	0951	R
0920	ES 9518	1051	R
1020	ES 9520	1151	R
1120	ES 9526	1251	R
1220	ES 9528	1351	R
plus other frequent service until 2050.			

DEPART Florence SMN	TRAIN NUMBER	ARRIVE Rome Termini	NOTES
1408	ES 9529	1540	R
1508	ES 9533	1640	R
1608	ES 9537	1740	R
1638	ES 9435	1810	R
1808	ES 9545	1940	R
1908	ES 9549	2040	R
plus other frequent service until 2208.			

Daily
R Reservations required
Distance: 197 miles (317 km)

On the south side of the square, you will see the **Loggia dei Lanzi,** which picked up a few other names, such as "Loggia dei Priori" and "Loggia della Signoria," since it was built in 1376. Statuary such as *Hercules and the Centaur* (1599) and *Rape of the Sabine Women* (1583), both by Giambologna, surround Cellini's *Perseus* (1545).

The **Galleria degli Uffizi** (Office Gallery) is, in fact, a converted office containing the priceless works of art acquired by the Medici family. Located on the right flank of Palazzo della Signoria, it has 45 exhibit rooms. Its vast collection includes the ancient sculpture *Medici Venus* from 300 B.C., Botticelli's *Primavera* and *Birth of Venus*, Leonardo da Vinci's *Adoration of the Magi*, and Michelangelo's *Holy Family*, plus an entire roomful of Rembrandts. *Hours:* 0815–1850 Tuesday–Sunday, admission €9.50. Visit www.uffizi.com.

This concludes your "quick" tour of the world-famous "City of Art, Florence," and it's time to taxi back to the rail station for the train back to Rome—unless, of course, you have succumbed to Florence's charms. It's a difficult decision to make. If you are still ambulatory, the walk back to the station will take about 20 minutes.

Day Excursion to

Naples (Napoli)

City by the Bay

Depart Rome Termini Station
Distance by Train: 134 miles (216 km)
Average Train Time: 1 hour, 35 minutes
City Dialing Code: 081
Tourist Information Office: Main Hall of Napoli Centrale Rail Station, in front of Platform 20 (English-speaking staff)
Tel: (081) 268779 or 206666; **Fax:** (081) 401961
www.comune.napoli.it
Hours: 0900–1800 daily

Naples (Napoli) is a world apart. There is no other place in Italy quite like it. In fact, there's no place that we have visited in the rest of the world quite like Naples. When you go there, you don't really see Naples—you feel it, hear it, and taste it. After you've been to Naples, you come away either loving it or hating it. You alone must be the judge.

Naples itself is a coalescing of gaiety and sadness. Its inhabitants, the Neapolitans, are expressive, noisy, and vivacious. They are imaginative, superstitious, and (about a third of them) unemployed, either by choice or by circumstance—it's difficult to determine which. But as a consequence, crime is rampant, so watch your wallets, pocketbooks, cameras, and other valuables.

But don't go to Naples in fear for your life; just be cautious. The Neapolitans don't want to harm you; they are only interested in your valuables. They want you to enjoy yourself and come back again—with more valuables. Deal only with official agencies. If you plan to take a city tour or sign up for a trip to **Vesuvius** and **Pompeii,** do it in an office, not on the street. Ignore the uniformed people who approach you on the street or in the rail station wearing badges proclaiming they are "official guides." There are several small shops on the square facing the station where you can buy one of those badges yourself.

Now for the fun part. Spaghetti was invented in Naples, as well as Neapolitan-style ice cream. Pizza first saw the light of day in Naples. If you can, enjoy a pizza in one of the pizzerias located in the old quarter of Naples. If you do, you'll probably not patronize your local pizza parlor for at least 30 days following your return home. The Neapolitan version of a Cajun fish-fry, *frittura di pesci*, is also well worth sampling. So much for tasting Naples.

You can't avoid hearing Naples. The musical style of Bel Canto is exclusively that of the Neapolitans. *Santa Lucia*, *Funiculi-Funicula*, and *O Sole Mio*! are but part of the repertory you will hear being played by hurdy-gurdies, all of it mixed in with the constant background noise of the crowded streets. Dray animals such as mules wear bells so that their presence can be acknowledged in the crowd.

Rome (Roma)—Naples (Napoli)

DEPART	TRAIN NUMBER	ARRIVE	NOTES
Rome Termini		Naples Centrale	
0626	IC 701	0829	R
0725	IC 1911	0938	R
0848	ES 9501	0955	R, Exc. Su
0926	IC 551	1129	R, Exc. Su
1053	ES 9509	1200	R

DEPART	TRAIN NUMBER	ARRIVE	NOTES
Naples Centrale		Rome Termini	
1700	ES 9552	1810	
1800	ES 9558	1907	R
2031	IC 560	2241	R
2142	ICN 796	2359	R, Exc. Su

Daily, unless otherwise noted
R Reservations required
Distance: 134 miles (216 km)

You will find the **Napoli Centrale** station in the city center and flanked by the two narrow-gauge railway stations serving the **Circumvesuviana Line** from Naples to **Pompeii** and **Sorrento.**

Money exchange, train information, and food services are all housed within the Napoli Centrale terminal. To the side of the main hall is a train information and reservations office. *Hours:* 0850–2000 daily.

Naples, a city with a population of more than one million, is just large enough so that unguided sightseeing can become difficult. Several reputable tour operators provide excellent service, such as the **Tourcar Travel Agency,** *Tel:* (081) 552 0429. The American Express Office located at Piazza Municipio 5/6 also provides tours under its travel agency. *Tel:* (081) 5518564; *Fax:* (081) 722242. Local trains leave the Napoli Circumvesuviana railway station for Pompeii and Sorrento. To reach this station, walk in the direction of the *Garibaldi* statue in the center of Piazza Garibaldi. Just before reaching the statue, turn left onto Corso Garibaldi and proceed to the station, which is close by. The train time from Naples to Pompeii averages about 25 minutes. To Sorrento, the average time is 60 minutes. Pompeii is 15 miles from Naples; Sorrento is 28. Check at the rail station for complete schedules. Eurail passes are not accepted on this line.

Day Excursion to

Pisa

New Slant on an Old Scene

Depart Rome Termini Station
Distance by Train: 208 miles (335 km)
Average Train Time: 2 hours, 39 minutes
City Dialing Code: 050
Tourist Information Office: In the station plaza, 16 Piazza Vittorio Emanuele II
Tel: (050) 42291
Hours: Monday–Saturday 0900–1900, Sunday 1030–1530
Tourist Information Office: Piazza del Duomo
Tel: (050) 560464
Hours: Monday–Saturday 0900–1800, Sunday 1030–1630
www.turismo.pisa.it
E-mail: info@turismo.pisa.it
Regional Information: Touristic Consortium of the Pisan Area, P.O. Box 215, 56125 Pisa
Booking Center: *Tel:* (050) 830253; *Fax:* (050) 830243
www.traveleurope.it or **www.turismo.toscana.it**
E-mail: pisa.turismo@traveleurope.it or info@pisaturismo.it
Notes: Take bus No. 1 from rail station plaza to Piazza del Duomo. The tourist information office is on the other side of the Leaning Tower.

Many consider Pisa to be the most beautiful city in Italy. Its location in the very heart of Tuscany may even entice you to make Pisa a base city for day excursions to its charming nearby villages. In only about an hour or so, you can venture by train or bus to other main art cities such as Lucca, Florence, Siena, Volterra, San Gimignano, and Arezzo.

Pisa is rich in artistic resources and possesses one of the loveliest architectural groupings in Europe. Known either as **Piazza dei Miracoli** (Square of the Miracles) or **Piazza del Duomo** (Cathedral Square), it contains, in addition to the famous **Leaning Tower** and the cathedral, the **Baptistery** and the Campo Santo (burial ground), each in its own stead a masterpiece of sculpture and architecture.

If you have never been to Pisa and actually stood and looked at the Leaning Tower, you are in for a surprise. Forget any photograph, painting, or motion picture you may have seen of the tower prior to your personal encounter. It is not an optical illusion—it really leans.

Ride bus No. 1 from Pisa's station plaza to Piazza dei Miracoli. Dismount from the bus on the southern end of the square—the direction in which the tower is leaning. You will have no doubt whatsoever that (1) the tower leans; (2) it's leaning in your direction; and (3) you had better get out of its way before it topples on you. No other work of art provokes the instinct of self-preservation like this one. You can spend hours gazing at it, but there is never a moment when you are not consciously aware of the trajectory it will take if it topples.

Rome (Roma)—Pisa

DEPART	TRAIN NUMBER	ARRIVE	NOTES
Rome Termini		Pisa Centrale	
0615	ES 9758	0826	R, M–F
0657	ES 9764	0946	R
0720	ES 9508	1028	R, 1
0835	ES 9408	1128	R
0957	IC 510	1300	R

DEPART	TRAIN NUMBER	ARRIVE	NOTES
Pisa Centrale		Rome Termini	
1455	IC 511	1803	R
1545	ES 2343	1948	R
1710	ES 9777	2003	
1911	ES 9781	2203	R
1932	R 3148	2240	R, 1
2051	ES 9788	2259	R

Daily
R Reservation required
1. Change trains in Florence (Firenze).
Distance: 208 miles (335 km)

Bonanno Pisano began construction of the tower in 1173, but the project was not completed until 1350. The primary reason for the delay in its completion was that the tower began to tilt when it reached its fourth level. With an annual increase of about 1.2 millimeters per year, the tower was closed to public access in 1990. Through sonar soundings of the ground, the foundation of an ancient village was discovered under the north side of the Leaning Tower. This explains why the north side has remained relatively stable, while the south side has sunk almost three-quarters of a meter. Various plans have been proposed to stabilize the tower. One plan is to use sonic waves to break up the ancient foundation under the north side so that it will sink at the same rate as the south. Another proposal requires a ring of steel to be inserted into the base of the landmark. Perhaps the Italian Public Works Ministry should expedite its plans. Studies reveal that the tower is nearly 17 feet off plumb.

For the best restaurants in Pisa, in the countryside, or by the sea, call the Touristic Consortium at (050) 830253 or inquire at the tourist offices.

When at last you can turn your attention away from the tower, you will realize that Piazza dei Miracoli holds some other fantastic sights that warrant your inspection. Among them is the cathedral, on which construction was initiated in 1063. The first work of art to catch your eye is the splendid bronze doors of its entrance. Inside the cathedral and opposite the pulpit, Lorenzi (according to legend) hung a bronze lamp on a chain so long that Galileo figured that it must be the first pendulum and proceeded to work out the theory of isochronism—one of the better "isms" existing today.

The astronomer and physicist Galileo (1564–1642) lived in Pisa and used the buildings of the **Piazza del Duomo** to conduct studies concerning the laws of gravity, the acceleration of falling bodies, and the movement of the pendulum. He used the Leaning Tower to work out his theories on gravity and acceleration and the cathedral for the accurate measurement of time.

Last of the edifices within the confines of the Piazza dei Miracoli is the building known as the **Camposanto** (Monumental Cemetery). It began when 53 shiploads of earth were transported from Calvary in the Holy Lands to the site and then surrounded by the building, which, after completion in 1283 by Giovanni Pisano, was frescoed by local Tuscan artists. The structure suffered damage during World War II bombings, but repairs have all but removed those scars.

During its days of prominence, Pisa was in close touch with the Orient. As a result, you'll note an Eastern flavor in its architecture. In the ninth century, the city was a naval power of considerable proportion. Pisa and its ally, Genoa, drove the Saracens out of Sardinia and Corsica in the 11th century. Pisa's powers, however, then went on the wane. No longer allied with Genoa, the city was taken by Florence in 1406, proving that, as is so often the case, your allies are not there when you really need them.

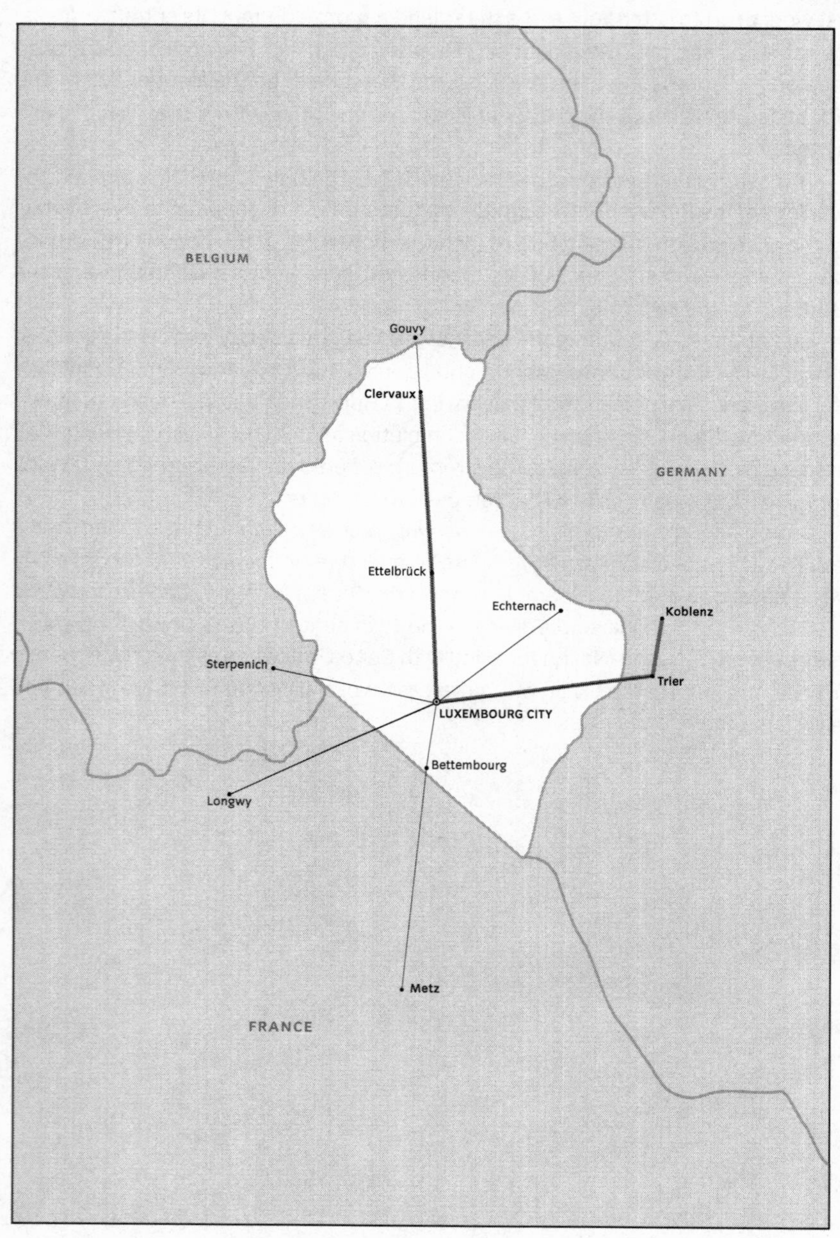
BELGIUM
Gouvy
Clervaux
GERMANY
Ettelbrück
Echternach
Koblenz
Sterpenich
Trier
LUXEMBOURG CITY
Bettembourg
Longwy
Metz
FRANCE

LUXEMBOURG

The Grand Duchy of Luxembourg is one of Europe's small countries—51 miles (82 kilometers) long and 32 miles (57 kilometers) wide, encompassing 999 square miles (2,586 square kilometers)—a little smaller than the state of Rhode Island. It is a constitutional monarchy with a population of about 400,000. Germany borders it to the east, France to the south, and Belgium adjoins it on the north and west. Luxembourg vies with Switzerland in the field of international banking. A substantial number of corporations doing business in the European community maintain accounts there.

The Grand Duchy once dominated an area nearly 300 times its current size. In more recent times, as well as in the past, Luxembourg's fate and fortunes have been linked with those of Belgium. The forces of French king Louis XIV conquered the city of Luxembourg in the middle of the 17th century. Subsequent fortifications built by the French and succeeding conquerors earned the city the title "Gibraltar of the North."

Luxembourg was overrun by the Germans during World War I, but its independence was restored by the Treaty of Versailles. It was occupied again by German forces during World War II. During the Battle of the Bulge in December 1944, the tides of war surged around Luxembourg. Liberated earlier by U.S. forces, the city was recaptured by the Germans, who executed many members of the Belgian and Luxembourgese underground before Luxembourg was again taken by the Allied forces.

For more information on Luxembourg, contact the Luxembourg National Tourist Office in North America:

New York: 17 Beekman Place, New York, NY 10022; *Tel:* (212) 935-8888; *Fax:* (212) 935-5896; **www.visitluxembourg.com;** *E-mail:* info@visitluxembourg.com or luxnto@aol.com

Banking

Currency: Euro (€)

Exchange rate at press time: €0.90 = U.S. $1.00

Communications

Country Code: 352

City codes are not used when dialing within Luxembourg.

Major Mobile Phone Companies: LuxGSM, Tango, Orange

Rail Travel in Luxembourg

The information service of **CFL, the Luxembourg national railways** (also gives country bus information), can be contacted by *Tel:* 24 89 24 89 (every day, 0700–1900 GMT) and by *Fax:* 49 90 44 70; www.cfl.lu (in French). The CFL accepts the multicountry Eurail passes. (See the Appendix for a detailed list of multiple-country and regional rail passes and prices.) If your travels are confined only to the Benelux countries, consider the **Benelux Pass** for unlimited rail travel throughout Belgium, the Netherlands, and Luxembourg.

Benelux Pass

	1st Class	2nd Class
5 days within 1 month	$446	$358
Youth: 5 days within 1 month	—	$234

Benelux Saverpass*

	1st Class	2nd Class
5 days within 1 month	$380	$304

*Prices are per person based on two people traveling together.

Base City: **LUXEMBOURG CITY**

www.lcto.lu
E-mail: touristinfo@lcto.lu

Arriving by Air

Luxembourg International Airport (*Tel:* 352 24640; www.luxairport.lu) is about 4 miles (6 kilometers) from the city center. Luxembourg, because of its central European location and convenient rail connections, attracts an increasing number of visitors from North America.

- **Airport–City Links:** Bus service from the airport terminates at the Luxembourg rail station. Municipal buses (Route 16) depart every 10 minutes Monday through Friday, every 20 minutes on Saturday, and every half-hour on Sunday from a platform about 50 feet outside the air terminal. Journey time, 25 minutes; you can check stops, timetables, fares, and extra transport like the City Night Bus or the City Shopping Bus at the website: www.autobus.lu. At present there is no underground or train service link, but there are very interesting plans proposed to link the airport to the railway station via a direct connection.
- **Taxis:** about €30 (supplements for nights, Sunday, and extra luggage). Journey time to city center: 15 to 20 minutes. All taxis are equipped with meters. No tips are expected. You must use designated pick-up points.
- **Tourist information at the airport:** *Tel:* 2464 0. *Hours:* 0400–2400 daily (except on holidays).

Arriving by Train

The city of Luxembourg is served by a single railway station located conveniently in the city center. Connections can be made directly to Belgium, France, Germany, Italy, the Netherlands, and Switzerland from the station. The downtown air terminal and the city bus terminal are clustered conveniently about the railway station, which, like the airport, has been modernized to handle an increasing number of passengers.

Luxembourg Central Station is actually located in what historians call the "new city." From 1855 to 1866, when the first rails were laid, the gorge of the Alzette River remained too wide to be bridged. Consequently, the rail station was established on the far side of the gorge opposite the city as it existed then, and the new section of the city began to develop around it.

The station has three platforms (*quais*) serving five tracks. Track 1 is served by Platform 1, which is directly connected to the station with level access to the platform. Trains arriving on the other tracks, however, require passengers to use an underground tunnel to reach the main station hall.

A system of elevators serves the outer train platforms. To access them, take the hallway off to the right of the main hall until you arrive at the entrance to the elevator service tunnel, just beyond the last ticket window and before reaching the baggage room.

The entrances to the elevators serving the train platforms are marked clearly, although it seems a bit confusing when you first use them. You descend from the train platform to a tunnel. There, you walk a short distance to another elevator, which you ascend to the station level; you then take another short tunnel into the main hallway.

- **Train information** is to your immediate left when exiting from the train platform area. *Hours:* 0600–2145 daily. *Tel:* 24 89 24 89.
- **Train seat reservations** for EuroCity, InterCity, and regular express trains can be made in the train information office. Sleeper reservations and rail pass validation may also be made here.

Tourist Information/Hotel Reservations

- *Office National du Tourisme,* Luxembourg Central Station, Place de la Gare. *Tel:* 42 82 82 20; *Fax:* 42 82 82 38. *Hours:* June 1–September 30: 0900–1900 Monday–Saturday, 0900–1230 and 1345–1800 Sunday; remainder of the year: 0900–1230 and 1345–1800 Monday–Saturday. Closed November 1, Christmas, and New Year's Day.

  The office is in the Central Station, on your right as you exit from the train platform area. In addition to making hotel reservations, information on youth hostels, camping grounds, and holiday flats and chalets available to tourists can be provided.

- *Luxembourg City Tourist Office (LCTO),* Place Guillaume II, P.O. Box 181, L-2011; *Tel:* 22 28 09; *Fax:* 46 70 70; www.lcto.lu/; *E-mail:* touristinfo@lcto.lu. *Hours:* April 1–September 30: 0900–1900 Monday–Saturday, 1000–1800 Sunday. October 1–March 31: 0900–1800 Monday–Saturday, 1000–1800 Sunday.

  The LCTO provides extensive services, such as guided city tours, tourist and cultural information, hotel and restaurant details, and offers telephone cards, maps, books, and souvenirs. Students attired in "Ask Me" T-shirts also walk about the streets of the city center to provide tourist information.

- **Hotel reservations** can also be made by the tourist information offices. There are numerous hotels on the side streets near the station in addition to some charming smaller hotels within reasonable taxi or city bus distances. The four-star **Best Western Hotel International** (*Tel:* 00 352 48 59 11; www.hotelinter.lu; *E-mail:* info@hotelinter.lu) and the **MAHC rive droit** (*Tel:* 352 2704 8371 www.maho.lu; *Email:* info@maho.lu) are across the street from the rail station. For those who prefer an American-style hotel with all the amenities, the **Sheraton Aerogolf** is located near the airport.

  Our choice is a small, quaint hotel with European-style charm and service—**Hôtel Italia** (20 rooms). Located at 15–17 rue d'Anvers, Hôtel Italia is near the rail station and features an excellent Italian restaurant. *Tel:* 48 66 26 1 or *Fax:* 48 08 07; *E-mail:* italia@euro.lu. Rates: €80–€115, single. Major credit cards are accepted.

Getting Around in Luxembourg City

The city center is condensed, and most sights are accessible on foot, despite the cliffs and ramparts that characterize this fortress city. For longer distances use Luxembourg's efficient network of buses (single fare, €2.00). Taxis are metered.

The most practical way of getting around Luxembourg on your own is to purchase a **LuxembourgCard.** You get free admission to more than 55 tourist attractions, free use of public transportation, and a 32-page guidebook to go along with it. The Luxembourg Card is valid from Easter through October.

Luxembourg Card Prices in Euros*

	Adult	Family (2–5 persons)
1 day	€11	€28
2 days**	€19	€48
3 days**	€27	€68

*10 percent reduction for persons older than age 60

** Within a period of two weeks

Train Connections to Other Base Cities from Luxembourg

DEPART	TRAIN NUMBER	ARRIVE	NOTES
		Amsterdam Centraal	
0610	IC 2129	1142	1
0810	IC 2131	1342	1
1009	IC 2133	1542	1
then hourly until 1709, then 1746.			
		Berlin Hauptbahnhof	
0831	RE 5111	1715	5
1931	RE 5133	0653+1	R, 5, Sleeper
		Bern (Berne)	
0612	RE 5107	1456	5
		Brussels (Bruxelles) Midi/Zuid	
Service is hourly from 0510 to 2007. Journey time is 2 hours, 50 minutes to 3 hours, 3 minutes.			
		Hamburg Hauptbahnhof	
0813	RE 5111	1613	5
1431	RE 5123	2213	5
		Lyon Part-Dieu	
0640	TGV 2855	1156	R, 6, Exc. Su
1309	TGV 2869	1856	R, 6
1709	TGV 2881	2256	R, 6
		Munich (München) Hauptbahnhof	
0612	RE 5107	1338	5
2031	RE 5135	0710+1	R, 5, Sleeper
		Nice Ville	
0640	TGV 2855	1556	R, 6, Exc. Su
1938	NZ 4749	0937+1	R, Sleeper
		Paris Gare de l'Est	
0640	TGV 2855	0850	R
1109	TGV 2865	1320	R
1310	TGV 2869	1521	R
1709	TGV 2881	1920	R
		Prague (Praha)	
1931	RE 5133	1128+1	R, 3, Sleeper
		Vienna (Wien) Hauptbahnhof	
0731	RE 5109	1909	R, 5
1102	IC 91	2312	R, 2
1615	IC 97	0734+1	R, 2, Sleeper

DEPART	TRAIN NUMBER	ARRIVE	NOTES
		Warsaw Centralna	
1831	RE 5131	1215+1	R, 3, Sleeper
		Zürich Hauptbahnhof	
1044	TGV 9879	1600	R, 4
2031	RE 5135	0805+1	R, 5

Daily, unless otherwise noted
R Reservations required
+1 Arrive next day
1. Change trains in Brussels.
2. Change trains in Zurich.
3. Change trains in Cologne (Köln).
4. Change trains in Basel.
5. Change trains in Koblenz.
6. Change trains in Paris.

Sights/Attractions/Tours

A basic city sightseeing tour by bus departs from platform No. 5 at the downtown bus terminal next to the rail station. The tour takes 2 hours and 15 minutes and departs every 20 minutes between 0940 and 1720 from the end of March to mid-November (on Saturday and Sunday only the remainder of the year). It includes the Old Town, the rail station district, the fortress ruins, the casemates (underground outside fortifications), European Center, and Luxembourg's version of Wall Street—the banking district. The tour fee for adults is €14; children ages 5 to 15, €7.

The **Bock and Pétrusse Casemates** are two unique networks of underground fortifications, one of the most interesting being the archaeological crypt in the Bock Casemates. This room presents an audiovisual show relating the history of the casemates. *Hours:* March 1–October 31: 1000–1800. Admission: €9 adults, €5 children. The Pétrusse Casemates are open Easter, Whitsunday, and during school holidays. Guided tours are 1100 to 1600 daily.

The **City Promenade** is a guided tour departing from the tourist office at Place Guillaume II at 1200 and 1400 daily (April through October), at 1300 Monday, Wednesday, Saturday, and Sunday (November through April) on foot. It encompasses the City Palace, the outside casemates, Place de la Constitution, the Government District, the Holy Ghost Plateau, the Corniche, the Monument of the Millennium, the Old Town, William Square, and the exterior of the Grand Ducal Palace. Cost: €9.00 adults, €7.00 students, €4.50 children.

Other interesting tours include the **Wenzel Circular Walk** and the **City Safari Discovery Tour** especially for kids and families. The Wenzel Circular Walk, or "1,000 years in 100 minutes," is rated as an "outstanding" cultural promenade. The tour includes the Bock promontory, Old Town Wenceslas ring wall, and the valley of the Alzette with its unique fortifications. The tour departs every Saturday at 1500 and Wednesday from Easter Saturday through October. Cost: €10.00 adults, €5.00 children. The City Safari tour operates daily except Monday at 1430. Cost: €6.00 per participant.

There are other tours by bus that take you through the Ardennes, or opt to see much of the area on your own during day excursions to Clervaux, Metz, and Trier.

"The soldier, above all other people," said Douglas MacArthur, "prays for peace, for he must suffer and bear the deepest wounds and scars of war." Such is the drama of 5,100 grave sites in the **American Military Cemetery** near the village of Hamm, 3 miles outside the city of Luxembourg. Among the crosses standing row upon row, you will see one marked George S. Patton, Jr., General, Third Army, California, December 21, 1945. Solemn in its simplicity, beautiful in the manner in which it attests to the American spirit, this cemetery must be seen. It is a moving, memorable moment. You can taxi there for about the same price as the airport-to-rail-station fare. Telephone for a return taxi.

Luxembourg's low value-added tax (VAT) makes it a bargain base city in comparison to some other European cities. Even residents of Luxembourg's neighboring countries purchase tobacco, alcohol, and fuel in the Grand Duchy because the taxes are lower.

Although hotel rates and restaurant prices are lower than those of most other European cities, the quality is not. Some Luxembourgers actually believe "the way to a man's heart is through his stomach," and they've made believers out of us. Try the smoked pork with broad beans or the delicate Ardennes ham cut paper-thin. For a real taste treat, try trout from the Moselle accompanied by a fine Luxembourg wine—all at popular prices.

Luxembourg abounds in international cuisine. One of our favorites is the **L'Hotel-Restaurant Italia** at 15–17 rue d'Anvers (*Tel:* 48 66 26 1; *Fax:* 48 08 07; *E-mail:* italia@euro.lu), which offers excellent Italian specialties. Phone ahead for reservations—it's popular with the local folks, too.

Day Excursions

Four day excursions have been selected for the Grand Duchy and its surrounding countries. Each is distinctly different in its points of interest. The day excursion to **Clervaux** takes you through the rugged north country of the Grand Duchy, where the World War II Ardennes campaign was contested bitterly in 1944. The day excursion to charming **Koblenz,** one of the oldest cities in Germany, is saturated with scenic views along the Moselle and Rhine Rivers. **Metz** measures up to a most interesting day excursion into France. The German city of **Trier,** founded by Augustus Caesar, provides an exciting opportunity to explore many Roman ruins and to titillate your taste buds with the most delectable Moselle wines.

Day Excursion to

Clervaux

Grand Duchy's Medieval Charm

Depart from Luxembourg City Central Station
Distance by Train: 38 miles (61 km)
Average Train Time: 54 minutes
Tourist Information Office: Clervaux Castle, B.P. 53, L-9701 Grand Duchy of Luxembourg
Tel: 92 00 72; **Fax:** 92 93 12
www.destination-clervaux.lu
Email: info@destination-clervaux.lu
Hours: March–October, 1000–1800 daily; November–April 1000–1200 and 1400–1600 daily
Notes: Start at the station by walking along the main street in the direction from which the train came. When you reach the town square, turn right and follow the paths and steps leading up to Clervaux Castle. The Clervaux tourist information office is located at the entrance to the castle in a towerlike structure on the right-hand side.

Clervaux is a medieval town nestled in the valley of the Clerf River, deep in the Ardennes of northern Luxembourg, through which runs the scenic rail route from Luxembourg through Liege in Belgium to Amsterdam in the Netherlands.

The scenic beauty of the train ride begins the moment you leave the Luxembourg station and the train crosses a viaduct high above the Alzette River. Take a seat on the left side of the carriage to best enjoy a spectacular view of the city of Luxembourg from the viaduct. Have your camera ready, and start shooting a moment after the train clears a short tunnel just beyond the rail station. The morning departure is best for photographing the ramparts of Luxembourg because the sun will be shining directly upon them at a rather low level at that time. You will pass the same scene on later departures; however, the sun will be at a higher angle, and the shadows will be less dramatic.

Clervaux is the fourth express-train stop en route after stops at **Mersch, Ettelbruck,** and **Kautenbach.** Beyond Ettelbruck, you enter the hilly and heavily wooded Ardennes, where the Battle of the Bulge was fought during World War II in December 1944. Some of the buildings along the right-of-way still bear the scars of this engagement. Don't be alarmed if you should spot a German or an American tank at a road intersection en route. The locals have intentionally placed it there.

The Clervaux railway station is a 15-minute walk from the town's main square. It's a delightful stroll along the river and easy to do with the aid of several maps posted along the way with "you are here" arrows to assist you.

Luxembourg City—Clervaux

Luxembourg–Clervaux

Departures hourly at 18 minutes past the hour, plus 1145, and others throughout the day.

Clervaux–Luxembourg

Departures at 45 minutes past the hour until 2245, plus 1615 and 2215.

Distance: 38 miles (61 km); journey time: 51–55 minutes

Clervaux is packed with points of interest. Three of the most prominent ones are the **DeLannoi Castle,** the **Benedictine Abbey of St. Maurice and St. Maur,** and the **parish church.** All three tower over the town and its surrounding countryside.

The DeLannoi family are some of Franklin Delano Roosevelt's maternal ancestors. The DeLannoi Castle has so much to offer that we recommend you concentrate on it first and see the rest of Clervaux's sites in the time remaining at the end of your visit. It houses the Battle of the Bulge museum, an exhibition of ancient Luxembourg castle models, and the world-famous **"Family of Man"** photo exhibition of Edward Steichen, an American citizen born in Luxembourg.

No one is quite certain about the castle's origins. There are several hypotheses: Some historians believe that it was built on top of an ancient Roman citadel; others speak of Celtic origins. In any event, it has been established that the oldest part of the castle dates from the 12th century.

There's an immediate impact upon entering the castle's outer courtyard. One of General Patton's tanks is parked there, along with its chief antagonist, a German Army 88-millimeter cannon. History buffs of all ages will enjoy climbing aboard the tank to inspect its armor and speculate as to the role it played during the liberation of Clervaux and the Battle of the Bulge. Bear in mind that by December 1944, the castle you see now was reduced to a burned-out hulk. The authentic restoration that has been accomplished by the townspeople of Clervaux and the Duchy of Luxembourg is laudatory.

The "Family of Man" exhibit and the castle model exhibit are just inside the first gate leading off the courtyard (*Hours:* 1000–1800 daily except Monday; closed January–February). The "Bulge" museum is located farther along toward the center of the castle off an inner courtyard.

Steichen considered the Clervaux castle an ideal location for his exhibition. The collection was given to the Grand Duchy of Luxembourg by the U.S. government in 1975, three years after Steichen's death.

Day Excursion to

Koblenz

Heart of the Rhineland

Depart from Luxembourg City Central Station
Distance by Train: 101 miles (163 km)
Average Train Time: 1 hour, 14 minutes
Germany Dialing Code: 49
City Dialing Code: 261
Tourist Information Office: Koblenz-Touristik, Bahnhofplatz 17, Postfach 201551, D-56068 Koblenz
Tel: (0261) 31304; **Fax:** (0261) 1004388
www.koblenz.de
E-mail: info-hbf@koblenz-touristik.de
Hours: Monday–Friday 0900–1730, Saturday 0900–1400, Sunday 1000–1600
Notes: To reach the tourist office, turn right as you exit the rail station, and you will find the tourist office on the ground floor of the rail station.

The Koblenz railway station is just far enough away from the meeting of the Moselle and Rhine Rivers and the city's major tourist attractions to cause a "walk or ride" decision. If you decide to ride into the city center, the tourist office can help you hail a cab or provide you with the city's bus schedule and fare information. If you are planning to stay in Koblenz, tourist-office staff can make hotel reservations at no charge. Be sure to pick up a map and the brochure *Koblenz . . . Tour of The Town's Heritage* before setting out.

Just as there is a subtle difference between Rhine and Moselle wines, so is there a difference between the scenic beauty of the two great rivers from which the wines take their names. At the rivers' confluence you will be able to enjoy both. Koblenz claims that it offers more than 2,000 years of history to its visitors—and all within the span of a few hours. The historical background of this city, in the very center of Germany's Rhineland, makes this no idle boast as its claim to Germany's most beautiful corner.

The area around Koblenz was settled originally by the Celts. Julius Caesar, dividing and conquering as he went, arrived with his legions and established domain along the Rhine's western banks. Roman tranquility thrived until the fifth century, when Rome's power weakened and the Franks took over.

Napoleon's memorable campaign against the Russians was inscribed on **St. Castor's fountain** in the city during 1812. In 1814 the tables were turned when the Russians captured the town and added a postscript, seen and approved, beneath the original inscription. At the **Deutsches Eck,** a monument erected at the confluence of the Rhine and the Moselle in 1897, the statue of the German emperor Wilhelm I was toppled into the Rhine by the U.S. Army Corps of Engineers in 1945.

The base of the monument was made as a memorial to German unity in 1953 by President Theodor Heuss. Since September 1993, Wilhelm I is back—in mini-model form on top of the monument.

You may want to spend several hours in Germany's oldest town and board a later train to Luxembourg City.

Luxembourg City—Koblenz

DEPART Luxembourg City	TRAIN NUMBER	ARRIVE Koblenz	NOTES
0612	RE 5107	0835	1
0831	RE 5111	1055	
0931	RE 5113	1155	1
1031	RE 5115	1255	1

DEPART Koblenz	TRAIN NUMBER	ARRIVE Luxembourg City	NOTES
1606	RE 5120	1840	1
1706	RE 5122	1929	M–F
1806	RE 5124	2029	
1906	RE 5126	2129	
2206	RE 5132	0031+1	1

Daily, unless otherwise noted
1. Change trains in Trier.
Distance: 101 miles (163 km)

If you choose to see Koblenz under your own foot power, guided by the city map, a 10-minute walk down the **Markenbildchenweg** brings you to the Rhine, and a left turn at that point sends you in the direction of the Deutsches Eck, where the Rhine meets the Moselle. The riverside gardens along the Rhine join up with those on the Moselle to provide a delightful 5-mile promenade along their banks.

If you plan to whiz around the city on wheels, bus No. 1, marked Rhine (Deutsches Eck), will deposit you on the promenade at a point opposite the **Rheinkran,** an antique building that once housed the harbor crane. The bus route takes you through the narrow streets of the old city along the Moselle and past the Deutsches Eck before reaching its final stop on the Rhine. Returning to the train station, the bus follows a more direct (and less interesting) route through the town's shopping areas. If your "walk or ride" decision is still up for grabs, we suggest you compromise by taking the bus outbound and returning on foot. From the river to the station, the bus is bannered HAUPTBAHNHOF. The bus ride takes about 15 minutes. Allow a little more time if you're walking.

Make the **Koblenz Weindorf** (Wine Village) a must-stop during your visit. It consists of four taverns clustered around a village square that, in turn, is enclosed within a real vineyard along the Rhine. The taverns are actual copies of half-timbered houses found in the notable German wine areas. Six hundred or more guests can be accommodated in the taverns and more than 1,000 outside when the weather is good—as it usually is.

The wine village was built on the occasion of the 1925 German Wine Exhibition. Since then, it has achieved fame for its products and romantic atmosphere. The village offers an excellent menu and wine list daily from 1100 to 2400. From November through March, an advance booking is required. Visit www.weindorf-koblenz.de.

Day Excursion to

Metz

Moselle Stronghold

Depart from Luxembourg City Central Station
Distance by Train: 39 miles (63 km)
Average Train Time: 53 minutes
France Dialing Code: 33
Northeast France Area Code: 3
Tourist Information Office: Office de Tourisme, 2 Place d'Armes, BP 80367, 57007 Metz, France
Tel: 387 55 53 76; **Fax:** 387 36 59 43
http://tourisme.mairie-metz.fr
E-mail: tourisme@ot.mairie-metz.fr
Hours: Monday–Saturday: 0900–1900, Sunday: 1000–1700 in summer, open until 1500 in winter
Notes: To get to the tourist office from the arrival gate, turn right and walk the length of the station hall to the departure gate (served by the northern underground passageway). The station's north end houses the train information office and faces General de Gaulle Square. Money can be changed in the post office, the huge red building in front of the station. Board either minibus line A or B at the bus terminal in front of the rail station. Get off at the Hotel de Ville (town hall) stop in front of the cathedral. The tourist office is on the right in Place d'Armes.

Throughout its 3,000-year history, Metz has been a great Roman city, a religious center of the Carolingian Empire, an independent republic, a part of Germany, and a bastion of France. Throughout the ages, various cultures have left their marks in the form of various architectural styles throughout the city.

Luxembourg City—Metz

DEPART Luxembourg City	TRAIN NUMBER	ARRIVE Metz	NOTES
0640	TGV 2855	0721	Exc. Su
0808	RE 88717	0857	M–F
1109	TGV 2865	1152	
1309	TGV 2869	1351	

DEPART Metz	TRAIN NUMBER	ARRIVE Luxembourg City	
1333	RE 86758	1423	
1508	TGV 2816	1553	
1708	TGV 2830	1753	
1803	RE 88988	1853	
1946	RE 88774	2047	Exc. Su
2109	TGV 2838	2153	M–F
2250	TGV 9898	2324	

Daily, unless otherwise noted
Distance: 39 miles (63 km)

Poised at the confluence of the Moselle and Seille Rivers, Metz claims one of the oldest churches in France, the fourth-century **St. Pierre-aux-Nonnains.** The center of attraction, however, is its Gothic cathedral of **Saint Etienne** (13th to 16th centuries). The cathedral has been described as the "apotheosis of light" due to the luminescent quality of its stained-glass windows—two of the largest surface stained-glass windows in the world. Its 300-foot-high nave is among the highest in France.

Metz further claims the largest railway station in eastern France. Due to its size, visitors arriving by rail may find the facilities somewhat confusing. When arriving from Luxembourg in the north, take the southern stairway rather than the northern one when transiting from the arrival platform to the main station hall via the underground passageway.

Obtain a map of Metz and a copy of *Transports Par Minibus*, which describes the two minibus lines from the tourist office. The two lines cover the city's major sights and shopping areas and terminate at the main railway station. The minibus stops throughout the city are marked with devices very similar in appearance to barber poles, to which are attached maps showing the course of the bus making that particular stop. Each pole is marked with the name of the stop, and inside the bus is a circular chart showing all of the stops that the bus makes. By noting first the name on the pole stop and then relating it to the map inside the bus, you can easily identify your position. Both minibus lines operate 0730 to 1930 daily except Sunday and holidays. A bus leaves the main railway station approximately every six minutes. Tickets are available in the bus.

Metz has many other interesting sights, such as the 14th-century **St. Louis market square** with its Italian influence. Its majestic buildings are constructed of yellow limestone, which gives them an aspect of light. The city's 18th-century theater, **Place de la Comédie,** is another typical example of this "brightness."

In August Metz goes "plum crazy." The golden mirabelle plum is celebrated in various deliciously edible forms—perhaps on a tasty tart or in a luscious, languid liqueur. Other gastronomic specialties include frog-legs pie, freshwater fish, and traditional stews, as well as not-so-traditional stews—snail stew.

Want to try a different type of city tour? Take a tour via Metz's **"Petit (little) Tourist Train"** (*Tel:* 387 55 53 76). It has departures at 1030, 1130, 1300, 1400, 1500, 1605, 1705, and 1805 daily April–September, and on Saturday and Sunday the remainder of the year.

The Metz tourist office proposes an audio-guided walking tour that covers the highlights of the city with an English narration. If you are sightseeing on your own in Metz, you should include the city's museum, with its Gallo-Roman collections and impressive 17th-century paintings by Dutch masters and artists of the French School. Also stroll along the city's Esplanade, on the banks of the Moselle River.

Day Excursion to

Trier

Germany's Oldest Town

Depart from Luxembourg City Central Station
Distance by Train: 32 miles (51 km)
Average Train Time: 41 minutes
Germany Dialing Code: 49
City Dialing Code: 651
Tourist Information Office: Trier Stadt und Land e.V., An der Porta Nigra, D-54290
Tel: (0651) 978 080; **Fax:** (0651) 978 0876
www.trier.de/tourismus
E-mail: info@trier-info.de
Hours: May–October: 0900–1800 Monday–Saturday, 1000–1700 Sunday; November–December: 0900–1800 Monday–Saturday, 1000–1500 Sunday; January–February: 1000–1700 Monday–Saturday, 1000–1300 Sunday; March–April: 0900–1800 Monday–Saturday, 1000–1500 Sunday
Notes: Money exchange is available in the tourist office, which is about a 10-minute walk from the rail station, or there is a taxi stand at the right-hand front of the station. On foot, proceed down Bahnhofstrasse, which runs from the station into Theodor-Heuss-Allee leading to the Porta Nigra. Located immediately

in back of the Porta Nigra monument. Walking tip: Avoid the din of traffic by using the park pathways on the left of the main thoroughfare.

Welcome to Germany's oldest city! "Before Rome, there was Trier." Although this is legend, it is also a historical fact. Evidence of human settlements as early as the third century B.C. has been discovered in and around the city of Trier. Further legend attributes the founding of Trier in 2000 B.C. to the Assyrians. But history more soberly attributes its roots to Emperor Augustus, who founded (or refounded) Trier in 16 B.C., thereby beginning Trier's role in Roman history.

In A.D. 293 Trier became the capital of Rome's province of Belgica Prima and the seat of the emperor's court. History records that no fewer than six Roman emperors held court here. The city's population swelled to about 80,000 citizens, and its cultural growth kept pace with its expanding population. Many magnificent edifices and archaeological finds attest to this growth today.

Trier came to be known as the second Rome. By the end of the third century A.D., it had become a capital of the western part of the Roman Empire. Its many monuments from that time attest to its greatness. The fourth-century Roman cathedral has among its treasures the "Holy Robe," said to have belonged to Christ. In ancient Roman records, Trier was among the first places north of the Alps to bear the name of "city."

Trier's pedestrian zone begins at the town's northern edge with its prize possession—the Roman gateway building, the **Porta Nigra** (Black Gate), built in A.D. 200. Known as the "northern gate of the Roman Empire," it takes its name from the dark patina that formed over its sandstone facade. It was transformed into a church during the 11th century, but Napoleon restored the building to its original appearance in 1804. Other Roman ruins still remaining are the **Barbara Baths** (A.D. 150), the **Imperial Baths** (A.D. 300), the **Forum Baths** (A.D. 100), the core of the **Cathedral** (A.D. 330/380), the **Amphitheater** (A.D. 100), and a bridge crossing the Moselle River.

Trier fell to the Franks in the fifth century, but the city's life did not end. During the thousand years that followed, churches, monasteries, convents, and mansions were built literally on top of, and around, its ancient structures. A cross, erected in A.D. 958 to signify Trier's right to conduct a market, marks the **Hauptmarkt** (Main Market) of today's city. On the other side of the coin, in 1818 a man was born in Trier whose ideas were in opposition to the free market concept; his name was Karl Marx.

Walks between the area of the Porta Nigra and beyond the Main Market will find you among stores galore, ranging from the quaint antiques shop to the eclectic gift emporium to the modern department store. Fine wines may be found in several locations (tastings offered, of course, prior to purchase), as well as rare Roman coins at the shop Haubrich. In 1993 Trier claimed the largest antique coin discovery with a find of more than 2,500 Roman gold pieces.

Trier is an appealing city. It probably can attribute much of this appeal to the fact that it has been an imperial residence since the days of the Caesars. Strolling through Trier, you will see examples of Renaissance, Baroque, and Rococo architecture standing side by side. More recently, during the 19th century, several impressive citizens' houses of outstanding architectural beauty were built along with many museums, including the Archaeological Museum, Bishop's Museum, Cathedral Treasury, the Karl Marx Museum, and the newest favorite, the Toy Museum.

Luxembourg City—Trier

DEPART Luxembourg City	ARRIVE Trier	DEPART Trier	ARRIVE Luxembourg City
0731	0825	1436	1529
0831	0925	1536	1629
0931	1025	1636	1729
1031	1125	1836	1929
1131	1225	1936	2029
1231	1325	2036	2129
1331	1425	2136	2229
		2236	2329
		2359	0105+1

Daily, including holidays
+1 Arrives next day
Distance: 32 miles (51 km)

There are three different types of tours for English-speaking tourists. From March through October you can ride in Trier's "biggest convertible." The **CityTour** bus departs Saturday from Porta Nigra at 1400. Journey time: about one hour. Fare: €11.50 adults; €7.00 children age 6 to 14. The **TrierTour** allows you to board the sightseeing bus at any one of the 13 bus stops. Air-conditioned buses run every 30 minutes, and you can get on and off to visit the sights whenever you please. Fare: €13.00 for one adult and up to two children. For a more detailed tour, we suggest the guided city walking tour, which includes a visit inside the **Palastaula** (Roman Imperial Throne Room). Tours in English depart Saturday at 1330 May–October. For more tour information, including summer boat trips down the Moselle, visit the tourist office.

The tourist office also offers the **Trier Card** (adult €9.90; family €21.00) valid for three consecutive days. The card provides free transport on city buses, free admission to museums (except during special exhibitions), fee reductions for Trier's Roman monuments, city walking tours (in English), and bus tours.

Not all of Trier's attributes are readily visible, for beneath the city in the storage cellars of its wineries there are vats and casks capable of holding more than three million gallons of the Moselle, Saar, and Ruwer wines produced annually in the area surrounding the city. If you would like to enjoy a gourmet meal with a glass of the grape, settle into the **Dorint Hotel** or the **Pfeffermühle restaurants,** or taste the

Mosel-Saar-Ruwer region wines and sparking wines at the Mediterranean-style eatery **Haus des Weines.** Wine tasting is also offered at the area's five wineries and at the vintners in Olewig.

Trier is abundant in festivals throughout the year. Celebrations include the Olewig Wine Festival, Trier Sparkling Wine Gala, Wine & Gourmet Festival in spring, and the Wine Forum, plus the Trier Summer Festival, Music Festival, and Christmas Market. Schedules are available from the tourist information office.

A small street to the side of the great cathedral in Trier is named Sieh um Dich (Look Around You)—an expression that depicts the city's greatness, for you can see 2,000 years of history in just about as many steps.

THE NETHERLANDS

Traditionally, when we think of the Netherlands, windmills, wooden shoes, wondrous flowers, and wheels come to mind. While these things probably will always be a part of Dutch traditions and landscape, there is another not-as-well-known facet to the Netherlands and its people—its important and enviable economic position in Europe and as one of the founding members of the European Union.

Dutch innovation and know-how are responsible for making the computer software Windows accessible for blind users through the use of a cordless mouse that uses sound instead of visual images. And the Netherlands is the only country with an Internet 2 Abilene link with the United States.

The Dutch seem to have an idea or an answer for just about everything. One Dutch company had an answer to automobile congestion and pollution problems by developing a new concept in public transport—People Movers—a combination of ski-lift design and the already existing airport-style people movers.

Another Dutch firm, Spectrum Buoca, has targeted another type of pollution—the acrid urine odor that plagues public facilities (particularly during hot weather). Biological Urine Odour Control Agent (Buoca) is a mixture of natural enzymes and bacteria that "eats" the smelly problem.

It doesn't take too long to discover that the Netherlanders are not only multitalented; they're also multilingual. The Dutch laughingly refer to their own language as "more of a throat condition than anything else" and readily join you in your native tongue. English is the primary second language spoken in the Netherlands, but French, Spanish, German, and many others are heard daily.

Although the Dutch are seemingly inventing the future, they are not forgetting their traditions. There are still about 1,000 working **windmills** that are functioning the same way they did more than a hundred years ago. A group of 19 windmills may be found at **Kinderdijk** in the province of South Holland, some of which you may tour inside. It's amazing—mills that were built in 1740 are still running.

Wooden shoes may not be worn very often anymore, but thanks to tourists, their production has continued. Now, almost any Dutch souvenir shop sells them, and a few farmers in some rural areas still don their wooden clogs when they work in the fields or stalls.

Wondrous flowers are, of course, still in generous supply in the Netherlands. Spanning about 70 acres, the **Keukenhof in Lisse** is the most famous and biggest

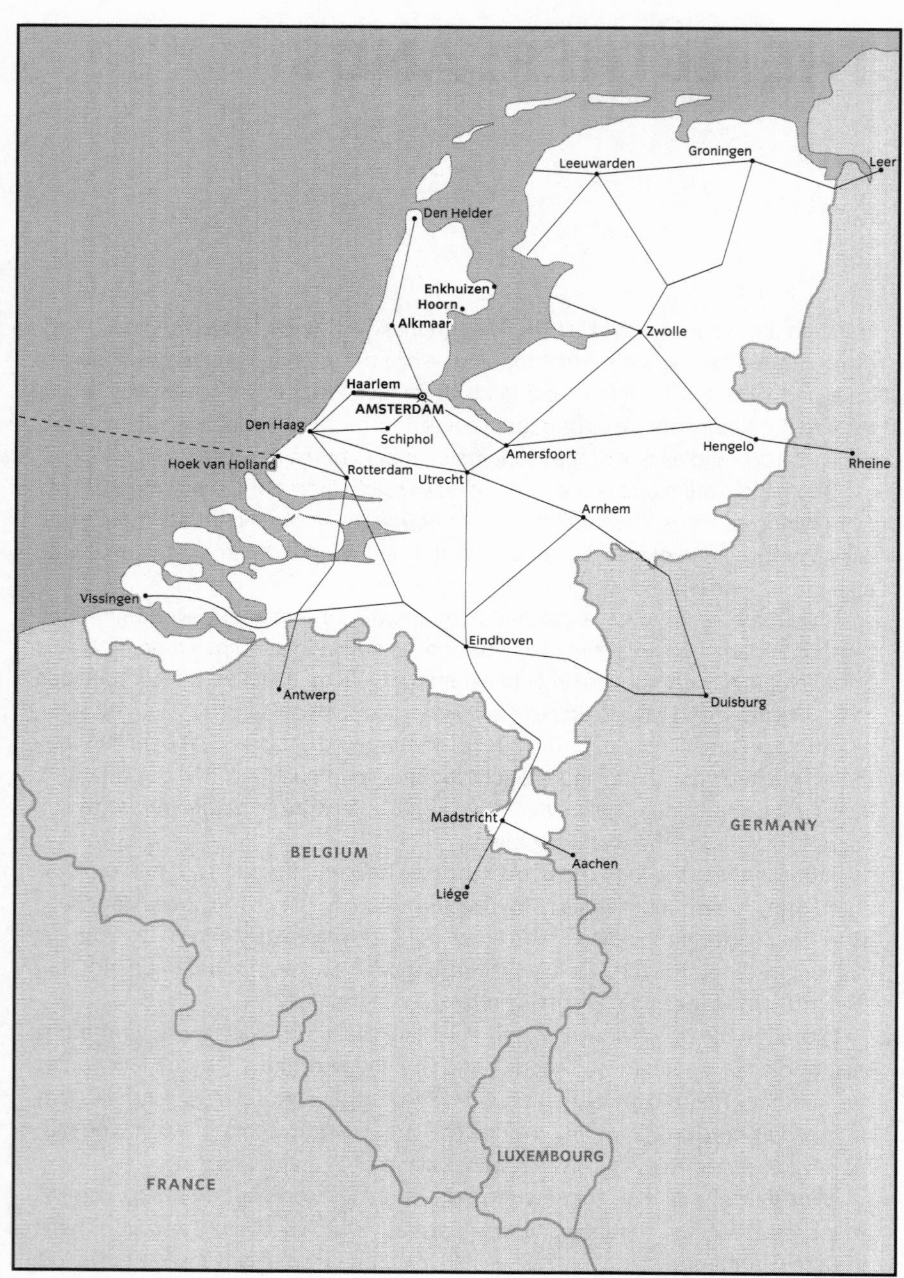
Leeuwarden
Groningen
Leer
Den Helder
Enkhuizen
Hoorn
Alkmaar
Zwolle
Haarlem
AMSTERDAM
Den Haag
Schiphol
Amersfoort
Hengelo
Rheine
Hoek van Holland
Rotterdam
Utrecht
Arnhem
Vissingen
Eindhoven
Antwerp
Duisburg
Madstricht
GERMANY
BELGIUM
Aachen
Liége
LUXEMBOURG
FRANCE

bulb show in the world. *Tel:* (252) 46 55 55; *Fax:* (252) 46 55 65; www.keukenhof.nl; *E-mail:* info@keukenhof.nl. *Hours:* March 22–May 20: 0800–1930 daily. More than 800,000 visitors can gaze upon some seven million bulbs. To get there, take a train to Leiden, and then take Express Bus No. 54. Admission: €15.00 adults; €7.50 children.

Wheels, wheels, wheels! The bicycle is a common mode of transport in its own right—there are more than twice as many bikes as cars! No less than 15,000 kilometers of marked routes, special paths, and bike lanes abound. More than 300 rail stations allow transport of bikes for a supplement. Many travelers hire a bike at the station. Contact the tourist office for bike rental agency information.

For more information on the Netherlands, contact the Netherlands Board of Tourism in North America:

> **New York:** 215 Park Avenue South, Suite 2005, New York, NY 10003. *Tel:* (888) GO HOLLAND (888-464-6552) or (212) 370-7360; *Fax:* (212) 370-9507; www.holland.com; *E-mail:* information@holland.com

Banking

Currency: Euro (€)

Exchange rate at press time: €0.90 = U.S. $1.00

Communications

Country Code: 31

For telephone calls within the Netherlands, dial a zero (0) preceding area code.

Major Mobile Phone Companies: KPN, T-Mobile, Vodafone

Rail Travel in the Netherlands

The Netherlands Railways (Nederlandse Spoorwegen, or NSB; www.ns.nl) has many of its own day excursions. Because the Netherlands is a very compact country, it is possible to take any one of the day excursions from any railway station within the country and return to your point of departure the same day. Frequent trains run to every part of the Netherlands, and most of the stations are linked with bus services and train taxis. To find out more about these day excursions, ask at the train information office in the Amsterdam Central Station or contact the Netherlands Board of Tourism.

Many Dutch cities, such as **The Hague** (Den Haag), **Rotterdam,** and **Utrecht,** are less than an hour away from Amsterdam. In just two hours, you could be in Antwerp, Belgium, shopping for diamonds. Add another 30 minutes, and you could hop on the fast Thalys train and have lunch in Brussels and then shop for lace. Continue your spree—the quaint town of **Delft,** where the world-renowned Delft blue pottery is made, is only 50 minutes' train time from Amsterdam.

The Netherlands Railways accepts the variety of **Eurail passes** and the **Benelux Pass.** A bonus for Eurail pass holders is a 30 percent discount on Stena Line high-speed ships (HSS) crossing from Hoek van Holland to Harwich, England.

Benelux Pass

	1st Class	2nd Class
5 days within 1 month	$446	$358
Youth: 5 days within 1 month	—	$234

Benelux Saverpass*	1st Class	2nd Class
2 people traveling together 5 days within 1 month	$380	$304

*Price per person

Base City: **AMSTERDAM**

www.iamsterdam.com
City Dialing Code: 20

One of the most unusual cities in Europe and built entirely on piles, Amsterdam is a "fun city"—fun to see, fun to be in. It is a pleasant, human city where handsome houses stand on quiet canals, shoppers walk uninterrupted on streets without vehicles, and street organs play in the parks (even on rainy afternoons). It is the kind of city that, when you are lost, sends a smiling old gentleman on his bicycle or a bevy of flaxen-haired schoolgirls to your rescue. Amsterdam is a patient city whose people listen as you attempt to read Dutch expressions from a phrase book—then respond in perfect English. Amsterdam is a city to fall in love with.

Though picturesque, by European standards Amsterdam is not an ancient city. In the 13th century it was a small fishing village tucked behind a protecting dam on the Zuider Zee. It wasn't until the 17th century that it emerged as northern Europe's most prosperous port. Dutch influence declined at the end of the 17th century, but Amsterdam survived in style, having been built on 90 islands linked by more than 1,200 bridges arching 165 canals. Although their interiors have been altered many times, the fronts of 17th-century houses along the canals remain unaltered.

As the Netherlands Board of Tourism states: "Amsterdam is to the Netherlands what New York is to the United States. It is the cuckoo in the Dutch nest, the strange bird with the big mouth, New York with a more easygoing nature. But that shouldn't be surprising. After all, New York was founded by Amsterdammers. Now you are invited to discover our Amsterdam."

Arriving by Air

Schiphol Airport, P.O. Box 7501, 1118 ZG Schiphol Airport, the Netherlands; Hello Port Schiphol Information *Tel:* 0900 0141 or 2079 40 800; www.schiphol.nl.

Amsterdam's Schiphol Airport, which ranks fourth largest in Europe after airports in London, Paris, and Frankfurt, is one of the most modern and efficient air terminals in the world. Schiphol handles more than 25.4 million passengers per year and has some of the best tax-free shopping in Europe. It was built to be convenient. At last count, the airport provides flights to more than 2,000 destinations in 85 countries by more than 90 airlines. After you have cleared customs, proceed to Schiphol Plaza to the **Holland Tourist Information** (HTI) center. *Hours:* 0700–2200 daily. There you can obtain all the information you may need for getting into downtown Amsterdam.

- **Airport–City links:** Rail service between the airport and Amsterdam's Centraal Station takes about 15 minutes and costs €6.80 one-way. Trains run approximately every 10 minutes from 0600 to midnight. If your destination is in the southern part of the city, you can board a train for the Zuid (South) Station as well. In fact, direct train service from Schiphol Airport to many other points in the Netherlands, such as The Hague, Rotterdam, and Delft, is available. Within Holland, *Tel:* 0900 9292 for bus, tram, subway, and rail connections, or for international train information, *Tel:* 0 0900 9296.
- **Schiphol Travel Taxi** provides a national taxi service that can be prearranged online (www.schiphol.nl). The third person receives a 35 percent discount, and children younger than age 12 are half fare. Fares are based on the postal code of your destination. From Schiphol to Amsterdam Centraal Station area, the adult fare is €25 (including luggage) one-way.

  Otherwise, a regular **taxi** may better serve your needs. A taxi takes about 30 minutes and costs about €35 to the Centraal Station area. Again, the HTI desk will be helpful. Taxis can be found just outside the Arrivals Hall.
- **Money exchange** services and ATMs are located in all three Arrivals Halls. *Hours:* 0800–2030 (Hall 1); 0600–2200 (Hall 2); 0700–2100 (Hall 3). The West Lounge has an ATM (bank cards only). The tourist office will also exchange money.
- **Duty-free shopping:** Amsterdam's Schiphol Airport Shopping Centre is actually three centers. The Plaza totals more than 50 shops with more than 120,000 different items. The shops are open from first to last flight departure. Duty-free shopping (See Buy Fly center) is available only to passengers departing Schiphol to destinations outside the European Union.

  Schiphol Plaza shopping is available to everyone, but normal VAT is payable. *Hours:* 0700–2200 daily.

Arriving by Train

The **Amsterdam Centraal Station** is the focal point of all rail, tram (trolley), bus, and Metro (subway) traffic within the city. All train service for the listed day excursions depart from, and arrive in, this station. Trams, buses, and the Metro (entrance) are available immediately in front of the station, the hub of Amsterdam's city-transportation network; practically everything in Amsterdam begins and ends here.

Although Amsterdam's Centraal Station abounds in digital train information displays, the station still provides train-departure information by separate directions on the standard train-departure posters with their yellow background. Rail service throughout the Netherlands is so dense—departures approximately every half hour—that these sectional timetables to Rotterdam, Utrecht, and other cities are most helpful.

Amsterdam's Centraal Station is virtually a city within a city, with many restaurants and shops operating over extended hours—a good place to stock up for a trip. It's also an originating point for long-distance express trains, including the Thalys train connections to Brussels and Eurostar to London, as well as the EuroCity network. This means lots of tourists—and tourists attract pickpockets. Watch when boarding the trains, particularly for people who are apparently traveling without luggage and are following you closely with only an empty shopping bag in hand. Chances are that they are "shopping" for your wallet and they plan to leave the train before it departs.

- **Money exchange** office "GWK" is on the street side of the station foyer. *Hours:* 0800–2200 Monday–Saturday and 0900–2200 Sunday. Money exchange is also possible at local banks. *Hours:* 1000–1600.
- **Tourist information** for all of the Netherlands, including Amsterdam, is available from the VVV Amsterdam Tourist Offices located inside Centraal Station at Platform 2 (Spoor 2). *Tel:* (0) 900 400 4040. *Hours:* 0800–2000 daily except 0900–1700 Sunday; or in front of the rail station (*Hours:* 0900–1700 daily); offices also located at tram stops Leidseplein (*Hours:* 1000–1900 daily) and Stationsplein (*Hours:* 0900–1900).
- **Train information** may be obtained in the office of the Netherlands Railways [information for trains within the Netherlands (*Tel:* 0900 9296), located on the far right of the main station hall as you exit from the trains]. This office has the familiar "i" sign. *Hours:* 0600–2300 daily. Take a number as you enter.
- **Seat reservations** as well as rail pass validation may be made in this office. Complete information about the Netherlands Railways day-excursion program is also available. Remember, when having your pass validated, write out the starting and ending dates on a piece of paper, and have the railroad representative agree to the correctness of the dates before the information is entered on your pass.

Tourist Information/Hotel Reservations

- *VVV Amsterdam Tourist Office:* P.O. Box 3901, 1001 AS, Amsterdam; *Tel:* (20) 5512525 or 0900 400 40 40. From abroad: *Tel:* 011 +31 (20) 5512525; *Fax:* 011 +31 (20) 625 28 69; www.iamsterdam.com; *E-mail:* info@actb.nl.

  Hours: 0900–1900 daily.

  Notes: Located immediately in front and slightly to the left as you exit Amsterdam's Centraal Station, in the Noord-Zuidhollands (NZH) Koffiehuis.

  This office can provide complete city and national information for all of the Netherlands. Hotel, hostel, camping, and apartment bookings can be made here.

Maps of Amsterdam are available for €3.00. You can also call 0900 400 40 40, Monday through Friday, 0900 to 1700, for information. Other VVV offices are located at Leidseplein, Stationsplein, and in the Centraal Station at Platform (Spoor) 2. A Holland Tourist Information center is located at Schiphol Airport Plaza.

- **Hotel reservations** can be made at the Holland Tourist Information (HTI) office at Schiphol Airport, at the VVV Amsterdam Tourist Office (aforementioned) in the Noord-Zuid Hollands Koffiehuis (NZH coffeehouse), in the VVV office in the Centraal Station at Platform 2, or at the Leidseplein and Stationsplein VVV offices. Hotel reservations may also be made before departure through Amsterdam Reservation Centre. *Tel:* 011 +31 20 201 88 00 (dialing from the United States, Monday through Friday 0900 to 1700 Europe time); *E-mail:* reservations@amsterdamtourist.nl.

For convenience, comfort, and cuisine all in one place, we recommend the **Victoria Hotel,** one of the Park Plaza Hotels Benelux.

- *Convenience*—centrally located in Amsterdam and across the street from Amsterdam Centraal Station. The hotel will even send someone to help with your luggage.
- *Comfort*—the stately Victoria Hotel, built in 1890, offers all of the modern "creature comforts," such as deluxe rooms, indoor heated swimming pool, beauty salon, and fitness room—even a free first-class train ticket to and from Schiphol Airport.
- *Cuisine*—fine French and international dinners in the Seasons Garden Restaurant.

Park Plaza Hotels Benelux are located either opposite from, next to, or very close to the central rail stations in Amsterdam, Utrecht, and Eindhoven in the Netherlands, as well as in Antwerp, Belgium. For reservations, *Tel:* +31 (20) 62 34 255; *Fax:* +31 (20) 62 52 997; www.parkplaza.com.

Getting Around in Amsterdam

GVB: located on square opposite Centraal Station; www.gvb.nl

Tel: 0900 9292 or 460 60 60

Hours: 0700–2100 Monday–Friday, 1000–1800 Saturday–Sunday

Amsterdam's public transportation system encompasses 17 tram lines, more than 30 bus lines, and 4 underground systems/light-rail lines, plus ferries and canal boats. The transport office, GVB (Gemeentevervoerbedrijf), is located in front of Amsterdam's Centraal Station in Noord-Zuid Hollands Koffiehuis. Check with this office for up-to-date information, for public transportation maps, and to purchase transport tickets.

There is a variety of transportation tickets available. The easiest way of traveling on GVB Transport's buses, trams, and metro is to purchase a **Day Ticket** that entitles you to unlimited travel for an entire day and evening. A single Day Ticket is €7.50. You can also purchase a ticket valid for up to nine days. Purchase Day Tickets from GVB Tickets & Info Desk (opposite the rail station), at metro stations, and at the VVV Amsterdam Tourist Board offices.

You can also purchase the **"Strippenkaart"** (strip tickets); strip tickets, however, require stamping with each use, and a single ticket is valid on all GVB forms of transport for one hour. To travel in one zone, you have to use two strips, plus one extra strip for each subsequent zone. The transport maps indicate how many zones you need to travel to your destination. Use the stamp machines, or the conductor can stamp your ticket. Tickets are not valid unless stamped and you are subject to a fine of €30 if you do not possess a valid ticket. For transportation information, *Tel:* 0900 92 92.

For **boat services** contact the tourist information office for details on the Canal Bus, Water Taxi, Artis Express Rederij Lovers, and the Museum Boat. Bicycle and water-bike rentals are also available.

The **I amsterdam Card** costs €47 for 24 hours, €57 for 48 hours, and €67 for 72 hours. It offers substantial discounts or free entry for various museums, including the Rijksmuseum, the Van Gogh, the Stedelijk Museum of Modern Art, and The Netherlands Maritime Museum. The pass also includes discounts on other attractions, excursions, and guided tours, *a three-day public transportation ticket for the price of a one-day ticket,* a 25 percent discount on Holland International's romantic Candlelight and Wine Cruises—even a free canal-boat cruise and discounts on the Museum Boat and the Canal Bus.

The I amsterdam Card is available in six languages at any of the VVV Amsterdam Tourist offices and at the Holland Tourist Information center at Schiphol Airport Plaza, or inquire at your hotel.

Sights/Attractions/Tours

If you'd like to see Amsterdam on foot, the VVV's color-coded signboards and map will guide you along six walking routes. More than 30 attractions are incorporated into the walking routes.

A boat trip on Amsterdam's canals is, undoubtedly, the most relaxing way to see the city. Canal-boat terminals line the city's pier-studded canals, many of which may be found immediately outside the station. The closest of these is the **Holland International** pier [*Tel:* (020) 622 77 88; www.hir.nl]. It is just across the bridge on the right. A canal tour costs €15.00 for adults and €7.75 for children age 4 to 12 and senior citizens older than age 65. Other tour-boat terminals are scattered throughout Amsterdam.

Train Connections to Other Base Cities from Amsterdam Centraal

DEPART	TRAIN NUMBER	ARRIVE	NOTES
		Berlin Hauptbahnhof	
0701	IC 141	1322	
1101	IC 145	1722	
1501	IC 149	2122	
		Bern (Berne)	
0805	ICE 105	1556	R, 1
1035	ICE 123	1856	R, 3
2031	CNL 40419	0724+1	R, 1, Sleeper
		Brussels (Bruxelles) Midi/Zuid	
0617	Thalys 9310*	0808	R, M–F
0817	Thalys 9322*	1008	R
0917	Thalys 9328*	1108	R, Exc. Su
and hourly until 2017.			
		Copenhagen (København) H.	
0701	IC 141	1822	R, 5
		Hamburg	
0701	IC 141	1213	5
1101	IC 145	1613	5
1501	IC 149	2013	5
		Luxembourg	
0617	Thalys 9310*	1150	4, M–F
0817	Thalys 9318*	1353	4
1117	Thalys 9340*	1653	4
1217	Thalys 9346*	1750	4
and hourly until 1817, then 2028.			
		Lyon Part-Dieu	
0817	Thalys 9322*	1400	R, 4
1017	Thalys 9334*	1600	R, 4
1317	Thalys 9352*	1956	R, 4
1717	Thalys 9376*	2344+1	R, 4
		Milan (Milano) Greco	
2031	CNL 40419	1037+1	R, 1, Sleeper
		Munich (München) Hauptbahnhof	
0635	ICE 121	1404	3, Exc. Su
1035	IC 123	1804	2
2031	CNL 419	0710+1	R, Sleeper
plus other departures.			

DEPART	TRAIN NUMBER	ARRIVE	NOTES
		Nice Ville	
0917	Thalys 9328*	2037	R, 4, Exc. Su
		Paris Gare du Nord	
0617	Thalys 9310*	0935	R, M–F
0817	Thalys 9322*	1135	R
1317	Thalys 9352*	1635	R
1517	Thalys 9364*	1835	R
1917	Thalys 9388*	2235	R
		Prague (Praha)	
1835	ICE 251	0928+1	R, 3, Sleeper
		Warsaw Centralna	
2028	ICE 61419	1215+1	R, 3, Sleeper
		Vienna (Wien) Hauptbahnhof	
0805	ICE 105	1909	R, 3
1035	ICE 123	2309	R, 3
1835	ICE 227	0820+1	R, 3, Sleeper
		Zürich Hauptbahnhof	
0805	IC 105	1600	R, 1
1035	ICE 123	2000	R, 3
1235	ICE 125	2204	R, 3
2031	CNL 40419	0805+1	R, 1, Sleeper

Daily, unless otherwise noted
R Reservations required
+1 Arrive next day
*Thalys high-speed train, supplement required
1. Change trains in Basel SBB.
2. Change trains in Düsseldorf.
3. Change trains in Frankfurt (Main) Hbf.
4. Change trains in Brussels.
5. Change trains in Osnabrück.

There are several canal cruise companies to choose from—all are excellent. During summer evenings, when the buildings along the canals are illuminated and the canal bridges are outlined by tiny lights, Holland International offers a Candlelight and Wine Cruise (€37.50)—the perfect way to end your day. Departs 2100 daily; reservations required. (Receive a 25 percent discount if you've purchased the I amsterdam Card.)

Amsterdam's old "inner city" is famous for its compactness. Most museums, markets, monuments, shopping streets, and other attractions are all within walking distance—or a short tram ride—from your hotel. Several of the city-center shops are open on Sunday—somewhat unusual when compared to the shopping hours for the rest of Europe. Amsterdam boasts the largest historical inner city in Europe, with more than 6,800 National Trust buildings.

The city has more than 60 museums, including the famous **Rijksmuseum** (*Hours:* 0900–1700 daily), where you can view Rembrandt's renowned *Night Watch*, along with an extensive collection of his other dazzling works. The South Wing is devoted to a wide-ranging overview of 18th- and 19th-century Dutch Impressionist art. All the paintings have explanations in English, and you can rent an audio guide that describes in English, German, or French the 200 most significant paintings in the collection. For more details visit www.rijksmuseum.nl or *E-mail:* info@rijksmuseum.nl. Tickets: €15 adults; younger than age 18 admitted free.

The **Van Gogh Museum** is also a must-see. For a preview check out www.vangoghmuseum.nl, or *E-mail:* info@vangoghmuseum.nl for more information.

One of the newest of Amsterdam's museums is appropriately named **"new Metropolis" Museum** or **"NEMO."** It is an interesting attraction, designed by Italian architect Renzo Piano, due to its location on top of one of the major tunnels leading into and out of Amsterdam. Plus its roof offers a spectacular view of the city. The building appears to rise from the water of the Oosterdok as a bow of a ship. A 21st-century public center for science and technology, this museum fits with our earlier statement, "The Dutch are inventing the future," by using up-to-date, hands-on techniques. Visit www.e-nemo.nl.

"Diamonds are a girl's best friend," and Amsterdam is a good place to see how a glassy little piece of stone can become the most beautiful, desirable gemstone in the world. With nine diamond factories to tempt you, we suggest taking a tour of the **Amsterdam Diamond Center,** located at Rokin 1–5. *Tel:* (020) 624 57 87; *Fax:* (020) 625 12 20; www.amsterdamdiamondcenter.nl. *Hours:* 1000–1900 Monday, Tuesday, Wednesday, Friday, and Saturday; 1000–2030 Thursday; 1100–1900 Sunday. Although free samples are not available, a diamond sure makes a great souvenir!

Dining in Amsterdam is an exercise in international cuisine. The expression "You can eat there in any language" is no exaggeration. First decide what type of food you want—Hungarian, German, Italian, Greek, Scandinavian, Japanese, or Indonesian—then select from among the many restaurants offering such dishes.

For more traditional Dutch bill-of-fare, try one of our favorites—**Haesje Claes** at Spuistraat 273-275. *Tel:* (020) 624 99 98; *Fax:* (020) 627 48 17; www.haesjeclaes.nl. *E-mail:* info@haesjeclaes.nl. Named after Lady Haesje Claes, this restaurant's slogan is "From canapes to caviar." Born in 1520 into a prosperous merchant family, Lady Haesje Claes was the founder and patron of the Public Orphanage, now the Amsterdam Historical Museum. Have a typical Dutch lunch or dinner in one of the eight chambers, each with its own special atmosphere. The salmon with lobster sauce is excellent.

Day Excursions

The *Europe by Eurail* day excursions described in this chapter are to **Alkmaar,** home of the world-famous cheese market; **Enkhuizen,** for its open-air Zuider Zee Museum, which depicts what Dutch life was like before the Zuider Zee was sealed off from the North Sea; **Haarlem,** for the Frans Hals Museum and more aspects of life in the Netherlands; and **Hoorn,** for browsing in a medieval market. These day excursions present a cross section of the Netherlands, from its rural to its sophisticated side.

Day Excursion to

Alkmaar

World-Famous Cheese Market

Depart from Amsterdam Centraal Station
Distance by Train: 24 miles (39 km)
Average Train Time: 30 minutes
City Dialing Code: 072
Tourist Information Office: Regio VVV Alkmaar, Waagplein 2-3, 1811 JP Alkmaar
Tel: (072) 548 8888; **Fax:** (072) 548 877
www.alkmaar.nl
E-mail: post@alkmaar.nl
Hours: Monday–Friday 1000–1700, closed weekends
Notes: An easy route to the town square and the tourist office is to follow the street, Geesterweg, running perpendicular to the front of the station and the VVV signs leading you across a bridge toward a large church (Church of St. Laurens). Pass the church on its left side, and pick up Lange Straat, still walking in the same direction. Pass the town hall, which will be on your right; 4 blocks farther, at a canal, turn left to the Weigh House, where the cheese market is held. The VVV office is located in the front of the Weigh House.

There is a cheese market in Alkmaar every Friday 1000 to 1230 the first Friday in April to the last Friday in September. But Alkmaar is such a picturesque town that it deserves a visit any day of the week at any time of the year. Trains run between Amsterdam and Alkmaar about every 15 minutes.

Alkmaar is famous not only for its cheese; it is steeped in Dutch history as well. It was at Alkmaar in 1573 that the Spanish were first compelled to retreat their occupying forces; hence, the Dutch expression "victory begins at Alkmaar." A festival is held annually on October 8 to commemorate the breaking of the Spanish siege.

Amsterdam—Alkmaar

Daily departures from Amsterdam Centraal Station every 12 and 42 minutes after the hour from 0642 throughout the day, last train at 2342; journey time 35 minutes.

Daily departures from Alkmaar Station at 12 and 41 minutes after the hour until 2241, and then the last train at 2351; journey time 35 minutes.

Distance: 24 miles (39 km)

Ask at the tourist office about seeing Alkmaar by canal, a popular way to see the town. Boats depart from Mient (near Waaggebouw). Adult fare, €6.00; children younger than age 12, €4.50. During the cheese market on Friday, boats sail every 20 minutes from 0930. During May, June, July, August, and September, they depart daily on the hour from 1100. In April, September, and October, they sail Monday through Saturday, every hour on the hour, from 1100, depending on the weather. The canal trip takes about 45 minutes. *Tel:* (072) 511 7750. Visit www.rondvaartalkmaar.nl.

The **cheese auction** is *the* thing to see in Alkmaar. The square explodes into a frenzy of color and activity as cheese porters trot across the square wearing red, blue, green, or yellow hats according to the group they represent. This auction has continued for more than 400 years and attracts thousands of tourists. It is not, however, merely a tourist attraction. It is a genuine auction, at which cheese merchants sample the product, bargain for the best price, and conclude the sale "on hand clap." From there the porters move the cheese to the Weigh House, where the weigh master checks the weight and calls it out in a loud voice; then the porters take the cheese from there to the buyers' warehouses.

Alkmaar's cheese makers founded their guild in 1622, only two years after the Pilgrims landed on Plymouth Rock. Unique in the curatorial world, Alkmaar's **Cheese Museum** attracts visitors from far and wide (*Hours:* mid-March–October: 1000–1600 Monday–Saturday; opens at 0900 on Friday). Visit www.cheesemuseum.com. Entrance fee: €4, but a **Dutch Museumpass** will get you in for free.

Another unique museum is dedicated to the history of beer production. Featuring the fine skills of brewmasters and covering 5,000 years of beer-making history, the **National Beer Museum De Boom** deals with all aspects down through the ages that have determined the various characteristics of beer, including the current Dutch favorite, pale lager. It is interesting to note that despite the complicated brewing equipment used today, the art of brewing has remained a natural process relatively unchanged from earlier times. *Hours:* April–September: 1300–1600 Monday–Saturday. *Tel:* (072) 511 3801; www.biermuseum.nl.

Both the Cheese Museum and the Beer Museum are but a few steps from the city square, where the cheese auction takes place.

Alkmaar is a charming town. It is crisscrossed by canals that, in turn, are spanned by humped stone bridges. The shining red roofs of its old houses are guarded by the towering vaults of the aged **St. Laurens Church,** constructed in 1520. Four blocks south of St. Laurens stands **Molen van Piet,** a windmill built in 1769.

There are an amazing number of things to do and see, among them a visit to the Municipal Museum, the Dutch Stove Museum, and the Hans Brinker Museum; on a Friday, take a look at the stately wooden gabled house complete with an embedded cannonball as a memoir of a war now past. Sample the famous Edam cheese at either lunch or dinner. Time moves slower in Alkmaar.

Day Excursion to

Enkhuizen

Zuider Zee Museum

Depart from Amsterdam Centraal Station
Distance by Train: 42 miles (62 km)
Average Train Time: 64 minutes
City Dialing Code: 228
Tourist Information Office: VVV-Enkhuizen e.o., Tussen Twee Havens 1, 1601 EM Enkhuizen
Tel: (0228) 31 31 64; **Fax:** (0228) 31 55 31
www.vvvenkhuizen.nl
E-mail: info@vvvenkhuizen.nl
Hours: 0900–1700 daily
Notes: After disembarking from the train, bear left approaching the railway station. As you round the station, you will see the VVV tourist office. The route is well marked; just follow the signs.

This day excursion from Amsterdam was made possible by the opening of the **Zuider Zee Open Air Museum** in Enkhuizen, east of Hoorn. Purchase museum tickets at the museum's ticket office. Admission: adults, €14.50; children age 4 to 12, €8.70; children younger than age 4 are admitted free. *Hours:* April–October: 1000–1700 daily. Visit www.zuiderzeemuseum.nl. The indoor portion, known as the **Binnen Museum,** is open throughout the year (except December 25 and January 1). Reduced entrance fees when the outdoor museum is closed. A visit to the Zuider Zee Museum begins with a 15-minute boat ride. After stopping at the VVV tourist office, walk along the right side of the boatyard in front of the rail station to its far end and board the launch at the pier. The boats leave every 15 minutes.

The museum was opened formally by Queen Beatrix on May 6, 1983, after 18 years of construction. It consists of 135 houses and workshops to depict the Zuider Zee culture before it was closed off from the North Sea in 1932 by the Afsluitdijk barrier dam. You will see a foundry, a steam laundry, a sail loft, and a smokehouse, to name but a few items. There are a fishing village on the quay and a town center complete with a church and a general store, where postcards, wooden shoes, and other souvenirs are for sale.

Snacks and various Dutch food specialties are also available, as are tours led by English-speaking guides. Check at the museum office for information. You will pass it just after the foundry.

Enkhuizen has succeeded in preserving its 17th-century character. The old center of the city contains a picturesque fisherman's quarter and a corresponding essential (a farmer's corner) from those days. Within the old seawall, which was constructed to protect the city from storms on the Zuider Zee, you will find a shopping center as well as sidewalk cafes and restaurants.

The last two Thursdays of July and the first two of August are the celebrations of Zuiderzeedag. Each Thursday brings a different theme, with old Dutch dancing groups, games for children, many types of music, a special market, contests, and much more.

Ever wonder how artisans build those beautifully detailed ship models inside glass bottles? A visit to the **Bottle Ship Museum** will reveal the secrets of this ancient sailors' handicraft. The world's largest collection of ships-in-a-bottle is housed in an early 17th-century building—the "Spuihuisje"—within easy walking distance of the Zuider Zee Museum. More than 500 models are contained in bottles ranging in size from small perfume bottles to a 30-liter wine flagon. Tickets may be purchased at the VVV office.

For the small-fry, Enkhuizen offers **Sprookjeswonderland** (Fairyland). Situated in a park setting, it contains a children's zoo with a deer park, a farm, and a "hugging" barn. *Hours:* mid-April to mid-October, 1000–1800 daily. Admission: €9.50. Visit www.sprookjeswonderland.nl.

The town of Enkhuizen is a living museum in itself. The Zuiderkerk, or Southern Church, with its spiraling tower and copper-clad roof, dominates the skyline of the city, assisted by the wooden bell tower of Enkhuizen's other church, the "Wester." Together with the ramparts and fortress walls, Enkhuizen ensures its future by preserving its rich past.

Amsterdam—Enkhuizen

Daily departures from Amsterdam Centraal Station at 9 and 39 minutes after the hour from 0709 until 2339; journey time about 57 minutes.

Daily departures from Enkhuizen Station at 24 and 54 minutes after the hour from 0524 until 2354; journey time 60 minutes.

Distance: 42 miles (62 km)

Day Excursion to

Haarlem

And the Frans Hals Museum

Depart from Amsterdam Centraal Station
Distance by Train: 12 miles (19 km)
Average Train Time: 15 minutes
City Dialing Code: 23
Tourist Information Office: Verwulft 11, 2011 GJ Haarlem
Tel: 0900 6161600; **Fax:** (023) 534 0537
www.haarlemmarketing.nl
Hours: 0930–1730 Monday–Friday, 1000–1700 Saturday; closed Sunday
Notes: The VVV tourist information office is situated on the south right-hand corner of the railway station as you exit. (The train bringing you to Haarlem is headed in a westerly direction as it enters the station.) The office is marked with an ample sign reading VVV HAARLEM and cannot be missed.

Haarlem is close to Amsterdam, and this trip has the shortest travel time of any day excursion described in this edition of *Europe by Eurail*. It is also one of the most interesting.

Haarlem remained relatively undamaged by both world wars. What you find there in the **Grote Markt** (Great Market), the old center of the town, has authentic origins dating from the 13th century. Haarlem was put to the sword in July 1573, when it fell to its Spanish besiegers and its citizens were butchered. Its devastation, however, was not on the scale that modern weapons could perpetrate.

With the release in 1976 of the motion picture ***The Hiding Place,*** the attention of the world was drawn to a quaint little watchmaker's shop established in 1837 at 19 Barteljorisstraat in the heart of Haarlem. It was here in the shop and home of a Christian, Opa ten Boom, and his family that Jewish refugees fleeing the wrath of Nazi Germany were hidden for a time during World War II. A hiding place was built in a bedroom where the refugees could go in case the Germans made a surprise inspection. The ten Boom family operated the refuge for more than 18 months, until they were betrayed on February 28, 1944.

At the time of the betrayal, six persons were concealed in the hiding place. They escaped while the Gestapo was still in the house. The ten Boom family, however, was imprisoned in a concentration camp for their acts of mercy. The ten Boom house is now a museum. Entrance is free, but a donation is always graciously appreciated. *Hours:* April–October: 1000–1530 Tuesday–Saturday; November–March: 1100–1500 Tuesday–Saturday. Visit www.corrietenboom.nl. Check with the VVV for directions and details.

Amsterdam—Haarlem

Daily departures from Amsterdam Centraal Station at 12, 27, and 42 minutes after the hour throughout the day; journey time, 16 minutes.

Daily departures from Haarlem Station at 02, 17, 32, and 47 minutes after the hour, throughout the day; journey time, 15 minutes.

Distance: 12 miles (19 km)

The old center of Haarlem is not so large as to require transportation to its points of interest, but the city bus system is available to assist if necessary. You will want to visit the Great Market and see the town hall and the **Church of Saint Bavo,** then proceed to the world-famous **Frans Hals Museum** and from there to the **Teylers Museum** before returning to the railway station.

The Great Market is actually the central square of Haarlem, in which the nobles of Holland staged their tournaments during the Middle Ages. Today, it is traditionally the social gathering place of the townspeople. A part of the town hall was once a hunting club. The Church of Saint Bavo houses a pipe organ that was once played by the 11-year-old Mozart.

On foot, head south from the station, crossing the Nieuwe Gracht (New Canal), and proceed to the city's central square, using the tower of the great church as your point of destination. As you enter the square, the church stands on your left, the town hall on your right. This square has been described as the most beautiful in the Netherlands. A pause here in one of the many restaurants, outdoor cafes, or ice-cream shops is recommended.

Time permitting, before leaving the Great Market, you may wish to visit the **Meat Hall** and the **Fish Hall.** No longer functioning by their descriptive names, both structures are now employed in the exhibition of modern visual art. The 17th-century architect Lieven de Key designed the Meat Hall, which is said to be one of the finest examples of Renaissance architecture in the Netherlands.

From the western end of the church, follow the street running south from the square to the **Frans Hals Museum,** just before the canal. This street has several names—Warmoesstraat, Schagchelstraat, and Groot Heiligland—appearing in that order as you move to the museum through one of the most heady 17th-century atmospheres to be found anywhere in Europe.

The Frans Hals Museum is a moving experience. *Hours:* 1000–1700 Tuesday–Friday, 1100–1800 Saturday and Sunday, adults €13. Visit www.franshalsmuseum.nl. Perhaps nowhere else can you find such a perfect combination of setting and display. The building is gorgeous; its inner courtyard is a magnificent example of 17th-century architecture. The versatility of the museum's collections is also unusual. In one section, the peak achievements of Haarlem's 17th-century painters may be viewed; in another wing of the museum, visitors may view an exhibition of modern Dutch art.

A left turn at the canal below the museum takes you to the **Turf Markt** on the Spaarne River, where another left turn takes you winding along the river to Holland's oldest museum, the **Teylers Museum,** just beyond Damstraat (Dam Street). Here you will be treated to a rich collection of drawings and paintings by Michelangelo, Raphael, Titian, and Rembrandt. The Coin and Medal Room displays Dutch coins and medals from the 16th to the 20th centuries. The museum also includes a collection of fossils and minerals.

Day Excursion to

Hoorn

Old Dutch Market

Depart from Amsterdam Centraal Station
Distance by Train: 26 miles (42 km)
Average Train Time: 39 minutes
City Dialing Code: 229
Tourist Information Office: Veemarkt 4, 1621 JC Hoorn
Tel: (0229) 252200; **Fax:** (0229) 215023
www.hoorn.nl
E-mail: info@vvvhoorn.nl
Hours: 1300–1700 Monday, 1000–1700 Tuesday–Friday, 1030–1700 Saturday; closed Sunday
Notes: To reach the tourist office, cross the main street in front of the railway station, bear right to the first street, then turn left to the next intersection. Here, you turn left, then take the second street on your right. Green signposts scattered along this route indicate the location.

Ever since its harbor slowly silted in the 18th century, the city of Hoorn has taken to relaxing—except on Wednesday from July to August, when it awakens with colorful markets and fun events.

In stalls grouped around the statue of Admiral Jan Pieterszoon Coen (founder of the East India Company) in the square the town calls **Rode Steen,** Hoorn's 17th-century crafts of clog making, net mending, basket weaving, and many others come to life while groups of folk dancers perform with musical ensembles. If you are not particularly fond of mingling with the crowd, this colorful spectacle may be viewed from the comfort of the **Old Dutch Tavern** on Rode Steen Square.

Although the Zuider Zee has been landlocked since the strait to the North Sea was sealed off in May 1932, Hoorn has managed to maintain its status of a port by establishing four harbor areas with more than 1,100 moorings for commercial and recreational watercraft. The pursuit of water sports, including sailboarding and waterskiing, may be observed—or participated in—throughout the season in Hoorn.

Amsterdam—Hoorn

Daily departures from Amsterdam Centraal Station at 9 and 39 minutes after the hour throughout the day beginning at 0709; last train at 2339; journey time: 42 minutes.

Daily departures from Hoorn Station at 20 and 50 minutes after the hour throughout the day, last train at 2350; journey time: 40 minutes.

Distance: 26 miles (42 km)

Steam-engine buffs will find interest in Hoorn, too. You can travel on a genuine **steam train** from Hoorn to Medemblik and back in old-fashioned coaches. The Netherlands Railways operates a day excursion, "Historical Triangle," during spring, summer, and fall. Starting either in Hoorn or Enkhuizen, a steam train plies between Hoorn and Medemblik and a boat between Medemblik and Enkhuizen. The VVV office in Amsterdam or the train information office in Amsterdam's Centraal Station can provide details for this triangle trip. Information for finding Rode Steen Square, as well as the departure point and tickets for the steam train to Medemblik, is also available in the Hoorn railway station.

On Wednesday you'll find the market area merely by following the crowd. At other times, follow the directions to the VVV tourist office (aforementioned).

Day excursions by train to Hoorn are popular trips out of Amsterdam in the summer. Local trains bear special markings (on Wednesday) from July through August, when the market is staged. Take these trains for a festive mood; but regular train service between Amsterdam and Hoorn runs about every half hour throughout the day, so you have the option of going and returning whenever you feel like it.

The steam train operates every day except Monday from April through the end of October; so Hoorn stages this market plus many other attractions on days other than Wednesday. In fact, the steam train continues to operate through September and October from Tuesday through Sunday. Visit www.museumstoomtram.nl.

Wednesdays during the summer are, of course, the times of high activity in Hoorn, but you may go there anytime throughout the year and spend an enjoyable day in this ancient town on the **Ysselmeer,** a freshwater lake that was once part of the Zuider Zee. It is one of Holland's loveliest cities. As an important 14th-century fishing harbor, it grew in stature until the 17th-century East Indies trade made it rich. The warehouses and mansions of the East India merchants that still line its streets make exploring the town on foot a sheer delight. You can obtain a street map with a recommended walking tour from either the VVV office or the ticket office in the railway station.

At Rode Steen Square you may inspect the 17th-century **Weigh House** and the **Westfries Museum,** which houses a collection of antiques, paintings, and objects associated with the city and its surroundings. The museum is crammed with beautiful paintings of Hoorn's citizen soldiers and other memories of Hoorn's "golden age" during the 17th century.

Stop at the 15th-century calligrapher's workshop. Here is where Hoorn's wealthy merchants had their contracts and correspondence penned prior to the invention of the printing press later in the century.

RUSSIA
Bodo
Fauske
Mo
Mosjoen
Grong
Steinkjer
SWEDEN
FINLAND
Trondheim
Östersund
Andalsnes
Röros
Tynset
Hamar
Dombås
Otta
Lillehammer
Myrdal
Bergen
Roa
Hønefoss
Kongsvinger
OSLO
Drammen
Charlottenberg
Kongsberg
Nordagutu
Moss
Stavanger
Skien
Neslandsvatn
Larvik
Kornsjø
Sira
Arendal
Egersund
Kristiansand

NORWAY

See, darling, how the departing day
On a scarlet pillow is laid away;
How the sun has set
In clouds of gold and violet.

—FROM THE POEM "BEAUTIFUL CLOUDS" (1839),

BY HENRIK WERGELAND

Norway—Land of the Midnight Sun (there seems to be more than one, including Finland and the state of Alaska). In the upper reaches of Norway during the summer, the sun never fully sets, generating extraordinary hues of scarlet, gold, and violet in the northern skies. The Norwegian Tourist Board succinctly describes a visit to Norway as "A nature so incredibly beautiful one can't help but feel spiritual. Overall, a vacation in Norway feels like a spa treatment. Norway will capture your heart and renew your spirit."

More than 30 percent of Norway's 155,000 square miles are covered by forests, rivers, and lakes, creating majestic landscapes and mystic fjords. Norwegian beauty and charm are not confined to its landscapes—they are reflected in its people.

Norwegian is the official language, but most Norwegians speak English, and some also speak French or German. Norwegians are friendly, fun, and eager to make visitors feel welcome.

Norway is a constitutional monarchy with a Parliament, known as "Stortinget," and has been a member of NATO (North Atlantic Treaty Organization) since 1949. Oil and gas are the cornerstone of its economy, and its people have one of the world's highest per capita incomes.

From art, beauty, and culture to hiking, skiing, and whale watching, Norway has something for everyone.

For more information on Norway, contact the Norwegian Tourist Board in North America:

New York: Innovation Norway, 655 Third Avenue, 18th floor, New York, NY 10017. *Tel:* (212) 885-9747; *Fax:* (212) 885-9710; www.goscandinavia.com

or www.norway.org; *E-mail:* info@goscandinavia.com or usa@innovation norway.no

Banking

Currency: Norwegian Kroner (NOK)

Exchange rate at press time: NOK 8.33 = U.S. $1.00

Hours: 0800–1530 Monday–Friday, closing at 1700 Friday, 0900–1200 on Saturday. Some banks are open longer than regular hours in larger cities. Most shorten hours during summer.

Communications

Country Code: 47

City codes are not used when dialing within Norway.

Major Mobile Phone Companies: Telenor Mobil, NetCom, Network Norway

Rail Travel in Norway

The **Norwegian State Railways** (NSB) successfully combines a comprehensive system (4,044 kilometers) of express and local rail service with bus and boat services. Visit www.nsb.no.

The NSB **"Norway in a Nutshell"** package tours incorporate various transportation modes, including travel on the Flåm Mountain Railway, to create a great day excursion. Telephone Scantours toll-free (800) 223-7226 or visit www.scantours.com.

Norway's trains traverse difficult geography; consequently, train speeds are limited to a maximum speed of 160 km/h. The rail connection between Gardermoen Airport and Oslo on the *Gardermoen Express,* however, is built for 200 km/h and takes only 19 minutes. Norwegian trains are known for cleanliness and comfort.

On the night trains, sleeper cars contain one, two, or three beds per compartment, and couchettes and/or reclining seats are available on some trains.

NSB accepts the multicountry variety of **Eurail passes,** including **Eurail Select Pass,** the **Eurail Scandinavia Pass** (for rail travel in Denmark, Finland, Norway, and Sweden), and the **Eurail Norway Pass**. Eurail bonuses include:

- 25 percent discount on the Color Line steamship fare between Norway and Denmark. Crossings: Kristiansand–Hirthals, Moss–Hirthals, Moss–Frederikshavn, Larvik–Frederikshavn, Larvik–Skagen.
- 25 percent reductions on ferry crossings (daytime) between Kristiansand and Hirtshals (Denmark) and between Larvik and Frederikshavn (Denmark).
- Ferry reduction of 25 percent on Flaggruten ANS: Bergen–Haugesund and Stavanger.

- Reduction of 30 percent on the Flåmsbana private railroad from Myrdal to Flåm.

Seat reservations are compulsory (NOK 20) on InterCity (ICE) trains and most other express trains. Supplement is charged for use of the ICE's "Bureau car" and for the "Saloon car," which includes a meal.

Eurail Norway Pass

DAYS Within 1 Month	ADULT 2nd Class	YOUTH 2nd Class
3 days	$284	$214
4 days	$307	$231
5 days	$339	$256
6 days	$386	$290
8 days	$428	$322

Children age 4–15, half adult fare; children younger than age 4 travel free (up to 2 children per adult). 50 percent discount on HSD boat Bergen–Haugesund–Stavanger; 30 percent discount on Flåm Line. Not valid on Airport Express train.

Base City: **OSLO**

www.visitoslo.com

Oslo, known as "the Viking Capital," is unique. If you love to bask in the sun, go to Oslo sometime between May and October, when more sunbeams fall on Oslo than on any other capital city in Europe north of the Alps. About half a million of Norway's four million people live in Oslo, and soaking up the sun is the thing to do in town during the summer. Sauna baths, of course, become the rage for the balance of the year.

Oslo is also Norway's business, cultural, and fun capital. Frequently referred to as the "Nightclub of the North," Oslo is Scandinavia's center for entertainment and night life. Artists and performers entertain into the wee hours of the morning.

Arriving by Air

Touted as "Europe's safest and most efficient airport," Oslo's international airport at Gardermoen is a beautiful example of contemporary Norwegian architecture. Located some 47 kilometers north of Oslo, the airport handles about 17 million passengers per year. There are daily direct flights to more than 30 European cities and hourly flights to Copenhagen and Stockholm. Visit www.osl.no.

- **Airport–City Links:** High-speed rail connections into Oslo on the Airport Express Train (*Flytoget*) take only 19 minutes. The rail station is located in the air terminal. Follow the pictographs. Long-distance train service provides connections to all parts of Norway and Scandinavia. *Tel:* 815 00 777. Visit www.flytoget.no. *Fare:* NOK 170.
- The taxi stand at Oslo Airport is on your right as you exit from the Arrivals Hall. Ask for Oslo Taxi service's "Airport Taxi" at the Taxi Information desk in the Arrivals Hall and expect to pay NOK 500 to NOK 600 for one to four persons. (To book in advance from the United States, *Tel:* 011 +47 02323.) All taxis are equipped with meters and accept all major credit cards.
- SAS Airport Bus departs every 20 minutes from 0400. Journey time: 35 to 40 minutes; to the Radisson SAS Scandinavia hotel, 50 minutes. *Tel:* 22 80 49 71. Visit www.flybussen.no.

Arriving by Train

Oslo has several suburban rail stations, but all international trains stop only at the **Oslo Sentralstasjon** (Oslo Central Station). You will see the station name frequently abbreviated as "Oslo S," or shortened to "Oslo Sentral."

Within the station, rail travelers can take advantage of a mini-market area amid a variety of kiosks selling everything from apples to zircons. The nostalgic market area stands on what was once known as the East Station. The East Station was devoted to steel rails, nail-spiked wooden platforms, and tiles bearing the patina of wear from countless passengers' feet as they hurried to and from the steam-hauled trains.

Oslo Sentral Station is a model of efficiency. Access from the train platforms to the station's main hall is by ramps. A shopping mall, Byporten ("City Gate"), is connected to Oslo Sentral and has more than 65 shops, 10 restaurants, and a hotel.

- **Baggage carts** are available for a NOK 10 coin. The coin is refunded if you return your cart to a rack when you are finished. Although the carts may be used on the ramps, they cannot be used on the station's escalators. You can, however, use the large passenger elevators located at either end of the main hall when moving from one level to another. The elevators are marked HEIS, which comes close to the word *hoist* in English. Follow the pictographs, and you will find every service you might need.
- **Baggage storage lockers** are located on a balcony to the right of the station's main exit. The locker area is open 0700 to 2300 daily.
- **Money exchange** facilities are located on the mezzanine level of the station, directly across from the ticket windows. Follow the currency exchange pictographs. *Hours:* June–September: 0700–1800 Monday–Friday, 0900–1500 Saturday. When the money exchange is closed, you can change money in the post office or at the tourist information office in Oslo opposite the City Hall.
- **Ticket offices** are on the left-hand side of the station. Domestic tickets are available 0600 to 2315 Monday through Saturday and 1000 to 1800 Sunday. The international ticket office is located next to the domestic ticket windows (open daily 0630 to 2200).
- **Tourist information office** is open 0700–2000 Monday–Friday, 0800–1800 Saturday and Sunday (until 2000 during the summer) and is located next to the money exchange office. It provides tourist information covering Oslo, hotel reservations, guesthouse and private accommodations, sales of the Oslo Pass, and sightseeing tours. To request information/accommodations in advance, write to Tourist Information, Oslo Sentralstasjon, Jernbanetorget 1, N0151, Oslo, or book accommodations online: www.visitoslo.com.

- **Train information** is located in Oslo Sentral's main concourse area on the left-hand side just prior to the moving walkways. *Hours:* 0700–2300 Monday–Saturday, 0700–2200 Sunday. If possible, get the information you need from the regular arrival and departure digital bulletin boards installed throughout the station. Departures carry the heading AVGAENDE TOG, and arrivals are labeled ANKOMMENDE TOG.
- **Train reservations** and rail pass validation are handled at window No. 4 in the ticket office of the main lobby. The ticket windows are marked BILLETTER, and any window can assist you if No. 4 is closed. This office can also make sleeping-car reservations.

Tourist Information/Hotel Reservations

Tourist Information Office: Fridtjof Nansens Plass 5, N–0160 Oslo; *Tel:* 24 14 77 00; *Fax:* 22 42 92 22

Hours: June–August: 0900–1900 daily; September: 0900–1700 Monday–Saturday; October–March: 0900–1600 Monday–Friday; April–May: 0900–1700 Monday–Saturday

Notes: The Tourist Information Centre is located opposite Oslo's City Hall; entrance is on Roald Amundsen Street.

The attitude of the personnel at the Information Centre is, "If we can't tell you what you need to know, we can tell you who can and where to go to get it." The Information Centre provides details on Oslo and its surrounding regions plus selected destinations throughout Norway; houses a nice cafe, interesting gallery, gift shop, and newspaper kiosk; and neighbors a restaurant serving "Norway's best food in a contemporary setting at an attractive price."

- **Hotel reservations** can be made in the tourist information office across from City Hall or in the one next door to the money exchange office in Oslo Sentral Station. This service is operated by Oslo Promotion. It will make reservations for you in hotels, pensions, and private homes (NOK 20 fee per booking). Oslo Promotion has an exceptional track record. Few, if any, are ever turned away though the entire town is "fully booked." Oslo is one of the few European cities where you can arrive without an advance reservation and still be reasonably certain of lodgings that night.

  Ask for the *Oslo Package* brochure. This package combines your hotel accommodations (choose from 42 selected hotels), including breakfast, and the Oslo Pass. Prices start from NOK 520 per person, per night, double occupancy, up to two children free in the same room as their parents.

  Be certain to ask for *The Official Guide for Oslo,* since it will aid you in seeing the various attractions in and around Oslo.

Train Connections to Other Base Cities from Oslo

Depart from Oslo Sentral Station

DEPART	TRAIN NUMBER	ARRIVE	NOTES
		Copenhagen (København) H.	
0701	IC 105	1428	R, 1, Exc. Su
1301	IC 117	2128	R, 1
		Hamburg	
0701	IC 105	2021	R, 1, 2, Exc. Su
		Stockholm Central	
0701	IC 105	1433	R, 1
1301	IC 117	2131	R, 1

Daily, unless otherwise noted
R Reservations required
+1 Arrive next day
1. Change trains in Göteborg Central.
2. Change trains in Copenhagen.

Getting Around in Oslo

Both tourist offices plus most Oslo hotels sell the **"Oslo Pass,"** which provides unlimited use of city transportation by bus, train, tram, suburban railway, and ferry within Oslo's boundaries as well as up to four fare-stages within **Akershus.** Online ordering is available at www.visitoslo.com. The card includes free admission to more than 50 attractions and museums, various sightseeing discounts, a free tour by boat (May through mid-August), discounts at local eateries such as Restaurant Dan Turell and Tryvannstua, and a surprise on the menu at Holmenkollen Restaurant and Brasserie 45. Reductions are also available at several shops (don't leave town without an authentic Norwegian sweater), ski lift tickets, theme parks, and even Oslo by Horse.

Oslo Pass

	Adult	Child*
24 hours	NOK 290	NOK 145
48 hours	NOK 425	NOK 215
72 hours	NOK 535	NOK 270

*Younger than age 16

Sights/Attractions/Tours

Visitors desiring personal-guide services can contact Guideservice or *Tel:* 22 42 70 20 for reservations and tariffs. Students, taxi drivers, and couriers are not permitted to arrange paid guided tours in Oslo and for the museums.

A variety of tours in and around the city is available. For details call at the tourist information office or consult your hotel. You may book the standard sightseeing bus tours, which normally take three hours to complete, or you may want to opt for one of the more specialized tours combining bus and boat transportation. You will find them listed in *What's On in Oslo* and *The Official Guide for Oslo and Surrounding Area*.

With so much good weather on hand, it is only natural that the majority of Oslo's sightseeing services concentrate their schedules into the summer months. In the period beginning with April and ending with October, a myriad of sightseeing opportunities are available to visitors. Fjord cruises from 50 minutes' duration to several hours are available. Likewise, there are land-and-water combinations to select from that include (among other attractions) a visit to the **Kon-Tiki Raft Museum,** a cruise on the **Oslofjord,** and a view from the top of the famous **Holmenkollen ski jump.**

The usual types of city bus tours are also available, along with a wide selection of things to be seen. There's an old adage that when the weather is nice, you will never find anyone home in Oslo. That is true. Chances are, you will find that many of the passengers on your tour bus or boat are townspeople enjoying the view along with you.

Information describing **Bygdoy** and many other attractions in Oslo is available at the tourist information office, at the Oslo Sentral Station, or from the Tourist Information Centre.

Visit Oslo's famous **Vigeland Park** while you are in town. Among the 193 granite and bronze statues by sculptor Gustav Vigeland, you will be able to examine *The Monolith*, the world's largest granite sculpture.

All members of the family will enjoy a visit to **Akershus,** a medieval castle built in the 12th century and reconstructed as a fortress during the 17th century. Standing at the front of Oslo's City Hall, you can see the fort off to your left. Akershus's military atmosphere is aided by the presence of two military museums. The **Norwegian Resistance Museum** chronicles Norway's struggle against the Nazis, and the **Norwegian Armed Forces Museum** traces the country's military history from the Vikings to World War II. The fort maintains a garrison of armed sentries who patrol the grounds in dress uniform and plumed headdress.

During your stay in Scandinavia's oldest capital—Oslo was established in 1050 by Harald Hardrade—you should plan to visit the world-famous ***Kon-Tiki*** raft, the polar vessel ***Fram,*** and the collection of Viking ships on exhibition at Bygdoy, across the harbor from the city hall. Each vessel bears a proud history in nautical accomplishments.

Day Excursions

When you consider that Norway is larger than the British Isles, you can readily appreciate why we deviate from our usual Base City–Day Excursion format for Oslo. An "out-and-back" excursion between Oslo and **Bergen** offers an almost limitless variety of travel modes and a visit to the fjord at **Flåm.**

Within our usual Base City–Day Excursion concept, we selected a variety of daytime trips that will permit you to see the beautiful fjords, lakes, and mountains without daily packing and unpacking.

A day excursion to the towns of **Larvik** and **Skien** takes you into Norway's seacoast towns for a look at some breathtaking scenery as well as a close look at the country's ports.

Hamar lies to the north of Oslo. Its day excursion affords inspection of the countryside surrounding the town and its extensive railroad museum.

The northernmost day excursion takes you to **Lillehammer,** site of the 1994 Winter Olympics and one of Norway's best-known summer-and-winter resorts.

Day Excursion to

Bergen

And the Fjord at Flåm

Depart from Oslo Sentral Station
Distance by Train: 293 miles (471 km)
Average Train Time: 6 hours, 40 minutes
Tourist Information Office: Vågsallmenningen 1, No. 5014 Bergen
Tel: 55 55 20 00; **Fax:** 55 55 20 01
www.visitbergen.com
E-mail: info@visitbergen.com
Hours: June–August: 0830–2200 daily; May and September: 0900–2000; rest of year: 0900–1600 Monday–Saturday
Notes: The tourist information office is located by the fish market harbor. There is a map in the station that will point the way. When you exit the main door of the rail station, continue straight ahead for about 600 to 700 meters. There is also an information desk at the ticket office in the rail station where you can obtain a city map and purchase the Bergen Card.

Bergen is Norway's second-largest city. It is beautifully framed by seven mountains. One cable car and one funicular terminate at mountaintop restaurants overlooking the city. Bergen has a fish market that also has live fish, a 16th-century town hall, and a 12th-century cathedral. **Troldhaugen** is the home of Edvard Grieg (1843–1907), the most distinguished Norwegian composer of the 19th century. The city has a 300-year-old wooden village **("Old Bergen"),** a symphony orchestra founded in 1765, and the oldest performing theater in Norway. Inseparable from the sea, Bergen also has the largest aquarium in northern Europe.

Founded in 1070 by King Olaf Kyrre, Bergen grew quickly as a commercial center, and during the 12th and 13th centuries, it was the capital of Norway. Built mainly of wood, the buildings were highly susceptible to fire, and the city suffered severe fires in 1702, 1855, and 1916. Bergen was badly damaged during World War II, when it was occupied by the Germans.

This excursion has more route options than a cat has lives. The variations are such that we can list only a few. The daily train service between Oslo and Bergen has three daytime trains and one overnight train in each direction. During summer, a fourth train operates daily except Saturday. The overnight trains haul sleeping cars between Oslo and Bergen.

Express boats cruise between Bergen and Flåm from mid-May to mid-September. As a result, many options are available in both time and mode. Before examining some of the options, let's look at the destinations and some of the reasons for going.

Flåm is the terminus of a famously spectacular railway—the **Flåm Railway** (Flåmsbanen). As the train journeys through the steep and narrow Flåm Valley, you're surrounded by astonishing waterfalls and mighty mountain peaks. The train slowly climbs 2,838 feet in only 12½ miles. From mid-April to mid-October, it makes a photo stop near the breathtaking Kjosfossen Waterfalls. The Flåm Railways is not included on rail passes; however, **holders of Eurail passes, Eurail Scandinavia Pass, and Eurail Norway Pass receive a 30 percent discount.** Visit www.flaamsbana.no.

Norway in a Nutshell

Oslo to Bergen

Daily all year. From $290 per person

Depart	**Oslo**	0825	By Train
Arrive	Flåm	1355	
Depart	Flåm	1500	By Boat
Arrive	Gudvangen	1715	
Depart	Gudvangen	1912	By Bus
Arrive	Voss	2000	
Depart	Voss	2114	By Train
Arrive	**Bergen**	2232	

Bergen to Oslo

Daily all year. From $242 per person

Depart	**Bergen**	0843	By Train
Arrive	Voss	0956	
Depart	Voss	1035	By Bus
Arrive	Gudvangen	1119	
Depart	Gudvangen	1200	By Boat
Arrive	Flåm	1410	
Depart	Flåm	1650	By Train
Arrive	**Oslo**	2235	

Contact Scanam World tours, Inc. USA for additional options. Oslo to Oslo same day is only available June through September. Scandinavian American World Tours, Inc. 108 N. Main Street, Cranbury, NJ 08512; *Tel:* 800 545 2204; *Fax:* 609 655 1622; www.scanamtours.com; *E-mail:* info@scanamtours.com.

Day Excursion to

Hamar

Heart of Norway's Lake Country

Depart from Oslo Sentral Station
Distance by Train: 78 miles (126 km)
Average Train Time: 1 hour, 45 minutes
Tourist Information Office: Gronnegata 52, 2304 Hamar
Tel: +47 40 03 2032; **Fax:** 6251 7551
www.hamarregionen.no
E-mail: post@hamarregionen.no
Hours: Monday–Friday 0900–1600

On September 17, 1976, en route to Hamar for the first time, we wrote, "This train passes through some of God's most beautiful countryside along one of His most beautiful lakes." That has not changed.

The countryside is the rich farmland of **Hedemarken,** and the lake is Norway's largest, **Lake Mjosa.** The lake is 75 miles long, and every foot of it is beautiful.

For a special treat cruise Lake Mjosa on the oldest operating paddle steamer in the world, the *Skibladner*, built in 1856. Ask the tourist office for excursion timetables and fares. For information in advance *E-mail:* skibladner@online.no; www.skibladner.no.

Hamar is situated on the eastern side of Lake Mjosa at its widest point. The train from Oslo traverses the river Vorma from Eidsvoll to Mirucsund, and then continues along the eastern shore of Lake Mjosa to Hamar. Watch for the bridge that the train crosses about 1 hour and 10 minutes out of Oslo. Station yourself on the right side of the coach for a spectacular view down the lake from the vantage point of the bridge as the train crosses.

It seems that you have hardly settled in your seat when the train glides to a stop in Hamar. Time will pass even more quickly here, for there is much to see and do in this most pleasant city. Two of its feature attractions are the **Hedmark Museum** and the **Norwegian State Railways Museum.** These are not stuffy old buildings crowded with relics. Both are spacious, outdoor areas with fascinating displays of what rural and railroad life was like in Norway's earlier times. Check with the tourist office regarding transportation to the museums. Both can be reached by public bus. If you prefer a taxi, you will find a taxi stand on your right when leaving the station.

Within the Hedmark Museum boundaries is the **Hamardomen,** enclosing the remains of a medieval cathedral built in 1152. Designed by architect Kjell Lund of Lund & Slaatto Arkitekter, Ltd., and completed in 1998, the glass-and-steel protective enclosure is a unique architectural and technical masterpiece. It is climate controlled to prevent any further deterioration of the cathedral's remains. The ruins reveal that it was one of the most magnificent churches in Scandinavia. History proves that the town of Hamar suffered along with the demise of the stately church. Years of civil strife and the Reformation nearly wiped out what was once a thriving city.

It was not until 1849 that Hamar once again enjoyed the status and charter of a town. Marking this return to status, the current Hamar Cathedral, replacing its medieval predecessor, was built in 1886.

The museum area also includes 40 buildings from the county of Hedmark. Most of them date from the 15th to the 18th centuries. One unusual building, the house of a Norwegian emigrant, was built in North Dakota in 1871 and moved to the museum in 1973.

The **Hamarstua Restaurant,** on the museum grounds, is open for business from mid-May through mid-September each year. From mid-June through mid-August, the museum is open from 1000 to 1700 daily. During the balance of the year, it is open for groups by appointment, and 1000–1600 Tuesday–Sunday. Visit www.hedmarksmuseet.no.

The railway museum rivals anything the Disney folks have come up with to date. If you are a railroad buff, don't miss this stop. Included in its collection of rolling stock are the old royal train, several "stagecoach" types, and even an old fourth-class (or, shall we say, no-class) wagon—without seats. Norway's first railway station is among the many buildings found on the 7½-acre tract covered by the museum. *Hours:* mid-August–June: 1100–1500, closed Monday; July–mid-August: 1000–1700. Visit www.norsk-jernbanemuseum.no.

Oslo—Hamar

DEPART Oslo Sentral	TRAIN NUMBER	ARRIVE Hamar	NOTES
0734	IC 307	0852	
0802	EX 41	0921	R
0934	IC 311	1052	
1034	IC 313	1153	Exc. Su
1134	IC 315	1252	

DEPART Hamar	TRAIN NUMBER	ARRIVE Oslo Sentral	NOTES
1500	IC 322	1626	Exc. Sa
1603	IC 324	1726	
1803	IC 328	1926	
2001	IC 332	2126	
2101	IC 334	2226	Exc. Sa

Daily, unless otherwise noted
R Reservations required
Distance: 78 miles (126 km)

When the Norwegian government closed the Aurskog-Hoeland railway in 1960, two steam locomotives and a selection of rolling stock from the narrow-gauge line were given to the railway museum together with many structures from this private railway that began operation in 1896. The museum also has 11 standard-gauge and 4 narrow-gauge engines—all in operating condition.

Hamar's railway museum is the oldest in Scandinavia, and it is also the oldest technical museum in Norway. No doubt it will still be in full operation during the Norwegian Railway Bicentennial in 2054.

Hamar is also a sporting town, and its Olympic halls can attest to that. Visit Hamar's **Olympia Hall,** the "Viking Ship," and the **Hamar Olympic Amphi Hall** (or the "Northern Lights Hall"). The Viking Ship is one of the largest sports halls in the world and was the architectural symbol of the 1994 Winter Olympics. The Northern Lights Hall is the world's largest wooden building. Check with the tourist office for opening times.

Day Excursion to

Larvik and Skien

Fjord Country

Depart from Oslo Sentral Station
Distance by Train: 120 miles (193 km) to Skien
Average Train Time: 2 hours, 30 minutes
Tourist Information Offices: Larvik: Larvik Tourist Office, Bolgen Culture house Sanden 2 NO-3264
Tel: 33 69 7100
www.visitlarvik.no
Hours: 0900–1530 Monday–Friday; closed weekends
Skien: Skien Tourist Information, Reiselivets Hus, Hjellen 18, 3724 Skien
Tel: 35 90 55 20; **Fax:** 35 90 55 30
www.grenland.no
E-mail: info@grenland.no
Hours: 0900–1530 Monday–Friday

If there's a fjord in your future, you'll probably find it on this day excursion. The greater part of that huge seaway known as the Oslofjord unfolds its grandeur as the train wends its way to Larvik and Skien. The sight of huge tankers and ocean liners miles from the ocean, plying between tree-covered mountains, is a breathtaking sight.

As the train leaves Larvik en route to Skien, you'll also leave the fjords but begin to travel in an area of beautiful lakes connected by streams running through a wooded countryside. This, too, is fascinating and well worth the trip.

Since a train departs the Oslo Sentral Station on the Oslo–Drammen–Larvik–Skien line every two hours throughout the day, you might consider leaving the train at any point that catches your interest and returning to board the train that follows to continue your journey. It's a nice option to take.

You'll need to seek out the local tourist information office in some of the places you elect to stop, and the train gives you an excellent preview of what each town has to offer as you approach. Basically, the route through Larvik takes you to typical Norwegian seafaring towns, and each seems to offer a different type of land- and seascape. In a sense, you'll be window-shopping, so be prepared to leave the train on impulse.

A summary of the cities the train passes follows. Be sure to take along a copy of the Norwegian State Railways schedule for this line in order to plan the follow-on portion of your trip as you go.

Drammen (40 kilometers from Oslo): Important center of Norway's timber and paper industries. There are many attractive buildings in town dating from the 17th century. Have your camera handy—the city covers the headwaters of the Drammensfjorden, where it joins the river, and the docks teem with seafaring activities.

A. Oslo—Larvik—Skien—Oslo

DEPART Oslo Sentral	TRAIN NUMBER	DEPART Larvik	ARRIVE Skien
0739	IC 807	0936	1018
0939	IC 811	1136	1218
1139	IC 815	1336	1418
1339	IC 819	1539	1618

DEPART Skien	TRAIN NUMBER	DEPART Larvik	ARRIVE Oslo Sentral
1425	IC 8240	1519	1721
1520	IC 8260	1619	1821
1620	IC 8280	1719	1921
1825	IC 8320	1919	2121
2025	IC 8380	2119	2321
other departures during week and seasonally.			

B. Oslo—Skien—Larvik—Oslo (circuitous route via Nordagutu)

DEPART Oslo Sentral	TRAIN NUMBER	ARRIVE Nordagutu	DEPART Nordagutu	TRAIN NUMBER	ARRIVE Skien	NOTES
0725	EX 715	0910	0929	R 2577	0959	R, M–F
1125	EX 723	1308	1506	R 2583	1536	R, M–F

DEPART Skien	TRAIN NUMBER	ARRIVE Nordagutu	DEPART Nordagutu	TRAIN NUMBER	ARRIVE Oslo Sentral	NOTES
1603	R 2584	1631	1641	EX 720	1825	R, M–F
1803	R 2586	1832	1842	EX 724	2025	R, M–F

See tables in section A above for return from Skien via Larvik to Oslo Sentral.

Daily, unless otherwise noted
R Reservations required
Distance: 120 miles (193 km) to Skien

Tonsberg (103 kilometers from Oslo): The oldest town in Norway and the seat for centuries of its Viking kings. The Oseberg Viking ship now resting in the Oslo Viking Museum was found in a nearby burial mound. The ruins of a Viking castle overlook the town.

Sandefjord (127 kilometers from Oslo): Home of the Norwegian whaling fleet. Regardless of your opinions about this industry, there's a whaling museum in town, and there's a spectacular whaling monument in the center of the town square. The coastline around Sandefjord is spotted with many islands and inlets, making it very photogenic.

Larvik (146 kilometers from Oslo): The city has its own fjord, which connects to the Lagen River. The beautiful lake country we mentioned begins immediately beyond its city limits. An interesting museum is housed in **Herregarden,** a 17th-century manor house built for the counts of Larvik. The building is one of Norway's best-preserved wooden structures. A world-famous mineral water, Farris, originates here. Many of the small fishing harbors along the coast are accessible by bus. For ferry service from Larvik to Frederikshavn, Denmark, *Tel:* 81 00 08 11.

Prior to your visit, write to the Larvik Tourist Office for interesting booklets describing the Larvik district tourist attractions. Otherwise, when in Larvik visit the tourist office at Storgate 48, across from the rail station.

Skien (193 kilometers from Oslo): Situated where the Skien River and Lake Hjelle meet, this city has been an active trading center since A.D. 900. Sawmills were an important part of its industry. The first began here in the 16th century. Skien is the birthplace of Henrik Ibsen (1828–1906), famous Norwegian playwright. Ibsen's well-constructed plays dealing realistically with psychological and social problems won him recognition as the Father of Modern Drama.

Brekke Park, which looks out over the river and the town of Skien, warrants a visit. There you will find the **Museum of Telemark and Grenland.** (Skien is the administrative center for the district of Telemark.) In the park there are a number of old houses from different parts of the district, including a reconstruction of Ibsen's childhood home, **Venstøp.** The **Telemark Canal** starts in Skien and stretches 105 kilometers into the country. Canal boats sail daily in the summer. For more information contact the Skien tourist office.

Rather than return to Oslo by retracing your route back through Larvik and the other coastal towns, you might want to return to Oslo via the main rail line running from Stavanger on the North Sea. Board train 2582, which departs from Skien at 1603 to Nordagutu, where you'll arrive at 1631. Look around Nordagutu, then board train EX 724 at 1842, bound for Oslo. You will arrive in the Oslo Sentral Station promptly at 2025.

Day Excursion to

Lillehammer

Norway's Vacation Center

Depart from Oslo Sentral Station
Distance by Train: 114 miles (184 km)
Average Train Time: 2 hours, 35 minutes
Tourist Information Office: Jernbanetorget 2, 2609 Lillehammer
Tel: 61 28 98 00; **Fax:** 61 26 96 55
www.lillehammer.com
E-mail: info@lillehammer.com
Hours: Summer: 0800–1800 Monday–Friday; 1000–1600 Saturday and Sunday. The remainder of the year, the office is open 0900–1600 Monday–Friday and 1000–1400 Saturday.
Notes: The office is in the rail station.

This day excursion is one of the most northerly of any appearing in *Europe by Eurail*. Thanks to its latitude, Lillehammer is a famous summer resort and an important winter-sports center as well, with more than 300 miles of prepared ski runs. Snow conditions for skiing are good from December until April, and the long summer evenings are perfect for enjoying the town's beautiful parks and recreation areas. No matter what the season, outdoors is how to enjoy Lillehammer.

If you have succumbed to the charm of Hamar, then you have already been introduced to the beauty of its Lake Mjosa. The train ride to Lillehammer will permit you to see the balance of the lake because Lillehammer lies 35 miles to the north of Hamar. Here, Lake Mjosa narrows to the Lagen River and, in doing so, provides a scenic blend of green forestlands and the special green color of the river. If you have ever wondered what most of the world was like before pollution, here is your answer.

Lillehammer served as the site for the 1994 Olympic Winter Games. The ski-jumps tower, with a view of the entire town, is open from late May to late September, 0900–1900; 1100–1600 remainder of the year. For those of us not in attendance at the 1994 games, the **Norwegian Olympic Museum** in Håkons Hall offers a chance to revisit them. Visit www.ol.museum.no. History of both summer and winter games plus the relevance of sport in society are highlighted from the beginning of the Olympics to present day. The exhibit is translated into four languages, including English; the entrance fee includes a ticket for Maihaugen Museum.

Among the city's attractions, the **Museum of Historical Vehicles** opens at 1000 from mid-June through mid-August and at 1100 the remainder of the year. Just north of Lillehammer you may visit **Lilleputhammer,** a scale model town of 62 miniature houses, where kids can romp at **Hunderfossen Family Park.** Ask the tourist office for details.

Oslo—Lillehammer

DEPART Oslo Sentral	TRAIN NUMBER	ARRIVE Lillehammer	NOTES
0834	IC 309	1045	R, M–Sa
0934	IC 311	1146	
1134	IC 315	1350	
1234	IC 317	1443	M–Sa
DEPART Lillehammer	**TRAIN NUMBER**	**ARRIVE** Oslo Sentral	**NOTES**
1512	IC 324	1726	
1713	IC 328	1926	
1758	EX 44	2004	R, Exc. Sa
1913	IC 332	2126	
2110	IC 336	2326	

Daily, unless otherwise noted
R Reservations required
Distance: 114 miles (184 km)

The city's stellar attraction is a 100-acre open-air museum known as **Maihaugen.** It is within easy walking distance of the tourist information office. The office can provide you with a city map as well as several brochures describing the Maihaugen Museum. The museum area is divided into three sections, and each depicts a different mode of Norwegian life. Its origins spring from the private collection of a dentist, Dr. Anders Sandvig.

As a young dentist just out of school, Dr. Sandvig came to Lillehammer in 1885. He soon learned that many of his patients preferred to pay him with products rather than cash. Sometimes it was a farm implement or a piece of furniture. Dr. Sandvig's practice grew, and so did his collection. Eventually, he laid out the museum area and began filling it with old buildings, which he acquired and transported to Lillehammer. Apparently, the museum business was more rewarding than dentistry, for Dr. Sandvig retired from the profession to run the museum personally, which he did until 1946, when he died at the age of 84.

The museum, founded in 1887, has 185 old buildings, with handicrafts sections of 60 workshops demonstrating skills of the local artisans. *Hours:* June–August: 1000–1700; September–May: 1100–1600, closed Monday. *E-mail:* post@maihaugen.museum.no; www.maihaugen.no. One of the most interesting objects of Norway's past on exhibit in the museum is the **Garmo Stave Church,** which was built in the Ottadal Valley area in the 11th century and reassembled at the museum in 1920. Another interesting exhibit is "Slowly We Conquered Our Country," Norwegian history from the Ice Age until tomorrow.

In the dock area of the city from mid-June to mid-August, you can see the ***Skibladner,*** a paddle-wheel steamer launched in 1856 and still in service today. Its nickname is *White Swan.* True to tradition, salmon and strawberries are served onboard. It is really difficult to accept the fact that the vessel is now more than 145 years old and is in as good a condition now as the day it was launched. Some things do get better with age!

Art lovers will not want to miss the **Lillehammer Art Museum,** one of the leading visual-art centers of Norway. Exhibits alternate between international and Norwegian art from the 1800s through today, with the core of the permanent collection composed of works by artists such as Dahl, Gude, and Munch. Guided tours run Saturday and Sunday 1400 to 1500 or by prearrangement with the museum. *Hours:* 1100–1600 daily. Tickets are NOK 100 for adults; free for children younger than age 16. Visit www.lillehammerartmuseum.com. *E-mail:* post@lillehammerart museum.com for further information.

After visiting Lillehammer, if you would like to return to Oslo via a different route, board the bus to **Gjovik** in front of the railway station at 1545. You arrive in Gjovik at 1625. Board the train for Oslo that departs at 1932. This train returns to Oslo by a different route and arrives in the Oslo Sentral Station at 2130. The train service is one class only, but it's always clean and neat.

The bus fare from Lillehammer to Gjovik is NOK 95. You will have time to do some fast sightseeing in this charming little town on the west shore of Lake Mjosa before departing on the 1902 train to Oslo.

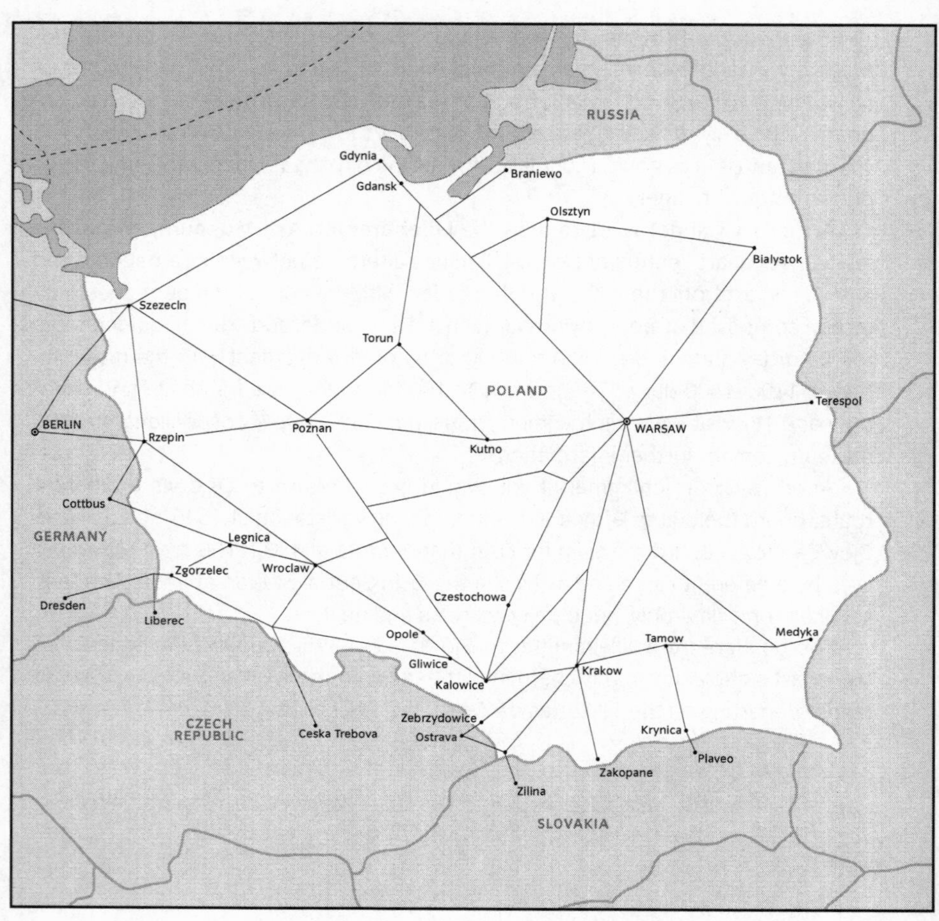

RUSSIA
Gdynia
Gdansk
Braniewo
Olsztyn
Bialystok
Szezecin
Torun
POLAND
Terespol
BERLIN
Rzepin
Poznan
Kutno
WARSAW
Cottbus
GERMANY
Legnica
Zgorzelec
Wroclaw
Dresden
Liberec
Czestochowa
Opole
Gliwice
Kalowice
Krakow
Tamow
Medyka
Zebrzydowice
Ostrava
CZECH REPUBLIC
Ceska Trebova
Krynica
Plaveo
Zakopane
Zilina
SLOVAKIA

POLAND

The history of Poland as a unified state dates back to at least 966. While it has had a tumultuous history since then, it is now a functioning democracy and the strongest economy in Eastern Europe. The country's location in Europe makes it an easy trip from Germany and the Czech Republic, or as part of a loop of eastern Europe. It is also an excellent gateway between western Europe and the east, with connections to Lithuania, Belarus, Russia, and the Ukraine.

Despite being defeated by Nazi Germany in 1939 (generally considered the start of World War II), occupied by both the Nazis and Soviets, and then governed as a Soviet client state until 1989, Poland has done a remarkable job of maintaining its history, culture, and historic sites. Poland has become increasingly popular as a tourist destination, with many castles, churches, and small towns of great history and beauty. There is great natural beauty in Poland, with opportunities for hiking and skiing in the Karkonosze Mountains, wildlife watching in the Białowie, a national park, and relaxing in the coastal resorts on the Baltic Sea.

For more information and pretrip planning tips, be sure to visit Poland's website, **www.poland.travel/en-us,** or contact the Polish National Tourist Office in North America: 5 Marine View Plaza, Suite 303B, Hoboken, NJ 07030; *Tel.* (201) 420-9910.

Banking

Currency: Złoty (zł)

Exchange rate at press time: 3.77 zł = U.S. $1.00

Hours: 0900–1600 Monday–Friday, 0900–1300 Saturday, closed Sunday. Banks in smaller towns may have shorter hours, although most have ATMs available.

Communications

Country Code: 48

For telephone calls within Poland, dial a zero (0) preceding area code.

Major Mobile Phone Companies: Orange, Polkomtel, T-Mobile, Play

Rail Travel in Poland

The Polish State Railway Company or Polskie Koleje Państwowe (PKP) owns and operates almost all of the nearly 20,000 kilometers of rail in Poland and accepts the **European East Pass;** the **Germany-Poland Pass;** and the national **Poland Pass.** (See the Appendix for a list of rail pass types and prices.) Remember to purchase your rail passes prior to your departure for Europe. Visit www.plk-sa.pl.

The aforementioned rail passes include the following discounts within Poland:

- Free travel on Przewozy Regionalne (operates some local servies and low-cost long-distance service).
- Free travel on KM Koleje Mazowieckie (a regional railway around Warsaw).
- 30% discount on the official fares on the ferry crossing from Gdynia–Helsinki/Rostock operated by Finnlines.

Eurail Poland Pass

DAYS Within 1 month	ADULT 1st Class	ADULT 2nd Class	YOUTH 1st Class	YOUTH 2nd Class
5 days	$198	$155	$141	$109
8 days	$280	$217	$198	$153
10 days	$317	$245	$222	$173
15 days	$439	$339	$308	$239

Younger than age 4 travel free. Youth younger than age 26.

Base City: **WARSAW (Warszawa)**

www.um.warszawa.pl
www.warsawtour.pl
City Dialing Code: 22

Arriving by Air

Warsaw Chopin Airport, *Tel:* (48) 22 650 4220 for information, including transport to the city center; www.lotnisko-chopina.pl.

- Located just 10 kilometers from the city center, Chopin Airport is the busiest airport in Poland, and handles around fifty percent of the passenger traffic in the country.
- **Airport–City Links:** Bus route 175 runs every 20 minutes Monday–Friday, every 30 minutes Saturday–Sunday, and takes you to the Centralna rail station in about 20 minutes. Fare 3.60 zł.
- Taxis are available just outside the arrivals area. Fare to the city center is about 60 zł; journey time, 20 to 30 minutes.

Arriving by Train

Warsaw Centralna is the main rail station in Warsaw, and it handles international service and most long-distance domestic traffic. There are suburban rail and light rail stations adjoining the main station. The Centralna station was built under Communist rule. It is not well laid out, and the government is considering options for its replacement. There are some shops and restaurants in the lower level of the station, but there are better places to eat and shop. There are relatively few English-speaking employees, so if you need tickets or railpass validation, be sure to write your dates, and have this confirmed before the pass is validated.

Tourist Information/Hotel Reservations

- Main Tourist Information Center: inside the Palace of Culture and Science, pl. Defilad 1. To get there from the train station, exit the east end of the

Centralna station (onto Emili Plater Street), turn left, and the large building across the street is the Palace of Culture and Science. *Tel:* 48 22 194 31, *Email:* info@warsawtour.pl. Open May–September daily 0800–2000; October–April daily 0800–1800.

Getting Around in Warsaw

The **Warsaw Card** is the recommended way to see all of the sights around the city. Most museums around the city grant free admission to the holder, and many galleries, hotels and shops offer a discount of between five and twenty percent. A 72-hour card is available for 159 zł. The card includes a map and booklet of the city indicating everywhere that accepts the card, which is available for purchase from the Tourist Information Centers.

Warsaw has a good public transport system that allows for efficient travel around the city. It uses a combination of trams, buses, light rail, and a single subway (Metro) line. Trams and buses are included for the 24-hour validation period on the card. If you choose not to purchase the card, single fare tickets range from 4.40 zł for a single fare to 15.00 zł for a travelcard good for a 24-hour travel period. Tickets are available from ticket vending machines, post offices, or from drivers, although they are able to refuse the sale if it will delay the departure, or you do not have exact change.

Sights/Attractions/Tours

Warsaw's most famous son continues to be the composer Fryderyk Chopin. Born in 1810, he moved with his family to Warsaw before he was a year old. It was in Warsaw that he was educated, recognized as a prodigy, and performed his first concerts. An excellent audio walking tour is available from the Tourist Office. You are guided along a series of 15 spots, each with a connection to the composer. Outside each location is a bench that plays a selection of Chopin's music. Other multimedia features are available at the benches if you have a smart phone with a data connection, although be sure of your data rates before using!

Stops along the tour include the **Chopin Family Drawing Room,** in the Czapski Palace. The Chopin family lived in the building as Fryderyk was becoming famous, and a portion of the family's residence has been refurbished to appear as it did when he was composing and practicing in the building. Open Tuesday–Sunday 1100–2000; www.chopin.museum/pl. Farther along the tour, the Łazienki Krolewskie Park, originally the Gardens of the Royal Summer Residence, are where Chopin played as a boy. The beautifully maintained gardens, ponds, and historical buildings are impressive and well attended by the locals. Open daily dawn to dusk. Historical buildings open 0900–1600, except Monday; www.lazienki-krolewskie.pl. The tour passes several historic churches, which are generally open, as long as services are not being conducted.

The Church of The Holy Cross, 3 Krakowskie Przedmiesci Street, is where the urn containing Chopin's heart (his body unable to be returned to Warsaw) is interned; www.swkrzyz.pl. Finally, you will arrive at ultimate goal of the tour, **The Fryderyk Chopin Museum.** The museum was recently remodeled and is now customizable to the visitor. The ticket you receive has a chip that guides you along one of several paths, each with varying levels of detail. This allows a music historian to have a much different experience than a young child. The museum, located at 1 Okólnik Street, is open Tuesday–Sunday, 1100–2000; www.chopin.museum/pl. Admission is 22 zł, and as the museum can only host a small number of visitors at once, advance purchased is recommended.

Be sure to not miss the **Old Town** area, a UNESCO World Heritage Site on the west bank of the Vistula river. The area was the original fortified town center of Warsaw, dating from sometime in the 13th century. While it was bombed, and then systematically destroyed by the Nazis during World War II, it was reconstructed as completely as possible after the war, with significant use of the original materials. The **Old Town Market Place,** once the center of town life, now has an excellent collection of galleries, small restaurants, and shops. Part of Old Town is the **Royal Castle,** originally built in the 15th century. In addition to the elaborate reconstructed chambers and halls, it now houses an impressive collection of artwork, including portraits by Rembrandt. Castle tours are 22 zł, with a discounted family rate available for those with children. The castle is open 1000–1800 Monday–Saturday and 1100–1800 Sunday, with reduced winter hours. Also housed at the castle is an impressive display of Polish coins, banknotes and medals, numbering over 15,000 pieces. Scattered around the Old Town area are numerous churches, statues, and monuments. As you wander the area, consider lunch from a vendor in the market and dinner at Bazyliszek, located on the Market Square. The excellent Polish food, combined with the authentic old world atmosphere, makes for a wonderful close to the day.

The **Museum of Independence** is a somber reminder of the turmoil and devastation that Warsaw and the Polish people have been through within the past 200 years. The museum consists of the Pawiak Prison Museum, and the Mausoleum of Struggle and Martyrdom. Together, they commemorate the unknown thousands of Polish patriots killed in struggles for independence against both Russia and Germany. The museum is about a half mile east of Old Town, along the Aleja Solidarnosci Road. Due to the subject matter, those under 14 years old are not admitted. Visit www.muzeum niepodleglosci.art.pl.

The **Royal Route** follows the original southward route out of Old Town. The route now connects a series of historic sites around Warsaw and the southern suburbs. It starts down Krakowskie Przedmiescie, one of the central avenues of Warsaw. It passes a series of churches and palaces, including the Presidential Palace, and runs by the campus of the University of Warsaw. There are impressive examples of architecture as you walk the route. Pick up a map of the route from the tourist office, but realize the complete route finishes about 7 miles from Old Town and consider stopping after visiting the Museum of Hunting and Horsemanship, or hop on a bus from there to the **Palace of Wilanów,** which is almost 5 miles farther.

With most of the city sitting on the river Vistula, a riverboat can provide a unique perspective on much of the city, including Old Town and the newly constructed National Stadium. The trip takes about 2 hours, with departures at 1000, 1200, 1400 and 1600. The riverboat operates only May–August, with weekend departures only in May and June. Boats depart from the Podzamcze dock, near Old Town on the west side of the Vistula.

Train Connections to Other Base Cities from Warsaw (Warszawa) Centralna

Depart from Warsaw Centralna Station

DEPART	TRAIN NUMBER	ARRIVE	NOTES
		Amsterdam Centraal	
1800	EN 446	1000+1	R, 3, Sleeper
		Berlin Hauptbahnhof	
0600	EC 46	1143	M–Sa
1000	EC 44	1543	
1400	EC 42	1943	
1800	EC 40	2307	Exc. Sa
		Brussels (Bruxelles) Midi/Zuid	
1800	EN 446	0935+1	R, 5, Sleeper
		Budapest Keleti	
0655	EC 103	1635	R, 1
0955	EC 131	1935	R
1255	EC 105	2235	R, 1
2125	D 407	0837+1	R
		Hamburg Hauptbanhof	
1000	EC 44	1821	4
1400	EC 42	2221	4
		Munich (München) Hauptbahnhof	
0600	EC 46	1841	R, M–Sa, 4
1255	EC 105	0058+1	R, 2, Sleeper
1400	EC 42	0710+1	R, 4, Sleeper
		Paris Nord	
1800	EN 446	1135+1	R, 5, Sleeper

DEPART	TRAIN NUMBER	ARRIVE	NOTES
		Prague (Praha)	
0955	EC 131	1739	R
2125	D 407	0638+1	R, Sleeper, Exc. Sa
		Vienna (Wien Westbahnhof)	
1255	EC 105	1951	R
2125	D 407	0702+1	R, Sleeper
		Zürich Hauptbahnhof	
1255	EC 105	0820+1	R, 2, Sleeper

Daily, including holidays, unless otherwise noted
R Reservations required
+1 Arrives next day
1. Change trains in Breclav.
2. Change trains in Vienna (Wien).
3. Change trains in Oberhausen.
4. Change trains in Berlin.
5. Change trains in Cologne (Köln).

Day Excursions from Warsaw

First up is a trip to the second largest city in Poland, **Kraków,** to visit the Old Town and be reminded of (relatively) recent history at Auschwitz. Next, travel to **Gdańsk,** where you can visit the beaches that much of northern Europe summers on and see where the first shots of World War II were fired. The third round-trip takes you to **Lublin,** the gateway to the East, and a university town known for its nightlife.

Other options abound. If you plan to spend longer in Poland, consider white-water rafting in the **Dunajec River Gorge** (south of Kraków), visiting the amazing **Białowieza Forest** (on the Belarusian border), or hiking in the **Tatra Mountains** (on the Slovakian border).

Day Excursion to

Kraków

Poland's Second Largest City

Depart from Warsaw Centralna
Distance by Train: 184 miles (297 km)
Average Train Time: 2 hours 45 minutes
City Dialing Code: 12
Tourist Information Office: Wyspianski Pavilion, Pl. Wszystkich Swietych 2
Tel: 48 12 616 18 86; **Fax:** (0421) 30 800-30
www.cracow.travel
E-mail: simwyspianski@infokrakow.pl
Hours: 0900–1700 daily
Notes: Exit the train station onto Pawia Street, and turn left. Turn right on Planty, and head into the plaza in front of the Juliusz Slowacki Theatre. The Tourist Information Office is in a booth in the plaza.

Kraków is the second largest city in Poland and is traditionally a hub of Polish cultural and academic life. While occupied by the Nazis during World War II, and serving as a regional capital, Kraków sustained relatively minor damage. While under Soviet control, the city was turned into an industrial center, with the significant academic community suppressed. Kraków also was the home of Karol Wojtyła, who in 1978 became the first non-Italian pope in over 500 years, Pope John Paul II.

Kraków's **Old Town** area can easily devour the entire day of your visit. The traditional walled center of the town, it has been an important trading spot since at least the 13th century. The **Main Market Square**, the largest medieval town square in Europe, is the gathering point for the entire city of Kraków. While the daily activity is impressive, the square also hosts numerous festivals throughout the year, including the Nativity Scene Festival in early December, the Juwenalia Student Festival in May, the Lajkonik Parade (recognizing the Tartar horseman that have ravaged Kraków throughout history), and the Festival of Military Bands. The square is surrounded by excellent cafés, pubs, restaurants and shops of all kinds. **St. Mary's Basilica,** which was re-built in the mid-fourteenth century from an even earlier version, is a cornerstone of the square. An impressive building in its own right, it is famous for one of the best preserved works of Gothic sculpture, a massive (almost 30 feet high) altarpiece constructed between 1477 and 1489 by Veit Stoss. A trumpet signal is also played from St. Mary's every hour, which cuts off before completion. The legend says that this is to commemorate a trumpeter who warned of approaching invaders but was killed before he could complete the tune. The church is open 1130–1800 Monday–Saturday, 1400–1600 Sunday, admission 10 zł. The main branch of the **Historical Museum of Kraków** is also located on the square and houses an array of artwork and memorabilia associated with the history of the city. Open 1000–1400 Tuesday–Sunday, admission 10 zł; www.mhk.pl.

The **Royal Road** of Kraków also begins in Old Town. This traditional route through the city has been used for hundreds of years as the procession route for coronations, funerals, and other affairs of state. Pick up the brochure at the tourist office, and follow the route past the remaining gates and fortifications of the old city, in front of churches and colleges before ending at the historic home of the Polish Monarchy, Wawel Hill and Castle. The dominating castle's prime was between the early 10th century and the early 17th century, when the center of Polish power moved to Warsaw. The castle is open 0930–1700, Tuesday–Sunday, admission 18 zł; www.wawel.krakow.pl. Advance reservations are suggested, as the number of visitors is limited.

The **Auschwitz-Birkenau Concentration Camp** is located about 70 km (44 miles) from Kraków. Many Americans do not realize that most of the implementation of Hitler's "final solution" took place outside the borders of Germany proper, in occupied countries. Auschwitz was one of the largest and most notorious concentration camps, and most prisoners never left the site. A visit here is deeply moving and disturbing, and not for the faint of heart. There are two separate camps, and visitors should allow at least 3–4 hours to see the camps and watch the short film showing the initial liberation of the camps. Visitors should take the train from Kraków to Oswiecim (about 110 minutes), and a local bus to the camp, or a bus direct from Kraków to the camp. While admission is free, visitors are required to have a guide at a cost of between 25 and 40 zł. Tours are available in multiple languages.

A brief 25-minute train ride outside of Kraków, in Wieliczka is the **Wieliczka Salt Mine.** For over 700 years, the mine was a major producer of salt for the region. A tour to the mines takes you almost 1,000 feet underground, and includes displays about the history of mining. Most striking are the many sculptures carved into the walls of rock salt. The older ones were completed by miners, but more recent ones were done by contemporary artists, and the carvings appear to have been carved out of granite, rather than salt.

Warsaw—Kraków

DEPART Warsaw	TRAIN NUMBER	ARRIVE Kraków
0650	TLK 1301	0909
0755	EIC 5300	1012
1055	TLK 5322	1328
and later service every two hours until 1950.		

DEPART	TRAIN NUMBER	ARRIVE
Kraków		Warsaw
1542	EIC 35100	1805
1737	EIC 3512	2005
1907	TLK 3112	2250
2008	IR 3106	2300

Distance: 184 miles (297 km)

Day Excursion to

Gdańsk

Markets and Seaports

Depart from Warsaw Centralna
Distance by Train: 201 miles (324 km)
Average Train Time: 4 hours 45 minutes
City Dialing Code: 58
Tourist Information Office: in the Railway Station
Tel: 48 58 721 32 88
www.gdansk.pl
E-mail: itpkp@gdansk4u.pl
Hours: 0900–1900 Monday–Friday, 0900–1700 weekends
Notes: Other tourist information offices located in the airport and near the central market area with similar open times.

Gdańsk, along with Gdynia and Sopot, form the Tricity area, in far northern Poland on the Baltic Sea. The area has a long history, and at times was primarily ethnically German (then known as Danzig) and closely aligned with the German states. Gdańsk is the primary seaport for Poland, and its shipyard was the birthplace of the Solidarity trade union, whose protests eventually hastened the downfall of Communism in eastern Europe. Gdańsk is home to a diversified industrial and educational base, and Sopot is a popular beach area for many northern Europeans.

Gdańsk operates a unique system of audio tour guides. Available for rental at the tourist offices, the small devices contain various facts and histories of historical sites around the area. The information begins playing automatically as you reach the site, and can be paused and continued at your own speed. The devices can be rented for as little as 12 zł, include a map, and are an excellent way to tour the city at your own speed.

Just a few blocks from the train station will find you near the **Dlugi Targ (Long Market)** area, a historical market area in the center of old Gdańsk. The wide open

Warsaw—Gdańsk

DEPART Warsaw	TRAIN NUMBER	ARRIVE Gdańsk	NOTES
0620	EIC 1501	0907	
0820	EIC 3500	1106	

DEPART Gdańsk	TRAIN NUMBER	ARRIVE Warsaw	NOTES
1800	EIC 5102	2040	
1951	TLK 51100	2255	
2332	TLK 83202	0335+1	Sleeper

+1 Arrives next day

Distance: 201 miles (324 km)

plaza contains many shops and restaurants, as well as historical buildings from as far back as the 16th century, although many were damaged during World War II and had to be reconstructed. Of particular interest is **Artus Court,** originally built as a meeting place for aristocrats and traders. It has been restored to look much as it did in the late 1700s, when it was used as a stock exchange, as well as a reception center for important visitors and concert hall. It is now a part of the Gdańsk History Museum. Visit www.mhmg.gda.pl.

If you are interested in military history, consider taking a bus or taxi to **Westerplatte.** This peninsula was the site of the opening of hostilities in World War II, as a German battleship moored close by on a "courtesy visit" to the harbor opened fire on the Polish garrison. German troops then attempted to take the strong point, held by fewer than 240 Polish soliders. While massively outnumbered, these men held out for over a week, in a siege that is still recognized as a source of pride and strength of the country.

The Gdańsk Standard **Tourist Card** (good for 24 or 72 hours), provides discounts for over 240 attractions throughout the Tricity area, with free admission to 24 of these. The MAX Card provides for the same discount, plus free public transportation in the city throughout the validation period. The cards are available at the tourist office, and range from 58 zł for a 72-hour MAX pass to 20 zł for a 24-hour Standard pass.

Located a 1-minute ferry ride across the Motława River from the old port of Gdańsk, the **Polish Maritime Museum** is worth a visit. Its impressive collection includes the earliest port crane anywhere in Europe, originally built in 1444 as both a lift for cargo and ship masts, and as a defensive gate for the city. The first ship built post–World War II in Poland for a Polish owner, the S.S. *Soldek* is preserved as a museum ship here, and there are numerous displays about the maritime history of the region and the Polish people as a whole. Open 1000–1600 Tuesday–Sunday, tickets are 12 zł and include the ferry ride. Visit www.cmm.pl.

Along the coast to the west of Gdańsk, toward the town of Sopot, are some of the most famous beaches in northern Europe. While the water and air temperature are never likely to compare with the Mediterranean, the water quality is excellent and the beach beautiful. If you travel in the summer months, expect to be surrounded by thousands of Europeans from all over Germany and Poland spending their summer vacation on the beach. If you decide to spend the night during high season, be sure to have reservations, as most hotels will be booked solid.

Given the relatively long travel time to Gdańsk, this could easily be a two-day trip, overnighting in Gdańsk before returning to Warsaw. For an excellent overnight experience, consider the **Hotel Willa Litarion,** located in the middle of old Gdańsk and less than a mile from the train station. Prices start around 200 zł a night, which includes breakfast; www.litarion.pl.

Gdańsk could also be your link to Scandinavia, as a ferry is available traveling between Gdańsk and Nynäshamn, just south of Stockholm. The ferry leaves at 1800 from either Gdańsk or Nynäshamn, arriving at 1200 the next day in the opposite city.

Day Excursion to

Lublin

Gateway to the East

Depart from Warsaw Centralna
Distance by Train: 109 miles (175 km)
Average Train Time: 2 hours 20 minutes
City Dialing Code: 81
Tourist Information Office: in the Railway Station
Tel: 81 532 1448
www.lublin.eu or **www.lrot.pl**
E-mail: info@lrot.pl
Hours: 0900–1800 Tuesday–Sunday
Notes: Tourist Office located in the Old Town area. Either take a taxi or the bus (2.40 zł) into Old Town from the train station.

The town of Lublin has long been known as the gateway to the east, located a mere 50 miles from the Ukrainian border. Over a century or more, this location has been both its source of strength and its greatest weakness. The location provided for a great deal of cross-pollination of scientific and social ideas, but also

Warsaw—Lublin

DEPART Warsaw	TRAIN NUMBER	ARRIVE Lublin
0650	TLK 82250	0924
0950	TLK 83104	1204

DEPART Lublin	TRAIN NUMBER	ARRIVE Warsaw
1826	TLK 31104	2045
1945	TLK 31108	2215
2025	TLK 28250	2305

Distance: 109 miles (175 km)

resulted in the town being invaded, and control of Lublin has changed hands many times. Since Poland joined the European Union, the city has become important as a cultural center, with a vibrant theater district, art scene, and a film-making tradition.

First, head into the **Old Town** area. This area remains the heart of the city, with narrow, cobbled streets and historical buildings at every turn. The **Castle of Lublin** and **Chapel of the Holy Trinity,** in the north side of Old Town, are a must visit. The castle dates from sometime in the 12th century and is now home of the Lublin Museum. The castle and the chapel contained within the house have paintings dating to 1418, which contain a unique mix of Western and Eastern Orthodox influences. The castle, which had fallen into disrepair by the 18th century, was rebuilt in the 1820s and went on to serve as a prison by whoever controlled Lublin until 1954, when it was converted to a museum; www.muzeumlubelskie.pl; admission 8.50 zł, open 1000–1600 Tuesday–Sunday. Other sites to visit in Old Town include the **Crown Tribunal** building, **St. Stanislas Dominican Basilica, St. Joseph Church,** and the old gates of **Grodzka** and **Cracow.**

At the east edge of Lublin, and easily accessible by bus (#23 or #156 buses) is the **Majdanek Concentration Camp.** Majdanek, one of a very few Nazi camps located near a city, was also one of the first camps liberated by the Allies, with the Red Army overrunning the camp in July 1944. An estimated 80,000 people, the majority Polish Jews, were killed at Majdanek. At the entrance to the camp is a haunting memorial, a sensation only reinforced as you visit the various buildings at the site and see the display of shoes confiscated from the victims of the camp. Majdanek is open 0900–1800 daily; admission is free, although guided tours are available; www.majdanek.eu.

During the summer, consider the **Tourist Trolleybus,** which leaves daily from Cracow Gate at 1400 and 1530. The tour guide will provide a running commentary on the route, which includes Old Town, Majdanek Concentration Camp, the Cathedral, and other attractions; 5 zł per person.

Lublin is a university town, with 6 state-run universities and several additional private universities. Close to 20 percent of Lublin's population are students, which probably has something to do with Lublin's reputation for having an excellent night-life. The clubs and bars are located both around the Old Town area and closer to the universities, which are concentrated west of Old Town.

When you pick the dates you will be headed to Lublin, check to see what festival will be underway. The city hosts over 20 festivals during the year, including a variety of musical, dance and film festivals, along with a storytelling festival.

PORTUGAL

Visitors to Portugal will find Old World traditions, charm, and culture well preserved. Each province retains its own heritage and individual characteristics, and its history can be traced through its medieval cities and ancient palaces, castles, and cathedrals.

An independent kingdom since 1143, Portugal is one of the oldest nations in Europe. In fact, 10,000-year-old cave paintings have been uncovered in the northern reaches of Portugal and are said to be Europe's greatest outdoor gallery of Stone Age art. In addition, Portugal's museums contain some of the finest collections in the world, reflecting its exposure to rich cultures explored by Portuguese navigators of the 15th and 16th centuries.

But Portugal is more than antiquity. Its geography is diverse, making it a popular holiday destination for travelers from all over the world. You will find wonderful white-sand beaches, crystal-clear mountain streams, and some of the finest golf courses in all of Europe. You'll even find fun and games at glamorous casinos and discos.

Portuguese is the national language, with English and French being the second languages. Though some words are similar to the Spanish language, Portuguese is its own language and not a Spanish dialect. According to the Portuguese National Tourist Office, Portugal is "a vision for the future." For more information about Portugal, contact the Portuguese National Tourist Office of North America: **www.visitportugal.com;** *E-mail:* info@visitportugal.com.

New York: 866 Second Ave. 8th floor, New York, NY 10017. *Tel:* (212) 354-4403 or (800) PORTUGAL; *Fax:* (212) 764-6137

Toronto: 60 Bloor Street, Suite 1005, Toronto, Ontario M4W 3B8, Canada. *Tel:* (416) 921-7376; *Fax:* (416) 921-1353

Banking

Currency: Euro (€)

Exchange rate at press time: €0.90 = U.S. $1.00

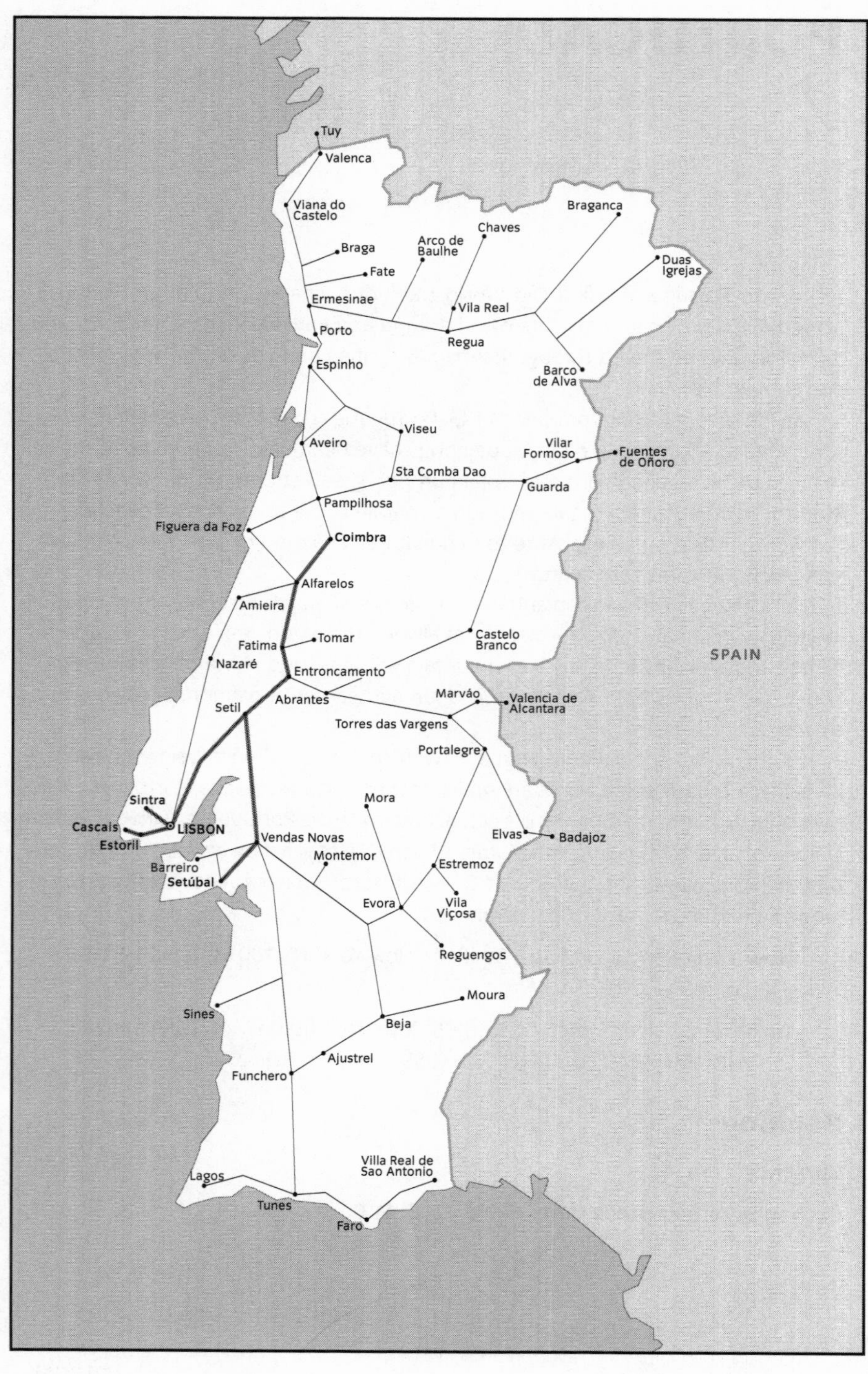

Tuy
Valenca
Viana do Castelo
Braga
Fate
Arco de Baulhe
Chaves
Braganca
Duas Igrejas
Ermesinae
Vila Real
Porto
Regua
Espinho
Barco de Alva
Viseu
Aveiro
Vilar Formoso
Fuentes de Oñoro
Sta Comba Dao
Guarda
Pampilhosa
Figuera da Foz
Coimbra
Alfarelos
Amieira
Fatima
Tomar
Castelo Branco
Nazaré
Entroncamento
SPAIN
Abrantes
Setil
Marváo
Valencia de Alcantara
Torres das Vargens
Portalegre
Mora
Sintra
Cascais
LISBON
Estoril
Vendas Novas
Elvas
Badajoz
Montemor
Barreiro
Setúbal
Estremoz
Evora
Vila Viçosa
Reguengos
Moura
Sines
Beja
Ajustrel
Funchero
Villa Real de Sao Antonio
Lagos
Tunes
Faro

Communications

Country Code: 351

Portugal Telecom operates the public telephones, including pay, Credifone, and TLP Card telephones. Use 00 before the country code to dial internationally from Portugal.

Major Mobile Phone Companies: TMN, Vodafone Portugal, Optimus

Rail Travel in Portugal

Portugal's rail system, **Caminhos de Ferro Portugueses** (CP), offers rail information by telephone. *Tel:* (808) 208 208 from 0700 to 2300 daily. Visit www.cp.pt.

The CP accepts **Eurail passes, the Eurail Portugal–Spain Pass/Portugal–Spain Saverpass,** and the **Eurail Portugal Pass.** Supplements are required on the AVE and Talgo high-speed trains. Children ages 4 through 11 travel at half the adult fare, and children younger than age 4 travel free on all the aforementioned passes.

Eurail Portugal Pass

Within 1 month	ADULT 1st Class
3 days	$179
4 days	$219
6 days	$289

Interregional trains commute through the various regions of Portugal, while CP's InterCity service links about 60 Portuguese cities to Lisbon or Porto. The express **Alfa** service connects Lisbon, Porto, and Braga with four trains in each direction conveying both first- and second-class service. Alfa and InterCity should be reserved at least 24 hours in advance.

Two other international train connections are available between Porto and Vigo (Spain) and between Lisbon and Badajoz (Spain).

Base City: **LISBON** (Lisboa)

www.visitlisboa.com
City Dialing Code: 21

Lisbon (Lisboa), Portugal's largest city, is the capital and primary gateway for visitors from North America. It's also the center of the country's rail network and the major industrial and commercial area.

Built on the terraced sides of the hills overlooking the harbor, languid Lisbon is an excellent gateway to the Iberian Peninsula and a good base for rail travel throughout Portugal.

Arriving by Air

Lisbon International Airport (Portela), 5 miles north of Lisbon. *Tel:* 21 841 3500; www.ana-aeroportos.pt.

- **Airport–City Links:** Metro (Red Line) to city center and Oriente Station runs every 5 to 10 minutes 0745–2015. Fare: €4.00, valid one day on all buses, trams, and city elevators (€6.00 for 2 way valid for 24 hrs). **City bus** lines 22, 44, 45, 83, 208, 705, and 745 are operated by CARRIS. Fare: €1.40. **Express Estoril-Cascais** bus operates hourly. Fare: €8.00.
- **Taxi fare** from the airport to the city center (journey time: 15 to 20 minutes) averages about €20 to €30, depending on your destination and how much luggage you have. Taxis are metered; a tip is appreciated. "Taxi Voucher," a system of prepaid travel vouchers for the number of zones covered by the journey, may be purchased in the Arrivals Terminal (*Tel:* 21 845 0660).
- Tourist information at the airport, *Tel:* 351 218 413 700. *Hours:* 0700–0000 daily. Look for the sign ASSOCIACÃO DE TURISMO DE LISBOA.

Arriving by Train

Lisbon has four stations and a ferryboat terminal and is the main gateway to other cities in Portugal. **Santa Apolonia Station** is Lisbon's international link and the western terminus of most European rail traffic. However, you can also arrive in Lisbon at the "Terreiro do Paço" south railway station, with the train departing from Vila Real St. Antónia to Barreiro (and then the ferry connection) if you come from Seville (Spain).

- **Money exchange** is on the left side as you exit from the trains, beyond Porta (Gate) 47.
- **Rail information** (CP) **and tourist information:** Turn to the right as you exit from the trains and walk past ticket window No. 1. *Hours:* 0900–2200.
- **Rail pass validation:** Porta (Gate) 47. *Hours:* 0800–1800 daily. Buses No. 9, 39, and 46 run from Santa Apolonia Station to the Rossio Station in downtown Lisbon. The fare may be minimal, but buses frequently are crowded, making it rather difficult for you and your suitcase to board the same bus at the same time. Because taxi fares are reasonable and metered, leave your forays on Lisbon's public transportation system for when your luggage is safely stowed in your hotel room.

Rossio Station, at Praça do Rossio (Rossio Square), is located in the heart of Lisbon in a lovely 19th-century Neo-Gothic building. It is on the immediate left of the Teatro Nacional D. Maria II (National Theater). Rossio Station serves as the commuter station to locations west of Lisbon (from Cacem Station to Figueira da Foz). Trains depart for Sintra on Tracks 4 and 5 every 20 minutes. Rossio Station, closed for three years for tunnel work, has now reopened, making the day excursion to Sintra much more convenient.

Campolide Station, the first station past Rossio, is the stop for the Alcantara commuter to Cascais or for travel to Azambuja.

Cais do Sodré Station is where trains from Estoril and Cascais terminate.

Terreiro do Paço Station is the ferryboat terminal for crossings to Barreiro Station on the east bank of the Tagus River. From Barreiro trains depart for cities in the Algarve.

Tourist Information/Hotel Reservations

Visit www.visitlisboa.com.

Available in rail stations, at Praça dos Restauradores in the Palácio Foz building (*Tel:* 21 03 12700; *Hours:* 0900–2000 daily); or at the Lisbon Airport and some hotels.

To reach Palácio Foz, take a taxi or bus No. 9, 46, or 39 to Praça dos Restauradores. It is opposite the post office, near Rossio Station. Palácio Foz (Foz Palace) has three main doors. Enter the one on the left marked TURISMO.

Hotel reservations can be made at the rail stations' combined train and tourist information offices.

Getting Around in Lisbon

Electric, cable car–like trams provide inexpensive and enjoyable transport to many parts of the city. Historic Belém, for instance, can be reached via Tram 15—an alternative to taking the train from Cais do Sodré Station.

Of super value is the **Lisboa Card,** which provides unlimited travel on the public transportation system (CARRIS), including buses, trams, and the recently remodeled metro (underground) system; free entry to 80 museums, monuments, and other attractions that normally charge admission; and discounts at certain shops. It is truly your "password" to the city.

The Lisboa Card is available at the Central Office, at Palácio Foz; at Jerónimos Monastery, Praça do Imperio; at the National Museum of Ancient Art, Rua das Janelas Verdes; Lisbon Airport, and at various CARRIS offices.

One-day Lisboa Card, €18.50; 48-hour card, €31.50; 72-hour card, €39.00.

Other value cards also may be purchased at the tourist information offices, including:

- The "Lisboa Restaurant Card," which offers no less than 10 percent discount on your bill at more than 40 restaurants within a 72-hour validity period. €6.15 single, €8.10 double (2 persons), €10.75 family (2 adults and 2 children age 14 and younger).
- The "Lisboa Shopping Card," which provides 5 to 20 percent discount at more than 200 shops. Valid for 24 hours, €3.70; 72 hours, €5.80.

Attractions/Tours

Tourist offices or your hotel can arrange for a sightseeing tour of Lisbon. Or ask the tourist office for the guide booklet *Lisboa Step by Step*, purchase a Lisboa Card, and conduct your own tour. Highlights of any tour will include the 16th-century **Jerónimos Monastery** and the **Tower of Belém** in the Belém district. Lisbon's more modern side can be seen by visiting the **Discoveries Monument** (Centro Cultural das Descobertas), inaugurated in 1960. Another symbol of Lisbon is the **25 de April Bridge** spanning the Tagus River, which is equal to the Golden Gate Bridge of San Fransisco in its structural beauty.

Completed for Expo '98, Lisbon's **Vasco da Gama Bridge** is a massive engineering feat. The bridge is 17 kilometers long—making it the longest bridge in Europe—1 kilometer longer than the one between Sweden and Denmark. Besides providing another modern symbol of Lisbon, it provides much-needed relief of traffic congestion crossing the Tagus River, especially during the summer. The **Vasco da Gama Steel Tower** (the tallest building in Portugal) and the impressive **Lisboa Oceanarium** contribute to the east side's modern attractions.

Lisbon has three distinct districts—the shopping areas clustered around **Rossio, Baixa,** and **Chiado;** the more ancient areas, such as the Moorish quarter **Alfama** and **Castelo;** and the "new Lisbon," with post-modern high-rise structures, **Amoreiras,** stretching out to the airport and to the north. Just five minutes from the airport is the Gare Intermodal de Lisboa multistation complex, also known as Oriental Station, which serves long-distance and suburban trains, the underground railway system, a bus and motor coach terminal, and a taxi stop. A day can easily be spent in any one of Lisbon's districts.

Train Connections to Other Base Cities from Lisbon (Lisboa)

DEPART Santa Apolonia	TRAIN NUMBER	ARRIVE	NOTES
		Madrid Chamartin	
2125	HOT 335	0840+1	R, 1, Sleeper
		Paris Gare Montparnasse	
2125	H 310/TGV 8542	1840+1	R, 2, Sleeper

Daily
R Reservations required
+1 Arrives next day
1. Hotel train.
2. Change in Hendaye.

Of particular interest to Western visitors is the Alfama district, which suffered the least damage during the Great Lisbon Earthquake of 1755 and has thereby been able to preserve much of its old facade and narrow, winding cobblestone streets. **St. George's Castle** offers a splendid view of the city. The tourist office has several excellent illustrated brochures describing Lisbon, one of which lists walking tours *From the Castle to Alfama via Mouraria*, where examples of Moorish and medieval architecture prevail. A city map is also available.

Spend at least one evening in Lisbon's famous nightlife district—**Bairro Alto.** It can be reached via the Elevador da Gloria, which operates from the west side of the Praça dos Restauradores at Calcada da Gloria. Dine in typical Portuguese restaurants/music bars, called "Fado houses," and listen to ***Fado*** (meaning "fate")—the plaintive, nostalgic, dramatic music of the *fadista* (Fado singer) that is unique to the Portuguese. Lisbon has its own type of Fado, which is considered to be more emotional and dramatic than that performed elsewhere.

Such Fado establishments are abundant in Lisbon, particularly in the Alfama and Bairro Alto districts. One of our favorites is **Adega Mesquita** at Rua Diário de Notícias, No. 107. Phone ahead for reservations: *Tel:* 21 321 92 80; *Fax:* 21 346 71 31; *E-mail:* adegamesquita@hed-web.com.

In Alfama on Largo do Chafariz de Dentro, visit **Casa do Fado e da Guitarra Portuguesa,** the Fado museum. According to the tourist office, "It gives an insight and enables one to better understand the development, identity, and soul of this incomparable form of urban musical expression that was born in Lisbon in the 19th century." *Hours:* 1000–1800 daily (last entry at 1730), closed Monday. *Tel:* 21 882 34 70. Visit www.museudofado.pt.

Day Excursions

Cascais and **Estoril,** resort towns along the beautiful beaches of Costa do Estoril, are frequented by celebrities, royalty, and just plain folk. **Coimbra** reveals Portugal's academic nature. This fine old university town was at one time the capital of Portugal. **Setúbal** is a city of beautiful beaches, hillside castles, and excellent seafood. Castle buffs and romantics will enjoy **Sintra,** with its ancient castles and nearby Cape Roca, the westernmost point of Europe.

Day Excursion to

Cascais and Estoril

Lisbon's Riviera

Depart from Lisbon Cais do Sodré Station
Distance by Train: 16 miles (26 km)
Average Train Time: 30 minutes
City Dialing Code: 21
Tourist Information Office: Avenida Clotilde, Edificio, Centro du Congressos, 3°A 2765-211-Estoril
Tel: 351214647570; **Fax:** 351214647576
www.estoril-portugal.com
E-mail: info@tourismoestoril.com
Hours: 0900–1900 Monday–Saturday, 1000–1800 Sunday

Portugal boasts miles and miles of sun-drenched, white-sand beaches. Probably the most famous stretch lies just to the west of Lisbon along the Costa do Estoril. Here the two resort towns of Cascais and Estoril offer a wide variety of scenes to suit everyone's tastes.

We recommend you make **Costa do Estoril** your first stop on your visit to this coastal area because Estoril is two stops before Cascais, which is the end of the rail line. Estoril has long been famous as a chic resort for royalty and a playground for the rich and famous. Besides the white-sand beach with its excellent facilities and seawater pool, the beautifully landscaped **Casino complex** of gaming rooms, restaurants, bars, and art gallery is a major attraction. But new, moderately priced hotels now make Estoril a major attraction for everyone.

Those who are sports minded can enjoy championship 18-hole golf courses that offer temporary memberships. **The Estoril Golf Course,** with its splendid seascape, has been home to the Portuguese Open. Tennis, horseback riding, and sailing are also available.

Cascais, which is only four minutes beyond Estoril, maintains a slightly lower-key atmosphere than its chic neighbor. Its beaches are smaller but more intimate. Reflecting the traditions of its fishing-village past, Cascais's Wednesday-morning and first and third Sunday market is well worth the trip from Lisbon. Locals in traditional garb hawk everything imaginable. Farmers' wives, suspicious of supermarket packaging, can be seen scrutinizing live chickens.

To reach the marketplace, bear to the right around the plaza in front of the rail station and continue to the right onto Avenue 25 de April. Two short blocks farther, and you will see the market—probably hear it, too. Bring your own market basket.

Worth visiting are the **Castro Guimarães Museum,** the **Sea Museum, Church of Cascais,** and **Marechal Carmona Park.**

Some rail travelers base themselves in a local resort hotel in or near Cascais or Estoril and then make day excursions into Lisbon for sightseeing or for continuing on with other day excursions. The fast and frequent rail service and the abundance of hotels to fit any budget make this concept a feasible one. The cosmopolitan nightlife is worth the stay. Cabarets, theaters, restaurants, and discotheques are all over the area. The **Estoril Casino** is the largest in Europe. *Hours:* 1500–0300 daily. *Tel:* 21 466 77 00. Visit www.casino-estoril.pt.

Lisbon (Lisboa)—Estoril—Cascais

Trains depart Lisbon's Cais do Sodré Station at 0530, 0600, then 3–5 trains per hour depart until 2130, and then every 30 minutes 2200–0130. Two to three trains per hour depart on weekends between 0530 and 0130.

Journey time:

Lisbon–Estoril, 28–33 minutes

Lisbon–Cascais, 32–40 minutes

Distance: 16 miles (26 km)

Day Excursion to

Coimbra

University Town

Depart from Lisbon Santa Apolonia Station
Distance by Train: 135 miles (218 km)
Average Train Time: 2 hours
City Dialing Code: 39
Tourist Information Office: Largo Toll, 3000–337 Coimbra
Tel: 239 488 120; **Fax:** 239 488 129
www.turismo-centro.pt
E-mail: info.coimbra@turismodocentro.pt
Hours: Summer (June–September): 0900–2000 Monday–Friday, 0900–1800 Saturday–Sunday; Winter (January–April and September–December): 0900–1800 Monday–Friday, 0930–1230 and 1330–1730 Saturday–Sunday
Notes: Trains from Lisbon stop at the Coimbra B Station, a short distance north of the city center. Either take a taxi to Largo da Portagem, or take a shuttle train into the main station. The tourist office is at the approach to the great bridge spanning the Mondego River. If you take the shuttle to the main station, walk 4 blocks away from the station, upstream along the river, until you come to the bridge approach.

Coimbra is one of Portugal's most charming cities, uniquely blending the old and the new. Site of the oldest university in Portugal, its ancient buildings seem to blend perfectly with the modern spirit of its students. Founded in 1290 in Lisbon, the university was transferred to its current site in 1537 to compensate for moving Portugal's capital from Coimbra to Lisbon.

Coimbra University sits on a hilltop overlooking the river. In keeping with tradition, many students wear black suits and capes, marked with ribbons in tones that denote their scholarship.

There is an air of antiquity surrounding Coimbra. It is the scene of the largest Roman archaeological site in Portugal. Coimbra's cathedral is said to be the finest Romanesque building in Portugal. Gothic tombs and an art collection are housed in this 12th-century monument.

An unusual attraction for "children" of all ages is the **Portugal dos Pequeninos** (Portugal of the Little Ones), in which you will find a miniaturized version of architectural styles of continental Portugal, Coimbra, Portuguese monuments, insular Portugal, and its overseas territories.

In the city center, you can visit the **monastery of the Holy Cross, Santa Cruz,** constructed in the 12th century. Later additions include a charming Renaissance sacristy and a magnificently carved facade. A pictorial record of the explorer Vasco da Gama's voyages adorns the choir loft.

Lisbon (Lisboa)—Coimbra

DEPART	TRAIN NUMBER	ARRIVE	NOTES
Santa Apolonia		Coimbra B (Junction)	
0730	IC 521	0928	M–Sa
0830	IC 511	1037	
0930	IC 721	1131	
1130	IC 523	1330	
1330	IC 513	1537	

DEPART	TRAIN NUMBER	ARRIVE	NOTES
Coimbra B (Junction)		Santa Apolonia	
1357	IC 522	1600	
1521	IC 512	1730	
1557	IC 722	1800	
1746	IC 126	1930	
1846	IC 128	2040	Exc. Sa
2021	IC 514	2230	
2146	AP 136	2330	Exc. Sa

Daily, unless otherwise noted
Reservations required on all trains
Distance: 135 miles (218 km)

Day Excursion to

Setúbal

Seaside and Castles

Depart from Lisbon Terreiro do Paço Ferry Terminal and Barreiro Station
Distance by Train: 18 miles (29 km) from Barreiro
Average Train Time: 35 minutes
City Dialing Code: 265
Tourist Information Office: Região de Turismo de Setúbal, Travessa Frei Gaspar, 10, Apartado 73, 2901 Setúbal
Tel: 265 539 120; **Fax:** 265 539 128
www.turismolisboavaledotejo.pt
E-mail: deleg.setubal@turismolisboavaledotejo.pt
Hours: 0900–1230 and 1400–1900 Monday and Saturday, 0900–1900 Tuesday–Friday, 0900–1230 Sunday
Town Hall Tourist Information: Praca do Quebedo; *Tel:* 265 534 222
Hours: 0900–1230 and 1400–1730 Monday–Friday

Notes: Take a taxi from the station to the regional tourist office (Região de Turismo de Setúbal) or to the tourist office in the Town Hall, located across from the park, Praca do Quebedo.

A day excursion to **Setúbal** begins at Lisbon's Terreiro do Paço Ferry Terminal with a 25-minute ferryboat ride across the Tagus River to Barreiro Station, where you board a southbound train to Setúbal. You may cross the 25 de April Bridge by train until Fogueteiro and board a bus to Setúbal or just ride the bus over both bridges.

Although Setúbal is Portugal's third-largest city, its location on the estuary of the Sado River provides a more restful, rural-type atmosphere. It can best be enjoyed from **Saint Philip's Castle,** which overlooks Setúbal from its highest point. The 16th-century castle was converted into a *pousada* (inn, or resting place), and it commands an impressive view of both land and sea. A local taxi can take you there. It's a perfect spot for a lunch in its fine restaurant or for an overnight stay.

Setúbal has a remarkable assemblage of monuments and grand old buildings. The **Church of Jesus** is said to be one of the most beautiful small churches ever built. Next door, the Town Museum displays a priceless collection of old masters. There are also a Maritime Museum and the Bocage Monument, which honors the city's great poet.

About 5 or 6 miles from Setúbal at the nearby seaport Sesimbra, the **Pousada do Castelo de Palmela** (Palmela Castle) offers a fantastic view of the surrounding countryside from high atop a hillside. Again, the best way to get there is via taxi.

Lisbon (Lisboa)—Setúbal

FERRY FROM	ARRIVE	DEPART	TRAIN NUMBER	ARRIVE
Lisbon Terreiro Do Paço Dock	Barreiro Pier	Barreiro Station		Setúbal Station
0715	0735	0758	R 17209	0828
0855	0915	0925	R 17215	0955

plus departures from Terreiro do Paço dock at 0615, 0745, 0805, 0955, and 1055 M–F.

DEPART	TRAIN NUMBER	ARRIVE	DEPART	ARRIVE
Setúbal Station		Barreiro Station	Barreiro Pier	Lisbon Terreiro do Paço Dock
1548	R 17232	1618	1630	1650
1718	R 17236	1748	1800	1820

plus hourly local service (2nd class) Setúbal–Barreiro Station at 48 minutes past each hour until 2348, and at 18 minutes past each hour until 1918 M–F.

Daily

Distance: 18 miles (29 km) from Barreiro

Day Excursion to

Sintra

Mountain Peaks and Palaces

Depart from Santa Apolonia Station
Distance by Train: 17 miles (28 km)
Average Train Time: 45 minutes
City Dialing Code: 21
Tourist Information Office: Praca da Republica 23, 2710–616 Sintra
Tel: 21 09 91 882; **Fax:** 916 355 799
www.cm-sintra.pt
E-mail: dtur@cm-sintra.pt
Hours: June–September: 0900–2000 daily; October–May: 0900–1800 daily (except January 1, Easter, May 1, and Christmas)
Notes: The main tourist office is about 1 kilometer from the rail station. Reach it by taxi or by boarding the bus Sintra Line No. 433, which leaves from near the station (at Correnteza). The bus stops a short distance from the National Palace of Sintra and the main tourist office. On foot, it is an interesting 15-minute walk.

According to the Sintra tourist information office, "Sintra is a location which is not to be talked about, its history discussed, or its countryside described—it is a location to be felt." **Sintra,** with its ancient castles and palaces towering above the countryside, is the former home of Portuguese kings. Surrounded by mountains and close by **Cape Roca,** the westernmost point of continental Europe "where the land ends and the sea begins," its beauty is unparalleled. This is the place Lord Byron termed "a glorious Eden," and it's all only 45 minutes from Lisbon by train.

There is public transportation to most of the places of tourist interest, except to the Gardens of Monserrate. Taxis and horse-drawn carriages are also available. Taxis do not have meters, but the fare usually includes a fixed amount of time to complete your sightseeing.

You'll probably want to visit the exquisite **Sintra National Palace** (Paço Real or Palácio da Vila) first. *Hours:* 0930–1730 (until 1900 May–September) daily, except closed on Wednesday, and there are no guides. There is a nominal admission charge (€9.50) to the palace grounds. Inside, it possesses the most extensive collection of *Mudejar azulejos*—colored glazed tiles—in the world.

Pena Palace's commanding position from the highest peak in the area makes it well worth the visit. *Tel:* 21 910 53 40; *Fax:* 21 910 53 41. *Hours:* October–March 1000–1800 daily, April–September 0945–1900 daily. Admission to the grounds, €7.50, Palace tours €14. Hungry? Try Pena Palace's 100-seat restaurant offering fine traditional and contemporary Portuguese cuisine.

The **Queluz Palace** captures the style of Versailles but on a smaller scale. It houses a gourmet restaurant in its former kitchen area. *Hours:* 0900–1800 daily, except closed Tuesday.

For a different experience, visit **Sintra Toy Museum** (*Hours:* 1000–1800 Tuesday–Sunday). Joao Arbués Moreira believed one could better understand the history of humankind through toys. He began his toy collection at the age of 14 with toys from his grandparents, parents, and others. As he acquired money, he began purchasing more toys. He spent a lifetime researching their manufacture and history and collected more than 20,000 different toys. You, too, can view this extraordinary collection at the Museu do Brinquedo, the Toy Museum, located in the old Sintra Fireman's Headquarters. *Tel:* 21 924 21 71; www.museu-do-brinquedo.pt. There's a toy restoration workshop, and the gift shop is a great place to purchase that special memento. Admission €5.00 adults, €3.00 children.

Lisbon (Lisboa)—Sintra

Trains run from Lisbon Rossio Station 2–4 times an hour, from 0620 to 0015.

Trains return to Lisbon Rossio Station 2–3 times an hour, from 0606 to 2306.

Trips average 39 minutes, distance: 17 mi (28 km)

SPAIN

Spain is a delightful dichotomy—futuristic in many ways, yet respectful of its rich history and tradition. Spain is among the most popular tourist destinations in the world.

From the *delicato* music of flamenco to swashbuckling matadors, Spain's culture and tradition are as widely varied as its geography. Flamenco is a genuine southern Spanish art form influenced by diverse cultures throughout Spain's history, including the Gypsies, the legendary Tartessos, and the Muslims.

Spain shares the Iberian Peninsula with its neighbor to the west, Portugal. France and the tiny country of Andorra lie to the north. Castilian Spanish is spoken throughout Spain, but Catalan, Valencian, Basque, and Galician are still spoken in their respective autonomous regions.

One social custom that visitors will notice immediately is that Spaniards get up later in the morning and usually stay out later at night than other Europeans. If you want to dance until dawn, you're visiting the right country. The nightlife in Spain is intensely zealous, with bars and discotheques remaining open until the wee hours of the morning, especially in the larger, more cosmopolitan cities of Barcelona and Madrid.

Arriving from North America, our base city Madrid is the primary gateway, with Barcelona being second. During summer, however, there are some direct flights to Malaga on the Mediterranean Sea.

For more information about Spain, contact the Tourist Offices of Spain in North America (**www.okspain.org**).

Chicago: 845 North Michigan Avenue, Suite 915 East, Water Tower Place, Chicago, IL 60611. *Tel:* (312) 642-1992; *Fax:* (312) 642-9817; *E-mail:* chicago@tourspain.es

Los Angeles: San Vicente Plaza Building, 8383 Wilshire Boulevard, Suite 960, Beverly Hills, CA 90211. *Tel:* (323) 658-7188; *Fax:* (323) 658-1061; *E-mail:* losangeles@tourspain.es

New York: 60 East 42nd Street, Suite 5300 (53rd Floor), New York, NY 10165-0039. *Tel:* (212) 265-8822; *Fax:* (212) 265-8864; *E-mail:* oetny@tourspain.es

Miami: 2655 LeJeun Rd., Suite 605, Coral Gables, FL 33134 *Tel:* (305) 476-1966; *Fax:* (305) 476-1964; *E-mail:* oetmiami@tourspain.es

FRANCE
PORTUGAL
MOROCCO
El Ferrol
La Coruña
Santiago de Compostello
Pontevedra
Viga
Tuy
Valenca
Lugo
Monforte
Orense
Avilés
Gijon
Oviedo
Leon
Astorga
Santander
Palencia
Venta de Baños
Valladolid
Zamora
Medina del Campo
Salamanca
Segovia
Vilar Formoso
Fuente
Fuentes de Oñoro
Avila
El Escorial
Villalba
Burgos
Arenda de Duero
Bilbao
Mirando de Ebro
Irun
San Sebastian
Hendaye
Alsana
Vitoria
Pamplona
Logrono
Castajón
Soria
Coscurita
Torralba
Ariza
Calatayud
Guadalajara
MADRID
Aranjuez
Algodar
Toledo
Castillejo
Cuenca
Plasencia
Cáceres
Marvão
Valencia de Alcantara'
Mérida
Elvas
Badajoz
Zafra
Huelva
Sevilla
Utrera
Cadiz
Algeciras
Ciudad Real
Cordoba
Campo Real
La Roca
Bobadilla
Malaga
Granada
Almeria
Guadix
Espeluy
Baeza
Jaen
Alcàzar
Manzanares
Albacete
Chinchilla
La Encina
Alicante
Murcia
Cartagena
Valencia
Jativa
Gandia
Alcoy
Castellon
Teruel
Caminreal
Tortosa
Pau
Canfranc
Ayerbe
Huesca
Tardiente
Zuera
Zaragoza
Pueblo de Hijar
Pobla de Segur
Lleida
Roda
Tarragona
St. Vicente
Sitges
BARCELONA
Blanes
Massanet
Gerona
Figueras
Port Bou
Cerbére
Ax-les-Thermes
Font Romeu
La Tour de Carol
Puigcerda

Toronto: 2 Bloor Street West, Suite 3402, Toronto, Ontario M4W 3E2, Canada. *Tel:* (416) 961-3131; *Fax:* (416) 961-1992; www.tourspain.toronto.on.ca; *E-mail:* toronto@tourspain.es

Other quality Internet sites include **www.tourspain.es** and **www.idealspain.com.**

Banking

Currency: Euro (€)

Exchange rate at press time: €0.90 = U.S. $1.00

Hours: 0900–1400 Monday–Friday, with some open 0900–1430 Saturday

Credit and ATM transfers at machines are the best exchange rate, since no commission is charged.

Communications

Country Code: 34

Major Mobile Phone Companies: Movistar, Vodafone, Orange, Yoigo

Public telephones are available most everywhere in Spain; they offer instructions in English and may be used to call most parts of the world. Some phones are equipped to take credit cards. Since calling from Spain to America is about 10 times more expensive than calling from America to Spain, it is advisable to access your American calling-card connection.

When in Spain, dial 00 to telephone outside of Spain. When calling Spain from abroad, include Spain's country code. It is then necessary to dial the provincial codes for each province. When calling within Spain, the provincial codes begin with 9.

Some provincial codes include Alicante, 96; Avila, 920; Barcelona, 93; Burgos, 947; Cordoba, 957; Madrid, 91; Malaga, 95; Seville, 95; Toledo, 925; and Valencia, 96.

Rail Travel in Spain

With **RENFE** (Red Nacional de Ferrocarriles Españoles, or Spanish National Railways), the trains in Spain run mainly on time—98 percent on time. Visit www.renfe.es. RENFE accepts the variety of Eurail passes, the **Eurail Portugal–Spain Pass, Eurail Portugal–Spain Saverpass,** and **Eurail Spain Pass,** but it deviates from the basic rail pass concept in that certain trains, such as AVE (*Alta Velocidad Espanola,* or Spanish High Speed) trains and Talgos operating on high-speed lines, are not included, but rail pass holders do receive substantial discounts. (Please see the Appendix for Eurail Portugal–Spain Pass and other Eurail products prices.) Special sightseeing/tour trains such as ***Al Andalus*** and the narrow-gauge FEVE are not included on the rail passes either, but tickets may be purchased separately.

Travel bonuses for holders of a Spanish Eurail pass include:

- 20 percent discount on ferry crossings operated by Grimaldi Ferries: Barcelona to Livorno, Cititavecchi, Savona and Porto Torres
- 20 percent discount on Baleria lines: Barcelona–Palma de Mallorca, Ciutadella, Ibiza, Mahon, and others
- 50 percent discount on FGC lines, including rack railways in Nuria and Montserrat, and cable lines in Gelida and Montserrat

The Spain Pass may be purchased for a minimum of three days of unlimited rail travel in Spain within a two-month period.

Eurail Spain Pass

Within 2 months	ADULT 1st Class	ADULT 2nd Class
3 days	$315	$253
4 days	$359	$289
5 days	$404	$324
6 days	$451	$362
7 days	$499	$400
8 days	$545	$437
9 days	$596	$477
10 days	$641	$514

The AVE and Talgo 200 trains require additional supplements. Children age 4–11 travel half price.

Not to be outdone by French high-speed TGVs and Germany's ICEs, RENFE's sleek **AVEs** are derivations of the French TGV (*train à grand vitesse*, or train of great speed) *Atlantique*. Dynamic RENFE has been "on the move" since the first AVEs cruised into service as the main rail link between Madrid and Seville due to the opening of the International Exposition of Seville—Expo 1992. Via AVE, the Madrid to Seville trip can be done in only 2 hours and 15 minutes.

Reservations for AVE trains are required. Choose Turista, Preferente, or Club Class. All three classes include television sets with individual earphones and four music channels, family areas with games for kids, facilities for the disabled, telephones, cafeteria, and a beverage machine. Club and Preferente Classes also include access to AVE club lounges, newspapers, and magazines. In-seat food/ beverage service is provided only in Club Class.

Ultramodern Talgo 200 trains link Madrid and Malaga in a little more than four hours. These gauge-changing, high-speed trains also have significantly reduced the travel time between Madrid and Cadiz/Huelva.

 *Remember—reservations are **required** on Spanish trains.*

The attractive blue and white **Euromed** (*Velocidad Alta Mediterranea* or Mediterranean High Speed) trains provide services on the Barcelona–Valencia–Alicante route with a cruising speed of 200 km/hour. These trains offer two classes of service—Preferente and Turista.

Base City: **BARCELONA**

www.barcelonaturisme.com
www.bcn.es
City Dialing Code: 93

Barcelona as it is today, the **New Barcelona,** was created only in 1874 by joining 27 separate municipalities. It has become Spain's most prosperous port and has developed a thriving industrial complex. The center of this new metropolitan area is the **Plaça de Catalunya,** a square rimmed with trees and highlighted by sculptures and fountains—and an abundance of pigeons. This square is where Old and New Barcelona meet.

Founded in ancient times by the Phoenicians and occupied by the Romans, **Old Barcelona** is composed of three districts: Barri Gótic, or the Gothic Quarter, and the Ribera and Raval districts. A visit to the History Museum in Plaça del Rei square provides insight to Barcelona's rich and ancient past.

At the other end of the spectrum, the World Trade Center (WTC) complex provides insight to Barcelona's promising future. According to the Tourist Office of Spain, the WTC Association (an organization of nearly 300 centers in almost 100 countries) was created "to stimulate world trade and to increase cultural exchange and the development of nations." This stunning waterfront complex solidifies Barcelona's position as a major portal to European and Mediterranean markets.

Arriving by Air

Barcelona Airport (*Tel:* 902 404 704; *Fax:* 93 478 4736; Email: bcninfofi@aena.es; www.aena-aeropuertos.es) is about 8 miles (13 km) from the city. Transportation to and from is easily available and inexpensive. Foreign currency exchange and ATMs are available in both Terminals A and B. Look for signs ARGENTARIA or LA CAIXA. Tourist information is also available in both terminals from 0900 to 2100 daily.

- **Airport–City Links:** Cercanias/Rodalie local line No. 1 **trains** connect travelers to Barcelona Sants Station in 17 minutes and depart every half hour from the airport 0530 to 2330 daily. The station is connected to the airport terminals by moving walkways. Follow the pictograms. Trains depart from track No. 1 in Barcelona Sants Station every half hour to the airport; Fare: €4.10 Monday through Friday; €4.00 weekends and holidays.

  The **Aerobus** service departs the airport every 10 minutes 0600 to 0105 Monday through Friday and 0630 to 0000 on weekends and holidays. Time en route is about 30 minutes. It stops at all three terminals on the way to and from Plaça de Catalunya. Aerobuses are equipped to handle wheelchairs. Fare: €5.90 one-way, €10.20 round-trip.

Approximate **taxi** fare from the airport to city center is €20–€30, depending on destination.

Arriving by Train

Barcelona Sants Station (Estacio de Sants), Plaça Països Catalans

The Sants Station is the center of Barcelona's transportation system. Most bus lines, all metro lines (through transfers), and both regional and long-distance trains are available here. The high-speed **Euromed** trains to Alicante, Castellón, Tarragona, and Valencia depart from the Sants Station, as well as direct trains to Montpellier for connections to Paris and Geneva on TGVs (French high-speed trains).

Twelve tracks are located beneath the main floor of the station, accessible by escalators or elevators. TV screens and a large display above the ticket windows show which trains leave from which platforms. There is a red desk, marked with an **M,** where you can purchase tickets for both the metro and bus systems. They can also provide metro and bus system maps.

- **Train information:** *Tel:* 902 920 320—24 hours, RENFE (Spain's national rail company) help line; *Tel:* 90 2240 505—passengers with disabilities; www.renfe.es. This easy-to-use website provides timetables for all travel originating in Spain (in English and Spanish).
- **Seat/sleeper reservations:** For same-day travel, go to the windows marked VENTA IMMEDIATE, which are on the right side of the station from the front entrance. For later travel, go to the VENTA ANTICIPADA windows on the left-hand side of the station. Usually, you need to take a number from the machine and watch for your number to appear on the digital display board. It will also indicate which window number you should go to. There are usually lines. We suggest you make your reservation as far in advance of your expected departure date as possible. **Rail pass validation** can be made at any of these windows.
- **Money exchange** may be made at the "kiosk" on the ground-floor level in the center of the station. *Hours:* 0800–2100 daily. There are also numerous ATMs scattered throughout the station—four of which are opposite the VENTA ANTICIPADA windows.
- **Tourist information** is available in the center of the station. For more extensive information and services, go to the one located at 17 Plaça de Catalunya.

Other RENFE stations include Barcelona França, Passeig de Gràcia, Plaça de Catalunya, Clot-Arago, and Sant Andreu Comtal. All of the day excursions detailed in this edition, however, may be visited by departing from the Sants Station.

Tourist Information/Hotel Reservations

- *Turisme de Barcelona Tourist Information Offices:*

  Plaça de Catalunya, 17 Pl. (basement)
  National calls: *Tel:* 906 301 282 (€0.39/minute)
  International calls: *Tel:* +34 93 285 3834
  Hours: 0930–2130 daily; closed January 1 and December 25
  www.barcelonaturisme.com
  E-mail: info@barcelonaturisme.com
  Located below street level

  Plaça Sant Jaume, 1
  Hours: 0830–2030 Monday–Friday, 0900–1900 Saturday, 0900–1400 Sunday/holidays

The tourist information offices can provide money exchange and hotel information and bookings. They also sell tickets for Barcelona Walking Tours, Bus Turístic, the theater, and other entertainment; they sell the Barcelona Card and city transport and phone cards; and they provide Internet service for a fee. In the summer, tourism officials in red shirts, known as the "Red Jackets," patrol the Las Ramblas and Barri Gótic areas, providing maps and information.

Getting Around in Barcelona

Transportation in and around Barcelona is plentiful and easy to use (www.tmb.net). The Barcelona Metro has six lines covering more than 86 kilometers and includes 123 stations. Trains run 0500 to 0000 Monday through Thursday, 0500 to 0200 Friday and Saturday, and 0500 to 0000 Sunday. Bus services generally run 0500 to 2200, although there is a special *Nitbus* (night bus) that runs 1000 to 0400. The price for a single bus or metro ticket is €2.15. A good deal is the 10-trip package for €10.30, which can be used on the bus and the metro, and it's transferable. Unlimited transfers can be made within 1 hour and 15 minutes. A two-day Travel Card for both metro and bus is €14.00; three-day, €20.00; four-day, €25.50; and five-day, €30.50.

The **Barcelona Card** is a real bargain. It provides free public transport, discounts at the city's major attractions, including museums, shops, and several restaurants, and discounts on the Aerobus to/from the airport, the Montjuic funicular railway and cable car, Tombbus and Tibibús, and more. Purchase at tourist information offices, airport Terminals A and B, and at the Sants rail station:

Barcelona Card Prices

	Adults	Children
2 days	€34	€13
3 days	€44	€19
4 days	€52	€25
5 days	€58	€29

Train Connections to Other Base Cities from Barcelona

Depart Barcelona Sants Station.

DEPART	TRAIN NUMBER	ARRIVE	NOTES
		Brussels (Bruxelles) Midi/Zuid	
1830	TGV 9726	0917+1	R, 1, 4, Sleeper
		Lisbon (Lisboa) Santa Apolonia	
1825	AVE 3180	0730+1	R, 2, 3, Exc. Sa, Sleeper
		Madrid Atocha	
0705	AVE 3072	0950	R
0900	AVE 3092	1145	R
1200	AVE 3122	1510	R
1525	AVE 3150	1755	R, M–F
2115	AVE 3412	0002+1	R
		Nice Ville	
0925	TGV 9702	1905	R, 5
		Paris Gare de Lyon	
0925	TGV 9702	1553	R
1830	TGV 9726	0804+1	R, 1, 6, Sleeper

Daily, unless otherwise noted
R Reservations required
+1 Arrive next day
1. Change trains in Perpignon.
2. Via Madrid. Arrive Madrid Chamartin Station. Transfer to Hotel Train 332; depart 2150.
3. Spanish TrenHotel train. Deluxe sleeping accommodations (including toilet and shower in the compartment) are available. Special fares applicable.
4. Arrive Paris Austerlitz 0652+1; transfer to Paris Nord, depart Thalys 9413 at 0746.
5. Change trains in Valence.
6. Arrive Paris Austerlitz.

Sights/Attractions/Tours

Barcelona is a beautiful and immensely varied city. **Las Ramblas,** the world-renowned main avenue of the "Old City," is one interesting part of an outstanding whole. An entire day can easily be spent wandering up and down this lively, fascinating street that stretches 2 kilometers between the Plaça de Catalunya and the port. Begin at the "Diagonal" metro sign on Plaça de Catalunya (near the tourist information office) and head down toward the harbor area. Along the way, watch the numerous entertaining street performers and peruse the variety of wares displayed on every available inch of pavement.

On your right is **La Bouqueria,** declared to be Barcelona's "best market." Farther on, to the right, you will see the **Gran Teatre del Liceu** (the rebuilt old opera house), where you can take a 40-minute tour that includes the Hall of Mirrors. The **Plaça Reial** is off to the left. Built on the site of a former Capuchin convent, this delightful square contains the *Fountain of the Three Graces,* designed by Antoni Gaudí, Barcelona's most famous "native son." If you're tired of walking, this is also a good spot (as is Plaça de Catalunya) to board the **Bus Turístic** (tourist bus) for a great overview of the city, complete with recorded commentary in multiple languages. You can hop on and off the double-decker bus along three sightseeing routes (44 stops) with the same ticket. Buses run every 5 minutes in summer (every 25 rest of the year) from Plaça de Catalunya. Fare: one day €27; two days €35; children (age 4 to 12), one day €16, two days €20.

Continuing on foot, the **Palau Güell,** designed by Gaudí as the palatial residence of Count Güell, will be on your right (closed on weekends/holidays). Near the harbor is the impressive **Mirador de Colón,** the Monument of Christopher Columbus. Take the elevator up 60 meters for an impressive panoramic view.

Like Las Ramblas, the **Barri Gótic (Gothic Quarter)** should not be missed. The most central metro stop is "Jaime I," but "Liceu" would also work. Within the Barri Gótic, you will find the **Picasso Museum** at Carrer Montcada, 15. *Tel:* 93 256 3000; www.museupicasso.bcn.es; *Hours:* 0900–1900 Tuesday–Sunday. You will also find **La Catedral,** the largest cathedral in Barcelona, located at Plaça de la Seu.

Via metro, another good stop is "Sagrada Familia," only a five-minute walk to **La Sagrada Familia**—the huge church designed by Gaudí. Although it is not finished (and has been under construction since Gaudí died in 1926), the church is breathtaking. Love it or hate it, it is well worth seeing. Another Gaudí-related sight, **Parc Güell,** is filled with mosaics he designed ("Vallarca" metro stop).

For a spectacular view, take the bus "Tibibús 2" from Plaça de Catalunya to **Plaça de Tibidabo** (or taxi—the metro does not run here), the highest point in Barcelona. Or take Tramvia Blau (blue tram). Board the rides in the amusement park for even more spectacular views. The park is open mid-March to the end of October.

Attention, shoppers! In terms of quality and quantity of a variety of fashions and products, Barcelona is truly a city of international standing. To make it easy to spend your euros, Turisme de Barcelona plotted out a remarkable 5-kilometer-long **shopping route,** which includes Port Vell, Las Ramblas, Eixample, and the shopping district of the Diagonal. Take the special "Tombbus" bus service (look for the Barcelona shopping line sign on the bus). Ask for more details at the tourist information offices.

Barcelona also offers an impressive zoo, the Olympic Village from 1992, museums and art galleries, more than 4 kilometers of beach (Barceloneta), and a selection of wonderful restaurants featuring local and international cuisine. Restaurants usually serve meals at much later times than other Europeans. Be prepared to eat your evening meals between 2100 and midnight.

Day Excursions from Barcelona

For a unique spiritual and cultural experience, take the metro from Plaça España to the Montserrat cable-car stop and board the cable car or funicular train up to the stunning Benedictine **Montserrat Monastery** (www.abadiamontserrat.net). Founded in the 11th century, it houses some 80 monks, who still live, work, and pray there. Montserrat, about 60 kilometers north of Barcelona, is also the home of the world's oldest boys' choir.

Other day excursions in this edition will take you to **Blanes,** also north of Barcelona, along the **Costa Brava** (Wild Coast), providing the breathtaking beauty of the Mediterranean coast and an opportunity to sample culinary delights from the sea. The citadel city of **Lleida,** stormed by Caesar's legions and conquered by the Moors, carries visitors far back into Spanish history. South of Barcelona along the beaches of Spain's Coasta Dorada (Gold Coast), picturesque **Sitges** attracts sun worshipers, gourmets, and wine connoisseurs alike. Farther south, the ancient city of **Tarragona**'s first-century Roman ruins stir the imagination.

Day Excursion to

Blanes

Beaches, Bikinis, and Boats

Depart from Barcelona Sants (suburban section) Station
Distance by Train: 42 miles (67 km)
Average Train Time: 1 hour, 10 minutes
City Dialing Code: 972
Tourist Information Office: Paseo Catalonia, 2
Tel: 972 330 348; **Fax:** 972 33 46 86
www.blanes.net
E-mail: turisme@blanes.cat
Hours: Winter: 1000–1500 Monday–Thursday, 1000–1400 and 1600–1800 Friday–Saturday, closed Sunday. Summer: 1000–1400 and 1600–2000 daily

The **Costa Brava** is a breathtaking, 90-mile stretch of rugged coastline blessed with fantastic beaches and hidden coves. And it all begins at Blanes. Blanes is best described as a typical Spanish coastal village, where fishing is still the primary industry. Blanes curves around the Mediterranean much like Cannes on the French Riviera, but it is not a "resort" in the usual, more commercialized sense. As with most Spanish fishing villages, the pace is slow and the people friendly.

The rail station serving Blanes is perched on a hill about a half mile from the center of the village and the sea. Buses marked ESTACION-BLANES will take you into town to the bus terminal at Plaça de Catalunya, near the sea.

Barcelona—Blanes

Trains depart Barcelona Sants daily, including holidays, from 0616, 0646, and every 30 minutes until 2046, then 2124, 2154, and 2224.

Trains depart Blanes to Barcelona Sants daily every 30 minutes until 2115, then 2155 (second class only).

Distance: 42 miles (67 km)

A stroll along the beach is delightful. It is fronted by fishermen's houses and dotted with boats lying at anchor in the curve of the bay. There is an auction of the day's catch each weekday evening at about 1700 at the breakwater. Blanes has plenty of fun-in-the-sun beaches, too.

Other diversions include Marimurta Jardi Botanie, a delightful botanical garden located near the breakwater where the fish auctions are held. Founded in 1924 by Karl Faust, the garden exhibits more than 4,000 species of regional and international flora. *Hours:* November–January: 1000–1700 daily; February, March, and October: 0900–1800 daily; April, May, and September: 0900–1900; June–August: 0900–2000.

From Blanes, other ports along this rugged and beautiful coast can be accessed by local buses, cars, or cruise boats. The Crucerus Line, which identifies its vessels with a blue whale at each bow, operates June through September. Boats sail north from Blanes to call at such places as **Lloret de Mar,** famous for its new hotels and exciting nightlife; **Tossa;** and **San Feliu de Guixols.** Obtain details and schedules from the tourist office.

Day Excursion to

Lleida (Lerida)

From the Coast to the Mountains

Depart from Barcelona Sants Station
Distance by Train: 114 miles (184 km)
Average Train Time: 2 hours, 46 minutes
City Dialing Code: 973
Tourist Information Office: Centre d'Informació i Reserves, 31 bis Major Street, 25007 Lleida
Tel: 902 25 00 50; **Fax:** 973 70 04 80
www.paeria.es or **www.turismedelleida.com**
E-mail: infoturisme@paeria.es
Hours: 1000–1400 and 1600–1900 Monday–Saturday, 1000–1330 Sunday and holidays
Notes: It's about a 15-minute walk from the rail station to the tourist information office. Exit the station and walk along Rambla de Ferran and Blondel Avenue to Major Street. A taxi can get you there in about five minutes.

A fast-moving Talgo or ELT (electrotren) diesel train takes passengers in comfort through the spectacular scenery of the rugged, steep slopes of Sierra de Montserrat in the Pyrenees to the Roman fortress city Lleida (Lerida). The train ride alone is worth the experience.

Be certain to make seat reservations well in advance of your day-excursion date, since the train's early morning departure does not allow sufficient time to make same-day reservations.

Your train stops briefly in Manresa, after which the scenery becomes more mountainous. Watch from the left side of the train as it approaches Lleida. The sight is unforgettable. Lleida's brooding **Seu Vella cathedral** stands as a sentinel atop a hill on the banks of the Segre River. The original cathedral makes Lleida's skyline very impressive.

Lleida served as an important Roman military outpost where Caesar's legions gathered to pursue their conquests. The Moors left a more lasting impression, which is reflected in the discernibly Mediterranean flavor of the city's marketplaces. Lleida's stormy history continued with Napoleon's attempts to annex it to France and with artillery fire during the Spanish Civil War.

Constructed in the 13th century on the former site of a mosque, Seu Vella was converted from a church to a military fortress in 1707 by Philip V and then burned and pillaged in the wars that followed. It was restored and reconsecrated in 1950. The **Seu Nova** (new cathedral) stands on Carrer Major, the main street of the old town. The ancient 15th- to 16th-century **Hospital de Santa Maria** is just opposite and houses many fine Iberian and Roman archaeological excavation exhibits. If you are up to it, scale the tower for a panoramic view of the plain surrounding Lleida.

Barcelona—Lleida (Lerida)

DEPART	TRAIN NUMBER	ARRIVE	NOTES
Barcelona Sants		Lleida	
0605	AVE 3062	0702	M–Sa
0800	AVE 3082	0857	
0920	AVE 8096	1028	
1000	AVE 3102	1057	
1200	AVE 3122	1257	

DEPART	TRAIN NUMBER	ARRIVE	NOTES
Lleida		Barcelona Sants	
1337	AVE 3113	1440	2nd class only
1431	AVE 3123	1530	
1600	AVE 8167	1708	Exc. Sa
1800	AVE 8187	1908	
2131	AVE 3193	2240	

Daily

A reservation is required for all trains that have numbers. A reservation purchased on-board the train costs more than one purchased in advance. Higher fares incorporating a supplement are payable for travel by Talgo and InterCity trains.

Distance: 114 miles (184 km)

Lleida's picturesque "Old Quarter" teems with interesting pedestrian streets of shops with colorful awnings and generally lower prices than you'll find in Barcelona. Take time to enjoy the simple yet high-quality cuisine of the region. Many dishes are flavored with olive oil of the Garrigues area—considered to be the best in the world. The annual **Agricultural Fair of Sant Miguel,** usually held at the end of September, shows off the best produce of the area. Top off your visit with a toast of one of the Costers del Segre wines.

Festival buffs will enjoy several of the other traditional celebrations of Lleida, including *Els Tres Tombs* (Feast of Saint Anthony) in mid-January, when the horses and cattle are led in procession through the streets of the city to be blessed; the *Aplec del Cargol* (Snail Feast), held on the first Sunday of May; and the Festival of the White Virgin, held in the beginning of October, when the city celebrates their patroness, the Madonna.

Day Excursion to

Sitges

Jewel on the Mediterranean

Depart from Barcelona Sants Station
Distance by Train: 25 miles (40 km)
Average Train Time: 30 minutes
City Dialing Code: 93
Tourist Information Office: Plaza Eduard Maristany 2, 08870, Sitges
Tel: 93 894 4251; **Fax:** 93 894 1521
www.stigestur.cat
E-mail: info@sitgestur.cat
Hours: 1000–1400 and 1600–1830 Monday–Friday; 1000–1400 and 1600–1900 Saturday; 1000–1400 Sunday
Notes: The tourist office is on the west end of the train station, by the taxi stand.

Only 25 miles (40 km) south of Barcelona, Sitges can be accessed by train from several stations in Barcelona, but Sants and Passeig de Gracia Stations are the most centralized. Sitges is one of the most cosmopolitan seaside resorts in Europe and a pleasant escape from Barcelona's summer heat.

Sitges, a member of the prestigious Jewels of European Tourism Club, boasts 17 golden beaches that stretch across 4 kilometers. It is also located in an important wine and "cava" champagne production area known as the Penedés region. Ask the tourist office about visiting the wine cellars in Vilafranca del Penedés and the Cava Cellars in Sant Sadurni de Noia.

Annually, Sitges hosts the national carnation show in June, when the town is awash with the brilliantly colored flowers. It coincides with the procession of Corpus Christi in June, one of the most renowned festivals in Spain, when streets are adorned with splendid carnation carpets, bands perform, and parades glide along narrow streets.

Fresh seafood is Sitges's specialty, but there are excellent meat and chicken dishes available as well at a multitude of fine restaurants. Typical Sitges dishes include *xato*, a salad of endive, tuna fish, salt-cod, anchovies, and olives, dressed with *nyora* peppers, roasted almonds, chilis, garlic, olive oil, more anchovies, and salt and vinegar. Or try *arros a la sitgetana*—rice with a delicious mixture of shellfish, sausage, pork, peas, and peppers, seasoned with saffron and almonds. Follow it all with a glass of Sitges's delicious dessert wine, *Malvasia de Sitges*.

The **Carnival** (usually the first week in February), **June International Theater,** and the **October Film Festival** attract a varied mixture of participants and spectators, including international celebrities.

Barcelona—Sitges

Trains depart daily from Barcelona Sants Station at 6 and 36 minutes after the hour from 0606 until 2206, then 2306; journey time to Sitges is 30 minutes.

Trains depart daily from Sitges at 29 and 59 minutes after the hour throughout the day until 2129, then at 2226; journey time to Barcelona Sants Station is 30 minutes.

All second-class local service.

Distance: 25 miles (34 km)

Other Sitges attractions include **Museu Romantic o Casa Llopis,** an outstanding exhibit of antique dolls housed in a refurbished 18th-century mansion; **Cau Ferrat,** the magnificent home of 20th-century artist Santiago Rusinol, which displays Rusinol's best work as well as art by El Greco, Casas, and Picasso; and the **Maricel del Mar Museum.**

Day Excursion to

Tarragona

City of Roman Spain

Depart from Barcelona Sants Station
Distance by Train: 53 miles (85 km)
Average Train Time: 50 minutes
City Dialing Code: 977
Tourist Information Office: Patronat Municipal de Turisme, 39 Carrer Major, 43003 Tarragona
Tel: 977 250 795; **Fax:** 977 245 507
www.tarragonaturisme.cat
E-mail: turisme@tarragona.cat
Hours: Summer: 1000–2000 Monday–Saturday, 1000–1400 Sunday; winter: 1000–1400, 1500–1700 Monday–Saturday, 1000–1400 Sunday
Notes: To reach the Patronat Municipal de Turisme, board a No. 2 bus across from the rail station. Get off at the Roman Wall, where you will see signs directing you to the tourist information office.

Tarragona can be reached via Barcelona's single-class suburban train system or by the faster, more stylish, and comfortable Talgo trains, which require seat reservations.

Barcelona—Tarragona

DEPART	TRAIN NUMBER	ARRIVE	NOTES
Barcelona Sants		Tarragona	
0633	R 15907	0738	2nd class
0733	R 15029	0837	2nd class
0800	EM 1081	0855	1, 2
0803	R 18051	0907	2nd class
0903	R 17501	1007	1, 2, M–Sa
plus other frequent service.			

DEPART	TRAIN NUMBER	ARRIVE	NOTES
Tarragona		Barcelona Sants	
1455	R 15402	1606	1, 2
1639	ALS 1142	1739	1, 2
1729	R 15042	1835	1, 2
1859	R 15036	2008	1, 2
1957	R 18058	2105	1, 2, M–Sa
2029	R 15016	2135	1, 2
2134	R 15138	2302	2nd class
2310	TLG 1202	2359	1, 2, Exc. Sa

Daily, unless otherwise noted

1. A reservation is required. A reservation fee paid to the conductor onboard the train costs more than one purchased in advance.

2. Higher fares incorporating a supplement are payable for travel by Talgo (TAL) and Inter-City (IC) trains. A special fare structure may apply for travel by EM trains (Euromed—200 km/hr high-speed trains, similar to AVE trains). Passengers wishing to travel on EM trains are advised to inquire at the Barcelona Sants Station before boarding.

Distance: 53 miles (85 km)

Tarragona is rich in antiquity. It was once considered a jewel in the crown of the Roman Empire, with more than one-quarter of a million inhabitants (more than twice the current population) enjoying all the privileges of Rome. Tarragona's enormous stone walls were constructed in the first century B.C. As with the great pyramids of Egypt, modern engineers still wonder how the ancient Iberians could position such massive blocks of stone. Its attractive seascape of azure water, gold-colored beaches, and flower-laden cliffs has attracted visitors for centuries.

St. Paul supposedly preached at the site of Tarragona's 12th-century cathedral, where a Roman temple to Jupiter once stood. Illustrations of his life are exhibited in the altar area.

A visit to the **Archeological Museum** is a journey into Tarragona's rich past, from Roman remains to reflecting the peoples who followed, including Visigoths, Moors, and Catalans. The penetrating stare of Medusa's eyes, cornices from the **Temple of Jupiter** (where the cathedral now stands), and age-old ceramics are on view. The museum operates on seasonal hours. Check with the tourist information office.

Hungry? While you're in the tourist office, ask for directions to the **Bufet el Tiberi Restaurant** at 5, Marti d'Ardenya, or the **Restaurant el Celler** and **Restaurant el Trull.** All three feature local specialties.

Base City: **MADRID**

www.esmadrid.com
City Dialing Code: 91

Madrid's central location in the very heart of Spain makes it a convenient base city and a major point of entry for Spain. Madrid, the capital of Spain, at first glance appears typical of any other modern capital that serves as a center for government and finance. But it is atypical of a busy metropolis in that the Spanish seem to move at a slower pace. They make time for friends and conversation, and as one Spanish writer noted, "Madrid is a city where no one is a stranger."

The Madrilenos are apparently connoisseurs of a variety of nightlife activities and have a flair for flamenco—the sensual, Gypsy-influenced form of singing and dancing. There are numerous specialized flamenco clubs in Madrid, including the Corral de la Moreria, Los Canasteros, and Torres Bermejas. It would appear that the Madrilenos never sleep!

According to the Spanish National Tourist Office, "Madrid has turned into the fable of Europe. It is called the capital of joy and of contentment. Describing our city in such terms means that it is welcoming, cordial, free, peaceful and universal."

Arriving by Air

Madrid's **Barajas International Airport,** about 9 miles (12 kilometers) northeast of the city.

- **Airport Information:** *Tel:* 91 902 404 704; www.aena.es
- **INFORIBERIA:** *Tel:* 91 902 400 500
- **Tourist Information:** Terminals 2 and 4, open daily 0900–2000. *Tel:* 913 058 656.
- **Airport–City Links:** Airport Bus (*Tel:* 902507850), a yellow bus service, runs from Barajas Airport to the Plaça de Colón (Columbus Square) about every 10 minutes 0600 to 0130. Journey time: about 30 to 60 minutes, depending on traffic; fare: €5. Take a taxi from Plaça de Colón to your hotel.
- **Metro, Line 8, Aeropuerto Stop,** goes to Nuevos Ministerios Station (city center financial district), where you transfer to other subway or commuter train lines to your final destination. Single-journey fare: €4.50. *Tip:* Purchase the 10-trip ticket, "Metrobus" (€12.20), for use on both the subway and city buses. *Tel:* 902 444 403 (*Hours:* 0900–2200).
- **Taxi** fare from the airport to city center is about €20–€30, and the trip takes 25 to 35 minutes, depending on traffic.

Arriving by Train

RENFE (Spanish National Railways)—For information on fares, schedules, and destinations (including AVE trains). *Tel:* 902 32 03 20; www.renfe.es. *International information:* 902 24 05 05.

Madrid's two main railway stations, **Chamartin** and **Atocha,** are connected by underground trackage via Madrid's metro system and by *Apeadero Cercanias* (local) trains or any through-trains scheduled to stop at both stations. The metro stop for Atocha Station is marked ATOCHA RENFE. Apeadero Cercanias stations also include **Nuevos Ministerios** in the government buildings area and **Recoletos** at the main post office. Rail passes are accepted on Apeadero Cercanias trains, but not on Madrid's metro.

Chamartin Station, San Agustin de Foxa Street, is Madrid's international station connecting with most European capitals, as well as the north, northeast, and south of Spain. The station is near the Chamartin metro stop, and buses Nos. 5 and 80 connect from the city and this railway station. High-speed AVE trains shuttle passengers quickly to and from **Seville** (about 2 hours and 15 minutes), with stops at **Cordoba** and **Ciudad Real.** Other fast trains depart to and arrive from various southern and southeastern Spanish destinations and from Portugal. There are 21 tracks.

- **Money exchange:** Opposite track Nos. 17 and 18. The sign reads CAJA ESPANA. *Hours:* 0830–1400 Monday–Friday. Banco Bilbao Vizcaya Argentaria, across from Track 12. *Hours:* 0800–2000 daily. ATM located next door.
- **Hotel reservations:** Opposite track Nos. 6 and 7. *Hours:* 0730–2300 daily. Nominal reservation fee. Be certain to ask for accommodations near one of the rail stations or close to public transportation. The check-in counter for Hotel Chamartin is near the luggage locker area.
- **Luggage lockers:** Available 0700 to 2230 daily. Follow the sign that indicates CONSIGNA AUTOMATICA.
- **Sala Club Intercity:** First-class lounge between entrances to track Nos. 13 and 14.

  Remember: Seat reservations are mandatory on all express and international trains.
- **Tourist information:** Opposite track No. 19 (*Tel:* 91 315 9976). *Hours:* 0800–2000 Monday–Friday, 0900–1300 Saturday.
- **Train information, seat reservations,** and **rail pass validation:** In the center of the station between track Nos. 11 and 12. *Hours:* 0830–2130. Take a number from the machine labeled RECOJA SU TURNO to reserve a place in line. Make certain the date (*fecha*) and departure time (*hora salida*) are correct on your reservation.

Puerta de Atocha Station—High-speed AVE and Talgo 200 trains connect Madrid with Andalusia from this station. A pleasant tropical garden and cafe provide a respite from the heat and noise. The local/suburban Cercanias trains depart from the lower level and connect with Chamartin Station. **Sala Club Intercity:** First-class lounge on the mezzanine level.

Principe Pio or Norte, near the Royal Palace on the west side of the city, links Madrid to cities in the north and northeast of Spain via the Cercanias, or suburban, trains. Other stations where you can board suburban-type Cercanias trains include **Nuevos Ministerios** and **Recoletos.** The variety of Eurail passes and the national Spain rail passes are accepted on these trains. Although considered "local" trains, they do extend to the surrounding countryside to our day excursions **Aranjuez** (Line C-3) and **El Escorial** (Line C-8a).

Tourist Information/Hotel Reservations

Madrid has several provincial and municipal tourist information offices. Four offices are most significant for *Europe by Eurail* readers:

- **Offina de Informacion de Turismo (municipal tourist office)**
  Plaza Mayor, 27
  Tel: 914544410; *Fax:* 91 480 2938; www.esmadrid.com; *E-mail:* turismo@esmadrid.com
  Hours: 0930–2030 daily
- **Barajas Airport**
  Tel: 915 881 636; www.aena.es; *E-mail:* bcninfofi@aena.es
  Hours: 0900–2000 daily
- **Chamartin Railway Station** (opposite track No. 19)
  Contact information same as Barajas Airport office.
  Hours: 0800–2000 Monday–Saturday, 0900–1500 Sunday
- **Puerta de Atocha Railway Station**
  Contact information same as Barajas Airport office.
  Hours: 0900–2030 daily

Hotel reservations: Chamartin Station, opposite track Nos. 6 and 7, as well as at the other tourist offices. Madrid is a large city, so be certain to ask for lodging near one of the rail terminals or close to public transportation.

Getting Around in Madrid

Madrid has an excellent metro and bus system, Consorcio de Transportes de Madrid (CTM). Visit www.ctm-madrid.es. A combined metro-bus single ticket is €2.00; a 10-trip ticket is €12.20. Tickets may be purchased at newspaper stands, tobacco stores, and all main bus and metro stops. The tickets are magnetically encoded.

Train Connections to Other Base Cities from Madrid

Depart from Madrid Chamartin Station.

DEPART	TRAIN NUMBER	ARRIVE	NOTES
		Barcelona Sants	
0730	AVE 3073	1040	R, 3
0930	AVE 3093	1234	R, 3
1130	AVE 3113	1440	R, 3
1500	AVE 3151	1730	R, 3, M–F
1800	AVE 3181	2030	R, 3
2030	AVE 3203	2340	R, 3, Exc. Sa
		Lisbon (Lisboa) Santa Apolonia	
2140	Hotel 332	0730+1	R, 1, Sleeper
		Paris Montparnasse	
0800	AVE 4087	2035	R, 2, Exc. Sa

Daily, unless otherwise noted

R Reservations required

+1 Arrive next day

1. Spanish TrenHotel train. Deluxe sleeping accommodations (including toilet and shower in the compartment) are available. Special fares applicable.
2. Change trains in Hendaye.
3. Depart Madrid Atocha.

The best transportation bargain is the **Tourist Travel Pass.** Pass holders can use any public transport in the Madrid region for an unlimited number of trips during the pass validity.

Madrid Tourist Travel Pass Prices

Numbers of Days	Price
1 day	€8.40
2 days	€14.20
3 days	€18.40
5 days	€26.80
7 days	€35.40

The **Madrid Card** makes sightseeing more convenient. It includes free admission to 40 museums in and around Madrid; use of Madrid Vision tour bus as often as you like; the Discover Madrid program, and much more. It also includes discounts in selected shops and restaurants. Prices: one day, €45; two days, €55; three days, €65; five days, €75 . Visit www.madridcard.com.

Sights/Attractions/Tours

Some "don't-miss" sights include **Puerta del Sol** (Gate of the Sun), the center of the old town and the terminus for the city's metro lines and many of the buses. Six of Spain's national freeways radiate from Kilometer Zero, a stone slab buried in the pavement from which all distances are measured in Spain. ***El Oso y el Madrono,*** the bush and the bear statue, is Madrid's emblem.

Proceed southwest along **Calle Mayor** to **Plaça de la Villa,** with two stunning buildings dating from the 15th century—the **Casa** (house) and the **Torre** (tower) **de los Lujanes.** Continuing to the right of Calle Mayor and beyond the Plaça de la Villa, turn into the alleyway leading to **San Nicolas de los Servitas** to visit Madrid's oldest church.

Going north along the **Calle del Arenal,** one can view a famous El Greco at the Church of San Gines or visit Joy Eslava, the city's trendy disco. Farther on are the Royal Palace and the Opera House.

Other significant landmarks include the **Palacio Real** (Royal Palace). *Tel:* 91 454 87 00; *Hours:* 1000–1800 Monday–Sunday. One of the best-conserved palaces in Europe, it's filled with paintings, frescoes, clocks, furniture, and porcelain. Metrostop: Opera; bus Nos. 3, 25, 39, and 148. **Plaça Mayor,** behind Calle Mayor, is an exquisite 17th-century arcaded square.

The incomparable **Prado Museum** at Paseo del Prado (*Tel:* 913302800; *Fax:* 91 330 28 56; www.museoprado.es. *Hours:* 1000–2000 Monday–Saturday, 1000–1900 Sunday, with free admission after 1800, and Sunday after 1700) houses more than 3,000 of the world's most precious works of art, including fine collections of the Spanish masters—Goya, Velazquez, El Greco, Murillo, and Zurbaran. General entry fee: €14. Metro stops: Banco de España and Atocha Stations; bus Nos. 9, 10, 14, 19, 27, 34, 37, and 45.

The **Thyssen-Bornemisza Museum,** in the Villahermosa Palace, features one of the world's most extensive private art collections. *Tel:* 91 369 01 51; www.museothyssen.org; *Hours:* Open Monday–Sunday 1000–1900. The **Reina Sofia National Art Museum** has a fantastic collection of 20th-century Spanish art, and the **National Chalcography Institute** includes 221 original copper and brass engraved plates by Goya.

If you plan to attend a bullfight in Madrid, remember what Ernest Hemingway wrote: "It is a tragedy; the death of the bull, which is played, more or less well by the bull and the man involved and in which there is danger for the man but certain death for the bull."

For people-watching visit several of Madrid's *chiringuitos*, a combination German-style beer garden and discotheque, and cafes that line the **Paseo de la Castellana** (which becomes Paseo del Prado as it nears the Prado Museum).

In the cuisine category, Madrid has some very old and very famous restaurants. The **Casa Botin** at 17 Calle Cuchilleros (*Tel:* 91 366 42 17; www.botin.es) is in the *Guinness Book of Records* as the oldest continuously operated restaurant and Hemingway's favorite for suckling pig and lamb. The **Zalacain** at Alvarez de Baena 4 (*Tel:* 91 561 48 40; www.restaurantezalacain.com) features Basque seafood and game.

Day Excursions

Aranjuez, Avila, El Escorial, and **Toledo** are four very different Spanish destinations easily accessed by train from Madrid.

Aranjuez and El Escorial are particularly picturesque. Aranjuez, on the fertile banks of the Tagus River, is set in a forested valley less than one hour's train journey south of Madrid. El Escorial is a village at the base of the Sierra de Guadarrama, one hour north of Madrid. Favorites of the royalty for centuries, they are now popular retreats for Madrilenos.

Avila and Toledo are cities with such different styles that they exemplify the diversity of this ancient land. Both are worth more than a day's visit to thoroughly explore and enjoy.

Burgos, home of El Cid, is about three hours' journey time from Madrid.

Day Excursion to

Aranjuez

Strawberries and Spanish Royal Retreat

Depart from Madrid Atocha Station
Distance by Train: 30 miles (49 km)
Average Train Time: 50 minutes
City Dialing Code: 91
Tourist Information Office: No. 9, Plaza de San Antonio, 28300 Aranjuez
Tel: 91 891 04 27; **Fax:** 91 891 41 97
www.spain.info
Notes: We recommend taking a taxi from the station to the tourist office, located near Palacio Real.

In the 18th and 19th centuries, **Aranjuez** was a favorite hangout for Spanish royalty. Now, it's a popular place for "regular" Madrilenos to gather on weekends. You may want to make this day excursion during the week to avoid the weekend crowds.

Madrid—Aranjuez

Madrid—Aranjuez
Frequent service beginning at 0713 with last train out at 2128.

Aranjuez—Madrid
Frequent service beginning at 0621 with last train out at 2132.

Average journey time: 30 to 45 minutes. All trains 2nd class only.

Reservations available (not required). A reservation purchased onboard the train costs more than one purchased in advance.

Distance: 30 miles (49 km)

Aranjuez has often been described as the "Oasis of Castille," in part because it nestles on the banks of the Tagus River that nurses dense groves of poplars, rich vegetation, and glorious crops of luscious strawberries and asparagus. Apparently, the jade green waters of the river favorably foster the growth of trees, as evidenced by the city's Circus of the Twelve Streets, a square from which 12 beautifully shaded avenues radiate.

The **Palacio Real** (Royal Palace) is a lavish palace that would vie with Versailles in extravagance. Its 18 magnificent rooms include the Porcelain Salon, the Throne Room, and the Museum of Royal Robes, which displays the court dress of sovereigns up to the 19th century. Another highlight is the grand staircase built during the reign of Philip V. *Hours:* Spring and summer: 1000–2000 daily; autumn and winter: it closes two hour earlier. Visit www.patrimonionacional.es.

The Farmer's Cottage, with its resplendent furnishings, can be reached through the Prince's Garden. The Casa de Marinos, the sailor's house that holds the royal vessels, displays Spain's dominant maritime history. And among the gardens, the Parterre Garden and the Jardin de la Isla (Island Garden) are most memorable.

You can purchase a combination ticket that includes a guided tour of the Royal Palace. The tours operate 1000 to 1800 April through September; 1000 to 1715 October through March. Note that all of the museums are closed on Monday.

Trains to Aranjuez depart every 20 to 30 minutes from Madrid's Atocha Cercanias Station. For a real treat, take the 19th-century ***El Tren del Fresa*** (the Strawberry Train). Yes, strawberries are served onboard by attendants in period costumes.

Day Excursion to

Avila

Walled City

Depart from Madrid Chamartin Station or Principe Pio
Distance by Train: 70 miles (112 km)
Average Train Time: 1 hour, 15 minutes
City Dialing Code: 920
Tourist Information Office: Casa de las Carnicerias san Segundo, 17 5001 Avila
Tel: 920211387; **Fax:** 920253717
www.turismoavila.com
Email: oficinadeturismodeavila@jcyl.es
Hours: May–September, 0900–2000 daily; October–April, 0900–1730 daily
RENFE at Avila Railway Station: *Tel:* 920 25 02 02
Notes: The tourist office is about a 20-minute walk. Follow the Paseo de la Estacion across from the station to the Paseo Rastro and the tourist office will be on the north side of the street.

Avila is the capital of the province of Avila, and at 1,127 meters it is the highest provincial capital in Spain and the best-preserved walled city in the world. The city is completely enclosed by 1.2 miles (2.5 kilometers) of 12th-century walls averaging 33 feet high and 10 feet thick, with 90 towers and 9 gateways. The enormousness of this project becomes apparent when you realize it was constructed in 1085.

Viewed from **Los Cuatro Postes,** an observation post on the Salamanca Road outside the city, Avila is a breathtaking sight nestled on the Adaja River against the mountains. From here, the walled city appears to be a fascinating giant stage all set for a medieval drama.

Avila is most remembered for Saint Teresa. Her presence is most evident in the convent **Nuestra Senora de Gracia,** built at the site of her parents' home; the Monastery de la Encarnacion, which depicts her lifestyle; and "Las Madres" (Monastery de San Jose), her first foundation.

Across the street from the tourist office is the **Gran Hotel Palacio Valderrabonos.** This former noble's residence is an excellent place to have lunch. Its door dates from the 15th century.

Other sights in Avila include the cathedral, which forms a part of the great wall, thus giving it the distinctive look of a fortress rather than a church. Its somewhat austere exterior is in contrast to its interior, which has many beautiful details. In the cathedral's museum, you may view a portrait painted by El Greco and a colossal silver monstrance, weighing nearly 200 pounds, made by Juan de Arfe in 1571.

The cathedral was begun in the 12th century in Romanesque style and finished in the 15th century with a facade of Gothic Towers, the Palacio de Polention, the Mansion de los Deanes, Mansion de Davila—all magnificent with art and architecture.

Madrid—Avila

DEPART Madrid Chamartin	TRAIN NUMBER	ARRIVE Avila	NOTES
0830	R 18921	0956	R
0905	IR 18061	1037	2nd class only
1108	IR 18903	1238	2nd class only
1220	R 18063	1404	1, 2nd class only
1335	IR 18905	1505	R
plus other frequent service.			

DEPART Avila	TRAIN NUMBER	ARRIVE Madrid Chamartin	NOTES
1600	IR 18004	1742	R
1700	IR 18012	1840	1, 2nd class only
1900	IR 18006	2052	1, 2nd class only
2000	R 18014	2144	R
2106	R 18908	2238	1, 2nd class only

Daily, unless otherwise noted
R Reservations required
Reservations required for all trains with categories (i.e., IC, TLG). A reservation fee paid to the conductor onboard the train costs more than one paid in advance. Higher fares incorporating a supplement are payable for travel by Talgo (TLG) and InterCity (IC) trains.
1. This train is a Castilla y León Exprés train; reservations are available.
Distance: 70 miles (112 km)

The cuisine of this area is fit for a king's palate. Trout from the Tormes River is renowned for its distinctive flavor; the roast suckling pig, lamb, or veal dishes are equally excellent and served with a hearty complement of vegetables, followed by *yemas de Santa Teresa*, small sweets made of egg yolks.

Nearby *paradors* offer unique accommodations for those who prefer to "base" themselves here. Paradors are historic buildings and palaces that the Spanish government has converted into hotels.

Day Excursion to

Burgos

Home of El Cid

Depart from Madrid Chamartin Station
Distance by Train: 211 miles (340 km)
Average Train Time: 3 hours
City Dialing Code: 947
Tourist Information Office: Plaça Alonso Martinez, 7 Bajo, 09003 Burgos
Tel: 947 20 31 25 or 20 18 46; **Fax:** 947 27 65 29
www.turismoburgos.org
E-mail: oficinadeturismodeburgos@jcyl.es
Hours: September 30–June 30: 1000–1400 and 1630–1931 daily; July 1–August 31: 1000–2000 daily
Notes: To reach the office on foot (about a 15-minute walk), exit the station and go straight ahead until you cross the Arlanzon River. Turn right and proceed along Paseo de la Isla Avenue to the arch where the walkway Paseo del Espolon begins.

Burgos is north of Madrid, approaching France, and on the crossroads to Portugal. Birthplace of the warrior El Cid, Burgos is the capital of Burgos province, one of the nine provinces of Castile and Leon.

El Cid and his wife, Ximena, are entombed in the **13th-century cathedral,** one of the world's outstanding examples of Gothic architecture. Its twin spires rise to greet you long before your Talgo train comes to a halt in the Burgos Station.

The nave of the cathedral and the ambulatory and portals of El Sarmental and Coroneria date from its beginnings in 1221. The latest additions, dating from the 16th century, include Diego de Siloe's *Golden Stairs*; the chapels of La Consolation, Santiago, and Navidad; and Juan de Vallejo's exquisite lantern.

Burgos was the site where the Castilians initiated their campaigns against the Muslims to reclaim Madrid in 1083 and Toledo in 1085. In the 20th century Generalissimo Franco used Burgos as his headquarters during the Spanish Civil War and here declared the cease-fire in 1939.

The **Casa del Cordon,** a 15th-century house so named from the huge cord of rope carved in stone fronting its entrance, forms the backdrop for **El Cid's statue.** It was here that Christopher Columbus was received in formal audience by the Spanish monarchs on his return from his second voyage to the Americas.

For lunch we suggest the **Ojeda Restaurant** at Calle Vitoria No. 5. It is quite pleasant to have a light snack or even a full meal at its outdoor tables in the summer. *Tel:* 947 20 90 52. Visit www.restauranteojeda.com.

Madrid—Burgos

DEPART	TRAIN NUMBER	ARRIVE	NOTES
Madrid Chamartin		Burgos	
0800	ALS 4087	1026	R
0905	R 18061	1319	R, 2nd Class
1220	IR 18063	1644	Exc. Sa

DEPART	TRAIN NUMBER	ARRIVE	NOTES
Burgos		Madrid Chamartin	
1714	R 18014	2144	2nd class
1933	ALS 4166	2206	

Daily, unless otherwise noted
R Reservations required
Reservation required for all trains with categories (e.g., IC, TLG). A reservation fee paid to the conductor onboard the train costs more than one paid in advance. Higher fares incorporating a supplement are payable for travel by Talgo (TLG) and InterCity (IC) trains.
Distance: 211 miles (340 km)

Day Excursion to

El Escorial

World's Eighth Wonder

Depart from Madrid Atocha or Chamartin Station
Distance by Train: 32 miles (52 km)
Average Train Time: 50 minutes
City Dialing Code: 91
Tourist Information Office: Calle Grimaldi 4
Tel: 91 890 53 13
www.patrimonionacional.es
Hours: October–March: 1000–1800 Tuesday–Sunday; April–September: 1000–2000 Tuesday–Sunday
Notes: The rail station is about 1 mile from town. Taxis are to the left of the station exit. A taxi ride to the town square or the tourist office costs about €3. Buses are also available that will take you to the town square.

El Escorial is the name of the village and the immense palace-monastery, both havens of Phillip II, who personally supervised construction of the monumental structure to commemorate his victory over France at St. Quentin in 1557. Part monastery, part palace, part cathedral, El Escorial reflects its builder's vanity. The monastery and palace are open 1000 to 1800 in summer, until 1700 in winter; closed on Monday.

El Escorial encompasses 8 acres and has 9 towers, 16 courtyards, 86 staircases, 1,200 doors, and 2,673 leaded-glass windows. A force of 1,500 laborers worked 21 years to complete it. Wear your best pair of walking shoes—you'll need them.

The **Hall of Battles** epitomizes Spain's aggressive history in paintings by Italian artists Castello, Grenello, and Tavorone. Priceless artworks by Borsch, Rembrandt, Tintoretto, and Titian are also displayed throughout the palace. Tapestries of Spanish country life woven from sketches drawn by Goya also hang on the walls.

Prior to mounting the Armada against England, King Phillip tried to bring England into the Spanish empire by marrying Mary Tudor, known as "Bloody Mary" for her overzealous persecution of English Protestants. Forty years later, just before his death, Phillip had become a religious fanatic. He returned to the palace to live as though in poverty in a sparse second-floor apartment, which provides stark contrast to its surroundings—one of the grandest palaces in Europe.

Two other attractions of interest are the **Casita del Principe** (the Prince's Cottage), which you pass en route to the station, and **Casita de Arriba,** a hunting lodge 2 miles farther on. Both are open 1000 to 1800 (1700 in winter); closed on Monday. Both were constructed by Charles III (1759–1788). His friendship with France and hostility toward Great Britain led to the alliance in support of the American Revolution.

Madrid—El Escorial

DEPART Madrid Chamartin	TRAIN NUMBER	ARRIVE El Escorial	NOTES
0633	R 18001	0709	M–F
0905	R 18061	0950	
1035	R 18011	1110	
1530	R 18907	1610	M–Sa
1835	R 18005	1910	
2112	R 18911	2151	Exc. Sa

DEPART El Escorial	TRAIN NUMBER	ARRIVE Madrid Chamartin	NOTES
1600	R 17104	1653	M–F
2001	R 18006	2052	
2103	R 18014	2144	

Daily, including holidays, unless otherwise noted
All trains 2nd class
Distance: 32 miles (52 km)

Day Excursion to

Toledo

City of History

Depart from Madrid Atocha Station
Distance by Train: 57 miles (91 km)
Average Train Time: 1 hour, 15 minutes
City Dialing Code: 925
Tourist Information Office: Puerta de Bisagra, 1, 45071 Toledo
Tel: 925 25 40 30; **Fax:** 925 25 59 46
www.toledo-turismo.com
E-mail: info@toledo-turismo.com
Hours: 0900–1800 Monday–Friday, 1000–1900 Saturday, 1000–1500 Sunday
Notes: Public bus service from rail station into town. Buses depart every 15 minutes. Bus stops first at the tourist information office at Puerta de la Bisagra before terminating in the main square, Plaça de Zocodover (Marketplace). There is also an information office at the city hall, in front of the cathedral.

Toledo is (as is Avila) capital of a province with the same name. Toledo province is defined by mountain ranges, rivers, and rich rolling valleys; it abounds with game, aromatic plants, and delicate white-leafed rock roses—all of which distinguishes Toledo from the other provinces of La Mancha with their monotonous, flat expanses.

Divided by the River Tagus, Toledo has the rich and varied history of most river towns, and in Europe's south that means conquests by Romans, Visigoths, Moors, and ultimately Christians, who declared it Spain's Imperial City. It was ruled by the legendary El Cid. The impact of such a diverse history earned Toledo the UNESCO "Heritage of Mankind" status, defining it as one of the richest historically, culturally, and monumentally endowed cities in Spain.

A Cretan named Domenico Teotocopulo arrived in Toledo in 1577. His arrival might have gone unnoticed, except that Señor Teotocopulo, better known as El Greco, happened to be a painter of some renown. El Greco painted and bequeathed his best to Toledo. The **Museum of Santa Cruz** and the **El Greco museum** as well as the cathedral honor the achievements of one of Spain's most creative artists.

Although Toledo's history may be complicated, its charm is definitely not. Wander the city's narrow cobblestone streets; visit its friendly cafes, which remain open late into the night; and taste its fresh fruits from the open market in the morning.

In 1226 King Ferdinand III laid the first stone in the **Cathedral of Toledo,** and today it is renowned for its art and architecture. The 13th-century fortress **Alcazar** was a Roman Pretorian Palace in the 3rd century.

Madrid—Toledo

DEPART Madrid Atocha	TRAIN NUMBER	ARRIVE Toledo	NOTES
0650	8062	0723	M–F
0920	8292	0953	
1120	8312	1153	
1220	8322	1253	

DEPART Toledo	TRAIN NUMBER	ARRIVE Madrid Atocha
1525	8153	1558
1725	8173	1758
1920	8193	1953
2130	8213	2203

Daily, unless otherwise noted
All train service to Toledo is second class only.
Reservations available on all trains (not required).
Distance: 57 miles (91 km)

Toledo also is well-known for its crafters who work steel into some of the finest blades for knives and swords. The distinctive black-on-gold designs embellishing the handles of blades have been carried over to jewelry and other accessories available in shops throughout the city.

Although there are numerous eateries, most visitors seem to gather in the main square, **Plaça de Zocodover** (Marketplace). Here, you will find cafes and bars to sample local sandwiches and tapas (appetizers).

The **Parador Conde Orgaz** and the **Hotel Alfonso VI** are exceptional accommodations in Toledo, if you choose to stay.

SWEDEN

Sweden is about the same size as the state of California or the country of Spain. It is half-covered by forests, dotted with nearly 100,000 lakes, and thousands of islands line its coastline. It is one of the largest and most prosperous countries in Europe and supports a large and efficient industrial complex. With a population of only 8.7 million inhabitants, however, it is not crowded, and its citizens enjoy a superb quality of life and one of the highest standards of living in the world.

Although Swedish, a Germanic language, is the language of the majority, Finland was a part of Sweden until 1809, and Finnish-speaking natives still occupy the northeastern area along with another minority group, the Sami (Lapp). Fortunately for English-speaking tourists, English is spoken by most Swedes who are involved in tourism, transportation, and international business.

From 1846 to 1930, approximately 1.3 million Swedes emigrated to North America. Thousands of visitors, including North Americans, trace their Swedish ancestry at the Swedish Emigrant Institute in Växjö, which houses and records memorabilia from that time period.

It is difficult to realize that only about a century ago, Sweden was one of the most backward countries in Europe. Today, Sweden is forward thinking—spending a large percentage of national output on industrial research and development. Since 1995, Sweden has played an important role as a member of the European Union. Sweden's strategic geographic location between the North Atlantic and Russia has affected its foreign policies and security strategies for all of Europe.

For more information about Sweden, visit **www.visitsweden.com,** *E-mail:* usa@visitsweden.com, or contact the Swedish Travel and Tourism Council:

New York: 655 Third Ave., Suite 1810, New York, NY 10017; *Tel:* (212) 885-9700; *Fax:* (212) 885-9710

Banking

Currency: Swedish Krona (SEK)

Exchange rate at press time: SEK 8.15 = U.S. $1.00

Hours: 1000–1500 Monday–Friday. Many are open until 1730 on Thursday. Banks in airports and major rail stations usually have longer hours.

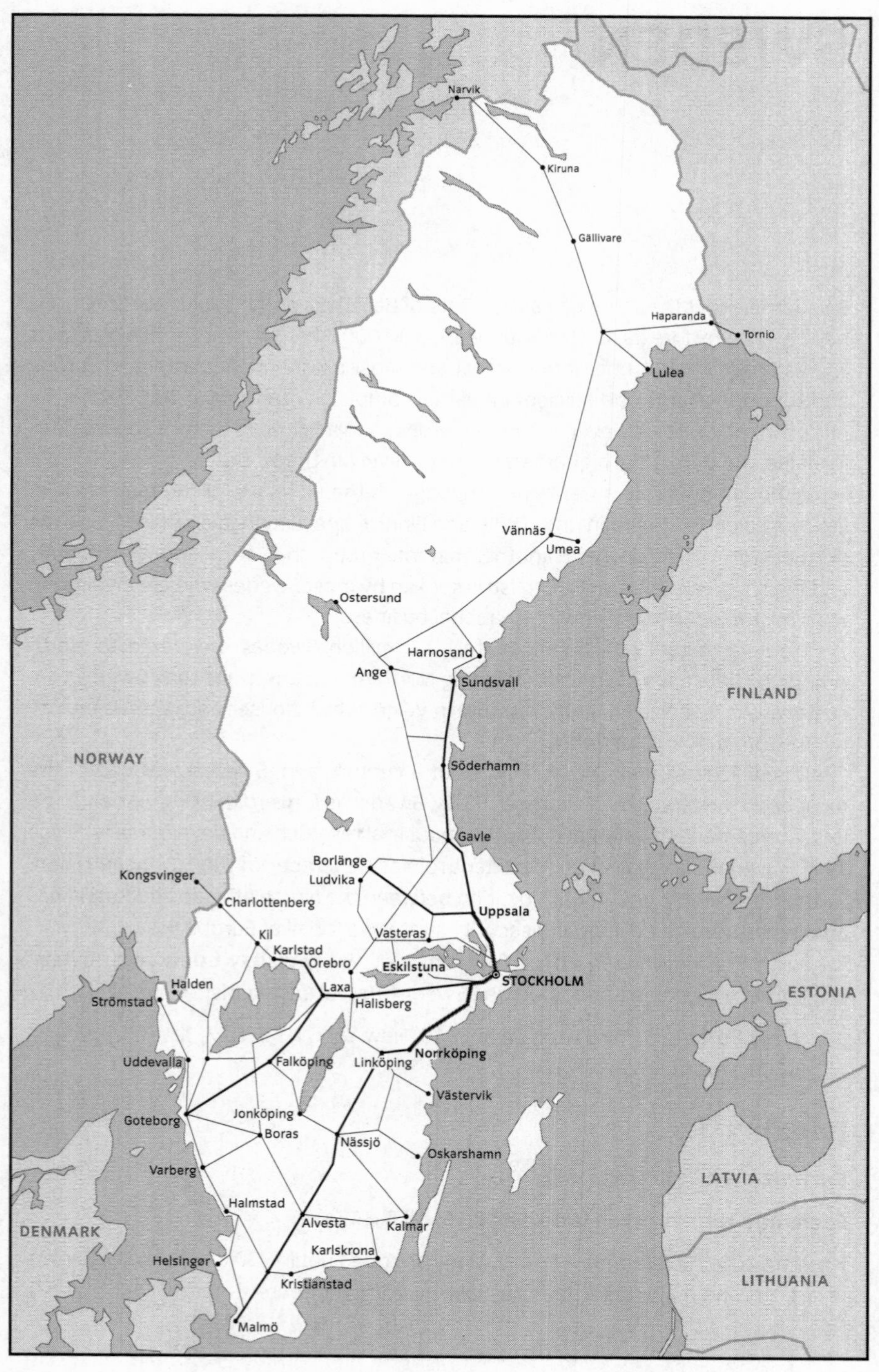

Narvik
Kiruna
Gällivare
Haparanda
Tornio
Lulea
Vännäs
Umea
Ostersund
Harnosand
Ange
Sundsvall
FINLAND
NORWAY
Söderhamn
Gavle
Borlänge
Ludvika
Kongsvinger
Charlottenberg
Uppsala
Vasteras
Kil
Karlstad
Orebro
Eskilstuna
STOCKHOLM
Halden
Strömstad
Laxa
Halisberg
ESTONIA
Uddevalla
Falköping
Linköping
Norrköping
Västervik
Goteborg
Jonköping
Boras
Nässjö
Oskarshamn
Varberg
LATVIA
Halmstad
Alvesta
Kalmar
DENMARK
Karlskrona
Helsingør
Kristianstad
LITHUANIA
Malmö

Communications

Country Dialing Code: 46

For telephone calls within Sweden dial zero (0) preceding area code.

Major Mobile Phone Companies: Telia, Tele2, Telenor

Rail Travel in Sweden

SJ AB, Central Station, SE-105 50 Stockholm; from outside Sweden, *Tel:* +46 771 75 75 75; within Sweden, *Tel:* 0771 75 75 75; www.sj.se.

SJ AB (Swedish Railways) operates about 7,000 miles of rail lines. SJ's X 2000 high-speed trains cruise at up to 125 mph (200 km/h) and serve most of the major cities in Sweden. In Business First Class, meals are served at travelers' seats. There is also a bistro car that serves sandwiches and hot and cold dishes, as well as some alcoholic beverages.

Linx AB (Ltd.) is an Inter-Scandinavian joint venture between SJ and NSB (Norwegian Railways). The new Linx trains (replacing X 2000 trains) link Oslo–Gothenburg with the Malmö/Copenhagen region (Øresund) and have improved travel time and comfort on the Oslo–Stockholm route. The combined rail and motorway connection via the 16-kilometer Øresund Bridge began in 2000. This major infrastructure brought the cities of Malmö, Sweden, and Copenhagen, Denmark, together to create the largest northern European market.

The Linx trains offer ergonomically correct seats, radio and music channels (ear plugs can be purchased), power outlets for laptops and mobile units, and even wireless Internet access. In Business Class, meals are served at travelers' seats; in Standard Class, you can buy cold or warm foods in the Linx Deli.

Sweden's **overnight trains** are among the best in Europe. The *Nordpilen* ("Northern Arrow"), which runs between Göteborg and Östersund/Storlien, even has a movie-and-Bistro carriage. Two films are shown each evening, as well as a free short film for the kids. The Stockholm–Östersund route also has a Bistro carriage. SJ offers four types of sleeping facilities: private compartment with two beds, shower, and toilet; shared two-berth compartment with shower and toilet in the corridor; shared three-berth with shower and toilet in the corridor; and shared six-berth couchette carriage with toilet and sink in the hallway. Night trains travel the following domestic and international routes: Göteborg–Östersund/Storlien–Göteborg; Malmö–Stockholm–Malmö; Malmö–Berlin–Malmö (www.berlin-night-express.com); and Stockholm–Östersund/Storlien–Stockholm.

Train platforms are referred to in Sweden as *spoors*. On most trains operated by the Scandinavian countries, drinking water is supplied at no charge. Train reservations are mandatory for trips of more than 90 miles on all X 2000/Linx and overnight trains.

SJ accepts the variety of **Eurail passes** (see list of European rail passes in the Appendix for prices and ordering information), **Eurail Scandinavia Pass,** and the

Sweden Pass. Pass prices do not include reservation fees, but a point-to-point ticket does.

Bonuses for pass holders include:

- 40 percent discount on Tallink-Silja Line: Stockholm–Helsinki, Finland (rail pass must be valid in Sweden and Finland), Stockholm–Turku
- Free ferry crossing on Scandlines: Helsingborg–Helsingør, Denmark (with valid rail pass in Sweden and Denmark)
- 20 percent discount on Stena Line: Göteborg–Frederikshavn, Denmark (no discount on cabin/couchette supplements)
- 50 percent discount on TT Line: Trelleborg–Travemünde, Germany
- 50 percent discount on TR-Line full-fare ferry crossing: Trelleborg–Rostock, Germany

Sweden Pass

Purchase online or in SJ rail stations. Valid for travel within Sweden and to/from Oslo and Copenhagen within a 1-month period. Valid on SJ, Linx, X 2000, and Connex trains; not valid on private railroads. Children younger than age 15 are free when accompanied by an adult (up to two children per adult paying passenger). Prices are in U.S. dollars. Prices do not include reservation fees, supplement for X 2000/Linx and InterCity trains, or couchette and sleeper fees.

DAYS Within 1 Month	ADULT 1st class	ADULT 2nd class	YOUTH 2nd class
3 days	$369	$286	$215
4 days	$396	$305	$231
5 days	$439	$339	$256
6 days	$497	$384	$289
8 days	$555	$428	$322

Child (age 4–15) fare 50 percent off adult fare. Youth younger than age 26.

Base City: **STOCKHOLM**

www.stockholmtown.com
City Dialing Code: 08

Stockholm declares intentions of retaining the old, then in the same breath states great love of progress and things modern; it provides visitors with the opportunity to experience Sweden's modern culture and to celebrate its ancient traditions.

Stockholm's **Gamla Stan** (Old Town) is located on a small island in the city center. Its narrow cobblestone streets wind their crooked ways over paths unchanged since the Middle Ages past houses bearing the same facades they had when they were built. But behind these old facades you find the most modern of business establishments and apartments whose decors rival those of similar dwellings anywhere in the world. With a delicate touch, Stockholm has made this dualism work in every way.

Another example is **Sergels Torg,** Stockholm's space-age city center. It is comfortably surrounded by other structures centuries older. Call it what you will, but most people call Stockholm absolutely beautiful.

Arriving by Air

Arlanda Airport lies 26 miles (42 kilometers) northwest of the city. *Tel:* (08) 797 60 00; www.swedavia.se. Tourist information is available in the arrivals areas.

Airport–City Links: Arlanda Express train service every 15 minutes to downtown Stockholm. *Tel:* 467 71 720 200 (within Sweden only); www.arlandaexpress.com; *E-mail:* info@atrain.se. Journey time: 20 minutes. Fare: SEK 260 adults one-way; SEK 130 seniors/students; children (four maximum) up to age 17, free when accompanied by an adult paying full fare; round-trip ticket valid for one month from date of purchase, SEK 490. Purchase tickets at LFV (Swedish Civil Aviation Administration) information desks in each terminal and at the Arlanda Express ticket office in Stockholm Central Station.

Flygbussarna Airport Coach departures are every 10 minutes at peak times. *Tel:* 46 0771515252; www.flygbussarna.se. Journey time: 40 minutes. Fare: SEK 105 adults one-way; SEK 198 adults round-trip; children (four maximum) up to age 17, free when accompanied by parents; Internet discounts available. Coaches terminate at Stockholm Cityterminalen (City Terminal).

Taxi stands are available outside each terminal. Average fare to Stockholm city center, SEK 435. The more expensive Airport Taxi can be pre-booked ahead of your arrival or at the "Flygtaxi" counters in the terminals. *Tel:* (08) 797 50 78. Taxi Stockholm: *Tel:* (08) 15 00 00.

Arriving by Train

Stockholm has several *suburban* stations, but international trains stop only at the main rail station in the center of the city, Stockholm Central. All excursions out of Stockholm depart from Stockholm Central Station.

Stockholm's Central Station is modern, well organized, and easy to move about in. International trains usually arrive on track No. 17 or 18.

- **Luggage carts:** Insert a SEK 10 coin in the lock; coin will be refunded upon returning the cart to a rack.

The Central Station is close to several major hotels and directly connected to the Stockholm subway (the *Tunnelbanan*). The main taxi stand is across the street from the railway station.

The station does an excellent job of moving its passengers to and from the trains. It also provides a full complement of services for the traveler. An arcade of shops, on the lower station level in the proximity of the exits from track Nos. 17 and 18, provides all types of foodstuffs, beverages, tobacco, newspapers, and so forth.

The *Konsum*—Sweden's answer to the American supermarket—is a good place to restock your larder. It is located in the same area within the station. There are also shops in the main station–concourse area where you may purchase food and soft drinks.

The station's food-service facilities range from a cafeteria to a restaurant with its own gambling casino. The cafeteria is located on the main level of the station to the far right as you stand looking into the station from the train exit. It can be identified by its sign, CAFE OASEN. Cafeteria service is continuous 0630 to 2330 Monday through Saturday and 0700 to 2330 Sunday; it is a good place to have breakfast, lunch, or dinner.

The **Centralens Restaurang** (restaurant) **Orientexpressen** has the previously mentioned casino. You'll see its sign on the right side of the station as you exit from the track area. The complex also includes a pub and a restaurant with good food at reasonable prices. The all-you-can-eat breakfast in the restaurant section is a real bargain. The restaurant has an expansive but relatively inexpensive luncheon-and-dinner menu featuring many Swedish specialties (closed during July).

Across the street from Central Station, along the street Vasagatan, you can find a number of excellent food facilities ranging from fast to fancy.

- **Train information** is displayed on digital boards and is readily available throughout the station, including key positions just inside the main entrance and again in the corridors leading to the track areas. The office is in the main concourse to the left of the main exit. *Hours:* 0600–2300 Monday–Saturday, 0700–2300 Sunday. Local train information, usually for commuter trains, is displayed by a bank of large-screen, closed-circuit television sets.

- **Train reservations** can be made in a large ticket office located in the main hall to the right as you proceed from the track area. A sign, FARDBILJETTER PLATSBILJETTER, identifies it. Take a queue number for seat reservations and sleeping-car accommodations. *Hours:* 0600–2200 Monday–Friday, 0600–1900 Saturday, 0800–2100 Sunday.
- **Rail pass validation** should be completed before making your first train trip. Operating personnel aboard the trains can validate the pass, but they are required to charge for the service. Validation is free in any regular railway station. In Stockholm's Central Station, use the window marked international tickets to the right of the main exit.
- **Money exchange** is located in the main station concourse and to the right of the main exit as you proceed from the track area. The office displays the regular pictograph sign plus one reading FOREX (exchange office). *Hours:* 0700–2100 daily.
- **Hotel reservations** can be made at Stockholm Information Service, located in the main station concourse next to the post office. Look for the sign HOTELLCENTRAL TURISTINFORMATION. *Tel:* (08) 789 24 90; *Fax:* (08) 791 86 66; *E-mail:* hotels@svb.stockholm.se. *Hours:* June–August: 0900–1900 daily; September–May: 0900–1800 daily. Advance booking is free. Advance payment is accepted to assure that the hotel or pension will hold your room until your arrival. If your accommodations are located some distance from the train station, this can be a welcomed service.
- **Tourist information** is available in the rail station at the same office, HOTELLCENTRAL TURISTINFORMATION, or in the main tourist center at Sweden House.

Tourist Information/Hotel Reservations

- *Stockholm Tourist Centre:* Vasagatan 14, 11120 Stockholm. *Tel:* (08) 508 285 08; *Fax:* (08) 508 285 09; www.stockholmtown.com; *E-mail:* touristinfo@stockholm.se. *Hours:* May–September: 0900–1900 Monday–Friday, 0900–1600 Saturday, 1000–1600 Sunday; October–April: 0900–1800 Monday–Friday, 0900–1600 Saturday, 1000–1600 Sunday

Inquiries about the "Sweden at Home" plan of meeting Swedes with similar interests should be made at this information office. The *Stockholm Guide* is excellent.

Getting Around in Stockholm

The city has excellent transportation facilities for sightseeing in Stockholm. The extensive network of bus and subway systems makes it easy to reach practically any point in the city from any other point.

Your key to using these city transportation facilities is the **Stockholm Card,** which provides free admission to 80 of the city's museums and sights, as well as free sightseeing by boat, free public transportation throughout the Stockholm area, a free bicycle sightseeing guide and free guidebook. Adult prices are SEK 495 for 24 hours, SEK 650 for 48 hours, SEK 795 for 72 hours, and SEK 1050 for 120 hours. Child rates are SEK 225 for 24 hours, SEK 265 for 48 hours, SEK 295 for 72 hours, and SEK 325 for 120 hours. For additional children there are reduced rates available. You can purchase the card online at www.stockholmtown.com and at the tourist information centers in Central Station and the Culture Center. It is sold undated and is stamped with the date and hour the first time you use it. With the card, you will be given a folder explaining its use and validation procedure.

Sights/Attractions/Tours

Gamla Stan—The Old Town dates from 1290 and is Stockholm's oldest and most enchanting area. Besides containing many historical sights, such as the world's oldest existing bank (since 1656), the Royal Palace, and Parliament, you'll also find unusual shops, art galleries, antiques stores, and more than 30 restaurants.

With the Stockholm Card in your pocket, you can expand your day-excursion itinerary to include places of interest in and near Stockholm. For example, you can make a day excursion to **Norrtalje,** with its quaint port, and have lunch aboard a vintage steamer permanently moored there. You can also ride one of the Stockholm Transit Authority (SL) buses to **Furusund,** a narrow passage for ships entering and leaving the city's harbor. You can have lunch in a quaint Inn at Furusund. During high season, May through August, sightseeing boats can take you to the outer archipelago.

Yet another alternative use for the card would be to take a bus ride to historic **Vaxholm** for a great Swedish lunch at the waterfront hotel overlooking the old fortress and shopping there at leisure. Stockholm has many museums to explore, so it is difficult to single out but a few recommendations. There is one, however, that we are sure you won't want to miss: the ***Vasa* Museum.** *Tel:* (08) 519 54800. Visit www.vasamuseet.se; *Hours:* June–August: 0830–1800 daily; September–May: 1000–1700 daily (until 2000 on Wednesday). Admission: SEK 130 adults; SEK 100 students; children up to age 18, free.

In 1628 Sweden proudly launched what was then the world's largest warship and pride of the nation, the *Vasa*. Carrying the name of the royal family, along with 64 cannon, this ship was presumed to be unconquerable. But Sweden's joy was short-lived. The *Vasa* capsized in the harbor during its maiden voyage. Raised in 1961, painstakingly restored, and now resting in a museum especially constructed

Train Connections to Other Base Cities from Stockholm

Depart from Stockholm Central Station

DEPART	TRAIN NUMBER	ARRIVE	NOTES
		Berlin Hauptbahnhof	
0821	X2 525	2055	R, 1, Exc. Sa
1221	X2 533	0640+1	R, 1, Sleeper
		Copenhagen (København) H.	
0621	X2 521	1148	R, 2, M–Sa
0821	X2 525	1324	R
1221	X2 533	1724	R
1621	X2 541	2148	R, 2
1821	X2 545	2348	R, 2, M–Sa
		Helsinki	
1700	Tallink-Silja Line Ferry	0945+1	R, 3
1730	Viking Line Ferry	1000+1	R, 4
		Oslo Sentral	
1106	X2 632	1609	R, Exc. Sa
1559	X2 639	2028	R, Exc. Sa

Daily, unless otherwise noted

R Reservations required. Seat reservations required on Swedish trains for journeys longer than 150 kilometers (90 miles).

+1 Arrive next day

1. Change trains in Copenhagen then Hamburg.
2. Change trains in Malmö.
3. Tallink-Silja Line ferries depart daily. Tallink-Silja Line docks are Stockholm Värtahamnen and Helsinki Eteläsatama. Refer to Appendix, Ferry Crossings, for details.
4. Viking Line ferries depart daily. Viking Line docks are Stockholm Stadsgarden and Helsinki Katajanokka. Refer to Appendix, Ferry Crossings, for details.

for its preservation, the warship is enthroned in the middle of a great hall, displayed in all its grandeur. The cobblestone ground floor suggests a quay, and the restored warship can be viewed from various perspectives from four levels.

Vasa is unique since it is the oldest fully preserved warship in the world. Films of the raising and restoration of the *Vasa* are shown hourly in the museum, and guided tours following the film are conducted in the summer.

Winter travelers plan ahead to experience Stockholm's annual winter festival, events, and activities.

Day Excursions

We have selected a group of day excursions that will give you an excellent cross section of life in Sweden. **Eskilstuna** is often referred to as "Sweden's Sheffield," although it bears little resemblance to its English counterpart. Next is a trip southward through Ostergotland, where the city of **Norrköping** will unfold its industrial lifestyles.

Uppsala brings another contrast, that of a university town. Admittedly, planning day excursions in Sweden is made somewhat difficult by the distances involved between the centers of population, but all of these are within reasonable travel times and well worth the visit.

Day Excursion to

Eskilstuna

Sweden's Steel Center

Depart from Stockholm Central Station
Distance by Train: 73 miles (117 km)
Average Train Time: 1 hour
City Dialing Code: 16
Tourist Information Office: Postal Address: Tullgatan 4, S-631 86, Eskilstuna.
Visiting Address: Stora Fristadshuset, Rothoffsvillan
Tel: (016) 7107000; **Fax:** (016) 149500
www.eskilstuna.se
E-mail: info@turism.eskilstuna.nu
Hours: Summer: 1000–1700 Monday–Friday, 1000–1400 Saturday and Sunday.
Winter: 1000–1700 Monday–Friday.
Notes: To reach the tourist office, exit by the front of the station and follow Drottninggatan Street 3 blocks to Rademachergatan. Turn left onto Rademachergatan and proceed until you see a cluster of red wooden houses. The one with the sign TURISTBYRÅ is the tourist office.

Eskilstuna is unique in that it has preserved its industrial birthplace in the midst of a great industrial expansion. In a quiet section in the center of Sweden's "steel town," the well-preserved **Rademacher Forges** stand today just as they have for almost the last 350 years. Be certain to include a visit to this area during your day excursion.

The forges were erected in 1658 under the supervision of Reinhold Rademacher. Originally 20 in number, 6 have been preserved as a tribute to the heritage of modern Eskilstuna. The entire area surrounding the forges was restored in 1959 to commemorate the city's tricentennial. Descendants of the "smiths" are still at work forming gold, copper, and iron into colorful trinkets for sale. In the spring and early autumn, there is also a handicraft market in the area. The **Faktori museet** is situated in the old Musket Factory nearby. The museum includes, among other things, the city's historical exhibition, "Mellan sjöarna" ("Between the lakes").

Eskilstuna is located in the most populous part of Sweden. Named after the 11th-century English missionary Sam Eskil, Eskilstuna is the center of the Swedish steel industry. Its parks and open-area squares, however, make it unlike any other steel town. A statue of Saint Eskil stands in the churchyard of **Fors Kyrka.** Both the statue and the church are worth a visit. If you continue your walk along the riverside, you will find another monument of Saint Eskil on your way to **Kloster Kyrka,** which is easily recognized by its two towers.

Eskilstuna's town charter dates from 1659. In 1971 five surrounding rural communities and the town of Torshälla merged with Eskilstuna. Torshälla is more than 650 years old. Its name was derived from the Nordic god, Thor, who was worshipped at offertory gatherings of the barbarians occupying Torshälla.

Parken Zoo (zoo park) in Eskilstuna ranks as one of Sweden's most visited tourist attractions. *Hours:* May and June daily 1000–1700, July and August 1000–1900, September 1000–1700. In addition to its zoological gardens, there are an amusement park known as the "Tivoli," a heated swimming pool with waterslides, "Phantom Land," "Flamingo Valley," and a petting zoo. The zoo is well-known for its collection of animals that are rare in Sweden, including the world's largest lizard, "the Komodo dragon," and a family of white tigers. The white tiger is thought to be extinct in the wild, but at Parken Zoo, several litters have been born since 1990. Visit www.parkenzoo.se.

The city is well endowed with works of art. The **Art Museum** (*Hours:* 1200–1600 daily) is especially proud of its collection of Swedish art from the 17th century to the present. Every three or four weeks, contemporary art exhibitions are changed.

Stockholm—Eskilstuna

DEPART Stockholm Central	**TRAIN NUMBER**	**ARRIVE** Eskilstuna
0629	R 901	0739
0755	R 915	0900
0855	R 919	1001
then hourly service at 55 minutes past the hour until 2255, plus 1622 and 1727.		

DEPART Eskilstuna	**TRAIN NUMBER**	**ARRIVE** Stockholm Central
1500	R 942	1605
1600	R 946	1705
1700	R 950	1805
1813	R 904	1920
2004	R 962	2109
2200	R 970	2305

Daily
Distance: 73 miles (117 km)

Be certain to visit **Tingsgarden,** the glass-making center located in the old town, where you can view glassblowing and glass painting. There is also a gift shop, cafe, and restaurant. The 18th-century surroundings are well preserved and have been declared a historical monument.

Sunbyholm Castle is located 8 miles outside Eskilstuna. Built by an illegitimate son of a Swedish king, it has been restored to its original splendor and a restaurant has been added. The area also has a harbor, good swimming beach, and the 1,000-year-old "strip cartoon"—the **Sigurd Carving** on stone—one of about 50 prehistoric monuments surrounding Eskilstuna. It illustrates some famous episodes from the ancient Icelandic saga of Sigurd the Dragon Slayer.

Day Excursion to

Norrköping

The Northern Cactus Center

Depart from Stockholm Central Station
Distance by Train: 101 miles (163 km)
Average Train Time: 1 hour, 17 minutes
City Dialing Code: 11
Tourist Information Office: Holmentornet, Dalsgatan 9, Uppler Norrkoping AB, S-60181, Norrköping
Tel: (011) 15 50 00; **Fax:** (011) 15 50 74
www.destination.norrkoping.se
E-mail: turistbyran@norrkoping.se
Hours: January 1–April 29 and September 9–December 31: 1000–1800 Monday–Thursday, 1000–1500 Friday, 1000–1400 Saturday, closed Sunday; April 30–June 20 and August 19–September 8: 1000–1800 Monday–Thursday, 1000–1600 Friday–Sunday; June 24–August 18: 1000–1800 daily
Notes: The tourist office is about a 10-minute walk from the rail station. Proceed down Drottninggatan. After crossing the bridge over the Motala River (Motala Ström), turn right onto Hamngatan and take another right onto Gamla Rådstugugatan. Pass Repslagaregatan and take the next right to Dalsgatan. The tourist office is located in the Industrial Landscape, opposite Louis De Geer Concert and Congress Hall.

If you want to experience, in the same day, two different forms of land transportation that span 100 years, now's your chance. Take the modern, high-speed X 2000 train (seat reservations required and supplement payable) from Stockholm Central in the morning and arrive in Norrköping in only 1 hour and 17 minutes. Then, for an excellent introduction to Norrköping that includes the charm of yesteryear, ride the 1902

Stockholm—Norrköping

DEPART Stockholm Central	TRAIN NUMBER	ARRIVE Norrköping	NOTES
0621	X 2000/521	0733	R, M–Sa
0721	X 2000/523	0833	R, M–F
0821	X 2000/525	0933	R
1021	X 2000/529	1133	R
1121	X 2000/531	1233	R
1221	X 2000/533	1333	R

DEPART Norrköping	TRAIN NUMBER	ARRIVE Stockholm Central	NOTES
1424	X 2000/534	1539	R
1524	X 2000/536	1639	R, M–F
1624	X 2000/538	1739	R
1743	R 296	1909	R
1824	X 2000/512	1939	R
1924	X 2000/544	2039	R
2024	X 2000/546	2139	R
2224	X 2000/550	2339	R, Exc. Sa

Daily, unless otherwise noted
R Reservations required on all X 2000 trains and for all journeys of more than 150 km on other trains. Special supplements payable on X 2000 trains.
Distance: 101 miles (163 km)

tram **Gamla Ettan,** "the Old Number One." There are only two cities in Sweden that still use the quaint, clean, and efficient tram system—Gothenburg and Norrköping.

Cactuses in Sweden? That's right. Just opposite the rail station, you may be surprised to see some 25,000 cactus plants in the Karl Johans Park. The plants are rearranged annually according to special motifs.

Norrköping is one of Sweden's most important industrial cities and is the eighth largest. If you proceed directly to the tourist office from the rail station, you'll be in the well-preserved **Industrial Landscape area** (Industrilandskapet). Take a ride on one of the yellow trams to experience yesterday's history in today's environment and to discover the unique Industrial Landscape where the old spinning mills have been transformed. Or take one of the many guided walks, such as "Johanna's Walk," to go back in time to 1910 and hear Johanna talk about life at that time.

The **Louis De Geer Concert and Congress Hall** is a prime example—it once was a paper mill. It no longer makes paper—it makes music—with performances by Norrköping's own symphony orchestra, as well as by many others. The hall is open to the public during the summertime, and guided tours are available.

One of Sweden's most beautiful industrial buildings sits in the middle of the Motala Ström (River). Shaped like an iron and called *strykjämet*, it houses the **Arbetets Museum** (the Museum of Work), with exhibitions, workshops, and a museum shop.

Tel: (011) 18 98 00; *Fax:* (011) 18 22 90; www.arbetetsmuseum.se. *Hours:* 1100–1700 Sunday–Monday; Tuesday 1100–2000, except for certain holiday weekends; no charge for admission. There's a spectacular view from the restaurant on the top floor.

Continuing in the old industrial area along the banks of the Motala Ström, visit the **Stadsmuseet** (City Museum) for a realistic view of life and the crafts and industries of 19th-century Norrköping. Visit www.norrkoping.se/stadsmuseet. *Hours:* 1100–1700 Tuesday–Friday (until 2000 Thursday), 1200–1700 Saturday and Sunday. No admission fee.

Farther along the banks of the Motala, you will come to an open-air museum, the **Färgargården** (Dyer's Workshop), which portrays the wool-dyeing processes of the mid-18th century. For a great midday snack, stop in the cafe for waffles—Swedish style.

Norrköping successfully blends its industrial history with some of nature's most beautiful assets. Its many parks and beautiful flower displays provide an atmosphere of contentment and tranquility.

Norrköping's history extends all the way back to the Bronze Age with the 3,000-year-old rock carvings in **Himmelstalundparken.** Guided tours of the rock carvings are available daily July 1 through August 1 at 1400. There are also special exhibitions, rock-carving trips, and boat trips on the Motala. The rock-carving museum, **Hällristningsmuseet,** is open 1000 to 1800 April–July, 1000 to 1600 August, and 1100 to 1600 October–November.

Only 25 kilometers north of Norrköping is the famous **Kolmårdens Zoo and Safari Park**—one of Europe's finest. Also, close to Norrköping, pleasure steamers ply the **Göta Canal** and the archipelago. Check with the tourist information office for more details on either of these great adventures.

Day Excursion to

Uppsala

University City

Depart from Stockholm Central Station
Distance by Train: 40 miles (66 km)
Average Train Time: 43 minutes
City Dialing Code: 18
Tourist Information Office: Kungsgatan 59, 75321 Uppsala, Sweden
Tel: (018) 727 48 00; **Fax:** (018) 12 43 20
www.uppland.nu
E-mail: info@destinationuppsala.se
Hours: 1000–1800 Monday–Friday, 1000–1500 Saturday; July–mid-August: Sunday 1000–1500

Notes: The tourist information office is a five-minute walk from the railway station. Exit the station and walk diagonally through the small park in front to the main street, Kungsgatan. Turn right, then turn left onto Vaksalagatan (the next crossing). When you reach the square (Stora Torget) where all the city buses meet, follow the street Drottninggatan and cross the small River Fyrisan. Turn right immediately after the bridge; the tourist office is identified by the traditional "i" sign.

No other town in Sweden has such a long recorded history as Uppsala. This is where Sweden began. As far back as the sixth century, it was the political and religious center of the expanding Swedish kingdom. According to the ancient legends, pagans from all reaches of the kingdom came to Uppsala every ninth year to feast and offer sacrifices until the 11th century, when Christianity began to take over. Legend has it that one of the kings of the period, King Aun, got all wrapped up in the nine-year cycle by sacrificing one of his sons each cycle. His tenth and last son put an end to old dad—and to the cycle, too!

Modern Uppsala won't remind you of Oxford or Heidelberg—or Bryn Mawr, for that matter. Uppsala is a university town with an academic environment distinctly its own. The city and the area surrounding it enshrine a great deal of Swedish history encompassing religion (pagan and Christian alike), academe, and politics. This composite results in a city of multifaceted interests, architecture, and customs.

Gamla Uppsala (Old Uppsala) lies 3 miles north of the current city center and is full of myth, legend, and history including the graves of the sixth-century Ynglinga Dynasty kings of Aun, Egil, and Adil (who worshiped the god Frej). (Take bus No. 2, 110, or 115.) The pagan religion of the Vikings persisted here well into the 11th century. A 12th-century church, heralding the advent of Christianity, then replaced the pagan temple. Some say the ancient mounds were part of the lost civilization of Atlantis. The area is now an open-air museum, accessible to visitors daily year-round. Visit the **Gamla Historical Centre** celebrating the archaeological finds. Hours vary—check with the tourist information office. Admission is SEK 70 for adults; children are admitted free. *Tel:* (018) 23 93 00; www.raa.se/gamlauppsala; *E-mail:* gamlauppsala@raa.se.

Uppsala Castle stands on a hill overlooking the city. Begun in the 1540s by King Gustav Vasa as a symbol of his power over the church, it was completed during the reign of Queen Christina. The king had cannon mounted on the castle pointing at the church. They still point that way today. Partially destroyed by fire in 1702, the castle has been restored. After the extensive renovation in 1994, you can now visit new parts of the castle on a 45-minute guided tour conducted in English at 1300 and 1500 from June 1 through August 27. You'll see the Hall of State and the castle church's uncovered altar wall.

The great **Hall of State** is frequently the scene of historic events. Both the coronation banquet for Gustavus Adolphus and Queen Christina's abdication took place within the castle's walls. *Hours:* June 17–August 27: 1000–1600 Tuesday–Friday, until 1800 Wednesday. A more restricted schedule is followed during the remainder of the year. Visit www.uppsala.se/konstmuseum.

Three-quarters of Uppsala was destroyed by fire in 1702. It was in the subsequent period of reconstruction that the character of the city changed. The university and its scholars began to dominate, and the reputation of the university spread throughout the civilized world. The current university building was opened in 1887.

Among the collections in Exhibition Hall of The Uppsala University Library (located on Dag Hammarskjolds vag 1) are the Silver Bible from the sixth century, medieval manuscripts, and musical notations by Mozart. Take bus No. 6, 7, 22, 26, or 52. *Tel:* (018) 471 39 00. Visit www.ub.uu.se. *Hours:* 0900–2000 Monday–Friday and 1000–1700 Saturday.

In Uppsala, Saint Erik, Saint Olof, and Saint Lars' church is usually referred to as **The Cathedral.** Two of its patron saints, Erik and Olof, were Christian kings in Scandinavia during the 11th and 12th centuries, when the Christians finally had the pagans on the run. Lars died a martyr's death in Rome in A.D. 258. Building of The Cathedral started in the late 13th century, and it took a century and a half to complete. It has been ravaged by fires, and its towers collapsed, but with Swedish determination it was restored. English-language tours of the Uppsala Cathedral are conducted several times a day in summer. Visit www.uppsaladomkyrka.se.

Stockholm—Uppsala

Note: In addition to trains shown here, there is local train service between Stockholm and Uppsala; get information at Stockholm Central Station.

DEPART Stockholm Central	TRAIN NUMBER	ARRIVE Uppsala
0811	R 812	0849
0911	R 816	0949
1011	R 820	1049

DEPART Uppsala	TRAIN NUMBER	ARRIVE Stockholm Central	NOTES
1611	R 849	1649	
1811	R 857	1849	
1911	R 861	1949	
2126	IC 2271	2221	R

Daily

R Reservations required

Seat reservations presumably not needed on regional trains since this trip is only 66 km, but passengers should check at the Stockholm Central Station before boarding these trains.

Distance: 40 miles (66 km)

SWITZERLAND

Switzerland is a year-round wonderland of astonishing beauty and one of the most multilingual countries in Europe. You can experience several different cultures encompassing four national languages—all within one neat little country. The German-speaking Swiss make up 65 percent of the population; French, 18 percent; Italian, 10 percent; and Romansch, 1 percent; and 70-plus dialects lend a special charisma to tiny villages and hamlets. And many Swiss can speak all four languages and English, too.

The diversity doesn't end there. From majestic snowcapped mountains to languid palm-fringed lakes, from cowbells and yodeling to craftsmanship and incredible feats of railroad engineering, Switzerland is surprising.

For more information about Switzerland, contact the Switzerland Tourism Offices of North America (**www.myswitzerland.com;** *E-mail:* info.usa@myswitzerland.com):

Chicago: 150 North Michigan Avenue, Suite 2930, Chicago, IL 60601; *Tel:* (312) 630-5840

Los Angeles: 222 North Sepulveda Boulevard, Suite 1570, El Segundo, CA 90245; *Tel:* (310) 335-5980; *Fax:* (310) 335-5982

New York: 608 Fifth Avenue, New York, NY 10020; *Tel:* (800) 794-7795; *Fax:* (212) 262-6116

Toronto: 480 University Avenue, Suite 1500, Toronto, Ontario M5G 1V2; *Tel:* (800) 794-7795; *Fax:* (416) 695-2774

Banking

Currency: Swiss Franc (CHF)

Exchange rate at press time: CHF 0.97 = U.S. $1.00

Hours: 0830–1630 Monday–Friday, closed Saturday and Sunday

Communications

Country Dialing Code: 41

For telephone calls within Switzerland, dial zero (0) preceding area code. You can buy a calling card for calls within Switzerland at any Swiss post office.

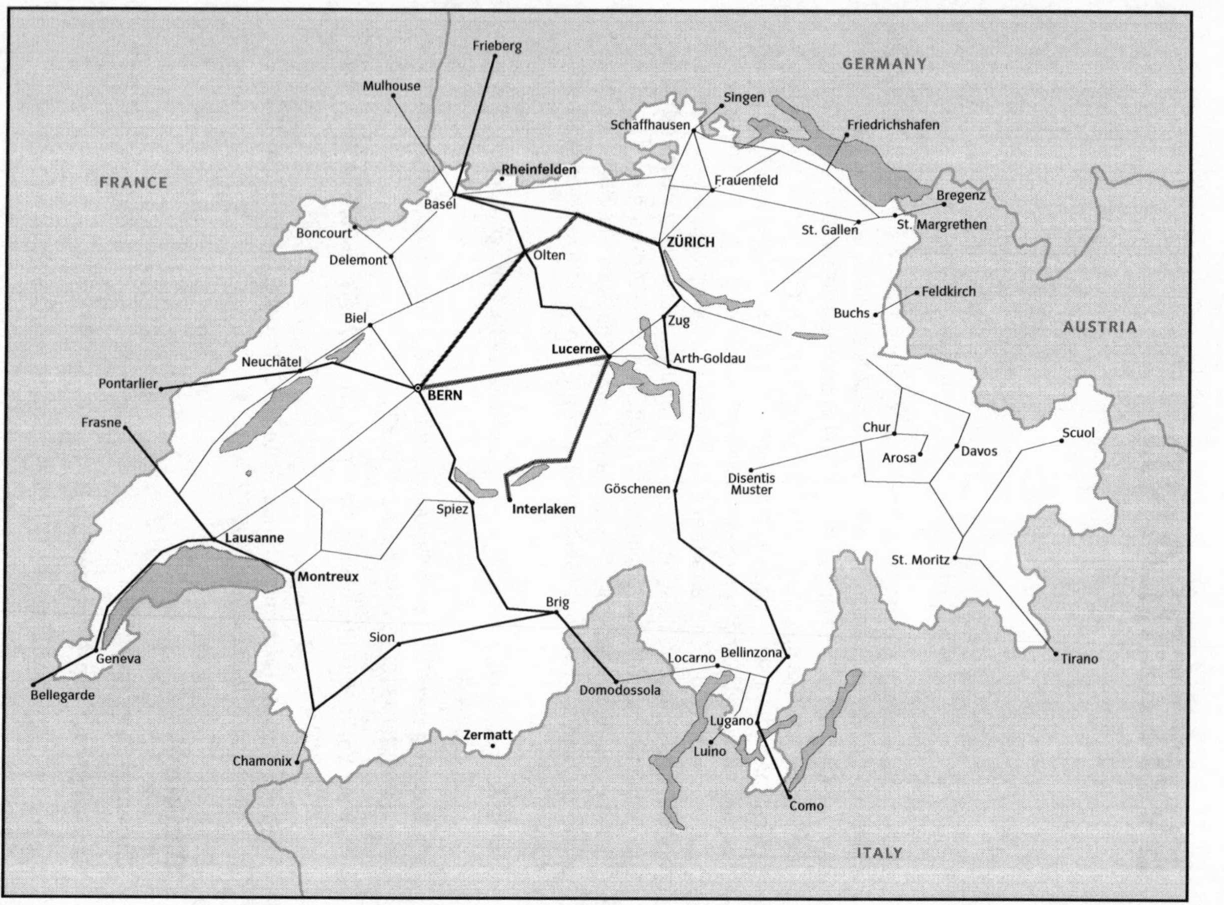

FRANCE
GERMANY
AUSTRIA
ITALY
Frieberg
Mulhouse
Rheinfelden
Basel
Boncourt
Delemont
Olten
ZÜRICH
Schaffhausen
Singen
Friedrichshafen
Frauenfeld
Bregenz
St. Gallen
St. Margrethen
Feldkirch
Buchs
Biel
Zug
Lucerne
Arth-Goldau
Neuchâtel
Pontarlier
BERN
Frasne
Chur
Arosa
Davos
Scuol
Disentis Muster
Göschenen
Spiez
Interlaken
Lausanne
Montreux
St. Moritz
Brig
Sion
Geneva
Bellegarde
Locarno
Bellinzona
Tirano
Domodossola
Lugano
Luino
Zermatt
Chamonix
Como

International calls can be placed from public phones at the post office and some major railway stations.

Major Mobile Phone Companies: Swisscom, Sunrise, Orange

Rail Travel in Switzerland

The Swiss are well-known for their excellence in clock production, and they know how to run a railroad with the same finesse—on time. Rail travelers from North America may take advantage of the **"Fly Rail Baggage Service"** program by checking their luggage through from their departure airport to one of the 60 railway stations in Switzerland offering the service (approximately $25). When returning to North America, visitors can also check their luggage through to their destination airport (CHF 20 per bag). American carriers do not allow outbound service from Switzerland.

According to the Swiss, only the "Man in the Moon" knows how dense the network of railroads in Switzerland *really* is. Although Switzerland is only 216 miles from north to south and 137 miles from east to west, more than 13,000 miles of train, bus, and boat routes make up the Swiss Travel System network. Even mountains don't stop the Swiss. They either tunnel through them or scale their heights with funiculars or cog railways. Switzerland has one of the longest railroad tunnels, the highest railroad, plus more bridges, tunnels, and other engineering works per square mile than any other country in the world. **ICN (InterCity Neigezug)** tilting trains have shrunk travel times on many routes, and frequency has increased to half-hourly service on most InterCity lines. Tilting trains and double-decker train equipment have also increased business, dining, family, and quiet-zone facilities.

The Swiss Federal Railways (SBB/CFF/FFS) accepts the following rail passes that can be purchased in advance of your departure for Europe: the 18-country variety of **Eurail passes,** the **Swiss Pass,** the **Swiss Card, Eurail Austria–Switzerland Pass,** and the **Eurail France–Switzerland Pass.** Visit www.sbb.ch or www.rail.ch.

Swiss Federal Railways provides the following **Eurail** bonuses:

- 20 percent discount on URh Rhine River boats: Constance–Schaffhausen
- Steamer services on lakes of Biel, Brienz, Geneva, Lucerne, Murten, Neuchâtel, Thun, and Zürich—free (seasonal)
- Alpnachstad–Mount Pilatus (see Lucerne section)—cable railway 35 percent discount
- Bürgenstock funicular—20 percent discount
- Free sailings on the Aare River, Biel–Solothurn (seasonal)
- Jungfrau Region Railways—25 percent discount
- 30 percent discount on funicular from Alpnachstad to summit of Mount Pilatus and on cable car from Kriens
- 25 percent discount on boats operated by BSB, SBS, and ÖBB on Lake Constance (May through October)

- Transportation Museum in Lucerne—35 percent off entrance fee
- Vitznau Rigi Railways—25 percent discount
- Stanserhorn funicular/cable railway—50 percent discount

The **Swiss Card** is valid for one free round-trip plus 50 percent discount for additional trips (except for some mountain railroads that offer 25 percent discount) within a one-month validity period. First class is $327; second class, $231. Children younger than age 16 travel free with parent. Children age 6 to 15 not accompanied by parent: half adult fare. Children younger than age 6 travel free.

The **Swiss Transfer Ticket** is great for skiers or for those who will stay in only one place. It provides for one round-trip ticket by rail between any Swiss airport or border town and any single destination in Switzerland. First class: $258; second class: $162. Children younger than age 16 can travel round-trip free when accompanied by at least one parent. Children age 6 to 15 not accompanied by a parent: half adult fare. Children younger than age 6 travel free.

Some of Switzerland's most scenic railroads (descriptions follow) accept Eurail passes; most private railroads, however, do not, although some offer discounts (aforementioned). Reservations are mandatory and cost extra. Remember to take along your passport for border crossings.

Some of Switzerland's most scenic routes by train include:

- **Bernina Express**—Chur–St. Moritz–Bernina Pass–Poschiavo–Tirano. Runs daily in the summer and only to and from Tirano in the winter. Trip is 2½ hours from St. Moritz or 4 hours from Chur. Visit www.rhb.ch.
- **Centovalli Railway**—Narrow-gauge railway connects Locarno with Domodossola (Italy). Runs all year. Scenic trip is 1½ hours. Visit www.centovalli.ch.
- **Glacier Express**—Zermatt–Brig–Andermatt–Chur–Davos/St. Moritz. Journey runs daily in summer and winter. Trip is 7½ hours and passes through 91 tunnels and over 291 bridges. Eurail passes valid only between Davos/St. Moritz and Disentis. You must purchase an additional point-to-point ticket for the portion from Disentis to Zermatt. Visit www.glacierexpress.ch.
- **Golden Pass**—Lucerne–Brünig Panoramic Express–Interlaken–Jungfraujoch–Salon bleu–Golden Pass Express–Montreux–Genève. Runs daily all year. Visit www.goldenpass.ch.
- **Swiss Chocolate Train**—Montreux–Gruyères–Broc–Montreux—a sweet delight for chocolate lovers and rail buffs. Ride in a vintage 1915 "Belle Epoque" or an ultramodern panoramic railcar and visit Cailler-Nestlé chocolate factory in Broc for chocolate sampling. Operates Monday, Wednesday, and Thursday June through October; Monday through Friday July and August.

Swiss Pass

Provides unlimited travel on the entire Swiss Travel System, including most of the private railroads, postal motor coaches, lake steamers, and urban transport systems in 35 cities. It also provides up to 25 percent discount on funiculars and cable cars.

Consecutive Days	**ADULT** 1st Class	**ADULT** 2nd Class	**SAVERPASS*** 1st Class	**SAVERPASS*** 2nd Class
4 days	$490	$306	$442	$276
8 days	$709	$393	$638	$389
15 days	$859	$476	$772	$472
22 days	$995	$552	$896	$550
1 month	$1,094	$607	$985	$605

*Price per person based on 2 people or more traveling together
Children younger than age 16: free with parent (including step or foster parent). Children age 6–15 not accompanied by parent: half adult fare. Children younger than age 6: free.

Swiss Youth Pass

Consecutive Days	1st Class	2nd Class
4 days	$367	$230
8 days	$532	$332
15 days	$643	$402
22 days	$746	$466
1 month	$820	$513

A discounted version of the Swiss Pass for those age 16–25.

Holders of first-class rail passes pay a reduced supplement of 28 CHF. Contact:

GoldenPass Services
GoldenPass Center
CH-1820 Montreux
Switzerland
Tel: 011 +41 (21) 989 8190 (from U.S.)
Fax: 011 +41 (48) 024 5245 (from U.S.)
www.mob.ch
E-mail: info@goldenpass.ch

- **William Tell Express**—Lucerne–Flüelen–St. Gotthard–Locarno/Lugano. Combination steamer and rail journey; includes gourmet Swiss lunch. Reservations compulsory; includes seats on the boat, train, journey documentation, and souvenir. Operates daily May through October. Visit www.lakelucerne.ch.

Rail travel note: A timetable bookshop is operated by the Swiss Federal Railways in St. Gallen, Switzerland, where you may purchase the current official timetables of many European countries, as well as a wide range of rail travel literature and rail maps. St. Gallen is one hour by train from Zürich in the direction of Austria and Germany. Call at Room 224 in the St. Gallen rail station or telephone 071 222 1021, extension 208, ahead of time for details.

Base City: **BERN** **(Berne)**

www.berninfo.com
City Dialing Code: 31

Bern (Berne) has the unique distinction of being the only city in Europe joined by all three of Europe's high-speed trains—the TGV from Paris, the ICE from Berlin, and the Cisalpino from Milan.

Bern, the federal capital of Switzerland, was founded in 1191 and is one of the few medieval cities that remains intact. Appropriately, Bern is a UNESCO World Heritage site. According to legend, it was named after the first animal caught in the area, a bear, and bears have played a part in its history ever since. The city's bear pits, now known as the Bear Park, where the animals are raised and displayed, are a must-see on any tour.

The most striking thing about Bern is its medieval appearance. Some of the buildings in the city's old town date from the 13th and 14th centuries. The low silhouette of its rooflines appears to be different from those of most of Europe's other cities with origins in the same era—and indeed it is, for there is a medieval ordinance still in effect today that mandates each roofline be at a different level from adjoining structures. This ancient architectural asset is most visible when you view the city from the Nydeggbrücke Bridge crossing the Aare en route to the bear pits. If you miss it, you'll have another opportunity when you view the city from the location of its rose gardens on the high bluff of the Aare's right bank.

Bern is a medieval city, yet it is a new city as well. Over the centuries, Bern's citizens have developed a remarkable means of combining modern living with the centuries-old facades of their surroundings. It is cosmopolitan, with more than 150 restaurants and a wide selection of hotels, museums, and concert halls. Modern Bern has grown well beyond the curve of the Aare and into the surrounding foothills. The main commercial, cultural, and political activities of the city, however, still take place in its old sector.

The Aare River embraces Bern in a great natural bend. Like the river, you too will embrace this ancient Swiss city once you have trod its cobblestone streets.

In summer Bern leads you to believe it is the geranium capital of the world as well as being the federal capital of Switzerland. These flowers bloom everywhere in an eye-dazzling display of color. Bern was once voted Europe's most beautiful city of flowers. You will be bewitched by Bern, beguiled by its bears, and satisfied with its sights.

Arriving by Air

Switzerland's international airports, Basel, Geneva, and Zürich, connect incoming flights with trains to Bern. Bern is only 1 hour and 26 minutes away from Zürich's airport and 1 hour and 52 minutes from Geneva's by comfortable passenger trains that depart daily from the airports every 30 minutes. In Zürich the rail station lies immediately beneath the airport's terminal. In Geneva the rail station and the airport terminal are connected by a plaza. At the Bern-Belp Airport (9 kilometers south of the City Centre), direct connections can be made to and from many European cities, as well as shuttle bus service directly to Bern's railway station.

Arriving by Train

Bern's modern rail station is a small city within a city, with an impressive array of facilities, including a spacious underground arcade that connects at its surface entrances with the city's fabled, arcaded shopping walkways. Direct rail transport from Bern to Amsterdam, Berlin, Brussels, Luxembourg, Milan, Paris, Rome, Venice, and Zürich is available.

More than 70 trains a day depart Bern for Zürich Hauptbahnhof; 34 of these continue on to the Zürich airport following the city stop. More than 40 trains a day depart Bern for Geneva. Upon arrival in Geneva, stay aboard, and eight minutes later you will be at the Geneva airport.

Bern's Railway Station. Parts of Bern's rail station have been rebuilt, making it a model of efficiency and functionalism. Trains are reached from its ground level via ramps, thus making the use of baggage carts practical.

With your baggage stacked in one of the station's baggage carts, leave the train platform by descending the ramp, then turn in the direction of track No. 1 and walk to the end of the passageway, where you will emerge into the station's underground arcade, with its myriad shops and services. You'll see the escalators directly ahead.

Escalators take you to the other levels of the station. Elevator service is also available. If you have your luggage on a cart, use the elevators. At street level you will find the **train information** and **Bern Tourismus** offices, plus additional facilities such as shops and restaurants. Snack bars and fruit stands prevail on the ground level; more extensive food-service facilities are on the upper levels, ending at the top of the escalators with a full-service restaurant.

- **Baggage storage.** Visitors burdened with baggage may want to use the coin lockers on the ground (train) level or find the area marked FLY BAGGAGE (baggage room) on the street level. Taxi service is available from the street level—follow the pictographs—but check with Bern Tourismus before attempting to use the public-bus and streetcar services. Their access ramps, fares, ticket machines, and so forth can be confusing.

  A suburban train station is located on the underground arcade level. To reach it, continue past the escalators that run to the street level and watch for its entrance on the left side of the passageway. This system is operated by a private

Swiss railroad. Swiss Passes are accepted, and Eurail passes are accepted by some private Swiss railroads such as RBS. Check prior to boarding the train.

The Bern station, like most of the major rail terminals in Switzerland, will accept your baggage and check it through the Zürich or Geneva airports directly to your U.S. port of entry (except if you're flying on American carriers). Trains for both airports depart the Bern station every 30 minutes throughout the day. Place your baggage on a train an hour or so in advance of your departure for the airport.

- **Money exchange** facilities, two of them, are located on the ground level of the station. Both may be reached by turning right, just before the elevators, as you come out of the passageway leading from the trains. Both will be on your right as you proceed into the station's arcade. The first office, marked CHANGE SBB, is operated by the Swiss railroads. *Hours:* Monday–Friday 0700–1930, Saturday 0700–1900, Sunday 0900–1900. There is also an ATM.

  There are several banks in the plaza surrounding the station. The rates of exchange are standard throughout the city each day, however, and the rail-station money exchange and ATM facilities are the most convenient.

- **Train information, reservations,** and **rail pass validations** can be obtained from the rail-reservations center immediately across the passageway from the tourist information office. Look for the blue "i" sign. *Hours:* 0900–1900 Monday–Friday, 0900–1800 Saturday. The center dispenses rail information, reservations, and other services, including validation of rail passes. Keep in mind that Eurail passes are accepted on all of the Swiss federal railways and certain lake steamers; on the other hand, they are accepted only on a few of the private railroads. To be certain, check your day-excursions plans with the train information office. For example, if you plan to ascend the **Jungfrau,** any of the Eurail passes or Swiss passes will take you to **Interlaken,** where you must purchase a ticket for the private railroads leading out of Interlaken to **Grindelwald** or **Lauterbrunnen** and **Wengen** en route to the Jungfrau. Pass holders will receive a discount.

- **Tourist information** and **hotel reservations** are available at **Bern Tourismus,** in the rail station complex. *Tel:* (031) 328 12 12; *Fax:* (031) 328 12 77; www.bern.com; *E-mail:* info@berninfo.com.

  Turn left coming off the escalator from the ground level, then right at the passageway leading to the street. The office will be a few steps farther on your right. It is identified by a green i sign. *Hours:* 0900–1900 Monday–Saturday, 0900–1800 Sunday. There is no fee for hotel reservations. For online bookings, visit www.bernetourism.ch.

  Ask Bern Tourismus for the booklets ***Bern Information*** and ***Bern Excursions,*** the latter being an informative publication listing more day excursions from Bern by rail, lake steamer, and postal buses.

Sights/Attractions/Tours

There are two excellent means of guided sightseeing in Bern: on foot or by comfortable motor coach escorted by a multilingual guide. The bus departs from in front of the railway station at 1100 daily April through October; November 1 through March 31 on Saturday only at 1000. The bus tour takes two hours, and tickets may be purchased at the tourist office for CHF 20; children age 6 to 16, CHF 10.

If interested in the walking tours, ask at the tourist office for the *Short City Sightseeing Map*. It leads you right through the heart of Bern's ancient walled city. The city's famed bear pits have been replaced by a **Bear Park,** which is free. The park is open for walkers looking for the bears 24 hours, with keepers and guides onsite 0800–1700, and area shops open 0830–1630. Visit www.baerenpark-bern.ch. In the center of Bern, be certain to take in the multimedia *Bern Show*. Performances are every 20 minutes, and it's free! From there you return to your point of departure by a different route. According to the map, the entire route can be covered in approximately one hour, but without any stops en route. Plan for a minimum of two hours and consider yourself lucky if you make it in three. (According to the tourist office, no one has ever returned within the hour.)

If interested in seeing Bern on foot with the help of a multimedia guide, ask at the tourist information office in the rail station or at the Bear Park about renting an **iPod audio guide** (available in five languages). You can choose between two routes, each with detailed directions and descriptions of the most interesting sights in Bern, and you have the freedom to tour at your own pace. Rental fees: up to 6 hours, CHF 18; up to 24 hours, CHF 25. Deposit required; charged to a credit card and refunded upon return of the iPod.

Be certain to see the ***Zeitglockenturm,*** the city's famous clock tower. It first began ticking in 1530, and it is still the city's official timepiece today. The clock's glockenspiel starts promptly at four minutes before the hour as accompaniment to a parade of armed bear figures following a rooster. It's quite a show. What makes it tick? Take the fascinating 50-minute guided tour, at 1430 daily May through October (July through August, also at 1130), inside the clock tower. Purchase tickets (CHF 15) at Bern Tourismus, from the tour guide, or at your hotel. Another option is the stroll through the **Old Town,** which includes visits to the cathedral and the clock tower. Tours depart daily April through September at 1100 from the station and cost CHF 20 (half price for children).

Train Connections to Other Base Cities from Bern (Berne)

DEPART	TRAIN NUMBER	ARRIVE	NOTES
		Amsterdam Centraal	
1404	IC 972	2156	1
2136	EC 56	0934+1	R, 2, Sleeper
		Berlin Hauptbahnhof	
0904	ICE 962	1728	1
1104	ICE 278	1928	
1304	EC 6	2128	
2004	ICE 984	0723+1	R, 2, Sleeper
		Brussels (Bruxelles) Midi/Zuid	
1204	IC 968	1901	R, 1
2136	EC 56	0832+1	R, 2, Sleeper
		Budapest Keleti	
2032	IC 733	0924+1	R, 4, Couchettes
		Hamburg Hauptbahnhof	
0604	IC 956	1335	1
1004	IC 964	1735	1
1204	IC 968	1935	1
1404	IC 974	2138	1
2136	EC 56	0837+1	R, 2, Sleeper
		Copenhagen (København) H.	
0804	IC 960	2222	1, 6
2136	EC 56	1422+1	R, 2, Sleeper, Exc. Sa
		Luxembourg	
1336	IC 1070	1735	1
1904	IC 982	2324	1
		Lyon Part-Dieu	
0534	IC 702	0922	R, 3
1034	IC 712	1426	R, 3, Exc. Sa
1134	IC 714	1522	R, 3
then 1534, 1734, 2134, and 2234.			
		Milan (Milano) Centrale	
0734	EC 51	1037	R
1334	EC 57	1637	R
1834	EC 59	2137	R
		Munich (München)	
0602	IC 805	1128	4
0802	IC 809	1328	4
1202	IC 817	1728	4
1702	IC 827	2245	4

DEPART	TRAIN NUMBER	ARRIVE	NOTES
		Paris Gare de Lyon	
0910	TGV 9214	1337	R
1336	IC 1070	1737	R, 1
1736	IC 332	2138	R, 1
		Prague (Praha)	
2004	IC 984	0928+1	R, 2, Sleeper
		Rome (Roma) Termini	
0734	EC 51	1440	R, 5
1834	EC 59	0717+1	R, 5, Exc. Sa
		Vienna (Wien)	
0932	IC 711	1830	R, 4
1332	IC 719	2230	R, 4
2032	IC 733	0635+1	R, 4, Sleeper
		Warsaw Centralna	
1704	IC 978	1215+1	R, 2, Sleeper
		Zürich Hauptbahnhof	

InterCity (IC) trains depart at 02 and 32 minutes past the hour. Journey time: 56 minutes; local trains depart at 39 minutes past the hour. Journey time: 1 hour, 18 minutes.

Daily, unless otherwise noted
R Reservations required
+1 Arrive next day
1. Change trains in Basel.
2. Change to sleeper (R) train in Basel.
3. Change trains in Geneva (Genève).
4. Change trains in Zürich.
5. Change to Eurostar Italia train (R) in Milan.
6. Change trains in Hamburg.

Another unusual feature of Bern is its **shopping arcades**—nearly 4 miles of them. They line the route of the walking tour suggested by Bern Tourismus and offer one of the finest selections of wares and food to be found anywhere in the world. The shopping arcades are completely covered, so they are weatherproof as well as traffic-free and totally delightful. On Tuesday and Saturday mornings, there are markets where Swiss farmers sell their meat and produce. Shop the city's arcades 0900 to 1830 Monday through Friday (until 2100 on Thursday), and 0900 to 1600 Saturday. Pick up a shopping guide at the tourist offices.

Or, if museums appeal to you, Bern has plenty to choose from, including the **Swiss Alpine Museum,** the **Museum of Communication,** the **Einstein House,** and even a **Museum of Psychiatry.**

For a view of Bern from an unusual perspective, take the **city tour by raft** on the River Aare (tickets cost CHF 78 for adults and CHF 39 for children). The 1½-hour rafting tour departs daily at 1700, reservations required, June through September, from Schwellenmätteli (indicated on the city map) and includes a 10-passenger raft, life jackets, paddles, and a guide.

Day Excursions

Bern is an ideal base for day excursions to almost any point in Switzerland. Geneva is 1 hour and 40 minutes to the west by train; you can reach Zürich to the east by rail in only 1 hour and 10 minutes. Travel north and, in the same amount of time, your train will set you down in Basel on the banks of the Rhine.

The five day excursions that we have selected reveal the natural grandeur of the country. The **Golden Pass** adventure takes you through Alpine surroundings, in the comfort of a vista-dome railcar, to Lake Geneva and a cruise on the lake before returning to Bern. The outing to **Interlaken** unfolds a panorama of towering peaks along the shore of the Lake of Thun, where again you have the opportunity of a lake cruise to conclude a memorable day.

Picture-postcard perfect, **Lucerne** will charm you with its scenery, cuisine, and ambience. Promenade along its ancient walkways, scale nearby Mount Pilatus, or cruise the Lake of Lucerne during your visit.

For a peek at a Disney-type setting that has been going strong since the 11th century, journey to **Rheinfelden,** where the mighty Rhine River swirls past a medieval backdrop that stirs the imagination. Or travel to Brig to catch the *Glacier Express* to **Zermatt,** where you can view the magnificent Matterhorn.

Day Excursion to

The Golden Pass

The Alps a la Train

Depart from Bern
Distance by Train: 65 miles (104 km) to Montreux
Average Train Time: 1 hour, 25 minutes
Tourist Information Office (Montreux): Place de l'Eurovision, CH-1820
Tel: 0848 86 84 84; **Fax:** (021) 962 84 94
www.montreuxriviera.com
E-mail: info@montreuxriviera.com
Hours: September 16–May 15: 0900–1200 and 1300–1730 Monday–Friday, 1000–1400 Saturday–Sunday; May 16–September 15: 0900–1800 Monday–Friday, 0930–1700 Saturday–Sunday

Dollar for dollar, or franc for franc, this day excursion is one of the best train-travel values in Europe. The Lucerne–Interlaken–Montreux rail route provides an exciting variety of landscapes and cultures. The Montreux–Bernese–Oberland Railroad (MOB) operates the **Golden Pass Panoramic Express.** Visit www.mob.ch. This train offers an unobstructed view of the breathtaking scenery between Zweisimmen and Montreux.

Before departure, check with Bern Tourismus. Inform them you are going on The Golden Pass trip and pick up the booklet *Bern Excursions*. (The booklet is usually available in the train information office as well.) Trains run through the Golden Pass rather frequently, and you may want to follow a different schedule. We selected the ***Golden Pass Panoramic,*** a luxury first-class train with panoramic-view windows and bar car on the portion of the route from Zweisimmen to Montreux and vice versa.

There is ample time for a leisurely lunch at the Majestic Hotel (located between the rail station and the city pier) in Montreux before boarding a lake steamer to Chillon. Disembark and go ashore to visit its famous castle. **Château de Chillon** is a beautifully restored 11th-century castle that was made famous by Lord Byron in his poetic story of the imprisonment of François de Bonivard. After touring the castle, board another lake steamer back to Montreux. Then, ride the funicular adjacent to the steamer dock to the **Lausanne** train station and board your train back to Bern. Whew! It's a day loaded with extras.

Check the weather report the night before embarking on this day excursion. The clearer the day, the better. You will be viewing some of the Alps' most spectacular scenery, and if it's shrouded in clouds, it just might spoil your day. To get the weather report in English, dial 162 on any Swiss telephone.

InterCity trains usually depart from the Bern railway station on Track 6, but double-check just to be sure. The destination of this train is **Brig,** and it makes a stop at **Thun** (pronounced "tune") before it arrives at **Spiez.** At Thun, the beautiful Lake of Thun comes into view. As you approach Spiez, you'll see Mount Niesen (7,750 feet) towering over this quiet town on the southwestern shore of the lake.

In Spiez you have 11 minutes to cross a platform to board the next train—time enough to enjoy the breathtaking view. **Zweisimmen,** the next stop and transfer point, lies almost halfway between Spiez and Montreux. When you depart Spiez, you will enter The Golden Pass.

The transfer at Zweisimmen places you aboard MOB's *Golden Pass Panoramic Express* on a narrow-gauge railroad, with Montreux as its destination. The best instruction here is to "follow the crowd" as you move between the standard- and narrow-gauge trains.

A regular stop is **Gstaad,** which, you may recall, is the alpine-resort retreat of many famous movie stars, including Elizabeth Taylor and Roger Moore. During his lifetime, Richard Burton frequented the area, and the late David Niven maintained a chalet there on a mountainside for many years. **Château d'Oex** (pronounced "day") is an alpine resort, too, but more at the family level, frequented by the Genevese when they grow tired of viewing beautiful Lake Geneva—possibly because it's flat.

Our "wood pile theory" can be tested—at least two-thirds of it—because you will be passing from a German-speaking area into one of French habitation. Based on research we have made during several decades of European rail travel, the theory is this: The Germans pile wood with precision, the Italians pile it artistically, and the French stack theirs with an air of independence. The two regular stops are Gstaad and Château d'Oex. Watch what happens to the wood piles between these two points. Gstaad, as the name may imply, is German; Château d'Oex lies in the French-speaking district.

Approaching Montreux, the train descends 2,000 feet to Lake Geneva in much the same manner as a jet airliner does when entering a landing pattern. It whirls through a series of hairpin curves for almost a half hour before coming to rest beside the main Montreux railway station. Have your camera handy, for you are going to see some sensational scenery during the descent.

Bern (Berne)—The Golden Pass

Depart Bern 0904	Train IC 961	Arrive Spiez 0932
Depart Spiez 0936	Train RE 4065	Arrive Zweisimmen 1019
Depart Zweisimmen 1025	Train D 3115	Arrive Montreux 1213

Other departures also available.

Lake steamers depart Montreux pier at 1240, 1440, 1640, also other departures; stop at Château de Chillon is 10 to 15 minutes after leaving Montreux. (Summer schedules.)

Lake steamers depart Château de Chillon for Lausanne-Ouchy dock at 1403, 1603, and 1708; journey time to Lausanne-Ouchy is 1 hour and 27 to 46 minutes; steamers also stop at Montreux 12 to 17 minutes after departing Château de Chillon pier.

Mainline trains depart Montreux Station for Lausanne at 18 and 53 minutes after the hour throughout the day; journey time to Lausanne is 21 minutes. There are other local trains that make several stops and take longer.

DEPART Lausanne Station	TRAIN NUMBER	ARRIVE Bern Hbf
1450	IC 2525	1556
1520	IC 725	1626
1550	IC 2567	1656
1620	IC 727	1726
1650	IC 2529	1756
1720	IC 729	1826
1750	IC 2531	1856
1820	IC 731	1926
2120	IC 737	2226

You have several options while visiting Montreux. You can extend your shopping and sightseeing in the city for 1 hour and 50 minutes if you forgo Chillon and yet board the same steamer for Lausanne and not miss any of your friends who may have elected to see the castle made famous by Lord Byron. If it's stormy on Lake Geneva, you can still keep to the schedule by proceeding to Lausanne by rail.

Chillon-bound passengers should scurry to the castle as quickly as possible after the lake steamer docks to ensure maximum use of the time ashore. The steamer proceeds on to the French port of St. Gingolph and then returns to Chillon. Check at the Chillon dock for its return time. Should you miss the boat, you still have another option. Hail a cab back to Montreux, then board the train for Lausanne to join your friends in the dining car en route back to Bern.

Day Excursion to

Interlaken

Lake of Thun Cruise

Depart from Bern
Distance by Train: 37 miles (59 km)
Average Train Time: 50 minutes
City Dialing Code: 33
Tourist Information Office: Interlaken Tourismus, P.O. Box 369, Höheweg 37, CH–3800 Interlaken
Tel: (033) 826 53 00; **Fax:** (033) 826 53 75
www.interlaken.ch
E-mail: mail@interlakentourism.ch
Hours: July–August: 0800–1700 Monday–Saturday, 1000–1600 Sunday; September: 0800–1800 Monday–Friday, 0800–1600 Saturday; October–April: 0800–1200 and 1330–1800 Monday–Friday, Saturday 0900–1200; May–June: 0800–1800 Monday–Friday, 0800–1600 Saturday
Notes: Interlaken Tourism Office is about a five-minute walk down the Höheweg (the grand promenade), which starts at the West Station and ends at Ost (East) Station. It's on the left-hand side next to the Hotel Metropole.

Interlaken can best be described as the cultural and social focal point of Switzerland's Alpine areas. The English poet Lord Byron is said to have exclaimed, "It's a dream!" at his first sighting of Interlaken and its surroundings. Nestled between the **Lake of Thun** and the **Lake of Brienz,** Interlaken (Latin for "between the lakes") began in the 12th century as a small cluster of buildings surrounding a monastery, traces of which can still be seen today.

The town's main thoroughfare, **Höheweg,** is lined with great hotels, shops, and even a grand casino that is set back from the main promenade and banked with such beautiful flowers that one might think it is a retirement home.

For Interlaken, the Höheweg plays the same part as does the Champs-Elysées for Paris or the Via Veneto for Rome—it is the boulevard, with the ambience for which the Swiss are famous. Just as in its larger counterparts, you'll find people on foot or aboard horse-drawn carriages taking in the sights along with those relaxing over coffee and pastries at the sidewalk cafes. Towering over this entire scene is the **Jungfrau** (www.jungfraubahn.ch), a massive mountain that tops out at 13,642 feet above sea level, a mere 11 miles south of Interlaken. On a clear day, the view is dazzling.

Bern (Berne)—Interlaken

There is hourly InterCity (IC) train service from Bern Hauptbahnhof to Interlaken West and Interlaken Ost (East) Stations; departures are at 04 minutes after the hour from 0704; journey time to Interlaken West is 47 minutes, and time to Interlaken Ost is 53 minutes.

Return hourly IC service departs Interlaken Ost on the hour and departs Interlaken West at 05 minutes after the hour; journey time to Bern from Interlaken West is 48 minutes.

Distance: 37 miles (59 km)

Lake of Thun Cruise

DEPART Interlaken Pier	ARRIVE Thun Dock	DEPART Thun Station	TRAIN NUMBER	ARRIVE Bern Hbf
1110	1323	1404	EC 52	1423
1210	1423	1504	IC 1074	1523
1410	1623	1633	IC 978	1652
1510	1723	1733	IC 980	1752
1810	2023	2036	IC 835	2054

Note: Interlaken Pier is approximately 100 meters from Interlaken West Station. Thun Dock is approximately 50 meters from Thun Station.

Believe it or not, the Jungfrau can be scaled by train. Beginning in Interlaken at the Ost (East) rail station, a private cog railroad terminates at the Jungfraujoch Station, at 11,333 feet, the highest rail terminal in Europe. The round-trip takes the better half of a day, and it should be made only in ideal weather. Furthermore, the round-trip fare is just as steep as the ascent, CHF 320.00 per person first class and CHF 298.40 for second class. Eurail passes do, however, provide a 25 percent discount. Plan your "assault" on the Jungfrau for a separate day after you have checked the weather—and your wallet. If both the weather—and your wallet—permit, you are in for an unforgettable journey over one of Europe's most remarkable routes: Interlaken Ost–Lauterbrunnen–Kleine Scheidegg–Jungfraujoch–Grindelwald–Interlaken Ost. Attractions on the Jungfraujoch include the Ice Palace and the Sphinx observation terrace, and you can dine at the "Top of Europe" Glacier Restaurant.

If you are lacking in time (or funds) but you *must* scale a mountain while in Interlaken, take the funicular running up to **Harderkulm,** which overlooks Interlaken to the south from 4,337 feet above sea level. On a clear day you can see both lakes surrounding Interlaken, as well as the Jungfrau. This can be done in about an hour for only CHF 43 per person. The Harderkulm Station is only a short walk from Interlaken's Ost (East) Station. Ask for directions at the tourist office.

Interlaken has two railway stations, west and east. Coming from Bern, you arrive first in the west station. Disembark here rather than riding another five minutes to the east station. Remember, however, if you are closer to the east station as your visit draws to a close, you can catch the same train from that point, too—but five minutes ahead of the west-station schedule.

An extra bonus offered with the Swiss Card is a 50 percent discount (25 percent with a Swiss Pass) on the **Brienz Rothorn Bahn,** Switzerland's oldest steam cog railway. Since 1892, it has climbed the 7,710 feet above sea level for a spectacular view from Rothorn Kulm. For further information *Tel:* (033) 952 22 22.

The Höheweg starts at the west station, and the grand promenade extends to the east station. With a city map in hand, courtesy of the tourist office, you are all set to tour the town. If walking isn't your forte, you may prefer to see the sights from a surrey. These horse-drawn vehicles are available just outside the west station. Rates vary and must be arranged with the driver.

There are more than 100 restaurants in Interlaken. We do have a favorite, although it's a bit off the beaten path—the **Hotel Rössli,** Hauptstrasse 10. *Tel:* (033) 822 78 16; *Fax:* (033) 822 96 16; www.roessli-interlaken.ch; *E-mail:* info@roessli-interlaken.ch. It is run by a friendly gentleman who worked in New York City restaurants for many years before he moved to the German district of Switzerland. The result is German-Swiss food served with a French flair and an American accent—rather unusual.

Interlaken is a good base for explorations of the entire **Jungfrau Region.** We suggest that you devote one day to Interlaken and its immediate area and check with the tourist office regarding other day-excursion possibilities. In addition to the rail ascent to the Jungfrau, you can reach the **Schilthorn** and lunch in the restaurant **Piz Gloria** (at 10,000 feet), where James Bond escaped the murderous intents of the opposition by skiing down the world's longest ski slope in the film *On Her Majesty's Secret Service*.

Wearers of pacemakers should be wary of the higher altitudes, but there's no reason to miss out on the fun around Interlaken. The **Swiss Open-Air Museum** at nearby **Ballenberg** (*Hours:* Mid-April–October: 1000–1700 daily) is an ideal alternative and easy to reach by either train or lake steamer departing from the city's east station. Ask for details at the tourist information office.

If the weather is agreeable, a cruise on the **Lake of Thun** before returning from Interlaken is a must. The ships depart from a pier that can be reached from either the west station by tunnel or the Bahnhofstrasse, where it intersects with the Höheweg alongside the station.

Day Excursion to

Lucerne (Luzern)

And Mount Pilatus

Depart from Bern
Distance by Train: 59 miles (95 km)
Average Train Time: 1 hour, 20 minutes
City Dialing Code: 41
Tourist Information Office: Zentralstrasse 5, CH–6003 Luzern
Tel: (041) 227 17 17; **Fax:** (041) 227 17 20
www.luzern.com
E-mail: luzern@luzern.com
Hours: November–March: 0830–1730 Monday–Friday, 0900–1700 Saturday, 0900–1300 Sunday. April: 0830–1730 Monday–Friday, 0900–1700 Saturday–Sunday. May–October: 0830–1900 Monday–Friday, 0900–1900 Saturday, 0900–1700 Sunday
Notes: The tourist information office is located in the railway station at track No. 3.

This day excursion is weatherproof. Rain or shine, Lucerne (Luzern) has much to offer. So much, in fact, that you may want to return again and again until you have seen it all—a challenging task.

Lucerne is in its glory on a bright, sunny day, when the city and its surroundings sparkle with a brilliance that defies description. At the northwestern end of Lake Lucerne, where the Reuss River resumes its swift quest for the Rhine, Lucerne's lakefront, rimmed by the mighty Alps, is an unforgettable sight. But a rainy day in Lucerne won't dampen your spirits one bit, for there are many things to see that are under cover.

The ***Kapellbrücke*** covered bridge is one example. A symbol of Lucerne, the bridge was built at the beginning of the 14th century, together with the Wasserturm (water tower) at its side. During the 17th century, artists painted a total of 112 pictures under its eaves, depicting Swiss history, particularly that of Lucerne and its patron saints. The bridge was destroyed by fire in 1993, but the bridge and the artwork were re-created.

The **Swiss Museum of Transport and Communications** is the largest and most modern museum in Europe—also one of the most visited. *Hours:* April–November: 1000–1800 daily, closes at 1700 remainder of the year. Visit www.verkehrshaus.ch. The museum is reached easily from the center of Lucerne by bus No. 6 or 8, which departs from the rail station every 6 minutes for the 10-minute trip, or by lake steamer to the Lido dock (variety of Eurail and Swiss passes accepted).

Its special attraction is the **Longines Planetarium** at Sternenplatz 3, and the museum also vividly traces the development of Swiss transportation, including rail, road, aeronautical, and water navigation. Kids from 7 to 77 will be fascinated by the operating scale model of the Gotthard tunnel railroad, and everyone will end up breathless following a visit to the museum's spectacular Swissorama and IMAX Filmtheater.

If you don't mind mixing fondue with frivolity, by all means eat at the **Stadtkeller Restaurant** at Sternenplatz 3, just 2 blocks north of the Kapellbrücke's right-bank entrance. It is "touristy," but if you like yodeling, alphorn blowing, cowbell ringing, beer drinking, and flag throwing, this is the place. At lunchtime, be there no later than 1130. It's a tour-bus lunch stop and fills up rapidly. *Tel:* (041) 410 47 33 for reservations. Visit www.stadtkeller.ch; *E-mail:* info@stadtkeller.ch. You can watch those poor, tired bus passengers try to determine what country they are seeing today.

Bern (Berne)—Lucerne (Luzern)

Depart Bern twice an hour, on the hour and at 36 minutes after the hour, until 2136, then 2232 and 2300.

Travel time 1 hour, 5 minutes to 1 hour, 27 minutes.

Other service requiring a change of trains at Olten available.

Depart Lucerne twice an hour, on the hour and 30 minutes after the hour, until 2300.

Travel time 1 hour, 5 minutes to 1 hour, 27 minutes.

Other service requiring a change of trains at Olten available.

Distance: 59 miles (95 km)

Lucerne (Luzern)—Pilatus

Via Pilatus cogwheel railway May–October. Discounts for rail pass holders on Pilatus Railway. Pilatus is 7,000 feet above sea level.

Train service from Lucerne to Alpnachstad throughout the day:
Departures at 0612, 0712, and continuing hourly at 12 minutes after the hour until 2312, then 2342; journey time is 15 to 20 minutes.

Trains depart Alpnachstad for Lucerne at 29 minutes after the hour until 2329; journey time is 18 to 22 minutes.

Distance 8 miles (13 km)

Alpnachstad—Pilatus Kulm rack railway—operates daily, weather permitting.

Depart Alpnachstad at 0810, 0850, 0935, 1015, 1055, 1135, 1220, 1300, 1345, 1425, 1505, 1550, 1630, 1710, and 1750; journey time is 30 minutes.

Depart Pilatus Kulm at 0845, 0930, 1010, 1050, 1130, 1215, 1255, 1340, 1420, 1500, 1545, 1625, 1705, 1745, and 1845; journey time is 40 minutes.

Distance: 3 miles (5 km) Pilatus cogwheel railway

For a sobering experience, follow up lunch with a visit to ***The Dying Lion of Lucerne.*** One of the world's most famous monuments, it was hewn from natural rock in commemoration of the heroic, fatal defense by Swiss guards of Louis XVI at the Tuileries in Paris at the beginning of the French Revolution in 1792. Mark Twain described the Lion of Lucerne as "the saddest and most poignant piece of rock in the world."

Next door, you will find Lucerne's **Glacier Garden Museum,** which contains remnants of Lucerne's prehistoric past that were discovered in 1872. Twenty million years ago, Lucerne was a subtropical palm beach on the ocean; 20,000 years ago, Lucerne was covered by more than a mile of glacial ice. Don't miss it.

On your way to the lion monument and the Glacier Garden Museum, you will pass one of Switzerland's most outstanding and attractive restaurants, the **Old Swiss House.** Built in 1859, the restaurant contains an antique collection of rare beauty. The oil paintings are all originals by famous artists. Call ahead for reservations [*Tel:* (041) 410 61 71; *Fax:* (041) 410 17 38; www.oldswisshouse.ch; *E-mail:* info@oldswisshouse.ch], because the Old Swiss House is frequented by the locals for its exquisite Swiss and French cuisine. Meals are served 0900 to 0030 Tuesday through Sunday. This Lucerne landmark should *not* be missed.

Visit **Mount Pilatus** as a side adventure during your Lucerne day excursion. Be certain to go on a clear day, for there is nothing more disappointing than a fog-shrouded peak. The world-famous Pilatus electric railway, with its maximum gradient of 48 percent, is the steepest cog railway in the world. Discounts are available for Eurail pass holders. It's best to purchase tickets at the tourist information office at Zentralstrasse 5. If you have a lot of time, you can take a lake steamer to **Alpnachstad.** For a breathtaking view and a beautiful way to end your day in Lucerne, descend Mount Pilatus in a cable car to **Kriens** and catch the bus to Lucerne. Check with the tourist information office for details and discounts available to rail pass holders.

Day Excursion to

Rheinfelden

Walled City on the Rhine

Depart from Bern
Distance by Train: 76 miles (122 km)
Average Train Time: 1 hour, 30 minutes
City Dialing Code: 61
Tourist Information Office: Marktgasse 16, CH–4310 Rheinfelden
Tel: (061) 835 5200; **Fax:** (061) 835 5253
www.tourismus-rheinfelden.ch
E-mail: tourismus@rheinfelden.ch
Hours: 1330–1830 Monday, 0800–1200/1330–1700 Tuesday–Friday, 0800–1200 the 1st and 3rd Saturday of each month
Notes: To reach the tourist information office, proceed downhill on Bahnhofstrasse (Station Street) to the bottom of the hill, where it meets Marktgasse, the pedestrian shopping area.

A medieval jewel set on the banks of the swift-moving Rhine River just above Basel, Rheinfelden stirs the imagination. Much of its wall and many of its watch towers are still standing, and they were erected back in the 11th century. An island on the Swiss side of the river's channel forms an important part of a bridge linking Switzerland to Germany. In the 13th century it was the site of the famed "Emperor's Palace" described by Schiller in the tale of William Tell. The castle is gone now, and the island serves mainly as a city park, but the swirls and eddies of the mighty Rhine continue to stimulate one's sense of the centuries of history that have unfolded there.

During World War II, the bridge over the Rhine was the center of intrigue and mystery. Many downed but uncaptured American and British aviators seeking the sanctuary of Switzerland attempted to flee Nazi Germany from there. Some made it; some were apprehended. We have talked with residents who still remember those days and the risks that were taken. One person recalled for us her perilous escape across the Rhine's waters in a rowboat.

Be certain to pick up a city map during your stop at the tourist office. Armed with the map, you can easily wind your way through the labyrinth-like streets to any point of interest and still find your way back to the train station in time for your return to Bern.

Check out the shops lining the Rhine. Here you can find bargains in jewelry, clothing, and sporting equipment. Most shops and restaurants are closed on Monday.

When your stomach (or your watch) tells you it's lunchtime, you have several excellent eating places to choose from in Rheinfelden. Our favorites are the **Hotel Schiff** at Marktgasse 58 and the **Café Confiserie Graf,** at Fröschweid 14, close to the river.

Bern (Berne)—Basel—Rheinfelden

DEPART Bern	TRAIN NUMBER	ARRIVE Basel	DEPART Basel	ARRIVE Rheinfelden
0704	ICE 372	0759	0813 (IR 1963)	0824
0804	IC 960	0859	0913 (IR 1965)	0924
0904	ICE 370	0959	1013 (IR 1967)	1024
plus other departures.				

DEPART Rheinfelden	TRAIN NUMBER	ARRIVE Basel	DEPART Basel	ARRIVE Bern
1534	IR 1974	1547	1559 (IC 977)	1656
1634	IR 1976	1647	1659 (IC 979)	1756
1734	IR 1978	1747	1759 (IC 371)	1856
and continuing at hourly intervals until 2234, plus other departures.				

Alternative route via Brugg:

DEPART Bern	TRAIN NUMBER	ARRIVE Brugg	DEPART Brugg	ARRIVE Rheinfelden
0634	IR 2161	0728	0742 (IR 2060)	0810
0734	IR 2163	0828	0842 (IR 2062)	0910
0834	IR 2165	0928	0942 (IR 2064)	1010
0934	IR 2167	1028	1042 (IR 2066)	1110

Alternative return route:

DEPART Rheinfelden	TRAIN NUMBER	ARRIVE Brugg	DEPART Brugg	ARRIVE Bern
1549	IR 2077	1619	1632 (IR 2178)	1726
1649	IR 2079	1719	1732 (IR 2180)	1826
1749	IR 2081	1819	1832 (IR 2182)	1926
1849	IR 2083	1919	1932 (IR 2184)	2026
1949	IR 2085	2019	2032 (IR 2186)	2126

Distance: 76 miles (122 km)

Rheinfelden is home of Switzerland's largest brewery, **Feldschlösschen.** Tours are available on an irregular basis. Excellent restaurants and beer stubes are located at the brewery.

Clustered about the bridge entrance are several eating places offering menus ranging from light snacks to full-course meals. Want to picnic by the Rhine? Pick up some cheese, bread, and wine at one of the market stalls and have your repast on the island as the Rhine provides the background.

Saline deposits were discovered under the town in 1844, and Rheinfelden quickly developed into an international spa. Its natural brine, which is one of the strongest in Europe, is piped from a depth of more than 600 feet to several bathing facilities in town. The tourist office can provide full details. The structures housing the pumps that bring the brine to the surface from the deep wells bear a striking resemblance to the original oil fields of western Pennsylvania, where oil refining first began in North America.

There is an unusual inside-outside saltwater swimming pool that you should see. You can reach it on foot by walking along the Rhine in an upstream direction. The brine-well structures may be seen nearby.

River steamers ply between Rheinfelden and **Basel.** Returning to Bern via Basel and a boat trip on the Rhine becomes an attractive option between May and September, when the service is in operation. Schedules are posted at the Schifflande (boat landing) opposite the island. Information on the steamer service to Basel, as well as cruises on the Rhine, is also available in the Rheinfelden tourist information office. Rhine steamers, unlike the lake steamers, do not accept rail passes, but the rates to Basel are nominal.

Day Excursion to

Zermatt

Via the Glacier Express

Depart from Bern
Distance by Train: 99 miles (160 km)
Average Train Time: 2 hours, 28 minutes
City Dialing Code: 27
Tourist Information Office: Zermatt Tourist Office, Bahnhofplatz 5, 3920 Zurich (located at the railway station)
Tel: (027) 966 81 00; **Fax:** (027) 966 81 01
www.zermatt.ch
E-mail: info@zermatt.ch
Hours: Open year-round: 0830–1200 and 1330–1800 Monday–Saturday, 0930–1200 and 1600–1800 Sunday

How about a cheese fondue luncheon in Zermatt while viewing the **Matterhorn?** A great place to have lunch is at the Winter Garden in the **Alex Hotel.** It is all glass and provides an endless view. *Tel:* (027) 966 70 70; *Fax:* (027) 966 70 90; www.hotelalexzermatt.com; *E-mail:* info@hotelalexzermatt.com. Located in the middle of the Alps at 1,620 meters (about 5,300 feet) above sea level, Zermatt can be visited very easily during your stay in Bern. Board the 0731 Cisalpino or the 0906 InterCity Express from Bern to Brig. In Brig you can connect with the *Glacier*

Express private railroad (reservations required) to Zermatt. A separate ticket must be purchased for the *Glacier Express* portion from Brig to Zermatt unless you have a Swiss Pass.

Taking the 0706 departure from Bern will have you in Zermatt at 0913; the later one at 0906 will still get you there in time for that luncheon at 1113. In fact, you could stay in Zermatt for an early dinner, too. There are more than 38 restaurants to choose from, offering specialty Swiss, Italian, French, and Asian cuisine. By leaving Zermatt at 1913 and changing trains in Brig, you could still be back in Bern at 2140—all in the same day!

Famous for its perfect snow conditions, Zermatt has the longest skiing season in the Alps. Summers offer exquisite scenery for hiking, walking, and golfing. If visiting between the end of June to the middle of August, you'll see the most famous goats in the world as they travel in and out of town along the main street. And Zermatt is car-free—only electric cars and horse-drawn conveyances are allowed.

Check with Bern Tourismus for information. The rail information office is across the hallway. Advance ***Glacier Express*** reservations can be made through railpass .com (*Tel:* 877-RAILPASS; *Fax:* 614-764-0711). Don't miss "God's perfect little place" at the foot of the Matterhorn.

Base City: **ZÜRICH**

www.zuerich.com
City Dialing Code: 1

Some describe it as a garden city by a lake. Others picture it as one of the most elegant cities in Europe. Statisticians term it the largest in Switzerland, and anyone engaged in international business knows it is a world center for industry and commerce. Bankers seem content in knowing that it all begins and ends right there. Zürich, known as "Downtown Switzerland," can be all things to all people.

Zürich is packed with surprising contrasts. A charming tree-shaded avenue named Bahnhofstrasse runs from the railway station to Lake Zürich, yet it houses the headquarters of the great world banks and some of the most elegant shops to be found in Europe. A few short blocks away, the scene yields to the Middle Ages around St. Peter's Church near the Limmat River, and the bridge that crosses the river leads into Niederdorfstrasse, the city's roistering nightclub area.

Zürich is a major hub for European rail transportation. Trains between Milan in the south, Munich in the east, and the great trunk line crossing Switzerland glide in and out of its Hauptbahnhof (central train station) in a never-ending procession.

Arriving by Air

Zürich's **Kloten International Airport** lies 10 miles northeast of the city. Flight information: *Tel:* 043 81622 11 (CHF 1.99/min.) Visit www.zurich-airport.com; *E-mail:* info@zurich-airport.com.

Zürich Airport has undergone extensive expansion, making it one of the largest shopping areas in Switzerland.

Airport–City Links

- **Train:** SBB trains depart every 10 to 15 minutes for Zürich Hauptbahnhof from 0602 to 0010; journey time: 10 minutes; one-way fare: CHF 10.00 first class, CHF 6.20 second class. Trains return from Zürich Hauptbahnhof to the airport every 15 minutes from 0526 to 2337. Also, direct rail connections are available from Zürich Airport to Basel, Bern, Constance, Geneva, Lausanne, Lucerne, St. Gallen, and Zug at least every 30 minutes, Lugano every hour.
- **Hotel Bus:** Many hotels offer shuttle bus service. The hotel guest pickup point is at the Arrivals Halls 1 and 2.
- **Regional Bus:** Bus connections available to towns and villages in the Zürich region. Bus terminal is opposite Parking Level 2.

- **Taxi:** Taxi queues are in front of the Arrivals Halls 1 and 2; journey time: 20 to 30 minutes; average fare to downtown Zürich: CHF 55 to CHF 60. Airport Taxi Reservations: *Tel:* +41 (0) 848 850 852.

Arriving by Train

Zürich Hauptbahnhof (main railway station) is one of the most up-to-date and complete railway stations in Europe. All EuroCity, InterCity, ICN, and express trains stop here. There are three other suburban terminals within the city. Train departures are displayed on digital boards.

The **Rail Travel Centre** is located on the same level as the trains, opposite Track 13. It contains all the elements required by the average rail traveler, including rail pass validation. The rail information desks are staffed by 25 to 30 multilingual rail travel specialists to assist you in obtaining train information, tickets, reservations, plus many other travel services. An efficient numbering system is used—just take a number from the machine upon entering. *Hours:* 0700–2030 daily.

- **Money exchange** office is located on the left side of the main Arrival Hall. *Hours:* 0630–2130. If you don't have Swiss francs upon arrival, stock up on them. Not only is Zürich expensive, but the Swiss prefer their francs.
- **Baggage lockers** are one level down using the escalators. Two levels down are the shops and food services.

Tourist Information/Hotel Reservations

- *Zürich Tourist Information:* Hauptbahnhof; Zürich 8021; *Tel:* (01) 215 40 00; *Fax:* (01) 215 40 44; www.zuerich.com; *E-mail:* information@zuerich.com.

  Hours: May–October: 0800–2030 Monday–Saturday, 0830–1830 Sunday; November–April: 0830–1900 Monday–Saturday, 0900–1800 Sunday.

  Hotel reservations: Tel: (01) 215 40 40; *Fax:* (01) 215 40 44; *E-mail:* hotel@zuerich.com.

  Notes: To reach the Zürich tourist office, exit from the trains, turning right at the end of the tracks, and proceed directly through the main hall. The office will be on your left. The tourist office can also make hotel reservations. A city map and a brochure describing the Zürich public transportation system are available.

Getting Around in Zürich

The *Ride with Us* brochure is particularly helpful because it explains how to use the self-service facilities of the city's transportation system, including rail (S-Bahn), trams, buses, and funiculars. The Swiss passes include travel on the city network, but the variety of Eurail passes are accepted only on the S-Bahn network. If you have any type of

Eurail pass, we recommend that you purchase a one-day or multiple-day pass to cover the remaining public transport network in Zürich:

- **Zürich Day Ticket**—24 hours within the city limits, CHF 8.60
- **Zürich Card**—A convenient bargain for getting around Zürich. Offers use of all forms of public transport within the greater Zürich area, including train, tram, boat, bus, or funicular, plus free admission to 43 museums, a complimentary drink in 24 restaurants, and several other discounts and bonuses. Purchase at the Zürich Tourist Information Office in the rail station; 24 hours, CHF 24 (children, CHF 16); 72 hours, CHF 48 (children, CHF 32).

Sights/Attractions/Tours

Obtain a copy of the brochure *Zürich City Tours and Excursions* from the tourist office. This brochure describes city sightseeing, excursions by motor coach or by trolley, cruises on the Limmat River as well as those on Lake Zürich, ascension of Mount Uetliberg for a panoramic view of the city and Alps, and how to see Zürich by night.

Escorted and unescorted tours are available at various times throughout the week during certain seasons of the year, so be sure to check with the train information office or the tourist office. Some of these excursions require rail pass holders to pay supplemental charges. Payment of these charges, along with reservations for the excursions, can be made at these offices.

For a relaxed "Classic Trolley Tour," board a vintage Swiss trolley. For this two-hour tour, you can sit and see the sights. Tours depart from the Hauptbahnhof at 0945, 1200, and 1400 daily. Fare: CHF 34; children up to age 16, half fare.

Lake steamers at the far end of the Bahnhofstrasse at the Schiffstation (boat station) offer several interesting cruises, including one to the eastern end of the lake to an interesting old Swiss town, **Rapperswil,** known as the "City of Roses."

Zürich has its share of cathedrals. The **Grossmünster Cathedral** stands brooding on the east bank of the Limmat River. The cathedral has a statue of Charlemagne, who is said to have built the original church. Almost opposite on the other side of the river stands the **Fraümunster Cathedral,** reached by crossing the Münsterbrücke (Cathedral Bridge). Here, you can view the cathedral's famously beautiful Chagall windows. Alongside the central station is the **Swiss National Museum.** On exhibition are authentic rooms of the 16th and 17th centuries, removed from their original sites and rebuilt within the museum. Zürich is not totally old in face. Its **Kunsthaus** (Fine Arts Museum) is an attractive, modern building with a magnificent collection of modern art.

There is no shortage of fine dining in Zürich. One of our favorite places that combines an elegant medieval atmosphere with fine Swiss cuisine and wines at reasonable prices is **Zunfthaus zur Zimmerleuten,** "Carpenters' Guildhouse," located at Limmatquai 40, along the Limmat River in the Old Town. You can get there on tram No. 4; get off at the Rathaus (Town Hall) stop. *Tel:* (01) 44 250 53 63; *Fax:* (01) 44 250 53 64; www.zunfthaus-zimmerleuten.ch; *E-mail:* info@zunfthaus-zimmerleuten.ch.

Train Connections to Other Base Cities from Zürich

DEPART	TRAIN NUMBER	ARRIVE	NOTES
		Amsterdam Centraal	
0800	ICE 76	1727	1
1200	ICE 72	2027	1
1400	IC 70	2156	3
2100	ICE 790	0856+1	R, 3, Sleeper
		Berlin Hauptbahnhof	
0600	ICE 78	1411	4
0800	ICE 760	1607	4
1000	ICE 74	1814	4
1200	ICE 72	2012	4
1300	EC 692	2126	3, Exc. Sa
2142	CNL 40478	0934+1	R, Sleeper
		Bern (Berne)	
Approx. 36 direct trains daily; most depart at 6 and 32 min. past the hour; average journey time, 1 hr 17 min.			
		Brussels (Bruxelles) Midi/Zuid	
1000	ICE 74	1735	R, 1
1400	ICE 70	2135	R, 1
2142	CNL 40478	0832+1	R, 2, Sleeper
		Budapest Keleti	
1040	RJ 165	2119	R
2140	EN 60467	0924+1	R, Sleeper
		Copenhagen (København) H.	
0800	ICE 76	2222	R, 8
2142	CNL 478	1422+1	R, 8, Sleeper
		Hamburg	
0600	ICE 78	1335	
0800	ICE 76	1535	
1200	ICE 72	1935	
2142	CNL 478	0836+1	R, Sleeper
		Luxembourg	
1200	ICE 72	1929	R, 3
1908	IR 2280	2324	R, 3
		Lyon Part-Dieu	
0832	IC 710	1322	R, 9, Exc. Sa
1032	IC 714	1522	9
1632	IC 726	2122	9
		Milan (Milano) Centrale	
0732	EC 13	1135	R
0932	EC 153	1335	R
1132	EC 17	1535	R

DEPART	TRAIN NUMBER	ARRIVE	NOTES
1532	EC 21	1935	R
1732	EC 23	2135	R
1932	EC 2504	2335	R
		Munich (München)	
0709	EC 191	1128	
0909	EC 193	1328	
1309	EC 195	1728	
1809	EC 197	2245	
		Nice Ville	
0932	IC 712	1905	R, 9
1334	TGV 9222	2237	R, 9
		Paris Lyon	
0734	TGV 9206	1137	R
1334	TGV 9222	1737	R
1734	IC 578	2138	R, 3
		Prague (Praha)	
0709	EC 191	1841	R, 6
1942	CNL 40470	0928+1	R, Sleeper
		Rome (Roma) Termini	
0732	EC 13	1540	R, 5
0932	EC 15	1740	R, 5
1532	EC 21	2340	R, 5
1840	RJ 363	0922+1	R, 5, Sleeper
		Vienna (Wien)	
0840	OEC 163	1630	
1440	RJ 169	2230	
2140	EN 60647	0635+1	R, Sleeper
		Warsaw Centralna	
0700	IC 760	2250	R, 3, Sleeper
1400	RJ 169	0700+1	R, 7, Sleeper

Daily, unless otherwise noted
R Reservations required
+1 Arrives next day
1. Change trains in Frankfurt (Main) Hbf.
2. Change trains in Cologne (Köln).
3. Change trains in Basel.
4. Change trains in Hannover.
5. Change trains in Milan.
6. Change trains in Linz.
7. Change trains in Vienna (Wien).
8. Change trains in Hamburg.
9. Change trains in Geneva.

Day Excursions

Zürich provides an alternative base city to Bern for those arriving via Zürich International Airport. The city's proximity to Lucerne and Rheinfelden decreases travel time for these day excursions when compared to Bern, but this time saving comes at a price. Zürich maintains a reputation for being one of Europe's most expensive cities. Budget-minded travelers may do well to use Bern as their base city and save Zürich for a day excursion and as a gateway city.

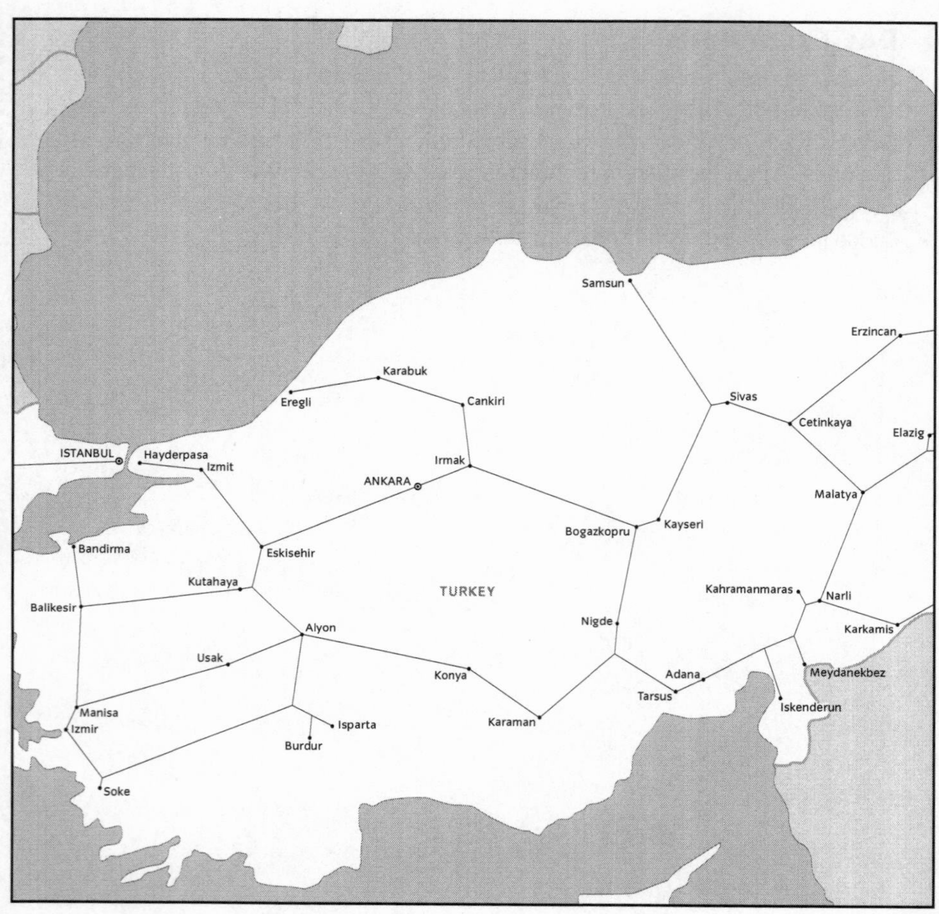

Samsun
Erzincan
Karabuk
Eregli
Cankiri
Sivas
Cetinkaya
Elazig
ISTANBUL
Hayderpasa
Izmit
Irmak
ANKARA
Malatya
Bogazkopru
Kayseri
Bandirma
Eskisehir
Kutahaya
TURKEY
Kahramanmaras
Narli
Balikesir
Nigde
Karkamis
Alyon
Usak
Konya
Adana
Meydanekbez
Tarsus
Manisa
Iskenderun
Izmir
Isparta
Karaman
Burdur
Soke

TURKEY

Given that Turkey's population is over 95% Muslim, most visitors are astounded to learn that Turkey is home to the majority of the Christian sites referenced in the New Testament of the Bible. For example, the Virgin Mary is said to have died in the Saint John's house, located near Ephesus, itself famous for its impressive Roman-era library and an outdoor theater thought to be the largest in the ancient world (seating for 44,000). In addition to the amazing historical and Biblical sites, visitors to Turkey can enjoy the thriving metropolis of Istanbul, which truly serves as a bridge between East and West. Further, the beaches on the Mediterranean and Aegean coasts boast sparkling blue water and a range of resorts, from modest to posh.

For more information and pretrip planning tips, check the Turkey Tourism website, **www.goturkey.com,** or contact Tourism Turkey: 821 United Nations Plaza, New York, NY 10017, *Tel:* (212) 687-2194, *Fax:* (212) 599-7568, *E-mail:* ny@goturkey.com.

Banking

Currency: Turkish Lira (TL)

Exchange rate at press time: 2.85 TL = U.S. $1.00

Communications

Country Code: 90

Major Mobile Phone Companies: Turkcell, Vodaphone, Avea

Rail Travel in Turkey

Unfortunately, it is nearly impossible to travel in Turkey solely by train, with the only major line running from Istanbul to the capital city of Ankara. For those wishing to see more of Turkey, the best option is to purchase low-cost airfare or rely on the generally excellent system of intercity buses. The Balkan Flexipass is good in Turkey, although it is generally only useful in the area immediately around Istanbul.

Base City: **ISTANBUL**

http://english.istanbul.com
City Dialing Code: 212

Arriving by Air

Istanbul Ataturk Airport. Istanbul's modern Ataturk Airport (www.ataturkairport.com) is situated on the European side of the city, only a short drive from the historic area of the city.

- **Airport–City Links:** A light rail connection is available between the airport and the Aksaray district of Istanbul, which houses the city's bus station. The trip takes between 30 and 40 minutes. Hava (www.havas.net/en) also operates shuttle services between the airport and major landmarks such as Taksim Square.

- **Money exchange, ATMs,** and **tourist information** are available in the International Arrivals area.

Getting Around in Istanbul

If you reserve a hotel in the historic district of Sultanahmet, you will rarely need to use public transportation, as the majority of the city's "must-sees" are within easy walking distance. That said, if you find it necessary to strike out from this area, the best bet is to use the aboveground tram system (www.istanbul-ulasim.com.tr). There are three major lines traversing the Sultanahmet area and the European side of the city, one from the airport into Sultanahmet on a northerly route, a second that hugs the coastline, and a third that splits the difference and offers the most accessibility to sites of interest.

Sights/Attractions/Tours

Istanbul is truly a magnificent city, as it literally straddles the divide between East and West. The Bosphorus Strait forms the boundary between Europe and Asia and cleaves the city in two. The European side is divided by another small waterway, which forms the famed "Golden Horn," a scimitar-shaped estuary that has served as a port for centuries. As noted, the most important tourist sites are clustered in the historic Sultanahmet District on the European side of the city, though there are fascinating sites on the Golden Horn as well. Unless you are spending a significant amount of time in the city, you should not feel obliged to cross to the Asian side.

Two of the most striking mosques in the world are the **Hagia Sophia** and the **Sultan Ahmet Mosque** (more commonly known as the "Blue Mosque"), both of which are located in the center of the Sultanahmet District. Construction of Hagia Sophia was completed in 537 and the massive edifice served as the cathedral of Constantinople until 1453, at which time it was converted into a mosque. The most impressive feature of the building is its gigantic dome, which is a staggering 102 feet in diameter. The mosque is open daily 0900–1900 (closed Monday) and entrance costs 30 TL. Immediately across a small plaza from the Hagia Sophia stands the "Blue Mosque." The name derives from the deep blue tiles that adorn the interior. Built between 1609 and 1616, the mosque boasts six minarets, a rarity for even the largest mosques throughout the world. The legend goes that the Sultan requested "altin" (the Turkish word for "gold") minarets, but the laborers heard "alti" (the Turkish word for "six"). There is no cost for entering the mosque, though it is closed during prayer times and it is necessary for women to cover their hair and shoulders as a sign of respect.

Nearby these two mosques looms **Topkapi Palace,** which was the primary residence of the Sultans for approximately 400 years. The palace is now a museum and home to such a dazzling array of treasures that it was designated a UNESCO World Heritage Site in 1985. Admission is 30 TL and the grounds and museum are open 0900–1845 daily (closed Tuesday). Audio tours are available for rent and an additional fee is charged for entrance to the harem rooms.

The **Basilica Cistern** is another must-see in the Sultanahmet District. The underground chamber is over 100,000 square feet in size and is refreshingly cool during the hot summer months. There are also two massive stone column bases carved to resemble Medusa. It was also featured prominently in the 1963 James Bond movie *From Russia With Love.*

On the Golden Horn side, **Dolmabahce Palace** is a stark contrast to the ancient Topkapi. In comparison to the Sultanahmet District, Dolmabahce is "new," in that it was completed in 1856 and served as the home for six sultans before the abolition of the Caliphate in 1924. The palace is much more Old European in appearance, boasting the world's largest crystal chandelier, weighing over 7.5 tons. Also of note, the founder of modern Turkey, Mustafa Kemal Ataturk, spent his last days in the palace, dying on November 10, 1938. The palace is open 0900–1600 (closed Monday and Thursday) and admission is 40 TL.

Base City: **ANKARA**

www.ankara.com
City Dialing Code: 312

Arriving by Air

Ankara Esenboga Airport, Ankara's modern Esenboga Airport (www.esenbogaair port.com) is approximately 18 miles north of the city.

- **Airport–City Links:** The two best options between Esenboga and the city center are a taxi or a shuttle bus run by Havas. The buses leave for the city center 25 minutes after flights arrive.

- **Money exchange, ATMs,** and **tourist information** are available in the International Arrivals area.

Getting Around in Ankara

Once settled in the city center, the best way to navigate around town is by taxi. Although there is a bus system, there are no maps, which makes choosing the appropriate bus nearly impossible. Taxis are relatively inexpensive, run on a clear meter system, and the cab drivers are well informed about local tourist attractions and major hotels.

Sights/Attractions/Tours

Ankara is Istanbul's significantly sleepier little sister. Although the city boasts a rich history steeped in Hittite and Roman lore, it was named the capital of the Turkish Republic in 1923. Since that time, it has become known as a largely government city, without significant cultural draw. That said, Ataturk's Mausoleum (Anitkabir) and a number of museums make this capital a worthy stop.

Anitkabir is the mausoleum of Mustafa Kemal Ataturk, the founder of modern Turkey who is still revered to this day. Completed in 1953, the mausoleum also houses an impressive museum showcasing both Ataturk's daily life and his heroic deeds during Turkey's War of Independence (1919–1923). Also interred on the grounds is Ismet Inounu, the second president of Turkey. The grounds are open 0900–1600 daily, with slightly longer hours in the summer.

The Museum of Anatolian Civilizations is housed in an old covered bazaar and hosts a large collection of sculpture and art from the Paleolithic Age (8000 B.C.)

through the Lydian Period (546 B.C.). In fact, the symbol of Ankara is an ancient Hittite rendering of a deer.

Day Excursion to

Cappadocia

UNESCO World Heritage Site

Depart from Ankara
Distance by Bus: 170 miles
Average Bus Time: 4 hours, 30 minutes
City Dialing Code: 384

The sprawling landscapes of Turkey's centrally located Cappadocia region were recognized as a UNESCO World Heritage Site in 1985 due to the beautiful vistas and unique geological formations. The best place to see both is the **Goreme Open Air Museum,** which is located in the center of the Goreme Valley and home to a collection of rock-cut churches dating as far back as the 11th century. A wide array of "fairy chimneys," large rock columns formed through erosion and wind, also loom over the museum. Two to three hours is sufficient to wander through this well-signed museum and learn about the fascinating history of the region. Nearby, the small town of Avanos specializes in red clay pottery and other artisanal works, and many artists have open workshops where you can watch them create their next masterpiece. There are a variety of underground cities in the area as well, most of which date back to the 8th century and some of which reach nearly 100 feet in depth. The largest and most popular of these is **Derinkuyu,** which boasts 11 floors and could hold more than 35,000 people with their livestock.

The most breathtaking way to experience the raw natural beauty of Cappadocia is with a hot air balloon ride. A variety of companies offer tours that usually leave at 0600 to take advantage of the cool air and gentle breezes. The balloons survey the landscape from a height of approximately 1,000 feet and the flight itself lasts about 90 minutes, with a traditional champagne toast upon landing. Prices €150–€200 per person, depending on the length of the flights and the associated amenities (breakfast, hotel-pick-up, etc.).

APPENDIX

Rail-Tour Itineraries

Three sample rail-tour itineraries are presented in response to readers' requests for sample itineraries combining several base cities and day excursions into a rail-tour package. These itineraries are similar to those used in previous tour programs and are considered "route-tested."

The base cities and day excursions in these itineraries are described elsewhere in this edition. Each itinerary may be completed with a 15-day Eurail Global Pass/Global Pass Saver or a 15-days-in-two-months Eurail Global Pass Flexi/Global Pass Saver Flexi.

Gateway cities are an important pretrip consideration. We have included airport information in base-city descriptions for your assistance. When suggested gateways are cities other than the rail-tour base cities, we have included rail schedules to assist in your planning, but as stated previously in this edition, our rail schedules are for planning purposes only. *Europe by Eurail* and its publisher cannot be held responsible for the consequences of either schedule or train changes occurring after press time or for inadvertent inaccuracies.

The following rail-tour schedules have been compiled on the basis of what we consider to be the best trains running at the best times; however, in almost every case, there are several other trains departing at other times that may be more convenient for your purposes. For this reason you may want to consult other schedules by contacting one of the companies listed in the Appendix.

Hotels suggested for the itineraries have been selected for their convenient locations near the railway stations and/or close to public transportation. Hotel price ranges are quoted in euros or local currencies for planning purposes only and are subject to change without prior notice. To convert the rates to U.S. dollars, consult the Foreign Exchange listing in the financial section of your hometown newspaper, contact your bank, or visit **www.oanda.com** and go to the cheat sheet for travelers page (you can print the rates for the countries on your itinerary and carry them with your other travel papers); another great site is **www.xe.com/ucc/** for universal currency exchanges.

Confirm hotel rates either through your travel agent or directly with the hotel. Most of the hotels listed have U.S. representatives through whom your travel agent can make reservations at no additional cost to you.

Europe à la Carte

A rail tour using the *Europe by Eurail* base cities Munich, Bern, and Paris is an adventure through the very heart of Europe.

Base Cities

Munich: Germany's fun capital. Plan ample time for shopping and sightseeing before beginning your exciting rail adventure. Allow for jet lag, too.

Bern: Medieval elegance in the heart of Switzerland. An all-weather shopping center. Save the sunny days for Bern's eye-filling day excursions.

Paris: The City of Light and everyone's "second" city is the only one of its kind. Mix Paris's pleasures with its unusual array of day excursions.

Gateways

Open Jaw: Munich inbound, Paris outbound. Discuss with your travel agent for professional advice. Other gateways include:

Frankfurt: ICE 721 to Munich departs 1554 and arrives 1907 or ICE 725 departs 1754 and arrives 2105. Return to Frankfurt on ICE 728, departing 0652 and arriving 1004 or ICE 690, departing 0810 and arriving 1208.

Amsterdam: ICE 105 to Munich departs at 0805; arrives Mannheim at 1223. Change to ICE 595, departing 1230 and arriving Munich 1528. Return to Amsterdam on ICE 626, departing Munich at 1255; arrive Frankfurt 1604. Change to ICE 122 Frankfurt to Amsterdam, departing 1629 and arriving 2027.

Paris: Depart Paris Est on TGV 9571 to Stuttgart Hbf at 0725; arrive Stuttgart at 1104 and change trains to ICE 1091 departing at 1116; arrive in Munich Hbf at 1327. Return to Paris on ICE 9573, departing Munich at 1054; arrive Stuttgart Hbf at 1247; change trains to TGV 9574, departing 1255 for arrival in Paris at 1635.

Base-City Hotels

Munich: Drei Lowen, 1 block from the station, is convenient, as is Best Western Hotel Cristal. Balance of hotels listed are clustered nearby. Hilton and Sheraton properties in suburbs have easy tram connections to city center.

Bern: Schweizerhof, on the station plaza, is tops in location, restaurant, and price. Hotel Baeren and Hotel Bristol are more economical and three minutes' walk to station. Other hotels listed are also within a short walk of station and maintain highest Swiss standards.

Paris: For economy and excellent location for rail travelers, choose Hotel Albert 1er, situated between Gare du Nord and Gare de l'Est. Holiday Inn Paris-Bastille, 1 short block away from Gare de Lyon's rail, Métro, and RER connections, has an excellent neighborhood-restaurant section.

EUROPE A LA CARTE BASE-CITY TRANSFER SCHEDULE

FROM	TO	DEPART	TRAIN NUMBER	ARRIVE	NOTES
Munich	**Zürich**	0717	EC 196	1153	R
Zürich	**Bern**	1202	IC 822	1258	R, 1
Bern	**Paris Lyon**	0910	TGV 9214	1337	R

EUROPE A LA CARTE DAY-EXCURSION SUGGESTIONS

BASE CITY	EXCURSION	DEPART	ARRIVE	DEPART	ARRIVE	NOTES
Munich	Berchtesgaden	0854	1130	1831	2115	2
	Garmisch-Partenkirchen	0832	0954	1805	1926	
	Innsbruck	0738	0923	1836	2023	
	Nuremberg	0755	0857	1828	1938	
	Salzburg	0818	0959	1915	2115	
Bern	Interlaken	0834	0928	2000	2052	
	Lucerne	0800	0900	1900	2000	
	Montreux, Golden Pass	0934	1109	1923	2056	R, 3
Paris	Annecy	0658	1117	1831	2212	R
	Rennes	0808	1025	1835	2054	R
	Fontainebleau	0919	0956	2000	2041	
	Lyon	0753	0955	1804	2007	R
	Rouen	0820	0948	1759	1910	

Note: All trains are daily.

R Reservations required or recommended

1. Half-hourly service Zürich–Bern.

2. Change trains in Freilassing.

3. Mainline trains depart Montreux for Lausanne at 19 and 54 minutes past the hour. IC 741 departs Lausanne at 1920, arrives in Bern at 2026.

Other departures available.

Europe a la Carte 15-Day Rail Itinerary

Day 1	Munich–Salzburg: Visit Mozart's birthplace and listen to Salzburg's sound of music.
Day 2	Munich–Garmisch–Partenkirchen: Home of the Winter Olympic Park and gateway to ascent of the mighty Zugspitze.
Day 3	Munich–Berchtesgaden: Explore salt mines, then soar to Hitler's ill-famed Eagle's Nest.
Day 4	Munich–Innsbruck: World famous for winter Olympics, with year-round exhilarating scenery.
Day 5	Munich–Nuremberg: Germany's leading toy producers spice activities with fresh gingerbread.
Day 6	Munich–Bern: Base-city transfer via Zürich.
Day 7	Bern–Interlaken: A day in alpine splendor; return to Bern by Lake of Thun steamer.
Day 8	Bern–Lucerne: A rain-or-shine outing with Mount Pilatus and Swiss cheese fondue.
Day 9	Bern–Montreux: A scenic rail trip with a visit to Château de Chillon.
Day 10	Bern–Paris: Base-city transfer via Geneva.
Day 11	Paris–Rouen: Visit historic site of France's Joan of Arc.
Day 12	Paris–Rennes: Half-timbered houses and a ride on the TGV *Atlantique*.
Day 13	Paris–Fontainebleau: Visit the scene where Napoleon ruled and later was vanquished.
Day 14	Lyon–Annecy: Breathtaking scenery, sparkling water, and a charming medieval marketplace.
Day 15	Paris–Lyon: City of contrast visited after exciting journey aboard TGV, one of the world's fastest trains.

Tour Tips: Make seat reservations immediately on arrival in Munich. At minimum, reserve all base-city legs. Reservations are obligatory on TGV and many EuroCity trains.

European Escapade

A more than passing acquaintance with some of Europe's most fascinating sights and cities. From gateway Luxembourg; you travel to Bern, Amsterdam, and Paris, with shopping in Brussels.

Base Cities

Luxembourg: Fortress city, steeped in European and American history. Virtually a tax-free city; save some money for Luxembourg shops.

Bern: Medieval settings in the heart of the Swiss Alps. Bern's arcaded walkways make shopping and sightseeing easy even in bad weather.

Amsterdam: Canals, cheese shops, diamond cutters, and Rembrandt's finest masterpieces await you.

Paris: City of Light. Mix Paris's pleasures with an array of action-packed day excursions.

Gateways

Discuss all gateway possibilities with your travel agent because the tour's circular itinerary provides a wide selection, including all of the base cities in this itinerary plus Brussels. Depart Brussels Central for Luxembourg at 0737 on EC 91 for arrival in Luxembourg at 1052; EuroCity or InterCity service returns you to Brussels at end of tour.

Base-City Hotels

Luxembourg: Pick a price. Most of the hotels listed are near the station. Book well in advance, particularly in summer tour season.

Bern: Schweizerhof for luxury, but the other listed hotels offer only a shade less at varying prices. All are within walking distance of the station.

Amsterdam: Victoria Park Plaza Hotel, a scant block from the station, is most convenient and highly recommended. Grand Hotel Krasnapolsky is just another stone's throw away but posh, with prices to match.

Paris: Best bargain and good location is Hotel Albert 1er between Gare du Nord and Gare de l'Est. Same for Holiday Inn Paris-Bastille, close to Gare de Lyon.

European Escapade 15-Day Rail Itinerary

Day 1	Luxembourg–Clervaux: An opportunity to visit site of World War II Battle of the Bulge.
Day 2	Luxembourg–Koblenz: A rail excursion along the Mosel to the Rhine in German wine country.

Day 3	Luxembourg–Bern: Base-city transfer via France.
Day 4	Bern–Interlaken: View of mighty Jungfrau and cruise on Lake of Thun highlight exciting rail tour.
Day 5	Bern–Lucerne: Sparkling highlights of Switzerland's lake city plus Mount Pilatus ascent.
Day 6	Bern–Milan: Cross into Italy for a delightful day of sightseeing in fascinating Milan.
Day 7	Bern–Amsterdam: Base-city transfer via Rhine.
Day 8	Amsterdam–Enkhuizen: Visit the Zuider Zee museum, depicting the Dutch battle with the sea.
Day 9	Amsterdam–Hoorn: Steam-engine ride from Hoorn to Medemblik; the old Dutch Market on Wednesday.
Day 10	Amsterdam–Alkmaar: World-famous cheese market and site of Dutch revolt against Spanish rule.
Day 11	Amsterdam–Paris: Base-city transfer via Brussels.
Day 12	Paris–Chartres: Palaces and castles abound along with Gothic Cathedral of Notre Dame.
Day 13	Paris–Rennes: Experience TGV *Atlantique* at 186 miles per hour.
Day 14	Paris–Fontainebleau: Visit palace where Napoleon relaxed with Josephine—and a few others.
Day 15	Paris–Lyon: "Newest" city of France, with Roman history, visited aboard one of the world's fastest trains, a TGV.

Tour Tips: Book all seat reservations when you arrive in Luxembourg. Depart Luxembourg (Day 2) on RE 5109 at 0726, arriving Koblenz at 0955. In Koblenz, board ICE 27 at 1048 for Mainz, arriving there at 1138. You'll get a great view of the Rhine from the train. Lunch in the Mainz Station restaurant and depart at 1303 and arrive in Bingen at 1334. Board the steamer ship from the Bingen pier at 1430. Then relax on the Rhine until reaching Koblenz at 1810. Service operates April through October. Have dinner at the Weindorf. Catch RE 5128 at 2006 back to Luxembourg (transfer in Trier), arriving at 2234.

En route to Amsterdam from Bern (Day 7), after departing Mainz, watch on the right-hand side of the train for spectacular Rhine scenery to Koblenz.

EUROPEAN ESCAPADE BASE-CITY TRANSFER SCHEDULE

FROM	TO	DEPART	TRAIN NUMBER	ARRIVE	NOTES
Luxembourg	**Bern**	0612	RE 5107	1456	R
Bern	**Amsterdam**	1104	ICE 278	2027	R, 1
Amsterdam	**Paris Nord**	0817	Thalys 9322*	1135	R
Paris Est	**Luxembourg**	0840	TGV 2809	1059	R

EUROPEAN ESCAPADE DAY-EXCURSION SUGGESTIONS

BASE CITY	EXCURSION	DEPART	ARRIVE	DEPART	ARRIVE	NOTES
Luxembourg	Clervaux	0818	0914	1845	1942	
	Koblenz	0831	1055	1906	2129	
Bern	Interlaken	0834	0928	2000	2052	
	Lucerne	0800	0900	1900	2000	
	Milan	0734	1037	1823	2123	R
Amsterdam	Alkmaar	0842	0920	1741	1819	
	Enkhuizen	0839	0936	1724	1823	
	Hoorn	0839	0915	1720	1753	
Paris	Annecy	0658	1117	1831	2212	R
	Rennes	0809	1025	1835	2054	R
	Chartres	0809	0925	1734	1850	
	Fontainebleau	0919	0956	2000	2041	
	Lyon	0753	0956	1804	2011	R

Note: All trains are daily.

R Reservations required or recommended

1. Change trains in Frankfurt.

*Thalys trains require supplement.

Scandinavian Splendor

Tour the Scandinavian capitals of Copenhagen, Helsinki, Oslo, and Stockholm, and board the Tallink-Silja Line's finest cruise ship for adventure on the Baltic.

Base Cities

Copenhagen: Jovial, entertaining, the fun capital of Scandinavia. Save it for the grand finale.

Helsinki: Daughter of the Baltic. A glittering gem set in a picture-book harbor. Make the best of your "shore leave" by enjoying every moment.

Oslo: Friendly, pleasant, and compact. Take the Bergen–Flåm excursion option if time permits.

Stockholm: Striking harbor skyline, a city of islands and waterways. Sightseeing must include a visit to Old Town, where it all began centuries ago.

Gateways

All the base cities have direct U.S. air service, even Helsinki. The circular nature of the tour's itinerary makes it possible to select any one of the aforementioned base cities as both the inbound and outbound gateway. Our choice would be Copenhagen; which is yours?

Base-City Hotels

Copenhagen: Palace Hotel gets the tourists' nod for convenient location, midrange rates, and so on. The Plaza, facing the station, is great but difficult to book in high season.

Helsinki: No listing because we recommend using the Tallink-Silja Line's accommodations for this tour's out-and-back day excursion, but we can recommend the *Presidenti* if you elect to extend your stay in Helsinki.

Oslo: The Grand Hotel features Old World elegance with modern conveniences—with the exception of price. The Hotel Nobel, with a wider rate range, is near the Grand Hotel.

Stockholm: Take your pick. All three hotels listed face Central Station. Price is probably the deciding factor. All have acceptable restaurants and are clean and well managed.

Scandinavian Splendor 15-Day Rail Itinerary

If Copenhagen is selected as the in-out gateway, spend jet-lag adjustment time there before validating your Eurail Global Pass, Eurail Select Pass, or Eurail Scandinavia Pass and leaving for Oslo.

SCANDINAVIAN SPLENDOR BASE-CITY TRANSFER SCHEDULE

FROM	TO	DEPART	TRAIN NUMBER	ARRIVE	NOTES
Copenhagen	**Oslo**	0832	R1026/R394	1652	R
Oslo	**Stockholm**	0701	IC 105	1428	R
Stockholm	**Helsinki**	1700	Tallink-Silja ferry	0945+1	R
Helsinki	**Stockholm**	1700	Tallink-Silja ferry	0945+1	R
Stockholm	**Copenhagen**	0821	X 2000/525	1324	R
		1221	X 2000/533	1724	R

SCANDINAVIAN SPLENDOR DAY-EXCURSION SUGGESTIONS*

BASE CITY	EXCURSION	DEPART	ARRIVE	DEPART	ARRIVE	NOTES
Copenhagen	Aarhus	0752	1043	1815	2105	R
	Helsingør	0813	0856	1703	1748	
	Odense	0855	1008	1824	1956	
	Roskilde	0830	0850	1857	1917	
Oslo	Hamar	0802	0921	1803	1926	R
	Larvik	0839	1036	1919	2121	2nd class
	Lillehammer	0834	1045	1913	2126	R
Stockholm	Eskilstuna	0855	1001	1813	1920	
	Norrköping	0821	0933	1624	1739	R
	Uppsala	0811	0849	1911	1949	R

*See appropriate base-city chapters for additional day-excursion suggestions.

Note: All trains are daily.

R Reservations required

+1 Arrives next day

Day 1	Copenhagen–Oslo: Scenic base-city transfer.
Day 2	Oslo–Larvik: Put a fjord in your future with an excursion to Larvik and on to Skien.
Day 3	Oslo–Hamar: Drink in the beauty of Lake Mjosa before exploring the rail museum in Hamar.
Day 4	Oslo–Lillehammer: Lillehammer can provide an insight into Norway's culture.
Day 5	Oslo–Stockholm: Colorful base-city transfer.
Day 6	Stockholm–Uppsala: Spend an interesting day in a city that dates from pagan times.
Day 7	Stockholm–Eskilstuna: See Sweden's "steel city" and visit 300-plus-year-old Rademacher Forges.
Day 8	Stockholm–Norrköping: Surprises such as cacti growing in Sweden await your arrival.
Day 9	Stockholm–Tallink-Silja Line cruise to Helsinki: Cruise the Baltic in luxury to Finland.
Day 10	Helsinki–Stockholm: Set sail again for Sweden after an exciting day ashore in Helsinki.
Day 11	Stockholm–Copenhagen: Arrive in Denmark's capital after overland rail through Sweden.
Day 12	Copenhagen–Aarhus: Ferry and rail transportation join to make an exciting day excursion.
Day 13	Copenhagen–Helsingør: A rail visit to north Zealand to inspect Hamlet's castle.
Day 14	Copenhagen–Odense: A rail visit to the birthplace of Hans Christian Andersen.
Day 15	Copenhagen–Roskilde: Five Viking ships await your inspection in Roskilde's museum.

Tour Tips: Make the Tallink-Silja Line cruise to Helsinki and back a highlight of your tour. Book a round-trip cabin and spend a carefree day ashore in Helsinki sans luggage. In Helsinki, ride Tram 3T for a quick view of this remarkable city. The Tallink-Silja Line can also arrange extended shore leave in Helsinki if desired.

Base-City Hotels and Information

All hotel rates, given in local currencies applicable at press time, are subject to change. The hotels listed are close to the railway stations and/or public transport facilities. The hotel's street location is below the hotel name.

When writing, the postal code, city, and country name should follow the hotel name and street address; for example, 1012 JS Amsterdam, The Netherlands.

Note: Most of the hotels listed offer a lower rate if you book online, and most offer lower rates on weekends.

Amsterdam Hotels

To telephone or fax the Amsterdam hotels from the United States, dial 011 +31, then the number listed below.

Grand Hotel Krasnapolsky ★★★★★ *Tel:* (20) 5549111
Dam 9 €175–475 *Fax:* (20) 6228607
1012 JS
Breakfast €19.50
www.nh-hotels.com; *E-mail:* nhkrasnapolsky@nh-hotels.com

Victoria Hotel ★★★★ *Tel:* (20) 6234255
Damrak 1–5 €189–390* *Fax:* (20) 6252997
1012 LG
Breakfast €16.50
*Some rate plans include breakfast buffet
www.parkplaza.com; *E-mail:* bookamsterdam@pphe.com

NH Amsterdam Centre ★★★ *Tel:* (20) 6851351
Stadhouderskade 7 €165–390
1012 VX
www.nh-hotels.com;
E-mail: nhamsterdamcentre@nh-hotels.com

Bern Hotels

To telephone or fax the Bern hotels from the United States, dial 011 +41, then the number listed.

Schweizerhof Bern ★★★★★ *Tel:* (31) 3268080
Bahnhofplatz 11 CHF 350–550 *Fax:* (31) 3268083
CH–3001
www.schweizerhof-bern.ch; *E-mail:* info@schweizerhof-bern.ch

Hotel Bern ★★★★ *Tel:* (31) 329 22 22
Zeughausgasse 9 CHF 130–405 *Fax:* (31) 329 22 99
CH–3011
www.hotelbern.ch; *E-mail:* reception@hotelbern.ch

Best Western Bristol ★★★★ *Tel:* (31) 3110101
Schauplatzgasse 10 CHF 150–340 *Fax:* (31) 3119479
CH–3011
Buffet breakfast included
www.bristolbern.ch; *E-mail:* reception@bristolbern.ch

City Am Bahnhof ★★★ *Tel:* (31) 3115377
Bahnhofplatz 7 CHF 169–350 *Fax:* (31) 3110636
CH–3011
Buffet breakfast CHF 18; continental breakfast CHF 9
www.fhotels.ch; *E-mail:* city-ab@fhotels.ch

Hotel Metropole ★★★ *Tel:* (31) 3299494
Zeughausgasse 26 CHF 155–255 *Fax:* (31) 3299495
CH 3000
www.hotelmetropole.ch; *E-mail:* info@hotelmetropole.ch

Copenhagen Hotels

To telephone or fax hotels in Copenhagen from the United States, dial 011 +45, then the number as listed.

The Palace Hotel ★★★★ *Tel:* 33 144050
Rådhuspladsen 57 DKK 1,100–2,350* *Fax:* 33 145279
DK–1550
*Some 5★ rooms available; rates include 25% VAT, service charge, and breakfast
www.palacehotel.dk; *E-mail:* palacecopenhagen@scandichotels.com

The Mayfair Hotel ★★★ *Tel:* 70 121700
Helgolandsgade 3 DKK 700–1,250 *Fax:* 33 239686
DK–1653
www.firsthotels.dk; *E-mail:* info@firsthotels.dk

First Hotel Excelsior ★★★ *Tel:* 33 245085
Colbjørnsensgade 11 DKK 432–1,280 *Fax:* 33 245087
DK–1652
www.firsthotels.dk; *E-mail:* info@firsthotels.dk

Luxembourg Hotels

To telephone or fax Luxembourg hotels from the United States, dial 011 +352, then the numbers as listed.

Note: Government of Luxembourg does not usually rate hotels.

Golden Tulip Central Molitor Hotel ★★★★ *Tel:* 489911
28 Avenue de la Liberté €110–210* *Fax:* 483382
L–1930
*Rates include buffet breakfast and taxes
www.hotelmolitor.lu or www.goldentulip.com; *E-mail:* reservations@goldentulipcentralmolitor.com

Best Western International ★★★ *Tel:* 485911
20 Place de la Gare €190–250* *Fax:* 493227
L–1024 (lower weekend rates)
*Rates include buffet breakfast and taxes
www.bestwestern.com; *E-mail:* info@hotelinter.lu

Munich Hotels

To telephone or fax Munich hotels from the United States, dial 011 +49, then the numbers as listed.

Atrium ★★★★ *Tel:* (89) 514190
Landwehrstrasse 59 €89–199 *Fax:* (89) 535066
D–80336
www.bestwestern.com; *E-mail:* info@atrium-muenchen.bestwestern.de

Best Western Hotel Cristal ★★★★ *Tel:* (89) 551110
Schwanthalerstrasse 36 €95–269 *Fax:* (89) 55111992
80336
www.cristal.bestwestern.de or www.bestwestern.com; *E-mail:* info@cristal.bestwestern.de

Drei Löwen ★★★★ *Tel:* (89) 551040
Schillerstrasse 8 €99–269* *Fax:* (89) 55104905
D–80336
www.hotel3loewen.de; *E-Mail:* info@hotel3loewen.de
*Breakfast included in rate

Hotel Germania ★★★ *Tel:* (89) 59046140
Schwanthalerstrasse 28 €65–140 *Fax:* (89) 591171
80336
www.hotel-germania-muenchen.de; *E-mail:* info@hotel-germania.net

Oslo Hotels

To telephone or fax Oslo hotels from the United States, dial 011 +47, then the numbers as listed.

Grand Hotel ★★★★ *Tel:* 23 21 20 00
Karl Johansgate 31 NOK 1,600–4,000 *Fax:* 23 21 21 00
N–0159
www.grand.no; *E-mail:* reservations-grand@rica.no

Best Western
Hotell Bondeheimen ★★★ *Tel:* 23 21 41 00
Rosenkrantz gate 8 NOK 795–1,675* *Fax:* 23 21 41 01
N–0159
*Breakfast included in rates
www.bondeheimen.com; *E-mail:* bookingoffice@bondeheimen.com

Norlandia Karl Johan Hotel ★★★ *Tel:* 23 16 17 00
Karl Johansgate 33 NOK 795–1,595 *Fax:* 23 42 05 19
N–0162
www.karljohan.no; *E-mail:* karljohan@bestwestern.no

Paris Hotels

To telephone or fax the Paris hotels from the United States, dial 011 +33, then the numbers as listed.

Hotel Ambassador ★★★★ *Tel:* (1) 44834040
16, Blvd. Haussmann €320–750 *Fax:* (1) 44834057
F–75009
www.marriott.com; *E-mail:* info.ambassador.paris@marriott.com

Hotel Albert Premier ★★★ *Tel:* (1) 40368240
162, rue LaFayette €99–239 *Fax:* (1) 40357252
F–75010
www.albert1erhotel.com

Holiday Inn Paris-Bastille ★★★ *Tel:* (1) 53022000
11, rue de Lyon €167–285 *Fax:* (1) 53022001
F–75012
www.holidayinn.com; *E-mail:* re@holidayinnparisbastille.com

55 Montparnasse Hotel ★★★ *Tel:* (1) 4542 8143
55, rue des Plaisance €72–215 *Fax:* (1) 4542 9787
F–75014
www.55montparnasse.com

Best Western Plaza Elysées ★★★ *Tel:* (1) 45639383
177, Blvd. Haussmann €189–289 *Fax:* (1) 45611430
F–75008
www.plazaelysees.com; *E-mail:* plazaelysees@plazaelysees.com

Stockholm Hotels

To telephone or fax the Stockholm hotels from the United States, dial 011 +46, then the numbers as listed.

Best Western Hotel Terminus ★★★★ *Tel:* (8) 440 1670
Vasagatan 20 SEK 1,500–2,190 *Fax:* (8) 440 1671
S–10125
www.terminus.se; *E-mail:* reservations@terminus.se

Sheraton Stockholm
Hotel & Towers ★★★★ *Tel:* (8) 412 3400
Tegelbacken 6, Box 195 SEK 1,350–2,795* *Fax:* (8) 412 3400
S–10123
*Breakfast included
www.sheratonstockholm.com; *E-mail:* sheraton.stockholm@sheraton
.com

Scandic Hotel Sergel Plaza ★★★ *Tel:* (8) 5172 6300
Brunkebergstorg 9 SEK 1,500–2,750 *Fax:* (8) 5172 6311
S–10327
Located by Central rail station
www.scandichotels.com; *E-mail:* sergel.plaza@scandichotels.com

Ferry Crossings

In addition to unlimited rail travel and other conveniences, Eurail provides rail pass holders with deck passage on ferries conveying train passengers within the Eurail countries. In some instances, passengers must detrain and board the ferries, but on most major rail lines, the passenger coaches are loaded directly onto the ferry. In either case, the ferries are equipped with amenities such as restaurants, bars, boutiques, and, when traveling between countries, money exchanges and tax-free shops.

Three major international ferry crossings exist; they are between Italy and Greece, Finland and Sweden, and Ireland and France. The distances are considerable and usually involve overnight travel. (Sleeping accommodations are extra.) Other ferry crossings of international importance to rail pass travelers include the lines between Ireland and Britain.

Italy–Greece and Vice Versa

If your rail pass is valid in Greece, you are granted free deck passage between Ancona or Bari, Italy, and Patras or Igoumenitsa, Greece, by **Superfast Ferries.** Rail pass holders are also granted free deck passage between Brindisi, Italy, and Corfu, Igoumenitsa, and Patras on ferries operated by **Hellenic Mediterranean Lines** and **Blue Star Ferries.**

You must present your rail pass to the shipping-company office in the port and have a ticket and a boarding pass issued before boarding. Reservation fees, port taxes, meals, reclining chairs, or sleeping accommodations are not included. Reclining chairs are a great bargain for the budget-minded traveler. During July and August there is a high-season surcharge of $20 (U.S.).

Superfast Ferries (www.superfast.com) operate daily, departing in the evening for arrival the following morning.

Italy–Greece

ROUTES	DEPART	ARRIVE	HOURS
Ancona–Patras	1630	1500	23.5
Via Igoumenitsa	1330	1130+1	21
Ancona–Igoumenitsa	1330	0600+1	13
Bari–Patras			
Via Igoumenitsa	1930	1300	16.5
Bari–Igoumenitsa	1930	0530+1	10.5
Bari–Corfu	1930	0430+1	9

Greece–Italy

ROUTES	DEPART	ARRIVE	HOURS
Patras–Ancona	1730	1630+1	22.5
Via Igoumenitsa	1430	1030+1	20
Igoumenitsa–Ancona	2000	1030+1	15.5
Patras–Bari			
Via Igoumenitsa	1800	0930+1	14.5
Igoumenitsa–Bari	0030	0930+1	9
Corfu–Bari	0200	1030	8.5

+1 Arrives next day.
Departures and arrivals in local time.
Schedules subject to change. Contact Superfast Ferries for bookings, prices for sleeping accommodations, exact sailing dates/times, and nondeparture dates due to ships' maintenance.
Bari routes operated by Blue Star Ferries.

Contacts:

Greece

Athens Superfast Ferries
157, C. Karamanli Av.
166 73 Voula, Athens, Greece
Tel: +30 (210) 891 9130; *Fax:* +30 (210) 891 9139
E-mail: info.Athens@superfast.com

Italy

F.LLI Morandi & Co.
Via XXIX Settembre 2/0
I-60122 Ancona
Tel: +39 (71) 20 20 33/4; *Fax:* +39 (71) 20 22 19
E-mail: morandi@superfast.com

United States

Amphitrion Holidays
1010 Rockville Pike, Ste. 401
Rockville, MD 20852
Tel.: +1 301-545-0999
Fax: +1 301-294-5324
Email: amphitrion-us@superfast.com

Minoan Lines

Italy–Greece		Greece–Italy	
DEPART	**ARRIVE**	**DEPART**	**ARRIVE**
Ancona	Patras via Igoumenitsa	Patras	Ancona via Igoumenitsa
1400	1300+1	1800	1430+1
Daily Exc. Thursday		Daily Exc. Wednesday	
DEPART	**ARRIVE**	**DEPART**	**ARRIVE**
Ancona	Igoumenitsa	Igoumenitsa	Ancona
1400	0700+1	2359	1430+1
Daily Exc. Friday		Daily Exc. Wednesday	

+1 Arrives next day.
Departures and arrivals in local time.
Schedules subject to change. Contact Blue Star Ferries for bookings, prices for sleeping accommodations, exact sailing dates/times, and nondeparture dates due to ships' maintenance.

Contact:
Minoan Lines
6–10 Thermopylon
185 45 Piraeus
Tel: +30 (21) 04145700; *Fax:* +30 (21) 04145755
www.minoan.gr
E-mail: booking@minoan.gr

Brindisi, Italy, Ferry Terminal: A 15-minute walk downhill to the Seno di Levante pier at the foot of Corso (Umberto), Corso Garibaldi, and Via del Mera, the streets leading to the waterfront. The terminal is on the right, just before the pier. It opens daily two hours prior to departure times.

Attenzione (That's "attention" in Italian): From the time you arrive in Brindisi until you are safely aboard the ferry, beware of "entrepreneurs" approaching you with offers to help. Many are garbed in official-looking uniforms or are wearing "Official Guide" headgear. They bear alarming messages such as, "I have bad news. All of the deck space for tonight's sailing has been sold out." Then they relate the good news: "You are fortunate in meeting me, for I can take you to an agency where a few cabins are still available." With that, he'll reach for your baggage unless, by now, you have interrupted his presentation with a firm, "No, thank you." If he insists, *polizia* (police) is another good word to inject into the conversation.

Patras, Greece, Ferry Terminal: To reach the terminal from the railway station, turn left as you exit the station. Walk along the street side of the quay approximately 300 yards, to the office marked Central Agency. Summer hours are 0900 to 2200 daily. Winter hours are 0900 to 1300 and 1700 to 2200. Report on day of embarkation only. No baggage checking is available.

Author's suggestion: The port cities of Brindisi and Patras are interesting, charming, and steeped in history. Why not take a day to see them at a leisurely pace? Plan to arrive a day before your scheduled ferry departure. Ask your hotel to call ahead for a reservation. Also ask the concierge to check on your ferry reservation. The address and telephone numbers of the city tourist information offices are posted in the Arrival Halls of the rail stations.

Finland–Sweden and Vice Versa

There are two competing ferry services between Helsinki and Stockholm: Tallink-Silja Line and Viking Line. Holders of Eurail passes, Eurail Select Pass (provided that Finland and Sweden were chosen as two of the three bordering countries), and Eurail Scandinavia Pass are valid for deck passage. Pass holders must pay extra for cabin space.

Crossing between Sweden and Finland, you may select between two routes: Stockholm–Helsinki direct; or Stockholm–Turku, with train connections or the Tallink-Silja Line express bus service between Turku and Helsinki. Our preference is the direct route between the two capitals because it gives you a few more hours aboard ship to enjoy the scenery, which is spectacular. Both routes traverse the breathtaking archipelago between the two countries.

Although your rail pass entitles you to travel on the ferry, you also need to obtain a boarding pass before embarking. If you need a boarding pass, you should be at the ferry terminal two hours before ship departure.

Tallink-Silja Line ferries depart daily from Helsinki Olympiaterminaali (Olympia Terminal) at Eteläsatama port at 1700 and arrive Stockholm Värtahamnen port at 0945 the next day. Tram 3B and 3T service, adjacent to the Olympia Terminal, connects with Helsinki city center. Shuttle bus service (extra charge) is available from Stockholm Värtan Terminal at Värtahamnen port to Ropsten Metro (underground/subway) station, where there are trains to Stockholm Central Station.

For more details, schedules, and/or to reserve cabin space, contact:

Tallink-Silja Line, Ticket Office
Erottajankatu 19
FIN-00130 Helsinki, Finland
Tel: +358 (0) 9 18041; *Fax:* +358 (0) 9 1804279
www.tallinksilja.com; *E-mail:* international.sales@tallinksilja.com

Silja Line's U.S. Sales Agent:
Borton Overseas
Scandinavi Specialist
5412 Lyndale Ave. South
Minneapolis, MN 55419
Tel: (612) 822-4640
www.bortonoverseas.com

Viking Line ferries depart Helsinki Katajanokka dock at 1730 daily. Arrive Stockholm Stadsgården dock 0945 the next day. From Stockholm, depart at 1645 for arrival in Helsinki at 1000 the next day. Tram 4 service operates daily between the vicinity of Viking Line Terminal and Helsinki city center; or bus No. 13 operates between Katajanokka Terminal–Helsinki rail station in connection with departure/arrival of ships. Bus service between Stockholm Stadsgården port and Cityterminalen (bus terminal) near Stockholm Central Station runs in connection with arrival/departure of ships. For information on Viking Line services or to reserve cabin space, contact:

Viking Line, Main Office
Monnerheimintie 14
FIN 00100 Helsinki
Tel: 358 (0) 9 12351; *Fax:* (358) (0) 9 647075
www.vikingline.fi

Viking Line U.S. Sales Agent
Borton Overseas
5412 Lyndale Avenue South
Minneapolis, MN 55419
Tel: (800) 843-0602; *Fax:* (612) 822-4755
E-mail: info@bortonoverseas.com
www.bortonoverseas.com

Train/Ferry Connections Helsinki—Stockholm via Turku

DEPART Helsinki	TRAIN NUMBER	ARRIVE Turku Harbor
0517	IC 941	0748
1657	IC 961	1923

Note: Arrives Turku Satama (harbor train station)

Tallink-Silja Line ferries depart Turku Harbor daily at 0815, arrive Stockholm Värtahamnen port 1815; depart Turku at 2015 for arrival at 0610 next day.

Viking Line ferries depart Turku Linnansatama dock daily at 0845, arrive Stockholm Stadsgården dock at 1855; depart at 2055 for arrival at 0630 next day. Bus service between Stadsgården port and Cityterminalen (bus terminal) near Stockholm Central Station in connection with arrival/departure of ships.

Ireland—Britain and Vice Versa

Stena Line, the world's largest international ferry company, operates on 16 routes in northwestern Europe, including the Irish Sea and the English Channel. Stena's HSS (High-speed Sea Service) ships cruise between Belfast in Northern Ireland and Stranraer in Scotland in only 105 minutes. Stena Line's Superferry service offers leisurely crossings with duty-free shopping, meals, and even a movie (on some routes). The Superferry *Koningin Beatrix* on the Rosslare–Fishguard route, capable of carrying 2,100 passengers and 500 automobiles, is the largest and most luxurious ferry to operate on the southern Irish Sea. Visit www.stenaline.com.

Irish Ferries can take you from Dublin to Holyhead, and P&O Irish Sea ferries serve on the Larne–Cairnryan route. Visit www.irishferries.com.

Coming from London by train requires a transfer to either a Stena Line or Irish Ferries ferry at Holyhead. The Stena Line ferries serve the port of Dun Laoghaire, a suburb of Dublin, where passengers can transfer to the center of the city by the local train service, DART.

Irish Ferries

	Dublin City—Holyhead		Holyhead—Dublin City		
VESSEL	**DEPART**	**ARRIVE**	**DEPART**	**ARRIVE**	**JOURNEY TIME**
Cruise Ferry	0805	1130			3 hrs, 25 min
Cruise Ferry			0240	0555	3 hrs, 15 min
Dublin Swift	0845	1045	1150	1339	2 hrs
Dublin Swift	1430	1630	1410	1725	3 hrs, 25 min
Cruise Ferry	2055	0020	1715	1915	2 hrs

	Rosslare—Pembroke		Pembroke—Rosslare		
VESSEL	**DEPART**	**ARRIVE**	**DEPART**	**ARRIVE**	**JOURNEY TIME**
Cruise Ferry	0845	1246	0245	0646	4 hrs
Cruise Ferry	2045	0046	1445	1846	4 hrs

Daily service. Schedules subject to change.

Stena Line to Britain

ROUTE	JOURNEY
Rosslare–Fishguard	3 hours, 30 minutes Superferry (twice daily)
Dublin–Holyhead	3 hours, 15 minutes Superferry (four times daily)
Dun Läoghaire–Holyhead	100 minutes HSS fast ferry (four times daily)
Belfast–Cairnryan	2 hours, 15 minutes Superferry (five times daily)

Ireland—France and Vice Versa

Trains connecting Dublin with the Irish Ferries services that sail from the port of Rosslare, south of Dublin, to the French ports of Cherbourg and Roscoff use Dublin's Connolly Station. A sign directing visitors to the nearby tourist information office on O'Connell Street is located on the right side of the concourse. Connolly Station is also the terminal in Dublin for trains arriving from Northern Ireland.

Eurail travelers are entitled to a 50 percent discount for deck passage on the Irish Ferries route between Rosslare and Cherbourg or Roscoff. Meals and sleeping accommodations are extra. Sailings operate April through September: Advance booking is highly recommended. Journey time between Rosslare–Cherbourg is 16.5 hours; between Rosslare–Roscoff, 18 hours. All passages are overnight. Check-in points are usually open two hours prior to sailing times. Passengers are requested to check in no later than one hour prior to sailing times.

For sailing schedules, cabin rates, availability, and reservations, visit www.irishferries.com or contact the Irish Ferries General Sales Agent, USA and Canada:

Scots-American Travel Advisors
825 13th Lane
Vero Beach, FL 32960
Tel: (772) 563-2856; *Fax:* (772) 563-2087
E-mail: info@scotsamerican.com
www.scotsamerican.com

24-hour Information line in Ireland: from the United States, dial 011 +44 01 6610715

Online bookings (in Euro dollars): www.irishferries.com

Rosslare Port, Irish Ferries Port Office *Tel:* 053 33158. Trains from Dublin and Limerick connect with the Irish Ferries on the Rosslare Harbor pier. There are no transfer costs.

Cherbourg Port, Irish Ferries Port Office *Tel:* +33 02 33 23 44 44. Taxi service available for transfer to/from Cherbourg's railway station to the Irish Ferries Terminal.

Roscoff Port, Irish Ferries Port Office *Tel:* +33 02 98 61 17 17. Rail connections available for Brittany, west coast, and southwestern France.

International Calling

The following chart provides the country codes and city codes you will need when calling from one country to another. The country codes should be used when dialing to that country from another country. In most cases you will also need to dial a city or area code prior to the local number.

Calling Europe from North America:
To use these codes from within North America, dial 011 + country code, city code, and the local number you wish to reach. If the European city code is prefaced with a "0," omit it when dialing from North America.

Communicating on the Go

If you have an AT&T or T-Mobile mobile phone in the U.S., check with your carrier to see if your phone can be used internationally. Often, your carrier will provide you with an "unlock" code (possibly for a fee) so that your phone can be used with a SIM (Subscriber Identification Module) Card from another carrier. This could allow you to buy a SIM, or a prepaid SIM, from the local carrier in the country or countries to which you travel. Verizon and Sprint phones, which use a separate technology, rarely work abroad. (Those that might are often labeled as "world phones.") Some prepay phones that you can buy will work across European borders, particularly if you remain within a few countries. We would recommend buying a prepaid cell phone or SIM card directly from the mobile company, or from a reputable shop. Most major train stations and airports now have one or more of this type of store. Check with the clerk in the store to see if the phone that you are thinking of buying will work throughout your itinerary. Buying prepaid phones in Europe is relatively inexpensive, with the phone being very inexpensive and additional minutes available for a small cost. You are probably best off not using this phone for international calls, unless you have read the fine-print regarding international rates associated with the phone and/or SIM card. There are other choices for a mobile phone, with several companies providing rental European phones, which can be shipped to you before you depart. Prices start around $50 for a week-long rental, not including airtime.

Depending on how long you will be gone, and how much you need to see loved ones back home, an Internet cafe and video conferencing may be the way to go. While there are several available services, Skype (www.skype.com) is the largest and most reliable one. If you use the service computer-to-computer only, it is only necessary to set up an account for free. Some Internet cafes will have Skype software and a webcam preinstalled on their computers, and your loved one(s) will need the same equipment on their computer back home. If you are planning on using Skype extensively, an inexpensive headset with a microphone may be an easily packable purchase to give some privacy and protect you from distractions. Of course, this assumes that you need to talk to your loved ones while you are gone. If you just need to check in, a few emails from internet cafes may be perfectly sufficient!

GMS rental from Cellhire includes free delivery of a fully tested and sanitized handset by high-end manufacturers such as Motorola, Ericsson, or Nokia and come with Voicemail as standard. You also get two batteries, a rapid charger, travel adapter, instruction booklet, and a return pack with a prepaid waybill. Call Cellhire toll-free at (866) CH ONLINE; online ordering and information, www.cellhire.com.

	COUNTRY/ CITY CODE
AUSTRIA	43
Vienna	1
Baden	2252
Innsbruck	512
Melk	2752
Salzburg	662
BELGIUM	32
Brussels	2
Antwerp	3
Bruges	50
Ghent	9
Namur	81
DENMARK	45
City codes not required. All points are 8 digits or 45 plus 121.	
FINLAND	358
Helsinki	9
Hanko	19
Lahti	3
Tampere	3
Turku	2
FRANCE	33
City codes not required; regional codes are included.	

	COUNTRY/ CITY CODE
GERMANY	**49**
Berlin	30
Dresden	351
Leipzig	341
Potsdam	331
Hamburg	40
Bremen	421
Hameln	5151
Hannover	511
Lübeck	451
Munich	89
Berchtesgaden	8652
Garmisch-Partenkirchen	8821
Nuremberg	911
Rothenburg	9861
(Romantic Road)	
Ulm	731
Koblenz	261
Trier	651
GREECE	**30**
Athens	21
Argos	751
Corinth	741
Patras	61
Piraeus	1
HUNGARY	36
Budapest	1
IRELAND	353
Dublin	1
Cork	21
Galway	91
Kilkenny	56
Killarney	64
ITALY	39
Milan	2
Bologna	51
Genoa	10
Venice	41
Rome	6
Anzio	06
Florence	55

COUNTRY/	CITY CODE
ITALY (con't)	**39**
Naples	81
Pisa	50
LUXEMBOURG	**352**
City codes not required.	
MONACO	**377 8**
No code required.	
THE NETHERLANDS	**31**
Amsterdam	**20**
Alkmaar	72
Enkhuizen	228
Haarlem	23
Hoorn	229
NORWAY	**47**
City codes not required.	
PORTUGAL	**351**
Lisbon	**21**
Cascais and Estoril	21
Coimbra	39
Setúbal	265
Sintra	21
SPAIN	**34**
When calling in Spain, use 9 before dialing city codes.	
Barcelona	**3**
Blanes	72
Lleida	73
Sitges	3
Tarragona	77
Madrid	**1**
Aranjuez	1
Avila	20
Burgos	47
El Escorial	1
Toledo	25
SWEDEN	**46**
Stockholm	**8**
Eskilstuna	16
Norrköping	11
Uppsala	18

	COUNTRY/ CITY CODE
SWITZERLAND	**41**
Bern	**31**
Interlaken	33
Lucerne	41
Lake Lugano	91
Rheinfelden	61
Zürich	1

Train Travel Terminology

English	French	Italian	German	Spanish
ON THE TRAIN:				
aisle	couloir	corridoio	gang	pasillo
car	compartement	vettura	wagen	vagón
couchette	couchette	cuccetta	liegeplatz	couchette
restaurant car	voiture-restaurant	carrozza -restaurante	speisewagen -restaurante	coche
seat	place	posto	sitzplätz	asiento
sleeper	wagon-lit	cabina	bettplätz	cama
sleeping	car voiture-lit	vagone letto	schlafwagen	coche-cama
smoking	fumeur	per fumatori	raucher	fumadores
nonsmoking	non fumeur	non fumatori	nichtraucher	no fumadores
table	table	tavolo	tisch	mesa
toilets	toilettes	tolette	toiletten	servicios
window	fenêtre	finestrino	fenster	ventana
IN THE STATION:				
entrance	entrée	entrata	eingang	entrada
exit	sortie	uscita	ausgang	salida
Gentlemen	Hommes	Signori	Herren	Caballeros
Information	Renseignements	Informazioni	Information	Información
Ladies	Femmes	Signore	Damen	Señoras
left luggage	consigne	depositato bagaglio	gepäckauf-bewahrung	consigna
lost and found	objets trouvés	oggetti smarriti	fundbüro	oficina de objeto perdidos
luggage	bagages	bagagli	gepäck	equipaje
luggage lockers	consigne automatique	armadietti per bagagli	schließfächer	consigna automática

English	French	Italian	German	Spanish
station	gare	stazione	bahnhof	estación
subway/ underground	Métro	Metropolitana	die U-bahn	Metro
track/platform	quai	binario	bahnsteig	andén
telephone	téléphone	telefono	telefon	teléfono
ticket office	guichet	biglietteria	fahrkarten-schalter	despacho de billetes
train	train	treno	zug	tren
AT THE TICKET WINDOW:				
arrival	arrivée	arrivo	ankunft	llegada
arrives	arrive	arriva	kommt	an llega
change at	correspondance	cambiare a	umsteigen in	cambiar en
first class	première classe	prima classe	erste klasse	primera clase
second class	seconde classe	seconda classe	zweite klasse	segunda clase
connection	correspondance	coincidenza	anschluß	conexión
departure	départ	partenza	abfhart	salida
departs	part	parte	fährt ab	sale
domestic tickets	billets	biglietti nazionali	fahrkarten inland	billetes nacionales
earlier	plus tôt	più presto	früher más	temprano
express	express	espresso	schnellzug	expreso
fast	rapid	rapido	schnell	rápido
from Rennes	(en provenance) de Rennes	(proviene) da Rennes	von Rennes	(procede) de Rennes
international tickets	billets internationaux	biglietti internazionali	fahrkarten ausland	billetes internacionales
not available	non disponible	non disponibile	nicht erhältlich	no disponible
later	plus tard	più tardi	später	más tarde
local service	service local	servizio locale	personenzug	servicio local
next train	prochain train	prossimo treno	nächst zug	próximo tren
reservation	reservation	prenotazione	reservierung	reservación
schedule/ timetable	horaires	orario	fahrplan	horari
supplement payable	avec con supplément	pagamento di supplemento	zuschlag-pflichtig	con pago de suplemento
to Oslo	vers Oslo, à destination de Oslo	a Oslo	nach Oslo	a Oslo
via	via	via	über	via

Passport Information

www.travel.state.gov

You can apply for a passport (in person if you are age 14 or older and do not meet the requirements to renew a previous passport by mail) at more than 8,000 facilities in the United States, including many post offices; federal, state, and probate courts; some libraries; and some municipal and county offices. Passport forms are also available for downloading from the Internet at www.travel.state.gov. You can enter your zip code to determine which passport application facility is closest.

Apply several months in advance if possible. It usually takes a minimum of six weeks. The National Passport Information Center (NPIC) operates an automated information number: (877) 487-2778. A recorded message describes the documents you need and the application process for obtaining a passport, as well as reporting the loss or theft of your passport.

Passport fees normally total $165 for a new passport and $140 for renewal or for those younger than age 16. For expedited service, send an extra $60 and pay for overnight delivery. This usually gets your passport to you in about two weeks. Or you can use one of the express passport services online, such as www.americanpassport.com or www.passportexpress.com. Be prepared to pay at least triple the normal passport fees, but they will get your passport to you in only one day after receiving the required documents.

If you are traveling within the next 14 days, or if you require a passport to obtain foreign visas within the next four weeks, you will need to make an appointment at a passport regional office. You may access the automated appointment system and general automated information (24 hours a day, seven days a week). Telephone (877) 487-2778 to make an appointment at a regional office or to talk to a customer service representative (normally available between 8:00 a.m. to 8:00 p.m. Monday–Friday; hours may be expanded during heavy calling periods). There is no charge to make an appointment. The regional offices' addresses follow.

Boston: Thomas P. O'Neill Federal Building, 10 Causeway Street, Suite 247, Boston, MA 02222-1094

Chicago: Kluczynski Office Building, 230 South Dearborn Street, Room 380, Chicago, IL 60604-1564

Connecticut: 850 Canal Street, Stamford, CT 06902

Dallas: 1100 Commerce Street, Suite 1120, Dallas, TX 75242

Denver: 3151 S. Vaughn Way, Suite 600, Aurora, CO 80014

Honolulu: Prince Kuhio Federal Building, 300 Ala Moana Boulevard, Suite I-330, Honolulu, HI 96850

Houston: Mickey Leland Federal Building, 1919 Smith Street, Suite 1100, Houston, TX 77002-8049

Los Angeles: Federal Building, 11000 Wilshire Boulevard, Room 1000, Los Angeles, CA 90024-3615

Miami: Omni Center, 1501 Biscayne Boulevard., Suite 210, Miami, FL 33132

Minneapolis: 212 3rd Avenue S., Minneapolis, MN 55410

New Orleans: One Canal Place, 365 Canal Street, Suite 1300, New Orleans, LA 70130-6508

New York: Greater Manhattan Federal Building, 376 Hudson Street, New York, NY 10014

Philadelphia: U.S. Customs House, 200 Chestnut Street, Room 103, Philadelphia, PA 19106-2970

San Francisco: 95 Hawthorne Street, Fifth Floor, San Francisco, CA 94105-3901

Seattle: 300 5th Avenue, Suite 600, Seattle, WA 98104

Tucson: 7373 E. Rosewood Street, Tucson, AZ 85710

Washington, D.C.: 1111 19th Street NW, Washington, D.C. 20524-1705

European Tourist Offices in North America

Austrian National Tourist Office—www.austria.info
E-mail: travel@austria.info

New York: P.O. Box 1142, New York, NY 10108. *Tel:* (212) 575-7723; *Fax:* (212) 944-6880

Toronto: 2 Bloor Street West, Suite 400, Toronto, Ontario M4W 3E2, Canada. *Tel:* (416) 967-3381; *Fax:* (416) 967-4101; *E-mail:* travel@austria.info.

Belgium Tourist Office—www.visitbelgium.com
E-mail: info@trabel.com

New York: 300 East 42nd Street, 14th Floor, New York, NY 10017.
Tel: (212) 758-8130; *Fax:* (212) 355-9726; *E-mail:* info@visitbelgium.com.

British Tourist Authority—www.visitbritain.com

New York: 551 Fifth Avenue, Suite 701, New York, NY 10176-0799.
Tel: (800) 462-2748 or (800) GO-2-BRIT; *Fax:* (212) 986-1188.

Chicago: 625 North Michigan Avenue, Suite 1001, Chicago, IL 60611-4977
Tel: (312) 787-0464; Fax: (312) 787-9641.

Czech Service Center—www.czech.tourism.com

New York: 1109 Madison Avenue, New York, NY 10028. *Tel:* (212) 288-0830 x101; *Fax:* (212) 288-0971.

French Government Tourist Office—www.francetourism.com http://us.franceguide.com/; E-mail: info.us@franceguide.com

For information on France by telephone, dial the Hotline, (514) 288-1904 for information requests.

New York: 825 Third Avenue, 29th Floor, New York, NY 10022-6903. *Tel:* (212) 745-0952; *Fax:* (212) 838-7855.

Chicago: Consulate General of France, 205 North Michigan Avenue, Suite 3770, Chicago, IL 60601. *Tel:* (312) 327-0290.

Los Angeles: 9454 Wilshire Boulevard, Suite 210, Beverly Hills, CA 90212. *Tel:* (310) 271-6665.

Montreal: 1981 McGill College Avenue, Suite 490, Montreal, PQ H3A 2W9, Canada. *Tel:* (514) 288-2026; *Fax:* (514) 845-4868.

German National Tourist Office—www.germany-tourism.de or www.cometogermany.com; E-mail: germanyinfo@germany.travel

New York: 122 East 42nd Street, 52nd Floor, Suite 2000, Chanin Building, New York, NY 10168-0072. *Tel:* 800-651-7010 or (212) 661-7200; *Fax:* (212) 661-7174; *E-mail:* gntonyc@d-z-t.com

Chicago: P.O. Box 59594, Chicago, IL 60659-9594. *Tel:* (773) 539-6303; *Fax:* (773) 539-6378; *E-mail:* gntoch@aol.com.

Toronto: 480 University Avenue, Suite 1500, Toronto, Ontario M5G 1V2. *Tel:* (416) 968-1685; *Fax:* (416) 968-0562; *E-mail:* info@gnto.ca.

Greek National Tourist Organization—www.greektourism.com; E-mail: info@gnto.gr

New York: 305 E. 47th Street, New York, NY 10017. *Tel:* (212) 421-5777; *Fax:* (212) 826-6940; *E-mail:* info@greektourism.com.

Hungarian National Tourism Office—www.gotohungary.com; E-mail: info@gotohungary.com

New York: 450 Fashion Avenue, #2601, New York, NY 10123. *Tel:* (212) 695-1221.

Irish Tourist Board—www.discoverireland.com; E-mail: info@irishtouristboard.com

New York: 345 Park Avenue, New York, NY 10154. *Tel:* (800) 223-6470 or (212) 418-0800; *Fax:* (212) 371-9052.

Toronto: 2 Bloor Street West, Suite 3403, Toronto, Ontario M4W 3E2, Canada. *Tel:* (800) 223-6470 or (416) 929-2777; *Fax:* (416) 929-6783.

Italian Government Tourist Board—www.italiantourism.com

New York: 630 Fifth Avenue, Suite 1965, New York, NY 10111. *Tel:* (212) 245-5618; *Fax:* (212) 586-9249; *E-mail:* enitny@italiantourism.com.

Chicago: 500 North Michigan Avenue, Suite 506, Chicago, IL 60611. *Tel:* (312) 644-9335; *Fax:* (312) 644-3019.

Los Angeles: 10850 Wilshire Boulevard, Suite 575, Los Angeles, CA 90024. *Tel:* (310) 820-1898; *Fax:* (310) 820-6357.

Toronto: 110 Yonge Street, Suite 503, Toronto, Ontario M5C 1T4. *Tel:* (416) 925-4882; *Fax:* (416) 925-4799; *Brochure Hotline:* (416) 925-3870.

Luxembourg National Tourist Office—www.visitluxembourg.com E-mail: info@visitluxembourg.com or **luxnt@aol.com**

New York: 17 Beekman Place, New York, NY 10022. *Tel:* (212) 935-8888; *Fax:* (212) 935-5896.

Malta National Tourist Office—www.visitmalta.com; E-mail: info@visitmalta.com

New York: Empire State Building, 350 Fifth Avenue, Suite 4412, New York, NY 10118. *Tel:* (212) 695-9520; *Fax:* (212) 695-8229.

Monaco Government Tourist/Convention Bureau—www.monaco-tourism.com; E-mail: info@visitmonaco.com

New York: 565 Fifth Avenue #23, New York, NY 10017. *Tel:* (800) 753-9696 or (212) 286-3330; *Fax:* (212) 286-9890.

Netherlands Board of Tourism—www.holland.com
E-mail: information@holland.com

New York: 215 Park Avenue South, Suite 2005, New York, NY 10003. *Tel:* (888) GO HOLLAND (888-464-6552) or (212) 370-7360; *Fax:* (212) 370-9507.

Northern Ireland Tourist Board—www.discovernorthernireland.com

New York: 551 Fifth Avenue, Suite 701, New York, NY 10176. *Tel:* (800) 326-0036 or (212) 922-0101; *Fax:* (212) 922-0099.

Toronto: 160 Bloor Street East, Suite 1150, Toronto, Ontario M4W 1B9, Canada; *Tel:* (416) 929-2777; *Fax:* (416) 929-6783.

Portuguese National Tourist Office—www.portugal.org
E-mail: tourism@portugal.org

New York: 866 Second Avenue, 8th Floor, New York, NY 10017. *Tel:* (212) 354-4403 or (800) PORTUGAL; *Fax:* (212) 764-6137.

Toronto: 60 Bloor Street, Suite 1005, Toronto, Ontario M4W 3B8, Canada. *Tel:* (416) 921-7376; *Fax:* (416) 921-1353.

Romanian National Tourist Office—www.romaniatourism.com
E-mail: infous@RomaniaTourism.com

New York: The Romania National Tourist Office, Department of Public Relations, 355 Lexington Avenue, 8th Floor, New York, NY 10017. *Tel:* (212) 545-8484; *Fax:* (212) 251-0429.

Scandinavian Tourist Boards of Denmark, Finland, Iceland, Norway, and Sweden—www.goscandinavia.com; E-mail: info@goscandinavia.com

New York: 655 Third Avenue, Suite 1810, New York, NY 10017-5617. *Tel:* (212) 885-9700; *Fax:* (212) 885-9710.

Tourist Office of Spain—www.okspain.org or www.spain.info; E-mail: oet ny@tourspain.es

New York: 60 East 42nd Street, Suite 5300 (53rd Floor), New York, NY 10165-0039. *Tel:* (212) 265-8822; *Fax:* (212) 265-8864; *E-mail:* oetny@tourspain.es.

Chicago: 845 North Michigan Avenue, Water Tower Place, Suite 915 E, Chicago, IL 60611. *Tel:* (312) 642-1992; *Fax:* (312) 642-9817; *E-mail:* chicago@tourspain .es.

Los Angeles: San Vicente Plaza Building, 8383 Wilshire Boulevard, Suite 960, Beverly Hills, CA 90211. *Tel:* (213) 658-7188; *Fax:* (213) 658-1061; *E-mail:* los angeles@tourspain.es.

Miami: 2655 Le Jeun Rd., Suite 605, Coral Cables, FL 33134. *Tel:* (305) 476-1966; *Fax:* (305) 476-1964; *E-mail:* oetmiami@tourspain.es.

Toronto: 2 Bloor Street West, Suite 3402, Toronto, Ontario M4W 3E2, Canada. *Tel:* (416) 961-3131; *Fax:* (416) 961-1992; *E-mail:* toronto@tourspain.es.

Switzerland Tourism—www.switzerlandtourism.com; E-mail: stnewyork@switzerlandtourism.com

Chicago: 150 North Michigan Avenue, Suite 2930, Chicago, IL 60601 *Tel:* (312) 630-5840.

Los Angeles: 222 North Sepulveda Boulevard, Suite 1570, El Segundo, CA 90245 *Tel:* (310) 335-5980; *Fax:* (310) 335-5982.

New York: 608 Fifth Avenue, New York, NY 10020. *Tel:* (800) 794-7795; *Fax:* (212) 262-6116.

Toronto: 480 University Ave., Suite 1500, Toronto, Ontario M5G 1V2; *Tel:* (800) 794-7795; *Fax:* (416) 695-2774.

To Purchase Passes

BritRail
www.britrail.com
Tel: (866) BRITRAIL

Eurail
www.eurail.com
E-mail: orders@eurail.com

Euro Railways
www.eurorailways.com
Tel: (954) 323-8389

European Rail Timetable
www.europeanrailtimetable.eu
Tel: 44 (0)1832 270198

Rail Europe
www.raileurope.com
Tel: (800) 622-8600

Airline Numbers and Websites

Dialing from the United States

Aer Lingus (EI)	800-IRISH-AIR/474-7424	www.aerlingus.com
Air Canada (AC)	888-247-2262	www.aircanada.ca
Air France (AF)	800-237-2747	www.airfrance.com
American Airlines, Inc. (AA)	800-433-7300	www.aa.com
Austrian Airlines (OS)	800-843-0002	www.austrianair.com
British Airways (BA)	800-AIRWAYS	www.britishairways.com
CSA Czech Airlines (OK)	800-628-6107	www.czechairlines.com
Delta Air Lines, Inc. (DL)	800-241-4141	www.delta.com
Finnair (AY)	800-950-5000	www.finnair.com
Icelandair (FI)	800-223-5500	www.icelandair.us
Lufthansa German Airlines (LH)	800-645-3880	www.lufthansa-usa.com
Olympic Airways (OA)	800-223-1226	www.olympicair.com
Scandinavian Airlines System (SK)	800-221-2350	www.flysas.com
Swiss International Airlines	877-359-7947	www.swiss.com
TAP Air Portugal (TO)	800-221-7370	www.tap-airportugal.pt
USAirways (US)	800-428-4322	www.usairways.com

Hotel Reservation Numbers

Dialing from the United States

Best Western International	800-937-8376	www.bestwestern.com
Choice Hotels International, Inc	877-424-6423	www.hotelchoice.com
Golden Tulip International	800-344-1212	www.goldentulip.com
Hilton Reservations Worldwide	800-HILTONS	www.hilton.com
Holiday Inns Worldwide	800-HOLIDAY	www.holiday-inn.com
Hyatt Worldwide Reservation Centres	800-233-1234	www.hyatt.com
InterContinental Hotels & Resorts	800-424-6835	www.ichotelsgroup.com
ITT Sheraton Corporation	800-325-3535	www.sheraton.com
Kempinski International	800-426-3135	www.kempinski.com
Leading Hotels of the World	800-223-6800	www.lhw.com
Loews Representation Int'l	800-223-0888	www.loewshotels.com
Marriott Corporation	800-228-9290	www.marriott.com
MinOtels Int'l	800-336-4668	www.minotel.com
Mövenpick Hotels Int'l	800-34-HOTEL	www.moevenpick-hotels.com
Preferred Hotels & Resorts Worldwide	800-323-7500	www.preferredhotels.com
Radisson Hotels, Int'l	800-333-3333	www.radisson.com
Ramada International Hotels & Resorts	800-854-7854	www.ramada.com
SRS World Hotels Service	800-223-5652	www.srs-worldhotels.com
Swissôtel	800-63-SWISS	www.swissotel.com

Airport—City Connections

Those arriving in many popular European cities will find direct rail service between central stations and airports at a growing number of European airports. Service includes:

STATION	AIRPORT	DISTANCE	TRANSPORT TYPE	BUS #	CITY TERMINAL
Alacant	Alicante	12 km	Bus services every 40 min.	C6	Plaça del Mar
Amsterdam	Schiphol	14 km	Train every 15 min.	—	Centraal Station
Athens (Athinai)	Eleftherios Venizelos	27 km	Train every 30 min.	—	Syntagma Station
Barcelona	Barcelona	10 km	Train every 30 min.	—	Barcelona Sants
Basel	Basel/Mulhouse/Freiburg	9 km	Bus every 15 min.	50 SBB	Station/Kannenfeldplatz
Belfast	Belfast International	26 km	Bus every 20 min.	300 (airbus)	Europa Buscentre, Glengall Street
Berlin	Schönefeld	18 km	S-Bahn train every 10 min.	—	Berlin Hbf
Berlin	Tegel	7 km	Bus every 10–20 min.	X9 & 109	Berlin Hbf
Bordeaux	Merignac	12 km	Bus every 10 min, 0500-0030	1+	Gare St. Jean
Bristol	Bristol	13 km	Bus every 10 min, 0600–1840	Airport flyer	Bus station, also Temple Meads Station
Brussels	Nationaal	12 km	Train every 20 min.	—	Midi/Zuid Station also calls at Central and Nord
Budapest	Ferihegy	16 km	Bus every 10 min.	200	Bus Station, Erzébet tér
Dublin	Dublin	11 km	Bus "Airlink" every 10–20 min.	747	Heuston Rail Station/ Busaras Bus Station
Düsseldorf	Düsseldorf	7 km	Train S7 (S-Bahn) every 20 min.	—	Hauptbahnhof
Florence (Firenze)	Firenze Peretola	7 km	Bus every 30 min.	ATAF 62	Santa Maria Station

STATION	AIRPORT	DISTANCE	TRANSPORT TYPE	BUS #	CITY TERMINAL
Frankfurt am Main	Frankfurt International	10 km	Train S8 (S-Bahn) 4–5 hourly	—	Hauptbahnhof
Gèneve	Gèneve	4 km	Train every 15 min.	10	Cornavin Station
Genova (Genoa)	Cristoforo Colombo	7 km	"Volabus" once per hour	—	Brignole and Principe Stations; Ferrari
Göteburg	Landvetter	25 km	Bus every 20 min. Mon–Fri; every 20–30 min. Saturday, Sunday, and holidays	—	City Air Terminal/Central Station
Grenoble	Lyon-Saint Exupery	91 km	Bus hourly, 0530–2330	Satobus	Gare routière (bus station)
Hamburg	Fuhlsbüttel	11 km	S-bahn train every 10 min.	51	Hauptbahnhof
Hannover	Langenhagen	13 km	S-Bahn train every 30 min.	S5	Bus station at Hauptbahnhof
Helsinki	Vantaa	19 km	Bus every 30 min.	615	City Air Terminal/Rail Station
Copenhagen (København)	Kastrup	12 km	Train every 10 min.	—	Central Station
Cologne (Köln)	Köln/Bonn	15 km	Train every 20 min.	S13	Hauptbahnhof
Lisbon (Lisboa)	Portela	7 km	Train every 10 min. 0700–2100	Red (vermelho) Line	Oriente Station
London	City	10 km	Train every 10–15 min.	—	Bank Underground Station
London	Gatwick	44 km	Train every 15 min.	Gatwick Express	Victoria Station
London	Heathrow	24 km	Train every 20 min.	Heathrow Express	London Underground/ Paddington Station
Luxembourg	Findel	7 km	Bus every 10–15 min.	16	Gare Centrale
Lyon	Saint Exupéry	25 km	Bus every 15 min. (Navette Aéroport)	—	Perrache Station, via Part Dieu

STATION	AIRPORT	DISTANCE	TRANSPORT TYPE	BUS #	CITY TERMINAL
Madrid	Barajas	12 km	Metro train, Bus every 10 min.	Line 8	Plaza Colón
Málaga	Málaga	7 km	Train every 30 min.	A	Málaga Station Centre-Alameda and RENFE Station
Marseilles	Marseilles/Provence	28 km	Bus every 20 min.	—	Gare St. Charles
Milan (Milano)	Linate	9 km	Bus every 10 min.	73	Piazza S. Babila/Milano Centrale Station
Milan (Milano)	Milano-Malpensa	45 km	Train “Malpensa Express” (FNM) every 30 min.	—	Cadorna rail stations
Münich (Munchen)	Strauss	37 km	Train, S-Bahn, every 10 min.	S1	Hauptbahnhof
Naples (Napoli)	Capodichino	7 km	Bus every 30 min.	3S	Piazza Garibaldi (Central Station)
Nice	Nice-Cote d'Azur	7 km	Bus every 20–30 min.	99	SNCF rail station
Oslo	Gardermoen	49 km	Airport Express Trains 3–6/hour	—	Central Station
Palma de Mallorca	Palma	11 km	Bus every 15 min.	1	Plaça Espana
Paris	Charles de Gaulle	25 km	RER train (Line B) every 10–20 min.	—	Gare du Nord/Châtelet les Halles and St. Michel Stations
Paris	Orly	15 km	RER train every 20 min. (Line C)	—	Austerlitz, St. Michel, Musée d'Orsay, and Invalides Stations
Pisa	Pisa (Galilei)	2 km	Train, 11 daily Bus every 10 min.	— 3	Pisa Centrale (trains continue to/from Firenze)
Porto	Pedras Rubras	17 km	Train every 20 min.	Line E	Campenhã rail station
Prague (Praha)	Ruzyne	17 km	Bus (CSA) every 30 min.	119	Dejvicka Rail Station
Rome (Roma)	Fiumicino	26 km	Train every 30 min.	—	Roma Tiburtina/Ostiense/ Termini stations

STATION	AIRPORT	DISTANCE	TRANSPORT TYPE	BUS #	CITY TERMINAL
Salzburg	Salzburg	5 km	Bus every 15 min.	2	Salzburg Bahnhof
Stockholm	Arlanda	44 km	Arlanda Express Train every 15 min.		Central rail station
Strasbourg	Entzheim	12 km	Train every 15 min.	—	Etiole Homme de Fer/Central Rail Station
Stuttgart	Echterdingen	14 km	Train S2, S3 S-Bahn every 15–20 min.	—	Hauptbahnhof
Turin (Torino)	Caselle	16 km	Train every 30 min.	—	Porta Nuova
Toulouse	Balgnac	8 km	Bus every 20 min.	11 Flybus	Gare Routière/Place Jeanne d'Arc
València	Manises	9 km	Train every 30 min.	—	Nord Rail Station
Venice (Venezia)	Marco Polo	13 km	Bus every 30 min. (summer/winter)	5	Pizzale Roma
Vienna (Wien)	Schwechat	17 km	Train every 30 min. Bus every 20–30 min.	—	Wien Mitte and Wien Nord Stations
Zürich	Zürich (Kloten)	12 km	Train 7 times per hour	—	Zürich Hauptbahnhof

In addition, rail service to other cities via the airport may be available.

Eurail Passes

Eurail passes entitle you to unlimited travel on Europe's extensive 100,000-mile rail network in 28 countries of Europe (England, Scotland, and Wales not included) as follows:

Austria • Belgium • Croatia • Czech Republic • Denmark • Finland • France • Germany Greece • Hungary • Ireland (Republic of) • Italy • Luxembourg • Netherlands • Norway Portugal • Romania • Slovenia • Spain • Sweden • Switzerland

Note: Prices are in U.S. dollars and are estimated conversions from euro prices, based on the exchange rate at press time. Please check with your retailer for updates. Prices may be slightly higher or lower. Prices listed for "additional rail days" are approximate.

Eurail Global Pass / Eurail Global Pass Saver

Eurail Global Pass: Consecutive-day travel on any or all days together at all times.

Eurail Global Pass Saver: Rail travel for two to five people traveling for the duration of the pass. Price is per person.

	ADULT 1st Class	EURAIL Youth Pass*	Eurail Global Pass Saver
15 days	$812	$528	$690
21 days	$1,046	$682	$891
1 month	$1,282	$838	$1,095
2 months	$1,816	$1,181	$1,543
3 months	$2,240	$1,457	$1,904

Children age 4–11, half adult fare; younger than age 4 travel free.

*Available for passengers age 12–25 on their first date of travel.

Eurail Global Pass Flexi / Eurail Global Pass Saver Flexi

Eurail Global Pass Flexi: Choose your travel days and use them within 60 days.

Eurail Global Pass Saver Flexi: Rail travel for two to five people traveling together at all times. Price is per person.

	ADULT 1st Class	Eurail Global Pass Saver Flexi
10 days in 2 months	$955	$813
15 days in 2 months	$1,254	$1,067

Children age 4–11, half adult fare; younger than age 4 travel free.

Eurail Global Pass Youth Flexi*

	2nd Class
10 days in 2 months	$623
15 days in 2 months	$817

*Available for passengers age 12–25 on their first date of travel.

Eurail Select Pass

The Eurail Select Pass gives travelers the option to customize a rail pass by choosing any three, four, or five bordering Eurail countries that are connected by train or by ship. The Select Pass covers Austria, Benelux (Belgium, the Netherlands, and Luxemburg as one country), Bulgaria/Serbia/Montenegro (as one country), Denmark, Finland, Czech Republic, Germany, Greece, Hungary, Italy, Norway, Portugal, Ireland (Republic of), Romania, Slovenia/Croatia (as one country), Spain, Sweden, and Switzerland.

Eurail Select Pass

Travel on any or all days for the duration of the pass in any three, four, or five adjoining Eurail pass countries.

DAYS	EURAIL SELECT PASS ADULT FIRST CLASS		
Within 2 months	3 Countries	4 Countries	5 Countries
5 days	$521	$573	$631
6 days	$576	$627	$686
8 days	$679	$730	$791
10 days	$788	$834	$891
15 days	NA	NA	$1,130

Eurail Select Pass Youth*

DAYS	EURAIL SELECT PASS YOUTH*		
Within 2 months	3 Countries	4 Countries	5 Countries
5 days	$341	$375	$411
6 days	$376	$408	$446
8 days	$442	$478	$516
10 days	$513	$544	$580
15 days	NA	NA	$736

*Youth price available for second-class travel passengers age 12–25. Children age 4–11, half adult fare; younger than age 4 travel free.

Eurail Select Pass Saver

For two or more persons traveling together at all times. Travel on any or all days for the duration of the pass in any three, four, or five adjoining Eurail pass countries.

DAYS	EURAIL SELECT PASS SAVER		
Within 2 months	3 Countries	4 Countries	5 Countries
5 days	$444	$489	$537
6 days	$490	$532	$583
8 days	$578	$621	$672
10 days	$669	$710	$758
15 days	NA	NA	$961

Children age 4–11, half adult fare; younger than age 4 travel free.

Eurail Regional Passes

Eurail Austria–Croatia–Slovenia Pass

	ADULT 1st Class	ADULT Saverpass*	YOUTH 2nd Class
4 days in 2 months	$308	$269	$224
Additional rail days (up to 6)	$43	$36	$28

Children age 4–11, half adult fare; younger than age 4 travel free. Youth age 12–25.
* Price per person for up to five people traveling together at all times.

Eurail Austria–Czech Republic Pass

Any four days unlimited first-class rail travel within a two-month period on national rail networks of Austria and Czech Republic. Purchase up to six additional rail days.

	ADULT 1st Class	ADULT Saverpass*	YOUTH 2nd Class
4 days in 2 months	$290	$248	$190
Extra rail days	$39	$334	$25

Children age 4–11, half adult fare; younger than age 4 travel free. Youth age 12–25.
*Price per person for up to five people traveling together at all times.

Eurail Austria–Germany Pass

DAYS Within 2 months	ADULT 1st Class	ADULT 2nd Class	ADULT Saverpass* 1st Class	ADULT Saverpass* 2nd Class	YOUTH 2nd Class
5 days	$465	$399	$399	$341	$344
6 days	$511	$438	$438	$375	$376
8 days	$610	$520	$520	$446	$448
10 days	$710	$603	$603	$521	$520

Children age 4–11, half adult fare; younger than age 4 travel free. Youth age 12–25.
*Price per person for 2–5 persons traveling together at all times.

Eurail Austria–Hungary Pass

	ADULT 1st Class	ADULT Saverpass*	YOUTH 2nd Class
4 days in 2 months	$290	$248	$190
Extra rail days	$39	$34	$25

Children age 4–11, half adult fare; younger than age 4 travel free. Youth age 12–25.
*Price per person for up to five people traveling together at all times.

Eurail Austria–Switzerland Pass

First-class rail travel in Austria and Switzerland for 4 to 10 days within 2 months. Saverpass is valid for 2 to 5 people traveling together.

	ADULT 1st Class	ADULT Saverpass*	YOUTH 2nd Class
4 days in 2 months	$448	$382	$314
Additional rail days (up to 6)	$49	$41	$35

Youth Passes are exclusively for those who are younger than age 26 on the first day of validity of their pass. Children age 4–11, half adult fare; under age 4 travel free.
*Price per person for up to five people traveling together at all times.

Balkan Flexipass

Valid for rail travel in Bulgaria, Greece, Macedonia, Montenegro, Romania, Serbia, and Turkey.

DAYS Within 1 month	ADULT 1st Class	SENIOR* 1st Class	YOUTH 2nd Class
5 days	$265	$212	$159
10 days	$462	$371	$277
15 days	$556	$445	$334

Children age 4–11, half adult fare; younger than age 4 travel free. Youth age 12–25.
*Senior age 60 and older.

Eurail Benelux–France Pass

DAYS Within 2 months	ADULT 1st Class	ADULT 2nd Class	SAVERPASS* 1st Class	SAVERPASS* 2nd Class	YOUTH 2nd Class
5 days	$505	$430	$430	$366	$330
6 days	$553	$471	$471	$410	$362
8 days	$641	$559	$546	$489	$418
10 days	$724	$637	$616	$555	$474

Children age 4–11 pay half adult fare; younger than age 4 travel free. Youth age 12–25.
*Price per person for up to five people traveling together at all times.

Eurail Benelux–Germany Pass

DAYS Within 2 months	ADULT 1st Class	ADULT 2nd Class	SAVERPASS* 1st Class	SAVERPASS* 2nd Class	YOUTH 2nd Class
5 days	$492	$370	$370	$299	$299
6 days	$543	$410	$410	$328	$328
8 days	$643	$481	$481	$387	$387
10 days	$748	$560	$560	$448	$348

Children age 4–11 pay half adult fare; younger than age 4 travel free. Youth age 12–25.
*Price per person for up to five people traveling together at all times.

Czech Republic–Germany Pass

DAYS Within 2 months	ADULT 1st Class	ADULT 2nd Class	SAVERPASS* 1st Class	SAVERPASS* 2nd Class	YOUTH 2nd Class
5 days	$455	$377	$374	$322	$322
6 days	$506	$418	$417	$357	$328
8 days	$593	$494	$492	$428	$391
10 days	$681	$570	$568	$495	$454

Children age 4–11 pay half adult fare; younger than age 4 travel free. Youth age 12–25.
*Price per person for up to five people traveling together at all times.

Eurail Denmark–Germany Pass

DAYS Within 2 months	ADULT 1st Class	ADULT 2nd Class	SAVERPASS* 1st Class	SAVERPASS* 2nd Class	YOUTH 2nd Class
4 days	$400	$328	$328	$255	$252
5 days	$450	$370	$370	$284	$284
6 days	$499	$410	$410	$310	$310
8 days	$602	$492	$492	$357	$357
10 days	$722	$549	$549	$403	$403

*Price per person for 2 to 5 people traveling together.
Children age 4–11 pay half adult fare; younger than age 4 travel free. Youth age 12–25.

European East Pass

Valid for rail travel in Austria, Czech Republic, Hungary, Poland, and Slovakia.

	1st Class	2nd Class
5 days in 1 month	$349	$238
Additional days	$42	$34

Up to 5 additional days can be added. Children age 4–11, half adult fare; younger than age 4 travel free.

Eurail France–Germany Pass

DAYS Within 2 months	ADULT 1st Class	ADULT 2nd Class	SAVERPASS* 1st Class	SAVERPASS* 2nd Class	YOUTH 2nd Class
4 days	$470	$424	$424	$384	$330
5 days	$521	$468	$468	$421	$363
6 days	$570	$514	$514	$455	$401
8 days	$667	$602	$602	$523	$470
10 days	$766	$691	$691	$602	$542

Children age 4–11 pay half adult fare; younger than age 4 travel free. Youth age 12–25.
*Price per person for up to five people traveling together at all times.

Eurail France–Italy Pass

DAYS Within 2 months	ADULT 1st Class	ADULT 2nd Class	SAVERPASS* 1st Class	SAVERPASS* 2nd Class	YOUTH 2nd Class
4 days	$435	$372	$372	$316	$285
5 days	$488	$416	$416	$353	$318
6 days	$536	$457	$457	$390	$350
7 days	$590	$502	$502	$427	$384
8 days	$643	$546	$546	$465	$420
9 days	$691	$587	$587	$501	$450
10 days	$739	$630	$630	$536	$482

*Price per person for up to five people traveling together at all times. Youth is under 26.

Eurail France–Spain Pass

DAYS OF TRAVEL Within 2 months	ADULT 1st Class	ADULT 2nd Class	SAVERPASS* 1st Class	SAVERPASS* 2nd Class	YOUTH 2nd Class
4 days	$435	$372	$372	$316	$285
5 days	$488	$416	$416	$353	$318
6 days	$536	$457	$457	$390	$350
7 days	$590	$502	$502	$427	$384
8 days	$643	$546	$546	$465	$420
9 days	$691	$587	$587	$501	$450
10 days	$739	$630	$630	$536	$482

*Price per person for up to five people traveling together at all times. Youth is under 26.

Eurail France–Switzerland Pass

DAYS Within 2 months	ADULT 1st Class	SAVERPASS* 1st Class	YOUTH 2nd Class
4 days	$471	$401	$330
5 days	$512	$435	$360
6 days	$572	$487	$401
7 days	$623	$529	$437
8 days	$674	$573	$472
9 days	$728	$620	$511
10 days	$779	$663	$546

Children age 4–11, half adult fare or saver price; younger than age 4 travel free. Youth younger than age 26.

*Price per person for 2 to 5 people traveling together at all times.

Eurail Germany–Poland Pass

DAYS Within 2 months	ADULT 1st Class	ADULT 2nd Class	SAVERPASS* 1st Class	SAVERPASS* 2nd Class	YOUTH** 2nd Class
5 days	$485	$414	$414	$350	$352
6 days	$532	$455	$460	$390	$390
8 days	$631	$543	$543	$461	$462
10 days	$725	$627	$627	$529	$529

*Price per person based on 2 to 5 people traveling together at all times.

**Younger than age 26.

Eurail Germany–Switzerland Pass

DAYS Within 2 months	ADULT 1st Class	SAVERPASS* 1st Class	YOUTH 2nd Class
5 days	$504	$431	$353
6 days	$555	$472	$391
8 days	$656	$560	$461
10 days	$756	$646	$532

*Price per person for 2 to 5 people traveling together at all times. One child (age 4–11) and one adult traveling together qualify for Saverpass.

Children age 3 and younger than travel for free; children age 4–11 travel for half the adult fare.

Eurail Greece–Italy Pass

	ADULT 1st Class	SAVERPASS* 1st Class	YOUTH 2nd Class
4 days in 2 months	$404	$345	$265
Additional rail days (up to 6)	$39	$34	$36

*Price per person for 2 to 5 people traveling together.
Children age 4–11 pay half adult fare; younger than age 4 travel free. Youth age 12–25.
Unlimited travel on the train networks of CH (Hellenic State railways) and Trenitalia, plus a return crossing between Ancona/Bari and Igoumenitsa/Patras on board the Superfast Ferries ships, or between Brindisi and Igoumenitsa/Corfu/Patras on board the Hellenic Mediterranean lines (HML) and Blue Star Ferries ships, for the period of validity of the pass.

Eurail Hungary–Croatia–Slovenia Pass

DAYS Within 2 months	ADULT 1st Class	SAVERPASS* 1st Class	YOUTH 2nd Class
5 days	$275	$234	$194
6 days	$303	$259	$214
8 days	$355	$303	$249
10 days	$408	$347	$286

Youth younger than age 26.
Children age 4–11, half adult fare; younger than age 4 travel free.
*Price per person based on 2 to 5 people traveling together at all times.

Eurail Hungary–Romania Pass

DAYS Within 2 months	ADULT 1st Class	SAVERPASS* 1st Class	YOUTH 2nd Class
5 days	$276	$235	$194
6 days	$302	$258	$213
8 days	$357	$303	$251
10 days	$408	$347	$286

Youth younger than age 26.
Children age 4–11, half adult fare; younger than age 4 travel free.
*Price per person for 2 to 5 people traveling together at all times.

Eurail Italy–Spain Pass

DAYS Within 2 months	ADULT 1st Class	SAVERPASS* 1st Class	YOUTH 2nd Class
4 days	$435	$372	$285
6 days	$536	$457	$350
8 days	$643	$546	$420
10 days	$739	$630	$482

Youth younger than age 26.
*Price per person for 2 to 5 people traveling together at all times.

Eurail Portugal–Spain Pass

	ADULT 1st Class	SAVERPASS* 1st Class
3 days in 2 months	$362	$308
Additional rail days (up to 7)	$50	$41

Purchase up to seven additional rail days. Children age 4–11, half adult fare; younger than age 4 travel free. *Price per person based on 2 to 5 people traveling together.

Eurail Scandinavia Pass

Valid for unlimited rail travel in Denmark, Finland, Norway, and Sweden.

DAYS Within 2 months	ADULT 2nd Class	ADULT SAVER 2nd Class	YOUTH 2nd Class	CHILD
4 days	$368	$313	$276	$159
5 days	$406	$345	$304	$174
6 days	$462	$394	$348	$198
8 days	$510	$434	$383	$219
10 days	$568	$483	$427	$243

Youth age 12–25. Child age 4–11; younger than age 4 travel free.

Eurail Country Passes

Austria Pass

The Austria country pass allows 15 days in which to use 3 to 8 travel days in either 1st or 2nd class.

	ADULT 1st Class	ADULT 2nd Class
3 days	$260	$184
4 days	$290	$204
5 days	$320	$225
6 days	$349	$246
7 days	$389	$267
8 days	$408	$287

Children age 4–11 pay half adult fare.

Benelux Pass

	ADULT 1st Class	ADULT 2nd Class	SAVERPASS* 1st Class	SAVERPASS* 2nd Class	YOUTH 2nd Class
5 days in one month	$446	$358	$380	$304	$234

Children age 4–11 pay half adult fare; younger than age 4 travel free. Youth age 12–25.
*Price per person for up to five people traveling together at all times.

Eurail Bulgaria Pass

	ADULT 1st Class	ADULT 2nd Class
3 days in one month	$159	$119
Additional rail days (up to 5)	$52	$41

Children age 4–11 pay half adult fare; younger than age 4 travel free. Youth age 12–25.

Eurail Croatia Pass

DAYS Within 1 month	ADULT 1st Class	ADULT 2nd Class	SAVERPASS* 1st Class	SAVERPASS* 2nd Class	YOUTH 2nd Class
3 days	$164	$130	$140	$112	$95
4 days	$218	$164	$187	$142	$110
6 days	$289	$218	$247	$186	$146
8 days	$343	$255	$293	$218	$164

Children age 4–11 pay half adult fare; younger than 4 travel free. Youth younger than 26.
*Price per person for 2 to 5 people traveling together at all times.

Czech Republic Pass

DAYS Within 1 month	ADULT 1st Class	ADULT 2nd Class	YOUTH 2nd Class
3 days	$173	$129	$87
4 days	$239	$179	$119
6 days	$336	$250	$167
8 days	$399	$296	$197

Children age 4–11 half adult fare; younger than age 4 travel free. Youth age 12–25.

Eurail Denmark Pass

DAYS Within 1 month	ADULT 1st Class	ADULT 2nd Class	YOUTH 2nd Class	CHILD 1st Class	CHILD 2nd Class
3 days	$238	$156	$118	$120	$82
7 days	$327	$214	$162	$164	$110

Child age 4–11; younger than age 4 travel free.

Eurail Finland Pass

DAYS Within 1 month	ADULT 1st Class	ADULT 2nd Class
3 days	$286	$193
5 days	$379	$256
10 days	$511	$345

Children age 6–16 half adult fare; younger than age 6 travel free.

France Railpass

Valid for 3–9 days of 1st- or 2nd-class travel within a 1-month period.

	ADULT	ADULT	SAVERPASS* ADULT	SAVERPASS* ADULT	YOUTH	YOUTH
	1st Class	2nd Class	1st Class	2nd Class	1st Class	2nd Class
3 days	$312	$253	$274	$222	$225	$191
4 days	$356	$290	$313	$256	$256	$218
5 days	$400	$327	$352	$290	$287	$245
6 days	$444	$364	$391	$324	$318	$272
7 days	$488	$401	$430	$358	$349	$299
8 days	$532	$438	$469	$392	$380	$326
9 days	$576	$475	$508	$426	$411	$353

Children age 4–11 half adult fare; younger than age 4 travel free. Youth younger than age 26.

*Price per person for 3 or more persons traveling together at all times.

German Railpass

DAYS Within 1 month	ADULT 1st Class Single	ADULT 1st Class Twin*	ADULT 2nd Class Single	ADULT 2nd Class Twin*	YOUTH 2nd Class
4 days	$403	$643	$298	$476	$239
5 days	$432	$691	$319	$512	$256
6 days	$476	$761	$352	$564	$282
7 days	$522	$835	$387	$619	$309
10 days	$658	$1,052	$486	$779	$390

Children age 4–11 half adult fare; younger than age 4 travel free. Youth younger than age 26.

*Twinpass prices are total for 2 people traveling together at all times.

Greece Railpass

DAYS Within 1 month	ADULT 1st Class	YOUTH 1st Class
3 days	$164	$146
4 days	$215	$193
5 days	$249	$222
6 days	$298	$266
7 days	$348	$310
8 days	$399	$355
9 days	$449	$401
10 days	$500	$445

Children age 4–11, half adult fare; younger than age 4 travel free. Youth younger than age 26.

Eurail Hungary Pass

	ADULT 1st Class	SAVERPASS* 1st Class	YOUTH 2nd Class
3 days within 1 month	$138	$118	$91
8 days within 1 month	$258	$219	$169

Children age 6–14, half adult fare. Youth age 15–25.

* Price per person for 2 or more persons traveling together at all times.

Eurail Ireland Pass

	ADULT 2nd Class	SENIOR 2nd Class	YOUTH 2nd Class
5 days within 1 month	$333	$251	$284

Children age 4–11, half adult fare; younger than age 4 travel free. Youth younger than age 26. Senior age 60 or older.

Eurail Italy Pass

DAYS Within 2 months	ADULT 1st Class	ADULT 2nd Class	SAVERPASS* 1st Class	SAVERPASS* 2nd Class	YOUTH 2nd Class
3 days	$310	$253	$265	$215	$205
4 days	$345	$280	$294	$239	$229
5 days	$384	$311	$327	$266	$255
6 days	$418	$339	$356	$289	$277
7 days	$458	$372	$390	$317	$304
8 days	$493	$401	$420	$342	$327
9 days	$531	$431	$452	$368	$352
10 days	$569	$462	$485	$394	$377

Children age 4–11 half adult fare; younger than age 4 travel free. Youth younger than age 26.

*Price per person for 2–5 persons traveling together at all times.

Eurail Norway Pass

DAYS Within 1 month	ADULT 2nd Class	YOUTH 2nd Class
3 days	$284	$214
4 days	$307	$231
5 days	$339	$256
6 days	$386	$290
8 days	$428	$322

Up to 2 children travel free with each adult pass; more than 2 children age 4–15 pay half adult fare; younger than age 4 travel free. Youth passes for students under 26 years old.

Eurail Poland Pass

DAYS Within 1 month	ADULT 1st Class	ADULT 2nd Class	YOUTH 1st Class	YOUTH 2nd Class
5 days	$198	$155	$141	$109
8 days	$280	$217	$198	$153
10 days	$317	$245	$222	$173
15 days	$439	$339	$308	$239

Younger than age 4 travel free. Youth younger than age 26.

Eurail Portugal Pass

DAYS Within 1 month	ADULT 1st Class
3 days	$179
4 days	$219
6 days	$289

Children age 4–11, half adult fare; younger than age 4 travel free (unless a separate seat is requested).

Eurail Romania Pass

DAYS Within 2 months	ADULT 1st Class	SAVERPASS* 1st Class	YOUTH 2nd Class
5 days	$201	$171	$161
10 days	$352	$301	$282

Children age 4–11 half adult fare; younger than age 4 travel free. Youth younger than age 26. *Price per person for 2 or more persons traveling together at all times.

Eurail Slovenia Pass

DAYS Within 1 month	ADULT 1st Class	ADULT 2nd Class	SAVER* 2nd Class
3 days	$106	$80	$69
4 days	$150	$113	$97
6 days	$211	$160	$136
8 days	$257	$193	$164

Children age 4–11 half adult fare; younger than age 4 travel free. *Price per person for 2-5 people traveling together at all times.

Eurail Spain Pass

DAYS Within 2 months	ADULT 1st Class	ADULT 2nd Class
3 days	$315	$253
4 days	$359	$289
5 days	$404	$324
6 days	$451	$362
7 days	$499	$400
8 days	$545	$437
9 days	$596	$477
10 days	$641	$514

Children age 4–11 half adult fare; younger than age 4 travel free. The AVE and Talgo 200 trains require additional supplements.

Sweden Pass

DAYS Within 1 month	ADULT 1st Class	ADULT 2nd Class	YOUTH 2nd Class
3 days	$369	$286	$215
4 days	$396	$305	$231
5 days	$439	$339	$256
6 days	$497	$384	$289
8 days	$555	$428	$322

Up to 2 free child passes with purchase of each adult pass; children age 4–15 half adult fare. Youth younger than age 26.

Pass does not include supplement on x2000 train.

Swiss Card (ideal for skiers)

Valid for one round-trip rail journey plus 50% discount on Swiss railways, lake steamers, postal buses, and most mountain railroads within a 1-month validity period.

	1st Class	2nd Class
1 month—1 round-trip	$327	$231

Children younger than age 16, free with parent. Children age 6–15 not accompanied by parent, half adult fare. Children younger than age 6 travel free.

Swiss Pass

Valid for consecutive-day unlimited travel. Choice of first class or second class. Free Swiss Family Card: Children younger than age 16 travel free when accompanied by at least one parent; half adult fare when not accompanied by parent. Includes travel on lake steamers, transportation on 35 city systems, postal and private bus lines.

CONSECUTIVE DAYS OF TRAVEL	1st Class	2nd Class	SAVERPASS* 1st Class	SAVERPASS* 2nd Class	YOUTH** 1st Class	YOUTH** 2nd Class
4 days	$490	$306	$442	$276	$367	$230
8 days	$709	$393	$638	$389	$532	$332
15 days	$859	$476	$772	$472	$643	$402
22 days	$995	$552	$896	$550	$746	$466
1 month	$1,094	$607	$985	$605	$820	$513

*Price per person based on two or more adults traveling together at all times; children younger than age 16 travel free when accompanied by a parent.

**For persons ages 16–25

Swiss Transfer Ticket

Great for skiers or for those who will stay in one place. Provides for one round-trip ticket from any Swiss airport to any Swiss destination within a 1-month period.

	1st Class	2nd Class
1 day in 1 month	$258	$162

Children younger than age 16 travel free when accompanied by at least one parent; otherwise, children age 6–15, half adult fare. Children younger than age 6 travel free.

Security

Rail Pass Security

Entitles traveler to a 100% reimbursement on the unused portion of the rail pass if lost or stolen while traveling in Britain or Europe.

$20.00 per pass

BritRail Passes

A BritRail consecutive-day or Flexipass allows unlimited travel on the entire British rail network spanning England, Scotland, and Wales. Prices are current as of press time, but are always subject to change without notice. Prices are estimates based on the exchange rate at the time of printing.

BritRail Consecutive Pass

Valid for consecutive days of rail travel throughout Britain (England, Scotland, and Wales).

	ADULT 1st Class	ADULT Standard Class	SENIOR 1st Class	YOUTH Standard Class	YOUTH 1st Class
4 days	$429	$289	$369	$235	$345
8 days	$615	$409	$525	$329	$495
15 days	$919	$615	$779	$495	$735
22 days	$1,165	$775	$989	$625	$935
1 month	$1,375	$919	$1,109	$735	$1,105

Senior 60+. Youth 16–25. Children 5–15, half adult fare. Children younger than age 5 travel free.

BritRail Family Passes

Receive one free child pass (age 5–15) of the same type when purchasing one adult or senior BritRail Consecutive Pass, BritRail Flexipass, or BritRail Pass + Ireland. Additional children pay half fare. Children under age 5 travel free.

BritRail Flexipass

Valid for unlimited rail travel in Britain for the days chosen within 2 months.

	ADULT 1st Class	ADULT Standard Class	SENIOR 1st Class	YOUTH 1st Class	YOUTH Standard Class
4 days in 2 months	$539	$365	$459	$435	$295
8 days in 2 months	$785	$525	$669	$629	$425
15 days in 2 months	$1,179	$795	$999	$945	$635

Senior age 60+. Youth 16–25. Children age 5–15, half adult fare. Children younger than age 5 travel free.

BritRail Pass + Ireland

Valid for travel in England, Scotland, Wales, Northern Ireland, and the Republic of Ireland.

	ADULT 1st Class	ADULT Standard Class
5 days within 1 month	$835	$569
10 days within 1 month	$1,489	$1,005

Children age 5–15, half adult fare; younger than age 5 travel free.

BritRail England Consecutive Pass

Unlimited consecutive-day rail travel in England (Scotland and Wales are not included on the England Pass).

	ADULT 1st Class	ADULT Standard Class	SENIOR 1st Class	YOUTH Standard Class	YOUTH 1st Class
4 days	$345	$235	$295	$189	$279
8 days	$495	$329	$419	$265	$395
15 days	$735	$495	$625	$395	$589
22 days	$935	$625	$795	$499	$749
1 month	$1,099	$735	$935	$589	$885

Youth 16–25; senior 60+. BritRail Family Passes must be requested so each child (age 5–15) can travel free with each adult/senior pass holder. Additional children are half regular adult fare.

BritRail England Flexipass

Unlimited four, eight, or fifteen days of flexible (nonconsecutive) rail travel in a two-month period throughout England (Scotland and Wales not included).

	ADULT 1st Class	ADULT Standard Class	SENIOR 1st Class	YOUTH 1st Class	YOUTH Standard Class
4 days	$435	$295	$369	$349	$235
8 days	$629	$425	$535	$505	$339
15 days	$945	$635	$805	$755	$509

Youth 16–25; senior 60+. Family passes allow one child to travel free with each adult.

BritRail London Plus Pass

A flexipass for a large section of southern England.

	ADULT 1st Class	ADULT Standard Class
2 days within 8 days	$245	$165
4 days within 8 days	$339	$259
7 days within 15 days	$419	$309

One child age 5–15 years travels free with each full paying adult. Ask for the free BritRail Family passes. Additional children age 5–15 pay half the full adult fare. Children younger than age 5 travel free. Now extended to Bristol, Bath, and Stratford-upon-Avon. Not valid on other services via Reading operated by Great Western Trains from Paddington Station. Travel on the London Underground is not included.

BritRail Freedom of Scotland Pass

	ADULT Standard Class
4 days within 8 days	$239
8 days within 15 days	$319

Includes transportation on all Caledonian MacBrayne and Strathclyde ferries to the islands of Scotland. Discounts on some P&O ferry routes. Children younger than age 5 travel free.

Gatwick Express

	1st Class	Standard Class
One-way	$48	$33
Round-trip	$94	$58

Travel by train from Gatwick Airport to London Victoria Station. Children 5–15, half adult fare.

Heathrow Express

	1st Class	Standard Class
One-way	$48	$35
Round-trip	$87	$57

Train travel from Heathrow Airport to London Paddington Station. Children 5–15, half adult fare.

London Pass

Entry to more than 70 major attractions, including Buckingham Palace (open August and September), St. Paul's Cathedral, and Windsor Castle, a 140-page *London Pass Guide Book*, commission-free currency exchange, free offers at restaurants, discounted telephone calls, and more. Available only with the purchase of another product.

	ADULT	**CHILD**
1 day	$82	$55
2 consecutive days	$114	$82
3 consecutive days	$122	$84
6 consecutive days	$162	$114

London Visitor Travelcard

Unlimited travel throughout all 6 zones of London on London Underground and buses. Three- or seven-day travel cards are available. Not valid on Heathrow Express, Gatwick, or Stansted Express.

	1 ADULT Standard Class	**1 CHILD** Standard Class
1 Day Central Zone	$16	$8
7 Days All Zones	$100	$50